Trekking in the
PATAGONIAN ANDES

Clem Lindenmayer
Nick Tapp

LONELY PLANET PUBLICATIONS
Melbourne • Oakland • London • Paris

www.lonelyplanet.com

your online travel community

350+ DESTINATION PROFILES · 5,000+ TRAVEL POSTS DAILY · 50,000+ MEMBERS

WEEKLY COLUMNS & INTERVIEWS · MONTHLY ADVISORIES · STORIES FROM AROUND THE WORLD

ONLINE SHOP · TRAVEL SERVICES · BEST TRAVEL WEBSITE: WEBBY AWARDS

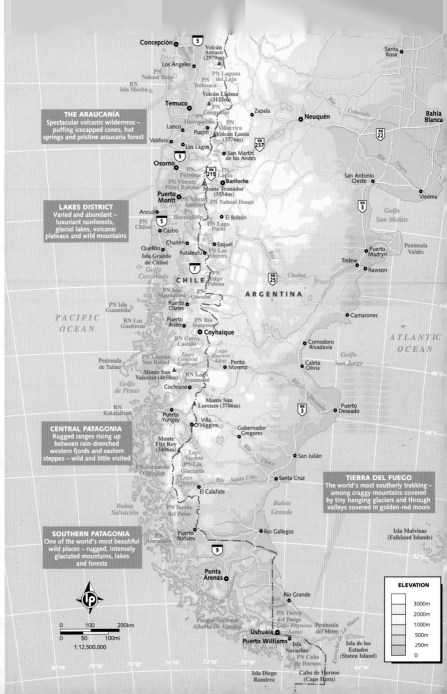

Concepción
Volcán Antuco (2979m)
5
Santa Rosa
Los Ángeles
RN Nahuel Buta
PN Laguna del Laja
PN Tolhuaca
Volcán Lluima (3125m)
PN Conguillío
Zapala
Neuquén
Bahía Blanca
Río Colorado

THE ARAUCANÍA
Spectacular volcanic wilderness – puffing icecapped cones, hot springs and pristine araucaria forest

Temuco
Lanco
PN Huerquehue
Pucón
PN Villarrica
Volcán Lanín (3776m)
RN 237
Valdivia
Los Lagos
San Martín de los Andes
Osorno
PN Puyehue
RN 215
PN Vicente Pérez Rosales
Bariloche
Monte Tronador (3554m)
PN Nahuel Huapi

LAKES DISTRICT
Varied and abundant – luxuriant rainforests, glacial lakes, volcanic plateaus and wild mountains

Puerto Montt
Ancud
PN Chiloé
5
PN Alerce Andino
PN Hornopirén
PN Lago Puelo
El Bolsón
San Antonio Oeste
Viedma
Golfo San Matías
Península Valdés
Castro
Chaitén
Quellón
Isla Grande de Chiloé
Golfo Corcovado
Futaleufú
Esquel
PN Los Alerces
7
PN Lago Palena
Puerto Madryn
Trelew
Rawson
Río Chubut
RN 25

CHILE

ARGENTINA

PN Isla Magdalena
PN Queulat
PN Isla Guamblín
PACIFIC OCEAN
PN Isla Guaitecas
Puerto Cisnes
Puerto Aisén
PN Río Simpson
Coyhaique
Camarones

RN Las Guaitecas
RN Cerro Castillo
Lago General Carrera
Lago Buenos Aires
Perito Moreno
Comodoro Rivadavia
Caleta Olivia
Golfo San Jorge
ATLANTIC OCEAN

PN Laguna San Rafael
Península de Taitao
Monte San Valentín (4058m)
Golfo de Penas
Cochrane
RN Lago Jeinimeni
Monte San Lorenzo (3706m)

RN Katalalixar
Puerto Yungay
Villa O'Higgins
Gobernador Gregores
Puerto Deseado
RN 3

CENTRAL PATAGONIA
Rugged ranges rising up between rain-drenched western fjords and eastern steppes – wild and little visited

Monte Fitz Roy (3406m)
Lago Viedma
San Julián
PN Bernardo O'Higgins
PN Los Glaciares
Lago Argentino
El Calafate
Río Santa Cruz
Santa Cruz
Bahía Grande

TIERRA DEL FUEGO
The world's most southerly trekking – among craggy mountains covered by tiny hanging glaciers and through valleys covered in golden-red moors

Bahía Salvación
PN Torres del Paine
RN Alacalufes
SOUTHERN PATAGONIA
One of the world's most beautiful wild places – rugged, intensely glaciated mountains, lakes and forests
Puerto Natales
9
Río Gallegos
Isla Malvinas (Falkland Islands)

Punta Arenas
Río Grande
PN Tierra del Fuego
Lago Fagnano (Kami)
Península del Mitre
Isla de los Estados (Staten Island)

ELEVATION
	3000m
	2000m
	1000m
	500m
	250m
	0

Ushuaia
Puerto Williams
Isla Navarino
PN Cabo de Hornos
Cabo de Hornos (Cape Horn)
Isla Diego Ramírez

0   100   200km
0   50   100mi
1:12,500,000

80°W   78°W   76°W   74°W   72°W   70°W   64°W
46°S
48°S
52°S

Trekking in the Patagonian Andes
3rd edition – November 2003
First published – April 1992

Published by
Lonely Planet Publications Pty Ltd ABN 36 005 607 983
90 Maribyrnong St, Footscray, Victoria 3011, Australia

Lonely Planet Offices
Australia Locked Bag 1, Footscray, Victoria 3011
USA 150 Linden St, Oakland, CA 94607
UK 72–82 Rosebery Ave, London EC1R 4RW
France 1 rue du Dahomey, 75011 Paris

Photographs
Many of the images in this guide are available for licensing from
Lonely Planet Images.
w www.lonelyplanetimages.com

Front cover photograph
Cuernos del Paine rising up above Lago Pehoé, Parque Nacional Torres
del Paine (Brent Winebrenner)

Small front cover photograph
Trekker wading in Lago Pehoé, Parque Nacional Torres del Paine
(Woods Wheatcroft)

ISBN 1 86450 059 X

Contents

The Maps

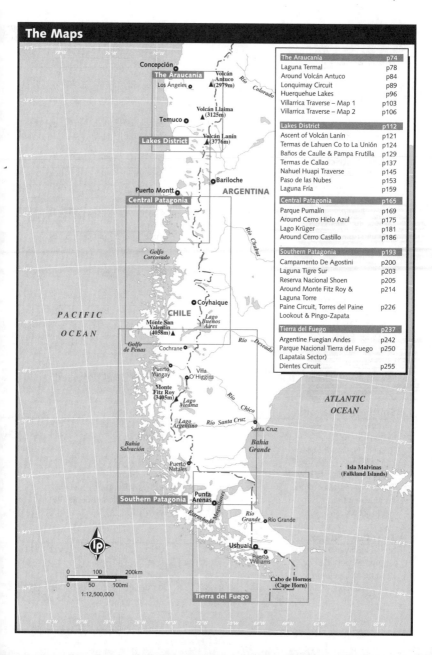

The Treks	Duration	Difficulty	Transport
The Araucanía			
Laguna Termal	6½–8¼ hours	moderate	bus
Around Volcán Antuco	3 days	moderate	bus & walk
Lonquimay Circuit	6 days	moderate–demanding	bus
Huerquehue Lakes	4 days	easy–moderate	bus
Villarrica Traverse	6 days	demanding	tour or taxi; bus
Lakes District			
Ascent of Volcán Lanín	3 days	demanding	bus
Termas de Lahuen Co to La Unión	2 days	easy	tour or taxi
Baños de Caulle	4 days	moderate	bus
Pampa Frutilla	2 days	easy–moderate	bus
Termas de Callao	3 days	easy	boat & bus
Nahuel Huapi Traverse	5 days	moderate–demanding	bus
Paso de las Nubes	2 days	moderate	bus & boat
Laguna Fría	2 days	easy–moderate	bus & walk
Central Patagonia			
Laguna Tronador	2½–3½ hours	easy–moderate	bus or tour
Sendero Alerces	30–40 minutes	easy	bus or tour
Cascadas Escondidas	1½–2 hours	easy	bus or tour
Around Cerro Hielo Azul	3 days	moderate	bus or taxi
Lago Krüger	4 days	moderate	bus
Around Cerro Castillo	4 days	moderate–demanding	bus
Southern Patagonia			
Campamento De Agostini	4 days	easy–moderate	bus
Laguna Tigre Sur	2 days	moderate	bus or taxi
Reserva Nacional Shoen	2 days	easy	bus, plane or b
Laguna Torre	2 days	easy	bus
Around Monte Fitz Roy	3 days	easy–moderate	bus
Torres del Paine Lookout	4½–6 hours	easy–moderate	bus
Paine Circuit	8 days	moderate–demanding	bus
Pingo-Zapata	2 days	easy	bus & van
Tierra del Fuego			
Sierra Valdivieso Circuit	4 days	demanding	van or taxi
Laguna Esmeralda	3–4 hours	easy	van or taxi
Paso de la Oveja	3 days	moderate	taxi
Dientes Circuit	5 days	moderate–demanding	boat or plane

The Authors

Clem Lindenmayer

Clem has spent much of the past two decades exploring the earth's wildest mountain regions. His trips have taken him to *almost* every continent – but he insists he still intends to trek across the trans-Antarctic mountains some day! He has always had a special fondness for the wild temperate lands of the Southern Hemisphere (and has also tramped extensively in Tasmania and New Zealand), returning regularly to the wilds of the Patagonian Andes. Clem has authored Lonely Planet's *Walking in Switzerland* and has coauthored *Hiking in the Rocky Mountains* and *Hiking in the USA*, and has also helped update our travel guidebooks on China, Southeast Asia and Europe.

Nick Tapp

Nick first picked up a rucksack while at university, some time last century, and was instantly converted. The career in medicine never eventuated but the outdoor habit stuck, and he has since walked, skied and/or climbed in five continents. This was his second trip to the Patagonian Andes. His first job in publishing, with Australia's *Wild* and *Rock* magazines, began in the packing room and ended in the editor's chair. His next, at Lonely Planet, led to the dizzy heights of publisher of outdoor activity guides. Nowadays he is a freelance editor, writer, photographer and dad based in Melbourne. He has coauthored two editions of Lonely Planet's *Walking in Italy*.

FROM THE AUTHORS
Clem Lindenmayer

Once again, I'm deeply grateful to all the staff of Chile's Conaf and Argentina's Administración de Parques Nacionales for their diligent assistance. In particular, I'd like to thank the following *guardaparques*: Jhon Bahamondez (Conaf, Villa O'Higgins), Luis Briones (Conaf, Puyehue), Mauricio Castell Cordero (Conaf, Conguillío), Fernando Grandón (Parque Pumalín, Chaitén), Marcos Mattus Lagos (Conaf, Villarrica), Felix Ledesma (Conaf, Huerquehue), Rodrigo Marín Suniga (Conaf, Conguillío), Daniel Martín (APN, Villa Futalaufquen) and Javier Subiabre (Conaf, Cochrane).

Thanks also to the following people: Rolando Alberto Alguilera (Gendarmería Nacional, Copahue), Aldi Banfield (Caviahue), Gabriel Bevacqua (El Bolsón), Denis Chevally (Punta Arenas), Alejo Contreras (DAP, Punta Arenas), Julio Contreras (Punta Arenas), Carolina Etchegoyen (Ushuaia), Nicolas La Penna (Chaitén), Cristián Mayorga (Puerto Williams/Valparaíso), Gabriela Neira Morales (Sernatur, Coyhaique), Alejandro Ouvello Bascur (Futaleufú), Patti (Hostal Pusaki, Puerto Williams), Alicia Petiet (Ushuaia) and Luis Turi (Ushuaia).

Finally, thanks aplenty to the ever-patient Lonely Planet team, including my fellow coauthor, the very eminent Nick Tapp.

Nick Tapp

Thanks to those many staff of Conaf in Chile and the Administración de Parques Nacionales in Argentina who helped me out with information, advice and encouragement, and to many other folk of the Andes – especially that special breed, the *refugieros* – who were only too keen to help spread the word. Thanks to my many temporary trail companions, foremost among them Andrew Bain, Tracey and Greg, Pete, Catherine, Kärsten and Klaus, Yasna and Adrian, and Christoph. Thanks to Clem of the Andes for so willingly taking on some hired help, and to Lindsay Brown and the team at Lonely Planet in Melbourne for their support. Finally, thanks to Amy, Oliver and, above all, Ely – who let me go and then let me come back.

This Book

The first two editions of *Trekking in the Patagonian Andes* were written by Clem Lindenmayer. Since then Clem has had the honour of having the mountains Cerro Clem and Montes Lindenmayer named after him by Chile's Ministerio de Bienes Nacionales (Ministry of National Resources). This edition was written by Clem Lindenmayer and Nick Tapp. Coordinating author Clem Lindenmayer wrote Facts about the Patagonian Andes, Watching Wildlife, Facts for the Trekker, Clothing & Equipment, Health & Safety, Travel Facts, Central Patagonia and Tierra del Fuego. Both Clem Lindenmayer and Nick Tapp contributed to the Araucanía, Lakes District and Southern Patagonia chapters. Some material from the fifth edition of *Chile & Easter Island* and the fourth edition of *Argentina, Uruguay & Paraguay* was used in this book.

FROM THE PUBLISHER

This edition of *Trekking in the Patagonian Andes* was commissioned at Lonely Planet's Melbourne base by Andrew Bain and Marg Toohey. The coordinating editor was Gabbi Wilson and the coordinating cartographer was Andrew Smith. Editorial assistance was provided by Andrew Bain, Nancy Ianni, Charlotte Keown, Nick Tapp, Fionnuala Twomey, Katrina Webb and Simon Williamson. Mapping assistance was provided by Barbara Benson. The book was laid out by John Shippick and the cover was designed by Wendy Wright. The language chapter was produced by Quentin Frayne and reviewed by resident Argentinian Gus Balbontin. The project was managed through production by Glenn van der Knijff.

Thanks

Many thanks to the travellers who used the last edition and wrote to us with helpful hints, advice and interesting anecdotes:

Tim Allman, Cameron Bell, Gabriel Bevacqua, P & F Black, Jose Blanco, Joseph & Isabelle Blandin-Taris, Justin Boocock, Peter Brazier, Ian Bunton, Anne Burgess, Alex Castillo, Alexander Caton, Dave Diperna, Jorg Droste, Sam Esmiol, Christine Fetterhoff, Montse Fontellas, B E Furmston, Amit Golander, Claudia Hanfland, Jeff Hankens, Sarah Hankinson, Deanna Harris, Justin Harrison, Imke & Andreas Hendrich, Kathryn Hiestand, Jock & Alan Hughes, Doris Hulbaklien, Leonie Janssen, Dion Keech, Roland Kienitz, Pavel Klejna, Tim Langmaid, Gil Liberman, Edgar Locke, Diedrik Lugtigheid, Rebecca Lush, Eoin McGrath, Elizabeth Maclaine-Cross, Arnout Meester, Pete Minor, Anna Moyers, Neal Neal, Robert Neumayr, Karin Obendorfer, Mandy Planert, Julie Wood Prosperi, Birgit Ruhfus, Andre Scherphof, Bogdan Siewierski, Diego Singer, Michael Stauch, Christine Sterbecq, Pete Syms, Silvia Ugarte, Xander Van der Burgt, Gunnar Vigerust, Marcus Vinicius Gasques, Phil Waring, Alun Williams

Trek Descriptions

This book contains 31 trek descriptions ranging from day trips to eight-day treks, plus suggestions for side trips and alternative routes. Each trek description has a brief introduction outlining the natural and cultural features you may encounter, plus information to help you plan your trek – transport options, level of difficulty, time frame and any permits required.

Day treks are often circular and are located in areas of uncommon beauty. Multiday treks include information on campsites, huts, hostels or other accommodations and where you can obtain water and supplies.

Times & Distances

These are provided only as a guide. Times are based on actual trekking time and do not include stops for snacks, taking photographs, rests or side trips. Be sure to factor these in when planning your trek. Distances are provided but should be read in conjunction with altitudes. Significant elevation changes can make a greater difference to your trekking time than lateral distance.

All quoted trekking times – unless the text says otherwise – are measured from the place where the last trekking time was given. The sum of these trekking times should more or less equal the number of hours quoted for the whole of that route description/trekking stage. In most cases, the daily stages are flexible and can be varied. It is important to recognise that short stages are sometimes recommended in order to acclimatize in mountain areas or because there are interesting features to explore en route.

Level of Difficulty

Grading systems are always arbitrary. However, having an indication of the grade may help you choose between treks. Our authors use the following grading guidelines:

Easy – a trek on flat terrain or with minor elevation changes, usually over short distances on well-travelled routes with no navigational difficulties.
Moderate – a trek with challenging terrain, often involving longer distances and steep climbs.
Demanding – a trek with long daily distances and difficult terrain with significant elevation changes; may involve challenging routefinding and high-altitude or glacier travel.

True Left & True Right

The terms 'true left' and 'true right,' used to describe the bank of a stream or river, sometimes throw readers. The 'true left bank' simply means the left bank as you look downstream.

Maps

Our maps are based on the best available references, often combined with GPS data collected in the field. They are intended to show the general route of the trek and should be used in conjunction with maps suggested in the trek description.

Maps may contain contours or ridgelines, in addition to major watercourses, depending on the available information. These features build a three-dimensional picture of the terrain, allowing you to determine when the trail climbs and descends. Altitudes of major peaks, passes and localities complete the picture by providing the actual extent of the elevation changes.

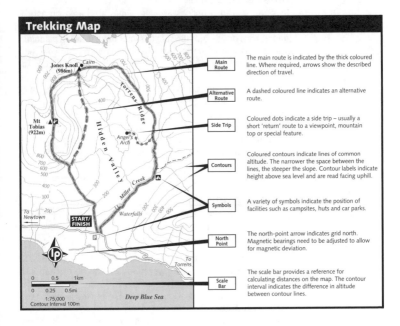

Route Finding

While accurate, our maps are not perfect. Inaccuracies in altitudes are commonly caused by air-temperature anomalies. Natural features such as river confluences and mountain peaks are in their true position, but the location of villages and trails is not always so. This may be because a village is spread over a hillside, or the size of the map does not allow for detail of the trail's twists and turns. However, by using several basic route-finding techniques, you will have few problems following our descriptions:

1. Always be aware of whether the trail should be climbing or descending.
2. Check the north-point arrow on the map and determine the general direction of the trail.
3. Time your progress over a known distance and calculate the speed at which you travel in the given terrain. From then on, you can determine with reasonable accuracy how far you have travelled.
4. Watch the path – look for boot prints and other signs of previous passage.

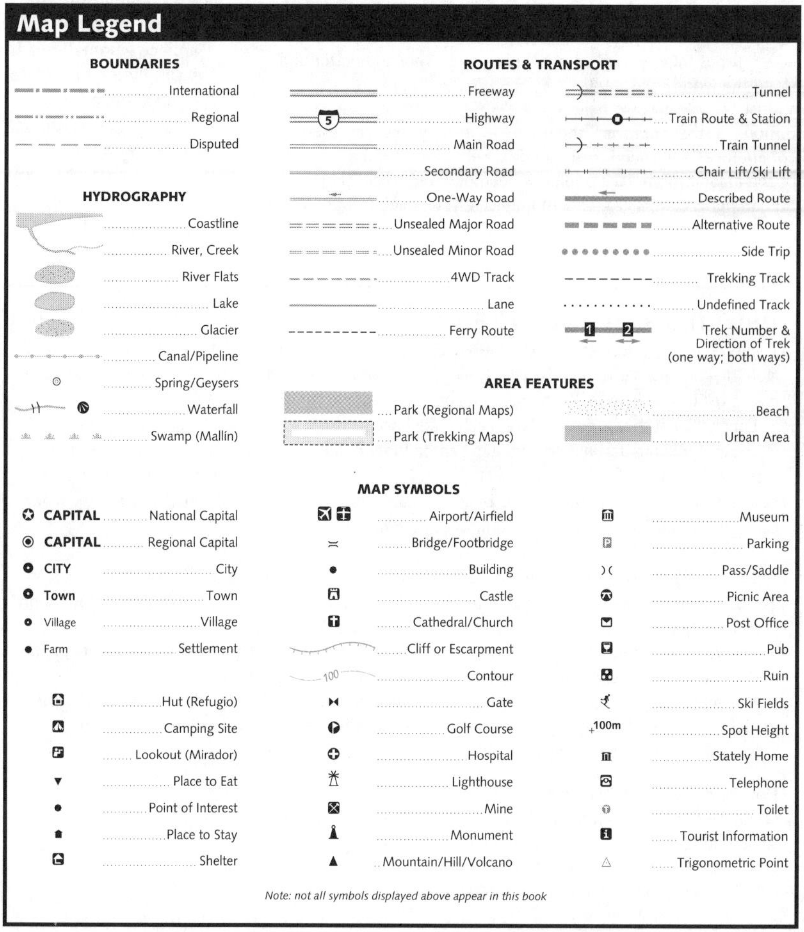

Map Legend

BOUNDARIES

International
Regional
Disputed

HYDROGRAPHY

Coastline
River, Creek
River Flats
Lake
Glacier
Canal/Pipeline
Spring/Geysers
Waterfall
Swamp (Mallin)

○ **CAPITAL** .... National Capital
◉ **CAPITAL** .... Regional Capital
● **CITY** .... City
● **Town** .... Town
● Village .... Village
● Farm .... Settlement

▣ .... Hut (Refugio)
▲ .... Camping Site
▣ .... Lookout (Mirador)
▼ .... Place to Eat
● .... Point of Interest
▲ .... Place to Stay
▣ .... Shelter

ROUTES & TRANSPORT

Freeway
Highway
Main Road
Secondary Road
One-Way Road
Unsealed Major Road
Unsealed Minor Road
4WD Track
Lane
Ferry Route

Tunnel
Train Route & Station
Train Tunnel
Chair Lift/Ski Lift
Described Route
Alternative Route
Side Trip
Trekking Track
Undefined Track
Trek Number & Direction of Trek (one way; both ways)

AREA FEATURES

Park (Regional Maps)
Park (Trekking Maps)
Beach
Urban Area

MAP SYMBOLS

✈ ♁ .... Airport/Airfield
✕ .... Bridge/Footbridge
● .... Building
▣ .... Castle
▣ .... Cathedral/Church
.... Cliff or Escarpment
.... Contour
ᴎ .... Gate
◐ .... Golf Course
⊕ .... Hospital
☆ .... Lighthouse
✕ .... Mine
▲ .... Monument
▲ .... Mountain/Hill/Volcano

▥ .... Museum
▣ .... Parking
)(........... Pass/Saddle
♠ .... Picnic Area
▣ .... Post Office
▣ .... Pub
▣ .... Ruin
⛷ .... Ski Fields
+100m .... Spot Height
▥ .... Stately Home
▣ .... Telephone
⊕ .... Toilet
▣ .... Tourist Information
△ .... Trigonometric Point

Note: not all symbols displayed above appear in this book

Foreword

ABOUT LONELY PLANET GUIDEBOOKS

The story begins with a classic travel adventure: Tony and Maureen Wheeler's 1972 journey across Europe and Asia to Australia. There was no useful information about the overland trail then, so Tony and Maureen published the first Lonely Planet guidebook to meet a growing need.

From a kitchen table, Lonely Planet has grown to become the largest independent travel publisher in the world, with offices in Melbourne (Australia), Oakland (USA), London (UK) and Paris (France).

Today Lonely Planet guidebooks cover the globe. There is an ever-growing list of books and information in a variety of media. Some things haven't changed. The main aim is still to make it possible for adventurous travellers to get out there – to explore and better understand the world.

At Lonely Planet we believe travellers can make a positive contribution to the countries they visit – if they respect their host communities and spend their money wisely. Since 1986 a percentage of the income from each book has been donated to aid projects and human rights campaigns, and, more recently, to wildlife conservation.

> Although inclusion in a guidebook usually implies a recommendation we cannot list every good place. Exclusion does not necessarily imply criticism. In fact there are a number of reasons why we might exclude a place – sometimes it is simply inappropriate to encourage an influx of travellers.

UPDATES & READER FEEDBACK

Things change – prices go up, schedules change, good places go bad and bad places go bankrupt. Nothing stays the same. So, if you find things better or worse, recently opened or long-since closed, please tell us and help make the next edition even more accurate and useful.

Lonely Planet thoroughly updates each guidebook as often as possible – usually every two years, although for some destinations the gap can be longer. Between editions, up-to-date information is available in our free, monthly email bulletin *Comet* (**w** www.lonelyplanet.com/newsletters). You can also check out the *Thorn Tree* bulletin board and *Postcards* section of our website, which carry unverified, but fascinating, reports from travellers.

Tell us about it! We genuinely value your feedback. A well-travelled team at Lonely Planet reads and acknowledges every email and letter we receive and ensures that every morsel of information finds its way to the relevant authors, editors and cartographers.

Everyone who writes to us will find their name listed in the next edition of the appropriate guidebook. The very best contributions will be rewarded with a free guidebook.

We may edit, reproduce and incorporate your comments in Lonely Planet products such as guidebooks, websites and digital products, so let us know if you don't want your comments reproduced or your name acknowledged.

How to contact Lonely Planet:
Online: **e** talk2us@lonelyplanet.com.au, **w** www.lonelyplanet.com
Australia: Locked Bag 1, Footscray, Victoria 3011
UK: 72-82 Rosebery Ave, London EC1R 4RW
USA: 150 Linden St, Oakland, CA 94607

Introduction

Unique in otherwise hot and humid South America, Patagonia is a distinct geographical region that lies completely within the cool temperate zone at the southernmost tip of the continent. The Patagonian Andes are shared between Chile and Argentina, and have an average height and climate similar to that found in New Zealand's Southern Alps or in the Coast Range of British Columbia.

Like many other countries in the New World, both Chile and Argentina have an extensive system of national parks and reserves. Along the 2000km length of the mountain chain dozens of parks and reserves protect areas of superb alpine wilderness.

The Patagonian Andes are increasingly popular among international trekkers, who value their outstanding natural and scenic beauty as well as their safe and hassle-free travelling. This book takes you through the Patagonian Andes' five distinct areas, each described in its own separate chapter.

The most northerly area (and where trekkers often begin their journey) is the Araucanía. Conical snowcapped volcanoes silhouetted by umbrella-like araucaria trees rise up intermittently along the great belt of the Andes. Most Araucanía treks lead around or up volcanoes (ranging from long-extinct to the world's most-active!), past hot springs or thermal fields with fumaroles and even geysers. Chile's Parque Nacional Villarrica is one of this area's major attractions.

The rich, green paradise of the Lakes District is often dubbed the 'Switzerland of South America'. Dozens of large glacial lakes splay out from both sides of the Andes through lush temperate rainforests into rich farmland. Huge ancient redwood-like alerce trees stand in rich temperate rainforest below grassy alpine meadows and craggy mountains. One of the highlights of the Lakes District is Parque Nacional Nahuel Huapi.

Central Patagonia is a remote, sparsely inhabited area of rugged ranges that is less visited due to its relative inaccessibility. This is an intensely glaciated landscape

with icefalls and deep U-shaped valleys fed by roaring glacier-fed rivers. Rare fauna inhabit the valleys. Trekkers generally avoid the notoriously wet central Patagonian coast and concentrate on the (slightly) more sheltered areas farther east, such as Reserva Nacional Cerro Castillo.

Southern Patagonia takes in a swathe of mighty summits from the great lone Monte San Lorenzo to the legendary massifs of Fitz Roy and Paine fringing the southern continental icecap (Hielo Sur). Uncomplicated yet spectacular treks lead to lookouts under and around the classic granite mitres and towers smothered in 'ice mushrooms'.

Tierra del Fuego is a fascinating subantarctic wilderness of jagged ranges crowned by countless hanging glaciers. Literally the world's most southerly, treks follow routes

– many originally formed over eons by wandering guanaco – across low passes that open out at the head of almost every moor-filled valley.

This 3rd edition of *Trekking in the Patagonian Andes* represents a solid update of the information in our last guidebook. It features some 31 detailed treks and outlines numerous other alternatives. New routes have been added, and some removed. We think this provides the best possible balance of the region's wonderful trekking options.

Facts about the Patagonian Andes

HISTORY

20,000 years ago – first humans cross into North America

13,000 years ago – first recorded settlements in southern Chile

8000 years ago – people cross Straits of Magellan to Tierra del Fuego

Before 7th century – early Mapuche culture established in southern Chile

16th century – Mapuche peoples spread eastward into present-day Argentina

1530s – first European expeditions into Patagonia searching for the legendary Ciudad de los Césares

1550s – Jesuit missionaries arrive; many killed by hostile Mapuche

1560s – Pedro de Valdivia conquers Mapuche lands south of Santiago and establishes many settlements

1578 – Sir Francis Drake probably first European to see Cape Horn (Cabo de Hornos)

1616 – Dutch mariner Willem Schouten 'discovers' and names Cape Horn

1619–20 – Ferdinand Magellan arrives seeking a trading route to India, sailing through and naming Straits of Magellan and Tierra del Fuego

1699 – massive Mapuche uprising sacks and burns cities; Spanish survivors flee

1820s – Chile and Argentina fight and win independence from Spain

1833 – naturalist Charles Darwin visits Patagonia in HMS *Beagle;* these journeys contribute to developing his theory of natural selection

1850s – service port of Punta Arenas prospers as the California gold rush and settlement of the North American west coast leads to a shipping boom around Cape Horn

1859–61 – opportunistic Frenchman Orélie-Antoine de Tounens proclaims independent 'Kingdom of the Araucanía and Patagonia' and organises a Mapuche rebellion, but is captured and deported

1865 – Basque, English, German and Welsh settlers establish settlements in northern Patagonia

1870s–1880s – Mapuche and Tehuelche tribes decimated in systematic military campaigns; remnants moved to reservations and settlers take former indigenous lands

1880s – explorers such as Hans Steffen, Luis Riso Patrón, Clemente Onelli and Francisco 'Perito' Moreno make extensive journeys into the Patagonian Cordillera to determine appropriate border between Chile and Argentina

1881 – Chile and Argentina sign treaty establishing common border as 'the highest peaks which divide the waters,' but this wording later causes bitter disputes due to the complex geography of Patagonia

1890s–1919 – many *estancias* (sheep ranches) established, but vast tracts of Patagonia fall under control of large landholders

1900s – work begins at Laguna San Rafael on shipping canal through Península de Taitao, but project abandoned after opening of Panama Canal in 1915

1902 – Chile and Argentina accept King Edward VII's proposed border running between major Patagonian peaks and across numerous 'international lakes'

1908–09 – Swedish botanist Carl Skottsberg travels south from Bariloche along the eastern foothills of the Andes to Tierra del Fuego

1920s – Americans William H Hudson, George G Simpson and Swede Otto Nordenskjöld explore Andes of central Patagonia

1922 – Francisco 'Perito' Moreno granted vast lands around Lago Nahuel Huapi, which he donates to establish Argentina's first national park

1925 – Parque Nacional Villarrica established in the Araucanía as Chile's first national park

1930s–1940s – Alberto Maria De Agostini explores the southern Cordillera, making first ascents of various important summits, and publishes classic mountaineering atlas of the Patagonian Andes

1931 – Club Andino Bariloche (CAB) founded largely by immigrants from the European Alps, soon becomes (and remains) largest mountain club in Latin America

1934 – Servicio (now Administración) de Parques Nacionales established to administer Argentine national parks

1937 – three vast national parks (Lanín, Los Alerces and Los Glaciares) declared in Patagonian Andes of Argentina

1940s–1950s – European immigrants set up mountain clubs (*clubs de montaña*) in some of the larger provincial cities along the Cordillera. Patagonia's highest still-unclimbed peaks including Monte Tronador, Monte Fitz Roy, Monte San Lorenzo, Monte San Valentín and Cerro Paine Grande conquered.

1949 – Cuerpo de Socorro Andino de Chile (Chilean Andean Rescue Corps) founded as Latin America's first mountain search and rescue organisation

1960s – British explorer Eric Shipton climbs in Tierra del Fuego and continental icecaps

1970s – military governments in Chile and Argentina murder thousands of people

1972 – Corporación Nacional Forestal (Conaf) established to administer Chile's national forests, parks and reserves

1982 – Argentina invades Falkland (Malvinas) Islands, but British forces recapture islands and Argentine military government collapses

1988 – Volcán Lonquimay in the Chilean Araucanía erupts spectacularly

1989 – 'Prince' Philippe Boiry of the 'Kingdom of the Araucanía and Patagonia' tours Mapuche and Tehuelche lands

1990s – Douglas Tompkins buys up lands in southern Chile to establish Parque Pumalín as world's first major private 'national' park

1990 – democratic government restored in Chile

1991 – Volcán Hudson in central Patagonia erupts violently, dropping ash over vast areas

1995 – international commission awards Argentina sovereignty to the Lago del Desierto region

1998 – Chile and Argentina sign accord to determine a mutually acceptable border through the Hielo Sur (southern continental icecap)

2003 – Néstor Kirchner, governor of Santa Cruz province, elected as Argentina's first Patagonian president

History of Trekking

In the first decades of the 20th century dedicated *andinistas* (mountaineers), following in the footsteps of explorers like Clemente Onelli and Perito Moreno, began to popularise the activities of climbing and trekking in the Patagonian Andes. European migrants in particular, most notably the Italian priest Alberto De Agostini (see the boxed texts 'Father Alberto De Agostini', and 'De Agostini's First Ascent', p202) and his accomplished contemporary, the Elsace-born Friedrich 'Federico' Reichert, who is also credited with introducing the sport of skiing to the region, organised numerous expeditions that culminated in many important first ascents.

Father Alberto De Agostini

Father Alberto De Agostini (1883–1960) was unquestionably Patagonia's most accomplished and respected early andinist. From his arrival in Punta Arenas as a newly ordained priest in 1910 until he finally retired to his native Turin almost 50 years later, the indefatigable De Agostini explored the Patagonian Andes, climbing, photographing and mapping these wild peaks and ranges. Somehow managing to coordinate his expeditionary activities with his clerical responsibilities, De Agostini made numerous first ascents throughout the Patagonian and Fuegian Andes, including in the areas of Nahuel Huapi, Fitz Roy, Torres del Paine and the Darwin Range (Cordillera Darwin).

In 1930 he accompanied a small group of andinists on a first east-to-west traverse of the vast Hielo Sur, the southern Patagonian icecap. In 1941 De Agostini and two members of the Club Andino Bariloche, Alex Hemmi and Heriberto Schmoll, became the first climbers ever to set foot on the summit of the mighty 3706m Monte San Lorenzo (see the boxed text 'De Agostini's First Ascent', p202). De Agostini was fascinated by the 2404m Monte Sarmiento – the third highest summit of the Fuegian Andes – and had made an early attempt on this majestic 'sphinx of ice' in 1913; in 1956 a climbing party organised by De Agostini finally achieved the first ascent of Monte Sarmiento.

De Agostini was also a skilled photographer whose extensive collection of photographs provides the earliest photographic record of the landscape and indigenous peoples of many parts of Patagonia and Tierra del Fuego. Today, quite a number of geographical features in Patagonia and Tierra del Fuego (including a fjord, a peak and even a national park) have been named in his honour. De Agostini wrote half a dozen books based on his experiences in the southern Cordillera, culminating in his outstanding *Andes Patagónicos*, which was the first serious mountaineering work ever published on the region.

The founding of the Club Andino Bariloche (CAB) in 1931 led to the construction of the region's first *refugios* (huts) and recreational trails in the mountains around Lago Nahuel Huapi. The renowned German-born Otto Meiling and the Austrian-Argentine Heriberto Schmoll were especially active CAB members, becoming the first to reach many summits on both sides of the Cordillera. Other mountain clubs were soon established, including Chile's Federación de Andinismo in 1942. New mountain hotels were built in the Araucanía and Lakes District, such as those around Lago Nahuel Huapi and Lago Villarrica.

In the past few decades the growth of trekking (and related activities) in the Patagonian Andes has brought prosperity to towns (like Pucón, San Martín and El Calafate) that lie close to the popular national parks *(parques nacionales)* or other wilderness areas. Today, 'ecotourism' increasingly benefits struggling agriculturally-based local economies. While national parks continue to develop new infrastructure such as trails and *refugios*, the focus is now on containing the impact of the greater numbers of visitors.

GEOGRAPHY

The Patagonian Andes can be divided into three latitudinally arranged zones, each roughly 600km in length and with a distinct geographical character. The mountains of Tierra del Fuego and its countless islands form an additional zone below the South American mainland.

The Araucanía & Lakes District

After reaching their greatest height of almost 7000m at the latitude of 30°S around Mendoza and Santiago, the character of the Andes changes in a gradual yet dramatic manner: the mountain passes and peaks become steadily lower and the Cordillera narrows. As rainfall increases, the dry, sparse vegetation of the north slowly changes into a fertile and perpetually green landscape of rich farming country and moist forests. Major rivers such as the Río Imperial and the Río Biobío descend from the main divide of the Cordillera through a wide and fertile

Definitions of Patagonia

In its widest definition, Patagonia comprises around one million square kilometres. The Patagonian region is just under one-third of the land area of both Chile and Argentina, but less than 5% of either nation's population actually lives there. Chilean Patagonia is geographically very different from Argentine Patagonia. While the coast of southern Chile is a wild and wet strip of densely forested mountainous country, the greater part of Argentine Patagonia is a broad semiarid plateau out of which rise eroded tablelands (called mesetas). It is only where these 'two Patagonias' meet, namely at the Patagonian Andes, that the area's continuity actually becomes apparent.

In Argentina, Patagonia officially includes all the land south from the Río Colorado (at 36°S). This vast area takes in the Argentine Lakes District in the provinces of Neuquén and Río Negro, as well as the provinces of Chubut and Santa Cruz and the territories of Tierra del Fuego and the Falkland (Malvinas) Islands.

To the west of the Cordillera the situation is less definite. In Chile, only the strip of land extending south from Puerto Montt (which Chilean geographers call the Sur Grande) is normally considered a true part of Patagonia, a definition that excludes the Chilean side of the Araucanía and Lakes District and usually also the island of Chiloé. Even this would come as a surprise to some Chileans, many of whom prefer to use the term Patagonia exclusively for the southern steppes of the Argentine also known colloquially as *la pampa*. However, the Araucanía and Lakes District on either side of the Andes show a very high degree of geographical homogeneity, and 'Patagonia' is used loosely in this book to include all the Chilean territory south of the Río Biobío (at roughly 37°S), in addition to the 'true' Patagonia of the Argentine steppes.

valley, which Chilean geographers call *el valle longitudinal*, before breaking out through the lower Coast Range (Cordillera de la Costa) to meet the Pacific Ocean.

On the western side of the mountains, the landscape is increasingly dominated by intense volcanic activity, and volcanoes are almost always the highest summits. Towering over the lower basalt ranges, their cones are scattered randomly along the line of the main divide between 36°S and 43°S, with one volcano roughly every 30km. The two highest peaks of this area, the extinct volcanoes Lanín (3776m) and Tronador (3460m), lie on the Argentine–Chilean frontier and form part of the Pacific–Atlantic watershed.

The centre of volcanic activity lies at the Andes' western edge, however, and for this reason most of the dormant and active volcanoes are west of the Cordillera in Chile. The perfect cone of Volcán Osorno (2652m) is known as the 'Fuji of the Andes' and is a great favourite among Chilean climbers and skiers. Small and major eruptions are quite common, and the inhabitants of towns and settlements close to volcanoes are continually on the alert. In places, lava flows have dammed rivers to create large new lakes, such as Laguna de la Laja, Lago Pirehueico and Lago Caburgua.

In 1988, Volcán Lonquimay had a minor yet highly spectacular eruption that continued for 13 months, creating the side crater known as Crater Navidad (see the boxed text 'The Christmas Crater', p92). Volcán Villarrica churns out smoke and gases constantly, and has erupted several times in the last generation or so. Literally hundreds of *termas*, or thermal springs, dot the countryside, most still undeveloped.

The southern part of the Araucanía takes in the beautiful Lakes District (known on the Chilean side as the Región de los Lagos, and on the Argentine side as the Corredor de los Lagos). With more than 20 great lakes gouged into the precordilleran landscape during the last ice age, and many hundreds of smaller lakes set higher up among snow-capped peaks, the Lakes District has often been promoted as the 'Switzerland of South America' – a title that very conveniently disregards the complete absence of volcanoes in the Alps.

Fertile volcanic soil and the area's mild and moist climate have made the Lakes District a prime agricultural region. Lush native rainforest still covers the higher ranges and large parts of the coast, but in the Chilean longitudinal valley, situated between the Pacific and the Cordillera, most of the original forested land has been cleared for farming and grazing. The mean level of the tree line is between 1700m and 2000m above sea level, with hardy alpine grasses covering the mountainsides to the permanent snow line some 300m to 400m higher up.

On the Chilean side of the Lakes District, the major lakes are situated mostly in the Andean foothills. Here, even the larger lakes are warm enough for swimming in summer (especially when compared with the chilled waters of the Pacific beaches). Chileans sometimes attribute the relatively warm water of their lakes to subterranean volcanic activity, but lower elevation (generally under 350m) is a more likely cause than thermal heating. The clarity of the water in the Chilean lakes can be surprising, often allowing visibility to depths of 15m or more. This seems to be due to the naturally low levels of nutrients in the water, which hinders the growth of algae.

In the adjacent Argentine Lakes District, the major lakes are deeper and more elevated (usually at least 750m) and, therefore, quite a few degrees colder. The Argentine lakes also tend to take a more classically glacial form, with fjord-like arms stretching westward deep into the Cordillera. Lago Nahuel Huapi is the best example of this.

Virtually the entire Argentine Lakes District lies within two vast national parks, Parque Nacional Lanín and Parque Nacional Nahuel Huapi. These parks straddle the eastern side of the Cordillera and are multi-use areas, with controlled harvesting of timber in certain designated sectors. There are eight or so Andean national parks in the Chilean Lakes District and the Araucanía. These parks are much smaller than those in Argentina, but have complete protection. The largest are Parques Nacionales Vicente Pérez Rosales and Puyehue, two adjoining parks which front Argentina's Parque Nacional Nahuel Huapi in the southern Lakes District. Nearby is another smaller park, Parque Nacional Alerce Andino, on the coast east of Puerto Montt. Chile's other important Lakes District parks are much further to the north. The national parks of Huerquehue and Villarrica are near the tourist town of Pucón, and the national park of Conguillío is east of Temuco. The most northerly area covered by this book, Parque Nacional Laguna del Laja is high up in the mountains just north of the Río Biobío. You'll also find there are large expanses of semiwilderness in the Chilean Lakes District outside the national parks.

Central Patagonia

South of the Chilean city of Puerto Montt at roughly 42°S the long western coastal plain begins to break up. The more or less continuous series of broad longitudinal valleys that further north are so much a characteristic of the Andes' western side, now disappear completely. After dropping briefly below sea level at the narrow straits of the Canal Chacao, the Coast Range continues for about 180km as the backbone of the great island of Chiloé, before suddenly fracturing into a wild maze of narrow channels and islands below 44°S. Known as the Archipiélago de los Chonos after their original inhabitants, these rainy and windswept islands are formed by the crests of the submerged Coast Range.

The islands of the Chonos considerably shelter the shipping lanes to as far south as 47°S, where the twisted-fist shape of the Península de Taitao juts out into the Pacific and blocks any further passage. Here, at the Laguna San Rafael, the Ventisquero San Rafael descends from the northern Patagonian icecap. The Ventisquero San Rafael is the world's 'most equatorial' (ie, closest to the equator) glacier that reaches the sea. At the Península de Taitao the Antarctic, Nazca and South American continental plates converge, making this remote and inaccessible peninsula a pivotal point of tectonic activity. Subaquatic volcanic eruptions occur off the coast, while on the peninsula itself the continental crust is gradually being pushed up and broadened.

Compared with areas of a similar latitude in the Northern Hemisphere, mean annual average temperatures on the coast are not only relatively warm, but also surprisingly constant. July (midwinter) has an average temperature of around 3°C as against the January (midsummer) average of 11°C. These climatic conditions have produced impenetrable temperate rainforests, where in places the continually cool temperatures even prevent fallen trees from rotting for hundreds of years. The coastal soils are leached and poor, and agricultural development is mostly limited to drier areas to the east that are sheltered by the coastal ranges. From about 41°S the main range of the Cordillera is increasingly dominated by hard granitic rock types. There are still isolated centres of intense volcanic activity down through the Patagonian Andes (almost entirely on the Chilean side) as far south as about 46°S, where in August 1991 Volcán Hudson erupted violently.

In Argentina, the central Patagonian Andes more or less correspond to the western strip of Chubut Province. In Chile this zone takes in the northernmost two-thirds of the XI Región, and includes the national parks of Queulat and Isla Magdalena as well as many other large national reserves (reservas nacionales), such as Cerro Castillo, Río Simpson and Lago Jeinimeini. On the Argentine side there are also two national parks, Los Alerces and the smaller Lago Puelo, while the so-called Comarca Andina del Paralelo 42 (or the 'Andean District of the 42nd Parallel') also offers outstanding natural scenery.

Of the four zones discussed here, the Andes of central Patagonia are by far the most thinly settled. Particularly in Argentina, transport and access are still the most difficult factors. Because of its remoteness, undeveloped infrastructure and wet weather, central Patagonia is rather more demanding of trekkers. Yet the greater difficulties involved in visiting the Andes of central Patagonia reflect the region's much wilder nature, and the extra hardship is well worth enduring.

Southern Patagonia

Below 46°S, volcanoes appear only sporadically and the Andes' average height once again increases. The climate becomes steadily more extreme and more heavily influenced by the closer proximity of the sea. Antarctic ocean currents with relatively low salt concentrations (caused by the enormous volumes of fresh water draining into the sea channels from glacier-fed rivers) and average temperatures of around 4°C drift along the coast. Fierce and almost perpetual storms drench and batter the ranges in southwestern Patagonia. Miserable weather is even more common here, and in the few isolated coastal settlements like Puerto Eden (at 49°S on Chile's Isla Wellington) two straight days without rain are quite rare. Annual rainfall in certain areas exceeds 8m, the highest levels of precipitation experienced anywhere outside the earth's tropical zone.

The Andes of southern Patagonia are covered by the most extensive area of glaciers outside the world's polar regions. Situated at an average elevation of around 1500m between 46°S and 51°S, two massive longitudinal sheets of glacial ice, many hundreds of metres thick, smother all but the higher peaks. Mountains within these frozen plateaus appear as rock islands (which mountaineers call nunataks), their summits projecting spectacularly from their white surroundings. Fed by extremely heavy snowfalls, these icecaps are kept from melting by almost continual cloud cover. Glaciologists have calculated that each snowflake that falls on these icecaps is trapped for 300 years or more before being finally released at the termination of a glacier.

The northern icecap is called the Hielo Patagónico (or Continental) Norte, 100km long and comprising almost 4500 sq km. The Hielo Norte is the smaller of the two icecaps and lies completely on Chilean territory. The 4058m Monte San Valentín, generally considered to be the highest peak in Patagonia (although the 4709m Volcán Domuyo, in the far northwest of Argentina's Neuquén Province, has a superior claim to this title), towers from its northeast flank. The largest icecap is the more southerly, the Hielo Patagónico (or Continental) Sur. The Hielo Sur comprises roughly 14,000 sq km and stretches about 320km from north to south. Although most of its mass is in Chile, some parts of the southern icecap's eastern fringe edge over the frontier.

Most of the highest peaks in southern Patagonia are associated with the great icebound ranges around the two main icecaps. It is here that Patagonia's classic peaks of over 3000m are found, and names like Cerro Torre, Monte Fitz Roy and Cerro Paine Grande are known to climbers all over the world. An exception to this is the great lone massif of Monte San Lorenzo (called Monte Cochrane in Chile), whose 3706m granite summit forms the Chile–Argentina border.

On the Andes' western side, glaciers from the inland icecaps slide down to calve in the deep fjords that extend far inland from the Pacific Ocean. To the east, huge glaciers of Alaskan proportions spill off east into enormous lakes fringing the Argentine pampas. Unlike those of the Argentine Lakes District far to the north, these lakes are low-lying, with an average altitude of just 200m above sea level. The most northerly of these is an 'international lake' known as Lago General Carrera on its Chilean side and Lago Buenos Aires on its Argentine side; it's the second largest natural lake in South America. At around 47°S, Lago General Carrera and the adjacent Península de Taitao both form a botanical and climatic division between the more temperate flora zone of central Patagonia and the frigid areas of the far south.

South of the Hielo Sur, the Patagonian Andes rapidly lose height. The higher peaks average little more than 1500m and are entirely within Chilean territory, stranded on offshore islands and peninsulas almost cut off from the mainland by canals and deep sounds channelled out by colossal glaciers during recent ice ages.

Large icecaps cover some of the higher and more exposed ranges, but never reach anything like the proportions of the Hielo Norte and the Hielo Sur. It is at Puerto Natales, on Seno Última Esperanza, that the dry zone of Patagonian steppes first extends westward right to the water line on the Pacific coast. Below the Península Brunswick, the most southerly point on the South American mainland, the Cordilleran islands connect with the intensely glaciated ranges of Tierra del Fuego. Here, on the Fuegian Peninsula, the Darwin Range (Cordillera Darwin) has a number of 2000m peaks that soar above the surrounding wild seas.

In Chile the zone of the southern Patagonian Andes takes in the southern third of the XI Región (chiefly the O'Higgins Province) and the mainland area of the XII Región (Magallanes). On the Argentine side, this zone corresponds fairly closely to the western part of Santa Cruz Province.

Tierra del Fuego

As they near the tip of the South American continent, the Andes swing around into an east–west line. For the first time in its entire length the Cordillera dips completely below sea level into the Straits of Magellan, only to surface again a little further south to meet the great island of Tierra del Fuego.

On Tierra del Fuego the mighty Darwin Range, situated on a great peninsula stretching 250km from west to east, forms the main range of the Andes. This entire Fuegian Peninsula is part of the remote Parque Nacional Alberto De Agostini, a wild area visited only by the occasional mountaineering expedition. The rugged and ice-cloaked peaks of the Chilean Fuegian Andes rise up directly from the icy seas to well over 2000m, sending numerous glaciers back down into deep fjords. Notorious for its poor weather, the Darwin Range can remain clouded in for months – seldom seen even from the passing fishing boats that trawl in the frigid Fuegian canals. To the west and south, many larger and smaller islands surround the Isla Grande, forming an intensely glaciated and storm-battered archipelago.

The Darwin Range peters out at its eastern end about 20km west of the Chile–Argentina frontier. The ranges that continue eastward into Argentine Tierra del Fuego have more modest elevations that rarely exceed 1500m. Although still exposed to winds from the south, the Argentine Fuegian Andes are somewhat sheltered from the wet westerlies. This produces a more moderate climate with lower precipitation levels, yet a decidedly subantarctic climate still prevails. Very small glaciers hang from the higher peaks and the permanent snow line lies at around 800m.

Cape Horn (Cabo de Hornos) is located less than 100km from Tierra del Fuego, and is usually regarded as the most southerly extension of the South American continent. However, although the Cordillera continues as a deep submarine ridge that reaches south as far as the Antarctic Peninsula, the rugged and windswept Staten Island (Isla de los Estados), due east of Tierra del Fuego, is the Andes' true point of southern termination. Geologically, Tierra del Fuego belongs to the Patagonian mainland, and the northern part of the island is essentially a continuation of Patagonia's arid steppes. The elongated form of Lago Fagnano (Kami), a deep glacial lake over 100km long, almost cuts Tierra del Fuego in two and more or less marks the halfway point between the dry flat north and the Fuegian Andes on the island's shattered southern coast.

When its numerous larger and smaller islands are included, over two-thirds of Tierra del Fuego is Chilean territory. Despite this, the Argentine sector has a considerably higher population and is more homogeneously settled. Apart from a few isolated estancias along the coast and south of Lago Blanco, the southern part of Chilean Tierra del Fuego is almost unpopulated and access is difficult.

GEOLOGY

The Patagonian Andes are largely composed of granitic rocks known as batholiths, which were formed over 100 million years ago as deep magma pushed up to the surface (a process known as intrusion). Today, this so-called Patagonian Batholith forms a vast belt of ranges stretching over 1000km, from southern Patagonia to northern central Patagonia. Generally, younger volcanic rocks predominate in the Lakes District and the Araucanía.

The Andes are a relatively young mountain chain, created over the last 70 million

Signs of a Glacial Past

Many of the world's finest treks are through landscapes, which have been – or are being – substantially shaped by glaciers. As a glacier flows downhill its weight of ice and snow creates a distinctive collection of landforms, many of which are preserved once the ice has retreated (as it is doing in most of the world's ranges today) or vanished.

The most obvious is the *U-shaped valley* ❶, gouged out by the glacier as it moves downhill, often with one or more bowl-shaped *cirques* ❷ at its head. Cirques are found along high mountain ridges or at mountain passes or *cols* ❸. Where an alpine glacier – which flows off the upper slopes and ridges of a mountain range – has joined a deeper, more substantial valley glacier, a dramatic *hanging valley* ❹ is often the result. Hanging valleys and cirques commonly shelter hidden alpine lakes or *tarns* ❺. The thin ridge, which separates adjacent glacial valleys, is known as an *arête* ❻.

As a glacier grinds its way forward it usually leaves long, *lateral moraine* ❼ ridges along its course – mounds of debris either deposited along the flanks of the glacier or left by sub-ice streams within its heart (the latter, strictly, an *esker*). At the end – or *snout* – of a glacier is the *terminal moraine* ❽, the point where the giant conveyor belt of ice drops its load of rocks and grit. Both high up in the hanging valleys and in the surrounding valleys and plains, *moraine lakes* ❾ may form behind a dam of glacial rubble.

The plains that surround a glaciated range may feature a confusing variety of moraine ridges, mounds and outwash fans – material left by rivers flowing from the glaciers. Perched here and there may be an *erratic* ❿, a rock carried far from its origin by the moving ice and left stranded when it melted.

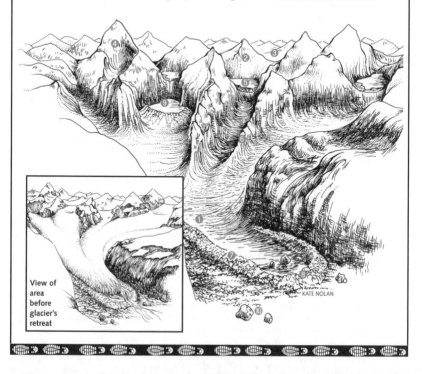

View of area before glacier's retreat

KATE NOLAN

years as the oceanic Nazca plate was slowly pushed under the continental South American plate. In Patagonia, the initial uplifting of the range was accompanied by intense volcanic activity. Clearly, these great volcanic eruptions must have been sudden, widespread and catastrophic for the existing vegetation. Forests of protoaraucaria and other coniferous trees were smothered below thick layers of volcanic ash. This is how the fascinating petrified forests found in the Chubut and Santa Cruz provinces of Argentina were formed. As the Cordillera gradually rose, the passage of moisture from the Pacific was blocked, drying out the land on the Andes' eastern side. Approximately two million years ago the Andes finally reached the elevation they have today. The mountain-building continues, and as a consequence the Andes experience a high level of seismic activity.

Over the last two million years the Cordillera has undergone several periods of intense glaciation during which much of its present topography was formed. At the height of these ice ages the entire Cordillera and a considerable part of the Patagonian lowlands were covered by an ice sheet many hundreds of metres deep. The glaciers released enormous quantities of moraine (debris) which was washed out from the mountains and deposited over the steppes of southern Argentina.

Approximately 14,000 years ago the last (Pleistocene) ice age began to end, and the glaciers that had intermittently covered most of the Andes retreated into the Cordillera. This natural global warming allowed the plants and animals to recolonise large areas previously under ice, and probably facilitated the arrival of the first humans not long afterward.

CLIMATE

The vast, unbroken stretch of ocean to the west and south of South America leaves the Patagonian Andes exposed to the saturated winds that circle the Antarctic land mass. The north–south line of the range forms a formidable barrier to these violent westerlies (known to English speakers as the Roaring Forties and the Furious Fifties), which dump staggering quantities of rain or snow on the ranges of the Patagonian Cordillera.

By Andean standards, the average height of the Patagonian mountains is relatively low, but they capture virtually all the airborne moisture and leave the vast Patagonian plains on the leeward side in a severe rain shadow. Nowhere else on earth do precipitation levels drop off so dramatically over such a short distance. Having left their moisture behind in the Andes, the now dry and cold westerly winds sweep down across eastern Patagonia towards the Atlantic, drying out the already arid steppes even more. The strong maritime influence makes for highly unpredictable weather in the Patagonian Andes. Particularly in spring or early summer, fine weather may deteriorate almost without warning, as violent westerly storms sweep in from the Pacific. During such disturbances snowfalls occur on all but the lowest ranges, even in midsummer.

As a rule, climatic conditions become steadily harsher the further south you go. This is reflected in the upper limit of alpine vegetation and the level of the summer snow line. Although there are major variations depending on many local factors such as exposure and precipitation, both the tree line and summer snow line drop dramatically.

The severe winds for which Patagonia has become notorious arise from strong low-pressure systems over the Argentine steppes. These low-pressure systems build up in summer as a result of the sun's warming effect and constantly draw in masses of moist air from the Pacific. As a general rule, winds become progressively stronger the further south you go, where very strong winds are a major nuisance and a real danger to trekkers and mountaineers in all high or exposed areas. Strong westerly winds are usually at their worst from November to January, but typically continue through to the end of April. Winter is surprisingly wind-free, with long periods of virtual stillness.

In southern Patagonia, where the climate is more heavily influenced by the subantarctic zone, extremely strong and incessant winds tend to blow westerly, but can vary

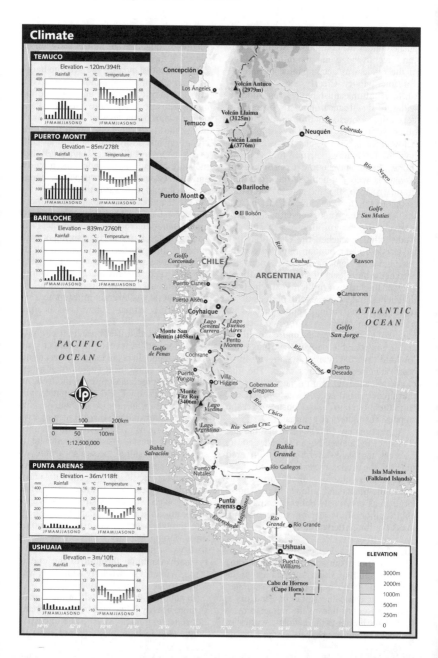

from northwesterly to southerly. West to southwesterly winds generally indicate an approaching cold front and imminent storms. If a new westerly storm is approaching, winds may again begin to turn southwesterly and very cold after only a few days of fine weather. On the other hand, a southerly airstream usually brings fine and stable conditions, although accompanied by very cold weather. Thunderstorms with lightning are unusual in the Araucanía and Lakes District and unheard of in southern Patagonia.

Long wispy streams of high cirrus cloud known as 'mares' tails', and heavy lens-shaped or lenticular clouds called 'hogs' backs' that hover above higher peaks are a possible (but by no means definite) indication of a breakdown in the weather. Local weather is generally more stable in northern Patagonia, with less wind and longer, warmer summers. From the Lakes District down to Aisén, signs of approaching bad weather often include strong, moist and suspiciously warm winds blowing in from the north. In northern areas isolated thunder storms sometimes build up in the mountains during hot summer weather. Storms of this type usually bring heavy rain but pass quickly. Areas of the Cordillera with an easterly aspect (generally on the Argentine side) also tend to have somewhat less severe weather, though frosts are more frequent because of higher valley elevations and a much more typically continental climate.

For more on climate see Weather Information (p52).

Seasons

Patagonia lies completely within the world's southern temperate zone. This means the year is divided into four very distinct seasons, as in North America or Europe. The seasons of the Southern Hemisphere are offset to those in the north by six months, which means that during the southern summer the Northern Hemisphere is experiencing its winter and vice versa.

Because of the peculiarities of the earth's rotation cycle, the seasons in the two halves of the globe do not have an identical pattern of daylight distribution. For example, Punta Arenas, situated between 53°S and 54°S, enjoys more summer daylight but less winter daylight than the English city of Manchester, which is located at precisely the same latitude in the Northern Hemisphere. Patagonia might therefore be expected to experience hotter summers and colder winters than comparable areas of Europe or North America. In high summer (late December) the maximum period of daylight ranges from around 15 hours in the far north at Laguna del Laja to 19 hours in Tierra del Fuego. See also When to Trek (p41).

ECOLOGY & ENVIRONMENT

Although the Patagonian Andes might at times give the impression of being a wholly pristine environment, serious degradation of ecosystems is occurring in many areas. The destruction of forest to create farmland or pastures, especially through fire-clearing (see the boxed text 'Fire in the Patagonian Andes', p26), has severely impacted on native animals such as pudu and *huemul*. Poorly regulated grazing of livestock on public lands (sometimes in national reserves and parks) consumes feed otherwise available to native herbivores. Poaching and illegal killing of animals deemed 'vermin', particularly pumas and foxes, is a serious problem in the Patagonian Andes. Introduced weeds, including blackberries, chrysanthemums, gorse and roses, have become serious pests in many areas, especially where the forest has been cleared or disturbed. Similarly, non-native European hares and rabbits have marginalised the native Patagonian mara to the point of near-extinction in the wild.

Until recently, the Patagonian Andes' rugged terrain itself often provided the best protection, as it discourages development – or even visitation. However, increasing road access is steadily changing this, particularly in Chile's Aisén region and Tierra del Fuego. It can be hard to convince local Patagonians – who live in a landscape formed entirely by the 'destructive' forces of glaciers, earthquakes and volcanoes – that nature may not be as robust as it appears.

Trekkers should always practise 'leave no trace' principles when in the mountains

– for more information see Responsible Trekking (p43).

Conservation

Environmental consciousness is growing in Chile and Argentina, and a number of conservation groups organise campaigns in opposition to over-the-top development or vandalistic forestry practices as well as positive campaigns to save native species.

In early 2003, citizens of the Argentine city of Esquel voted overwhelmingly (albeit in a nonbinding referendum) to block a planned gold mine in the nearby Andean foothills. This Canadian-backed project

would almost certainly pollute water in local rivers.

For more than a decade, conservationists and Mapuche activists – whose people are literally being flooded from their homes – have been waging a losing battle to stop Endesa, Chile's power company, from proceeding with its gigantic hydroelectric project on the Río Biobío. The first major dam is already operational, but if the scheme is eventually completed it will leave a series of six long reservoirs on what was once the southern Andes' most magnificent white-water river.

Chilean conservationists are also deeply concerned about the massive US$2.7 billion Alumysa project planned for Puerto Aisén (near Coyhaique), which involves building hydroelectric dams to power an aluminium smelter. Alumysa's sulphur emissions would produce acid rain – endangering local forests and fisheries – and 660,000 annual tonnes of useless toxic residue that could not be properly disposed.

Organisations dedicated to conservation and education include:

Allianza Aysén Reserva de Vida (W www .noalumysa.cl) Active in Chile's Aisén (Aysén) region.

Comité Nacional Pro Defensa de Fauna y Flora (Codeff, ☎ 02-2747461, W www.codeff.cl) Luis Uribe 2620, Ñuñoa, Santiago. Chile's leading nongovernment conservation organisation. Organises summer schools and tours in natural areas; publishes various (Spanish) periodicals.

Defensores del Bosque Chileno (Defenders of the Chilean Forest, W www.elbosquechileno.cl) Works to protect Chile's remaining native forest areas.

Fundación Vida Silvestre Argentina (☎ 011-4331 3631, fax extension 24, W www.vidasilvestre .org.ar) Defensa 251 Piso 6 'K' (C1065AAC) Buenos Aires. Argentina's leading non-government conservationist organisation; owns nature reserves throughout Argentina.

Patagonia Land Trust (W www.patagonia landtrust.org) Founded by Kristine McDivitt Tompkins and Douglas Tompkins (founders of Parque Pumalín). Raises funds to acquire ecologically significant areas of (especially Argentine) Patagonia.

Fire in the Patagonian Andes

It would be difficult to overstate the devastation that forest fires can cause in the Patagonian Andes. Particularly in the colonisation of southern Chile, fire was frequently used as a means of clearing land for farming and grazing. Often strong winds would whip the flames out of control, resulting in enormous fires that soon became impossible to contain. It was not uncommon for such fires to remain burning throughout the whole summer, laying waste to vast tracts of valuable forest as they spread.

During the worst periods of the 1930s and 1940s smoke and ash from forest fires in Chile's Aisén region were deposited as far away as Argentina's Atlantic coast. Some 20,000 sq km of virgin forest in the southern Andes were destroyed in this way. Even today, forests of dead trees are the enduring landmarks of many regions, and scar entire mountain ranges.

Slow regeneration after forest fires makes soil erosion a severe problem in Patagonia. The destruction of the forest along the middle course of the Río Aisén in Chile caused the river to silt up so badly that the city of Puerto Aisén became useless as a port. Fire is also partly responsible for the alarming decline in numbers of some animal species, most particularly the *huemul* and pudu.

If you must light a campfire, please exercise special care (see Responsible Trekking, p43).

[Continued on page 37]

WATCHING WILDLIFE

FAUNA

South America was once an isolated continent with quite different bird and mammal life, including a diverse range of marsupials (whose last stronghold is now Australia). However, with the creation of a natural land bridge at the Isthmus of Panama some three million years ago, large-scale migration of more sophisticated North American placental mammals occurred. For this reason, South American wildlife is generally more closely related to the fauna of regions further north.

In addition, many newly introduced species of animal, including pigs, horses, hares, rabbits, beavers, exotic red deer and even reindeer now run wild and have altered local ecosystems.

Mammals

Due to their shyness, nocturnal habits and increasing rarity, many of Patagonia's native animals are seldom seen. Sightings tend to be unexpected and fleeting – sometimes you'll have to be content with finding the odd dropping or hoof print. Trekkers are almost assured of seeing guanacos and foxes, however, and have a fair chance of spotting a *coipo*, *huillín*, pudu, tucotuco or vizcacha. If you managed to sight a puma or the rare *huemul* in the wild it would be the highlight of your trip.

Small Mammals

The browny-grey **mouse opossum** (*monito del monte*; *kongoi* in Mapuche) is one of the southern Andes' few surviving marsupials, and the female nurtures her young in a belly-pouch. Its Spanish name, literally 'little monkey of the mountains', alludes to its tree-dwelling lifestyle and highly adapted, monkey-like hands with four fingers and an opposing thumb to facilitate climbing. The mouse opossum feeds on fruit and insects in summer, then in winter goes into a seasonal torpor (hibernation) living on fat stored in its tail.

LPP

Mouse opossum

An aquatic rodent, the **coipo** has prominent, sharp front teeth useful for chomping herbs and roots. It burrows under the banks of lakes and slow-flowing streams (below water level to deter predators) and rarely comes out before dusk. Once trapped almost to extinction for its pelt, the coipo is now protected by law. (Ironically, coipos raised on fur farms in Louisiana, USA, have escaped into the wild, where they are a major pest.)

The omnivorous **Patagonian skunk** (known locally as the *zorrino* or *chingue*) has typical skunk features: a black coat with a white back stripe, a bushy tail and a rounded, pointed snout. Like its cousins, the Patagonian skunk protects itself by ejecting an acidic liquid with a powerfully unpleasant odour from its tail.

Standing just 45cm and weighing only 9kg, the **pudu** is the world's smallest deer. This shy animal lives in the dense rainforest of the Araucanía and Lakes District, where it is occasionally spotted scurrying through the underbrush. The male has pointed, branched horns.

HUGH D'ANDRADE

Pudu

27

WATCHING WILDLIFE

Half a dozen species of **tucotuco**, relatives of the hamster, are found throughout the Patagonian Andes and Tierra del Fuego. The tucotuco has powerful incisor teeth, which it uses to burrow through the earth.

The endangered **mara**, also called the Patagonian hare (*liebre patagónico*), is not a true hare at all but another larger relative of the hamster that inhabits the Patagonian steppes.

The **vizcacha** (also called *chinchillón*, and related to domesticated chinchillas), is a burrowing animal that resembles a bearded squirrel. It weighs under 1kg and has thick soft yellow to greyish fur and a brush-like tail. Vizcachas build extensive burrows in steep, rocky terrain. Older members of the colony watch for approaching predators and let out a shrill warning at the slightest sign of danger. Preferring grass shoots, moss and lichens, the diet of the vizcacha is strictly vegetarian.

Larger Herbivores

The **guanaco** is found mainly on the Patagonian steppes, but in Tierra del Fuego it also inhabits mountain areas. A member of the camel family (and closely related to the alpaca and llama), the guanaco is a sleek but powerful deer with a brownish-white body and long neck. Guanaco herds have been drastically reduced on the steppes, but the animal manages to hold its own due to continuing human persecution of its main predator, the puma.

Guanaco

The **huemul**, an agile deer, was once abundant in the southern Andes, but forest fires and competition from grazing livestock have devastated its numbers, which are now, most optimistically, estimated at 5000. The *huemul* is brown with a black snout, reaches 1.5m in length and stands just over 1m at the shoulder. The bucks discard their two-branched antlers each year after mating.

In Chile, the **Huemul Project** (W *www.salvemosalhuemul.cl*) is underway to save the *huemul* from extinction, and in Argentina it has been declared a 'living natural monument'. Your best chances of seeing *huemul* are in parts of central and southern Patagonia.

Predators

Several small native cats are found in Patagonia. The shy **Geoffroy's cat** (*gato montés*, literally 'mountain cat') is a maximum of 1m from head to tail tip, and lives mainly in areas of dense closed forest, hunting birds, rodents and occasionally even small pudu.

Only slightly larger than your common domesticated pussycat, the **huiña** (*kodkod* in Mapuche) lives in northern Patagonian forests. Well camouflaged with its reddish-yellow fur covered in dark grey spots, the *huiña* preys largely on birds.

The **huillín**, or southern river otter, inhabits inland waterways and coastal areas of Patagonia. Growing to over 1m in length and weighing 10kg at maturity, its long tail and broad, short paws make the *huillín* an excellent swimmer and diver, while its thick, oily fur insulates it from cold water. It burrows into river banks or lake shores, venturing out at dusk in search of crabs and mussels which it locates using its sensitive whiskers.

Huemul

HUGH D'ANDRADE

The small **Azara's fox** or pampas fox (*zorro gris; chilla* in Mapuche) is a greyish animal that prefers open country. It is mainly vegetarian, but supplements its diet with insects and tiny rodents. Azara's fox itself has few natural enemies, apparently due to its highly unpalatable flesh. The larger **Patagonian red fox** (*zorro culpeo* or *zorro colorado*) lives primarily in lightly forested country. It has a reddish-brown fur coat, for which it was trapped extensively. A subspecies, known as the **Fuegian fox** (*zorro fueguino*) is found on Tierra del Fuego.

HUGH D'ANDRADE

Puma

The adaptable **puma** is found anywhere on the Patagonian mainland where there is natural protection from its only enemy – people. The puma's coat is a uniform sandy-brown, except for the dirty-white muzzle, and it reaches over 2m from head to tail in length. The puma typically preys on guanaco or pudu, but because it sometimes also takes livestock it is often (illegally) killed by ranchers. Not surprisingly, the puma is wary of humans, so trekkers will be lucky to glimpse this mainly nocturnal animal. Having said that, the mark of puma paw prints – about the size of a man's fist – are quite often seen in soft earth or snow. Essentially the same animal as the North American cougar (or mountain lion), the puma is not normally considered a danger to humans.

Birds

With almost 5% of the world's bird species, Patagonia is a bird-watcher's paradise. The region's rich feathered fauna includes numerous native species of cormorants, ducks, eagles, gulls, hawks, hummingbirds, parrots, pigeons, woodpeckers and swans – a good many of which are endemic to Patagonia. A powerful pair of binoculars and a good field guide are essential items for the amateur ornithologist.

Forest Birds

The **chucao**, whose onomatopoeic Mapuche name represents its distinctive two-syllable 'chuckling' call, is a tiny orange-red breasted bird that lives and nests in understorey thickets, feeding mainly on insects. The *chucao* is naturally curious, and if you stand still for a moment it will often hop over for a closer look at you.

Several species of hummingbird (*picaflor*) are native to the forests of the southern Andes, where they feed largely on the nectar of flowers. The tiny **green-backed firecrown** (*picaflor chico*) inhabits moist lower-level forests even as far south as Tierra del Fuego, while the **white-sided hillstar** (*picaflor cordillerano*) is found at higher elevations. The metallic greyish-green **giant hummingbird** (*picaflor gigante*) lives in the Araucanía and northern Lakes District.

Pairs of **Magellanic woodpecker** (*carpintero negro*) can frequently be seen (or heard) chipping away energetically at tree trunks and branches in the Andean forests. These birds are pitch-black, except for the male's striking red head.

WATCHING WILDLIFE

Larger Birds

Often seen circling in pairs high in the sky in wild places like Parque Nacional Nahuel Huapi and Isla Navarino, the **Andean condor** has a wingspan of over 2.5m. This otherwise ugly vulture is black except for white feathers on its collar and wing tips. The condor is a voracious carrion eater – a single bird weighing just 8kg can eat a guanaco carcass in a week – and builds its nest in the protection of inaccessible rock ledges.

The **ñandú**, or rhea, is a 1.5m-tall flightless ostrich that roams the Patagonian steppes, laying its eggs (which the male incubates until they hatch) in scrub. Ñandú avoid their numerous enemies by abruptly changing direction as they flee, and trekkers (particularly in the Fitz Roy or Torres del Paine areas) may spot one as it zigzags off.

Birds of Prey

These birds can often be spotted sitting on branches or circling above as they watch for prey – typically other birds and small mammals. Several species of caracara (carancho) are found in the southern Andes, including the **white-throated caracara** (carancho cordillerano), recognisable by its black head and back, white breast and underbelly and yellow beak, and the brownish **crested caracara** (traro), most common in southern Patagonia.

Ñandú

HUGH D'ANDRADE

The **red-backed hawk** (aguilucho) and **rufous-tailed hawk** (aguilucho de cola rojiza) are common in most areas.

Waterbirds

Found throughout Patagonia, the **black-necked ibis** (bandurria) is a large omnivorous bird with a long curved beak and reddish-yellow neck. A gregarious bird, it is often seen in flocks noisily picking over moist pastures for grass seeds, insects, worms, lizards or frogs. The black-necked ibis has a distinctive dull-toned call not unlike a car horn.

The **black-necked swan** (cisne de cuello negro) is a large white swan with the characteristic elongated neck, which is black except for a strident red tip just behind the bird's bill. This adaptable swan inhabits both salt and freshwater areas and has extremely oily feathers, enabling it to remain in the water for several weeks at a time. The goslings can occasionally be seen riding tucked between the wings and body on the backs of adult birds.

Black-necked swan

JUSTINE MURLER

Of the dozen or so native ducks in Patagonia, one of the most interesting is the **flightless steamer duck** (quetru vapor or quetru no volador), so named because it is able to move with surprising speed across water by flapping its small underdeveloped wings in a circular 'paddling' motion. This is a large ground-dwelling bird of a blackish-grey colour, weighing up to 6kg. It mostly inhabits the southern islands or other coastal areas where there are fewer predators.

The remarkable **torrent duck** (pato de torrentes) lives along mountain rivers and has a streamlined body and feet that allows it to dive into rapids for fish and insects without being dragged along by the current.

HUGH D'ANDRADE

Ashy-headed goose

Common to the moist meadows of southern Patagonia is the **upland goose** *(caiquén)*, identifiable by the white and grey feathers of the gander (male) and the coffee-black plumage of the female, and the closely related **ashy-headed goose** *(canquén* in Chile; *cauquén* in Argentina). The ashy-headed goose is a light-brown bird with a short beak that has a sharp point ideal for cutting through grasses.

FLORA

The vegetation of the Patagonian Andes can be divided into four zones – temperate, highland, alpine and continental – determined by distance from the coast and altitude. There is no definite transition point between these zones, but the temperate rainforest and highland forest zones become gradually lower with increasing distance south.

The **temperate** zone is covered in so-called Valdivian rainforest *(bosque valdiviano* or *selva fría)*, made up of mixed evergreen tree species, and occupies all lower areas west of the Cordillera with strong coastal influence (and heavy rainfall). This is the most diverse of the four zones, and includes virtually all the important species. In the Araucanía and Lakes District, temperate rainforest is species-rich and grows from sea level up to about 1400m. In the far south, however, the rainforests are composed of only a few species – dominated by *coigüe de Magallanes* (also called *guindo)* – and only found close to sea level in sheltered locations.

Above the temperate zone is the **highland** zone, which is covered by so-called Magellanic forest *(bosque magellánico)*. Although very attractive, these subalpine forests have a poorer range of species, with deciduous southern beech species (chiefly *lenga*) dominating. Especially in southern Patagonia, where there is little undergrowth, mosses and herbs make an attractive 'park lawn' type landscape.

Above the highland forest is the **alpine** zone, an often narrow, thinly vegetated area extending up as far as the bare rock almost to the permanent snow line. Tundra species, including many alpine wild flowers, are found here.

The highland zone merges with the **semiarid continental** zone on the Patagonian Andes' lower eastern sides. Here, sparse steppe-like

The Gondwana Connection

The flora of Patagonia shows similarities to the vegetation found in other regions of the Southern Hemisphere. This is due to their common geographical past, when the earth's southern landmasses were joined in a single supercontinent called Gondwana. When Gondwana began to split up 100 million years ago, plants were left stranded on each of the newly isolated 'continental islands', and gradually evolved to form separate – but still closely related – species and genera. In particular, visitors from New Zealand and Tasmania will be struck by the close resemblance of some species (such as southern beech) to their own native floras.

vegetation, such as tough, slow-growing tussock grasses known as *coirón* and thorny 'saltbush' plants called *mogotes*, is found. Sporadic clusters of low trees (especially *ñirre*) and *calafate* scrub grow in sheltered places and along the river courses.

Wild Flowers

Although they are generally less spectacular than in comparable areas of the Northern Hemisphere (such as the Alps or the Rocky Mountains), the range of wild flower species that can be found in the Patagonian Andes is arguably more diverse and interesting. The best time to see wild flowers in the Patagonian Andes is December, although there is always something in bloom. Following are just a few of our favourites.

Delightful **añañucas** are found in the volcanic soils of the Araucanía and Lakes District. Growing from an onion-like bulb, these perennials produce large pink or red goblet-shaped flowers at the end of a long succulent stem. *Añañuca* cultivars are widely sold by florists as hippeastrums (its old botanical name) throughout the world.

Possibly also familiar are the flamboyant orange **amancays** (known to gardeners as alstroemerias), which typically grow in drier sunny clearings or along roadsides. *Amancay* means 'eternal love' in the Mapuche language, because according to indigenous folklore it is the reincarnation of a Mapuche girl who sacrificed herself in order to save her lover. Growing on similar sites to the *amancay* is the pink or orange daisy-like **mutisia** *(clavel del campo)* that clings to bushes using leafy tendrils.

Colonising fallen trunks in the moist temperate rainforests of the Araucanía and Lakes District, are the **botellita** (little bottle) and **estrellita** (little star), which both have vine-like creepers that produce red flowers true to their descriptive names.

Another climbing rainforest plant found in the Patagonian Andes is Chile's national flower, the **copihue**, which has beautiful delicate pink flowers with a yellow stamen.

The hardy **ourisia** thrives on waterlogged sites beside streams or lakes, forming delicate, strikingly red flowers which mature into small heavy seeds that sink back into the water.

Mapuche Herbal Medicine

A remarkable variety of wild plants have traditionally been used by the Mapuche for medicinal purposes. An extract from the stems of the giant fern, or *quilquil*, can be used to treat eye problems, while the leaves and pods of the *notro* contain natural agents that alleviate toothache and inflamed glands. *Nalca* roots have a gum high in tannin that acts as a stimulant, and the bark of the *radal* tree is a natural purgative. Native tobacco, or *petrem*, was used for both medicinal and ceremonial purposes – and probably also for the odd recreational puff.

Shrubs

These woody plants grow as heaths, form thickets or stand on slopes and meadows. Following are some of the main species found in Patagonia.

Thickets of thorny **calafate** grow throughout the Patagonian Andes, most commonly in the far south. The *calafate* has attractive bright-yellow flowers that by late February turn into sweet, seedy, purple berries that prompt plenty of Paine trekkers to pause and pick.

The original species of all the world's fuchsia cultivars, **chilco** grows in the cool, humid rainforest, typically by waterfalls or streams. Its distinctive flowers, a major source of nectar for hummingbirds, have bright-red sepals and bluish-purple petals.

The remarkably vigorous **nalca** (also called *pangue* in Mapuche) thrives in wet locations. Reaching up to 3m in a single growing season, it produces an enormous 1m-wide 'elephant ear' leaf, at the end of which are a half-dozen thorny succulent stems that can be eaten (see Wild Food, p45). With the first frosts, the *nalca* dies back to overwinter under a thick insulating mulch of its own dead foliage.

A distant relative of Australia's waratah, the **notro** or Chilean firewheel *(ciruelillo)*, is a large bush that grows on sunny sites, producing attractive red elongated flowers that develop into seed pods among its leathery oval-shaped leaves.

Native bamboo, separate species of which are known as **quila** and **colihue**, grows in all areas covered by temperate rainforest, except for the far south. In tall mature forest, where the understorey is starved of light, *quila* is reduced to a few straggly canes, but as soon as the forest is disturbed – such as by a falling tree – the pale-green canes of this vigorous opportunist spread out horizontally to colonise the opening. *Quila* regrowth is normally the first stage of regeneration after a forest fire or landslide, when it can form impenetrable thickets up to 6m high. The traditional Mapuche 'trumpet' *(trutruca)* is made by hollowing out a thick *colihue* cane. *Colihue* canes are also used for furniture or basket weaving. Also see the boxed text 'The Quila Cycle', (p102).

Trees

The superb forests of the Patagonian Andes are definitely one of the region's most appealing features. With several dozen larger common species, only the most important are listed below.

Southern Beech

Andean-Patagonian vegetation is characterised by the southern beech (genus *Nothofagus*). Seven species are found in the Patagonian Andes, and, although many other tree species may also be present, southern beech forms the basis of the forest in virtually all areas.

Three evergreen species of southern beech known as *coigüe* (*coihue* in Argentina) are mostly found at lower elevations. The vigorous and adaptable common **coigüe** *(coigüe común)* has larger and more serrated leaves and grows (often in a distinct 'stratified' form) to well over 50m, often attaining a truly massive girth.

At least as widespread is **coigüe de Magallanes** (*guindo* in Mapuche, especially in Argentina), which can be identified by its smaller leaves. The distribution of both these *coigüe* species overlaps considerably, and novices may find it difficult to distinguish the common *coigüe* from *coigüe de Magallanes*.

A third species **coigüe de Chiloé** has scaly, almost triangular leaves of a lighter colour. As its name suggests, its distribution is centred on the large island of Chiloé, but *coigüe de Chiloé* can sometimes also be found in the forests on the adjacent mainland.

Of the deciduous species of southern beech, **lenga** is easily the most common, and grows in a variety of forms. Its 3cm-long leaves have neat, rounded double-indentations; in early summer their soft light-green colour gives the tree an 'airy' feel, while in autumn the leaves turn a beautiful golden red. In the mountains of the Araucanía and Lakes District, *lenga* is rarely found below 1000m, but in the far south of Patagonia and Tierra del Fuego *lenga* often grows as low as sea level. At lower altitudes *lenga* grows to be a full-sized tree up to 40m in height, but it also commonly grows right up to the tree line, forming low impenetrable thickets. Under the extreme conditions of altitude, *lenga* takes on an attractive 'bonsai' appearance.

Ñirre (*ñire* in Argentina) is a small southern beech species – found throughout Patagonia – that occupies difficult sites, from dry semisteppe to waterlogged *mallín* (an area periodically inundated, and typically covered by open swamp vegetation) country. Ñirre only occasionally grows large enough to earn the title of a tree proper, when it is easily mistaken for *lenga* – particularly in autumn when its leaves turn the same golden-

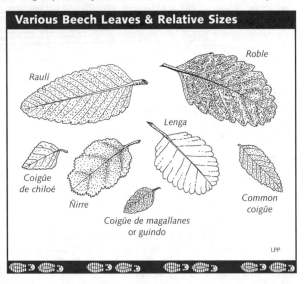

Various Beech Leaves & Relative Sizes

Rauli

Roble

Coigüe de chiloé

Lenga

Ñirre

Coigüe de magallanes or *guindo*

Common coigüe

LPP

red hue; *ñirre* is easily distinguished from *lenga* by its crinkled, irregular leaves and much coarser bark.

Another lovely deciduous southern beech species found only in the forests of the Araucanía and northern Lakes District, **rauli** rarely grows above 1000m. It has leathery, almost oval-shaped leaves of up to 15cm long and reaches a height of up to 40m. *Rauli* prefers the zones of lower temperature, often forming pure forests or growing in loose association with its near relative, the roble. Being relatively fast-growing, it is an ideal species for use in reforestation programs, and gives a much-prized red-grained timber.

Roble (often called *pellín*), has a straight untapered trunk reaching up to 35m. Roble has a similar distribution pattern to the *rauli*, although it is found somewhat farther south, seeming to grow best at an altitude of around 600m. As its Spanish name indicates, roble has distinctive 'oak-like' leaves with serrations.

Other Broadleaf Trees

The **arrayán** thrives in wet coastal rainforests or along lakes and rivers. Covered with smooth almost luminescent cinnamon-red bark that peels off leaving strips of white, the *arrayán* tree typically produces multiple trunks and beautiful, dimpled, twisted branches. In January the tree is covered in white flowers that develop into edible purple berries.

Sacred to the Mapuche people, **canelo** (*fuñe* in Mapuche) is a beautiful rainforest tree belonging to the magnolia family. It grows in moist areas throughout the Patagonian Andes, reaching a height of 30m and a diameter of 1m. *Canelo* has thick, light-green elongated leaves that grow out radially around the branchlets, and in November is covered with fragrant white flowers. The bark of the *canelo* (meaning 'cinnamon') is rich in vitamin C, mineral salts, essential oils and natural antibacterial substances, and at one time it was exported from Chile.

Tepa (a relative of southern Australia's sassafras) is a tall, straight tree with thick, serrated leaves that, when crushed, give off an intense, delicious aroma – somewhere between eau de cologne and fresh basil!

The Araucaria Nut

Rich in complex carbohydrates, the nuts of the araucaria (*piñones* in Spanish; *ngülla* in Mapuche) were mainstay of the Pehuenche (a large tribe of the Mapuche) people. In autumn (March), the Pehuenche would venture high into the mountains to collect the araucaria nuts, which they mostly dried and pounded into a kind of flour that could be used to thicken stews or baked in small bread-like loaves. The flamboyant *cachaña*, or austral conure (parakeet species), lives almost exclusively on araucaria nuts, as do dozens of insect species.

Conifers

The **araucaria** (*pehuén* in Mapuche; 'monkey puzzle' tree in English) typifies the Araucanía and northern Lakes District, where it grows from an altitude of about 1000m right up to the tree line. The araucaria is inextricably linked with the Araucarian (or Pehuenche) people, a large Mapuche tribe whose staple diet was the araucaria nut. The graceful umbrella-like conifer produces these nuts inside a large cone – the size and shape of a pineapple – that drop to the ground when the cone splits open in autumn (March). Individual trees have been measured at 50m in height and 2000 years of age. The Chilean national park authority, Conaf, has adopted the araucaria as its official symbol.

Reminiscent of North American redwoods, the **alerce**, or *lahuén*, is an extremely slow-growing conifer that can – after thousands of years – attain a diameter of 4m and a height of almost 60m. These majestic trees have green scaly branchlet-leaves and a reddish spongy bark. The wood is extremely durable – alerce shingles last up to 100 years – and is in high demand. Although it's illegal to cut down living trees, some clandestine felling does occur. Most important alerce forests are now protected within national parks such as Alerce Andino and Los Alerces.

Several species of **mañío** (often spelt *mañi*), members of the coniferous *Podocarpus* genus, grow in the forests of the Lakes District. *Mañío* is recognisable by its distinctive waxy elongated leaves and unpalatable red fruit. It grows to be a very large, attractive tree with a reddish-brown trunk that is often deeply twisted, although it yields excellent timber.

Alerce

The hardy but slow-growing conifer, **Cordilleran cypress** (*ciprés de la cordillera*), produces male and female flowers on separate flattened, scaly branchlets, and when the trees are in bloom (in October) large puffs of pollen blow around the forests. Preferring a drier 'continental' climate, Cordilleran cypress is most widespread in the Argentine Araucanía and Lakes District, where it forms glorious tall, pure-stand forests fringing the eastern foothills of the Andes. The tree is also present on the Chilean side of the Andes in dry highland areas such as Parque Nacional Laguna del Laja in the northern Araucanía.

The world's most southerly conifer, **Guaitecas cypress** (*ciprés de las Guaitecas*) – in stark contrast to the related Cordilleran species – thrives in waterlogged ground in the intensely wet coastal areas of western Patagonia, most notably in the remote Archipiélago de las Guaitecas. The tree looks similar to, though it is much smaller than, the alerce, but does not have the same reddish bark.

[Continued from page 26]

NATIONAL PARKS & RESERVES

Both Chile and Argentina have a well-organised system of national parks, which are areas that enjoy maximum protection. There are also many other reserves that have somewhat less protection, which in Chile are called national reserves.

Patagonia's first national park – and one of the first in Latin America – originated from a large tract of land around Lago Nahuel Huapi that was given to the Argentine explorer Francisco 'Perito' Moreno for his services to the national boundary commission. Perito Moreno donated this land back to the nation to form today's Parque Nacional Nahuel Huapi, which at 7580 sq km is easily the largest national park on either side of the Andes in northern Patagonia. Soon afterward, the first Chilean national parks were established, with the establishment of Parque Nacional Villarrica in the Araucanía in 1925, and Parque Nacional Vicente Pérez Rosales in the Chilean Lakes District the following year. In 1937, three more vast national parks – Lanín, Los Alerces (including today's separate Lago Puelo) and Los Glaciares – were declared in the Argentine Patagonian Andes.

Since then, a large number of new parks and reserves have been established in the region. The most recent is the 3450-sq-km Parque Pumalín, a unique private 'national' park that consists of lands purchased by Douglas Tompkins and the Conservation Land Trust (against vehement opposition from pro-development politicians). Such nongovernment parks and reserves are a growing trend, as individuals and organisations, such as the Patagonia Land Trust, buy up (often struggling) properties that have ecologically significant features.

There are now many dozens of national parks, provincial parks and national reserves in the greater Patagonian Andes (including 22,000 sq km in the Araucanía and Lakes District) with a combined area of well over 100,000 sq km. By far the largest parks are in Chile, where the roughly 26,000-sq-km Parque Nacional Bernardo O'Higgins covers much of the Hielo Sur and the fjords or glaciated islands along the west coast of southern Patagonia. Two adjoining areas, the 21,500-sq-km Reserva Nacional Las Guaitecas, which takes in the Península de Taitao, and the 17,420-sq-km Parque Nacional Laguna San Rafael, which includes the entire Hielo Norte, are similar in size and character. To the south in Chilean Tierra del Fuego is the 22,000-sq-km Parque Nacional Alberto De Agostini. These stupendously large wilderness areas have savage terrain and weather, however, and are inaccessible by land; there are almost no trails or other infrastructure. Argentina's largest park in southern Patagonia is Parque Nacional Los Glaciares, which abuts the Chilean parks of Bernardo O'Higgins and Torres del Paine.

Park & Reserve Administration

In Chile, national parks, national reserves and forest reserves are all administered by the Corporación Nacional Forestal, or **Conaf** (☎ 02-6966677, fax 6715881; Ⓦ *www.conaf .cl; 5th Floor, Oficina 501, Av Bulnes 285, Santiago)*. In Argentina, national parks are managed by the Administración de Parques Nacionales, or **APN** (☎ 011-4312 0257, 4311 0303; Ⓦ *www.parquesnacionales.gov.ar; Av Santa Fe 690, 1059 Buenos Aires)*. The Conaf and APN rangers *(guardaparques)* work

---

Sendero de Chile

The ambitious Sendero de Chile (Chilean Trail) project envisions a 7500km foot track running the whole length of Chile – from the town of Visviri, on the Chile–Peru border, right down to Cape Horn. Transiting some 17 national parks and 21 national reserves, the route will link the country's most attractive natural and historical sites. Its designers plan to integrate existing trails wherever possible, but major new sections will need to be cut. Currently, only around 100km of the trail are open, but when – or perhaps, if – it is eventually completed the Sendero de Chile will be the world's longest continuous walking track.

For more information, go to Ⓦ www.senderodechile.cl.

with very limited resources and generally do an excellent job.

Conaf and the APN have information centres *(centros de informes)* or ranger stations *(guarderías)* at, or close to, popular parks and reserves. Contact and address details are given in the regional chapters under Gateways, Access Towns or Nearest Towns. Even if you do not speak enough Spanish to converse with staff, it is generally well worth visiting the local information centre or ranger office before you set out on your trek.

Most Argentine, and some Chilean, national parks have restricted areas *(reservas naturales estrictas)* where public access is strictly controlled, and generally allowed only under the supervision of national park personnel. (Also see Permits & Fees, p43.)

POPULATION & PEOPLE
The Argentinians

The Argentinians (who now number some 37 million) are a cultured and sophisticated people largely of European stock. Waves of

The Mapuche

According to their mythology, the Mapuche – whose name in their own language means simply 'people of the land' – were born of a struggle between the ocean and the mountains. This is an unmistakable reference to the Mapuche heartland – southern Chile's longitudinal valley (which they called Lelfun-Mapu) – a region afflicted by repeated earthquakes, tidal waves, volcanic eruptions and floods.

Archaeological evidence suggests that by 1500 years ago the Mapuche already existed in southern Chile as a distinct ethnic group, and by the 16th century their population was probably approaching one million. In pre-Columbian times the Mapuche strongly resisted incorporation into the vast central Andean empire of the Incas (who called them Aukas, hence the term Araucarians), and later waged a relentless guerrilla war against the Spanish invaders. At the time of the arrival of the Spanish the Mapuche nation consisted of various loose tribal groupings, such as the Huilliche (People of the South), Pehuenche (Araucaria Nut-Eating People of the Mountains) and Lafquenche (People of the Coast). Their adoption of the horse in the mid-16th century, however, led to a major expansion of the Mapuche language and culture as they migrated eastward into the northern Patagonian steppes. By the end of the 18th century the Mapuche had largely replaced other (ie, non-Mapuche) indigenous peoples.

The Mapuche traditionally lived in small clustered settlements consisting of *rucas* – oval-shaped huts with a timber or bamboo frame and a thatched roof with smoke holes for simple ventilation. Small scale horticulture, fishing, hunting and the gathering of wild foods – most importantly the nuts of the araucaria tree (or *pehuén*) – kept them well fed and clothed; some Mapuche tribes also practised animal husbandry, herding small flocks of llamas for meat and wool.

The Mapuche were skilled artisans whose handicrafts included pottery, the weaving of plant and animal fibres into cloth, grinding of stone tools and weapons, wood carving and metallurgy – most particularly silverwork. They have long been renowned for their expertise in making silver jewellery. The Mapuche had an intimate knowledge of the native plants, a great many of which had ceremonial or medicinal significance.

In the decentralised Mapuche social structure there was no overall chief. Clan heads *(lonkos)* made everyday decisions and in times of war were collectively responsible for electing military commanders. Originally the Mapuche were polytheistic, believing in a hierarchy of gods and goddesses. The Andes, which they called Pire Mapu (Land of Snows), were the abode of the Pillanes, the spiritual ancestors of all Mapuche tribes. Dreams were held to be the means of communicating with the supernatural, and sorcerers *(calcus)* and shamans *(machis)* – who could be male or female, but who must have suffered a prolonged serious illness – were responsible for the interpretation of dreams. They also diagnosed sicknesses, which they treated with herbal remedies or rituals.

immigrants have given Argentine society a cosmopolitan flavour unique among Latin American nations. Italians immigrants were easily the most numerous, and their influence is found throughout the country. There are also strong and recognisable elements of British, German and Yugoslav influence. Argentinians are outgoing and passionate, with a strong artistic flair. They tend to say what they think with little hesitation, and have a strong sense of identity and national pride.

The Chileans

Bordered by the Atacama Desert in the north and the mighty Cordillera to the east, Chile is geographically cut off from the rest of South America, and Chileans (around 15 million people) sometimes refer to their isolated country as *el último rincón del mundo*, or 'the last corner of the world'. The result of this isolation was that Chile's European and indigenous peoples mixed gradually to create an overwhelmingly mestizo population. The population has been modified relatively little by new arrivals, and the European immigration that shaped Argentina's growth did not occur on anything like the same scale in Chile. Politics notwithstanding, the Chileno is typically a cool-headed and modest person, not given to overly exuberant behaviour. This slightly reserved nature is sometimes considered a sign of their introversion, yet the people of Chile are friendly and hospitable and they possess a sharp and ironic sense of humour.

The Patagonians

Around two million people live in the region of greater Patagonia (including the Chilean Araucanía and Lakes District). The lower average height of the Cordillera in Patagonia has traditionally encouraged movement between the two countries, even in precolonial times. Especially noticeable to the visitor is the high proportion of people in Patagonia with distinctly indigenous features.

For more than a century, Chileans have migrated east to seek work on Argentine *estancias* or as labourers in the towns. A great number of the migrants were Chilotes, the mixed-race inhabitants of the island of Chiloé, who also established settlements along the west Patagonian coast. A large percentage of the inhabitants of certain Argentine provinces are actually Chilean nationals or their children.

SOCIETY & CONDUCT
Traditional Culture

The trans-Andean territory of the Araucanía and Lakes District remains the stronghold of the once mighty Mapuche people. Depending somewhat on definition, the Mapuche today still number around 250,000, most of whom live on the Chilean side of the Cordillera.

Mapuche culture has experienced something of a revival in recent years, with an increase in published literature and even the establishment of pharmacies selling traditional herbal medicines. Some sections of the Mapuche and Tehuelche population have maintained their traditional religious beliefs, although most have (at least nominally) adopted Christianity.

Social Graces

Wearing shorts is fine when you are trekking, but is not the done thing in restaurants or similar venues. While male trekkers take their shirts off in hot weather, public nudity is unacceptable in Chilean and Argentine society. Never skinny-dip (swim nude) unless you are somewhere very remote – not directly accessible even via a foot track. Taking off your shoes in public situations (such as on long-distance bus trips) is frowned on.

Local campers, especially at organised camping grounds, are often more interested in partying than enjoying the scenery – if this bothers you, moving may be a better option than complaining. On the trail, always greet others you meet – a simple *¡hola!* will suffice – and yield to trekkers going uphill. Respect private property, and where routes cross private land be on your best behaviour.

Facts for the Trekker

SUGGESTED ITINERARIES

Unless you arrive very early, trek solidly without rest days and finish your last trek absurdly late, there won't be time to complete all – or even most – of the treks in this guidebook in one summer season. In other words, you will have to plan your trip according to your own preferences – the Table of Treks (p4) gives a basic overview of the alternatives. Remember, bad weather or missing a transport connection may disrupt your itinerary. Don't forget to allow time for some relaxing and sightseeing.

Two Weeks

Even if the extra expense of flying is not an issue, it's probably best to concentrate on one region of either country to avoid losing too much time in transit. Unless you desperately want to visit the Torres del Paine and/or Los Glaciares areas (as indeed many trekkers do), the Chilean Araucanía and/or Lakes District are recommended. The Huerquehue Lakes, Baños de Caulle, Pampa Frutilla and Termas de Callao are ideal treks.

One Month

You'll still have to concentrate on a few areas, and leave the rest for your next trip. Perhaps do routes on both sides of the Araucanía and Lakes District, including in Parque Nacional Nahuel Huapi, or travel south to the Torres del Paine and Fitz Roy areas. It's probably best to avoid less accessible areas like central Patagonia and Isla Navarino.

Two Months

This is probably the minimum period necessary to properly experience the Patagonian Andes, though you'll still have to be fairly disciplined with your time. Consider adding several longer treks like the Lonquimay Circuit, Villarrica Traverse, Nahuel Huapi Traverse, Around Cerro Castillo and the Dientes Circuit.

Highlights

Scenery 'On the Rocks'

Letting your eyes wander across the cracked, crevassed expanse of Glaciar Grey as you trek the Paine Circuit (p223). Speculating about when the next block will crash off the icefalls into Laguna del Tranquilo (p201).

Turning on the Heat

Trekking across a rolling plateau of pumice dunes past puffing fumaroles to bubbling mud pots and gushing geysers near the Baños de Caulle (p126). Standing beside the remarkable steaming Laguna Termal (p75), or just lying back in a hot tub by a rushing stream at the Termas de Callao (p135).

Eating Out

Collecting potfuls of pine nuts that drop from old araucaria trees beside Lago Paimún and boiling them up for a delicious exotic feast as you trek from Termas de Lahuen Co to La Unión (p122). Stopping to snack at *calafate* thickets loaded with sweet tangy berries on the Pingo-Zapata trek (p232).

Watching Wildlife

Sitting quietly under graceful *lengas* while pairs of black Magellanic woodpeckers tap away noisily at the trunks in Parque Nacional Huerquehue (p93). Surprising a pair of *huemul* caught in the act of browsing on alpine herbs on the Laguna Tigre Sur trek (p203). Watching *ñandú* ostriches zigzag across the Patagonian steppes that fringe the soaring Paine Massif in Parque Nacional Torres del Paine (p217).

Land's End

Heaving yourself up the last few hundred paces through scoria and snow to reach the 3776m top-of-the-world summit of Volcán Lanín (p118) – almost 1000m above anything else in sight. Scanning the misty southern horizon toward the legendary islands of Cape Horn from Paso de los Dientes on Isla Navarino (p249).

Four Months

This will give you a full-spectrum Patagonian experience, but since you'll probably arrive in early summer (December) you should pay some attention to snow conditions – which may initially still be a problem on higher routes. You will have enough time to include many treks between Parque Nacional Laguna del Laja and Tierra del Fuego. It will never be long enough, of course, but don't worry – you'll be back.

WHEN TO TREK

Trekking is only possible in the Patagonian Andes for a maximum period of six months – from early November until late April. In colder years, snowfalls may close trails a month earlier or later. Although each month has its own particular charms and drawbacks, for a balance of convenience and weather, February and March are the best two months for a trekking trip to the Patagonian Andes.

The Patagonian summer lasts from early December to late February, and often brings quite hot weather, particularly in the Araucanía and Lakes District. During the busy local holiday season (January to mid-February), transport and accommodation are often heavily booked. On the other hand, tourist services and public transport in some areas start to wind down after the end of February. Another seasonal problem is the *tábanos*, swarms of blood-sucking horseflies that harass trekkers on low-level routes in the Araucanía and Lakes District. *Tábanos* are generally at their worst during January.

The early autumn (fall) period, from March to mid-April, typically brings cooler but more stable weather. The red-gold colours of deciduous native trees make this an especially pleasant time to trek. Toward the middle of May the days become short and temperatures fall steadily, yet conditions are often still suitable for trekking in the Araucanía and Lakes District. Parties undertaking treks at this time should be equipped for possible heavy snowfalls.

WHAT KIND OF TREK?

Trekking in the Patagonian Andes is rather different from trekking in areas such as the Alps or the Himalayas. Most routes go through (semi) wilderness areas in national or provincial parks and reserves where there are no mountain villages and only the occasional remote farm.

Despite a steady improvement in track construction and maintenance in recent years, trails are often unreliably waymarked and poorly routed – often leading directly up the slope rather than ascending in switchbacks. They can be muddy and heavily eroded, especially where used by livestock. Dense vegetation usually makes trekking off trails very difficult below the tree line. Although in some areas there are mountain huts *(refugios)*, it is always advisable – and usually essential – to carry a tent and full trekking gear.

Routes described in this guidebook are suited mainly to self-reliant trekkers.

ORGANISED TREKS

This guidebook aims to give trekkers all the information necessary to undertake treks independently, but those less confident in (unfamiliar) mountain terrain may opt to join an organised trekking tour. An increasing number of local and foreign operators organise guided treks (as well as many other outdoor-adventure activities) in the Patagonian Andes. Some of the best are listed below.

Organised Treks Within Chile & Argentina

Andes Mountain Expediciones (☎ 02-5821122, fax 2341092, ⓦ www.andesmountain.cl) Nuestra Señora del Rosario 1411, Vitacura, Santiago, Chile. This company offers 15-day trips to Torres del Paine and Los Glaciares (US$2300) and 20-day trips to the Chilean Lakes District (US$2950). It also specialises in mountaineering trips.

Anticura Expediciones (☎ 063-212630, ⓦ www.anticura.com) Anfión Muñoz 327, Valdivia, Chile. This group runs three- and four-day trips in the Chilean Lakes District (eg, to Lago Constancia and Volcán Casablanca from around US$300 per person).

Patagonia-Argentina (☎ 011-4815 2952, ⓦ www.patagonia-argentina.com) 956 Libertad, Local 15B, Buenos Aires (1012), Argentina. Patagonia-Argentina organises adventure tours in northern and central Patagonia from US$480.

Patagonia Adventure Trip (☎/fax 011-4345 6375, W www.patagoniaadventuretrip.com) Room 161, 6th Floor, Maipu 42, C1084ABB, Buenos Aires, Argentina. This company runs short trips of up to seven days in Torres del Paine, Los Glaciares and Tierra del Fuego.

Patagonia Guide Service/Salvaje Corazón (☎/fax 067-211488, W www.patagoniaguideservice .com) Casilla 311, Coyhaique, Chile. This company organises trips in central Patagonia from around US$90 per day.

Tromen Expedicions y Aventuras (☎ 011-4328 4875, W www.tromenweb.com.ar) Maipu 216, Buenos Aires, Argentina. This outfit offers 20-day trekking and climbing tours (including ascents of volcanoes Domuyo, Lanín and Villarrica) in the Argentine and Chilean Araucanía.

Trek Operators Abroad

Prices, unless stated, exclude airfares to/from South America.

Australia

Willis's Walkabouts (☎ 08-8985 2134, fax 8985 2355, W www.bushwalkingholidays.com.au) 12 Carrington St, Millner, NT 0810. This company organises excellent six- to eight-week trips to Patagonian Andes.

Canada

World Expeditions (☎ 613-2412700, fax 2414189, W www.worldexpeditions.com) 78 George St, Ottawa, Ontario, K1N 5W1. World Expeditions runs 20-day trips to southern Patagonia (C$4780 including airfares).

Continental Europe

Alpin Travel (☎ 081-7202121, W www.alpin travel.ch) Seestrasse 60, Postfach 14, 8880 Walenstadt, Switzerland. This travel group runs 16-day trekking tours including the Paine Circuit and Fitz Roy area (Sfr2730).

Hauser Exkursionen (☎ 89-2350060, fax 235 00699, W www.hauser-exkursionen.de) Spiegel-strasse 9, D-81241 München, Germany. This company does 22-day trekking trips to the volcanoes of the Chilean Araucanía and Lakes District and of southern Patagonia, Tierra del Fuego and Monte Aconcagua (€3690).

United Kingdom

Andean Trails (☎ 0131-4677086, W www.andean trails.co.uk) The Clockhouse, Bonnington Mill Business Centre, 72 Newhaven Rd, Edinburgh EH6 5QG, Scotland. Andean Trails offers 17- and 20-day tours of southern Patagonia and Chilean Lakes District (around UK£1450).

Andes (☎ 01556-503929, fax 504633, W www .andes.org.uk) 37a St Andrew St, Castle Douglas, Kirkcudbrightshire, DG7 1EN, Scotland. This company runs 21-day trekking trips to southern Patagonia (UK£1595) as well as climbing trips to six volcanoes in the Chilean Araucanía.

Footprint Adventures (☎ 01522-804929, W www .footprint-adventures.co.uk) 5 Malham Dr, Lincoln, LN6 0XD, England. Footprint Adventures offers a variety of four- to 12-day trekking tours of areas including the Chilean Lakes District, southern Patagonia and Tierra del Fuego (UK£400 to UK£1200).

Ramblers Holidays (☎ 01707-331133, W www .ramblersholidays.co.uk) Box 43, Welwyn Garden City, AL8 6PQ, England. Ramblers Holidays offers 20-day tours of southern Chile and Argentina (from around UK£2650 including airfares).

United States

Aventuras Patagonicas (☎ 888-203 9354, fax 303-417 0789, W www.patagonicas.com) PO Box 11389, Jackson Hole, WY 83002. This adventure group does 18-day trekking tours to Torres del Paine and Los Glaciares (US$3300) as well as several other climbing and skiing tours in Patagonia.

Go-Active (☎ 800-462 2848, 510-527 1555, fax 527 1444, W www.backroads.com) 801 Cedar St, Berkeley, CA 94710-1800. Go-Active runs luxury 11-day trips to the Chilean and Argentine Lakes District (from US$3998).

Latin American Escapes (☎ 800-510 5999, W www.latinamericanescapes.com) PMB#421/712 Bancroft Ave, Walnut Creek, CA 94598. This company organises four-day to two-week trips to Torres del Paine and Fitz Roy.

Patagonia Mountain Agency (☎/fax 907-789 1960, W www.mountainagency.com) PO Box 210516, Auke Bay, AK 99821. This agency does two-week trekking tours of southern Patagonia (US$2200).

Southwind Adventures (☎ 800-377 9463, 303-972 0701, fax 972 0708, W www.southwind adventures.com) PO Box 621057, Littleton, CO 80162. Southwind Adventures does trips of Patagonian parks and Tierra del Fuego (17/23 days from US$4155/6245).

Wilderness Travel (☎ 800-368 2794, fax 510-558 2489, W www.wildernesstravel.com) 1102 Ninth St, Berkeley, CA 94710. This group runs trips to Torres del Paine and Glaciar Moreno (15 days from US$3495).

GUIDES & PORTERS

Apart from organised trips run by operators like those listed above, trekkers do not normally use or need guides in the Patagonian Andes (although climbers often engage a mountain guide). The use of porters to carry gear and supplies is virtually unheard of in Patagonia, although some routes (such as multiday horse riding trips outside national parks) can be done with pack animals.

PERMITS & FEES

Some Argentine national parks charge an entry fee of US$4 (valid for one week). In others, such as Parque Nacional Los Glaciares, there is no fee. Entry fees are not normally charged to Argentine provincial parks.

In Chilean national parks and reserves, the fee also ranges from nothing to as much as US$11 in Parque Nacional Torres del Paine – the only national park where foreigners must pay a different (higher) price than Chileans. Officially, trekkers are required to obtain permission – though usually not a permit as such – to hike in all Argentine national parks and in many of those in Chile. In general, the more heavily visited national parks take trekking permits most seriously. Refer to the Permits & Regulations headings in each trek description for more information.

A small (but possibly increasing) number of farm owners within or at the edge of national parks charge a 'toll' to cross through their property, ranging from US$4 to around US$12. Such is the case of Fundo El Caulle (p127), which includes excellent infrastructure for trekkers.

RESPONSIBLE TREKKING

As the wilderness areas of the Patagonian Andes are receiving increasing numbers of visitors, trekkers should aim to leave no trace as they move through the mountains by following the simple rules outlined below.

Rubbish

- If you've carried it in, you can carry it back out – everything, including empty packaging, citrus peel and cigarette butts, can be stowed in a dedicated rubbish bag. Make an effort to pick up rubbish left by others.
- Sanitary napkins, tampons and condoms don't burn or decompose readily, so carry them out, whatever the inconvenience.
- Burying rubbish disturbs soil and ground cover and encourages erosion and weed growth. Buried rubbish takes years to decompose and will probably be dug up by wild animals who may be injured or poisoned by it.

Human Waste Disposal

- If a toilet is provided at a camp site, please use it.
- Where there isn't one, bury your waste. Dig a small hole 15cm deep and at least 30m from any stream, 50m from any paths and 200m from any buildings. Take a lightweight trowel or a large tent peg for the purpose. Cover the waste with a good layer of soil.
- Contamination of water sources by human faeces can lead to the transmission of giardia, a human bacterial parasite.

Camping

- Always seek permission before you camp near a farm or house.
- Use a recognised site rather than create a new one. Keep at least 30m from watercourses and paths. Move on after a night or two.
- Do not dig trenches – choose a site that is naturally well drained.
- Leave your site as you found it – with minimal or no trace of your use.

Washing

- Don't use detergents or toothpaste in or near streams or lakes; even if they are biodegradable they can harm fish and wildlife.
- To wash yourself, use biodegradable soap and a water container at least 50m from the watercourse. Disperse the waste water widely so it filters through the soil before returning to the stream.
- Wash cooking utensils 50m from watercourses using a scourer or gritty sand instead of detergent.

Fires

- Ideally, trekkers should refrain from lighting campfires, which have severely degraded many popular camping areas (and are now banned completely in a growing number of national parks).
- If you must light a fire, use a safe existing fireplace rather than making a new one. Don't surround it with rocks – they're just another visual scar – but clear away all flammable material for at least 2m. Keep the fire small (under 1 sq m) and use a minimum of dead, fallen wood.

- Never leave a fire unattended.
- Never light a campfire in areas with peat soils. Peat largely consists of organic matter that is often quite dry and porous, making it difficult to extinguish once ignited.
- Ensure that the fire is completely extinguished before you leave the site. Spread the embers and drown them with water. Scatter the charcoal and cover the fire site with soil and leaves.

Access

- Many of the treks in this book pass through private property (although this may not always be obvious) where public access is freely permitted. If you are in any doubt, however, ask a local person before entering private property.

ACCOMMODATION

Apart from the seasonal vacation rush from January to mid-February, finding somewhere to stay is usually not too difficult even in out-of-the-way places. In larger towns and tourist centres, there is generally quite a range of accommodation. The local tourist office usually has the most up-to-date list of accommodation alternatives from the more humble *casas de familia* (family houses) to the most expensive hotels.

Camping

Camping is very popular in Chile and Argentina.

Camping Grounds In Argentina especially, organised camping grounds are widespread and generally offer good value. They normally have flush toilets, hot showers and a *quincho* (common shelter for rainy weather). However, camping grounds fill up quickly in the busy summer holiday season and can get noisy. In Argentina they generally charge per person (around US$3), but in Chile charges are often per site (up to US$12).

'Wild' Camping The term 'wild' camping means pitching your tent outside established camping areas or camping grounds. All Argentine and some Chilean national parks have now banned wild camping, and only allow camping at park-designated sites along the trails. During the busy summer

holiday period, when cheap accommodation is scarce, wild camping close to roads and towns is common among local backpackers, though it calls for some discretion – see Responsible Trekking (p43).

Refugios

In certain areas, mountain huts exist for the benefit of trekkers. Called *refugios* ('refuges' in Spanish), some huts are just draughty wooden shacks with a dirt floor. Other *refugios*, such as those in the mountains around San Carlos de Bariloche (commonly known as Bariloche) or in Parque Nacional Torres del Paine, are comparable in standard to mountain huts in New Zealand or Europe, with a fee payable to the resident hutkeeper. (Note that some hostels call themselves *refugio* although they are not really 'huts' at all.)

The better *refugios* offer bunk beds from around US$4 (as on the Nahuel Huapi Traverse) to around US$15 (as on the Paine Circuit), and usually serve meals from around US$3. *Refugios* can quickly become overcrowded in wet weather or during the holiday season, and it is recommended to carry a tent even in areas where there are good *refugios*.

Hostels

Hostels (often called *albergues* in Spanish) offer dormitory accommodation from US$6 per person, which usually includes breakfast. Some hostels also offer cheap individual rooms.

Many hostels are affiliated with Hostelling International (HI) or the loose Chilean Backpackers (**w** www.backpackers-chile.com) network. Some hostels only operate during the busy summer holiday period (particularly January), and may use schools or other public buildings as dorms.

Useful hostel organisations include:

Hostelling International Chile (☎ 02-2333220, fax 2332555, **w** www.hostelling.cl) Av Hernando de Aguirre 201, Oficina 602, Providencia, Santiago

Hostelling International Argentina (☎ 011-4511 8712, fax 4312 0089, **w** www.hostels.org.ar) Florida 835, Piso 3, Oficina 319b, C1005AAQ, Buenos Aires

Casas de Familia & Hospedajes

These usually offer the cheapest rooms available to travellers. A *casa de familia* is a private home that lets out a spare room or two to travellers, sometimes only during busier holiday periods. *Hospedajes* offer similar accommodation, but tend to be more permanent. Both are generally very good value for money. Prices are normally charged per person, ranging from around US$5 to US$8 with breakfast.

Residenciales & Pensiónes

Although they are usually also family-run concerns, *residenciales* and *pensiónes* are more upmarket and (*pensiónes* especially) generally offer better facilities and more privacy. Depending on price, rooms may even have their own bathroom. Prices per person typically start at around US$10 with breakfast.

Hotels & Hostales

In Chile and Argentina, the terms hotel and *hostal* (not to be confused with hostel) are usually used for the most upmarket accommodation, but sometimes quite cheap places also call themselves hotels. 'Real' hotels offer rooms that have at least a bathroom with hot water, and probably a private telephone. In larger towns there are many mid-range hotels, but international-style luxury accommodation is rarely found outside the main cities. Hotels and *hostales* tend to charge upwards of US$20 per person.

FOOD
Local Food

Fish and seafood are the great speciality of Chilean cuisine. Shellfish were first eaten by the Indians of the west Patagonian coast, and today oysters, mussels and clams form the bases of various traditional soups and casseroles. *Curanto*, originally a dish from Chiloé, is a rich potpourri of various kinds of seafood, beef or chicken cooked with vegetables such as pumpkin and potato. A cheap and universal Chilean takeaway food is the *empanada*, a pastry filled with anything from sweetened maize or vegetables to minced meat.

Salmon farming is booming along Chile's southern coast, and salmon is served widely in restaurants. In the Fuegian islands, king crabs, known as *centollas,* are harvested.

Argentine food is typified by meat dishes, especially roast lamb and beef. Argentina is famous for its *asados*, where a whole sheep or calf is grilled on a vertical spit around a large open charcoal fire. Italian-style food is also excellent in Argentina. Pasta and real pizza – Chileans think pizza is a sort of lightly toasted cheesy bread sandwich – are served in restaurants throughout the country.

On the Trek

The longer the trek, the more carefully you should plan your meals. When selecting food, try to balance bulk and weight against nutritional value. The daily weight of food will probably come to at least 700gm per person. Always carry two days' extra rations for unplanned side trips, emergencies or slower-than-expected progress.

Dehydrated foods such as rice and noodles are compact and keep well, but they can take up to 20 minutes to cook. Packet soups are lightweight, tasty and need only a few minutes' cooking time. With potato flakes you just need to add boiling water. See the boxed text 'Trekking Food' (p46) for more recommendations.

Some trekkers make up their own high-energy mix of dried fruit and nuts (known as gorp or scroggin) to be eaten during breaks. It's a good idea to carry some additional fruit and vegetables. Note, however, that it is prohibited to take unprocessed dairy and agricultural products across the border from Argentina into Chile – an important consideration if you intend doing a trek immediately after crossing into Chile.

At *refugios* and popular camp sites, rats and mice will often nibble at unattended food (or anything else vaguely edible). As rodents may carry the hantavirus (see Health & Safety, p67) – and can easily chew through your expensive pack or tent – it is best to store food suspended in a sturdy bag from a ceiling beam or tree branch.

Cooking Fire is neither a reliable nor environmentally friendly means of cooking in the wild. For this reason all trekkers should carry a stove – see Stove (p57). Choosing foods that cook quickly will save fuel.

Trekking Food

Cheese *(queso)* Excellent in Argentina; try the delicious *pepato*

Condensed milk *(dulce de leche* or *manjar)* Caramelised condensed milk eaten as a spread for bread and cakes

Dried fruits *(frutas secas)*

Dulce de batata & dulce de membrillo A semisolid dessert made from sweet potato and quince, respectively

Fruitcake *(pastel de pascua)* Full of calories and if packed carefully won't crumble too much; just the thing for a sunny southern Christmas day

Home-made chocolates Especially good in San Carlos de Bariloche, San Martín de los Andes, Calafate and other towns in southern Argentina

Instant cereals containing dextrine *(cereales dextrinados instantáneos)* These are nutritious, lightweight, easy to prepare and taste surprisingly good. One local brand is Blevit.

Muesli A nourishing mixture of grains that requires no cooking

Mushrooms *(callampas)* Dehydrated mushrooms available in small packets

Mussels *(cholgas)* Available dried at markets in Chile

Packet soups Try interesting flavours like *chochlo* (corn), *marisco* (seafood) and *lenteja* (lentils)

Pasta and spaghetti *(fideos)* A wide range is available in Argentina

Porridge *(harina tostada)* Toasted wheat flour mixed with milk to form a kind of instant porridge

Walnuts *(nueces)* Especially good in Chile

Wholemeal bread *(pan integral)* Available in larger supermarkets and occasionally health-food stores in most larger centres of Chile and Argentina

Buying Food Try to buy all necessary food (and other supplies) in a larger regional centre, where prices will generally be lower, quality better and range wider. With the exception of certain specialised freeze-dried products, a similar range of food suitable for backpacking is available as in Australasia, Europe or North America.

Although farms near the start of (and sometimes along) many trekking routes sell home-baked bread, cheese or eggs, it is unwise to depend on local food supplies. Trekkers should carry enough food to last the whole trek.

Wild Food Along many trails native and introduced plants provide occasional treats. These wild foods can only supplement your diet, and should not be depended on.

Berries The most common treats are the abundant native berry species. February and March are the best berry producing months. None of the edible-looking fruits that grow in Patagonia are poisonous (although many are unpalatable).

Blackberries Introduced European blackberries (*moras* in Spanish). They grow along trails in the Araucanía and Lakes District, ripening in March.

Calafates Seedy, purple-blue berries that grow on thorny bushes in southern Patagonia and Tierra del Fuego. A traditional folk song claims 'whoever eats the *calafate* comes back to Patagonia for more'.

Chauras Red to white berries that grow on heath-like bushes. *Chauras* are usually at their best when found just above tree line.

Frutilla de Magallanes A red 'strawberry' (but with a more raspberry flavour) found half-buried in moist soil in southern Patagonia and Tierra del Fuego.

Murtas Mildly sweet, bland red berries with a scaly skin. *Murtas* grow in forest clearings in the Araucanía and Lakes District, ripening in March; they are sold at local markets.

Wild strawberries Related to cultivated strawberry, but berries are smaller and less abundant.

Other Wild Foods Several other Patagonian wild foods are interesting – both from a culinary and botanical viewpoint.

Nalca Thick, succulent stems of the *nalca*. It tastes vaguely similar to celery, though sourer, and can be stewed with sugar like rhubarb. The harder skin of soft thorns must be stripped off.

Pan del indio Round, rubbery growths on the trunks and branches of southern beech. They look like champignons and have a musty fungal taste.

Piñones Starchy nuts of the araucaria tree found in the Araucanía and northern Lakes District. They fall in late summer. Roasted or boiled *piñones* taste like a chestnut with a slightly resinous aftertaste.

DRINKS
Alcoholic Drinks

Chile is world renowned for its outstanding wines, particularly the smooth mellow reds. Argentine wines are not bad either, but not quite as good as their trans-Andean counterparts. Bottled beer is sold widely, and has a fuller flavour than the local draft beer (known as *chopp*) available in restaurants.

Nonalcoholic Drinks

Bottles of carbonated mineral water and durable 1L cardboard cartons of fruit juice are cheap liquid refreshments, but are too heavy to be carried for long in your backpack.

On the Trek

Packets of sweet, flavoured drink powders (such as Tang) are available in local supermarkets and make a refreshing source of glucose on the trek. Herbal teas, including the native *boldo* and *manzano*, are available in tea bag form and are ideal for an after-dinner brew. Trekkers are likely to be offered *yerba mate*, a high-caffeine beverage that is a national obsession in Argentina and quite popular in southern Chile.

WOMEN TREKKERS

The culture of machismo can be rather trying at times, especially in Argentina – where men sometimes whistle or make lewd 'compliments' to women walking alone – though it tends not to be truly intimidating.

With the exception of the larger urban centres, Patagonia is at least as safe for women travellers as Europe, North America and Australasia. Although attitudes to women are still not as progressive as those in most Western countries, Chilean and especially Argentine women are independent and self-assertive by Latin American standards. Even on longer routes it's not uncommon for local women (generally in pairs or small groups) to trek unaccompanied by men.

TREKKING WITH CHILDREN

The Patagonian Andes' rugged terrain and weather generally makes these mountains unsuitable for trekking with children under nine years of age. As most overnight treks require packing a full range of camping gear, it is impractical, and at times unsafe, for parents to carry the additional weight of a tired, bored child on their backs.

Overnight trekking with younger children should be limited to shorter-distance routes and day treks. Treks rated easy or easy–moderate, including Termas de Lahuen Co to La Unión, Pampa Frutilla, Laguna Torre and routes in the Lapataia area of Parque Nacional Tierra del Fuego (see Table of Treks, p4) are suitable for children.

Children walk slower and need more frequent rest stops than adults. The distance and duration of the trek you choose should be based on the children's capabilities, rather than your own with a bit taken off.

Remember that children are very sensitive to environmental extremes. This makes them more prone to hypothermia, heatstroke, heat exhaustion and sunburn. It's important to bring a good range of clothing for varying conditions.

Keep in mind that spectacular views and 'interesting' geological formations are usually more of an adult pastime. Carry plenty of food and drinks, including the children's favourites. Children like to carry their own packs and gear – adjustable day-packs are suitable, and half-length sleeping bags (used by mountaineers) are of better quality than most sleeping bags made for kids.

Lonely Planet's *Travel with Children* has lots of practical advice on this subject.

DANGERS & ANNOYANCES

Although you should never get too complacent about security, Chile and Argentina are unquestionably safer places for foreigners than certain countries immediately to their north. Serious incidents such as assaults are rare outside large cities, and almost unheard of in the countryside.

The risk of robbery can be minimised by wearing an inconspicuous money belt under your clothes. In busy places such as bus and train stations, keep cameras and other valuables out of sight and avoid putting your bag down. Don't pack valuables in the top of your pack and use small padlocks to deter petty theft (such as when staying at hostels). On the whole trekkers are an honest and upright bunch, so you're less likely to be a victim of theft or other crime up in the mountains.

MAPS

Mapping in Chile and Argentina is mainly carried out by the military. Both countries have a separate central mapping authority called the Instituto Geográfico Militar (IGM). Almost all other locally produced maps are (to a greater or lesser extent) based on IGM maps of either country.

It is almost impossible to buy IGM topographical maps outside the national capitals, so if you are passing through Buenos Aires or Santiago be sure to buy all maps there. It is, however, possible to order IGM maps either by mail or online, but delivery time within the respective country may take up to two weeks.

Unfortunately maps of large sectors of the southern Cordillera at any useful scale are still not available. Maps of a scale less than 1:100,000 – the next size downward is usually 1:250,000 – are generally unsuitable for accurate ground navigation. In Argentina topographical maps are sometimes only updated every few generations, so some key maps are now woefully out of date.

Small-Scale Maps

Small-scale maps that give an overview of a wide area are very useful for planning your trip. A problem with many such locally produced maps, however, is that they tend to feature only one side of the Andes – a Chilean map will often give poor coverage even to adjacent areas in Argentina, and vice versa.

Both the Chilean IGM and the Argentine IGM (see Large-Scale Maps, p9) produce their own separate 1:250,000 series of maps that cover the entire Patagonian Andes.

The **Chilean JLM Mapas** (☎/fax 02-364808; General de Canto 105, Oficina 1506, Providencia, Santiago) publishes a range of regional maps that cover all of the Patagonian Andes, including the 1:450,000 *Lagos Andinos – Temuco a Bariloche* (the Araucanía), the 1:250,000 *Ruta de los Jesuitas – Puerto Montt a Bariloche* (Lakes District), the 1:1,100,000 *Camino Austral* (central Patagonia) and the 1:1,250,000 *Patagonia Sur – Tierra del Fuego*. The excellent *Turistel Sur* and *Turistel Sur Argentina* tourist guidebooks to southern Chile and southern Argentina are worth buying just for their detailed colour maps.

Large-Scale Maps

Large-scale maps that cover a smaller area in more detail are essential for serious navigation in the back country. Even where navigation is straightforward, a map of the surrounding area will increase your appreciation and enjoyment of the landscape.

Chilean Maps The **Chilean IGM** (☎ 02-4606863, fax 4608294; ⓦ www.igm.cl; Dieciocho 369, Santiago), near Toesca metro station, is open Monday to Friday from 9am to 5.30pm.

The Chilean IGM has divided the country into 12 sections (secciones), or mapping zones, given a letter from A to L. All Chilean treks in this book are within the (southern) mapping zones G to L. The standard IGM series covering southern Chile is scaled at 1:50,000. Generally these are topographically quite accurate, though trekking routes are often not properly indicated. Maps in the 1:50,000 series cost around US$11. Photocopies of out-of-print maps are available the next working day for the same price.

At the IGM sales office (salón de ventas) folders of maps can be viewed freely. To order, quote the map's name, number and mapping zone (eg, *Volcán Puyehue*, No 27, Sección H). All maps can be ordered online from the Chilean IGM website.

In some areas, most notably the Chilean Araucanía, **Conaf** (☎ 02-6966677, fax 671 5881; W www.conaf.cl; 5th Floor, Oficina 501, Av Bulnes 285, Santiago) has produced excellent colour maps of many popular national parks and reserves, including Reserva Nacional Malalcahuello-Nalcas and Parque Nacional Nahuel Buta, at scales between 1:35,000 and 1:110,000. These are available free (after you have paid the park or reserve entry fee), and are accurate enough for navigation.

Argentine Maps The **Argentine IGM** (W www.geoargentina.com.ar; Av Cabildo 381; (1426) Buenos Aires) is open Monday to Friday from 8am to 1pm.

The 1:100,000 map series covers the Patagonian Andes of Argentina. Unfortunately, many maps are hopelessly out of date and show topographical information poorly, especially in the important provinces of Río Negro and Neuquén. The 1:100,000 maps cost around US$8 per map. Colour photocopies of out-of-print maps are available while you wait for US$15 (US$5 in black and white).

To buy Argentine IGM maps, first view and order them at the adjacent map library (mapoteca), then pay when you pick them up at the sales counter. In theory, maps can be purchased online, but the Argentine IGM website has had recurring problems in this regard.

Trekking Maps For some of the most popular trekking areas (including the parks of Nahuel Huapi, Los Glaciares and Torres del Paine as well as the Argentine Fuegian Andes), contoured topographic maps produced specifically for trekkers by independent cartographic publishers are available. Many are published by the Buenos Aires–based **Zagier & Urruty** (☎ 011-4572 1050; W www.patagoniashop.net) or **Sendas & Bosques** (☎ 02972-427836; W www.sendasybosques.com.ar) in San Martín de los Andes. Some maps produced by JLM Mapas (see Small-Scale Maps,) include large-scale insets that may also be of use to trekkers.

PLACE NAMES

Much of the Spanish nomenclature in Patagonia is repetitive. The southern Cordillera seems to have an endless number of lakes with names like 'Laguna Verde' or 'Lago Escondido', and rivers called 'Río Blanco' or 'Río Turbio'. Many land features bear the names of battles or heroes from the wars of independence, such as Cordón Chacabuco, Lago O'Higgins and Cerro San Martín.

Nomenclature often shows indigenous origins, particularly in the Araucanía and Lakes District, where place names are largely based on local Mapuche dialects. Some of the more common Spanish and Mapuche words found in place names are listed in the Language section (p273). See also the Glossary (p280) for an explanation of various common terms used in the route descriptions.

USEFUL ORGANISATIONS

The following organisations may be of help or interest to trekkers in the southern Andes.

Mountain Clubs

Provincial centres, particularly in Argentina, often have some kind of mountain club. Usually calling themselves *club andino* or *club de montaña*, these local mountain clubs tend to be small and have informal arrangements (in some cases they are centred around just a few enthusiasts). Mountain clubs that can give advice to trekkers are listed in the regional chapters under Gateways or Access Towns.

The three most important mountain clubs in Chile and Argentina are listed below. They publish periodical journals (in Spanish) on recent club activities and exploits, and organise mountaineering courses.

Centro Andino Buenos Aires (☎ 011-4381 1566, W www.caba.org.ar) Rivadavia 1255, Planta Baja, Oficinas 2/3, (1033) Buenos Aires, Argentina
Club Andino Bariloche (☎ 02944-527966, W www.clubandino.com.ar) 20 de Febrero 30, San Carlos de Bariloche, Río Negro, Argentina
Federación de Andinismo de Chile (☎ 02-2220888, fax 6359089; W www.feach.cl) Almirante Simpson 77, Santiago, Chile

Mountain Guides & Schools

The following organisations conduct courses in climbing and arrange mountain guides.

Asociación de Guías de Montaña (☎ 02944-4525248, Ⓦ www.aagm.com.ar) Casilla de Correo 90, (8400) San Carlos de Bariloche, Río Negro, Argentina

Escuela Nacional de Montaña (☎ 02-2220799, Ⓦ www.enam.cl) Almirante Simpson 77, Santiago, Chile. Organises climbing courses in association with the Federación de Andinismo de Chile.

South American Explorers

The South American Explorers *(SAE;* ☎ *607-277-0488;* Ⓦ *www.samexplo.org; 126 Indian Creek Rd, Ithaca, NY 14850, USA)* is a non-profit organisation that supports travellers to South and Central America. The SAE collects member's trip reports and publishes *South American Explorer* (see Magazines, p51), included in membership (US$50 annually). A short online newsletter is available free from the SAE website.

DIGITAL RESOURCES

Ⓦ **www.andeshandbook.cl** Background information on principal peaks and mountain ranges throughout the Chilean Andes.

Ⓦ **www.aventurarse.com** Trip reports and general tips on a wide range of outdoor activities in Chile and Argentina.

Ⓦ **www.bienes.gob.cl** Chile's Ministerio de Bienes Nacionales (Department of National Resources).

Ⓦ **www.conama.cl** Comisión Nacional del Medio Ambiente (National Commission of the Environment), the Chilean government agency.

Ⓦ **www.elexploradorweb.com.ar** Trip reports and general tips on outdoor activities in Argentina.

Ⓦ **www.lonelyplanet.com** Links to the Thorn Tree bulletin board and Postcards, where you can catch up on postings from fellow travellers. Also has travel news and the subwwway section links you to the most useful travel resources elsewhere on the Web.

Ⓦ **www.vientoblanco.cl** Informal Chilean mountain club with trip reports and good links.

BOOKS
Lonely Planet

Chile & Easter Island gives comprehensive practical information for all travellers to Chile, including details on its national parks and reserves. *Argentina, Uruguay & Paraguay* is a great guide providing major coverage of Patagonia. Budget travellers covering a large part of the continent should look for *South America on a shoestring*.

Trekking in the Central Andes is invaluable if you're planning on heading further north to do some trekking. If you're planning your first big trip, you may want to check out *Read This First: Central & South America*. Another indispensable companion is the *Latin American Spanish phrasebook*.

Natural History

In English *Árboles Nativos de Chile*, by Claudio Donoso Zegers, is a handy little field guide (co-published by Conaf) to the native trees of Chile with text in English and Spanish.

Field Guide to the Birds of Chile, by Braulio Araya M and Guillermo Millie H, contains accurate illustrations and some good colour photographs of the 339 species of bird found in Chile.

Fungi of the Andean-Patagonian Forests, by Irma Gamundi and Egon Horak (Vazquez Mazzini Editores, Buenos Aires), is an English-language guide to native fungi of the (Argentine) Patagonian Andes; it includes edible species of mushroom. The book is available locally (US$8).

Natural Patagonia/Patagonia Natural: Argentina & Chile, by Marcelo D Beccaceci, is an outstanding bilingual guide with wonderful photographs and text on Patagonian wildlife and geography.

Patagonia: Natural History, Prehistory and Ethnography, by Colin McEwan et al, contains photos and Victorian accounts of encounters with 'savages', including notes from the young Charles Darwin.

In Spanish *Apuntes Sobre la Fauna Argentina*, by Raul Leonardo Carman, focuses on Argentina's animals and contains excellent colour photos. *Arbustos Nativos de Chile*, by Claudio Donoso Zegers, is a companion to Carman's work. This booklet deals with the species of bushes commonly found throughout Chile.

Aves de Magallanes, by Claudio Venegas, covers birds that are found in Chile's XII Re-gión (Magallanes), but is useful for the Patagonian Andes in general. The colour illustrations are of a high standard.

Guía de Aves de Patagonia & Tierra del Fuego, by Tito Narosky, is a recent field guide that covers birds of (especially Chilean) Patagonia and Tierra del Fuego.

Flora Silvestre de Chile: Zona Araucanía, by Adriana E Hoffmann, is a comprehensive field guide by an eminent Chilean botanist that details 250 trees and shrubs of the Araucanía and Lakes District.

Plantas Altoandinas, by Adriana E Hoffmann et al, is another superb guide to high-alpine flora of the southern Andes.

Classics

Voyage of the Beagle, by Charles Darwin, (first published in 1839) is Darwin's remarkably insightful account of his journey to South America that was crucial to his development of the theory of natural selection.

Idle Days in Patagonia, by William Henry Hudson, was first published in 1917. In his classic book this famous British ornithologist recounts his travels in Patagonia in the first decades of the 20th century. Hudson – that's as in Volcán Hudson – also wrote half a dozen other books about his bouts of birding in (southern) South America.

Attending Marvels: A Patagonian Journal, by George Gaylord Simpson, (first published in 1930) is another title by a well-known US scientist who spent considerable time reconnoitring the Patagonian Andes.

Andes Patagónicos, by Alberto De Agostini, (first published in 1941) was a ground-breaking historical atlas of the central and southern Patagonian Andes by the region's most renowned mountaineer (see the boxed texts 'Father Alberto De Agostini', p16, and 'De Agostini's First Ascent', p202). Editions are available in Spanish and Italian only.

Land of the Tempest, by Eric Shipton, is an account of this famous explorer's expeditions in the southern Andes in the 1960s.

In Patagonia, by Bruce Chatwin, is an engaging introduction to the people who inhabit the vast Patagonian steppes.

Buying Books

Except in the national capitals and some of the larger (especially tourist) centres, bookstores stock a very limited range of titles. (Note that local bookstores, or *librerías*, often specialise as much in stationary and office products as in books – sometimes they sell almost no books at all!) In Chile books are expensive, though of high print quality.

Locally printed books generally have fairly small print runs, and therefore tend go out of stock quite quickly. If you see a title that takes your fancy, buy it right away to avoid later disappointment.

Santiago & Buenos Aires

El Ateneo (☎ 011-4325 6801, Florida 340 • ☎ 011-4813 6052, Santa Fe 1860) Has two bookstore branches in Buenos Aires with a wide selection of titles in English and Spanish.

Feria Chilena del Libro (☎ 02-6327334, W www .feriachilenadellibro.cl) Paseo Huérfanos 623, Santiago

Librería ABC (☎ 011-4314 8106) Córdoba 685, Buenos Aires. Stocks books in English and German.

Librería Manantial (☎ 02-6967463) Plaza de Armas 444, Santiago

Librería Platero (☎ 011-4382 2215, W www .libreriaplatero.com.ar) Talcahuano 485, Buenos Aires. Has a wide range of 'Argentina'.

Librerías Turísticas (☎/fax 011-4963 2866) Paraguay 2457, Buenos Aires. Offers a range of guidebooks and maps.

MAGAZINES

Andes y Montañas (W www.andesymontanas.cl) is a Chilean quarterly focusing mainly on trekking and climbing (Spanish, US$5 per issue).

Outdoors (W www.outdoors.cl) is a bimonthly that covers virtually any kind of outdoor activity on the west side of the Cordillera (Spanish, US$5 per issue).

Aventura Sur (W www.aventurasur.com) is another bimonthly featuring trips in the wilds of Argentina (Spanish, US$4 per issue).

Aire y Sol (W www.aireysolrevista.com.ar) is an Argentine monthly with articles ranging from sport-fishing and hunting to trekking and climbing in the Andes (Spanish, US$3.50 per issue).

South American Explorer is an English-language quarterly published by South American Explorers (p50) with articles on anything generally South American – from scientific research, local culture, history and adventure travel to book reviews (annual subscription US$22).

WEATHER INFORMATION

Weather in the Patagonian Andes is so fickle and localised that official forecasts should only be considered as a general indication of what to expect on your trek.

The best up-to-date weather forecasting for the southern Andes is available (in Spanish) from the **Dirección Meteorológica de Chile** (W *www.meteochile.cl*) and the **Servicio Meteorológico Nacional de Argentina** (W *www.meteofa.mil.ar*). Their websites give a three-day outlook for the administrative regions and provinces of each country (click on 'Prognóstico', then the appropriate region or province) as well as an overview of recent precipitation levels and temperatures around the country (click on 'Climatología').

The Santiago daily *El Mercurio* is available throughout Chile and contains (in the newspaper's 'C' section) a national four-day weather report covering all of the country's 12 regions. The information is presented in enough graphic detail to make the overall weather outlook fairly clear even to people with little knowledge of the Spanish language. Regional newspapers also include local weather forecasts, although they rarely give anything longer than a two-day outlook.

Taking Photos Outdoors

For trekkers, photography can be a vexed issue – all that magnificent scenery but such weight and space restrictions on what photographic equipment you can carry. With a little care and planning it is possible to maximise your chance of taking great photos on the trail.

Light & Filters In fine weather, the best light is early and late in the day. In strong sunlight and in mountain and coastal areas where the light is intense, a polarising filter will improve colour saturation and reduce haze. On overcast days the soft light can be great for shooting wild flowers and running water and an 81A warming filter can be useful. If you use slide film, a graduated filter will help balance unevenly lit landscapes.

Equipment If you need to travel light carry a zoom in the 28mm–70mm range, and if your sole purpose is landscapes consider carrying just a single wide-angle lens (24mm). A tripod is essential for really good images and there are some excellent lightweight models available. Otherwise a trekking pole, pack or even a pile of rocks can be used to improvise.

Camera Care Keep your gear dry – a few zip-lock freezer bags can be used to double wrap camera gear and silica-gel sachets (a drying agent) can be used to suck moisture out of equipment. Sturdy cameras will normally work fine in freezing conditions. Take care when bringing a camera from one temperature extreme to another; if moisture condenses on the camera parts make sure it dries thoroughly before going back into the cold, or mechanisms can freeze up. Standard camera batteries fail very quickly in the cold. Remove them from the camera when it's not in use and keep them under your clothing.

For a thorough grounding on photography on the road, read Lonely Planet's *Travel Photography*, by Richard I'Anson, a full-colour guide for happy-snappers and professional photographers alike. Also highly recommended is the outdoor photography classic *Mountain Light*, by Galen Rowell.

Gareth McCormack

PHOTOGRAPHY

Few trekkers will want to go without a camera. Film is relatively expensive throughout Chile and Argentina, but is available at the duty-free zone *(zona franca)* in Punta Arenas and – for only slightly less than the normal retail price – in the free port of Ushuaia. Most serious outdoor photographers prefer to use slide film. Agfa, Fuji (pronounced 'foo-he' in Spanish) and Kodak slide film is available in larger regional centres. Having film developed is expensive, so it may be best to get it developed in Chile or in your home country (but see Airport & Border Security,). All types of camera batteries can be bought locally.

Film & Equipment Restrictions

The photographing of military and some telecommunications installations is prohibited in Chile and Argentina for security reasons. Of course, the ban only applies from close range.

Photographing People

Especially in the countryside of Chile, it is considered very bad manners to photograph a person without first asking permission. If you are unable to ask, at least be discreet. Usually a person will consent, but may ask you to send them a copy of the photo – so make sure it's a good shot!

Airport & Border Security

Checked baggage on both international and national airlines is now routinely x-rayed in Chile and Argentina. Increasingly, the luggage of bus passengers (less often of private vehicles) arriving in Chile is also scanned as they pass through customs. You should remove all film, both new and exposed, as the intensity of these scans will damage film.

Clothing & Equipment

Your clothing and equipment will be – at times, quite literally – your life support system. Give careful thought to the gear you bring to the Patagonian Andes. For the Spanish names of items, see the Language chapter (p273).

CLOTHING

Making the right choices in clothing will ensure you stay more comfortable on the trek. Modern outdoor garments made from new synthetic fabrics (which are breathable and actively remove perspiration) are better for

Check List

This list is a general guide to necessary equipment and optional extras for your trek. Important considerations for selecting appropriate clothing and equipment are given later.

Clothing
- [ ] boots and spare laces
- [ ] gaiters
- [ ] hat (warm), scarf and gloves
- [ ] jacket (waterproof)
- [ ] overtrousers (waterproof)
- [ ] runners (training shoes), sandals or thongs (flip flops)
- [ ] shorts and trousers or skirt
- [ ] socks and underwear
- [ ] sunhat
- [ ] sweater or fleece jacket
- [ ] thermal underwear
- [ ] T-shirt and shirt (long-sleeved with collar)

Equipment
- [ ] backpack with liner (waterproof)
- [ ] first-aid kit*
- [ ] food and snacks (high-energy), and one day's emergency supplies
- [ ] insect repellent
- [ ] map, compass and guidebook
- [ ] map case or clip-seal plastic bags
- [ ] pocket knife
- [ ] sunglasses
- [ ] sunscreen and lip balm
- [ ] survival bag or blanket
- [ ] toilet paper and trowel
- [ ] torch (flashlight) or headlamp, spare batteries and globe
- [ ] water container
- [ ] whistle (for emergencies)

Overnight Treks
- [ ] cooking, eating and drinking utensils
- [ ] dishwashing items
- [ ] matches, lighter and candle
- [ ] portable stove and fuel
- [ ] sewing/repair kit
- [ ] sleeping bag and bag liner/inner sheet
- [ ] sleeping mat
- [ ] spare cord
- [ ] tent, pegs, poles and guy ropes
- [ ] toiletries
- [ ] towel (small)
- [ ] water purification tablets, iodine or filter

Optional Items
- [ ] altimeter
- [ ] backpack cover (waterproof, slip-on)
- [ ] binoculars
- [ ] camera, film and batteries
- [ ] emergency distress beacon
- [ ] GPS receiver
- [ ] groundsheet (lightweight)
- [ ] mobile phone**
- [ ] notebook and pen/pencil
- [ ] swimming costume
- [ ] travel alarm clock
- [ ] trekking poles

*see the First-Aid Check List p61
**see Mobile Phones p264

trekking than anything made of cotton or wool. Trekkers should practise 'layering' to cope with changing temperatures (see the boxed text 'The Layering Principle',). All trekkers should carry at least one very warm fibre pile or woollen sweater. This will retain much of its insulating ability even if it gets wet. Thermal underwear can be worn in the sleeping bag or in cold conditions. Gloves or mittens are also recommended.

Especially above the tree line in volcanic areas of the Araucanía and the Lakes District, summer can get quite hot and you should wear lighter clothing such as shorts and short-sleeved shirts. Regardless of what the weather conditions are when you set out, you should always carry warm clothing in case the weather suddenly deteriorates.

Wet-Weather Clothing

A waterproof and windproof rain jacket with a hood is an essential piece of clothing that *must* always be carried – even on shorter treks. Trekkers experienced in the Patagonian Andes sometimes prefer totally impervious rubberised rainwear (such as sailing jackets) to 'breathable' garments, because the latter tend to leak after a few hours in heavy rain or as they age. Waterproof ponchos, usually large enough to slip over a pack, are popular with local trekkers. Ponchos don't offer the same protection from the elements as tailored rainwear, however, and tend to catch on branches as you pass. A pair of waterproof overtrousers is also highly recommended, although trekking in wet overtrousers is tiring and water tends to run down into your boots; wearing gaiters helps prevent this.

Footwear

Trekking boots should be robust (for strong ankle support) but have a flexible midsole (rather than a steel shank) with an insole that supports the arch and heel. A waterproof, breathable inner lining will help keep your feet dry, although its effectiveness will gradually decrease as the boots wear. In the boggy terrain of the west Patagonian archipelago and Tierra del Fuego, local trekkers often prefer walking in rubber boots, though it's probably not worth bringing quality rub-

ber boots with you unless you intend doing a lot of trekking in those areas. Impregnate boots with a waterproofing agent to protect the leather and keep your feet dry. It is important to ensure that your boots are properly worn-in before you begin any serious trekking.

Some other lightweight alternative footwear, such as running shoes or a pair of durable sandals, should also be carried – use them when wading streams.

Gaiters

Many of the treks described in this guidebook follow rough routes or partially overgrown foot tracks. Wearing gaiters *(polainas)* to protect your lower legs from vegetation is often advisable, especially if you wear shorts.

The Layering Principle

The layering principle involves adding or peeling off extra clothing as you start to feel cold or hot. This allows the body to maintain a comfortable and constant temperature. Ideally, garments should be made from synthetic fabrics that wick away perspiration. On summer days, the base layer may be all you feel like wearing, though all layers should be carried in your pack.

For the upper body, the base layer is typically a light vest or T-shirt made of synthetic 'thermal' fabric. The second layer is a long-sleeved shirt, and the third layer can be either a synthetic fleece sweater or a 'pile' jacket that continues to wick away moisture. The outer shell consists of a waterproof jacket that also protects against strong cold winds.

For the lower body, shorts will probably be most comfortable in midsummer, though some trekkers prefer long pants (trousers) – light, quick-drying fabric (no more than 30% cotton) is best. As 'long john' type underwear can't be easily removed, it is not recommended except when conditions are expected to remain very cold for the whole day (such as from mid-autumn). Waterproof overpants form the outer layer for the lower body.

Headwear

For maximum protection from that burning Patagonian sun, wear a broad-brimmed hat that keeps the sun off your face, ears and neck. Baseball caps have only a face visor and are *not* recommended – least of all when worn in the 'cool' backward position. As up to 50% of all body heat is lost via the head, a woollen cap (beanie) or balaclava should be worn in cold or windy weather.

EQUIPMENT
Backpack

A pack that weighs on your shoulders as you trek is not just uncomfortable, it may be doing permanent injury to your back. The only good packs are those with robust, easily adjustable waist-belts that can comfortably support the entire weight carried, effectively transferring the load off your shoulders and onto your hips. The shoulder straps should serve only to steady the pack. Convertible packs that can be zipped up to look like hand luggage should be avoided, since they compromise trekking comfort. Carry a spare 'quick-clip' buckle for your pack belt in case the others break; good quality pack buckles are hard to find in this part of the world.

Packs with at least 70L of volume are best. Removable day-packs that attach to the top of the pack are a convenient innovation, but side pockets – which tend to get caught on bushes, bus racks etc – are not recommended. Locally available backpacks are generally good only as replacements for a lost or damaged pack. Despite manufacturers' claims, packs are never completely waterproof, and you should keep the contents dry either by packing everything inside a large, robust internal plastic bag like a garbage bag and/or by using a well-fitting pack cover.

For day treks or side trips, a small day-pack or 'bumbag' should hold all you need, though it's sometimes hard to justify the additional weight and bulk when your main pack can serve the same purpose.

Tent

Good tents are difficult to buy in this part of the world, and (even in the few areas where reliable huts exist) it's always advisable to carry a tent. Serious trekkers should therefore bring a tent with them. A high-quality tent, more than any other piece of equipment, is well worth the extra cost. Remember that your tent may provide the only available shelter in an emergency, so make sure it is absolutely waterproof and able to withstand the windy conditions you will surely encounter.

Modern mountain tents are supported by flexible (usually aluminium) poles, and come in a great variety of compact 'tunnel', lightweight 'single-hoop' or more robust 'dome' designs. Most tents are two-skin (with a waterproof outer fly), and two-person models typically weigh under 3kg. Breathable single-skin tents are lighter but tend to be much more expensive. Vestibules (porches) are useful for stashing gear or for placing a lighted candle, and can be used for cooking in rainy weather.

Of course, a tent also serves as alternative accommodation, making travel more flexible, and even between treks camping out is cheaper and often more pleasant than staying in hotels or *pensiónes*. An inconspicuous colour – a dull fawn or olive blend is best – will allow you to camp more discreetly.

Sleeping Bag & Mat

Sleeping bags should have a rating of at least -10°C. For treks in the far south or early or late in the season anywhere, bags with an even lower rating are preferable. Using a fleece liner or sleeping with additional clothing may be a practical alternative. Note, however, that the temperature ratings for sleeping bags are notoriously unreliable.

Most people prefer down-filled bags, as they are more compact and give better insulation for their weight and bulk. But if your down bag gets wet two days into a six-day trek, you're in for some uncomfortable nights – so make sure it stays dry. Bags with synthetic fill are bulkier and heavier, but have the advantage of retaining insulating properties even when wet. A design that allows good ventilation (such as a zip opening at the foot end) will improve comfort on warmer nights.

For sleeping comfort and insulation, some kind of lightweight mattress is essential. Closed foam cell mats weigh no more than a few hundred grams, but are bulky and awkward to pack. Reasonably priced Chinese versions are locally available. Thermarest-type inflatable mattresses are heavier and much more expensive, but offer greater sleeping comfort and take up less room in the pack. To avoid punctures clear the ground of any sharp matter (such as araucaria needles and *calafate* thorns) before setting up the tent.

Stove

In all trekking areas, fire is neither a reliable nor an environmentally sound means of cooking, and some national parks and reserves have now banned the lighting of campfires altogether. For this reason all trekking parties must carry a camp stove. At least one cooking pot should be carried. Fair quality aluminium and stainless steel utensils are available in both Chile and Argentina, but those who value the strength and light weight of titanium pots should bring their own. A pot-gripper is also a handy device.

It is highly illegal and irresponsible to carry any kind of stove fuel – whether alcohol, petrol or gas canisters – in checked or hand luggage on aircraft. Anyone caught doing so may face criminal charges or forfeit their ticket or both.

Multifuel Stoves The most practical stoves are multifuel stoves – those that can burn a range of fuels like petrol (gasoline), kerosene or white gasoline. However, they tend to be sootier and more prone to blockages due to contaminated fuel. They also require some care and experience to use and maintain.

Petrol (gasoline) is known as *bencina* in Chile and *nafta* in Argentina, while kerosene is called *parafina* or *kerosén*. Locally sold petrol is often full of impurities, so it's best to filter it before use. *Bencina blanca* and *nafta blanca* are the local terms for white gasoline. In Chile, white gasoline is available at every second pharmacy or hardware store, but prices per litre can vary from US$1.25 up to US$3 (when sold in 250ml containers). White gasoline can be harder to find in Ar-

gentina, however, where it is usually sold as industrial solvent *(solvente industrial)*.

Gas Stoves Butane gas stoves use disposable canisters and are popular among local backpackers. They are safe and virtually foolproof, and make a good alternative to the somewhat more hazardous liquid fuel stoves. However, gas stoves won't operate effectively in low temperatures. Gas canisters are often available even in small towns, where they are usually sold in hardware stores.

Alcohol Stoves Alcohol (spirit) burning stoves are slower and less efficient, requiring more fuel to be carried, but are safe, clean and easy to use. Alcohol burning stoves often come as a complete cooking kit, with integrated compact pots, pans and kettles. In both Chile and Argentina, industrial alcohol is widely and cheaply available in larger supermarkets or hardware stores.

Sunglasses

Sunglasses should be carried on all higher treks, particularly early in the season when snowfields may have to be crossed. Sunglasses suited to trekking have preferably yellow- or brown-tinted UV-Polaroid lenses that block out all UV, and most infrared, rays and reduce glare off snow or water surfaces. Mountaineering (glacier) sunglasses are robust but tend to be poorly ventilated and uncomfortable in hot conditions.

Binoculars

Compact lightweight binoculars (8 x 25 or 10 x 25) are a must for bird- and animal-watchers, and are also useful for surveying the route ahead. Inexpensive brands are available locally.

Ice Axe & Crampons

An ice axe and crampons may be necessary if you intend climbing the higher summits (such as Volcán Lanín or Monte Tronador) early in the season, but for general summer and autumn trekking the considerable weight of ice-climbing equipment is hard to justify.

[Continued on page 60]

NAVIGATION EQUIPMENT

Maps & Compass

You should always carry a good map of the area you are trekking in (see Maps, p48), and know how to read it. Before setting off on your trek, ensure that you understand the contours and map symbols, plus the main ridge and river systems in the area. Also familiarise yourself with the true north–south directions and the general direction in which you are heading. On the trail, try to identify major landforms such as mountain ranges and gorges, and locate them on your map to give you a better understanding of the region's geography.

Buy a compass and learn how to use it. The attraction of magnetic north varies in different parts of the world, so compasses need to be balanced accordingly. The entire area of Patagonia is within the South Magnetic Equator (SME) zone, and only compasses balanced for South American countries or southern Africa are suitable. Compasses set for magnetic conditions in Australasia, Europe or North America tend to give inaccurate readings. If buying a compass in South America, check whether the needle dips down at one end when held horizontally, as this indicates improper balancing. Magnetic deviation in the Southern Andes is minimal, ranging from close to 8°E in parts of the northern Araucanía to about 14°E in the islands around Cape Horn. 'Universal' compasses are available that function correctly anywhere in the world.

How to Use a Compass

This is a basic introduction to using a compass and will only be helpful if you are a proficient map reader. For simplicity, it doesn't take magnetic variation into account. Before using a compass we recommend you obtain further instruction.

1. Reading a Compass

Hold the compass flat in the palm of your hand. Rotate the **bezel** so the **red end** of the **needle** points to the **N** on the bezel. The bearing is read from the **dash** under the bezel.

2. Orientating the Map

To orientate the map so that it aligns with the ground, place the compass flat on the map. Rotate the map until the **needle** is parallel with the map's north–south grid lines and the **red end** is pointing to north on the map. Identify features around you by aligning them with labelled features on the map.

3. Taking a Bearing from the Map

Draw a line on the map between your starting point and your destination. Place the edge of the compass on this line with the **direction of travel arrow** pointing towards your destination. Rotate the **bezel** until the **meridian lines** are parallel with the north–south grid lines on the map and the **N** points to north on the map. Read the bearing from the **dash**.

4. Following a Bearing

Rotate the **bezel** so that the intended bearing is in line with the **dash**. Place the compass flat in the palm of your hand and rotate the **base plate** until the **red end** points to **N** on the bezel. The **direction of travel arrow** will now point in the direction you need to trek.

1	Base plate
2	Direction of travel arrow
3	Dash
4	Bezel
5	Meridian lines
6	Needle
7	Red end
8	N (north point)

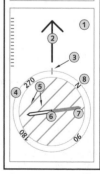

5. Determining Your Bearing

Rotate the **bezel** so the **red end** points to **N**. With the compass flat in your hand, rotate the **base plate** until the **direction of travel arrow** points in the direction in which you have been trekking. Read your bearing from the **dash**.

Global Positioning System (GPS)

Originally developed by the US Department of Defense, the GPS is a network of more than 20 earth-orbiting satellites that continually beam encoded signals back to earth. Small, computer-driven devices (GPS receivers) can decode these signals to give users an extremely accurate reading of their location – to within 30m, anywhere on the planet, at any time of day, in almost any weather. GPS receivers will only work properly in the open. The signals from a crucial satellite may be blocked (or bounce off rock or water) directly below high cliffs, near large bodies of water or in dense tree cover and give inaccurate readings.

Remember that a GPS receiver is of little use without an accurate topographical map. The receiver simply gives your position, which you must then locate on the local map. To assist GPS users with navigation, latitude and longitude are given for points on some treks. Note that some maps in Chile and Argentina show only the metric Universal Transverse Mercator (UTM) grid, in which case you will have to calibrate your GPS receiver – a simple process – so that it gives readings in UTM coordinates.

When buying a GPS receiver, consider its weight, bulk and battery life. Cheaper hand-held GPS receivers cost as little as US$100, while new compact models, such as Casio's Pro Trek costing around US$400, are integrated within a (bulky) wrist watch that allows you to take readings more conveniently. GPS receivers are more vulnerable to breakdowns (including dead batteries) than the humble magnetic compass – a low-tech device that has served navigators faithfully for centuries – so don't rely on them entirely.

Altimeter

Altimeters determine altitude by measuring air pressure. Because pressure is affected by temperature, altimeters are calibrated to take lower temperatures at higher altitudes into account. However, discrepancies can still occur, especially in unsettled weather, so it's wise to take a few precautions when using your altimeter.

1. Reset your altimeter regularly at known elevations such as spot heights and passes. Do not take spot heights from villages where there may be a large difference in elevation from one end of the settlement to another.

2. Use your altimeter in conjunction with other navigation techniques to fix your position. For instance, taking a back bearing to a known peak or river confluence, determining the general direction of the track and obtaining your elevation will usually give you a pretty good fix on your position.

Altimeters are also barometers and are useful for indicating changing weather conditions. If the altimeter shows increasing elevation while you are not climbing, it means the air pressure is dropping and a low-pressure weather system may be approaching.

[Continued from page 57]

Trekking Poles

Trekking poles give stability and absorb jolting on steep descents. They can help prevent knee pain (see Knee Strain, p63), but tightly gripping the poles for long periods tires the hands. Better designs have wrist straps that largely eliminate this problem. Snow baskets can be fitted to some models, allowing their use in snowy conditions.

Buying & Hiring Locally

It can be difficult to buy high-quality trekking equipment at a reasonable price in both Chile and Argentina. This applies particularly to tents, though less to rainwear and thermal garments, which are more widely available. It's therefore advisable to bring all necessary gear with you. Fishing/hunting suppliers normally have a small range of general outdoor gear, which may serve as emergency replacements. Otherwise, check at larger hardware stores or supermarkets.

Specialist outdoors stores can be found in Santiago and Buenos Aires as well as in centres close to popular trekking areas such as Bariloche, El Calafate, San Martín and Puerto Natales – some are included in the regional chapters. Gear available for hire at some places includes tents (US$10), backpack (US$7), stoves (US$5), ice axe (US$5), crampons (US$5). These daily rates are approximate. In Santiago try:

Andes Gear (☎ 02-2457076, W www.andesgear
.cl) Ebro 2794, Las Condes

Lippi (☎ 02-2256803, fax 2231472, W www
.lippi.cl) Av Italia 1586, Ñuñoa. Santiago's best-established outdoor gear outlet.

Patagonia Sport (☎/fax 02-2229140, W www
.patagoniasport.cl) Almirante Simpson 77, Providencia

In Buenos Aires try:

Camping Center (☎ 011-4794 5534, W www
.camping-center.com.ar) Blas Parera 3145 (cnr Panamericana & Pelliza)

Rupal Mountaingear (☎ 011-4702 9017, fax 4702 1445, W www.rupalnet.com) 11 de Septiembre 4555 (1429)

Vagabundo (☎ 011-4790 3469) Blanco Encalada 2679

Health & Safety

There are few real health hazards in southern Chile and Argentina, and standards of hygiene are high. In Patagonia only a handful of diseases and organisms can do you any real harm, and even these are mostly confined to areas outside the mountains themselves. (In the vast South American tropical zone to the north, however, conditions are very different; travellers intending to go to those regions should acquire a good basic knowledge of tropical diseases and conditions.)

PREDEPARTURE PLANNING

For travel in Patagonia only common sense health precautions need to be taken. It's wise to have a thorough medical checkup before you begin your journey. Having a dental checkup is also a good idea.

Health Insurance

Unless your own domestic health insurance covers you, it's essential that your travel insurance includes comprehensive medical coverage. Some policies offer lower and higher medical expenses options, but the higher one is chiefly for countries with very high medical costs, such as the USA. Make sure you have adequate health insurance. See Travel Insurance (p260).

Physical Preparation

Some of the treks in this book are physically demanding and most require a reasonable level of fitness. Even if you're tackling the easy or easy–moderate treks, it pays to be relatively fit, rather than launch straight into them after months of fairly sedentary living. If you're aiming for the demanding treks, fitness is essential.

Unless you're a regular trekker, start your get-fit campaign at least a month before your visit. Take a vigorous trek of about an hour, two or three times per week and gradually extend the duration of your outings as the departure date nears. If you plan to carry a full backpack on any trek, carry a loaded pack on some of your training jaunts.

First-Aid Check List

Following is a list of items you should consider including in your first-aid kit – consult your pharmacist for brands available in your country.

Essentials
- [ ] adhesive tape
- [ ] bandages and safety pins
- [ ] elasticated support bandage – for knees, ankles etc
- [ ] gauze swabs
- [ ] nonadhesive dressings
- [ ] paper stitches
- [ ] scissors (small)
- [ ] sterile alcohol wipes
- [ ] sticking plasters (Band-Aids, blister plasters)
- [ ] thermometer (note that mercury thermometers are prohibited by airlines)
- [ ] tweezers

Medications
- [ ] antibiotics – consider including these if you're travelling well off the beaten track; see your doctor, as they must be prescribed, and carry the prescription on you
- [ ] antidiarrhoea and antinausea drugs
- [ ] antifungal cream or powder – for fungal skin infections and thrush
- [ ] antihistamines – for allergies, eg, hay fever; to ease the itch from insect bites or stings; and to prevent motion sickness
- [ ] antiseptic (such as povidone-iodine) – for cuts and grazes
- [ ] cold and flu tablets, throat lozenges and nasal decongestant
- [ ] painkillers – eg, aspirin or paracetamol (acetaminophen in the USA) – for pain and fever

Miscellaneous
- [ ] calamine lotion, sting relief spray or aloe vera – to ease irritation from sunburn and insect bites or stings
- [ ] eye drops – for washing out dust
- [ ] rehydration mixture – to prevent dehydration, eg, due to severe diarrhoea; particularly important when travelling with children

Immunisations

Chile and Argentina require no immunisations for entry from any country, but if you are visiting neighbouring tropical countries consider prophylaxis against typhoid, malaria and other diseases.

First Aid

Trekkers should know what to do in the event of a serious accident or illness. Consider taking a basic first-aid course (preferably tailored to outdoor recreation) before you go.

Although detailed first-aid instruction is outside the scope of this guidebook, some basic points are listed under Traumatic Injuries (p68). Prevention of accidents and illness is as important – read Safety on the Trek (p70) for more advice. You should also know how to summon help should a major accident or illness befall you or someone with you – see Rescue & Evacuation (p72).

Travel Health Guides

A number of books provide good information on travel health.

Lonely Planet's *Healthy Travel: Central & South America* is the best all-round guide to carry. It's compact, detailed and well-organised. Also published by Lonely Planet is *Travel with Children*. This recently updated book includes advice on travel health for younger children.

Medicine for the Outdoors by Paul S Auerbach is a lay person's reference, giving brief explanations of many medical problems and practical treatment options.

Digital Resources

You can find a number of excellent travel health sites on the Internet. Some recommended sites are:

Centers for Disease Control and Prevention (W www.cdc.gov) US government agencies with a vast amount of relevant information.
International Society for Infectious Diseases (W www.isid.org) World organisation representing numerous agencies and individuals that work in infectious disease research.
Lonely Planet (W www.lonelyplanet.com/sub wwway) Links to the World Health Organization and many other useful sites.

Wilderness Medical Society (W www.wms.org) Nonprofit organisation dedicated to promoting outdoor and emergency knowledge and research.

STAYING HEALTHY
Hygiene

Maintaining a high standard of general hygiene, such as washing your hands frequently, particularly before handling or eating food, will reduce your chances of contracting an illness.

Water

Even in towns and cities in Chile and Argentina, water is rarely a health problem. In remote, lightly visited mountain areas, water taken from springs or small streams close to a spring source is almost certain to be fit for drinking untreated provided there is no other source of contamination upstream – such as a farm or camping area.

However, the high concentration of trekkers in popular national parks such as Torres del Paine and Nahuel Huapi is beginning to seriously affect the quality of water, even in lakes and streams well away from trails. As water from such sources may contain harmful pathogens (especially those causing giardiasis, amoebic dysentery and hydatid cysts), it is wise to sterilise it. Don't collect water downstream from abandoned mines or other human infrastructure such as ski resorts as it may contain toxic impurities that cannot be removed by standard methods of purification. It is advisable not to rely on just one method of water purification.

Water Purification Normally, boiling water is the simplest way of treating it for human consumption. Due to the generally low elevations of treks in the Patagonian Andes, boiling water for five minutes should be long enough to kill all pathogens. If boiling is your main method of purification, carry plenty of stove fuel.

Chemical sterilisation using chlorine drops or tablets (Drinkwell, Puritabs, Steritabs or other brand names) will kill many, but not all, pathogens. Iodine is very effective in purifying water and is available in tablet form (such as Potable Aqua), but follow the directions carefully and remember that too much iodine can be harmful. Adding vitamin C (which is an additive in drink powders such as Tang) to iodised water eliminates the unpleasant taste and colour of iodine, but wait until the iodine has had time to work.

Many trekkers carry a pump-filter (such as those made by Katadyn, MSR or PUR) that are capable of removing water contaminants. Ensure that the unit you buy filters out pathogens like giardia.

Food

Food in Chile and Argentina is (almost) invariably prepared and served to a high sanitary standard. Salad greens and other fresh vegetables are generally safe to eat. On your treks, don't dump food scraps around camp sites as this will attract rodents. See also the section on hantavirus (p67).

Nutrition Poor nutrition and heavy exercise is an unhealthy combination that will eventually compromise your immune system, so it's particularly important that trekkers eat well. As backpacking food tends to be dried or canned – and probably less nutritious than your regular off-the-trail diet – it's a good idea to carry some supplementary fresh fruit and/or vegetables, even on longer treks. Many trekkers also take multivitamin tablets.

Common Ailments

Blisters Trekkers can generally avoid getting blisters by properly wearing in boots before their trip. Ensure your boots fit comfortably, with enough room to move your toes – boots that are too big or too small will cause blisters. Socks should also fit properly. Wear only special padded hiking socks, and check that there are no seams across the widest part of your foot. If you feel a blister coming on, treat it sooner rather then later. Apply either a simple sticking plaster or a 'second skin' plaster made specifically for the treatment of blisters.

Fatigue Trekking accidents tend to occur in the latter part of the day. After many hours'

hard walking, trekkers are often impatient to reach their destination and may fail to notice a steady decline in their concentration and balance. This not only detracts from the appreciation of the trek, but in bad weather or in dangerous terrain it becomes life-threatening. If you're still on the track by midafternoon, make a deliberate effort to slow down and take regular rest stops. Keep your blood-sugar level up by snacking frequently on high-energy foods such as chocolate.

Knee Strain Even in very steep terrain, tracks in the Patagonian Andes often drop directly down a slope rather than moderating the descent with switchbacks – not only causing erosion but knee pain. Long, steep descents put a heavy strain on the knees. Knee strain occurs as the leg bends sharply to compensate for the lower step, transferring weight onto the bent knee and pulling the kneecap backward against the joint – ouch!

Trekkers can reduce knee strain by developing a proper technique of descent; take short, controlled steps with the legs in a slightly bent position, placing your heels on the ground before the rest of the foot. Even on narrow paths, try to descend diagonally down the slope rather than straight downhill. Trekking stocks take much of the load off the legs, and are recommended for trekkers susceptible to knee pain.

Everyday Health

Normal body temperature is up to 37°C (98.6°F); more than 2°C (4°F) higher indicates a high fever. The normal adult pulse rate is 60 to 100 per minute (children 80 to 100, babies 100 to 140). As a general rule the pulse increases about 20 beats per minute for each 1°C (2°F) rise in fever.

Respiration (breathing) rate is also an indicator of illness. Count the number of breaths per minute: between 12 and 20 is normal for adults and older children (up to 30 for younger children, 40 for babies). People with a high fever or serious respiratory illness breathe more quickly than normal. More than 40 shallow breaths a minute may indicate pneumonia.

Warning

Self-diagnosis and treatment can be risky, so you should always seek medical help. An embassy, consulate or five-star hotel can usually recommend a local doctor or clinic. Although we do give drug advice in this section, it is for emergency use only. Correct diagnosis is vital.

Note that we have used generic rather than brand names for drugs throughout this section – check with a pharmacist for locally available brands.

MEDICAL PROBLEMS & TREATMENT
Environmental Hazards

Trekkers are more at risk from environmental hazards than most groups. However, the risk can be significantly reduced by applying common sense – and reading the following sections.

Altitude The potentially fatal condition known as acute mountain sickness (AMS) is caused by the lack of oxygen and the lower atmospheric pressure at high altitudes. This prevents the lungs from passing enough oxygen into the blood.

For trekkers, the generally lower elevation of the Andes in Patagonia virtually eliminates the danger of altitude sickness (known as *soroche* or *puna*). However, the threat of AMS is significantly greater to mountaineers in Patagonia as they tend to get to higher altitudes, ascend more quickly and stay there for longer periods. In the treks featured in this book, altitude sickness is extremely unlikely except perhaps for the Ascent of Volcán Lanín (altitude 3776m).

Lack of oxygen at high altitudes (over 2500m) affects most people to some extent. The effect may be mild or severe and occurs because the air pressure is reduced, and the heart and lungs must work harder to oxygenate the body.

Sun Protection against the sun should always be taken seriously, particularly in the rarefied air and deceptive coolness of the mountains where sunburn occurs rapidly.

Sunburn is a particular problem in the Patagonian Andes in spring and early summer (mid-November to mid-January), when the sun's intensity is greatest but there is still plenty of snow to reflect UV.

Slap on the sunscreen and a barrier cream for your nose and lips, wear a broad-brimmed hat and protect your eyes with good quality sunglasses with UV lenses, particularly when trekking near water, sand or snow. If, despite these precautions, you get yourself burnt, calamine lotion, aloe vera or other commercial sunburn relief preparations will soothe.

Snow Blindness This is a temporary painful condition resulting from sunburn of the surface of the eye (cornea). It usually occurs when someone walks on snow or in bright sunshine without sunglasses. Treatment is to relieve the pain – cold cloths on closed eyelids may help. Antibiotic and anaesthetic eye drops are not necessary. The condition usually resolves itself within a few days and there are no long-term consequences.

Heat Although Patagonia has a cool climate, heat exhaustion may occasionally become a real concern, especially in exposed volcanic country above the tree line. One way trekkers can avoid the heat is by getting an early start, then taking it easy during the hottest part of the day.

Dehydration & Heat Exhaustion Dehydration is a potentially dangerous and generally preventable condition caused by excessive fluid loss. Sweating combined with inadequate fluid intake, diarrhoea, vomiting, and high fever are all common causes of dehydration in trekkers. The first symptoms of dehydration are weakness, thirst and passing small amounts of very concentrated urine. This may progress to drowsiness, dizziness or fainting on standing up and, finally, coma.

Dehydration and salt deficiency can cause heat exhaustion, so ensure that your body gets sufficient liquids – a minimum of 3L a day is recommended. Salt deficiency is characterised by fatigue, lethargy, headaches, giddiness and muscle cramps, and is best treated with salt tablets.

Heatstroke This is a serious, occasionally fatal, condition that occurs if the body's heat-regulating mechanism breaks down and the body temperature rises to dangerous levels. Long, continuous periods of exposure to high temperatures and insufficient fluids can leave you vulnerable to heatstroke.

The symptoms are feeling unwell, not sweating very much (or at all) and a high body temperature (39°C to 41°C). Where sweating has ceased, the skin becomes flushed and red. Severe, throbbing headaches and lack of coordination will also occur, and sufferers may become confused

or aggressive. Eventually they will become delirious or convulse. Hospitalisation is essential, but in the interim get victims out of the sun, remove their clothing, cover them with a wet sheet or towel and then fan continually. Give fluids if they are conscious.

Cold Too much cold can be just as dangerous as too much heat. The Patagonian Andes are renowned for their unpredictable weather. A sudden storm can drench unprepared trekkers with cold, heavy rain or sleet – exactly the sort of conditions that typically cause hypothermia.

Hypothermia Also known as exposure, hypothermia is a real and ever-present threat to trekkers anywhere. Hypothermia

The 'Ozone Hole'

The ozone layer in the middle atmosphere – at between 8km and 50km – prevents most of the sun's harmful ultraviolet (UV) radiation from reaching the earth's surface, keeping the planet habitable for animals and plants. The alarming discovery that certain artificial compounds, especially chlorinated fluoro-hydrocarbons (CFCs), were destroying this protective ozone layer, led to the 1992 Montreal Protocol banning CFCs and (later) bromine-containing halons. CFCs are very long-lived, however, and remain in the atmosphere for decades.

Extremely low winter temperatures over the polar regions allow CFCs to break down atmospheric ozone much faster than in the temperate and tropical zones. As Antarctica experiences a much colder winter than the North Pole, ozone depletion is much more severe in the Southern Hemisphere.

In Patagonia the most critical period is during the (southern) spring months, especially in mid-October, when a vast area of ozone-depleted atmosphere – the so-called 'ozone hole' – expands northward. In bad years, the edge of the ozone hole has reached as far north as 42° over South America (the latitude of the cities of Puerto Montt and El Bolsón). The ozone hole soon weakens and contracts, however, and by mid-November it only covers part of Antarctica.

While the ozone hole remains a worrying phenomenon – very slight increases in UV levels could still seriously effect sensitive species or even upset whole ecosystems – the danger to people has been grossly exaggerated in some rather irresponsible media reporting.

A key factor to consider is that the *natural* level of UV radiation at higher latitudes is low compared to tropical regions. Furthermore, UV radiation rises progressively with increasing altitude. The Patagonian Andes lie far outside the tropics, of course, and treks are generally at relatively low elevations. (Trekkers in elevated tropical regions like the Himalayas or the Peruvian Andes are exposing themselves to much higher levels of UV radiation than in the Patagonian Andes.) In any case, although the ozone hole has receded toward Antarctica by the time the Patagonian trekking season gets under way (in early December), normal UV radiation is still greater because the sun itself is higher in the sky. This is the reason – and not ozone depletion – why trekkers in the Patagonian Andes must give proper attention to UV protection.

NASA's Total Ozone Mapping Spectrometer website at W http://jwocky.gsfc.nasa.gov gives UV readings around the planet and information on ozone depletion in general.

occurs when the body loses heat faster than it can produce it, causing the core temperature to fall.

It is surprisingly easy to progress from very cold to dangerously cold due to a combination of wind, wet clothing, fatigue and hunger, even if the air temperature is above freezing. Key signs of hypothermia include exhaustion, slurred speech, numb skin (particularly toes and fingers), shivering, irrational or violent behaviour, lethargy, stumbling, dizzy spells, muscle cramps and violent bursts of energy. Irrationality may take the form of a sufferer complaining of being hot and trying to undress.

To treat hypothermia, first get the victims out of the wind and/or rain, remove their clothing if it's wet and replace it with dry, warm garments. Give them hot liquids – not alcohol – and some simple sugary food. Do not rub them but place them near a fire or in a warm (not hot) bath. This should be enough for the early stages of hypothermia, but if it has gone further it may be necessary to place the victim in a warm bed or sleeping bag and get in with them.

Frostbite If you trek in very cold conditions, such as early or late in the season and/or at high elevations, there may be a (minor) risk of frostbite.

Frostbite refers to the freezing of extremities, including fingers, toes and nose. Signs and symptoms of frostbite include a whitish or waxy cast to the skin, or even crystals on the surface, plus itching, numbness and pain. Warm the affected areas by immersion in warm (not hot) water or with blankets or clothes, only until the skin becomes flushed. Frostbitten parts should not be rubbed and blisters should not be broken. Pain and swelling are inevitable. Seek medical attention immediately.

Infectious Diseases

Diarrhoea Simple things like a change of water, food or climate can all cause a mild bout of diarrhoea, but a few rushed toilet trips with no other symptoms is not indicative of a major problem. More serious diarrhoea is caused by infectious agents transmitted by faecal contamination of food or water, using contaminated utensils, or directly from one person's hand to another. Paying particular attention to personal hygiene, drinking purified water and taking care of what you eat, as outlined earlier in this section, are important measures to take to avoid getting diarrhoea on your trek or travels.

Dehydration is the main danger with any diarrhoea, particularly in children or the elderly as it can occur quite quickly. Under all circumstances *fluid replacement* (at least equal to the volume being lost) is the most important thing to remember. Weak black tea with a little sugar, soda water, or soft drinks allowed to go flat and diluted 50% with clean water are all good.

With severe diarrhoea a rehydrating solution is preferable to replace lost minerals and salts. Commercially available oral rehydration salts (ORS) are very useful; add them to boiled or bottled water. In an emergency you can make up a solution of six teaspoons of sugar and a half teaspoon of salt to 1L of boiled or bottled water. You need to drink at least the same volume of fluid that you are losing in bowel movements and vomiting. Urine is the best guide to the adequacy of replacement – if you have small amounts of concentrated urine, you need to drink more. Keep drinking small amounts often and stick to a bland diet as you recover.

Gut-paralysing drugs such as diphenoxylate or loperamide can be used to bring relief from the symptoms, although they do not actually cure the problem. Only use these drugs if you do not have access to toilets, eg, if you *must* travel. These drugs are not recommended for children under 12 years, or if you have a high fever or are severely dehydrated.

In the following situations antibiotics may be required: diarrhoea with blood or mucus (dysentery), any diarrhoea with fever, profuse watery diarrhoea, persistent diarrhoea not improving after 48 hours and severe diarrhoea. These suggest a more serious cause of diarrhoea and gut-paralysing drugs should be avoided. In these situations, a stool test may be necessary to diagnose what bug is causing your diarrhoea, so you should seek medical help urgently. Where this is not possible, the recommended drugs for bacterial diarrhoea (the most likely cause of severe diarrhoea in travellers) are norfloxacin 400mg twice daily for three days or ciprofloxacin 500mg twice daily for five days. These are not recommended for children or pregnant women. The drug of choice for children would be co-trimoxazole with dosage dependent on weight; a five-day course is given. Ampicillin or amoxycillin may be given in pregnancy, but medical care is necessary.

Two other causes of persistent diarrhoea in travellers are giardiasis and amoebic dysentery.

Giardiasis This is caused by a common parasite, *Giardia lamblia*. Symptoms include stomach cramps, nausea, a bloated stomach, watery, foul-smelling diarrhoea and frequent gas. Giardiasis can appear several weeks after you have been exposed to the parasite. The symptoms may disappear for a few days and then return; this can go on for several weeks.

Seek medical advice if you think you have giardiasis, but where this is not possible, tinidazole or metronidazole are the recommended drugs. Treatment is a 2g single dose of tinidazole or 250mg of metronidazole three times daily for five to 10 days.

Amoebic Dysentery This is characterised by a gradual onset of low-grade diarrhoea, often with blood and mucus. Cramping abdominal pain and vomiting are less likely than in other types of diarrhoea, and fever may not be present. It will persist until treated and can recur and cause other health problems. If you think you have amoebic dysentery, you should seek medical advice; treatment is the same as for giardiasis.

Fungal Infections Sweating liberally, probably washing less than usual and going longer without a change of clothes mean that long-distance trekkers risk picking up a fungal infection, which, while an unpleasant irritant, presents no danger.

Fungal infections are encouraged by moisture, so wear loose, comfortable clothes, wash when you can and dry yourself thoroughly. Try to expose the infected area to air or sunlight as much as possible and apply an antifungal cream or powder like tolnaftate.

Rabies This fatal viral infection is not currently found in Patagonia, although there have been outbreaks in northern regions of both Chile and Argentina in recent years (where it is carried mainly by the freetailed bat).

Rabies is found in many countries. Many animals can be infected (such as dogs, cats, bats and monkeys) and it is their saliva which is infectious. Any bite, scratch or even lick from an animal should be cleaned immediately and thoroughly. Scrub with soap and running water and then apply alcohol or iodine solution. Medical help should be sought promptly to receive a course of injections, which can prevent the onset of symptoms and death.

Tetanus This disease is caused by a germ which lives in soil and in the faeces of horses and other animals. It enters the body via breaks in the skin. The first symptom may be discomfort in swallowing, or stiffening of the jaw and neck; this is followed by painful convulsions of the jaw and whole body. The disease can be fatal. It can be prevented by vaccination, so make sure your shots are up to date before you leave.

Hantavirus The potentially deadly hantavirus (known locally simply as *la hanta*) is spread through the saliva and faeces of the native long-tailed rat, whose populations are known to rise dramatically after unusually wet winters. Since its recorded appearance in the mid-1990s near El Bolsón, hantavirus seems to have spread through parts of southern Chile and adjacent areas of Argentina. Most effected are Chile's VII (or Biobío) Región and the VIII (or Maule) Región.

Hantavirus causes the disease known as Hantavirus Pulmonary Syndrome (HPS).

The early symptoms of HPS are fever and muscle aches one to five weeks after infection, followed by shortness of breath and dry coughing. The disease then progresses rapidly and treatment is urgent. The antiviral drug Ribaviron (Virazole) is effective in treating HPS, but only when given early. Of the currently 100 or so annual human cases of HPS in Chile (and perhaps a dozen more in Argentina), around 25% are fatal.

It's wise to cover your nose and mouth with a cloth or breathing mask before entering *refugios* (huts) that have been closed for any period of time, then ventilate the building thoroughly by leaving the windows and door open for at least 30 minutes before you settle in. If available, apply a strong solution of chlorine and water to the floor and other places that may have been contaminated by rodents – Corporación Nacional Forestal (Conaf) supplies *refugios* with chlorine powder for this purpose. Be particularly careful with hygiene. Keep cooking pots and food out of contact with benches, and wash your hands regularly.

Hydatid Cysts The hydatid tapeworm is a 6mm-long tapeworm that forms cysts in the entrails of sheep (though it may also infect cattle or pigs). The eggs of the hydatid are generally passed on to humans through contact with dogs that have fed on the entrails of infected animals. So-called hydatid cysts occur when the parasite establishes itself in organs of the body – especially the liver or lungs – and develops gradually over a number of years. This condition (known in Spanish as *hidatidosis)* is extremely serious, and requires surgery to remove the cysts.

To control hydatids, an extensive government program is now underway to educate farmers not to allow their dogs into areas used for slaughtering animals, to dispose of entrails properly and to treat dogs regularly with antiparasitic drugs. Hydatids were once found all over the world, but these simple precautions have largely eradicated this disgusting parasite from countries as far apart as Iceland and New Zealand.

It is advisable not to pet suspect dogs – such as those on more remote farms – or other canines that may be infected with hydatids, and to properly boil, filter or sterilise all water when passing through grazing country. Washing hands thoroughly before handling food will also greatly reduce the likelihood of infection. In wilder (especially forested) mountain areas, however, the risk of contracting hydatids is virtually nil.

Traumatic Injuries

Sprains Ankle and knee sprains are common injuries among trekkers, particularly when crossing rugged terrain. To help prevent ankle sprains, wear boots that have adequate ankle support. If you do suffer a sprain, immobilise the joint with a firm bandage and, if feasible, immerse the foot in cold water. Distribute the contents of your pack among your companions. Once you reach shelter, relieve the pain and swelling by keeping the joint elevated for the first 24 hours and, where possible, by putting ice on the swollen joint. Take simple painkillers to ease the discomfort.

If the sprain is mild, you may be able to continue your trek after a couple of days. For more severe sprains, seek medical attention as an x-ray may be needed to find out whether a bone has been broken.

Major Accidents Falling or having something fall on you, resulting in head injuries or fractures, is always possible when trekking, especially if you are crossing steep slopes or unstable terrain. Following is some basic advice on what to do in the event of a major accident. If a person suffers a major fall:

• Make sure you and other people with you are not in danger.
• Assess the injured person's condition.
• Stabilise any injuries, such as bleeding wounds or broken bones.
• Seek medical attention – see Emergency Communications (p72) for more details.

If the person is unconscious, check whether they are breathing – clear the airway if it is blocked – and check whether they have a pulse (feel the side of the neck rather than the wrist). If they are not breathing but have a pulse, you should start mouth-to-mouth resuscitation immediately. In these circumstances it is best to move the person as little as possible in case their neck or back is broken.

Check for wounds and broken bones – ask the victim where they have pain if they are conscious, otherwise gently inspect them all over (including their back and the back of the head), making sure to move them as little as possible. Control any bleeding by applying firm pressure to the wound. Bleeding from the nose or ear may indicate a fractured skull. Don't give the person anything by mouth, especially if they are unconscious.

You'll have to manage the person for shock. Raise their legs above heart level (unless their legs are fractured); dress any wounds and immobilise any fractures; loosen tight clothing; keep the person warm by covering them with a blanket or other dry clothing; insulate them from the ground if possible, but don't heat them.

Some general points to bear in mind are:

- Simple fractures take several weeks to heal, so they don't need fixing straight away, but they should be immobilised to protect them from further injury. Compound fractures need urgent treatment.
- If you do have to splint a broken bone, remember to check regularly that the splint is not cutting off the circulation to the hand or foot.
- Most cases of brief unconsciousness are not associated with any serious internal injury to the brain, but as a general rule of thumb in these circumstances, any person who has been knocked unconscious should be watched for deterioration. If they do deteriorate, seek medical attention straight away.

Cuts & Scratches

Even small cuts and grazes should be washed and treated with an antiseptic such as povidone-iodine. Infection in a wound is indicated by the skin margins becoming red, painful and swollen. More serious infection can cause swelling of the whole limb and of the lymph glands. The patient may develop a fever, and will need medical attention.

Burns

Immerse the burnt area in cold water as soon as possible, then cover it with a clean, dry, sterile dressing. Keep this in place with plasters for a day or so in the case of a small mild burn, longer for more extensive injuries. Seek medical help for severe and extensive burns.

Bites & Stings

Blood Suckers The Patagonian Andes are completely free of ticks. Leeches are common in the wet rainforests of archipelagic Chile, however, although they are not dangerous to your health. Leeches can easily be removed by applying salt, stove fuel or direct heat, though the skin around the bite often remains itchy for a few days afterward. Small biting gnats, insects that are locally known as *petros* or *pilmes*, tend to be found in lowland areas grazed by livestock. There are also mosquitoes, but they are generally less bothersome than in other moist areas of the world. Mosquitoes in Patagonia are not carriers of malaria or any other known disease.

Tábanos A collective term for several species of horsefly – but particularly the large and voracious red-black ones – *tábanos* are the scourge of the Patagonian Andes. *Tábanos* generally appear for about six weeks, from Christmas until late January, first in the forests of the Araucanía and the Lakes District, and later in central Patagonia. They are far less common in southern Patagonia. Spells of hot, dry weather typically bring out swarms of frenzied *tábanos*, when regular insect repellents don't work for long, if at all.

Trekkers are likely to hear various homegrown methods for keeping the insects at bay. Some people say you should never wear dark (particularly blue) clothing, as this attracts the insects, while others claim that eating fresh cloves of garlic – until your sweat and blood taste noxious – acts as a natural repellent. When *tábanos* are out in force, however, the only sure method of avoiding them is to trek well above the tree line, but you've got to come down some time!

Spiders Two species of spider are found in lowland areas (particularly on farms) of northern Patagonia.

Chilean Recluse Spider The venomous Chilean (or brown) recluse spider, or *araña del rincón* in Spanish, is a pale-yellow to reddish-brown 4cm-long spider, often identifiable by a violin-shaped marking on its head. It is found in Chile and Argentina to as far south as 43°S (about the latitude of Chaitén and Esquel) in dark, sheltered sites both in buildings and outside. As its name suggests, the Chilean recluse spider is shy and unaggressive and will only bite when threatened.

The spider's extremely toxic, necrotising venom causes intense pain, and the skin around the bite becomes red, swollen and blistered – sometimes eventually gangrenous. Chills, fever, nausea, muscle ache or other flu-like symptoms are common. In around 2% of cases, haematuria (blood in the urine) heralds acute renal failure and death. The Chilean recluse spider is responsible for several fatalities each year, so even suspected spider bites should be treated urgently – within a maximum time of 72 hours. Treatment is normally with cortisone and antihistamines. An antivenin exists, but it is not fully tested and its use remains controversial.

Black Widow Known as *araña de trigo* in Spanish, the black widow spider – the same species found in parts of the USA – is also found in the Araucanía and Lakes District. The black widow female is up to 1cm in length with long legs and a round abdomen with red markings on its underside and back, while the male is smaller with red and white stripes on its abdomen.

A black widow's bite is distinguished by a double puncture wound. Its venom is neurotoxic, blocking the transmission of nerve impulses, but is rarely fatal. Symptoms are similar to an attack of angina pectoris, with heart pain reaching into the left arm, rapid pulse rate and cold skin, but can be satisfactorily treated with calcium injections. If treated properly and promptly, the victim will completely recover.

Women's Health
Women's health issues can be a bit trickier to cope with when you are on the trail.

Pregnancy If you are pregnant, see your doctor before you travel. Even normal pregnancies can make a woman feel nauseated and tired. In the third trimester, the size of the baby can make walking difficult or uncomfortable.

Thrush (Vaginal Candidiasis) Antibiotic use, synthetic underwear, tight trousers, sweating, contraceptive pills and unprotected sex can each lead to fungal vaginal infections, especially when travelling in hot, humid or tropical climates. The most common is thrush (vaginal candidiasis). Symptoms include itching and discomfort in the genital area, often in association with a thick white discharge. The best prevention is to keep the vaginal area cool and dry, and to wear cotton rather than synthetic underwear and loose clothes. Thrush can be treated by clotrimazole pessaries or vaginal cream.

Urinary Tract Infection Dehydration and 'hanging on' can result in urinary tract infection and the symptoms of cystitis, which can be particularly distressing and an inconvenient problem when out on the trail. Symptoms include burning when urinating, and having to urinate frequently and urgently. Blood can sometimes be passed in the urine. Drink plenty of fluids and empty your bladder at regular intervals. If symptoms persist, seek medical attention because a simple infection can spread to the kidneys, causing a more severe illness.

SAFETY ON THE TREK
Although trekking is generally one of the safest mountain activities, trekker injuries and deaths do occur – despite most serious accidents being preventable. Above all, trekkers should avoid getting themselves into dangerous situations, especially when trekking off-trail. Falls due to slipping on wet grass, loose scree, mossy rock or icy paths are among the most common hazards.

Watch for signs of impending bad weather and descend or seek shelter if conditions start to look threatening. Trekkers should always carry a completely waterproof rainjacket (and preferably overpants) regardless of how good the weather seems when they set out. Avoid crossing exposed areas in poor weather and don't camp in any spot that has no natural shelter. Even in areas where there are *refugios*, carrying a tent will ensure you always have shelter in an emergency. Also carry basic supplies, including food containing simple sugars (such as chocolate) to generate heat quickly, and lots of fluid to drink.

Bamboo

Bamboo (known as *quila* or *colihue*) grows in the understorey of all but the most southerly temperate rainforests. Where tracks have been slashed through clusters of bamboo, sharp cut-off canes are left sticking out of the ground. These make potentially dangerous obstacles as there is a risk of slipping and falling onto the stumps. Walk very carefully where any track leads through bamboo, especially on steep muddy descents.

Crossing Rivers

Only a few of the treks described in this guidebook involve a serious river crossing, as most larger streams have bridges. However, a serious wade may be necessary in late spring and early summer (mid-November to late December) when thawing snow swells streams, or after heavy summer rain. Remember that while heavy rain quickly makes rivers impassable, mountain stream levels fall almost as fast as they rise. Fast-flowing glacial streams call for the greatest caution as fine sediment often clouds the water, making it difficult to gauge the depth. Streams of glacial origin usually reach their highest level in late afternoon (after the sun's intensity has begun to wane), so a morning crossing will always be easier.

Trekking parties should nevertheless be well practised in river-crossing techniques. The safest place to cross a river is usually just downstream from a long pool. Undo the waist buckle and loosen the shoulder straps of your pack so that you can easily slip it off if you stumble or are swept off your feet. Groups should undertake a serious wade by linking arms and moving together in a line at right-angles to the current. Lone trekkers should use a sturdy pole (or an improvised tree branch) for support, leaning sideways into the current.

Dogs

On the whole, Patagonian pooches are a placid breed, but never pat sheepdogs – they are workers, not pets, and don't like being touched by strangers. At times trekkers have to pass by farmhouses guarded by decidedly unfriendly dogs. If you are suddenly confronted by an aggressive dog, remember that you are encroaching on its territory. You should avoid eye contact – which the animal would interpret as a territorial challenge – and retreat discreetly or make a wide circle around the farmyard. Picking up hard projectiles in

---

Trek Safety Basic Rules

- Allow yourself more than enough time to complete each leg of the trek before nightfall, especially late in the season when days are shorter.
- Always be prepared to turn back if you don't feel confident about continuing.
- Avoid going alone – two is the minimum number for safe trekking in the mountains.
- Inform a responsible person – especially a *guardaparque* (national park or reserve ranger) – of your trekking route, and try to stick to your plans. Register your arrival by signing the *refugio* (hut) or summit logbook (if available).
- Carry an accurate topographical map, compass or Global Positioning System (GPS) receiver and whistle (perhaps also a mirror or reflector).
- Check the latest weather forecast before setting off and, while you trek, keep a careful watch on the weather.
- Never leave trails in foggy conditions. With care, most trails can be followed even in thick fog – otherwise wait until visibility improves.

front of a snarling canine should earn you instant respect. If this signal fails to make the dog back off, however, the recommended course of action is to let them have it!

Bites from farm dogs should be treated seriously, as the animals may carry parasites that cause hydatid cysts (p68) or possibly even rabies (p67).

Rockfall

Even a small falling rock could shatter your hand or crack your skull, so always be alert to the danger of rockfall. Trail sections most obviously exposed to rockfall lead below cliffs fringed by large fields of raw scree – don't hang around in such areas. If you accidentally loosen a rock, loudly warn any other trekkers who may be below you.

Rescue & Evacuation

As help might be many days away, trekkers should aim to be as self-reliant as possible. In case of an emergency, rescues may be carried out by national park, (border) police or military personnel. **The Cuerpo de Socorro Andino de Chile** (w www.socorroandino.cl; e jefatura@socorroandino.cl) is a special volunteer organisation that carries out mountain rescues in the Andes of Chile. Its website features an online registration form (avisos de salida) where you can register details of your party members and intended route.

In most circumstances, evacuation by helicopter will not be an option. If a helicopter is available you may be required to give some kind of assurance of payment – ensure that your travel insurance covers this. Particularly in remote and sparsely populated areas (such as central Patagonia), your best first option may be to seek assistance at a nearby farm or ranch (estancia).

Emergency Communications Public telephones exist only where there is other substantial infrastructure – rarely at trailheads. Although mobile (cell) phones occasionally work in parts of national parks or reserves close to regional towns, the mobile network is far too limited to be a reliable form of emergency communication.

Satellite (world) phones can be used from virtually anywhere, but are extremely expensive to own and operate (see Telephone, p264). Larger estancias, ranger stations (guarderías) and staffed refugios – such as those in the national parks of Nahuel Huapi and Torres del Paine – usually have a two-way radio that can be used in an emergency situation.

Flashing a mirror is a good way to attract attention of people far away. Although it may not be recognised as such, you could try using the international distress signal. It consists of six whistles, six calls, six smoke puffs – ie, six of any sign you can make – followed by a pause (equalling the length of time taken to make the six signs) before you repeat the signal. If your distress call is understood, you might receive a reply consisting of three signals, each separated by a long pause.

The Araucanía

The Araucanía extends southward from the Río Biobío to the snows of Volcán Villarrica. Like the Lakes District, which shares many of its typical features, the Araucanía is extremely active volcanically, and offers a fascinating variety of natural phenomena such as thermal springs, volcanoes and mountain lakes. The area is the heartland of the Araucarian, or Mapuche, people, who relied heavily on the edible nuts of the araucaria 'pine' for food. These glorious trees still grow throughout the Araucanía, where they are protected by the region's many national parks and reserves.

GATEWAY
Temuco (Chile)
The largest city in the Araucanía, Temuco (population 220,000) is on the Panamerican Hwy 675km south of Santiago, and is the jumping-off point for trips to the national parks of Villarrica, Huerquehue, Conguillío, Nahuel Buta as well as Reserva Nacional Malalcahuello-Nalcas. The small Conaf-administered Cerro Ñielol nature reserve borders the town (access via Calle Prat), and is ideal for a short 'urban trek'.

Information The **tourist office** (☎ 045-211969; *Bulnes 586*) is opposite the Plaza de Armas. The regional headquarters of **Conaf** (*Corporación Nacional Forestal;* ☎ *045-298100, 045-298210;* e *temuco@conaf.cl; 2nd floor, Bilbao 931*) are in Temuco. Anglers can buy a Chilean fishing licence at the regional office of **Sernap** (*Servicio Nacional de Pesca;* ☎ *045-238390; General Mackenna 215*). **Lhotse** (☎ *045-247697;* w *www.lhotse.terra.cl; San Martin 349*) makes outdoor clothing and sells some mountaineering equipment.

Places to Stay & Eat The small HI-affiliated **Residencial Temuco** (☎ *045-233721; 2nd floor, Rodríguez 1341; dorm beds US$9*) includes breakfast in its bed rates. Other places to say in Temuco are the **Hostal Aldunate** (☎/fax *045-231128; Aldunate 864;*

CHRIS BARTON

Gazing out over old lava flows and the Pucón Valley from the Volcán Villarrica summit

- Standing beside Laguna Termal (p75), the steaming, hot crater lake on Volcán Copahue

- Glissading down snow after a successful ascent of Volcán Lonquimay (p87)

- Backstroking out into the cool, tranquil waters of Lago Verde in Parque Nacional Huerquehue (p93)

- Pitching the tent on tundra meadows under the smoking, snowcapped Volcán Villarrica (p100)

dorm beds with shared bathroom US$10) and **Hotel Turismo** (☎ *045-210583; Claro Solar 636; singles/doubles from US$15/28*).

Hotel Oriente (☎ *045-233232; Manuel Rodríguez 1146; singles/doubles with shared bathroom US$11/19, with private bathroom US$18/33*) is also good value. The historic **Hotel Continental** (☎ *045-238973; Varas 709; singles US$19-40, doubles US$31-44*) has hosted numerous eminent people. **Hotel de la**

Frontera (☎/fax 045-200400; Bulnes 733; singles/doubles US$50/60) has an indoor pool.

Restaurante El Turista (☎ 045-238056; Puesto 32) offers sound Chilean fare. The **Quincho de la Empanada** (☎ 045-216307; Aldunate 69) serves traditional Chilean cuisine.

Getting There & Away Numerous flights to Santiago (US$85) are offered by **Lan-Chile** (☎ 045-211339; Bulnes 687). **TAN** (☎ 045-210500; Portales 840) flies to/from Neuquén (US$70) in Argentina.

Although an increasing number of long-distance buses leave from **Terminal Araucario**

(☎ 045-255005; Ortega), north of the town centre, many bus companies use their own terminal closer to town. There are frequent departures to destinations along the Panamerican Hwy between Santiago and Puerto Montt. International buses run several times weekly to Zapala and Neuquén (via Paso de Pino Hachado) and to Junín and San Martín de los Andes (via Paso Mamuil Malal) in Argentina.

Buses to regional destinations leave from the **Terminal de Buses Rurales** (☎ 045-210494; Balmaceda & Pinto), including to Curacautín, Cherquenco and Melipueco.

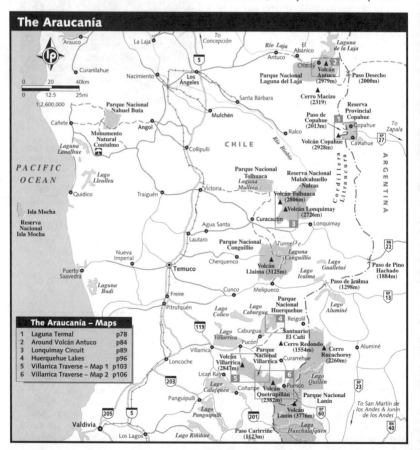

The Araucanía

The Araucanía – Maps

1	Laguna Termal	p78
2	Around Volcán Antuco	p84
3	Lonquimay Circuit	p89
4	Huerquehue Lakes	p96
5	Villarrica Traverse – Map 1	p103
6	Villarrica Traverse – Map 2	p106

Parque Provincial Copahue

The 105-sq-km Parque Provincial Copahue lies in the remote northwest of Argentina's Neuquén province. The park takes in the eastern slopes around Volcán Copahue (2928m), an exploded volcano cone with two very new side craters. Volcán Copahue is highly active, and erupted spectacularly in June 2000, sending a cloud of smoke 600m into the air and depositing a layer of grey ash on the nearby villages of Caviahue and Copahue. The eruption also released quantities of sulphur-rich water into Lago Caviahue (also called Lago Agrio) that turned the lake green.

The hot springs and mineral waters of Copahue ('place of sulphur' in the Mapuche language) are probably the most highly regarded of any in the southern Andes. Since pre-European times the Mapuche have journeyed up to Volcán Copahue to collect the lake water, which they believe to have special health and healing properties. (Bottles of Copahue water are even sold at regional markets such as in the Chilean city of Los Ángeles.)

The reserve is entirely above 1500m, and has a cold winter with heavy snowfalls (around 5m in Copahue) and dry, hot summers. Most of the reserve is above tree line, although light araucaria forest covers the slopes above Caviahue. In summer, sheep are grazed on the sparse, mostly unfenced highland pastures surrounding the park.

ACCESS TOWN
Zapala (Argentina)

The town of Zapala (population 35,000) lies on the dry, windswept steppes, 186km west of Neuquén at the junction of Ruta Nacional 22 and Ruta Nacional 40. Apart from the 112-sq-km Parque Nacional Laguna Blanca, 30km southwest of town (a park centred around Laguna Blanca, a lake with outstanding bird life), Zapala has little to offer.

Zapala's **tourist office** (☎ 02942-421132; *Av San Martín & Almirante Brown*) is open daily. The local **APN office** (*Administración Parques Nacionales;* ☎ 02942-431982; *e* lagun *ablanca@zapala.com.ar; Ceballos 446*) can advise on Parque Nacional Laguna Blanca.

Places to Stay & Eat Free camping can be found at **Camping Municipal** (☎ 02942-422095; *Calle Sapag*), south of the rail line. **Residencial Coliqueo** (☎ 02942-421308; *Etcheluz 159; singles/doubles US$12/20*) and **Hotel Pehuén** (☎/fax 02942-423135; *Etcheluz & Elena de la Vega; singles/doubles US$13/20*) offer excellent value.

El Chancho Rengo (☎ 02942-422795; *Av San Martín & Etcheluz*) is popular for coffee and light meals. **La Zingarella** (☎ 02942-422218; *Houssay 654, between Paraguay & Chile*) offers home-style cooking.

Getting There & Away The airline **LADE** (☎ 430134; *Uriburu 397*) flies once weekly to Neuquén (US$20), Bariloche (US$26), El Maitén (US$35) and Esquel (US$44).

Buses run two-hourly between Zapala and Neuquén (US$7), from where there are many regional air and bus connections. There are also several daily buses to Junín (US$5.50) and San Martín de los Andes (US$9), and several weekly departures to/from Temuco (US$25) in Chile. Albus and Aluminé Viajes run daily buses to Laguna Blanca (US$2) and Aluminé (US$6). Ticsa runs buses north to San Juan and San Luis three times weekly, while TAC connects to Mendoza (US$20).

Laguna Termal

Duration	6½–8¼ hours
Distance	25km
Difficulty	moderate
Start/Finish	Copahue
Nearest Towns	Copahue (p76), Caviahue (p76)
Transport	bus
Summary	A circuit up to a remarkable warm steaming lake that fills the small eastern crater of Volcán Copahue.

Surrounded by small glaciers, fumaroles and hot springs, Laguna Termal's temperature fluctuates, depending on the season and level of volcanic activity, between 20°C and 40°C. Its water, which drains subterraneously – as the source of the Arroyo Caviahue (Río Agrio) – is acidic and rich in trace minerals.

This trek involves an ascent/descent of 700m. Also described is the marvellous side trip up to Volcán Copahue and two very interesting alternative route options.

Along the route are several tiny *refugios* (huts) built by the Argentine Gendarmería Nacional. These *refugios* are intended for bad-weather and emergency use only. Two of them are in such poor condition that they provide very limited shelter.

PLANNING
When to Trek
The trek can normally be done from mid-January until mid-April. Before mid-January much of the track is likely to be snow-covered (and possibly impassable without ice axe and crampons).

Maps
The only available topographical map that covers the area at any useful scale is the Chilean IGM 1:50,000 map *Volcán Copahue* (Section G, No 44). Although this map shows detail well, it has some topographical errors and outdated information, including the position of most foot tracks and minor roads.

Permits & Regulations
Trekkers do not require permits, but parties should leave names and details of their intended route with the **Gendarmería Nacional** (☎ 02948-495055) at the entrance to Copahue. Camping is not permitted in Parque Provincial Copahue apart from in the upper Arroyo Caviahue (Río Agrio).

Warning
Particularly on windy days, acrid fumes rising from Laguna Termal can be overpowering due to sulphur dioxide gas (which attacks your airways). Approach the lake cautiously – don't even consider swimming in it. Less experienced trekkers are advised to go with an organised tour (see Caviahue).

NEAREST TOWNS
Copahue and Caviahue (w www.cavia hue-copahue.com.ar) are on Ruta Provincial 26, respectively 139km and 120km from Zapala. In recent years, a 21km village-to-village half-marathon known as the Desafío de Volcán Copahue (or Copahue Challenge) has been held each February. It can be hard to change money here, so bring plenty of cash.

Copahue
Copahue (2030m) is a small thermal springs resort, standing on the northeastern side of its namesake volcano among steaming, sulphurous pools (including a bubbling hot mud pool, the popular Laguna del Chancho).

The village centres around the large, modern **Complejo Termal Copahue** (☎ 02948-495049; *Ortiz Velez*), which offers a wide range of curative bathing programs. **Hospedaje Codihue** (☎ 02948-495031; *singles/doubles US$18/36*) offers rooms with full board. Or try the **Hotel Santa Mónica** (☎ 02948-495027/12; *Arturo Fernandez 125; singles/doubles US$15/30*), behind the Complejo, or the **Hotel Termas** (☎ 02948-495141; *singles/doubles from US$25/50*) – both hotels include breakfast only.

Café La Humedad, opposite the Complejo entrance, has good food and coffee, while **Parrillada Nito** (☎ 02948-495040; *Sambojara*), next door, does *asado* roasts.

Getting There & Away During summer, Centenario operates one bus daily in either direction between Neuquén (US$13) and Caviahue/Copahue via Zapala (US$8), departing from Neuquén at around noon and back from Copahue at around 9am. The bus gets into Copahue at roughly 6pm.

Caviahue
The ski village of Caviahue (around 1600m) lies on the western shore of Lago Caviahue (Lago Agrio) at the southeast foot of Volcán Copahue. A popular day trek from Caviahue goes up past the waterfall known as Cascada Escondida to Laguna Escondida. **Caviahue Tours** (☎/fax 02948-495107; e *caviahuetur@ infovia.com.ar; Av Costanera & Volcán Copahue*) organises treks from both villages

(including to Laguna Termal/Volcán Copahue for US$18/25 per person).

Places to stay in Caviahue include the **Hotel Lago Caviahue** (☎/fax 02948-495074, 02948-495110; e hotellcaviahue@infovia .com.ar; Av Costanera Quimey Có; rooms per person from US$20), which includes breakfast, and **Hotel Farallón** (☎ 02948-495087; singles/doubles from US$35/50). **Del Cerro**, in the Hotel Farallón, serves meals.

The bus to Copahue (see Getting There & Away, p76) arrives in Caviahue about 20 minutes before it reaches Copahue. The 19km road between Caviahue and Copahue is unsurfaced and often very dusty.

THE TREK (see map p78)

From the Hotel Valle del Volcán at the upper (southwest) edge of the village, cross the little footbridge and climb briefly past a life-size statue of the Virgin. The well-worn foot track leads across a sparsely vegetated plain towards the exploded cone of Volcán Copahue, dipping down to lush, green lawns by the northern shore of the **Lagunas Las Mellizas'** western 'twin'. From here, it's worth making a 200m detour northwest to the **Paso de Copahue** (2013m), where an orange marker (hito) indicates the Argentina–Chile border. The pass looks down into the headwaters of the Río Queuco, a tributary of the Río Biobío.

Follow a path along the lake's north side past black-sand beachlets and gushing springs on its opposite shore to reach the start of a steam pipeline, one to 1¼ hours from the village. The roaring of steam from the subterranean Copahue Geothermal Field (see the boxed text) entering the vapoducto and irregular explosive blasts of discharging steam can be heard along much of the trek.

Cross the lake outlet – farther downstream is a wide, easy ford – then cut up southwest over snowdrifts past a tarn to meet a 4WD track at the edge of a small waterlogged mallín (wet meadow). Turn right and follow this rough road up around left (or take a vague trail marked with white paint splashes to its right until you come back to the road on a rocky ridge below a wooden cross). The 4WD track continues westward up through a barren volcanic moonscape to end under a tiny glacier on the east flank of Volcán Copahue, 1¼ to 1½ hours from the pipeline. (Guided treks usually begin from here.)

Ascend southwest over bouldery ridges, crossing several small mineral-and-meltwater streams. To the northwest, in Chile, the ice-smothered Sierra Velluda and the near-perfect snowy cone of Volcán Antuco rise up majestically. From the third streamlet (with yellowy, sulphur-encrusted sides), cut along the slope below a hot spring then climb to the top of a prominent grey-pumice spur that lies on the international border. Ascend the spur until it becomes impossibly steep, then traverse up rightward over loose slopes into a gap to reach **Laguna Termal**, 1¼ to 1½ hours from the end of the 4WD track (3½ to 4¼ hours from Copahue).

Filling Volcán Copahue's eastern crater, this steaming hot lake feeds itself by melting the snout of a glacier that forms a

Copahue Geothermal Field

Centred between the Lagunas Las Mellizas, the 1.2-sq-km Copahue Geothermal Field (Pozo Geotérmico Copahue) is a subterranean reservoir of highly pressurised steam. The field is replenished each spring as melting snow seeps through the porous earth (eventually) to a depth of almost 1300m, where it vaporises as it comes into contact with hot rock. At temperatures of up to 200°C, a 'pressure-cooker effect' then forces the steam up to the surface.

A 670kW geothermal power station built in 1988 generates electricity that is transmitted as far as Loncopué, more than 50km away. In a unique project completed in 1999, steam is also transported to Copahue by a 3km pipeline (vapoducto), whose pipes and valves roar and hiss like a jet-powered locomotive. When it reaches the village, the steam is ducted through a sophisticated network of coiled pipes laid under each street, heating the concrete paving so they remain snow-free even in midwinter.

massive rim of ice above its back wall. Sulphurous fumes often force trekkers to retreat from the lake, but these high slopes also grant a wonderful vista across the vast basin (where both villages are visible) between the horseshoe-shaped Lago Caviahue (Lago Agrio) and the elongated Lago Trolope to the northeast. From here, more experienced trekkers can continue up to the summit of Volcán Copahue (see Side Trip).

Either return from Laguna Termal via your ascent route (in three to four hours), opt for the Alternative Route back to Copahue via Arroyo Caviahue (Río Agrio) and Ruta 26 (p79), or take the Alternative Finish to Caviahue (p79).

Side Trip: Volcán Copahue Summit

2¾–3½ hours return, 8km,
200m ascent/descent

This is the normal route to the top of Volcán Copahue – other, more difficult ascent

possibilities exist from the volcano's south side. The route is demanding and may not be passable without ice axe (and perhaps crampons) until mid-January.

From Laguna Termal, ascend steeply northwest along the right side of the rim, turning left to reach the edge of the glacier. The route cuts southwest across the (crevasse-free) ice, then heads over left to a gap in the main ridge. At this point, it's worth detouring a short way back north past a **refugio** *(GPS 37° 51.515 S, 71° 09.822 W)* – of similar design and condition to Refugio Lopetegui – to a spectacular **lookout** high above Laguna Termal. Skirt on around to the left just above the snowy basin (the remains of the ancient, exploded crater), then make a short climb to the small summit of **Volcán Copahue** (2928m), which is marked by a wooden cross with a tiny shrine and an orange border-marker.

From here you get a superb panorama of dozens of distant and closer volcanoes,

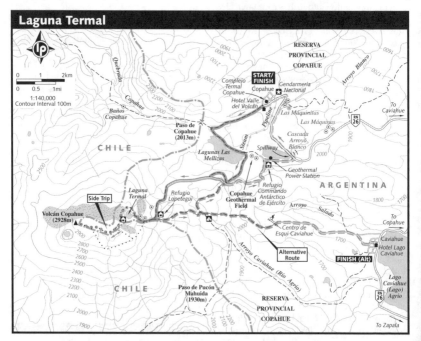

including Volcán Callaqui directly to the southwest. A round, blue crater-lake (usually snow-filled early in the season) sits right below you, above wild Chilean valleys forested with araucarias that contrast sharply with the dry terrain on the Argentine side.

Return via the ascent route.

Alternative Route: via Arroyo Caviahue (Río Agrio) & Ruta 26
3–4 hours, 13.5km, 700m descent

From Laguna Termal drop back via the spur (400m past where you joined it) to reach **Refugio Lopetegui** *(GPS 37° 51.508 S, 71° 08.785 W)*. Although it could serve as a life-saving bivouac, this tiny, semiruined A-frame hut stands half-buried in the pumice at around 2475m on a little shelf. The dimpled form of Volcán Llaima is recognisable to the southwest, in Chile.

Head down northeast through a bare basin before cutting rightward over a minor saddle. The trail (marked with cairned stakes) descends on to the right, then turns left at a track junction (see Alternative Finish) to ford the small Arroyo Caviahue (Río Agrio), 50 minutes to 1¼ hours from the lake.

Continue eastward over fine, eroding glacial-volcanic moraines on a shelf above the stream. The route turns northeast again as it skirts a minor depression to cross the *mallín* and intersect with the 4WD track (mentioned in the main route description), 25 to 30 minutes from the Arroyo Caviahue (Río Agrio).

Follow this dirt road northeast past the A-frame **Refugio Commando Antárctico de Ejército** *(GPS 37° 50.402 S, 71° 06.326 W)* to the east lake of the Lagunas Las Mellizas, continuing along its southern shore past the noisy geothermal power station to reach Ruta 26, 50 minutes to one hour from the *mallín.* Turn left and proceed across the outlet spillway bridge above the Cascada Arroyo Blanco and on uphill past the thermal area of Las Maquinitas to arrive back in Copahue after a final 50 minutes to 1¼ hours.

Alternative Finish: Caviahue
3–4 hours, 12km, 1130m descent

From Laguna Termal descend via Refugio Lopetegui to the turn-off *(GPS 37° 51.147 S,*

71° 08.049 W) as described in the Alternative Route. Turn right and head down to spring-fed meadows dotted with *llaretas* (green, lawn-like mounds) along the Arroyo Caviahue (Río Agrio). Follow cairns across the stream (where **camping** is permitted only among the bare rubble), cutting east over a scoria plain to the left of a boulder field.

After reaching a marker pole by a square rock block, the route drops leftward across a reddish mineral spring. Continue east through waterlogged meadows and over a bare ridge, then sidle around southeast above the upper basin of the Arroyo Salado to reach the **Centro de Esquí Caviahue**. From this small ski field, a road leads 5km downvalley through beautiful araucaria forest to Caviahue (p76).

Parque Nacional Laguna del Laja

Parque Nacional Laguna del Laja lies east of the Chilean city of Los Ángeles, just north of the Río Biobío and almost abutting the border with Argentina. Although it covers little more than 100 sq km, the park includes several distinctive features: the near-perfect cone of Volcán Antuco, the classic multiarmed lake of Laguna de la Laja, and – both just outside the park boundary – the biologically rich *bofedal* (high marsh) of Los Barros and the impressive, glaciated Sierra Velluda range. With altitudes ranging from 1000m to almost 3000m above sea level, this park is a varied and surprisingly compact Andean wilderness.

At the centre of the park is the 2979m cone of Volcán Antuco, just one of the region's many dormant volcanoes. Its name is made up of the Mapuche words *antu*, meaning 'sun', and *co*, meaning 'water'. The tiny summit caldera still steams and puffs out sulphuric gases but – for the moment – is otherwise fairly quiet. Immediately to the southwest is the Sierra Velluda, a spectacular range that rises to 3585m. Choked by hanging glaciers and icefalls, these nonvolcanic peaks contrast sharply with Antuco's smoother contours.

At the eastern foot of Volcán Antuco lies Laguna de la Laja. This large lake is the source of the Río Laja, the major river of Chile's Chillán region, whose famous Salto del Laja waterfall can be found far downstream on the Carretera Panamericana. The lake's interesting form, with several narrow arms, was created by the volcano's 1873 eruption when masses of lava blocked the Río Laja, impounded its waters and drowned the valleys upstream. Unfortunately, hydroelectric development has disturbed the lake's natural shoreline (which is around 1400m above sea level), but its setting among lofty peaks still makes a dramatic scene.

NATURAL HISTORY

Because of its climate, height and recent volcanic activity, the park is relatively sparsely vegetated, but one feature of its flora is Cordilleran cypress *(ciprés de la cordillera)*. Known to the Mapuche as *lahuén*, this small coniferous tree thrives in the dry alpine conditions, and can be seen on the mountainsides surrounding the approach road to the park. There are also small areas of evergreen *coigüe* forest and, higher up, deciduous *ñirre* scrub.

Another feature of the area's botany is its hardy wild flowers, which, in spring and early summer, grow sporadically in the loose volcanic earth. Some of the most attractive are the alpine violets, whose delicate blooms often produce a 'desert-garden' effect. There are also specialised succulents, including the *maihuén*, a rather atypical member of the cactus family. The *maihuén* grows in large spiny mounds that look a bit like closely mown lawns (though you wouldn't want to sit on them), from which clustered, bright-yellow flowers emerge in early summer. The pink-petalled *mutisia volcánica*, the white, vaguely carnation-like *estrella de la cordillera* and several bulbous rhodophilias are among the rarer local plant species.

It's interesting to observe the regeneration patterns since Volcán Antuco's last catastrophic eruption. This has proceeded only gradually, but in places islands of original vegetation have been left untouched within the desolate fields of lava.

Condors and other birds are the most visible native fauna. Other animals are seldom seen, although pumas, foxes, vizcachas and some interesting lizards and frogs exist in and around the park.

CLIMATE

Parque Nacional Laguna del Laja, the most northerly area covered in this book, has a climate more like the mountain areas further to the north. The seasons show a marked annual contrast, with hot, dry summers and cold winters. Most of the year's precipitation falls in winter as snow. The average mid-winter snow depth at the park information centre (approximately 1200m above sea level) is 2m, but this increases with elevation. Skiing is possible, and there's a small ski village at around 1400m on the northwestern slopes of Volcán Antuco.

The warmer weather of spring quickly melts away the snow cover, however, and by late January the largest patches of snow remain only above approximately 2000m. Volcán Antuco and the Sierra Velluda cause a rain shadow on the eastern edge of the volcano, producing drier conditions in that sector of the park.

PLANNING
When to Trek

The best months to trek in Parque Nacional Laguna del Laja are December (when the wild flowers are best) and April (when there is little snow and conditions are not so hot). Before mid-November much of the park, including the Around Volcán Antuco route (p82), is still snowbound. From mid-December until late January, *tábanos* (bloodsucking horseflies) can be bothersome at lower elevations. On the other hand, trekkers will find the going hot and dusty in January and February. Cooler yet snow-free conditions can generally be expected from late March until early May.

Maps

The entire park is covered by one Chilean IGM 1:50,000 map, *Laguna de la Laja*

(Section G, No 21). Although this map indicates topographical detail very well, some higher areas are left uncontoured and the trekking routes themselves are not shown.

Information Sources

Conaf's Centro de Información Ambiental (information centre), 700m uphill from the Guardería Chacay, was not functioning when we researched this edition, but the *guardaparque* at the administration centre is enthusiastic and knowledgeable.

Permits & Regulations

An entry fee of US$1 per person is payable at the park entrance gate (Portería El Álamo), but may be waived (or simply overlooked) if you don't arrive with your own vehicle.

There are few restrictions on camping in the park, but trekkers are asked to give special consideration to sanitation and to make sure all garbage is carried out.

Park authorities may insist that trekkers ascending Volcán Antuco (see Other Treks, p109) be accompanied by a local guide, but this is not really enforced.

ACCESS TOWN
Los Ángeles (Chile)

This unassuming regional capital lies a short distance north of the Río Biobío, just outside Chile's Araucanía region. Los Ángeles is a transit point for Laguna del Laja and Tolhuaca national parks as well as many other

---

Laguna del/de la Laja

Many visitors find the name Parque Nacional Laguna *del* Laja confusing, since the lake itself is called Laguna *de la* Laja. The reason for this is that the park's Spanish name refers as much to the Río Laja as to the lake, and thus might be translated as 'Lake of the *River* Laja National Park'. The Spanish word *laja* means 'smooth rock', and was first given to a section of the Río Laja far downstream – you won't see too much smooth rock in Parque Nacional Laguna del Laja!

---

potential trips into the nearby Cordillera. The city is just west of the Panamerican Hwy and is easily reached from the north or south.

Perhaps the best source of information is the **Automóvil Club de Chile** (☎ 043-314209; *Caupolicán 201*). **Inter Bruna** (☎ 043-313812; *Caupolicán 350*) changes money, and there are numerous **ATMs**.

Spot the alerce tree in the elegant, leafy Plaza de Armas, which was remodelled in 2000–01.

Places to Stay & Eat Much of Los Ángeles' accommodation is along the Panamerican Hwy, but the most reasonable options are in town.

Residencial El Angelino (☎ 043-325627; *Colo Colo 335; rooms per person US$10*) is a great place with very clean, cheerful rooms.

Hotel Villena (☎ 043-321643; *Lautaro 579; rooms with bathroom US$20*) is a well-kept, rambling place with a good restaurant. Room rates include breakfast.

Hotel Mariscal Alcázar (☎/fax 043-311725; **w** *www.hotelalcazar.cl; Lautaro 385; singles/doubles/triples from US$31/39/50*), at the northeast corner of the Plaza de Armas, is airy and comfortable, though the rooms are not huge.

Supermarkets for provisions include **Las Brisas** (*Villagrán 558*), opposite Terminal Santa Rita bus station, and **Tucapel** (*Colón 600 • Alemania 100*) which has two stores.

Café Prymos (*Colón 400*) is a reliable spot for breakfast, coffee or sandwiches. **Julio's Pizza** (*Colón 452; pizzas US$3-6*) serves good pizzas, pasta and other dishes. **Bife Sureño** (*Lautaro 681; mains US$4-6*) does meat, meat and more meat in mellow surroundings.

Getting There & Away Los Ángeles has two main bus stations. The long-distance **Terminal Santa María** (*Av Sor Vicenta 2051*) – and the separate, shinier Tur-Bus terminal – is a taxi ride northeast of town. In the centre of town is the **Terminal Santa Rita** (*Villagrán & Rengo*), for buses to local destinations.

There are frequent buses between Terminal Santa María and Puerto Montt (US$13, eight hours), Temuco (US$6, four hours) and Santiago (US$12, eight hours). Bus companies operating on these routes all have offices at the terminal, and include **Biobío** (☎ 043-314621), **Igi Llaima** (☎ 043-321666), **Cruz del Sur** (☎ 043-317630), **Fénix Pullman Norte** (☎ 043-322502), **Buses Jac** (☎ 043-317469), **Unión del Sur** (☎ 043-316891), **Tur Bus** (☎ 043-328062) and **Jota Be** (☎ 043-363037). Jota Be also runs to Angol, the gateway to Parque Nacional Nahuel Buta, via Renaico (US$2, 1½ hours).

Destinations served from Terminal Santa Rita include El Abanico, near the entrance to Parque Nacional Laguna del Laja (see Getting to/from the Trek, p83).

Around Volcán Antuco

Duration	3 days
Distance	40.5km
Difficulty	moderate
Start/Finish	Guardería Chacay
Nearest Town	Los Ángeles (p81)
Transport	bus & walk

Summary Crunch over lava that looks as though it solidified yesterday, see hanging glaciers and cool off in a highland lake on this circuit through the wildest parts of Parque Nacional Laguna del Laja.

This circumnavigation of Volcán Antuco is the only long trekking possibility in the park. The trek crosses bare lava flows and loose volcanic earth for virtually the entire distance. It involves a climb from Guardería Chacay (1115m) to a 2054m pass, and the route is largely unmarked, though fairly straightforward. In the central section there is no real track and deep snow may lie well into January. The long final section is along an easily navigable dirt road. Fine summer weather can make the going unpleasantly hot, in particular lower down.

The trek can be done in two very long days, but parties should plan to take three days. An ascent of Volcán Antuco, on either the northern or southeastern side (see Other Treks, p109), would take an additional day. An easy but spectacular one-hour return walk can also be made from opposite the

Conaf information centre to the nearby waterfalls of Salto Las Chilcas and Salto El Torbellino on the Río Laja, where at various points the subterranean flow of water from Laguna de la Laja and Volcán Antuco gushes from the porous ground.

The circuit can be trekked in either direction, but the recommended way to do it is anticlockwise.

PLANNING
What to Bring
As there are no huts along the route, this trek cannot be done safely without a tent. Conaf has plans to construct a basic emergency shelter below the pass on the southwestern slopes of Volcán Antuco at some time in the future, but this would not alter the need for a tent. Some wide tent pegs such as snow pegs would be useful in the loose volcanic soil, though fallen *quila* (bamboo) canes make a satisfactory substitute.

Permits & Regulations
No permit is required for this trek, but the standard rules apply regarding signing in and out. Visitors can sign in at the Guardería Chacay or (better) at the adjacent administration centre, and should sign out on completing the trek.

NEAREST TOWN & FACILITIES
See Los Ángeles (p81).

Parque Nacional Laguna del Laja & Around
The nearest stores are in El Abanico and Antuco, and there are kiosks beside the turn-off to the park for limited last-minute purchases, but Los Ángeles is by far the best option for buying supplies. Just before the turn-off, near the village of El Abanico, is the **Hotel Malalcura** (☎ 043-313183).

Within the park itself, on the banks of the Río Laja about 1km up the road from the Portería El Álamo, is the **Centro Turístico Lagunillas** (camping per site US$8, 6-person cabins US$60). This privately run camping ground offers good self-contained cabins and sheltered, rather dusty camp sites. There are hot showers and a kitchen for guests. For information and reservations call **Hostería Manantiales** (☎ 043-314275), at the Salto del Laja on the Panamerican Hwy.

Higher up at the small ski village of Volcán Antuco is the **Casino Club de Esquí/ Refugio Antuco** (*dorm beds around US$10*). Although much busier in winter, the *refugio* is open year-round and serves meals and drinks. Also here is **Refugio Digeder** (☎ 041-229054; *dorm beds US$10*), which is operated by the city of Concepción's Dirección General de Deportes y Recreación and *may* be open in summer.

GETTING TO/FROM THE TREK

Parque Nacional Laguna del Laja is 90km by road east of Los Ángeles (p81). There is no public transport the whole way to the park, but there are regular **ERS** (☎ 043-322356) buses from Los Ángeles' central bus station, Terminal Santa Rita, via Antuco to El Abanico, a village near the turn-off to the park (US$2, 1½ to two hours, up to six daily). These stop at the turn-off. The first leaves at 8.30am (10am at the weekend), and the last return bus from El Abanico departs at around 7.15pm.

From the El Abanico turn-off the road leads 11km up beside the Río Laja to the Guardería Chacay, a minor ranger station adjacent to the park administration centre at Chacay. This stretch can be walked in three or four hours, but there is enough friendly traffic during the busy tourist season to make successful hitching reasonably certain. The trek described here begins at the *guardería*.

THE TREK (see map p84)
Day 1: Guardería Chacay to Estero Los Pangues Camp
1¾–2½ hours, 4.5km

Follow the path (signposted 'Sendero Meseta Los Zorros y Sierra Velluda') from just above Guardería Chacay due south up the slope past clusters of Cordilleran cypresses. Head up a steep, eroding, reddish ridge to reach a signposted junction at the edge of a tiny plateau overlooking the Río Laja after 30 to 45 minutes. From here an easy side trip goes to Meseta de los Zorros (see Side Trip).

To continue, take the left branch (marked 'Sierra Velluda') up over the low, sparsely vegetated ridges until you come to a lava flow. The path first skirts left along the edge of the lava, then follows a scrubby lead amid the mass of solidified slag before heading across broken rock, marked by cairns and *quila* wands, directly towards a prominent hanging glacier high up on the Sierra Velluda. Eventually the rock ends and the trail continues across volcanic sand to reach the small but fast-flowing Estero Los Pangues after one to 1½ hours. Here you meet another foot track coming up the north bank of the stream.

Go briefly downstream until you find a place to cross the Estero Los Pangues, then head towards tall *lengas* at the foot of a ridge coming down from the Sierra Velluda to **camp** after a further 15 minutes or so. The ground is loose and sometimes dusty (see What to Bring, p82), but water is close by and the views directly up to the Sierra Velluda, which towers above a wide grassy bend in the stream, are spectacular.

Side Trip: Meseta de los Zorros
40 minutes–1 hour return, 2.5km

From the signpost at the edge of the plateau, take the right branch (marked 'Meseta Los Zorros') and follow the track down through light forest to the lovely grassy meadow of Meseta de los Zorros (shown on IGM maps as Los Pangues), set among moss-draped Cordilleran cypress and *coigüe* trees. There are good views across the valley towards the adjacent rocky range. Just below, the spectacular torrent of the Estero Los Pangues washes black volcanic scoria out from the mountains. Camping is possible on the grass, and a track continues down into the lower Estero Los Pangues valley. Retrace your steps to the signpost.

Day 2: Estero Los Pangues Camp to Los Barros
3¾–5½ hours, 13km

Backtrack to cross again to the north side of the Estero Los Pangues, then head upstream, tending southeast, across the scoria towards the obvious low point between the

THE ARAUCANÍA

Around Volcán Antuco

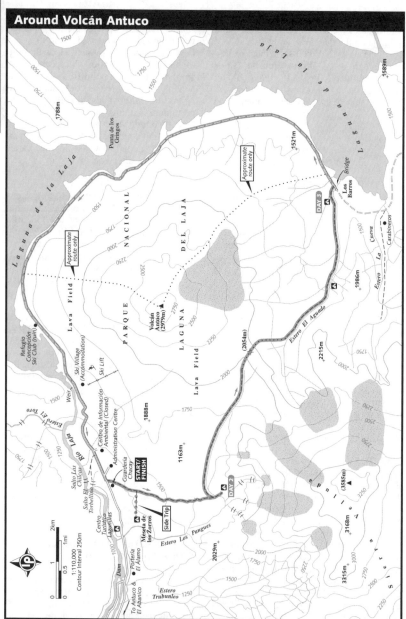

Sierra Velluda to your right and the majestic cone of Volcán Antuco. Marked only by occasional cairns, the track stays within earshot of the Estero Los Pangues, for the most part avoiding the vast expanse of broken volcanic rock. After you pass a steep ridge descending from the Sierra Velluda, the tiny upper valley widens to reveal more glaciers up to the right.

Make your way across a broad, rusty-red alluvial wash to the head of the now tiny stream. From here on, winter avalanches have mostly erased any markings leading up to the pass, but the best option is probably to ascend a loose-rock ridge that goes up steeply between two eroded gullies. Where this peters out, sidle rightward to arrive at the **pass**, two to three hours from camp.

The pass lies at 2054m, and gives wonderful views ahead down the valley to the southern arm of Laguna de la Laja and the ranges along the Chile–Argentina frontier. Hidden behind a bluff from the pass itself is the impressive glacier-clad eastern face of the Sierra Velluda's 3585m main summit.

The pass is likely to be snowed over and corniced well into January, so it may be necessary to traverse leftward along the ridge top for 500m or so before dropping down into the small basin below the pass. Snowdrifts here in early summer provide good glissading. Later in the season a faint trail sidles to the left before directly descending the steep, loose-earth slopes to the banks of the milky **Estero El Aguado** after one to 1¼ hours. If coming in the other direction, look out for a large cairn opposite a chasm with a waterfall before you reach the head of the valley. This points directly to the pass. In the upper Valle El Aguado occasional grassy patches among *ñirre* thickets on the true right (south) bank of the stream (which is easily waded) make nice alternative **camp sites.**

Proceed downstream through the sparsely vegetated Valle El Aguado. Away from the moister ground near the stream, the growth consists only of low shrubs and small vegetated mounds. The dusty path follows the northern bank, crossing several clear streams that emanate from the snow on Volcán Antuco's southern slopes. As you approach a

lone araucaria, stay close to the stream to avoid a boggy area over to the left, then continue a short way to reach a small wooden bridge at **Los Barros** after 45 minutes to 1¼ hours. Here, the flat shoreline of Laguna de la Laja is periodically inundated when the lake rises. Just upstream of the bridge, by a ford in the broad, shallow Estero El Aguado, is a good **camp site**. Goats and cattle graze hereabouts, so you may wish to treat the water, which is best taken from a clear tributary stream that crosses the dirt road between the ford and the bridge.

Day 3: Los Barros to Guardería Chacay
4¾–7 hours, 23km
There are no permanently running streams along this hot and sandy section, so it's advisable to carry water from camp. (The lake itself is not always easily accessible, though its water is generally safe to drink.) There is modest traffic along the rough, narrow road – mostly sport fishers or the odd truck from the summer-only *estancia* at the southern end of the lake – so it may be possible to hitch a ride.

Head off northward around the western side of Laguna de la Laja, through a volcanic desert caused by the eroding sand and the rain shadow of Volcán Antuco and the Sierra Velluda. In the heat of the late afternoon occasional meltwater streams may flow down from the volcano's upper slopes. Across the turquoise waters of Laguna de la Laja impressive bare eroding crags drop straight down to the shore, while mountains further to the north and south are heavily forested. The road dips and rises constantly, passing the curiously named narrow of **Punta de los Gringos** after two to three hours. There is reasonably good **camping** and opportunities for a cooling swim around the shore, although the ground is quite muddy in places.

Make your way around northwestward into an enormous lava flow (responsible for damming the Río Laja to create the lake) and on past the derelict Refugio Concepción Ski Club. The road continues through this raw landscape, soon bringing the peaks of the Sierra Velluda back into view, and passes a weir built over the lake outlet just before reaching the Volcán Antuco **ski village** (see Nearest Town & Facilities, p82) 1¾ to 2½ hours on. This small winter sports centre consists of 20 chalets scattered around the base of a ski lift.

Follow the road as it winds steadily down into the upper Valle Laja. Just after crossing a small brook the road passes a (signposted) turn-off leading a few minutes left through *coigües* to the park information centre – closed when we researched this edition – to arrive back at the Guardería Chacay after a final one to 1½ hours.

Reserva Nacional Malalcahuello-Nalcas

The 313-sq-km Reserva Nacional Malalcahuello-Nalcas lies 120km northeast of Temuco. It consists of the two contiguous reserves (managed jointly), whose boundary runs across the summit of Volcán Lonquimay (2726m).

Although a large forest reserve was originally established around the volcano in 1931, much of this land was later given to colonists. From the early 1930s until the mid-1940s, uncontrolled forest fires ravaged a quarter of Malalcahuello-Nalcas. Then, in the 1950s, the area was extensively logged (partly for sleepers used in the construction of the now disused railway line to the town of Lonquimay). In the early 1960s, exotic conifers were planted.

Even though almost half the forest has been burnt or logged in the past, today the reserve is a surprisingly wild – but easily accessible – wilderness that offers some outstanding shorter and multiday treks.

NATURAL HISTORY

The superb araucaria tree most typifies the local vegetation, and at higher elevations it is the dominant tree in most locations. In the past the local Pehuenche people visited these highland forests in autumn to collect the rich supply of araucaria nuts (known in local Spanish as *piñones*), from which they prepared a starchy meal. Also well represented among the forest trees are a number of *Nothofagus* species, including the common *coigüe, coigüe de Magallanes, lenga* and *raulí*. Unfortunately, exotic Douglas firs (introduced from North America) are gradually supplanting native forest in some areas on the reserve's periphery.

Growing in the sandy volcanic soil among the araucarias you'll find the *quellén*, a native wild strawberry whose yellow-white flowers mature into edible berries by March. The striking, deep-red flowers of the *notro* bush grows on sunny sites. Common mountain wild flowers found in the reserve include the *añañuca*, which produces several pink flowers in an elongated goblet form growing from a single succulent stem, the *violeta del monte*, a yellow subalpine violet species, and *capachitos*, attractive yellow, white or pink flowers of the genus *Calceolaria*. Tough native tussock grasses endure in less exposed places above tree line.

The local fauna includes the elusive puma and its much smaller feline cousin, the *huiña*, as well as the pudu and the tree-dwelling mouse opossum *(monito del monte)*. At times trekkers may sight falcons or even Andean condors circling the ridge tops, and native ducks like the red shoveller *(pato cuchara)* and the Chiloé wigeon *(pato real)* around the lakes and rivers. The black Magellanic woodpecker *(carpintero negro)* inhabits the forests.

CLIMATE

Annual precipitation levels in Malalcahuello-Nalcas average almost 3000mm, mostly falling in winter as snow. Normal midwinter (July–August) snow cover is around 2m near Refugio Pewen, but down the valley of the Río Cautín snow does not normally remain for much longer than a week. The warmer weather of spring (October–November) quickly melts away the snow cover, however, and by late January few areas below around 2300m have any snow. Summer weather is typically pleasantly hot, though long periods of dry weather are fairly uncommon.

ACCESS TOWN
Curacautín (Chile)

Curacautín (population 12,700) is close to Parque Nacional Conguillío and Reserva Nacional Malalcahuello-Nalcas. There is a tourist information booth at the bus terminal, on the Plaza de Armas.

Hostal Rayén *(☎ 045-881262; Manuel Rodríguez 1040; rooms per person US$8)* offers basic rooms with breakfast included. Or try **Hotel Turismo** *(☎ 045-811116; Tarapacá 140; singles/doubles US$13/20)*. There are simple **restaurants** around the Plaza de Armas.

Getting There & Away Erbuc runs around 10 daily buses from Temuco to Curacautín (US$2.50). The trip takes about two hours via Lautaro, or 2½ hours via Victoria. Buses running between Temuco and Zapala via Paso de Pino Hachado pass through Curacautín.

Lonquimay Circuit

Duration	6 days
Distance	95.5km
Difficulty	moderate–demanding
Start/Finish	Malalcahuello (p87)
Transport	bus
Summary	A varied round-the-mountain trek through a fascinating volcanic landscape formed by very recent eruptions.

Largely following long-disused logging roads dating from the 1950s, this trek crosses several minor saddles and two passes to make a circumnavigation of Volcán Lonquimay. The route leads through beautiful araucaria and *lenga* forests, skirts a vast scoria field and passes small lakes dammed by a lava flow before climbing past a crater that formed in the volcano's 1989 eruption.

The route is marked by steel stakes variously coloured to distinguish each trail section. It is probably best done in a clockwise direction. Combined with Day 1 only, the Alternative Route (p93) forms a much shorter (19.5km) circuit suitable as a day trek.

Another option is to start – or better end – the trek at the Refugio Pewen (see Day 4, p91), from where it may be possible to get a ride with staff back to Malalcahuello (13km).

PLANNING
When to Trek

The trek is best undertaken between mid-December and late April. Early in the season the route may be severely snowed over and tricky to cross without an ice axe and crampons. The trails are virtually snow-free by mid-January.

Maps

Two Chilean IGM 1:50,000 maps, *Malalcahuello* (Section G, No 64) and *Lonquimay* (Section G, No 65) cover the trek but do not indicate any of the tracks. Conaf has produced a 1:80,000 colour-contoured map available free from the Malalcahuello office. It shows official tracks accurately and is good enough for basic navigation. (Note that it gives only UTM – Universal Transversal de Mercator – coordinates so you may have to reset your GPS receiver.)

Permits & Regulations

Permits are not required to trek in the reserve, though all parties should inform staff at the Conaf office of their intended route. Camping is permitted at any existing site but, due to high fire danger, trekkers should avoid lighting campfires.

NEAREST TOWN
Malalcahuello

The scattered village of Malalcahuello lies on Ruta 181 (R-89), 31km east of Curacautín and 15km west of Lonquimay. Its interesting Mapuche name (usually pronounced mal-al-ka-**way**-yo) is derived from Spanish and means 'horse corral'. The old train station was recently converted into a tourist centre. The **Conaf administration centre** *(☎ 045-97103720)*, 200m east of the village entrance, can give information on Reserva Nacional Malalcahuello-Nalcas.

Hospedaje Los Sauces *(☎ 09-8837880; rooms per person US$5)* – cut left from the disused rail line – has basic rooms with breakfast included, and serves other meals. **Hostal La Nahuelcura** (☎ *045-9321633, 9191083; cabins US$18*) also has a restaurant.

Getting There & Away Erbuc buses running between Curacautín (p87) and the village of Lonquimay pass by Malalcahuello up to four times daily in either direction. The last bus back to Curacautín (US$2.50, 40 minutes) passes at approximately 6.50pm.

THE TREK
Day 1: Malalcahuello to Upper Río Coloradito
4–5½ hours, 11km, 950m ascent

Carry some water, as the central part of this section (although well shaded) has no running water.

Walk to the Conaf administration centre, 200m east of the village entrance. After signing in, follow a rough road (marked with numbered, blue-tipped stakes) from the upper left side of the Conaf office around west through pastures, past a disused wooden aqueduct and waterwheel to reach a fork above a sawmill. Turn right and head up into roble forest that goes over into stands of *rauli* and fragrant *tepa* as you climb steadily higher beside a rushing little stream. The track leads on around northwest through exotic Douglas firs to end at a wire fence (the reserve boundary), 50 minutes to 1¼ hours from the Conaf office.

Here continue northeast up a broad spur under tall *coigües* to cross a tiny stream (the first water for some time) after 30 to 45 minutes. The route makes a long, winding, upward traverse high above the valley of the Río Coloradito through araucaria and *lenga* forest (and large snowdrifts earlier in the season) to reach a narrow, open strip between bands of forest just below the main ridge *(GPS 38° 26.445 S, 71° 34.551 W)*, 45 minutes to one hour on.

Pick up yellow paint markings and stakes guiding you diagonally across the eroding slope, then cut up right to gain the ridge top fringed by *lenga* forest after 15 to 20 minutes. (Alternatively, just take a route directly over this rockier section of the ridge.) There are clear views southward to the snow-capped Sierra Nevada and Volcán Llaima as well as ahead to Volcán Lonquimay. The track rises and dips northward along the 1700m contour line between sparse grassy tundra and the uppermost *lengas* and araucarias, before dropping away left into a broad bamboo gully. Continue on down into the forest past **camp sites** around a tiny, soggy meadow grazed by timid cattle, 30 to 45 minutes from where you first reached the ridge top.

Rise over a minor embankment and on across spring-fed streamlets to a fork. Bear left (the right-hand way short-cuts west directly across the tundra of the upper Río Coloradito to join Day 2) and descend steadily past superb old araucarias to meet a disused road below the clearing of an old logging camp, 40 to 50 minutes from the soggy meadow. There are **camp sites** here on sloping lawns or (better) by the nearby stream.

Walk five minutes along the old road and pick up a foot track on the right 40m before it fords the upper **Río Coloradito** (see also Alternative Route, p93). The track climbs the east bank of the small stream to intersect with the trail from Portezuelo Colorado (see Day 5) near a large araucaria just above tree line in the broad tundra basin. Descending trekkers should cut briefly down to find the trail where it enters the forest, 50m from the stream *(GPS 38° 25.005 S, 71° 35.631 W)*. There are fair **camp sites** just downstream on the opposite side of the Río Coloradito.

Day 2: Upper Río Coloradito to Estero Laguna Verde
5½–6¾ hours, 17km, 750m ascent

Hop across the small upper Río Coloradito and sidle northwest gently upward through bamboo scrub along tree line. Where you encounter some shallow gullies, cut around briefly rightward above a stand of araucarias to cross a deeper (often snow-filled) gully. **Camp sites** can be found in a hollow 150m around to the left. Head around northward on a vague route that zigzags up through the bare scoria scattered with *cuye eldorado* (a hardy oxalis species). The terrain gradually levels out as you head into the **Portezuelo Huamachuco** (1715m), a

Lonquimay Circuit

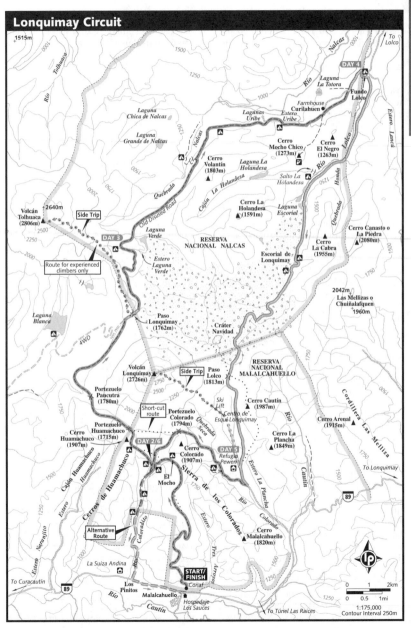

1:175,000
Contour Interval 250m

very broad pass between Volcán Lonquimay and Cerro Huamachuco, 50 minutes to 1¼ hours from the upper Río Coloradito. Here the trek exits Reserva Nacional Malalcahuello.

Drop rightward into an old lava field towards an isolated red-rock outcrop. The route follows a shelf covered in alpine grasses and pinkish-purple *añañucas* overlooking the upper basin of the Estero Huamachuco, dipping across a small ravine. Climb around north via a broad scoria gully where large snowdrifts often lie well into January, then continue over a barren plain and climb to cross the lava-choked watershed slightly above (right of) **Portezuelo Pancutra** (1780m), 1¼ to 1½ hours from Portezuelo Huamachuco. From here you get a first direct view northward to Volcán Tolhuaca.

Descend 1.2km northwest along the left edge of a rugged lava field just where it fringes the forest, then (when you reach cream-coloured bluffs up to your left) start heading rightward. Watch carefully for old paint markings and sporadic orange-tipped marker stakes that guide you through narrow sections of sandy scoria between the broken black rocks. The route moves diagonally up the slope before beginning a northeast traverse at approximately 1800m to avoid the roughest terrain. Down to your left, the lava extends into a wild, enclosed basin almost to the shore of a small unnamed lake fed by a spectacular 300m waterfall plummeting from the névés of Volcán Tolhuaca.

Stay high as you continue across bouldery terrain above stands of araucarias then cut left slightly downhill over sparse scoria tundra full of tucotuco burrows to meet an old 4WD track on the broad **Paso Lonquimay** (1762m), two to 2½ hours from Portezuelo Pancutra. This old road switchbacks up from **Laguna Blanca**, a larger lake that remains unseen behind a forested ridge. The pass opens up a great view northeast towards Volcán Callaqui and Volcán Copahue, both more than 40km away.

Turn right and follow the rough old road (impassable even to 4WD vehicles) on northward into Reserva Nacional Nalcas. Early

in the season, large snowdrifts across the old road ahead may be tricky to cross. The route winds down into araucaria and *lenga* forest above a vast expanse of old and more recent lava flows – the younger rock distinguishable by its reddish tint – stretching across the northern slopes of Volcán Lonquimay to pass **camp sites** shortly before the old road bridge (still passable to pedestrians) over the Estero Laguna Verde, 1¼ to 1½ hours from Paso Lonquimay.

Side Trip: Volcán Tolhuaca Summit
6–8 hours return, 15km,
1045m ascent/descent
The ascent of Volcán Tolhuaca via its southeast side is not much harder than Volcán Lonquimay (see Day 4 Side Trip, p92), but generally requires an ice axe (and probably crampons). The ascent can begin from Paso Lonquimay by following the ridge northwest or by cutting up from the first hairpin bend you encounter 3km north of the pass. The route initially climbs via a spur, avoiding rocky outcrops as it cuts up rightward over snowfields to the crater.

Descend by the same route.

Day 3: Estero Laguna Verde to Río Lolco–Estero Lancú Confluence
4¾–6¼ hours, 21km, 300m ascent
Contour high above Laguna Verde, a tarn at the edge of the lava (it's glimpsed through the trees but is difficult to reach), before rising gently over the scenic **Portezuelo Nalcas** watershed (1660m) after 25 to 30 minutes. The often heavily eroded old road makes a long downward traverse northeast towards distant snowy ranges on fire-cleared slopes high above the roaring Quebrada Nalcas. When you reach the first hairpin bend (marked by a large cairn) after 50 minutes to 1¼ hours, continue straight ahead. (The road itself winds down 15 to 20 minutes to attractive **camp sites** by the Quebrada Nalcas.)

A graded but sometimes overgrown foot track now rises briefly before descending into mixed forest, gradually turning eastward as it crosses side streams and **camp sites** in occasional tussock-grass clearings. Head on smoothly down under bluffs up to your right through *ñirre* scrub dotted with anemones, purple-flowered vetches and yellow *capachitos*, crossing a minor watershed to pass the reedy, mosquito-plagued Lagunas Uribe, 1¾ to 2½ hours after leaving the old road. Jump across the small Estero Uribe and climb along a minor ridge, then drop back right to make an easy wade of the (now larger) Estero Uribe, 25 to 30 minutes on. There are **camp sites** along the stream's southern bank.

Head on through meadows beside the cascading stream towards the striking, pyramid-shaped Cerro Maravilla (2178m) in the Cordillera Lancú to the east. The path drops gently into roble forest scattered with pineapple-like bromeliads as it continues over slopes that look out north across the marshy plains of the Río Nalcas, before cutting down to the lush boggy pastures of **Curilahuen** (an enclave of private land in the reserve), 30 to 40 minutes from the second Estero Uribe crossing.

Continue eastward through 2m-high spiny *chacay* bushes to the right of a wire fence (marking the boundary of this enclave). The route passes a small corral and old farm shacks (from where a blue-marked trail leads off southwest 3km to the 1273m lookout peak of **Cerro Mocho Chico**), tracing the fence line around northeast across a scrubby stream to meet a 4WD track (the access to Curilahuen) after 25 to 30 minutes.

Turn right and follow the rough road (directly past the left trail turn-off going 1.2km to Laguna la Totora) to meet the Río Lolco near its confluence with the Estero Lancú after 15 to 20 minutes. Excellent **camp sites** can be found in daisy meadows a short way upstream along the west bank of the Río Lolco, but fires are not allowed.

Day 4: Río Lolco–Estero Lancú Confluence to Refugio Pewen

6–8 hours, 26km, 880m ascent,
180m descent

This rather long section follows a road proper for the entire distance. It can be broken into two leisurely days by camping lower down on the northern approach to Paso Lolco.

Follow the road across the Río Lolco out of the reserve – an iron gate on the east side of the bridge blocks public vehicle access – to reach the Malalcahuello–Lolco road after five to 10 minutes. (If coming from the other direction, this turn-off is about 100m upvalley from a blue farmhouse on the north side of the Estero Lancú.) You are now within the private property of the **Fundo Lolco**, where camping is prohibited.

Turn right and follow the often rough dirt road steadily up through roble and *coigüe* forest above the rushing river to re-enter Reserva Nacional Nalcas after one to 1½ hours. The gradient eases as you continue five to 10 minutes past a short turn-off to **camp sites** on moist clover lawns near the **Salto la Holandesa**, a waterfall at the edge of a recent red lava flow.

Proceed up opposite the enormous expanse of lava fringing the Río Lolco, which has been forced into a narrow course between the raw, broken-up rock and the valley's steep, forested eastern slopes. In places the lava has dammed the (now small) river to create tarns in whose clear, greenish waters submerged trees are still visible. Parts of the old road itself may be flooded early in the season (though construction of a basic road slightly higher up is planned), but sections of foot track generally allow easy passage. Head on upvalley to reach **Laguna Escorial**, a larger and deeper lake also hemmed in by the lava, 30 to 45 minutes on from the Salto la Holandesa.

Climb on into *lenga* forest past **camp sites** by a shallow tarn down left before crossing a final streamlet (your last water for some time) flowing down from the bare ridges. At a sharp curve, ignore an older road that continues off right, alongside the lava, and ascend left through the last araucarias. The road winds its way up through the desolate moonscape, granting good views across the volcanic basin to Volcán Tolhuaca and up to the northeastern face of Volcán Lonquimay, finally curving slightly downward into Paso Lolco (1813m), three to four hours from Laguna Escorial.

From the pass, a rough and poorly marked route (1½ hours, 4km return) leads around northwest up over loose black-sand slopes above a deep scoria basin to the rim of **Cráter Navidad** (see the boxed text 'The Christmas Crater'), from where you can look down into the raw core of this young crater. Another high-level route cuts up left over Cerro Cautín to rejoin the road lower down.

The road drops south over heavily eroding volcanic ash into the basin of the Río Colorado, passing the (right) turn-off to the tiny Centro de Esquí Lonquimay by the short driveway to Refugio Pewen, one to 1¼ hours from the pass. Also known as Refugio Volcán Lonquimay, **Refugio Pewen** (☎ 02-1963549; W www.pewen.com; dorm beds/private rooms per person US$8/18; breakfast/lunch/dinner US$2/4/6), is a small mountain lodge that stands at tree line (around 1600m) among graceful araucarias. This warm refugio has electricity and hot water. The refugio, whose name is the modern Mapudungan (Mapuche language) spelling of the word pehuén, or 'araucaria', makes an excellent base for climbing Volcán Lonquimay (see Side Trip). Or if you want to end the trek here it may be possible to get a ride with staff back down to Malalcahuello (13km).

The Christmas Crater

On 25 December 1988, Volcán Lonquimay suddenly erupted, blasting ash and smoke 8000m into the atmosphere. While the spectacle aroused considerable public attention, vulcanologists were less surprised by the eruption itself than by its creation of a new 'parasitic' crater on the northeast side of Volcán Lonquimay. Promptly dubbed Cráter Navidad, or 'Christmas Crater', for the next 13 months this side crater continued expelling volcanic debris, building a cone over 100m-high until it finally petered out. Cráter Navidad – though certainly not the volcano as a whole – is now thought to be extinct. This was the first time in Chile that the full birth-to-extinction cycle of a volcano had been observed. Considering the size of the eruption, its impact on the local ecology was relatively minor.

Side Trip: Volcán Lonquimay Summit
6–8 hours return, 16km,
1100m ascent/descent

This route up the southeast side of the volcano that has dominated (at times blocked) your views is the highlight one of the circuit. Although rated moderate–demanding, the climb is surprisingly uncomplicated, but early in the season (before January) snow higher up may make it advisable to carry an ice axe. Follow the road up to the Centro de Esquí Lonquimay and head up beside the ski lift. The route continues up the ridge northwest over a snowdrift before ascending a steeper spur that leads to the summit. The sensational panorama takes in dozens of key peaks in the Araucanía, including the now familiar Sierra Nevada, Volcán Llaima and Volcán Tolhuaca as well as more distant landmarks like Volcán Lanín to the south.

Descend by the same route.

Day 5: Refugio Pewen to Upper Río Coloradito
2½–3 hours, 9.5km, 175m ascent

Walk 800m down the (now well-graded) road and take a (right) trail turn-off by a Conaf information board and map. Head northwest onto a sparse scoria plain and cross (normally dry) stream gullies of the upper Río Colorado to reach the ruins of a small log cabin, 30 to 40 minutes from the refugio. Attractive **camp sites** can be found nearby among the araucarias.

Don't take the dead-end route going off left across a stream, but watch for occasional yellow-tipped marker stakes leading northward along the edge of forest. The trail cuts left to avoid a deeply eroded gully, following this streamway around northwest along an undulating grassy shelf dotted with yellow orchids, purplish-white vetch and other alpine wild flowers to a tiny spring. Continue 100m past a small stand of araucarias, then cross the tiny stream and climb northwest up loose scoria slopes towards the obvious pass between Volcán Lonquimay and the low, pinkish summit of Cerro Colorado to reach **Portezuelo Colorado** (1794m), 1¼ to 1½ hours from the ruined log cabin. This pass gives views east to the bare ridges of Cerro Cautín and southwest to Volcán Llaima. A short-cut route traverses west across the slope to Portezuelo Huamachuco.

Descend southwest through a broad dry gully towards Cerro Huamachuco. Treading carefully, as burrowing tucotucos have created ground hollows that sink under your weight, head left down around an old lava field. The route (confused in places by diverging cattle pads) cuts down across a stream gully among the grassy alpine herbage, recrossing the stream some way down. Move rightward to meet the small upper Río Coloradito, which splashes over lava slabs as you follow it down to reach the trail junction (see Day 1), 40 to 50 minutes from Portezuelo Colorado.

Day 6: Upper Río Coloradito to Malalcahuello
3–4½ hours, 11km, 950m descent
Retrace your steps as on Day 1 or opt for the Alternative Route described below. Both variants could be combined with Day 5 for a longer day's trekking.

Alternative Route: via Los Pinitos
2¼–3¼ hours, 9.5km, 600m descent
This is a quicker and less steep variant back to Ruta 181 (R-89). Combined with Day 1 only, the Alternative Route forms a shorter circuit suitable as a day trek.

Head down into the forest from the upper Río Coloradito along the true left (east) bank of the river to meet the old road (see Day 1). Follow it directly right to ford the small stream, then drop smoothly past excellent **camp sites** (but no fires allowed) around a grassy clearing among araucarias on your left. The rough road descends through *coigüe* and *rauli* forest logged and/or burnt decades ago to reach another attractive clearing just uphill from a locked gate (marking the reserve boundary), 50 minutes to 1¼ hours from the upper Río Coloradito. There is a Conaf information board and map here. This is also an attractive spot for **camping** (but a fire ban also applies here).

The road continues down past the first farmhouses (watch out for dogs!) to cross the river on a bridge, levelling out before it intersects with Ruta 181 (R-89) at Los Pinitos, a further 50 minutes to 1¼ hours on. There is a bus shelter here, and **La Suiza Andina** (☎ 045-1973725, 09-8849541; ⓦ www.suizaandina.com; camping per person US$4, dorm beds US$8, self-contained cabins US$25, doubles with private bathroom & breakfast US$40), a Swiss-owned hostel, is 400m to the right (west).

Turn left and walk along the highway directly past the **Restaurante-Hostería Piedra Santa**, through rich dairy pastures picked over by honking flocks of black-necked ibis to reach Malalcahuello after 35 to 50 minutes.

Parque Nacional Huerquehue

Parque Nacional Huerquehue (where-**kay**-way) lies to the east of Lago Caburgua, 35km northeast of Pucón. This 125-sq-km park – soon to be expanded eastward to include an additional 100 sq km – is a gentle landscape of numerous lovely lakes nestling into small plateaus (averaging 1300m). Craggy ranges approaching 2000m and clothed in a thick mantle of rainforest tower above the lakes. The lowest point in the park is the eastern shore of Lago Tinquilco, a deep, 3km-long glacial lake with tiny beaches.

Apart from some wonderful treks, swimming and fishing in the lakes are popular activities. The surface water in Lago Tinquilco reaches around 20°C in summer, and although the higher lakes in the central part of Huerquehue are generally a few degrees cooler they are fine for a quick dip. Several developed hot springs surrounding the park, including the Termas de Río Blanco (visited on the Huerquehue Lakes trek, p95).

NATURAL HISTORY
The park's Mapuche name means 'place of the thrushes', a reference to the austral thrush, or *zorzal*, which inhabits this densely

forested area. Among other bird life in the park is the ubiquitous *chucao*, whose chuckling calls resound throughout the undergrowth of the forest floor. The area is also home to the large Magellanic woodpecker, or *carpintero negro*, and its smaller relative, the *carpintero chico*. The tiny native deer, or pudu, is occasionally spotted scurrying through the underbrush.

As in much of the Araucanía, the araucaria tree, or *pehuén*, dominates the more elevated areas, often forming pure stands. These beautiful conifers fringe the shores of the higher lakes, and their distinct umbrella-like form stands out on the ridge tops. The southern beeches *lenga* and *coigüe* are also present. Lower down, the forests are dominated by *tepa*, identifiable by its serrated, deliciously fragrant leaves, and the coniferous *mañío*. Lower elevations also favour *boldo*, whose oval-shaped, leathery leaves are often used to make a hot infusion that is taken like tea. A parasitic plant called the *quintral* lives on the *boldo*, and unsuspecting observers might mistakenly assume its more flamboyant white, red-tipped blooms belong to the *boldo* (whose flowers are actually pale yellow).

Wherever the forest is fully mature, the understorey is quite open and surprisingly sparse, featuring epiphyte species such as the *botellita* and the *estrellita*. Typically seen growing on tree trunks, these two climbing vines produce fine red flowers that brighten up the shady forest floor.

Quila grows in small clusters anywhere that receives even a few stray rays of direct sunlight. Around the shores of Lago Tinquilco you will also see the graceful *arrayán*, a water-loving myrtle species with smooth, almost luminescent orange bark.

CLIMATE

Huerquehue is in a climatic transition zone between the warm temperate lowlands and the cooler Andes. The Lago Tinquilco area has a moderate climate with a mean annual temperature of 11.5°C. Precipitation is concentrated between the winter months of May and September – when the upland area above 1300m receives heavy snowfalls – and annual levels reach a relatively moderate 2000mm in the ranges of central Huerquehue.

ACCESS TOWN
Pucón (Chile)

The outdooring and ski resort of Pucón (population 10,000) lies on the eastern shore of Lago Villarrica directly below the perfect cone of Volcán Villarrica, close to the national parks of Huerquehue and Villarrica.

Information Pucón has a helpful public **tourist office** (☎ 045-441916; O'Higgins 669) as well as the private **Cámara de Turismo** (☎ 045-441671; Brasil 115), which also sells annual fishing licences (US$3). The **Conaf office** (☎ 045-441261; Camino Internacional 1450), at the eastern edge of town on Ruta 119 (towards Puesco), can advise on trekking and climbing in the area.

Almost a dozen companies in Pucón run guided climbing, trekking and other outdoor-adventure tours in the surrounding mountains. Several of the best are **Anden Sport** (☎ 045-441048; ⊠ www.andensport.cl; O'Higgins), **Politur** (☎ 045-441373; ⊠ www.politur.com; O'Higgins 635) and **Trancura** (☎ 447-498575; ⊠ www.trancura.com; O'Higgins 211).

Places to Stay & Eat The HI-affiliated **Hostería ¡ecole!** (☎ 045-443201; ⊠ www.ecole.cl/english/hosteria.htm; Urrutia 592; dorm beds from US$7, singles/doubles US$17/30) runs regular climbing trips to Volcán Villarrica, and has an excellent **vegetarian restaurant**. **La Tetera** (☎ 045-441462; ⊠ www.tetera.cl; Urrutia 580; singles/doubles with shared bathroom from US$16/24, doubles with private bathroom from US$33) offers better rooms and runs the excellent **Traveller Café** downstairs.

Getting There & Away From the **bus terminal** (☎ 045-441923; Uruguay & Palguín) there are roughly hourly buses to Villarrica (30 minutes) and Temuco (three hours) as well as local buses to Puesco, Reigolil (via Curarrehue) and Lago Tinquilco (at Parque Nacional Huerquehue). International buses running between Temuco and San Martín de los Andes (via Paso Mamuil Malal) pass through Pucón daily.

LanExpress (☎ 600-5262000) flies four times weekly between Santiago and Pucón (US$74, some flights via Temuco).

Huerquehue Lakes

Duration	4 days
Distance	42.5km
Difficulty	easy–moderate
Start/Finish	Guardería Tinquilco
Nearest Town	Pucón (p94)
Transport	bus

Summary This out-and-back trek explores a delightful lakeland plateau on the way to remote hot springs.

The subalpine lake basin above Lago Tinquilco can be visited fairly easily as a day trek. This multiday out-and-back route includes some less visited areas beyond these popular lakes. All tracks are well maintained and variously marked with yellow and (later) blue stakes. There are signposts at all important junctions. Faster trekkers may opt to walk to the Termas de Río Blanco in a single day, then return the next day.

PLANNING
When to Trek
The trek can normally be done from mid-November at least until the end of April. Note, however, that *tábanos* are out in force (especially in hot weather) from late December to early February.

Maps
The entire park area is covered by the Chilean IGM's 1:50,000 *Nevados de Caburgua* (Section G, No 96). Although topographically very accurate, this map does not show any trekking routes. Conaf has produced a simpler contoured map at a scale of 1:38,000, *Parque Nacional Huerquehue*, which is available free when you pay your entry fee. The Conaf map in-dicates the main paths with a fair degree of accuracy, and most trekkers will find it good enough.

Permits & Regulations
The entrance fee to Parque Nacional Huerquehue is US$3/1 per adult/child, payable at the Guardería Tinquilco.

There is a ban on camping in Parque Nacional Huerquehue, except at the Conaf camping ground on Lago Tinquilco and at Camping Renahue (all other nearby camping grounds are outside the park boundaries). Fires are not permitted *anywhere* in the park (including at the Conaf camping ground and *refugio*).

NEAREST TOWN & FACILITIES
See Pucón (p94).

Around Lago Tinquilco
Conaf's **Guardería Tinquilco**, about halfway around the lake's southeastern shore, administers the park. The **interpretation centre**, 300m past the *guardería*, has exhibits on local flora and fauna. The 24-site **Conaf camping ground** (*Jan-Feb sites US$12, Mar-Dec sites US$8*) sits among beautiful *arrayán* trees along the lake shore near the Guardería Tinquilco. To access the Lago Tinquilco area see Getting to/from the Trek.

GETTING TO/FROM THE TREK
The trek starts at Guardería Tinquilco, 35km from Pucón.

In January and February, Buses Jac runs two buses daily from Pucón to Guardería Tinquilco, leaving Pucón at 8.30am and 4pm and returning from Guardería Tinquilco at 10am and 5pm (US$2, 40 minutes). At other times, there is only the morning bus on Monday, Wednesday, Friday and Saturday.

There are also several daily buses from Pucón that run (via Caburgua) only as far as Paillaco, from where it's a 7km (two-hour) mostly uphill walk to Guardería Tinquilco.

Campers can park cars for free near the Guardería Tinquilco, but vehicles must otherwise be left at the private car park near Refugio Tinquilco (US$1.50 per day).

THE TREK
Day 1: Guardería Tinquilco to Camping Renahue

3¾–5¼ hours, 11km, 640m ascent

Follow the dirt road past the information centre to **Camping & Hospedaje El Rincón** (☎ 09-6463025, 7915767; *terraced sites per tent US$11, rooms per person US$7*), at the northeast corner of Lago Tinquilco. Prices include firewood for campers and hot showers. El Rincón has a small **restaurant**.

Proceed around the northern side of Lago Tinquilco to reach a small car park where the transitable road ends. Here, cross the lake's main inlet stream on a little footbridge into the clearing where Refugio Tinquilco stands, 25 to 30 minutes from the *guardería*. **Refugio Tinquilco** (☎ 02-7777 673, 09-5392728; ⓦ *www.tinquilco.cl; dorm beds US$7, rooms US$26, rooms with private bathroom US$32, breakfast/lunch/dinner US$2/4/4*) is a superb wooden hut among tall *tepa* and *mañío* trees. Sheets for dorm beds costs US$1.50 extra. A trail leads down past the sauna to a beachlet on the lake. **Camping Olga** (☎ 045-441938; *sites US$7*), five minutes walk past Refugio Tinquilco, has secluded lakeside sites and

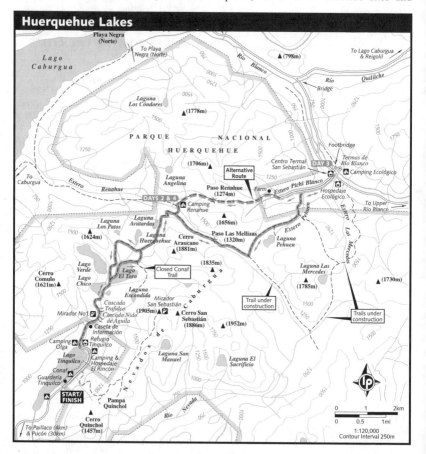

Huerquehue Lakes

Climbing Volcán Villarrica (2847m)

SHANNON NACE

An isolated araucaria tree in the Araucanía

NICK TAPP

Forest of araucaria trees at Laguna Huerquehue, Parque Nacional Huerquehue

VLADIMIR LIBA

Camping at Los Barros below the glaciated Sierra Velluda, Parque Nacional Laguna del Laja

Lava landscape from Volcán Antuco's 1873 eruption, Parque Nacional Laguna del Laja

offers hot showers for US$1. It is open only in January and February.

Cut up rightward to rejoin the (now rougher) vehicle track, and climb mostly gently to the **Caseta de Información**. This is a Conaf checkpoint on the national park boundary, where a friendly *guardaparque* will register your details. The track continues up quickly past the turn-off leading 400m to the **Cascada Nido de Águila**, 30 to 45 minutes from the *guardería*. This mossy-ferny waterfall lies within lovely forest of *mañío* and *tepa* whose trunks are often smothered by *estrellitas* and *botellitas*.

Continue up to the minor lookout point known as the **Mirador No 1**, where Lago Tinquilco comes back into view below, then on past the turn-off down to **Cascada Trafulco**, a more spectacular long cascade splashing over smooth granite rocks. The stepped path begins a steeper winding ascent past the **Mirador No 2** (1094m) to finally reach **Lago Chico**, 50 minutes to 1¼ hours from the Cascada Nido de Águila.

Cross the outlet of Lago Chico on a footbridge, then walk smoothly around the eastern shore through stands of *coigües* and araucarias to an intersection just after crossing the lake's first inlet (flowing down from Lago El Toro).

Take the right branch to pass by a tiny pebble beach on the southwest tip of **Lago El Toro** a few minutes on. The path rises and dips gently along the western side of Lago El Toro (past a connecting trail left to Lago Verde and short right turn-offs to several scenic points by the lake) to reach a picturesque little inlet at its northern shore, 45 minutes to one hour after crossing the Lago El Toro outlet. Ignore an old trail here (now closed by Conaf) that leads off right to Laguna Seca and Laguna Escondida.

Head up northeast through the forest to reach a trail junction on a tiny, flat shelf among stands of araucarias after 15 to 20 minutes. Just 50m along this left (northwest) branch is **Laguna Huerquehue**. Although not one of its prettier lakes, this shallow tarn has at least given the park its name.

Follow the (now blue-marked) trail northeast along the edge of a long, thin *mallín*

then drop gently through a saddle past the tiny, murky Laguna Avutardas and come onto fire-cleared slopes high above the Estero Renahue. This spot grants a sudden (and the only) glimpse downvalley to the blue waters of Lago Caburgua before you begin a steep winding descent through regenerating *notro* and *colihue* scrub, then ease rightward into the forest to reach a track intersection by a little stream, 50 minutes to 1¼ hours from Laguna Huerquehue.

Head down across the stream to arrive at **Camping Renahue**, below high ridges on a grassy lawn between the two small branches of the upper Estero Renahue, after 10 minutes. This is the only place where camping is permitted within the national park, apart from the Conaf camping ground at Lago Tinquilco. There is fee of US$12 per site (good for *two* nights), payable at Guardería Tinquilco before you depart. The only facilities at Camping Renahue are fireplaces, a pit toilet and an extremely basic *refugio*.

An easy three-hour return side trip can be made up to **Laguna Angelina** by following a path across the stream and climbing gently northwest.

Day 2: Camping Renahue to Termas de Río Blanco (via Paso Las Mellizas)

2½–3¼ hours, 9.5km, 250m ascent, 575m descent

Return to the junction above the camping area described in Day 1. Continue left (southeast) into a tiny side valley across a gully of coarse boulders swept down from impressive overhanging crags on the terraced northeast face of Cerro Araucano (1881m). The path climbs moderately into clearings among the young *coigües*, crossing the stream shortly before reaching Paso Las Mellizas, 35 to 45 minutes from the turn-off. This forested pass lies at 1320m, close to the park's geographic centre.

Cut through a tiny clearing across a trickling stream, then continue southeast gently down to reach a junction after 15 to 20 minutes. (The right branch, signposted 'Descampe Vega', continues southeast down to Laguna Las Mellizas.)

Head left (northeast) slightly uphill through highland araucaria-*lenga* forest, crossing another watershed before coming out onto open slopes high above the Estero Pichi Blanco. Traverse down through meadows scattered with red-berry *chauras* towards ranges on the other side of the Río Blanco to reach the turn-off to **Laguna Pehuen** *(GPS 38° 07.332 S, 71° 38.499 W)*, 20 to 30 minutes from the last junction. The (20-minute return) detour through the *quila* to this picturesque lake is highly recommended.

The path descends on gently northeast along a broad ridge to reach a junction at the forest edge, 20 to 30 minutes on. Continue left (the right branch goes across to Laguna Las Mercedes) and drop north over slopes overlooking the enclosed basin of the Río Blanco. The trail makes an increasingly steep descent over regenerating fire-cleared slopes scattered with crimson-flowered *notro*. It becomes indistinct lower down, but just cut through wild rose bushes left of the Estero Pehuen to join the road along the Estero Pichi Blanco (just upvalley from a rustic farmhouse with fruit trees) after 25 to 35 minutes.

Follow this often rough road down above the stream's southern side to cross the **Estero Pehuen** after five minutes. The valley narrows as you proceed through *mañío* and fragrant *tepa* to meet the road along the Río Blanco immediately above **Termas de Río Blanco**, 20 to 30 minutes on.

Termas de Río Blanco

Beside the small, icy Río Blanco lies Termas de Río Blanco, isolated, almost undeveloped hot springs. As accommodation is extremely limited (less than a dozen beds), it is advisable to carry a tent if you come on a weekend. There is a charge of US$3 per person per day to use the hot springs – this includes the *piscina* (swimming pool) and *pozos* (a concrete tub and makeshift rock pools of varying warmth). There is one (public) telephone at the Termas.

Centro Termal San Sebastián *(☎ 17121-1968799; camping per person US$4, 6-person cabins US$40)*, on the river's left (southern) side, has an open, steaming *piscina* in a streamside meadow. Meals are available.

A short way up the road, across the Estero Las Mercedes, is the simple **Hospedaje Ecológico** *(doubles per person US$5.50)*, which has no phone or electricity. Room rates include breakfast and meals cost from US$3.

Across a footbridge from the *piscina*, on the opposite (right) bank, are the *pozos*. Just upstream lies **Camping Ecológico** *(site for up to four persons US$4)*.

Day 3: Termas de Río Blanco to Camping Renahue

2¾–3½ hours, 9.5km, 575m ascent, 250m descent

Retrace your steps as described on Day 2 (or opt for the Alternative Day 3).

Instead of returning to Guardería Tinquilco from the Termas de Río Blanco, some trekkers continue 18km on along the little-transited road south to Reigolil (via the turn-off 4km downvalley), from where there are bus connections back to Pucón.

Alternative Day 3: via Paso Renahue

2½–3 hours, 7.5km, 540m ascent, 215m descent

This is a more direct but somewhat less scenic alternative to backtracking along the route described in Day 2.

Head back up along the Estero Pichi Blanco past where the trail on Day 2 meets the road (five minutes after crossing the Estero Pehuen) and ford to reach a farmhouse. Walk through the farm gate, crossing a side stream to pick up a stock track. This often heavily eroded route leads westward, ascending steeply before beginning a more gentle upward sidle through slopes of mature araucarias to Paso Renahue (1274m). Drop southwest through alternating fire-damaged and intact forest to arrive back at Camping Renahue.

Day 4: Camping Renahue to Guardería Tinquilco via Laguna Los Patos & Lago Verde

3¾–5 hours, 12.5km, 640m descent

Retrace you steps to the junction near Laguna Huerquehue as described on Day 1. Go right, following this somewhat less trodden trail for 15 to 20 minutes northwest to a (right) turn-off. This leads a few minutes to the **Laguna Los Patos**, another tiny tarn surrounded by araucarias.

The main trail continues around southward, sidling down along the left side of a ridge past a left turn-off to Lago El Toro (signposted 'Renahue') to reach a little beach on the southeast shore of **Lago Verde** after 25 to 30 minutes. Surrounded by forested ridges crowned by the umbrella-like outlines of araucarias, this tranquil lake is perfect for swimming in hot weather. Continue across the outlet footbridge and make your way down to the junction at Lago Chico, 10 to 15 minutes on. Now backtrack again as described on Day 1.

Parque Nacional Villarrica

The 610-sq-km Parque Nacional Villarrica lies at approximately 39°S, 30km southeast of Pucón. Created in 1925 (from a forest reserve originally set aside in 1912), it is the oldest and one of the most accessible national parks in Chile. The park stretches along a broad volcanic range running southeast from Volcán Villarrica as far as the 3776m summit of Volcán Lanín on the Chile–Argentina border. This extensive plateau was created several thousand years ago when Volcán Quetrupillán exploded. A number of attractive alpine lakes lie within this stark lunar landscape of lava flows, scoria and pumice.

The park's major attraction, and most obvious feature, is Volcán Villarrica, a classic 2847m volcanic cone covered by recent and older lava flows. These show the fascinating battle of natural forces, as the local vegetation struggles to survive against recurring, intense volcanic activity. The upper slopes of Volcán Villarrica are covered by névés and glaciers and its northern slopes have been developed for winter skiing.

NATURAL HISTORY

The lower slopes of Parque Nacional Villarrica are clothed by rich virgin forests, where montane southern beech species such as *rauli*, roble and the evergreen *coigüe* predominate up to an elevation of approximately 1000m. Above this altitude *lenga* and *ñirre*, alpine species of southern beech, coexist with superb forests of araucaria trees.

The araucaria is often found in pure stands that form tree line (at around 1600m above sea level). Typical southern Andean wild flowers, such as the *añañuca*, a species recognisable by its pink goblet-like flowers, and the Chilean field orchid, or *orquídea del campo*, are well represented. Hardy shrubs, including the *michai*, a thorny member of the *Berberis* genus (similar to the *calafate*) with yellow flowers, and *chauras* thrive on the upper slopes of these volcanic mountains. Usually present in alpine herb fields of the Araucanía are numerous species of yellow groundsels, or *senecios*. The volcanic soils also favour the *brecillo*, a small shrub that produces edible purple berries (often seen in the scats of native foxes).

The shy native fauna is seldom seen in Parque Nacional Villarrica, though it is much easier to spot birds. A bird common in the park is the Chilean pigeon, or *torcaza*, a large grey bird that the Mapuche call *conu*. Although this species seemed dangerously close to extinction in the early 1960s, populations of Chilean pigeon have recovered dramatically in recent decades. The austral parakeet, or *cachaña*, feeds largely on araucaria nuts, which it splits open with its sharp beak. The luxuriant forests also provide an ideal habitat for the Magellanic woodpecker, or *carpintero negro*, which can often be seen tapping about the tree trunks.

CLIMATE

Parque Nacional Villarrica's elevated topography ensures it has higher average precipitation levels and lower temperatures than the surrounding Araucarían lowlands. Reaching nearly 4000mm annually (concentrated between May and early September), precipitation is highest on the western slopes of Volcán Villarrica, which lie directly in the path of the moist Pacific airstream. The winter period brings frequent and heavy snowfalls above 1000m.

THE ARAUCANÍA

Villarrica Traverse

Duration	6 days
Distance	81km
Difficulty	demanding
Start	Refugio Villarrica (Centro de Ski Pucón)
Finish	Puesco (p101)
Nearest Town	Pucón (p94)
Transport	organised tour or taxi; bus
Summary	A classic longer trek along the rugged volcanic spine of Parque Nacional Villarrica.

The Villarrica Traverse (*'Traversía Villarrica'* in Spanish) is an incredibly scenic, high-level trek that 'traverses' virtually the whole length of the national park, giving you constantly changing views. The route first leads around Volcán Villarica's glacier-shrouded southern sides, then heads along a complex volcanic plateau of alpine lakes, small calderas and lava flows that extends as far as Volcán Lanín. The mostly rocky, open terrain provides some sensational vistas, although the route dips repeatedly into beautiful highland araucaria and *lenga* forests.

The Villarrica Traverse is marked by coloured – yellow, red and then green – stakes that identify various sections of the trail. The guided ascent of Volcán Villarrica (see Other Treks, p109) is itself an unforgettable experience, and can be done on the first day of the trek.

PLANNING
When to Trek
Early in the season, snow may still cover large areas of the route. Summer (December–February) can be surprisingly hot. From about late December until early February, bothersome *tábanos* are out in force in the forests, although they are almost absent above tree line.

Maps
Conaf has produced a 1:110,000 colour-contoured map that, for the most part, shows routes correctly. Most trekkers will

Volcán Villarrica

The indigenous Mapuche people knew Volcán Villarrica by the name of Rucapillán, meaning 'house of the spirits', and believed the mountain to be the abode of their ancestors. The volcano is extremely active and unpredictable. From the crater rim, molten magma is visible deep down in the core and at times red-hot lava spurts up. Volcán Villarrica smoulders constantly, emitting a trail of smoke visible from all over the northern Lakes District. At night, the summit has an eerie, glowing orange halo.

The volcano has experienced repeated catastrophic eruptions over the centuries, most recently in 1971, when a 4km-wide fracture opened, releasing massive lava flows that destroyed the small township of Coñaripe and only just spared Pucón. Smaller eruptions are even more common – such as in September 1996, when Volcán Villarrica shot out columns of thick gaseous smoke that covered its northwest slopes in a fine layer of ash.

Both despite and due to its continuing activity, Villarrica is the most climbed – and studied – mountain in Chile. Seismic and volcanic activity are now carefully monitored, and any increase can result in 'closure' of the mountain until activity subsides. Residents surrounding the volcano live in a permanent state of alert, ready to evacuate their homes with little notice.

The Proyecto de Observación Villarrica (**W** www.povi.org) is a scientific organisation that studies Volcán Villarrica.

find it detailed enough for the Villarrica Traverse.

Otherwise, four 1:50,000 Chilean IGM maps cover the trek: *Pucón* (Section G, No 104), *Curarrehue* (Section G, No 105), *Liquiñe* (Section G, No 113) and *Paimún* (Section G, No 114). An additional map, *Villarrica* (Section G, No 103) is optional. These maps do not show the track (or Laguna Blanca) but they are topographically accurate.

Permits & Regulations

Visitors to Parque Nacional Villarrica pay an entry fee of US$2 per day or US$4 for an indefinite longer stay in the park. The fee can be paid at either Guardería Rucapillán or Guardería Chinay. Apart from several Conaf-organised camping grounds, camping is only permitted in the park at least one hour's walk from the nearest road. Trekkers are strongly encouraged to carry a stove rather than lighting fires.

NEAREST TOWN & FACILITIES

See Pucón (p94).

Puesco

The Villarrica Traverse finishes at the tiny village of Puesco, which has an altitude of 700m, and is the last Chilean settlement on Ruta 119 (the international road across Paso Mamuil Malal) before the border. Conaf's Guardería Puesco, just down from the *aduana* (customs post), is responsible for park's eastern sector. Puesco has no accommodation or camping – not even a proper store. **Hospedaje Agricultor** *(camping per person US$4, 4-/6-person cabins US$17/22)* at Piedra Mala, 2km north of Puesco below the peak known as La Peineta, has a camping ground by the river (maximum two persons per site) and cabins with gas stove and hot showers.

Getting There & Away From Puesco, **Buses Regionales Villarrica** *(☎ 045-411871)* runs buses to Pucón on Monday, Wednesday and Friday at 7am, which return to Puesco at around 3pm the same day. From Curarrehue, 24km north of Puesco, there are up to five local buses each day to Pucón.

Buses also run daily in either direction between Junín and San Martín de los Andes in Argentina and Pucón and Temuco in Chile. International buses arriving from Argentina (at around 10.30am) can be boarded if there are vacant seats. It's unlikely, however, that you'll be allowed to get on a bus heading into Argentina (these generally arrive in Puesco around noon) unless you have booked and are already on the passenger list – although it's certainly worth asking.

GETTING TO/FROM THE TREK

The trek begins at Refugio Villarrica (also known as Centro de Ski Pucón), a ski lodge (closed in summer) roughly 18km from Pucón on the northwest side of Volcán Villarrica. There is no public transport, but taxis can be chartered up to Refugio Villarrica for – depending on your bargaining skills – around US$12. You can walk to Refugio Villarrica from Pucón in around five hours. A dozen or so local outdoor-adventure companies organise guided ascents of Volcán Villarrica. In fine weather in the main tourist season (January and February) several guided parties are likely to make the climb each day. These trips include transport by the companies' own minibus to/from Refugio Villarrica, and if there is extra space in the minibus they will take you to the start of the trek for around US$5 (one-way).

It is also possible to start the trek roughly midway from the Termas de Palguín, Fundo El Mocho or Camping Chinay along the Palguín Bajo–Coñaripe road (see Day 3), which may be reached from Pucón via taxi (US$20 to US$25). A local bus from Pucón to Curarrehue or Puesco goes past the turnoff at Palguín Bajo, from where it is a pleasant 3½-hour walk up the valley to the Termas de Palguín and another 1½ hours to the Fundo El Mocho.

The trek ends in Puesco.

Warning

Although the Villarrica Traverse is well marked and well trodden, it is a long, high-level route almost entirely above tree line. There are no *refugios*, so all trekkers must carry a sturdy tent. The central section is very exposed. Deep winter snow often remains well into January, but among the extensive fields of lava the going can be very hot. Bad weather or low cloud can quickly move in to make navigation difficult. Finding water is often hard as the earth is very porous and streams tend to flow underground (and/or streams stop running overnight because of the cool night temperatures).

THE ARAUCANÍA

THE TREK
Day 1: Refugio Villarrica to Estero Ñilfe
4½–6¼ hours, 11.5km, 350m ascent
Early in the day and/or late in the season, only larger streams (highlighted in bold text) can be relied on to have running water.

The road ends at a car park beside Refugio Villarrica (a winter ski lodge that's closed in summer), a short way above tree line at around 1500m. Walk 200m back down the road to the start of the track (signposted 'Challupén') on the first bend near a large tin shed. Follow yellow-tipped, metal marker-stakes southward across the first eroded gully – the **Zanjón Correntoso** – rising over mostly dry stream beds on the open slopes of hardy Andean heath and wild flowers to the cross the **Zanjón Molco**, 25 to 30 minutes from the *refugio*. There is fair **camping** by this stream among the bare rock.

The well-formed track climbs on steadily leftward through lava fields and occasional snowdrifts and on to sparse tussock-grass ridges as the shining blue waters of Lago Calafquén gradually move into view down to the southwest. Cut back down around through a rocky gully between the lava, into the scrub, to reach the **Zanjón Voipir**, 1¾ to 2¼ hours from the Zanjón Molco. There is a good view up this sediment-filled stream (flowing underground in places) to the snowy crown of Volcán Villarrica.

Head on across another trickling gulch into mature *lenga* and araucaria forest whose *quila* understorey has died back (a curiosity of its life cycle; see the boxed text 'The Quila Cycle'). The trail passes a signposted turn-off going down to Villarrica township (33km – a useful exit route in bad weather) just before it drops into the **Zanjón Pino Huacho**, 50 minutes to 1¼ hours from the Zanjón Voipir. A wooden pipe ducts water from a tiny spring trickling out of the sandy embankment at the base of the canyon.

On the other side, continue left (ignoring a minor path going along the left bank) and begin an undulating traverse through more beautiful forest and pockets of red-flowered *notro* scrub. The route passes a signposted

trail turn-off (leading down 28km to the town of Lican Ray) to reach the **Zanjón Challupén** after 30 to 40 minutes. Cut 300m left, diagonally up through this wide streamway that (when flowing) washes scoria down from the slopes of Volcán Villarrica.

Pick up the trail on the other side and head 200m through lava rock before you cut away rightward (ignoring a rough, paint-marked

The Quila Cycle

Numerous species of native bamboo of the *Chusquea* genus grow in the moist, temperate Valdivian rainforests of Patagonia. Even for botanists, these species are difficult to differentiate, although most members of the genus – but particularly the most abundant species, *Ch. quila* – are commonly known by the Mapuche name of *quila*. Quila is an extremely vigorous and aggressive plant, often smothering smaller trees as it spreads out to monopolise sunnier sites in the forest.

Like many other bamboo genera found throughout the world, *quila* flowers only at the end of its reproductive cycle. In a given area, up to 90% of the *quila* may be on the same cycle – approximately 25 years for most species – which results in the *quila* blooming over wide areas simultaneously. Once the plants have produced fruit they die off, leaving a mass of dry canes which present a worrying fire hazard that lasts for many years. The flowering of the *quila* is also noted with apprehension by locals, because mice and rats multiply out of control as they gorge on the nutritious fruit. Once this food source is exhausted, the rodents move out of the forest into the surrounding farms and villages.

Quila can barely survive in a mature, closed rainforest because too little sunlight reaches the ground, yet its regrowth is particularly vigorous after fires, which destroy the shade of the forest canopy and release nutrients. This has led some botanists to theorise that *quila* may actually have evolved its die-back cycle as a way of 'provoking' fires, in order to create new openings in the forest.

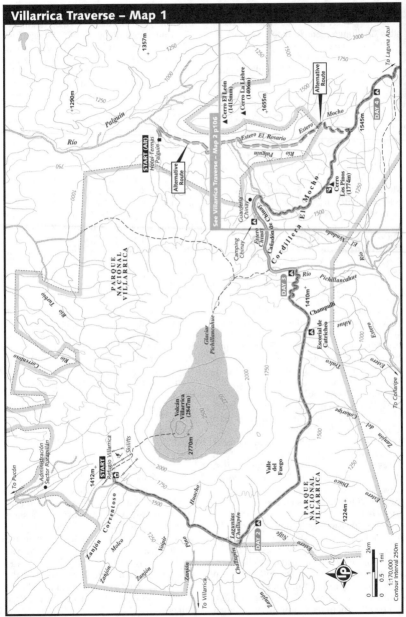

Villarrica Traverse – Map 1

route going off left to a glacier) back into the trees to reach the ponds known as the **Lagunitas Challupén** (approximately 1250m), 30 to 40 minutes on.

Climb on southeast over a minor forested ridge, descending across a dry gully to jump an unnamed stream (with reasonable **camp sites** on tiny terraces along its south side). The trail continues briefly through *ñirres* to arrive at the **Estero Ñilfe** (*GPS 39° 27.486 S, 71° 58.712 W*), a permanent glacial stream 40 to 50 minutes from the Lagunitas Challupén. These open slopes give a clear view south towards the snowcapped double-summit of Volcán Choshuenco and Volcán Mocho, rising behind forested ranges. The best **camp sites** are sheltered by low *lengas* on the stream's north bank.

Day 2: Estero Ñilfe to Río Pichillancahue
4–5½ hours, 16.5km, 330m ascent, 35m descent

Follow yellow marker-stakes across a broad tundra basin scattered with *chaura*, yellow groundsels and other tiny wild flowers under glaciers on Villarrica's southwest face. Traverse past recent lava flows in the area known as the **Valle del Fuego** (Valley of Fire), over a minor crest, then cut across an upper channel of the Estero Diuco. (Confusingly, a Conaf sign here call this gully 'Zanjón del Coñaripe'.)

The trail (well defined by lines of stones on either side) climbs slightly north of east to reach a saddle (1516m) between a reddish side crater (2006m) and another smaller cone (1646m), 1¼ to 1¾ hours from the **Estero Ñilfe**. From here you get the first clear views southeast towards the exploded crater of Volcán Quetrupillán and the majestic 3776m ice-encrusted cone of Volcán Lanín behind it.

Descend via a ridge leading around to the right and cross a trickling stream, then climb over a steep grassy ridge to meet the **Zanjón del Coñaripe** (as labelled on the Conaf map, although the Conaf sign here calls it 'Estero Tralco'), after 15 to 25 minutes.

Cut up leftward across the stream through a deep, sometimes snow-filled, trench

towards a white-paint circle on a rock, then head eastward into the **Escorial de Catricheo**. The trail avoids the worst of this large field of black scoria, following an easy route through gaps in the coarse, gnarled rock that resembles petrified tree trunks. Down to the right, mushroom-like araucarias stand silhouetted against the classic outline of Volcán Lanín.

Climb to a ridge top under crevassed icefalls on the southern sides of Volcán Villarrica, descending on rightward through sparse alpine tundra strewn with tiny yellow, star-like *quinchamalí* to meet a grassy stream near a basalt bluff. The route continues quickly over a crest (marked by a pole) to cross the **Estero Aihue** (*GPS 39° 28.630 S, 71° 53.149 W*), one to 1½ hours from the Zanjón del Coñaripe. A scenic but unsheltered **camp** could be made downstream on the grassy flats within the canyon.

Sidle on around leftward past a prominent red ridge coming off Villarrica to reach a cluster of araucarias just above the normal tree line at Champulli (wrongly shown on the IGM map), after 20 to 30 minutes. These slopes overlook the wild upper valley of the Río El Vendado. Disregarding trails that descend right, traverse around northeast, slightly upward past grassy mountainsides scattered with pink *añañucas* opposite Volcán Quetrupillán. The foot track crosses a series of small, steep stream gullies (usually snow-filled at least until mid-December) before finally cutting down into the *lenga* scrub (*GPS 39° 28.239 S, 71° 52.122 W*), 35 to 45 minutes on.

A steep, switchbacking descent through tall forest leads to the **Río Pichillancahue** after a final 30 to 40 minutes. There is no bridge here, but this large stream can usually be forded with little difficulty a short way upstream. There are excellent **camp sites** located among *coigüe* forest on the true left (east) bank of the river, but be particularly careful with campfires as large amounts of dead *quila* here could set the whole area ablaze. Glaciar Pichillancahue is visible through the trees at the head of the valley.

Day 3: Río Pichillancahue to Upper Estero Mocho

5½–7 hours, 16.5km, 1150m ascent, 700m descent

The path leads five minutes downstream along the east bank, then climbs left over a low ridge to come out at the Palguín Bajo–Coñaripe road after 15 to 20 minutes. The trail turn-off is signposted 'Challupén' *(GPS 39° 28.284 S, 71° 51.221 W)*. Turn left and follow this often rough – almost 4WD-standard – road up through araucaria forest (past a left trail turn-off leading 3km north-west to a lookout under Glaciar Pichillan-cahue) to cross a pass at 1264m on top of the main Villarrica range after 30 to 40 minutes.

Follow the winding road down for 30 to 40 minutes past a Conaf picnic area and **Camping Chinay**. About 1km upvalley from the Guardería Chinay, this Conaf camping ground has 10 organised sites (around US$10) with tables and fireplaces among lovely araucarias and *lengas*; there is also a toilet block with cold showers. The road descends through rich forests of mixed southern beech species, crossing and re-crossing the rushing **Estero Chinay** to reach Conaf's **Guardería Chinay**, near the park boundary, after a further 25 to 35 minutes. Advise the officious *guardaparque* of your arrival. Some people may choose to start or finish their trek here.

Walk 50m past a swing gate on the road and turn off right at a red-marker stake. This trail quickly crosses the stream on a foot-bridge, then heads rightward over a minor crest to ascend slopes ablaze with red *notro* (Chilean firewheel) bushes. The gradient eases only briefly as you pass a short side trail down to a fresh spring (your only source of water for some time). Climb on steeply southward, through regenerating fire-cleared forest high above the Cañadón de Chinay, to finally reach grassy alpine slopes that give welcome views across the upper valley of the Río El Vendado to araucaria-clad ranges and volcanoes. The path traces the scrub line along the right side of the ridge, then cuts up left along a streamlet to a rocky gap (1688m) in the Cordillera El Mocho, 2¼ to three hours from Guardería Chinay.

Don't descend from the gap, but climb 15 to 20 minutes along the bare ridge to a flat **lookout** at 1758m that gives a marvellous panorama of the five surrounding volcanoes – Villarrica, Quetrupillán, Lanín, Mocho and Choshuenco – as well as many more distant summits. The route traverses left below Cerro Los Pinos (1774m), following the scrubby ridge down into forest to intersect with an unsignposted trail coming up from the Fundo El Mocho (see Getting to/from the Trek, p101) on a broad saddle (around 1435m) among araucarias, 1½ to two hours from the lookout.

Climb gently on for 25 to 30 minutes until the ridge finally ends by a small stream at the edge of the gently tilted plateau on the western side of Volcán Quetrupillán. Here, pleasant **camp sites** can be found a short way right along the stream among the shelter of the scrub. The familiar puffing summit of Volcán Villarrica dominates the skyline to the northwest.

Alternative Start: Termas de Palguín

4½–6 hours, 12km, 880m ascent

This route is easier and shorter (but less scenic) than the track via the Cordillera El Mocho.

The **Termas de Palguín** *(☎/fax 045-441968)* are 12km from the turn-off on Ruta 119. The **Hotel Termas Palguín** *(rooms per person with full board US$50)* was reconstructed after the historic building burnt down in 1998. Day visitors can use the hot baths for US$5.50 and eat in the hotel **restaurant**; camping is possible nearby. (Trekkers coming downvalley from the Guardería Chinay – 3.5km and one to 1¼ hours – should turn right just after crossing the Río Palguín.)

From the Termas de Palguín, follow the Palguín Bajo–Coñaripe road upvalley for 1¼ to 1½ hours to a Y-fork (recognisable by the signpost 'Al Parque 3km') and take the left branch. Cross almost immediately through the large entrance gate to the **Fundo El Mocho** *(camping per person US$2)*, whose owners now charge a US$1.50 fee to cross this private property. Parking costs US$2.

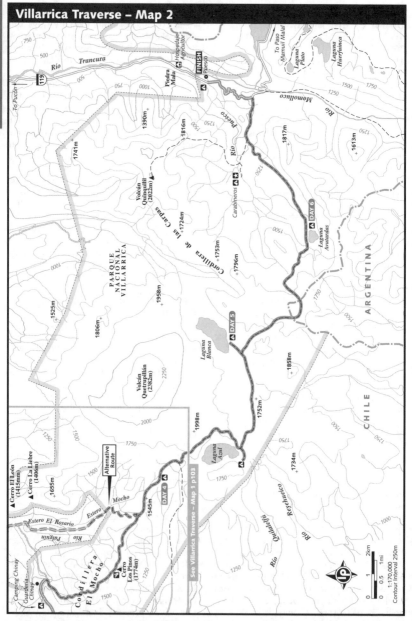

Villarrica Traverse – Map 2

119
To Pucón
Río Trancura
750
500
500
1000
750
1000
Hospedaje Agricultor
Piedra Mala
FINISH Puesco
To Paso Mamuil Malal
Laguna Plato
Laguna Huerfánica
1390m+
1816m+
1741m
Volcán Quinquilil (2022m)
Río Puesco
Río Momolluco
1250
1250
1500
1750
1817m
1613m+
1750
1250
Carabineros
+1724m
Cordillera de las Carpas
+1753m
+1796m
1500
DAY 6
Laguna Aviutardas
1500
PARQUE NACIONAL VILLARRICA
+1958m
ARGENTINA
1525m
1000
1806m+
DAY 5
Laguna Blanca
1750
CHILE
Volcán Quetrupillán (2382m)
2250
+1858m
1752m+
1734m+
Alternative Route
+1998m
Laguna Azul
1750
1750
Cerro El León (1415mm)
Cerro La Liebre (1406m)
+1655m
2000
1750
1500
1500
Estero Mocho
DAY 4
1545m
See Villarrica Traverse – Map 1 p103
1750
1000
Río Reyehueico
Río Quitaleya
Estero El Rosario
Río Palguín
Camping Chinay
Guardería Chinay
Cordillera El Mocho
Cerro Los Pinos (1774m)
1750
1250
1500
1250
2km
1mi
0   0.5   1
0   1
1:170,000
Contour interval 250m

Follow the road across the **Estero Rosario** just above its confluence with the Río Palguín, then through fields and past a group of farmhouses. Where the road fords the stream near the **camping area**, continue through the burnt-out clearing ahead. Climb gently into the forest past a gate (the national-park boundary) before picking up a path diverging right 300m on, 1½ to two hours from the Palguín Bajo–Coñaripe road.

Ascend steeply through the *coigües* to a broad ridge, then follow this a short way up leftward to cross a stream (a tiny tributary of the Estero Mocho below). The path climbs on via a spur, past old lichen-covered araucaria to join the main trail in the forested saddle at around 1435m, 50 minutes to 1¼ hours on. Now continue as described in Day 3.

Day 4: Upper Estero Mocho to Laguna Blanca

3¾–5 hours, 13.5km, 150m ascent

Head out over the open plateau to the left of a rounded rock bluff (an old volcanic plug). The track leads southeast over alpine grassland and raw volcanic scoria through a stream gully (filled with snow early in the season, but dry later in the summer) to cross the tiny source of the **Río Llanchahue** after 30 to 40 minutes.

Follow the path five to 10 minutes downstream to where a marker stake (*GPS 39° 30.763 S, 71° 45.181 W*) indicates where to begin climbing left. (Ignore another path that continues downstream, ie, southwest, and eventually meets the Palguín Bajo, Coñaripe road.) Markings guide you up roughly south over tussock-grass ridges with sporadic clusters of wild orchids, then rightward up sparsely vegetated slopes into a rocky gap, 40 to 50 minutes on. From here there are more fine volcanic vistas towards the north.

Sidle southwest to get your first glimpse of the dark-blue lake directly below to your right, then cut back up southeast (left) on to the ridge. Here, the giant of the region, Volcán Lanín, and the lower, double cone of Volcán Choshuenco and Volcán Mocho (off to the south) come back into view, while

Andean condors drift around above you. Maintain a high route over the coarse slopes and snowdrifts that persist well into summer, then drop down to the right in zigzags along a loose-earth ridge to reach the southeast shore of **Laguna Azul** (shown on IGM maps as Laguna *de los* Patos), 50 minutes to 1¼ hours from the gap. This impressive lake lies in a deep trough whose outlet stream was dammed by the large lava flow nearby. There are **camp sites** here among the *lenga* scrub and less sheltered spots exist across the small outlet on the grassy saddle a short way below the ruins of a *refugio*.

From the southeastern shore of Laguna Azul, head east between the broad band of lava and the ridge you descended. Occasional paint markings and small tree branches propped up with cairns lead easily through the broken rock. Climb over a minor crest, then cut through another regenerating lava field and continue northeast along a broad, barely vegetated ridge to a barren, rocky area. Edge down to the right of this into a silt-filled stream bed before making your way left for 500m. (Winter snow tends to accumulate here, and the meltwater may temporarily form a shallow lake.)

At this point head up northeast, immediately left of a tiny stream, to reach a narrow sandy gap, 1½ to two hours from Laguna Azul. From here you get a view across the desolate moonscape to **Laguna Blanca**, a small lake lying at just above 1600m. Drop down the eroding slopes into the barren basin (if the gap is dangerously corniced, climb briefly around left) then head directly northeast across the raw, undulating plain to arrive at Laguna Blanca, 15 to 20 minutes on. Scenic, but only semisheltered, **camp sites** can be found among boulders on the southern shore of this starkly beautiful alpine lake.

Day 5: Laguna Blanca to Laguna Avutardas

3½–4¼ hours, 11km, 400m ascent

Return to the main trail and head on around to the right into a dry gully. Follow the gully until it turns eastward, then climb away around the eastern rim of a small extinct crater. Continue on generally south towards the distant twin peaks of Volcán Choshuenco and Volcán Mocho, before crossing leftward over a small spur marking the Chile–Argentina frontier. The path sidles around slopes overlooking the wild, forested valley of the Río Blanco in Argentina, dips into a bare bowl-like basin, then ascends northeast to reach a pass *(GPS 39° 34.191 S, 71° 40.280 W)*, back on the international border, 1½ to two hours from Laguna Blanca. (The Conaf map tactfully – but erroneously – shows this section of the route *inside* Chilean territory!)

At 1838m, this often windy ridge top is the highest point on the traverse, and looks out northeast (into Chile) towards 2022m Volcán Quinquilil, the major summit of the jagged Cordillera de las Carpas. Beyond the valley of the Río Puesco, further over to your right, stands an impressive saw-shaped range, which locals call La Peineta (The Comb). You can also enjoy the last clear views of Volcán Lanín over to your right.

Drop to the right, then ease down leftward beside the stream on to a wet shelf of shallow pools and alpine bogs, vegetated by water-loving plants such as native yellow buttercups known as *madecos*. Pick up the path at the left-most (north) edge of the shelf where the stream tumbles over a low escarpment, before descending in a few quick switchbacks. The route doubles back rightward to cross the stream below the waterfall.

Continue upward under the cliff face across another waterlogged area into *lenga* scrub to reach an open ridge top separating two branches of the upper Río Puesco, 50 minutes to 1¼ hours from the pass. Up to your right, more small cascades tumble over the escarpment, while there are enticing glimpses of a welcoming lake down in the valley below you.

Follow the ridge to just before a rock knob, then watch out for markings on the right that indicate where the trail starts its steep descent southeast. Drop via narrow snow chutes that lead you down into taller forest to finally come out on a marshy meadow grazed by noisy flocks of black-necked ibis at the western corner of **Laguna**

Avutardas (shown on IGM maps as Laguna *Los* Patos), after 25 to 30 minutes.

Make your way directly east, bounding across babbling brooks to pick up the trail again at the edge of the trees. This sometimes indistinct track sidles through the forest above the lake's north side, before cutting rightward to **camp sites** on an open grassy clearing at the eastern end of Laguna Avutardas, a final 20 to 30 minutes on.

Laguna Avutardas lies at around 1450m, and is enclosed on three sides by steep forested ranges. It has a narrow sandy beach, and in hot weather the water is just right for a leisurely dip (and also gives some respite from the voracious swarms of *tábanos* that infest this area in late December and January). As an increase in visitor numbers is beginning to impact severely on this once pristine area, please light fires only in existing fireplaces and carry out all rubbish.

Day 6: Laguna Avutardas to Puesco
3¾–5 hours, 12km, 775m descent

Rejoin the trail and continue gently down northeast through tall *lenga* forest and *quila*, crossing a small stream to reach a *mallín* after 20 to 30 minutes. Make your way 500m through the middle of this scrubby strip before moving rightward to where the route re-enters the trees *(GPS 39° 34.109 S, 71° 37.047 W)*. Continue northeast, rising and dipping over low ridges, before you drop down through *coigüe* forest scattered with *quellén* (wild strawberries) and long-abandoned farm clearings to meet a disused old road, 1½ to two hours from the *mallín*.

(From here, a 4km orange-marked route leads off left to ford the Río Puesco before it climbs to the summit of Volcán Quinquilil. It is possible to **camp** near the crossing, although sites are less than ideal unless you wade the knee-deep river.)

Turn right and follow this rough track through *ñirre* and *notro* scrub. The old road (closed to all motorised vehicles) sidles gently down in an almost easterly direction above the raging Río Puesco, crossing through a remnant cherry orchard to pass a small house just before it intersects with Ruta 119 (the international road between Pucón and Junín de los Andes), one to 1½ hours on. (This junction is signposted 'A Quetrupillán'.) Go left here and descend northward through the forest of *rauli* and *roble*, watching out for unmarked short-cut trails that lead down more directly between the road's numerous hairpin bends to arrive at Puesco (p101) after a final 40 to 50 minutes.

For reasons of courtesy, present your papers at the customs office here. Make sure the staff realise that you have not just crossed from Argentina (although they may want to inspect your gear anyway).

Other Treks

VOLCÁN DOMUYO (ARGENTINA)

By strict definition, the 4709m summit of Volcán Domuyo, in the Cordillera del Viento in the remote northern corner of Argentina's Neuquén province, is the highest point in the Patagonian Andes. It is one of the few volcanoes entirely within Argentina that has significant geothermal activity, including fumaroles, geysers and thermal springs.

Volcán Domuyo can be climbed in around five days return from its south side. Although technically straightforward this remote, high-alpine ascent, with the associated dangers of altitude sickness (see Health & Safety, p61), requires proper experience, equipment (including ice axe and crampons) and planning. **Albus** (☎ 02942-432108) runs daily buses from Zapala to Chos Malal, roughly 110km south of Domuyo, but access to the volcano itself is by private (preferably 4WD) vehicle only. Some outdoor companies (eg, Huemul Turismo in San Martín, p117) organise guided ascents.

Unfortunately, to date no topographic map of the area has been published at a useful scale.

ASCENT OF VOLCÁN ANTUCO (CHILE)

The 2979m cone of Volcán Antuco ends in a crater just 40m in diameter, which sometimes emits gases and steam. This summit grants a superb panorama that includes the upper Valle Laja to the west and the Sierra Velluda to the south. Across Laguna de la Laja lie Volcán Chillán (3122m) to the north and the ranges extending into Argentina to the east.

Volcán Antuco can be climbed from several points. One route starts 4km past the ski village

on the volcano's northern slopes, beyond the lava flow. It is steep and direct, and takes around eight hours return. A less steep and somewhat faster route goes up the southeastern slopes from Los Barros. There is no trail to follow on this route.

Beware of a dangerously crevassed glacier on the volcano's upper southern slopes. Depending on snow conditions, crampons and an ice axe are generally advisable (sometimes essential) before about mid-January, and cannot be hired at the park.

The ascent is more strenuous when there is no snow covering the loose earth. Inexperienced trekkers should inquire at the park administration centre or the Centro Turístico Lagunillas (see Nearest Town & Facilities, p82) for a guide.

PARQUE NACIONAL CONGUILLÍO (CHILE)

The 612-sq-km Parque Nacional Conguillío (usually pronounced con-**gee**-yo) lies east of Temuco. Its key features are Volcán Llaima's distinctive twin summits at 2920m and 3125m, and spectacular Laguna Conguillío, a large lake below the towering Sierra Nevada. The park **administration centre** (☎ 045-272402) is on the southern shore of Laguna Conguillío, where there is also a **camping ground** *(sites US$12, 4-/6-person cabins US$45/60).*

There is no public transport to Laguna Conguillío. A twice-weekly (Monday and Friday) bus from Curacautín will only get you to Guardería Captrén at the park's northern entrance gate – still 16km from the administration centre. Otherwise, hiring a vehicle, chartering a taxi or taking an organised tour are the only options. Taxis from Curacautín can be arranged through **Taxis Alameda** *(☎ 045-882699),* which shuttles trekkers to trailheads such as Laguna Blanca (US$20, 22km) or Laguna Conguillío.

Lack of public transport, prohibition of camping anywhere except at Laguna Conguillío and relative difficulty of (longer) routes generally makes the park less attractive for trekking. However, several interesting treks are described below.

La Baita *(☎ 045-416410; W www.labaita conguillio.cl),* at the park boundary on the Melipueco–Conguillío road, organises guided treks and climbs in the area.

Laguna Captrén

The easy 3½-hour trek to the lovely Laguna Captrén begins a short way west of the administration centre. The trail leads 5km northwest through beautiful forest then skirts the shore of Laguna Captrén. The lake was created when a lava flow dammed a stream, and drowned trees are still visible in its waters.

Sierra Nevada

The 18km, 6½- to 8½-hour return trek to the Sierra Nevada leaves from Playa Linda, on the southeast shore of Laguna Conguillío. A well-graded track climbs a broad spur through araucaria and *lenga* forest to the base of the Sierra Nevada, then ascends along a ridge before cutting left to a lookout with wonderful views across the lake to Volcán Llaima.

A difficult (and somewhat hazardous) two-day continuation leads north across two deep stream gullies before dropping left to the **Baños El Toro**, a hot spring in a rustic shed (US$3). From here, either simply follow a dirt road out to the Curacautín–Lonquimay highway (Ruta 181) or continue down the Río Blanco to the Curacautín–Conguillío road (where the twice-weekly bus stops).

Use the Chilean IGM's 1:50,000 map *Volcán Llaima* (Section G, No 75).

Ascent of Volcán Llaima

Volcán Llaima's distinctive double-cone summits present few technical difficulties, and are a popular goal for local andinists. Llaima is best climbed from its western side, where there are two *refugios*, the **Centro de Ski** (☎ 045-562313; [W] www .skiaraucarias.cl) and **Refugio Llaima del Colegio Alemán de Temuco** (☎/fax 045-1970515; [e] refugiollaima@dstemuco.cl). Both *refugios* offer dorm beds for around US$7 in summer, and can organise ice-climbing equipment and transport from Cherquenco village (21km, around US$15 each way). There are frequent buses to Cherquenco from Temuco. Use the Chilean IGM's 1:50,000 map *Laguna Quepe* (Section G, No 74).

PARQUE NACIONAL HUERQUEHUE
Pampa de Quinchol & Mirador San Sebastián

From the road 500m north of the Guardería Tinquilco, a well-graded, 3km path winds up steep slopes to the grassy alpine ridge top known as the Pampa Quinchol (three hours return). From here an easy 1km loop cuts around clockwise along the southern side of the ridge through a smaller saddle to meet the main track again lower down. A more demanding 6km (3½ hour return) route leads northeast up a craggy ridge to the Mirador San Sebastián. This lookout offers amazing views across Huerquehue's lakes to numerous summits of the Araucanía. Carry plenty of water on the Mirador climb.

PARQUE NACIONAL VILLARRICA
Ascent of Volcán Villarrica

Volcán Villarrica is Chile's most climbed high summit, despite the fact that Conaf now requires everyone – apart from properly trained mountaineers and guides, who must present adequate proof of their qualifications – to make the ascent with an approved guide.

Almost a dozen outdoor-adventure companies in Pucón (p94) organise guided ascents of Volcán Villarrica from around US$30 (which covers equipment, lunch and transfers).

The climb begins from Refugio Villarrica (Centro de Ski Pucón) at 1420m. A well-trodden track ascends to the upper chairlift station at 1882m. (Participants of guided climbs often opt to ride the chairlift.) The route leads up a steep ridge past the minor outcrop of Piedra Negra and a rocky rib known as the Pingüinera (2247m). It continues up over broad snowfields to make a final steep ascent to the 2847m summit. Approach the rim cautiously to avoid noxious fumes and be alert to sudden changes in wind direction.

The 1:50,000 Chilean IGM map *Pucón* (Section G, No 104) covers Volcán Villarrica but the summit area is omitted (due to clouds on the aerial photographs!). Conaf's 1:110,000 free colour map of the park shows the route.

PARQUE NACIONAL LANÍN
Lago Quillén to Lago Ñorquinco

This trek explores the remote northern sector of Parque Nacional Lanín, crossing two high passes that connect three beautiful lakes. As camping is not permitted between each stage, it requires two very long days.

The route leads north from the eastern end of Lago Quillén, crossing the Arroyo Malalco and switchbacking up through a pass (at around 1850m) on the eastern side of the Cordón de Rucachoroi. It then descends to meet a road on the south shore of Lago Rucachoroi, where there is a **camping ground**. From here the route heads northwest up the Arroyo Calfiquitra and across a watershed at Mallín Chufquén before again descending to Lago Ñorquinco via the Arroyo Coloco. There is another **camping ground** here.

It is possible to extend the trek by continuing along the scenic, lightly transited Ruta 11 (either hitching or walking) to Moquehue, then trekking on around the south side of Lago Moquehue to Villa Pehuenia. In summer there are several daily buses from San Martín de los Andes (p117) to Zapala via Aluminé, from where there are connections to Villa Pehuenia and Moquehue.

Two old Argentine IGM 1:100,000 maps, *Lago Ñorquinco* (Neuquén, No 3972-23) and *Quillén* (Neuquén, No 3972-29), cover the area (but not the track). Sendas y Bosques' 1:200,000 map *Parque Nacional Lanín* shows the route clearly.

Lakes District

The luxuriant rainforests of the Lakes District contain the greatest diversity of plants and animals found anywhere in Patagonia. The Lakes District's outstanding scenery includes large glacial lakes, volcanic plateaus, fresh, clear streams and wild mountain passes, making this area a real delight to explore. Of particular interest are ancient alerce forests, a conifer that reaches gigantic proportions, and the pudu, a native midget deer species. The area's obvious appeal and easy accessibility have helped it become the premier trekking region of Chile and Argentina, and this is reflected in the number of Lakes District treks featured in this book.

GATEWAYS
Osorno (Chile)

The city of Osorno is on the Panamerican Hwy, roughly halfway between Temuco and Puerto Montt. It is an ideally located trekking base for trips to the national parks of Puyehue and Vicente Pérez Rosales in the central Chilean Lakes District. **Sernatur** *(Servicio Nacional de Turismo;* ☎ *064-237 575)* has a tourist office in the Edificio Gobernación Provincial on Plaza de Armas. The local **Conaf office** *(Corporación Nacional Forestal;* ☎ *064-234393)* is at Martínez de Rozas 430.

Places to Stay & Eat The **Residencial Ortega** *(*☎ *064-232592; Colón 602; rooms per person US$9)* has simple clean and airy rooms with breakfast included. **Hospedaje Millantué** *(*☎ *064-242480; Errázuriz 1339; singles/doubles US$22/38)* is across from the bus terminal and offers fair value for money. **Hotel Villa Eduvijes** *(*☎ *064-235023; Eduvijes 856; singles/doubles US$28/48)*, a few blocks south of the bus terminal, is clean and friendly.

Dino's *(*☎ *064-233880; Ramírez 898)* serves excellent cakes and coffee. **Bocatto** *(*☎ *064-238000; Ramírez 938)* serves pizza, sandwiches and very good ice cream.

HIGHLIGHTS

CHRIS BEAL

The view over lakes Nahuel Huapi and Perito Merino on the Nahuel Huapi Traverse

• Gazing up at the majestic cone of Volcán Lanín from the shores of Lago Paimún on the trek from Termas de Lahuen Co to La Unión (p122)

• Standing among bubbling mud pools and gushing geysers among scoria dunes on the Baños de Caulle trek (p126)

• A steaming hot tub at the end of a day's trekking in the remote rainforested valley of the Termas de Callao (p135)

• Contrasting views of craggy Cerro Catedral and hulking Monte Tronador from high on the Nahuel Huapi Traverse (p142)

Getting There & Away There are daily flights to/from Santiago with **LanChile** *(*☎ *064-236688; Matta 862, Block C)* for US$94. Buses to local and regional destinations leave from the **Terminal de Buses Rurales** *(*☎ *064-232073; Mercado Municipal,*

Lakes District

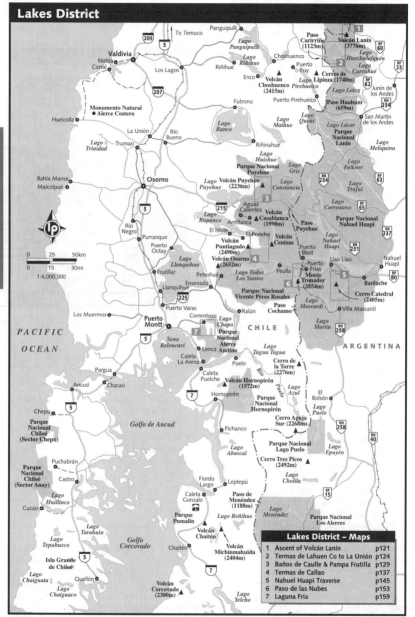

205 To Temuco
Panguipulli
Lago Panguipulli
Valdivia
Niebla
Corral
Los Lagos
207
Hueicolla
Monumento Natural
Alerce Costero
La Unión
Río Bueno
Trumao
Lago Trinidad
Bahía Mansa
Maicolpué
Osorno
Río Negro
Purranque
Puerto Octay
Frutillar
Llanquihue
Lago Llanquihue
Los Muermos
Puerto Varas
Puerto Montt
Ensenada
Petrohué
Correntoso
225
Lenca
Caleta La Arena
Ancud
Chacao
Pargua
Chepu
Parque Nacional Chiloé (Sector Chepu)
Parque Nacional Chiloé (Sector Anay)
Puchabrán
Castro
Lago Huillinco
Cucao
Lago Tarahuín
Lago Tepuhueco
Isla Grande de Chiloé
Lago Chaiguata
Lago Chaiguaco
Quellón

Riñihue
Enco
Choshuenco
Puerto Fuy
Lago Riñihue
Volcán Choshuenco (2415m)
Futrono
Lago Ranco
Riñinahue
Lago Maihue
Puerto Pirehueico
Paso Carirriñe (1123m)
Volcán Lanín (3776m)
Cerros de Lipinza (1740m)
Pirehueico
Lago Pirehueico
Lago Lolog
Paso Huahum (659m)
Lago Quení
Lago Lácar
San Martín de los Andes
Junín de los Andes
Parque Nacional Lanín
Lago Meliquina
Lago Huechulafquén
Lago Currhué

Lago Huishue
Parque Nacional Puyehue
Lago Puyehue
Volcán Puyehue (2236m)
Lago Gris
Lago Constancia
Lago Falkner
Lago Traful
Lago Correntoso
Parque Nacional Nahuel Huapi

Aguas Calientes
Antillanca
Volcán Casablanca (1990m)
Lago Rupanco
El Islote
El Poncho
Vulcán Puntiagudo (2490m)
Volcán Osorno (2652m)
Volcán Cenizas
Paso Puyehue
Puerto Blest
Peulla
Puerto Frías
Monte Tronador (3554m)
Lago Nahuel Huapi
Llao Llao
Nahuel Huapi
Bariloche
Cerro Catedral (2405m)
Villa Mascardi
Lago Mascardi

Lago Todos Los Santos
Parque Nacional Vicente Pérez Rosales
Rálün
Paso Cochamó
Lago Chapo
Parque Nacional Alerce Andino
CHILE
Lago Tagua Tagua
Lago Martín
ARGENTINA

Seno Reloncaví
Caleta Puelche
Puelo
Volcán Hornopirén (1572m)
Hornopirén
Parque Nacional Hornopirén
Pichanco
Cerro de la Torre (2276m)
Lago Azul
El Bolsón
Lago Puelo
Cerro Aguja Sur (2268m)
Parque Nacional Lago Puelo
Lago Epuyén
Cerro Tres Picos (2492m)
Lago Cholila

Golfo de Ancud
Fiordo Largo
Leptepú
Caleta Gonzalo
Paso de Menéndez (1188m)
Parque Pumalín
Lago Reñihue
Volcán Chaitén
Chaitén
Volcán Michinmahuida (2404m)
Lago Menéndez
Parque Nacional Los Alerces

Golfo Corcovado
Volcán Corcovado (2300m)
Lago Yelcho

PACIFIC OCEAN

0   25   50km
0   15   30mi
1:4,000,000

Route markers: 205, 5, 207, 5, 215, 5, 225, 5, 7, 5, 7, RP 60, RP 23, RP 62, RN 234, RN 234, RP 63, RP 65, RN 237, RN 231, RN 80, RN 258, RN 258, RN 40, RP 15

Lakes District – Maps

1	Ascent of Volcán Lanín	p121
2	Termas de Lahuen Co to La Unión	p124
3	Baños de Caulle & Pampa Frutilla	p129
4	Termas de Callao	p137
5	Nahuel Huapi Traverse	p145
6	Paso de las Nubes	p153
7	Laguna Fría	p159

Errázuriz & Prat), two blocks west. Long-distance buses use the **main terminal** (☎ 064-234149; Errázuriz 1400), near Angulo. The larger companies, including **Igi Llaima** (☎ 064-234371) and **Tas Choapa** (☎ 064-233933), have frequent departures north and south along the Panamerican Hwy to Puerto Montt, Temuco and Santiago, as well as daily buses to Bariloche and other Argentine destinations.

Bariloche (Argentina)

Apart from being the largest Argentine city in the Patagonian Andes, San Carlos de Bariloche, commonly known as Bariloche, is also easily the most touristy. It can be expensive but is nevertheless very attractive. On the southeastern shores of Lago Nahuel Huapi in the southern Lakes District, Bariloche is the gateway to Argentina's superb Parque Nacional Nahuel Huapi.

Information All trekkers should pay a visit to the **Club Andino Bariloche** (CAB; ☎ 02944-527966; w www.clubandino.com .ar; 20 de Febrero 30; open 9.30am-1pm & 4.30pm-8.30pm Mon-Sat, 4.30pm-8.30pm Sun), which sells trekking maps and is a great source of information. The **administration centre** (☎ 02944-423121; e pnint@bariloche.com.ar; San Martín 24; open 9am-2pm Mon-Fri) for Parque Nacional Nahuel Huapi is uphill from the Centro Cívico.

The city website is w www.bariloche.com.

Supplies & Equipment Bariloche has several small outlets for outdoor clothing and equipment. One of the best is **Patagonia Outdoors** (☎/fax 02944-426768; w www.patagonia-outdoors.com.ar; Elflein 27). Try **Grupo García Pinturería** (cnr Gallardo & Rolando), a paint shop, for solvente (white gas), and outdoor-gear suppliers for gas canisters.

Supermarkets, including **Todo** (San Martín 281 • Neumeyer • Elflein), which has several branches around town, **Uno** (Moreno 350) and **La Anónima** (Quaglia) are open late six or seven days a week. **Feria Naturista** (Elflein 55) is good for bulk wholefoods. **Del Turista** (Mitre 239) and **Fenoglio** (Mitre & Rolando)

are institutions in a town that prides itself on its chocolate.

Places to Stay & Eat Bariloche has a **municipal tourist office** (☎ 02944-423022, 423122; e securismo@bariloche.com.ar; Centro Cívico; open 8am-9pm daily) that keeps a database with accommodation prices, including listings for places outside of town.

La Selva Negra (☎ 02944-441013; Av Bustillo Km 2.9; camping per site US$3), 3km west of town on the road to Llao Llao, is the nearest camping ground. Other sites between Bariloche and Llao Llao include **Camping El Yeti** (☎ 02944-442073; Av Bustillo Km 5.8; camping per site US$2) and **Camping Petunia** (☎ 02944-461969; Av Bustillo Km 13.5; camping per site US$2).

Albergue Patagonia Andina (☎ 02944-421861; w www.elpatagoniaandina.com.ar; Morales 564; dorm beds US$4, doubles from US$10) is just three blocks uphill from the CAB, and rates include sheets, towels, use of the kitchen and Internet access.

Hostel 1004 (☎ 02944-432228; e 1004 hostel@ciudad.com.ar; San Martín 127, 10th floor; floor space US$2.50, dorm beds US$4, doubles US$9.50) is in the Bariloche Center Building and there's a great view; BYO sleeping bag. A free shuttle ferries guests from Hostel 1004 to the more sylvan **La Morada** (☎ 02944-442349; w www.lam oradahostel.com; Cerro Otto Km 5; dorm beds US$4.50, doubles with/without bath US$6.25/5.50), just out of town.

Hostería El Ciervo Rojo (☎ 02944-435241; e ciervorojo@ciudad.com.ar; Elflein 115; singles/doubles from US$20/25) is one of Bariloche's many hosterías (family-run hotels). Book in advance to stay at this pleasant place.

La Andina (Elflein 95; pizzas US$2-5) is a friendly place with good food where followers of the Deportivo La Coruña football (soccer) team will feel right at home.

Días de Zapata (Morales 362; mains US$2.50-5) does good, filling Mexican food.

El Boliche de Alberto Pastas (Elflein 49) serves generous portions of tasty pasta and is easier to get into than its popular namesake parrilla (grill restaurant), around the corner in Villegas.

Getting There & Away Bariloche is the Patagonian Andes' best connected city for air services, with flights to/from Buenos Aires (US$80, 2¼ hours, several daily), El Calafate (US$105, 1¾ hours, nine weekly) and many other large cities throughout Patagonia. The main local carriers are **Aerolíneas Argentinas** (☎ 0810-222-86527; Mitre 185), **Southern Winds** (☎ 02944-423704; Quaglia 262, Bldg 13) and **LADE** (☎ 02944-423562; Mitre 531).

The **bus terminal** (☎ 02944-426999; Ruta Nacional 237) is out of town to the east; it's where most local and long-distance bus services originate and terminate, and the long-distance bus companies all have offices there. Numerous buses daily run south along Ruta 258 to El Bolsón (US$3, two hours) and Esquel (US$7, 4½ hours), as well as north to San Martín (US$7, 4½ hours) and Buenos Aires (US$35, 23 hours). There are also daily buses to Osorno (US$11, five hours) and Puerto Montt (US$11, seven hours) in Chile with **Tas-Choapa** (☎ 02944-426663; Moreno 138). A more scenic route into Chile, with **Cruce de Lagos** (W www.crucedelagos.cl), crosses the lakes of Nahuel Huapi, Frías and Todos Los Santos, using a combination of launches and buses to reach Puerto Montt (US$140, one to two days).

Puerto Montt (Chile)

Sprawling along the sheltered northern shore of the wide bay known as Seno Reloncaví, Puerto Montt is the gateway to the national parks of the southern Chilean Lakes District and the Great Island of Chiloé. This booming port city has many fine examples of southern Chilean wooden and corrugated iron architecture, although these are rapidly giving way to less characteristic modern buildings.

Information Puerto Montt's **municipal tourist office** (☎ 065-261700, ext 823; Antonio Varas & O'Higgins; open 9am-1pm & 3pm-6pm Mon-Fri, 9am-1pm Sat Mar-Dec, 9am-9pm daily Jan-Feb), in a kiosk across from the plaza, is more helpful than **Sernatur** (☎ 065-252720; open 8am-4.30pm Mon-Fri, 9.30am-6.30pm Sat & Sun Nov-mid-Mar), on the west side of Plaza de Armas. **Conaf** (Ochagavía 464) has its main regional office here, but the **local office** (☎ 065-290711; Amunátegui 500) is helpful for information on nearby national parks. The **Argentine consulate** (☎ 065-253996; Cauquenes 94) is near the corner of Cauquenes and Varas.

Places to Stay & Eat Local buses from the bus terminal will drop you at **Camping Paredes** (☎ 065-258394; camping per site US$14), 6km west of town on the road to Chinquihue, which has pleasant sites and hot showers.

Camping Anderson (☎ 09-789-8998; camping per person US$3), further out on the road towards Panitao, on the shores of the Bahía de Huequillahue, is somewhat remote and inconvenient; sites include hot showers. Buses Bohle departs from the bus terminal for Panitao six times daily Monday to Saturday.

Residencial Los Helechos (☎ 065-259525; Chorrillos 1500; per person US$7), just west of the bus terminal, is good value and comfortable, and has rooms with private bathroom for a little more. Add US$2 for breakfast.

The friendly **Residencial La Nave** (☎/fax 065-253740; Antonio Varas & Ancud; rooms from US$14) is a short walk from the bus terminal. It has small but comfortable rooms and a good, unpretentious **restaurant**.

Hostal Pacífico (☎ 065-256229; Mira 1088; singles/doubles US$23/43) is one of the better choices, with clean rooms that are quiet despite the noisy street. A large breakfast is included, and staff are patient and helpful.

Supermarkets close to the bus station include **Las Brisas** (Diego Portales 1040 • Antonio Varas 995) and **Ahorremas** (Antonio Varas 1070).

El Piso Catalán (Quillota 185; meals US$2-5) serves excellent-value menúes (fixed-price meals) in a low-key, artistic dining room.

Pizzería Di Piazza (Gallardo 118; pizzas US$3-12) does good pizzas and also some hearty pasta dishes.

Balzac (Urmeneta 305; meals US$10-15) is more formal and serves fine seafood and international cuisine.

Getting There & Away There are up to five flights daily with **LanChile** (☎ 065-253315; O'Higgins 167, Bldg 1B) from Puerto Montt to Punta Arenas (US$140 one-way, 2¼ hours) and up to nine daily to Santiago (US$150 one-way, 1½ hours). **TAN** (☎ 065-250071; O'Higgins 167) usually flies twice weekly to Bariloche (US$73 one-way) and Neuquén (US$114 one-way), but Argentina's economic woes have disrupted service.

Puerto Montt's waterfront **bus terminal** (☎ 065-253143; Portales & Lillo) gets busy and chaotic – watch your belongings or leave them with the *custodia* (left-luggage office) while sorting out travel plans. In the trekking season, bus trips to Punta Arenas and Bariloche can sell out, so book in advance. Numerous bus companies, all with offices at the terminal, go to Santiago (US$11 to US$23, 13 to 16 hours, several daily), stopping at various cities along the way; departures are usually between 8pm and 10pm. For trips to Punta Arenas (US$50, 30 to 36 hours), try **Cruz del Sur** (☎ 065-254731; Antonio Varas 437), **Queilen Bus** (☎ 065-253468) or **Turibús** (☎ 065-253345). **Tas-Choapa** (☎ 065-254828), **Río de La Plata** (☎ 065-253841) and Cruz del Sur travel daily to Bariloche (US$19, eight hours) via the Cardenal Samoré pass, east of Osorno. Andesmar goes to Bariloche three times weekly.

At the **Terminal de Transbordadores** (Ferry Terminal; Av Angelmó 2187) you'll find ticket offices and waiting lounges for **Navimag** (☎ 065-253318; [W] www.nav imag.cl). Navimag's M/N *Magallanes* sails each Monday to Puerto Natales, a popular three-night journey through Patagonia's canals; book at **Navimag's Santiago office** (☎ 02-4423120, fax 2035025; El Bosque Norte 440, 11th floor, Las Condes), or make a reservation via the Internet and confirm with the Santiago office. Fares (which include meals) vary according to the season, class of accommodation and view, but in the high season (November to March), per-person one-way fares range from US$275 for a berth to US$1590 for an AAA single cabin.

Parque Nacional Lanín

The 3790-sq-km Parque Nacional Lanín forms a 180km-long strip of wilderness stretching south through the Andes of Neuquén Province.

The 3776m Volcán Lanín – from which the park takes its name – dominates the skyline throughout the entire area. This mighty volcano divides the park into northern and southern zones. The northern zone – which theoretically belongs to the Araucanía region – covers about one third of the park's area, and is centred around the elongated, fjord-like Lago Quillén. The much larger and broader zone to the south of the great volcano forms a band of more rugged mountains. From this, three other major glacial lakes – Lago Huechulafquén, Lago Lolog and Lago Lácar (along with several other very sizeable water bodies of glacial origin) – splay out up to 100km eastward, almost as far as the Patagonian steppes.

Until the late 19th century the vast area of the park was inhabited by the Pehuenche people. The lifestyle of this large Mapuche tribe was integrally linked with the annual harvest of *ñulli* (pine nuts; also known as *piñones* in Spanish) from the region's extensive montane forests of coniferous araucaria trees. Two Pehuenche Indian reserves within the park, at Rucachoroi and Curruhuinca, are all that remain of the former Pehuenche lands. The Mapuche reservations of Curruhuinca and Rucachoroi – fragments of the vast territory formerly held by the indigenous people – are located within the park, and are fittingly called *reducciones*.

NATURAL HISTORY

Argentina's richest forests of southern beech grow in Parque Nacional Lanín. The evergreen *coigüe* (spelt *coihue* in Argentina), is present mainly at the lowest elevations. Two deciduous species of southern beech are dominant in the subalpine forests, *rauli* and roble (or *pellín*), and are absent in the Andean–Patagonian forests further south. *Rauli* has long leathery, almost oval-shaped leaves, while its close relative, the roble, has distinctive oak-like leaves with deep serrations.

In the alpine zone (roughly above 1000m), two other deciduous southern beech species, ñirre (spelt ñire in Argentina) and lenga, are found. The two trees are easily distinguishable: the leaves of the lenga have rounded double notches, while those of the ñirre have irregularly crinkled edges. Lenga grows right up to tree line in low, weatherbeaten scrub (known in local Spanish as bosque achaparrado). In autumn the mountainsides are aflame with colour as these mixed deciduous beech forests turn a beautiful golden red.

Various parasitic plants attack the southern beeches, embedding their roots in the branches or trunk of a host tree and drawing off its sap. Common parasites are the liga, or injerto native mistletoes, the quintral, whose nectar-filled red flowers attract many species of hummingbird, and the llaollao, a fungus that deforms the wood into a large, knotted growth on which round spongy balls form.

Cloaking the northern zone of Parque Nacional Lanín are extensive forests of umbrella-like araucaria, or pehuén, a unique tree with long branches covered in sharp scales. In autumn the araucaria yields head-size cones containing starchy nuts, which were the staple food of the local Pehuenche tribes (who called the nuts ñulli). Particularly in the park's southern zone, forests of Cordilleran cypress, with occasional stands of maitén (a native willow-like species), spread across the less watered Andean foothills.

As always in the Patagonian Andes, numerous species of native wild flower can be identified. The bright spots of yellow scattered around the floor of montane forests could be the delicate violeta amarilla, a yellow species of violet whose unusual colour belies the name of this large, worldwide genus of flowers, or perhaps the yellow topa topa, which resembles a large pea flower. Two pretty white species are the centella, a native anemone, and the cuye eldorado, an oxalis species that has long been a favourite of gardeners in the British Isles. The cuye eldorado grows low to the ground

on well-drained and exposed mountainsides above tree line – typically in otherwise bare volcanic soils – and has pale blooms with pinkish edges.

Parque Nacional Lanín is one of the last habitats of the tunduco, an extremely rare species of native rat. A member of an ancient rodent family (the so-called octodontids), the tunduco typically inhabits quila and colihue thickets, feeding on the roots and shoots of these bamboo species. Other mammals found in the park include the monito del monte (or mouse opossum), pudu, coipo, viscacha and the rare Andean deer known as the huemul. These animals are variously preyed on by the puma, the Patagonian red fox, the huillín and huiña.

Well represented are tapaculos, small ground-dwelling birds that include the chucao, the huet-huet and the churrín, or Andean tapaculo, which all find shelter in bamboo thickets, forest underbrush or alpine heathland. Unmistakable because of its absurdly long tail (about double the length of the bird's body) is Des Murs' wiretail, or colilarga.

CLIMATE

Parque Nacional Lanín has a continental climate ranging from subalpine to alpine, with a relatively low proportion of rainfall outside the spring-to-autumn period. Summers are warm to hot, particularly in the park's northern (Araucanía) sector, while winters are crisp and white, particularly on the higher ranges. The areas immediately east and north of Volcán Lanín lie in a marked rain shadow created by the volcanic range extending east from Volcán Villarrica. From an annual maximum rainfall of 4500mm on the snowy upper slopes of Volcán Lanín, precipitation levels drop away sharply to well under 1000mm near the dry plains bordering the eastern fringes of the park. Towards the south, in the moist temperate forests of the park's mountainous western sectors, annual precipitation is around 2500mm.

PLANNING

The APN Intendencia in San Martín de los Andes (p117) can give up-to-date advice and information (including weather forecasts) on trekking and climbing in Parque Nacional Lanín.

An entry fee of US$3 applies but is payable only when you enter via an APN *portada* (entrance gate). Camping is not permitted outside organised camping grounds and established en route camping areas.

Maps & Books

A 1:200,000 double-sided colour trekking map, titled *Parque Nacional Lanín* and published by **Sendas y Bosques** (W *www .sendasybosques.com.ar*), covers the entire park. It shows most official trails and, although its scale is a bit too small for comfortable navigation, it is the only widely available quality map. Sendas y Bosques also publishes *Parques Nacionales Lanín y Nahuel Huapi*, a Spanish-language trekking guidebook to the Argentine Araucanía that includes some information in English. Both publications are available in local bookshops and outdoor-supply shops.

ACCESS TOWN
San Martín de los Andes
(Argentina)

The outdoor-sports and tourist centre of San Martín de los Andes lies at the eastern end of Lago Lácar in the southern part of Parque Nacional Lanín. There are well-developed skiing facilities nearby on Cerro Chapelco.

Information San Martín's **tourist office** (☎ 02972-425500; W *www.turismosmandes .com; San Martín & Rosas*), across from Plaza San Martín, is well organised and sells fishing licences. Across the plaza, the **APN Intendencia** (☎ 02972-427233; *Emilio Frey 749; open 9am-1pm Mon-Fri, daily Jan & Feb*), which is the administration centre for Parque Nacional Lanín. **Cerro Torre** (☎ 02972-429162; e *cerrotorre@smandes .com.ar; San Martín 960*) sells and rents trekking and climbing gear, and organises guided climbs of Volcán Lanín.

Places to Stay & Eat Accommodation options in San Martín de los Andes include

HI-affiliated **Puma Youth Hostel** (☎ 02972-422443; e *puma@smandes.com.ar; A Fosbery 535; dorm beds US$6*), **Residencial Los Pinos** (☎ 02972-427207; *Almirante Brown 420; rooms with breakfast per person US$12*) and **Hostería Las Lucarnas** (☎ 02972-427085; *Coronel Pérez 632; singles/doubles with breakfast US$20/35*).

Getting There & Away Travelling by air, **Aerolíneas/Austral** (☎ 02972-427218) flies almost daily from San Martin de los Andes to Buenos Aires (US$123 one-way), while **LADE** (☎ 02972-427672) flies approximately weekly to Bariloche (US$20 one-way), Neuquén (US$30 one-way) and Buenos Aires (US$110 one-way).

From San Martín de los Andes' **bus terminal** (☎ 02972-427044; *Villegas & Juez del Valle*) there are frequent departures north to Zapala (all services are via Junín, with some via Aluminé) and Neuquén, as well as south to Bariloche. There are also buses that run via Paso Mamuil Malal to Temuco in Chile at least daily. Buses Lafit runs several times weekly, via Paso Huahum to Puerto Pirehueico (US$8) in Chile, from where there are (scenic but unreliable) ferry/bus connections that take you on to Puerto Fuy and Panguipulli.

From January to early March only, **Empresa KoKo** (☎ 02972-427422) runs several buses daily to Puerto Arturo on Lago Lolog (from where a popular two-day trek heads north via Portezuelo Auquinco to Lago Curruhue). A number of travel companies, including **Huemul Turismo** (☎ 02972-422903; W *www.huemulturismo .com.ar; San Martín 881*), **Lucero Viajes** (☎ 02972-428453; e *luceroviajes@smandes .com.ar; San Martín 946*) and **Tiempo Patagónico** (☎ 02972-427113; *San Martín 950*), run tours (most days in summer) to Quila Quina, Termas de Lahuen Co, Termas de Queñi and Lagos Huechulafquén and Paimún, which are the only form of public transport to/from many of the treks in Parque Nacional Lanín. **Remises del Bosque y Andes** (☎ 02972-429110; *Villegas 944*) will shuttle trekkers to trailheads for reasonable rates.

LAKES DISTRICT

Ascent of Volcán Lanín

Duration	3 days
Distance	25km
Difficulty	demanding
Start/Finish	Guardería Tromen
Nearest Towns	Junín de los Andes (p119), San Martín de los Andes (p117)
Transport	(international) bus

Summary A climb to the top of a majestic volcanic cone that gives a tremendous panorama of the Lakes District and Araucanía.

Towering over the northern Lakes District, Volcán Lanín rises from a base plain of around 1100m to a height of 3776m. Viewed from any other direction than the east, Volcán Lanín's thick cap of heavily crevassed glacial ice makes it look almost impossible to climb, but up its eastern side is a strenuous, though straightforward ascent route. In fact, Lanín is probably the highest summit in Patagonia safely attainable without ropes.

Lanín's Mapuche name means 'Dead Rock', as the Mapuche people believed that anyone who climbed the mountain would be killed by evil spirits (although, today, freezing winds and glacier crevasses are generally a greater danger).

PLANNING
When to Trek

Although winter ascents of Volcán Lanín are not unheard of, the summit is normally tackled between November and mid-April. All climbers must carry an ice axe and crampons so ascents early in the season are generally easier because the remaining snowpack provides a more stable surface than the often loose volcanic earth underneath. Remember, however, that after midday the snow often becomes soft and slushy, making the going tiring uphill and hazardous on the descent.

The volcano's exposed, steep slopes are definitely no place for tents, so all trekkers must stay at one of the three unstaffed *refugios* on Lanín, which are all roughly halfway up the mountain.

The *refugios* provide good, basic shelter (free of charge) but it is essential to carry your own means of cooking and a warm sleeping bag. The ascent of Volcán Lanín is a popular excursion, and in the peak holiday season (January to mid-February) the number of climbers on the mountain may exceed the huts' comfortable capacity.

What to Bring

It is now mandatory for all trekkers to carry the items listed below.

• ice axe and crampons
• waterproof jacket
• mountain sunglasses
• sleeping bag
• stove
• sturdy boots (suitable for snowy conditions)
• headlamp
• medical kit

You can hire an ice axe (around US$3 per day) and crampons (around US$5 per day) in San Martín or, less reliably, in Junín. Climbing ropes are not required, but wearing gaiters to protect your shins and keep rocks and snow out of your boots is advisable.

Maps

The best map available is the Chilean IGM 1:50,000 map, *Paimún* (Section G, No 114). This map provides good topographical information on Volcán Lanín, but does not show huts, ascent routes or the correct position of glaciers. JLM Mapas' 1:250,000 map, *Pucón – San Martín de los Andes* (No 07), includes an inset scaled at 1:65,000 that accurately shows the route and *refugios*.

Permits & Regulations

All parties must receive authorisation to climb the volcano from the *guardaparque* (national-park ranger) at the Guardería Tromen. Trekkers without proper ice-climbing gear (see What to Bring) will not be permitted to make the ascent. Be sure to inform the ranger on your return, too.

Camping is not permitted anywhere on or around the base of Volcán Lanín apart from at the Guardería Tromen and the camping area at the southern shore of Lago Tromen.

Warning

The trek involves a total ascent of almost 2700m (from around 1100m to 3776m) over loose earth and/or snow slopes. Trekkers should be physically fit, carry basic ice-climbing gear (see What to Bring, p118) and have some experience in mountainous terrain. Although the ascent route itself (apart from the summit) is not exposed to the worst of the westerlies, strong, freezing winds can pick up at any time and with little warning. Attempt the summit only in perfect weather. As you climb, watch for changing conditions and be prepared to descend if conditions deteriorate. Lanín is high enough to cause altitude sickness (p64), so be alert to symptoms in yourself and your companions. Although the route does not cross glaciers, there are dangerous, heavily crevassed glaciers near the summit – keep to the route.

NEAREST TOWNS & FACILITIES

See San Martín de los Andes (p117).

Junín de los Andes (Argentina)

Although it's not an especially interesting place, Junín de los Andes, 41km north of San Martín, does make a good base for trips in the north of Parque Nacional Lanín.

Junín's helpful **tourist office** (☎ 02972-491160; e turismo@jandes.com.ar; Padre Milanesio 596) is on Plaza San Martín. At the same address (but facing Coronel Suárez) is the local **APN office** (☎ 02972-491160). **Club Andino Junín de los Andes** (CAJA; ☎ 02972-491637; Padre Milanesio 568, Local 12) can give you information on climbing and trekking in the region – ask about hiring ice-climbing gear.

Hostería Chimehuín (☎ 02972-491132; Coronel Suárez & 25 de Mayo) has rooms from US$10 per person. **Ruca Hueney** (☎ 02972-491113; Padre Milanesio 641) has a varied menu.

From Junín's **bus terminal** (☎ 02972-492038) there are frequent departures to all of the region's major centres, including San Martín de los Andes (some via Aluminé) and Zapala. Empresa San Martín, Igi-Llaima and JAC all have (almost) daily buses to Pucón and Temuco, which run via Tromen and Paso Mamuil Malal.

Tromen Area

The remote locality of Tromen consists of a **Gendarmería Nacional** customs post and the **APN's Guardería Tromen** (☎ 02972-427204/10; e laningparque@smandes.com.ar) on Ruta Provincial 60, which continues 4km across Paso Mamuil Malal into Chile. Free camping is allowed near the *guardería* (ranger station), but much better is the beautiful free camping area 3km away on the southern shore of Lago Tromen. There is no nearby store or accommodation.

GETTING TO/FROM THE TREK

This trek begins and ends at Guardería Tromen. A number of bus companies, including Empresa San Martín, Igi-Llaima and JAC, run buses almost daily to/from Temuco and Bariloche, San Martín or Zapala.

In January and February, **Alquimia** (☎ 02972-491355; Padre Milanesio 840) in Junín de los Andes runs minibuses from Junín to Tromen (US$15) daily, subject to demand. Otherwise, **Julio Villanueva** (☎ 02972-491375) in Junín runs shuttles to Tromen for US$60 one-way.

After clearing customs, trekkers arriving directly from Chile can disembark at Tromen. If you do this, it might be worth reserving a seat with the bus company for the trip back out, even if you have to pay a bit extra, to ensure you have an onward seat when you return.

Trekkers intending to cross the border after the climb should note that they are not normally permitted to board a Chile-bound bus in Tromen unless their names are on the official passenger list. It's important that you have a ticket to Chile – with a definite arrangement to join that bus – before you get to Tromen; this can be organised in San Martín de los Andes or Junín de los Andes. The road is remote and carries only light traffic, so hitching is an unreliable transport option and we don't recommend it as a rule.

LAKES DISTRICT

THE TREK
Day 1: Guardería Tromen to Refugio CAJA
4½–5½ hours, 7km, 1518m ascent

As there is unlikely to be any running water for most of today's sweaty climb, fill up your canteen at the camping area when you sign in at Guardería Tromen (1142m). Pick up the trail behind the Gendarmería Nacional building and follow this roughly southwest through attractive forest of *lenga*, then across a plain of volcanic sand to cross the **Arroyo Turbio** after 30 to 45 minutes. (Early in the day this stream may carry little or no water here, but Lanín's melting névés and glaciers normally produce a steady flow by late afternoon.)

You will notice the **Espina de Pescado**, a long, lateral moraine ridge that snakes around to the right above the stream. Climb this 'spine', following the narrow ridge top as it steepens and curves slightly rightward past an old secondary crater on the left to reach the **Sendero de las Mulas** turn-off going off right (see Alternative Route), one to 1½ hours from the Arroyo Turbio.

Keep to the craggy ridge line, where unstable rock calls for careful footwork and minor detours are necessary to negotiate small outcrops. The route climbs up alongside a long, broken-up glacier down to your left to arrive at the red- and orange-painted **Refugio RIM-26**, two to 2½ hours on. Built at 2450m along the Espina de Pescado route by the Regimiento de Infantería de Montaña, the *refugio* is on ground that was left almost level after the recession of the nearby glacier. It has capacity for up to 10 people. Afternoon meltwater can be collected from the glacier, but take care not to get too close to where the ice falls away abruptly. Tread cautiously on dirt-covered ice, and save enough water for the next day.

Just above the *refugio*, pick up a vague trail leading up beside the glacier, following this up to where the rock rib disappears. The route continues up for 100m, before leaving the ridge line and heading right through an area of broken-up rock rubble to reach the much more rustic **Refugio CAJA** after 25 to 35 minutes. The rustic tin-roofed hut stands at 2660m on a low, flat ridge. Built and owned by the Club Andino de Junín de los Andes, this smaller civilian *refugio* has space for up to eight people. Collect water from a small névé just around to the west.

Alternative Route: via Sendero de las Mulas
5½–7 hours, 9km, 1518m ascent

The Sendero de las Mulas (literally 'mule track') is a longer but less strenuous route that follows a trail proper (rather than the much steeper Espina de Pescado). It is a better option for slower or less fit trekkers.

From the turn-off, the trail turns away westward, winding and switchbacking up repeatedly through the scoria to finally reach **Refugio BIM-6** after two to three hours. This comfortable *refugio* (built by the Batallon de Ingenieros de Montaña) is situated at 2350m and sleeps up to 15 people. The path continues its serpentine course, rising around slightly leftward to arrive at **Refugio CAJA** after a further one to 1½ hours.

Day 2: Refugio CAJA Return (via Summit of Volcán Lanín)
7–11 hours, 11km, 1116m ascent/descent

This final section climbs over – when not snowbound – extremely unstable scoria slopes. The steep and loose earth makes a frustratingly unstable trekking surface, and you need to step very carefully to avoid slipping. Do not try for the summit unless the weather is good. Allow yourself plenty of time. There is no running water higher up, so carry plenty (at least a litre per person).

Head up the initially gentle slope over large patches of snow, passing between the two larger permanent snowfields (about 400m over from the glacier), where the gradient begins to steepen. As the ground becomes looser, often giving way as you step, keep an eye out for marker stakes and paint splashes on rocks. Layers of volcanic rock have weathered unevenly to produce very low ridges that lead up the slope. These are much more stable and, if winds are not too strong, they may make for easier climbing.

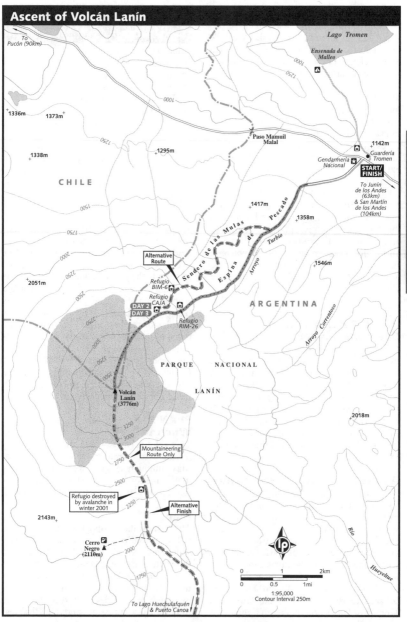

Ascent of Volcán Lanín

To Pucón (90km)

Lago Tromen

Ensenada de Malleo

1336m
1373m

1250
1000

Paso Mamuil Malal

1295m

1142m

Guardería Tromen

Gendarmería Nacional

START/ FINISH

CHILE

1338m

To Junín de los Andes (63km) & San Martín de los Andes (104km)

1417m

1358m

1500

Pescado

Sendero de las Mulas

Espina de

Arroyo Turbio

1546m

Alternative Route

2000

1750

2051m

2250

Refugio BIM-6

Refugio CAJA

DAY 2
DAY 3

Refugio RIM-26

ARGENTINA

Arroyo Correntoso

2750

3250

3000

PARQUE

NACIONAL

Volcán Lanín (3776m)

LANÍN

2018m

3250
3500

Mountaineering Route Only

2750

2500

Refugio destroyed by avalanche in winter 2001

2250

Alternative Finish

2143m

Cerro Negro (2110m)

2000

1750

Río

Hueyelue

To Lago Huechulafquén & Puerto Canoa

0   1   2km
0   0.5   1mi

1:95,000
Contour Interval 250m

Although strenuous, the route is now straightforward. In the last stages before you reach the summit, a scramble over rock ledges leads up past the impressive seracs of a glacier that descends westward. Follow a few rock cairns left on to the small névé leading up to the summit of Volcán Lanín, which – atypically for a volcano – is not topped with a wide caldera. The relatively small summit is capped by glacial ice which falls away sharply on the south side. Sometimes small crevasses open up and, particularly in early summer, you should be extremely careful on the summit.

Llaima, Villarrica, Tronador and many other major peaks of the Lakes District and Araucanía regions are visible from the summit of Lanín. Directly north and south are the large lakes Tromen and Huechulafquén, and a number of beautiful smaller lakes lie on the northwestern slopes of the volcano. In clear conditions you might even be able to make out Chile's Pacific coast far to the west.

Retrace your way back to Refugio CAJA.

Day 3: Refugio CAJA to Guardería Tromen
4–7 hours, 7km, 1518m descent
Retrace your steps as on Day 1. Fit and fast trekkers often prefer to descend the whole way from the summit to Guardería Tromen on their – long – second day. Despite the slope's steepness, the loose volcanic earth breaks your fall. This often makes the going easier. If the sustained descents are painful for your knees, opt for the Sendero de las Mulas route.

Alternative Finish: Puerto Canoa
9–12 hours, 17km, 2850m descent
Experienced climbers can opt for an alternative and more difficult descent route leading southeast to the ruins of a *refugio*. At an elevation of 2400m, it was destroyed by an avalanche in the winter of 2001. From there, a path goes on southward down the Arroyo Ruc Leufu to Puerto Canoa, near La Unión (p123) on Lago Huechulafquén. Once down, be sure to report back to the Guardería Tromen or the Guardería Puerto Canoa.

Termas de Lahuen Co to La Unión

Duration	2 days
Distance	26km
Difficulty	easy
Start	Termas de Lahuen Co (p123)
Finish	La Unión (p123)
Nearest Towns	Junín de los Andes (p119), San Martín de los Andes (p117)
Transport	guided tour and/or taxi

Summary An uncomplicated trek from remote, unspoilt hot springs to the scenic shores of Lago Paimún under the spectacular cone of Volcán Lanín.

This A-to-B style 'destination' route leads from the Termas de Lahuen Co along disused roads (not used by vehicles since the 1960s), over abandoned pastures and past an old sawmill to the last remaining farmlets on the southern shore of Lago Paimún. The gradual regeneration of vegetation cleared by settlers (known as pobladores in Spanish) in the early decades of the last century is visible along much of the trek. Many of the quila thickets flowered and died in 2000, leaving meshed dry canes (see the boxed text 'The Quila Cycle', p102). Introduced wild boar and red deer are quite abundant along this route but, being wary of humans, they are seldom seen.

PLANNING
When to Trek
This relatively low-level trek is normally passable from mid-November until mid-May, although seasonal weather conditions may make road access to the trailheads difficult (especially to Termas de Lahuen Co).

Maps
The best available topographical map is the (Chilean) IGM's 1:50,000 map *Paimún* (Section G, No 114), which does not show the route and is not available locally. The (Argentine) IGM's 1:100,000 map, also titled *Paimún* (Neuquén, No 3972-34), is extremely out of date but still shows the route fairly accurately. Sendas y Bosques'

1:200,000 map *Parque Nacional Lanín* also covers the trek and is sold locally.

Permits & Regulations
Permits are not necessary, but trekkers should leave the details of their intended route with the appropriate APN office (either in San Martín or at Guardería Carilafquen). Camping is permitted only at the park-authorised Camping Libre Aila on Lago Paimún.

NEAREST TOWNS & FACILITIES
See San Martín de los Andes (p117) and Junín de los Andes (p119).

Termas de Lahuen Co
These remote, but popular hot springs (once known as the Baños de Epulafquen) lie at 930m, just off Ruta Provincial 62, 350m past (ie, west of) the APN's Guardería Carilafquen. The rustic bath shed is open from 9am to 12.30pm, and from 2pm to 9pm; entry costs US$1. (The steaming overflow pools outside are not recommended.)

Camping Termas (☎ 02972-426066), just past the *guardería*, is open from early December to late April, and charges US$2 per person (including hot showers) for sites.

Getting There & Away The Termas de Lahuen Co are an 80km, 2½-hour drive northeast from San Martín de los Andes (p117) via Ruta Provincial 62 (which continues 7km over Paso Carirriñe into Chile). The last 20km of the road is narrow and sometimes rough, but still passable for non-4WD vehicles except in wet or snowy conditions.

Termas de Lahuen Co is not accessible by public transport, but throughout the summer season (generally from mid-December until mid-March) various travel agencies in San Martín run organised tours to both the Termas and to the eastern end of Lago Paimún (which make a stop at the chapel in La Unión, where the trek ends). Most agencies are quite happy to drop off trekkers, but will probably charge you the full price for each tour.

La Unión & Puerto Canoa
La Unión is the name given to the picturesque narrows where Lago Paimún drains into Lago Huechulafquén, at the western end of Ruta Provincial 61.

Near the farmhouse on Lago Paimún's western shore is **Camping Ecufué** *(camping per person US$1)*, which has no facilities. The owners run the **Balsa La Union** 'ferry', and will row you across the 50m-wide narrow for US$1 per person, including your pack.

On the eastern shore of La Unión, you can summon the ferry by ringing the makeshift gong beside the picnic area, about 200m south of a rather incongruous Austrian-style chapel and Gendarmería Nacional post. Near here, a road turn-off goes 3km north past **Restaurante Mawizache**, which serves quality meals, and **Camping El Rincón** *(camping per person US$1)*, which has no facilities, to **Camping Piedra Mala** *(camping per person US$2)* situated on a black-sand beach.

At nearby Puerto Canoa is an APN *guardería* and the **Hostería Refugio Pescador** *(☎ 02972-491132; rooms per person about US$15)*.

To access La Unión, see Getting There & Away under Termas de Lahuen Co.

THE TREK (see map p124)
Day 1: Termas de Lahuen Co to Camping Libre Aila
4–5¼ hours, 16km, 350m ascent/descent
From the Termas, follow the road across the **Río Oconi** uphill through lush, tall rainforest to where the **Senda Paimún** *(GPS 39° 47.821 S, 71° 39.222 W)* departs on your right after one to 1¼ hours. This path drops directly northeast to ford the very small Arroyo Burriquete, then continues smoothly downvalley (often on a long-disused road) to reford the stream after 45 minutes to one hour. There are few views apart from glimpses of the bald ridge tops around Cerro Huecuifa up to your right, but it is pleasant trekking through mixed stands of *ñirre*, araucaria, *lenga* or *raulí* with a – largely dead – *quila* understorey (see the boxed text 'The Quila Cycle', p102).

Continue on through the forest to reach **Pampa Grande** – cleared farmland that is gradually regenerating after it was abandoned decades ago. Guided by occasional blue or yellow markings where stock trails confuse the route, head along the right (eastern) side of these scrubby meadows to encounter a rusted old locomotive (once used to power a local sawmill) near the southeastern corner of **Lago Paimún**, one to 1¼ hours from the second ford.

The track climbs rightward, passing below a square of living poplars (the former site of a farmhouse) before it begins an undulating traverse along Lago Paimún's southeastern side, where wild flowers such as pink *mutisias* and orange *amancays* grow. Do not

descend at a small sloping shelf dotted with *calafate* and rose bushes (from where there are the first clear views across the lake to Cerro Caquituco and ahead to the stunning glacier-capped southwest face of Volcán Lanín), but contour directly along the slope.

You can then either short-cut down left across cattle pastures (in places infested by *pega-pega*, whose annoying prickly seeds attach to clothing) to reach **Camping Libre Aila** on the lake shore, 1¼ to 1½ hours from the old locomotive, or continue a short way on to **Arroyo Rimeco** and follow the stream's left (west) bank down, which takes five to

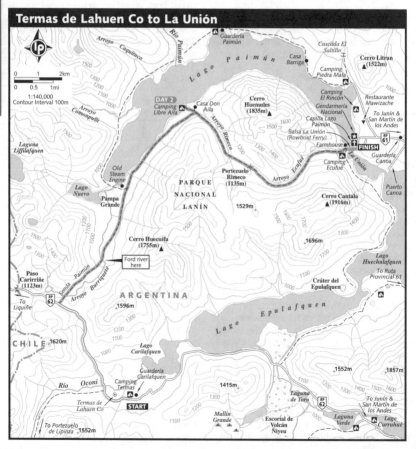

Termas de Lahuen Co to La Unión

10 minutes longer. The idyllic (free) camp site here is under araucarias beside a tiny beach, from where you can admire the glowing, red summit of Volcán Lanín in the evening light.

Day 2: Camping Libre Aila to La Unión

2¼–2¾ hours, 10km, 255m ascent/descent

Follow a trail up the stream past a short turn-off that crosses to the *casa* (house) of Don Aila (whose family established this small farm in the 1940s) before beginning a steeper southeastward ascent. The gradient eases as you head through a series of tussock-grass meadows among low *ñirres* to cross the now tiny Arroyo Rimeco. Climb gently across – probably without noticing it – the broad, flat, forested saddle of **Portezuelo Rimeco**, one to 1¼ hours from the lake shore. Virtually the only views around here are of black Magellanic woodpeckers tapping about the highland *lenga* forest (where the *quila* understorey has also largely died back).

The path dips gradually through mature stands of araucarias, where wild pigs plough up the ground as they forage for *piñones*, then traverses the valley's right (southern) slope well above the rushing Arroyo Ecufué, opposite Cerro Huemules. Descend more steeply through *coigüe* forest into little meadows (frequented by mountain caracaras spying small prey) under the rugged ridges of Cerro Cantala. There are also new views of the southern face of Volcán Lanín. Finally, the route switchbacks down to arrive at a farmhouse on the west side of **La Unión** (p123), 1¼ to 1½ hours from Portezuelo Rimeco.

From here, a worthwhile 18km, four- to five-hour side trip leads south around the shore of Lago Huechulafquén to **Crater del Epulafquen**, a tiny extinct volcano.

Parque Nacional Puyehue

Situated to the east of the Chilean provincial city of Osorno, Parque Nacional Puyehue (pooh-**yay**-way) consists of 1070 sq km of forested wilderness stretching from the eastern shores of Lago Puyehue and Lago Rupanco as far as the Chile–Argentina frontier. Its Mapuche name translates as 'place of the puye', after a small native fish abundant in the freshwater lakes and rivers of the Lakes District.

The 2236m Volcán Puyehue and a fascinating broad volcanic plateau stretching out to its northwest are the park's central features. Volcán Puyehue experienced a major eruption in 1960, spewing great quantities of pumice and ash over its once forested upper slopes. Volcán Puyehue has remained dormant since then, and vulcanologists suspect that the area's centre of geothermal activity may be shifting north to nearby Volcán Carrán, a much younger and lower volcano that has erupted a number of times in recent decades. The combination of intense volcanic activity and high precipitation levels gives rise to numerous hot springs, including Chile's premier spa resort, Aguas Calientes/Termas de Puyehue at the park's western extremity. There are also numerous other small, undeveloped thermal springs in the area.

NATURAL HISTORY

Luxuriant temperate rainforest – the most species-rich ecosystem found anywhere in the Lakes District – blankets the slopes surrounding Volcán Puyehue and Volcán Casablanca. The chief botanical ingredients of these so-called Valdivian forests are several southern beech species, the three *mañíos* as well as *ulmo* and fragrant *tepa*. *Tineo*, which has attractive fern-like branchlets with serrated opposing leaves, is also common, and there are even examples of the coniferous alerce and Guaitecas cypress. The often very thick forest understorey nurtures species such as the *chilco* – the progenitor of countless fuchsia cultivars grown in gardens throughout the world – whose nectar attracts the green-backed firecrown, a tiny hummingbird.

Half-a-dozen or so species of the genus *Baccharis* grow as small upright bushes that produce fluffy, pale-yellowish flowers, including the *pañil*. Bushes of *murta*, whose five-petalled, bell-shaped, pinkish-white flowers develop into small, edible (if somewhat bland) berries that ripen in January, are found at the edge of forest clearings.

The flowering trees and shrubs support an abundance of insects. Two native beetles are the beautiful, multicoloured *coleóptero* and the carnivorous *peorro*, a large carabid whose black, shell-like abdomen has a luminescent, reddish-green sheen. The *peorro* crawls about tree trunks sniffing out ants and other tiny prey. Also remarkable is the *neuroptera*, a well-camouflaged predatory insect with pale-green wings that resemble the leaves of *quila*. One extraordinary butterfly is *Eroessa chilensis*, a living fossil whose evolutionary development has remained almost static for millions of years; it is found in close association with the thorny *tayu*, or *palo blanco*, an ancient tree species that has also changed little over time.

Often seen in the park is the house wren, known locally as the *chercán*, which has a yellow underbody and coffee-coloured, black-striped wings and tail. Also quite common is the austral thrush, which migrates up from the Pacific coast to spend the summer foraging for insects, seeds and berries in the rainforests of Puyehue. It has a brownish head and wings, a white breast and its beak and legs are yellow. The black-winged ground dove, or *tórtol cordillerana*, lives in the forests of the montane zone above 600m.

The less conspicuous mammalian wildlife includes the vizcacha, *monito del monte* (mouse opossum), pudu, puma and the small, grey Azara's fox.

CLIMATE

The park's proximity to the high mountains along the continental divide produces a very wet climate, even by the standards of the southern Lakes District. Precipitation levels start at around 4000mm annually in Anticura and Aguas Calientes on Puyehue's western edge, rising progressively towards the east. At elevations above 1000m, winter snows begin to accumulate after May, when

skiing is possible at the alpine resort of Antillanca on Volcán Casablanca. By early summer (December) snow cover is mostly confined to areas above 2000m, although large wind-blown drifts remain in many places.

Baños de Caulle

Duration	4 days
Distance	50km
Difficulty	moderate
Start/Finish	Anticura (p127)
Nearest Town	Osorno (p111)
Transport	bus

Summary A marvellous trek to a thermal field with steaming fumaroles, geysers and undeveloped hot springs on a high, barren volcanic plateau.

This trek takes you into a stark, but spectacular landscape of dune-like ridges of pumice and enormous black lava flows to the northwest of Volcán Puyehue, where steaming fumaroles *(azufreras*, or volcanic steam vents) break through the ground in places, depositing sulphurous crystals over the bare earth. Geysers gush out among pools of perpetually boiling water and bubbling mud pits, and thermal springs provide naturally heated bathing high above tree line.

PLANNING

Although described below as an out-and-back route, this trek can be done as a circuit via the Ruta de los Americanos or as a one-way traverse by continuing north to Riñinahue (see Alternative Finish: Riñinahue, p131).

When to Trek

The trek can be done from December to mid-April, although this can vary somewhat depending on seasonal (snow) conditions.

Maps

Two Chilean IGM 1:50,000 maps cover this trek: *Volcán Puyehue* (Section H, No 27) and *Riñinahue* (Section H, No 17), but do not show the route. Fundo El Caulle has produced a quality 1:40,000 – *not* 1:50,000 as it claims – map based on the IGM maps (although it does not show grid coordinates), which is available at the El Caulle entrance.

Permits & Regulations

Permits are not required, but all trekking parties should register at Conaf's Guardería Anticura before setting out. The US$1.50 entrance fee to Parque Nacional Puyehue is only charged to those entering the park's Aguas Calientes sector.

See also Fundo El Caulle under Nearest Towns & Facilities.

NEAREST TOWNS & FACILITIES

See Osorno (p111).

Anticura

The locality of Anticura (a Mapuche name meaning 'rock of the sun') is 94km east of Osorno on the international highway Ruta 215 (which runs via Paso de Puyehue to Bariloche in Argentina). The **Guardería Anticura** (☎ 064-234393) is on the south side of Ruta 215. Opposite, north of the highway, are the Conaf information centre (which also has a store selling basic supplies), and the **camping ground** *(tent sites with hot showers US$6; 4-person cabins with gas cooking & hot water US$12)*.

A worthwhile short trek from Anticura goes to the **Salto del Indio**, a churning, 6m-high waterfall on the Río Golgol (where legend has it that a Mapuche fleeing slavery in a gold mine eluded the colonial Spaniards by hiding behind the cascading curtain of water).

Warning

The trek crosses an exposed and unvegetated plateau well above tree line where it is surprisingly easy to become disoriented during bad weather or misty conditions. The loose pumice is shifted constantly by wind, rain and snow, making the trodden path harder to follow. Wooden stakes marking the route are often pushed over by the elements – please firmly re-erect any fallen marker stakes you encounter.

In summer, Buses Puyehue, at the company's terminal at the eastern end of Mercado Municipal in Osorno, runs two daily buses to/from Anticura (US$3.50, 1½ hours). These leave Osorno at 10.30am and 3pm, and return at 12.10pm and 4.30pm. International buses running from Osorno's main bus terminal, via Paso Puyehue to Bariloche, will normally carry passengers travelling only as far as Anticura (or back) if there are spare seats.

Fundo El Caulle

The start and finish of the Baños de Caulle trek leads through **Fundo El Caulle** *(Ⓦ www.elcaulle.com)*. A peculiarity of land ownership in Chile, the area of this 270-sq-km private property overlaps extensively with national park territory. El Caulle now operates mainly as an ecotourism business and runs regular guided (especially horse-riding) trips in the Puyehue area.

At the El Caulle *entrada* (entrance gate), on Ruta 215, 2km west of Anticura, trekkers pay a US$12 flat fee – regardless of how long they remain on the property. As El Caulle built and/or maintains most of the infrastructure (including tracks, picnic tables, signposts and a free *refugio*), this payment is not unreasonable. A new **hostería** is under construction near the El Caulle entrance gate and it will charge from around US$10 per person per night.

THE TREK (see map p129)
Day 1: Anticura to Refugio El Caulle

3¼–4½ hours, 10.5km, 1070m ascent

After signing in at the *guardería*, walk for 25 to 30 minutes northwest along the highway and across the Río Golgol bridge to reach the entrance gate to **Fundo El Caulle**, where trekkers must sign in and pay an entry fee. Here, you can also buy maps and basic supplies (including homemade bread and cheese).

Head along the dirt road directly past a (left) trail turn-off (signposted 'Miradores') near the new **hostería**, before turning around to the right through the pastures past the El Caulle administration building. The

LAKES DISTRICT

road passes a (right) trail turn-off (sign-posted 'Saltos del Río Golgol') to reach a trail junction immediately before **Campamento Los Ciervos**, 15 to 20 minutes from the entrance gate. There are idyllic tent sites with tables and fireplaces here on grassy meadows by a small stream.

Turn left and climb gently along a rougher bulldozed track through the forest to reach a large flat clearing scattered with blackberry bushes and fringed by *ulmos*, 20 to 25 minutes on. Follow white-tipped wooden posts past **Campamento de Perdida** to glimpse a gushing waterfall in the rainforest up to the left before you cut right into the trees.

A foot track leads up steadily northeast to cross a trickling streamlet under high cliffs, continuing up across a second streamlet (the last water until the end of Day 1) after one to 1½ hours. Contour briefly around eroded gullies before beginning a steep, strenuous and sustained ascent over slopes of unstable volcanic earth. Make a final climb through pleasant, open *lenga* forest to emerge onto grassy alpine meadows, and sidle 300m ahead to arrive at **Refugio El Caulle** (also called Refugio Volcán Puyehue), 1¼ to 1¾ hours after crossing the second streamlet.

The refugio (*GPS 40° 36.904 S, 72°08.525 W*) stands at tree line, just under 1400m, in a very scenic spot at the base of Volcán Puyehue. This new but very basic hut sleeps up to 16 people and has a slow-combustion stove (the nearby wood shed is regularly stocked by Fundo El Caulle). The **camp sites** here (with picnic tables and benches) receive heavy usage throughout the summer, so please use the pit toilet provided and light campfires only in existing fireplaces. The tiny stream in the nearby gully tends to flow underground, but higher up it often stays running. Due to the possibility of faecal contamination, avoid collecting water from anywhere below the hut and camp sites unless you can properly treat it.

Day 2: Refugio El Caulle to Baños de Caulle

3¼–4½ hours, 14.5km, 350m ascent

Head to the right of a stream gully over grassy meadows dotted with daisy bushes,

following staked cairns moderately northeast to reach the track turn-off up to the **Mirador Volcán Puyehue** (see Side Trip, p130) at roughly 1600m on the volcano's bare upper slopes, 35 to 45 minutes from the *refugio*. From here, you can enjoy an excellent panorama of the major volcanic peaks to the south: Osorno (the magnificent cone to the southwest), Puntiagudo, Casablanca and Tronador (the high, irregular, ice-covered mountain to the southeast). Lago Puyehue is below to the west.

Continue left (northwest) along the **Sendero Los Baños**, which makes a long, undulating ascent around the steep, rocky mountainsides across ravines (many filled with snow until late summer) and small ridges. Well-marked by cairned bamboo stakes, the track turns gradually northeast, giving views of the amazing **Río de Lava**, an enormous black lava flow that looks like a petrified glacier. Head on below puffing fumaroles on Volcán Puyehue's northwest side, through the broad, snow-smothered saddle of **Portezuelo Puyehue** (around 1730m), 1½ to two hours from the *mirador* (lookout) turn-off.

The route dips northeast into the barren, rolling plateau on the volcano's northern side to reach a sturdy steel signpost (*GPS 40° 33.545 S, 72° 07.439 W*) at 1635m marking the fork where Ruta de los Americanos departs right (see Alternative Finish, p131), 15 to 20 minutes on.

Continue left along the Sendero Los Baños, which leads gently down slightly northwest (towards Volcáns Mocho and Choshuenco in the distance), over dune-like slopes of grey pumice, skirting the right (east) side of a deep, green stream gully to reach another signpost (*GPS 40° 32.526 S, 72° 07.556 W*) at around 1525m after 25 to 30 minutes. From here, a multiday route departs right (north) to Riñinahue (see Alternative Finish, p131).

The Sendero Los Baños now turns westward, winding around past some extinct fumaroles. It then cuts down left to cross the stream gully at its confluence with another stream a short way below **Campamento Baños Antiguos** (*1430m; GPS 40° 32.374 S,*

Approaching Cerro López (2076m) above lakes Nahuel Huapi and Perito Moreno

Still waters of Laguna Fría in the Andean foothills of Parque Nacional Alerce Andino

Volcán Lanín (3776m) towering over the northern Lakes District in Parque Nacional Lanín

Looking toward Refugio Segre (Italia) beside Laguna Negra on the Nahuel Huapi Traverse

Windswept camp site near Refugio Otto Meiling on a side trip on the Paso de las Nubes trek

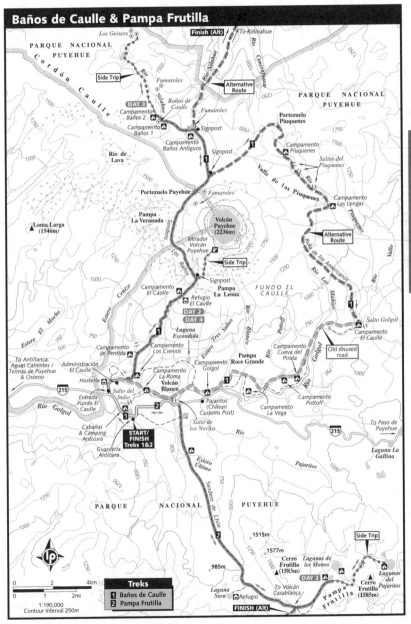

Baños de Caulle & Pampa Frutilla

LAKES DISTRICT

PARQUE NACIONAL PUYEHUE

Los Geisers

Finish (Alt)

To Riñinahue

Cordón Caulle

Río Nilahue

Alternative Route

Side Trip

Fumaroles

Baños de Caulle

PARQUE NACIONAL PUYEHUE

Campamento Baños 2

DAY 3

Fumaroles

Portezuelo Piuquenes

Campamento Baños 1

Signpost

Campamento Piuquenes

Campamento Baños Antiguos

Signpost

Valle de los Piuquenes

Saltos del Piuquenes

Río de Lava

Signpost

Campamento Las Lengas

Portezuelo Puyehue

Fumaroles

Pampa La Veranada

Volcán Puyehue (2236m)

Alternative Route

Loma Larga (1546m)

Mirador Volcán Puyehue

Ruta de los Americanos

Río Los Mellizos

Estero El Mocho

Estero Cenizo

Sendero Los Baños

Side Trip

Campamento El Caulle

Refugio El Caulle

Signpost

Pampa La Leona

FUNDO EL CAULLE

Río Blanco

Campamento Cueva del Pirata

Salto Golgol

Campamento El Caulle

DAY 2 / DAY 4

Old disused road

Laguna Escondida

Estero Tres Saltos

Campamento de Perdida

Campamento Los Ciervos

Pampa Roce Grande

Río Pulhoti

Río Golgol

Campamento Golgol

Administración El Caulle

To Antillanca / Aguas Calientes / Termas de Puyehue & Osorno

Hostería

Campamento La Ruma

Volcán Blanco

Campamento Pottoff

215

Salto del Indio

Pajaritos (Chilean Customs Post)

Campamento La Vega

Entrada Fundo El Caulle

START/ FINISH Treks 1&2

Salto de los Novios

215

Río Golgol

Cabañas & Camping Anticura

Río

To Paso de Puyehue

Guardería Anticura

Estero Último

Sendero de Chile

Laguna La Gallina

PARQUE NACIONAL PUYEHUE

Pajaritos

1515m

Side Trip

1577m

Cerró Frutilla (1583m)

Lagunas de los Monos

Lagunas del Pajaritos

985m

DAY 2

Cerró Frutilla (1585m)

Laguna Seca

Refugio

To Volcán Casablanca

Pampa Frutilla

FINISH (Alt)

Treks
1 Baños de Caulle
2 Pampa Frutilla

0   2   4km
0   1   2mi

1:190,000
Contour Interval 250m

72° 08.117 W) after 15 to 20 minutes. There are secluded, semisheltered camp sites just upstream around these former hot springs (which dried up many years ago).

Head northwest over the desolate terrain, crossing a (cold) side stream of the upper Río Nilahue to reach **Campamento Baños 1** *(GPS 40° 32.113 S, 72° 08.964 W)*, beside the river at the start of the small **Baños de Caulle** thermal field after 20 to 25 minutes. This tiny, flat area has a few poorly sheltered tent sites by the track. A dug-out 'bath' hidden among the ferns and *nalcas* here is often uncomfortably tepid but bathers regulate the hotter springs emerging directly from the rocky river bed by building shallow pools. (Avoid a larger and very warm hot spring slightly downstream, however, as it mixes erratically with the river water.)

The path continues a few minutes upstream along the river's true right (west) bank to the **Campamento Baños 2**, by a warm stream coming from the left. There is better camping here, although these sites are often occupied by guided horse-riding tours from El Caulle. This side stream can be followed for five or 10 minutes up to where various other bathable hot springs arise.

The track continues northward to Los Geisers (see Side Trip).

Side Trip: Mirador Volcán Puyehue
2½–3½ hours return, 3.5km,
630m ascent/descent
This side trip continues from the junction above the *refugio* signposted simply 'Crater' and cuts up northeast to the left of a spur. The most popular route climbs (virtually straight up) across snowdrifts in a minor basin, then curves around to the left to gain a ridge leading to the highest point (2236m) on the volcano's rim overlooking the ice-filled crater. Snow-corniced cliffs drop away into the crater, so be careful where you tread. From the rim there is a superb view of the surrounding country-side, with the double summit of Volcán Choshuenco now also visible towards the northeast, as well as Lago Rupanco to the southwest.

Side Trip: Los Geisers
3–4 hours return, 11km,
120m ascent/descent
This easy trek to a small field of bubbling mud tubs, effervescent pools and geysers is a must.

From the Baños de Caulle, trek a short way upstream along the true right (west) bank of the Río Nilahue, briefly following then crossing a side stream. The route heads northwest through a pumice gully, before cutting across a sparse plain to make a (sometimes knee-high) wade through a larger spring-fed side stream, 25 to 30 minutes from Campamento Baños 2.

The main path – evidently routed more for the convenience of horse-riders – crosses and recrosses the now very small Río Nilahue several times as it leads on upstream past fumaroles on the slopes over to the right. A less-prominent track saves trekkers either time or wet feet by continuing along the true right (ie, west) bank until crossing at the shallow, uppermost ford *(GPS 40° 30.741 S, 72° 09.943 W)*, after 20 to 25 minutes.

Ascend away right (northwest), where the river emerges in several clustered cold springs to the top of a minor ridge overlooking an undrained depression normally filled by a shallow, murky lake. Follow the ridge rightward (north) and then cut down to the far end of the boggy basin. There, make a quick, steep climb to the right high above the lake, continuing northeast to a point *(GPS 40° 29.770 S, 72° 09.556 W)* directly above the steaming, sulphurous thermal field of **Los Geisers**, 45 minutes to one hour from the final upper Río Nilahue crossing. For your own safety, and to preserve the delicate formations, be careful where you tread while you explore this fascinating area.

Return via the same route.

Days 3 & 4: Baños de Caulle to Anticura
5½–8 hours, 25km
Retrace your steps as on Day 2 and Day 1. Fitter and faster parties can opt to do both sections in one long day.

Alternative Finish: via Ruta de los Americanos
3 days, 49km

Although it is 24km longer, the Ruta de los Americanos is an excellent alternative to backtracking via Refugio El Caulle. (It is also more interesting and challenging than the other alternative route to Riñinahue.) The route is lightly used and is not always well marked, so careful navigation and route-finding are needed. Fundo El Caulle is establishing well-spaced camping areas along the way.

Retrace your steps (as on Day 2) to the signposted trail junction just northeast of Portezuelo Puyehue, then head northeast via a narrow, snowy gap and a broad ridge to **Paso Piuquenes** (around 1425m). The route then drops southward along the western side of the Río Piuquenes, climbing high above the **Saltos del Piuquenes** (several waterfalls spilling over escarpments), before turning southwest to cross a series of stream gullies on the tundra-covered eastern slopes of Volcán Puyehue.

Watch for where a foot track enters the largely dead upper scrub *(GPS 40° 35.537 S, 72° 03.711 W)* and descend through the forest to meet a disused road on the northern side of the **Río Golgol**. The old road continues west through superb tall rainforest that gradually gives way to cow pastures before you reach **Campamento Los Ciervos** (see Day 1).

Alternative Finish: Riñinahue
3 days, 36km

This easier alternative is more straightforward, although generally less scenic, than the Ruta de los Americanos.

From Baños de Caulle retrace your steps (as on Day 2) to the signposted trail junction east of Campamento Baños Antiguos, then head northward between two branches of the Río Nilahue. The route drops steeply right to cross the eastern branch before climbing to join a disused road. Continue along a broad ridge separating the Río Nilahue from the **Río Contrafuerte**, before fording and refording the latter river several times due to recent landslides. The often muddy trail continues through the wet rain-

forest to meet a rough road shortly before reaching a farmhouse (the owner here charges a 'transit fee' of US$4 – watch out for aggressive dogs).

The road steadily improves as it crosses the Río Nilahue (not far above its confluence with the Río Contrafuerte) and the Río Los Venados, passing dairy farms and patches of forest. **Camp sites** can be found in attractive meadows scattered with wild blackberry bushes. Proceed past the picturesque **Laguna Pocura**, from where there are daily buses to Riñinahue. Otherwise, continue through the scattered settlement of Quirrasco to intersect with the Futrono–Lago Ranco road, then turn left and head a short way on to Riñinahue. This village has two *hosterías* and several daily buses to the town of Lago Ranco. At Riñinahue, free **camping** is possible on the southeastern shore of Lago Ranco – ask permission before camping on private property.

Pampa Frutilla

Duration	2 days
Distance	38km
Difficulty	easy–moderate
Start/Finish	Anticura (p127)
Nearest Town	Osorno (p111)
Transport	bus

Summary A straightforward out-and-back trek up to one of the Chilean Lakes District's most extensive *coirones*, or natural highland pastures.

Pampa Frutilla, whose lowest point lies at just over 1200m, is an attractive subalpine plateau at the northeastern foot of Volcán Casablanca. Its Spanish name (meaning 'strawberry field') refers to the native Chilean strawberry, or *quellén*, which grows among tussocky grasses of Pampa Frutilla. The *quellén's* sweet, little red berries begin to ripen in late January.

The trek follows an old road built by the Chilean military in the late 1970s during the period of confrontation with Argentina. Now quite impassable to motorised vehicles, the road forms a section of the Sendero de

Chile, or the Chilean Trail (see the boxed text 'Sendero de Chile', p37) – a planned extension will eventually take it from Pampa Frutilla up to Volcán Casablanca.

PLANNING
When to Trek

The trek can normally be done between late November and late April. In January, *tábanos* (native horseflies) are likely to be out in force at lower elevations, but you will leave most of them behind as you climb through the damp, dim forest.

Maps

Two Chilean IGM 1:50,000 maps, *Volcán Puyehue* (Section H, No 27) and *Volcán Casablanca* (Section H, No 36) cover the trek.

Permits & Regulations

Trekkers are required only to sign in before they depart and sign out after they return. Although Pampa Frutilla currently receives a moderate number of visitors, please be mindful of 'leave-no-trace' principles in order to keep this beautiful area pristine.

THE TREK (see map p129)
Day 1: Anticura to Lagunas de los Monos

6–7½ hours, 19km, 875m ascent

After signing in at the Guardería Anticura, walk 3km east up the Ruta 215 for 40 to 50 minutes past the **Salto de los Novios** (waterfall) to a right turn-off signposted '**Sendero de Chile**' *(GPS 40° 39.679 S, 72° 08.634 W).* Follow a dirt road 10 minutes south to a car park in a tiny meadow of daisies and foxgloves. (When the missing bridge across a large stream between the Río Anticura and the Río Pajaritos is repaired or replaced, it will be possible to trek to this point directly from the Guardería Anticura via the Sendero de Chile.)

Continue along the old road (now not passable by vehicles) fringed by stinging nettles, elephant-ear *nalcas* and red-flowered *escallonia* bushes. The track leads southeast, rising only very gently up through moist forest of *tiaca* and fragrant *tepa*. After one to 1½ hours

you reach an open grassy field offering views of the snowy tops of Volcán Casablanca to the south as well as to Volcán Puyehue back north – a welcome respite from the temperate jungle. Ideal **camp sites** can be found here.

Cross the **Estero Ultimo** as you re-enter the forest – this stream is the last water source for some time – and begin a steady but moderate climb through well-spaced stands of common *coigüe* with a dense understorey of fuchsias and *quila*. In places, the scarlet flowers of creeping *estrellitas* light up the dark, mossy trunks, but there are no views until the track leads up under a jagged ridge over to your left. The track rises into stands of *coigüe de Magallanes* that gradually give way to highland *lenga* forest, passing an unmarked turn-off (shortly after the route makes a rightward curve) that goes off southwest down to a rustic *refugio* by the aptly named **Laguna Seca**, two to 2½ hours from Estero Ultimo.

The old road cuts up around to the left, skirting the side of the ridge as it ascends through *ñirre* scrub into grassy rolling tundra dotted with tasty white *chauras*. There are great vistas southeast along the wild, densely forested basin of the Río Negro as far as the mighty Monte Tronador massif. Make your way around eastward across a broad **pass** (around 1330m), before shortcutting down left to rejoin the old road. There are new views across the alpine meadows of **Pampa Frutilla** immediately below to Cerro Frutilla and further southeast to the remarkable horn of Cerro Pantojo.

Continue left across a normally dry, eroding stream bed to reach scenic, semisheltered **camp sites** at the forest fringe by the upper lake of the **Lagunas de los Monos**, two to 2½ hours from the Laguna Seca turnoff. The larger, lower (northeast) lake can be reached in five minutes by cutting over in a northeasterly direction; its southeastern shore is suitable for **camping**. Pairs of Andean gulls frequent these lakes.

Side Trip: Lagunas del Pajaritos

2–3 hours return, 10km, 120m ascent

From the upper of the Lagunas de los Monos, cut 1km southeast across the open meadows, then turn around left and follow a narrow extended clearing within the lenga forest *(GPS 40° 44.774 S, 72° 02.027 W)* until it ends. Here, pick up the sometimes slightly overgrown track leading northeast over a crest to reach a small stream (which drains into the lower of the Lagunas de los Monos), crossing and recrossing the stream as it heads up into an eroding, gravelly canyon. At a small, isolated stand of *lengas*, cut up steeply rightward then traverse well above the stream, past where it divides into several branches to a ridge top. From the ridge top the nearby **Cerro Frutilla** (1585m) can be climbed in around two hours return.

The route skirts around to the left into a minor **pass** (around 1335m) covered with *brecillo*, 45 minutes to one hour from Lagunas de los Monos. Head around left onto a scoria embankment, then cut down southeast through the forest to reach the **Lagunas del Pajaritos** after 25 to 30 minutes. These beautiful aqua-blue lakes offer excellent **camping** on grassy meadows (which extend well to the southeast of the lakes). Return via the same route.

Day 2: Lagunas de los Monos to Anticura
5–6½ hours, 19km, 875m descent
Retrace your steps as on Day 1.

Alternative Finish: Antillanca via Volcán Casablanca
6½–9 hours, 18km, 1020m ascent
This difficult traverse across Volcán Casablanca is suited only to trekkers with excellent navigational and route-finding abilities. Before January, an ice axe (and perhaps also crampons) may be advisable.

Return to the small pass above Pampa Frutilla (see Day 1), then cut down southwest through the light forest and across the uppermost streamlets of the Río Negro basin. The route climbs westward via open volcanic ridges to the summit of Volcán Casablanca, whose views do not disappoint. The descent normally leads via **Crater Rayhuén** (a small side crater) then along a dirt road to reach the tiny ski village of Antillanca on the volcano's western slopes,

18km by road from the hot-springs resort of Aguas Calientes. In summer, you can stay at Antillanca's **Refugio Buschmann** *(☎ 02-6551881; singles/doubles from US$23/31).* (Note that downhill traffic from Antillanca is only permitted from noon to 2pm and then after 5.30pm; uphill traffic to Antillanca is only permitted from 8am to noon and then from 2pm until 5.30pm.)

Alternatively, trekkers can follow an 11km trail from Crater Rayhuén northwest via Conaf's rustic **Refugio Bertin** to Aguas Calientes.

Parque Nacional Vicente Pérez Rosales

Created in 1926, the 2510-sq-km Parque Nacional Vicente Pérez Rosales is the second-oldest national park in Chile and the largest in the Chilean Lakes District. The park fronts the Argentine border, where it meets the even larger Parque Nacional Nahuel Huapi, and these two national parks, together with the adjoining Parque Nacional Puyehue, form the largest tract of trans-Andean wilderness in the Lakes District. The park's name is homage to the Chilean businessman and mining magnate Vicente Pérez Rosales, who was also an accomplished writer and the founder of Puerto Montt.

Situated at roughly 41°S, Parque Nacional Vicente Pérez Rosales centres round the 221-sq-km Lago Todos Los Santos, which, at only 184m above sea level, is the park's lowest point. This fjord-like lake is ringed by some of the highest and most prominent volcanic peaks of the southern Lakes District. They form an arc running eastward from the perfect cone of Volcán Osorno along the volcanic peaks of Puntiagudo, Cenizas and Casablanca to the majestic Monte Tronador at the lake's eastern end. Ranges also extend westward along the southern side of Lago Todos Los Santos as far as Volcán Calbuco.

Apart from Lago Pirehueico, some distance to the north, Lago Todos Los Santos is the only major low-level lake on the Chilean side that stretches deep into the Andes. The lake lies deep within a glacial trough, not at the termination of a former glacier's path (like nearby Lago Llanquihue). Immediately following the last ice age, Lago Todos Los Santos was joined with Lago Llanquihue in an enormous body of water, but subsequent eruptions of Volcán Osorno and Volcán Calbuco divided them into separate lakes. Todos Los Santos is unique among the large lakes in that, apart from the access road to Petrohué at its outlet and the isolated road between Peulla and Puerto Frías at its eastern end, no roads penetrate its wild, densely forested shoreline.

The lake's name, which means 'All Saints Lake', was given to it by Jesuit missionaries, who, from the early 17th century – when the whole of the Lakes District was still under the control of hostile Mapuche tribes – journeyed across its waters en route from Argentina to Chiloé.

NATURAL HISTORY

The heavy rainfall and mild weather of Vicente Pérez Rosales support dense, lush Valdivian rainforest whose predominant trees are *coigüe*, *tepa*, *mañío*, *ulmo*, *canelo*, *olivillo* (or *teque*), *lingue* and *avellano*. Less common tree species include the *lleuque*, a podocarp related to the *mañío* that grows on moist slopes above 600m. The *lleuque's* small yellow fruit have the appearance of tiny lemons. Another is the *fuinque*, a small tree of the proteaceae family with yellow flowers. The *maqui* is a very small tree typically found in stands (so-called *macales*) at the edge of the forest. It has oval leaves on a reddish stem and produces edible purple berries, from which the Mapuche made an alcoholic drink called *tecu*.

The rainforest understorey harbours great botanical diversity. The park is an important refuge for the *ciprés enano*, an extremely rare dwarf member of the podocarp family that is almost identical to the pygmy pine of New Zealand. This tiny, prostrate conifer grows in montane swamps, often largely hidden by other nearby plants. More common is the *quilquil*, a common species of tree fern typically found growing in stream gullies. The *quilquil* looks like a small palm, hence its other common name of *palmilla*. In small clearings you'll find several species of *ñipa*, which are recognisable by their red or pinkish tubular flowers that end in five outturned petals. Another distinctive bush (sometimes growing to a small tree) is the *chaquihue* (also called *polizonte*), whose large, leafy twigs produce bright-red, rounded, pod-like flowers. The *chaquihue* prefers wet sites, such as along streams or wetlands.

The park's lush vegetation makes it a veritable paradise for birds, of which parrots and nectar-eating hummingbirds are especially plentiful. The *choroy*, a large green parakeet most easily identified by its long curved beak, dwells in these forests. The *run run* is a species of tyrant flycatcher that typically frequents wetlands, lake shores and riverbanks; apart from its yellow beak the male *run run* is black, while the female has a coffee-coloured upper body and a pale-yellow breast with dark longitudinal stripes. The *yeco*, also called *bigua*, a large black cormorant widely distributed throughout the moist coastal areas of southern South America, often visits Lago Todos Los Santos, where it finds plenty of fish and small amphibians to feed on. This large waterbird is an excellent diver and can often be seen perched on a log or rock with its wings outstretched.

The tiny brown *monito del monte*, or mouse opossum, inhabits these temperate rainforests along with its marsupial cousin, the *rincholesta*. The *rincholesta* is a rare nocturnal insectivore that was only discovered by science – although the indigenous Mapuche people certainly knew about it – in the 1950s. Other mammals common to the forests of Vicente Pérez Rosales include the pudu, *coipo*, *huiña*, Patagonian red fox and puma.

Numerous native fishes are found in the park's lakes and rivers. The main species are *pejerrey*, *puyen*, Patagonian perch and *peladilla*. More plentiful are introduced salmon and trout. The peculiar Darwin's frog (*sapo partero* as it's known in Spanish or midwife frog), first zoologically classified by Charles Darwin, also inhabits the park's ponds, lakes and rivers. After fertilisation, the male frog incubates and hatches the eggs inside his own mouth, from which the fully developed froglets – not tadpoles – emerge after three weeks.

CLIMATE

In this extremely wet coastal climate, annual rainfall averages 2500mm at Ensenada on the park's western extreme, and rises steadily towards the east. Precipitation levels around Paso de Pérez Rosales on the Chile–Argentina frontier reach over 5000mm – the highest levels in the Lakes District. Moderated by the lake's low elevation and proximity to the Pacific coast, average annual temperatures around the shore of Lago Todos Los Santos are a relatively high 12°C. The hottest summer days rarely exceed 30°C. Conditions are less mild at higher altitudes in the surrounding ranges, where winters regularly bring heavy snowfalls.

PLANNING
When to Trek

Unless you're planning to go above tree line, treks in Parque Nacional Vicente Pérez Rosales can generally be done between early November and early May. The hot weather between mid-December and late January usually brings out the *tábanos*, which can be a particular nuisance in locations below tree line.

Permits & Regulations

There are few restrictions on trekking in Parque Nacional Vicente Pérez Rosales. No permit is required but, where possible, inform the park authorities of your intended trekking route and the names of all members in the party. There are a number of small enclaves of freehold land within the park, and although the trekking routes are public rights of way, trekkers should respect private property. Some recognised camp sites are also on private land and an increasing number of property owners levy a small charge for camping. Wild camping is permitted, but use discretion when choosing your camp site.

Termas de Callao

Duration	3 days
Distance	40km
Difficulty	easy
Start	El Rincón
Finish	El Poncho
Nearest Towns	Petrohué (p136), Osorno (p111)
Transport	boat & bus

Summary Trek through dense temperate rainforest with volcano views and soak in a hot tub on this traverse between two major lakes.

The relatively remote Termas de Callao lie hidden behind Volcán Puntiagudo in the Valle Sin Nombre. These delightful natural hot springs emerge from the ground just beside the small Río Sin Nombre, which flows into Lago Todos Los Santos. Small farms blend into the forest along the river. The trek reaches its highest point at a forested pass around 800m, then descends to finish along the shore of tranquil Lago Rupanco.

The trek generally follows horse trails kept in condition by the local inhabitants, and all larger streams are bridged. Along the central section of the route between the Termas de Callao and Laguna Los Quetros, however, fallen trees obscure the way in places, so careful route-finding is occasionally required. Throughout this trek, where the earth is composed of friable pumice, the path rapidly erodes to form deep trenches, revealing the history of previous local volcanic eruptions in the layers of the soil. In places where the trenches have become too deep the path has been rerouted or reinforced with logs.

Trekkers are strongly advised to walk in a south-to-north direction, as there is no reliable way of getting out from El Rincón (on the remote northern shore of Lago Todos Los Santos) once you arrive.

PLANNING
When to Trek
Because of their low elevation and relatively sheltered aspect, the Termas de Callao can be visited from late spring until late autumn (late October to early May) when other walks may be out of condition. However, the summer months (December to February) are the best time to do the trek. An additional day could be spent enjoying the attractive valley around the springs.

What to Bring
There is only one *refugio* along the route. Although it is possible for fit and fast parties to do the trek without carrying a tent, this is not recommended.

Puerto Montt (p114) or Puerto Varas (depending on which way you approach the trek) is the logical place to buy supplies before the trek. Farms along the trek often sell home-baked bread and other produce.

Maps
The JLM Mapas *Ruta de los Jesuitas* map (No 15) includes a 1:50,000 (approximately) map of the Termas de Callao sector of Parque Nacional Vicente Pérez Rosales. It and the two Chilean IGM maps on which it appears to be based – *Volcán Casablanca* (Section H, No 36) and *Peulla* (Section H, No 44) – show the walking track but suffer from omissions and errors regarding the exact route.

NEAREST TOWNS
See Osorno (p111).

Petrohué
This tiny tourist village situated at the western end of Lago Todos Los Santos is the usual departure point for boats across the lake. Conaf has a **park administration centre** here and also a **visitor centre** with information on local flora and fauna, and there is a small **store** where you can buy last-minute snacks.

On the other side of the Río Petrohué are **Hospedaje Küschel** *(camping per person US$5, rooms per person US$10)* and one or two *casas de familia*. Boats from the dock

at Petrohué shuttle backpackers across the river (US$0.50). The other option is the cosy, comfortable **Hotel Petrohué** *(☎/fax 065-258042; singles/doubles from US$44/67)*, which has an expensive **restaurant**.

You can get to Petrohué from Puerto Montt by catching a minibus to Puerto Varas on Lago Llanquihue – these leave throughout the day from the eastern end of Puerto Montt's main bus terminal (US$0.80, 30 minutes) – changing in Puerto Varas for Petrohué (US$2, one hour).

GETTING TO/FROM THE TREK
The trek begins at El Rincón (also known as Puerto Callao) in an inlet on the northern shore of Lago Todos Los Santos, about halfway across the lake.

There is no regular transport to El Rincón, so it is necessary to charter a boat to get there. In summer, boats wait for passengers at the dock in Petrohué. The starting price for a boat to El Rincón is about US$55, so try to find other trekkers to share the cost. The trip takes about two to three hours, depending on the type of boat as well as the direction and speed of the winds. It should also be possible to charter a boat to El Rincón from Peulla (p153), a village on the lake's remote eastern shore. Remember, once you reach El Rincón the only way out is the route described.

The walk finishes at El Poncho, a small scattering of holiday houses on the southern shore of Lago Rupanco. Buses leave El Poncho for Osorno (US$3, twice daily) at 6.30am and 3.30pm.

THE TREK
Day 1: El Rincón to Refugio Termas de Callao
3–4 hours, 12km

From behind the tiny sandy beach of El Rincón, where your boat lands, make your way uphill through a clearing that would make a pleasant **camp site** and over a minor crest looking back over Lago Todos Los Santos. (There is also good camping on the scenic flats where the Río Sin Nombre enters Lago Todos Los Santos, 15 to 20 minutes west around the lakeside via a good

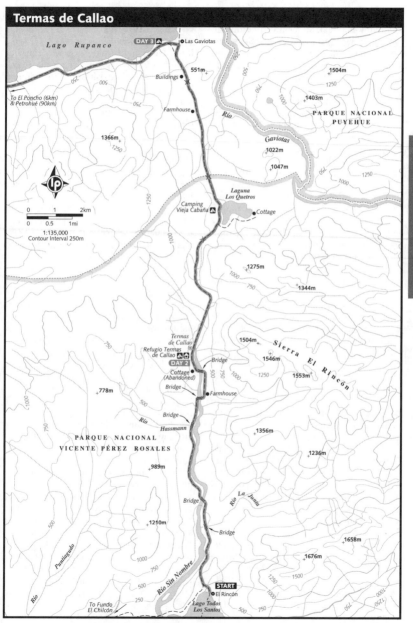

Termas de Callao

Lago Rupanco

DAY 3

Las Gaviotas

Buildings

551m

1504m

1250

To El Poncho (6km)
& Petrohué (90km)

Farmhouse

1403m

Río

PARQUE NACIONAL
PUYEHUE

Gaviotas

1022m

1366m

1047m

1250

0   1   2km
0   0.5   1mi

1:135,000
Contour Interval 250m

Camping
Vieja Cabaña

Laguna
Los Quetros

Cottage

1275m

1344m

1504m

Sierra El Rincón

Termas
de Callao
Refugio Termas
de Callao
DAY 2

1546m

1553m

Bridge

Cottage
(Abandoned)

Bridge

Farmhouse

778m

Bridge

Río
Hassmann

1356m

PARQUE NACIONAL
VICENTE PÉREZ ROSALES

1236m

989m

Bridge

Río La Junta

1210m

Bridge

1658m

1676m

START
El Rincón

To Fundo
El Chilcón

Río Sin Nombre

Lago Todos
Los Santos

LAKES DISTRICT

trail.) Continue through semicleared fields. A good horse track sidles down northward through *ulmo* forest above the **Río Sin Nombre**, which rushes through a deep gully on your left, to cross the **Río La Junta** side stream after 40 to 50 minutes. If you don't trust the rickety suspension bridge, wade the shallow water slightly downstream.

Follow the sometimes muddy path for 20 to 25 minutes to cross the Río Sin Nombre itself on another precarious suspension bridge and continue upstream. The path dips and rises along the river's steep-sided western bank before it climbs away left past a farm (with produce for sale) and crosses another suspension bridge over a large side stream, the **Río Hassmann**, after a further one to 1¼ hours. Here, the trail goes briefly left, upstream, then climbs back to the right and proceeds on through the rainforest. 'Termas' signs direct you through a bamboo-scattered clearing and back across the Río Sin Nombre to reach a farmhouse 35 to 45 minutes on.

The farmhouse (where you can buy farm produce) stands in full view of the majestic volcanic plug summit of Volcán Puntiagudo to the west. You should pick up the keys to the *refugio* and hot springs, and pay your dues, at the farmhouse. You can arrange to leave the keys at the *refugio* to save backtracking to the farm.

The route now leads along the eastern bank of the Río Sin Nombre, crossing once more before it passes an abandoned, shingled, wooden cottage and arrives after a final 30 to 40 minutes at **Refugio Termas de Callao** *(camping per tent US$4, refugio per person US$4)*. This excellent hut built from native timbers stands on private land and has a wood stove, a sink, bamboo furniture and space for six people. There is very attractive **camping** just below the refugio. The **thermal baths** are just down by the river in a little shed with two tubs inside. The water is piping hot and very relaxing and use of the hot baths is US$2 per person. The scenic valley is enclosed by high, densely rainforested granite peaks on either side, which makes it an excellent spot to stop for a day.

Day 2: Refugio Termas de Callao to Las Gaviotas
4–5¼ hours, 16km

From the *refugio* make your way upvalley through scrubby pastures along the river's western bank before rising into the rainforest. Bear leftward at the second (probably dry) major side stream you come to, carefully following the route through an area of fallen trunks, then on through tiny grassy patches.

After 40 to 50 minutes the well-maintained path turns away from the Río Sin Nombre and begins climbing gently northwest beside a cascading stream, through a forest of gnarled *mañío* and fragrant-leafed *tepa*.

Cross the stream and ascend along a steep spur through dense thickets of bamboo until the gradient eases, 50 minutes to 1¼ hours on. The path briefly follows the ridge top northward through montane *coigüe* and *ulmo* forest, dropping down steeply to cross a stream, then climbing again, before it makes a proper descent northeast along fire-cleared pastures where the southwestern corner of **Laguna Los Quetros** comes into view. Continue around the lake's reedy western shore to reach **Camping Vieja Cabaña** *(camping per tent US$4)*, which has a pit toilet, beside a small stand of alerce trees after 40 to 50 minutes. There is a picturesque farm cottage on the opposite side of Laguna Los Quetros, which lies in a basin that drains subterraneously through the porous volcanic soil. The lake and camping area are on private land attached to the cottage, and the owner rows across the lake to collect fees.

Follow the prominent horse track, in places massively reinforced with logs, up around the northwest side of the tranquil lake into the forest and over a low watershed. Make your way down beside a stream (a small tributary of the Río Gaviotas) towards the snowy cap of Volcán Casablanca. The path descends steadily through clearings, giving way to open hillsides, to pass the first farmhouse at the edge of a broad green bowl after 1¼ to 1½ hours. Horses, cattle and flocks of noisy black-necked ibis graze on these choice Lakes District pastures.

Skirt northwestward through a series of gates in the middle of the fields into a minor saddle high above Lago Rupanco. With the volcano and shimmering lake ahead of you, drop down past wooden cottages, neat vegetable gardens and a rural school to reach a trail fork on grassy slopes scattered with blackberry bushes after 30 to 40 minutes. Five minutes further down, the left-hand branch meets a wide track along the black-sand shore of Lago Rupanco, while the right-hand path goes down almost to the village of **Las Gaviotas** at the lake's south-eastern corner. Las Gaviotas has no accommodation or store, and there is no particular reason to go right into the village unless you need a public telephone, which it *does* have. There is a nice **camping ground** *(camping per tent US$3)*, with picnic tables and firewood provided, a 10- to 15-minute walk west, near where a stream enters the lake; a landowner collects the fee. Other **camping** possibilities exist along the black-sand beach a short way from where you meet Lago Rupanco.

Day 3: Las Gaviotas to El Poncho
2¼–2¾ hours, 12km
Follow the dark, sandy shore west through the front yards of lake-side holiday houses. The wide, graded track rises and dips around the often very steep banks of Lago Rupanco, past rustic shacks and through patches of forest fringed by blackberry bushes. Cross a large, dry gully and head up to the left, past the remains of a suspension footbridge, just before you come out above a lovely lake-side pasture after one to 1¼ hours.

The trail climbs away left over scrubby slopes high above the lake, bringing into view the bare volcanic ridges surrounding Volcán Puntiagudo to the south. Drop down behind more holiday houses around a broad tranquil bay, its western side now scarred by an unsightly road extension, to cross a major stream on a sturdy log bridge, 30 to 40 minutes on. On the far side of this bridge the dirt road begins. Follow this around the bay, past a *kiosco* (kiosk) and across the Puente Río Blanco, then past the exclusive

Bahía Escocia Fly Fishing Lodge, to reach the tiny settlement of **El Poncho** after a final 40 to 50 minutes. El Poncho itself has a small **store** and a bus stop but little else.

Parque Nacional Nahuel Huapi

Parque Nacional Nahuel Huapi (nah-**well**-**wah**-pee) lies to the west of the popular tourist centre of Bariloche in the southern Argentine Lakes District. Formally established in 1922, Nahuel Huapi is the oldest of Argentina's national parks. The original park (whose title was Parque Nacional del Sur) comprised a vast tract of land first granted to the pioneering explorer Francisco Pascasio Perito Moreno for his services to the Argentine Boundary Commission. Perito Moreno donated it back to the nation on the condition that it be turned into a national park. Additional areas were later incorporated into Parque Nacional Nahuel Huapi to create what remains by far the largest national park on either side of the Andes in northern Patagonia.

The area of the modern-day park formed a large part of the Mapuche heartland, and tribes lived around the eastern shores of the great lake. There are several low Andean passes in the park, such as Paso Vuriloche (near Pampa Linda) and Paso de Pérez Rosales, which linked the many Mapuche tribes on either side of the Cordillera. These passes were later used by Christian missionaries as a safe route to Chiloé. Today, Nahuel Huapi's rugged interior is more easily accessible via an extensive network of well-maintained pathways – as well as numerous rougher, unmarked routes – supported by many excellent alpine *refugios*. The park is a wonderfully scenic area of forests and lakes set among craggy ranges.

Parque Nacional Nahuel Huapi's northern boundary fronts Parque Nacional Lanín. From there it stretches southward to the southern edge of the Argentine Lakes District at roughly 42°S. The park includes 7580 sq km of prime wilderness, whose heart and hub is the 557-sq-km Lago Nahuel Huapi itself. With its numerous fjord-like branches (which reach a maximum depth of 454m), Lago Nahuel Huapi is the finest example of a major glacial lake anywhere in northern Patagonia. This enormous lake lies at 765m above sea level – the lowest point within the northern four-fifths of the park, which is drained by the Río Limay and is therefore part of the Atlantic basin.

Numerous other sizable lakes lie in the deep valleys surrounding Lago Nahuel Huapi. The largest of these are Lago Traful and Lago Espejo to the north, and Lago Mascardi in the park's most southerly zone, which drains westward via the Río Manso and Río Puelo into the Chilean Pacific. Approximately 20% of the park's area is covered by water.

The other dominant feature of Parque Nacional Nahuel Huapi is the icy crown of Monte Tronador. At 3554m above sea level – at least according to most Argentine maps – Monte Tronador is the highest point within the entire Lakes District, and stands almost 1000m above its nearest rivals. The loftiest of Monte Tronador's several summits, Pico Internacional, marks the Argentina–Chile frontier. This massif is smothered by some 60 sq km of névés, glaciers and icefalls, and is the only significant glacially active area found in the park.

Parque Nacional Nahuel Huapi is one of the few areas in Patagonia where the Andes are more extensive and rugged on the Argentine side than on the Chilean side. (Although individual volcanoes do form higher summits in Chile, the ranges surrounding them are relatively low.) This is particularly evident in the mountains to the south of Lago Nahuel Huapi, where the 2405m Cerro Catedral – the highest nonvolcanic peak in the Lakes District – rises up in craggy, steeple-like columns. Many other peaks in the area surpass 2000m. There are no real glaciers left on this eastern side of the park, but in many places intense frost shattering has formed large scree slides on the higher slopes.

The name Nahuel Huapi is usually translated from the Mapuche as 'island of the tiger'. This refers to the spotted South American jaguar, or *yaguarete*, whose vast range once included northeastern Patagonia.

NATURAL HISTORY

Three main types of forest are found in Parque Nacional Nahuel Huapi: wet temperate (Valdivian) rainforest in the park's most westerly valleys, deciduous alpine forest at higher elevations, and coniferous forest in the drier eastern sectors of the park.

Of these, the rainforest is easily the most species diverse, with several dozen different types of trees forming the canopy, including alerce (or *lahuén*), *arrayán*, *avellano*, *canelo*, *ciprés de las Guaitecas*, *coigüe*, laurel, *mañío*, *olivillo* (or *teque*), *tineo* and *ulmo*. The deciduous forest of the highland valleys is dominated by *lenga* mixed with *ñirre* and occasional *luma blanca*, a bush of the myrtle family. The *lenga* forest is interspersed with areas of *mallín* (wet meadow) country where the local drainage is poor, but the mountainsides are barren and sparsely vegetated above 1700m.

Parque Nacional Nahuel Huapi has some of the best-preserved coniferous forests in the southern Andes. These are composed of *ciprés de la cordillera*, a graceful cypress species that forms pure stands on the dry and exposed ranges around the eastern side of Lago Nahuel Huapi.

Parque Nacional Nahuel Huapi is renowned for its alpine and subalpine wild flowers. One of the most lovely and widespread species is the *amancay*, or *liuto*, which is typically found in forest clearings, where its orange blooms carpet the ground. Various members of the *mutisia* genus, collectively known by the popular name of *clavel del campo* (carnations of the countryside), are climbing opportunists that produce orange, pinkish-white or purple daisy-like flowers. They often grow along sunny roadsides or where the forest has been disturbed.

Hidden among the rocks on drier slopes, you may spot the *estrellita de la cordillera*, a small composite perennial whose flowers have numerous white clustered petals.

Capachitos, various herb-like plants with yellow flowers, are also found here. The *cuye colorado* is a small alpine shrub with clam-like leaves; its white flowers have pink-tipped petals around a yellow centre. Other common wild flowers include the *coxinea*, an annual that grows as a single reddish stalk crowned by a clustered head of tubular yellow flowers with five crimson petals, and a ground orchid whose flowers have a bluish tinge. The *chupa sangre* (literally 'bloodsucker') is a spiky cushion-like plant, found still further to the east where the park fringes the semiarid Patagonian steppes.

Ground-dwelling birds, such as the *chucao*, *churrín* and *huet-huet*, inhabit the forest floor, where *picaflores* (hummingbirds) flutter madly around nectar-yielding flowers. The forests also provide the habitat for the *carpintero negro*, or black woodpecker, which can often be seen chipping away at tree trunks; the *torcaza* (or *conu*), a large grey pigeon; and the austral parakeet *cachaña*. Countless waterbirds, including native ducks such as the *quetru*, *pato cuchara* and *pato real*, live in the park's extensive lakes and rivers.

Mammals sometimes spied in the rainforest are the shy pudu, the world's smallest deer and the *monito del monte*. The puma and the far smaller *huiña* are the main terrestrial predators, while the amphibious *coipo* and the carnivorous *huillín* inhabit the waterways of the park. North American red deer have multiplied greatly since their introduction early in the 20th century, and this is a major factor in the increasing rarity of the *huemul*, or Andean deer.

Parque Nacional Nahuel Huapi is the only place where the rare *tucotuco colonial*, which was only discovered by science in 1983, is known to exist. It is a small rat-like creature, and unlike other members of this large South American genus, it lives in big colonies. On the rare occasions when it leaves the warren, the *tucotuco colonial* gives out a peculiar cheeping call that sounds more like that of a bird than a mammal. Two other species of tucotuco also inhabit the park.

CLIMATE

The park's relatively high elevation and isolation from the Pacific (whose nearest point is roughly 150km from Llao Llao on Lago Nahuel Huapi) means that a cool and dry 'continental' climate prevails. At low elevations, mean temperatures in winter are around 2°C and in summer they're around 18°C. Summers tend to be relatively dry and most of the annual precipitation occurs in winter and spring, when areas above 1000m are covered by a thick mantle of snow.

The high ranges on the international frontier – most of all, Monte Tronador – cause a typical rain-shadow effect, with steadily diminishing precipitation levels towards the east. It is very wet close to the main continental divide, and the eastern sectors of Parque Nacional Nahuel Huapi are semiarid. For example, Puerto Frías, on the border with Chile, has an annual average rainfall of around 4000mm, while the Cerro Catedral area receives less than 2000mm and the eastern outskirts of Bariloche less than 800mm.

PLANNING
When to Trek

As most scenic routes in Parque Nacional Nahuel Huapi take you well up into the mountains, there's not much scope for trekking before mid-November or any later than the first half of May. The period from December to April offers the best chance of encountering favourable conditions. Early- and late-season trekkers are cautioned that if there is any breakdown in the weather it is likely to bring snowfalls on the ranges. In the main summer tourist season (January and February) the trails and *refugios* are crowded with trekkers.

Books

Several publications of interest to Spanish-reading trekkers are available from bookshops in Bariloche. *Fauna del Parque Nacional Nahuel Huapi*, by Claudio Chehébar & Eduardo Ramilo, is a booklet dealing with the animals, birds and reptiles found in the park. *Las Montañas de Bariloche*, by Toncek Arko & Raúl Izaguirre, is a locally produced guidebook covering treks

LAKES DISTRICT

in the mountains around Bariloche. *Trekking en Bariloche*, published by the CAB, gives a history of mountain rescue in the Nahuel Huapi region and includes information on trekking routes.

Permits & Regulations

A fee of US$3.75 is levied when visitors enter Nahuel Huapi through an official park entrance gate. This fee does not apply if the road is a public right of way, as in the case of the Villa Catedral and Llao Llao roads, but visitors to the park's Pampa Linda, Río Manso or Lago Steffen sectors will have to pay it.

Camping within the park is allowed only at designated camping areas. In most cases these are clearly indicated on trekking maps and by official signs at the park-approved camping areas themselves. Away from the more travelled trails, however, wild camping is generally tolerated as long as trekkers take care of their surroundings (see Responsible Trekking, p43). Lighting fires is prohibited throughout the park.

Nahuel Huapi Traverse

Duration	5 days
Distance	36.5km
Difficulty	moderate–demanding
Start	Villa Catedral (p143)
Finish	Puente López
Nearest Town	Bariloche (p113)
Transport	bus

Summary A classic trek with a challenging middle day that hops over passes and mountain ridges amid some of the finest scenery in the Argentine Lakes District.

This spectacular route offers ever-changing scenery of craggy mountain summits, lovely alpine lakes, waterfalls and beautiful forests. Not surprisingly, it's one of the most popular treks in Argentina.

PLANNING

The full traverse can be done in four to five days. A further one or two days will allow you time to rest or do short side trips. You can also do many shorter variations on the trek, including:

- a three-day circuit known as the Circuito Chico, which combines Day 1 (or the Alternative Route via Arroyo Van Titter), Day 2 and the Alternative Route: Refugio San Martín (Jakob) to Ruta Nacional 79
- a shorter circuit that combines Day 1 and (in reverse) the Alternative Route via Arroyo Van Titter, either as a long day walk or in two short days
- a combination of Days 1 to 3, plus the exit route down the Arroyo Goye (Alternative Route: Refugio Segre (Italia) to Colonia Suiza), which makes a trek of three or four days length

Most sections of the route are well marked and well trodden, and route-finding is relatively straightforward. The exceptions to this are Day 3, between Refugio San Martín and Refugio Segre, where trekkers must navigate carefully, and some places, especially on Days 2 and 4, where the terrain is too rocky and/or steep to hold a proper path.

Many other tracks intersect with the traverse route, allowing you to shorten or vary the trek as you like. On all stages of the trek it is possible to walk out in one day. Less experienced parties are advised to opt for the Circuito Chico variation mentioned above.

Apart from Day 3, which is rated demanding, and Day 4 (moderate–demanding) all sections are of a moderate level of difficulty.

When to Trek

Many sections of this trek are well above tree line. The route's relatively high altitude generally makes it unsuitable for inexperienced trekking parties until around the beginning of December, although in places snow may remain right through the summer. The area is somewhat sheltered by the mountains to the west (chiefly Monte Tronador), and bad weather tends to be slightly less extreme than on the other side of the Andes. Nevertheless, many parts of the route are very exposed to the elements, so if conditions are poor you should wait for the weather to improve.

What to Bring

There are four *refugios* along the route, which makes it possible to do the trek without carrying a tent. Nevertheless, for greater safety and in case the huts are overcrowded, trekkers are advised to carry a tent. Particularly during spells of poor weather in January and February, the *refugios* can quickly fill to (over) capacity. All of the *refugios* are open at least from early December until mid-April.

The *refugios* offer basic dormitory accommodation, with little or no bedding apart from, perhaps, a mattress. Trekkers must therefore bring a sleeping bag. With the exception of Refugio López, the *refugios* belong to the CAB, although they are generally run by a private concessionaire who acts as a *refugiero* (hut keeper). The *refugios* all charge an overnighting fee, and there's an additional charge if you use the cooking facilities. Simple meals, refreshments and supplies are available from all of the *refugios*.

The deep and steep-sided valleys often require heavy climbs and descents through loose rock or scree; wearing gaiters or long pants that cover the tops of your boots will make the going more comfortable.

Maps

Recommended is the contoured 1:50,000 *Trekking 1* map in the Refugios, Sendas y Picadas series, which is an extract (with additional topographical information) from the larger-format 1:100,000 Refugios, Sendas y Picadas *Parque Nacional Nahuel Huapi* colour map. This latter map covers a much wider area and is perhaps a better alternative if you plan further treks elsewhere in the park. Both are available from the CAB in Bariloche. Unfortunately, both these maps are inaccurate in a few short (but very important) sections of the route.

Permits & Regulations

Trekkers attempting Day 3 from Refugio San Martín (Jakob) to Refugio Segre (Italia) are asked to fill out a form at Refugio San Martín before they leave and hand it in on arrival at Refugio Segre. The *refugiero* at

San Martín will advise staff at Segre by radio to expect you. At the same time, trekkers are strongly advised to view the photos of the day's route held at Refugio San Martín.

NEAREST TOWN & FACILITIES

Bariloche (p113) is the best place to buy all provisions.

Villa Catedral

The trek begins at Villa Catedral, a ski village about 20km by road from Bariloche. Villa Catedral has a number of ski lodges which may accept guests in summer, including the **CAB hostería** *(dorm beds US$3)*. Ask at the **CAB information booth** in Villa Catedral for other accommodation options. Kiosks in the village are OK for last-minute supplies such as chocolate and film. There's also a selection of **restaurants** and **snack bars**.

Throughout the trekking season there is a regular bus service from Bariloche to Villa Catedral (US$0.75, 30 to 40 minutes, nine daily). Buses depart from the bus terminal at the eastern edge of Bariloche and call in at the centre, including two stops on Moreno and one opposite the national park administration centre on San Martín, then proceed along either Av de los Pioneros or Av Bustillo. The first bus leaves Bariloche at 7.30am and the last at 8pm, all returning almost immediately from Villa Catedral. Buy tickets beforehand from **Buses 3 de Mayo** *(Moreno 480)* or on board.

Colonia Suiza

Colonia Suiza, at or near the end of the trek and two of the popular alternative routes, was originally settled by Franco-Swiss farming families in the first decades of the 20th century and is today a modest lake-side holiday village. A number of the original houses remain, and the locals sell homemade fruit preserves and chocolates.

Colonia Suiza has two public camping grounds, both with hot showers: the cramped and dusty **Camping Goye** *(☎ 02944-448627; camping per person US$1.50, dorm beds US$2.50)*, near the No 10 bus stop, and the more spacious **Camping Huenei Ruca**

(☎ 02944-427471; camping per person US$1.50), where you can pitch your tent right on the shore of Lago Perito Moreno. **Restaurante Heidi** (☎ 02944-448492) offers camp sites, lodging and a restaurant. For a feed, there's also the woody **Fundo Colonia Suiza** (menú US$3) in the village centre.

Bus Nos 10 and 11 run frequently between Colonia Suiza and Bariloche (US$0.70, one hour, 12 daily).

GETTING TO/FROM THE TREK

The trek begins at Villa Catedral (p144) and ends at Puente López (López Bridge), a picnic area and kiosk on the road between Llao Llao and Colonia Suiza, 22km west of Bariloche. The No 10 or No 11 bus to Bariloche (US$0.70) passes this point five or six times a day. You can walk from Puente López to Colonia Suiza in 30 to 40 minutes by following the bitumen 150m along to the right, then turning off southeast (ie, to the right) along an unsurfaced road.

THE TREK (see map p145)
Day 1: Villa Catedral to Refugio Frey

2¾–4 hours, 8.5km

This exhilarating high-level route may be impassable because of snow and ice early (and sometimes late) in the season, in which case the Alternative Route via Arroyo Van Titter (p146) will be the only safe way to reach Refugio Frey. Fortunately, much of the higher option is exposed to the sun so the snow tends to melt away fairly early. If in doubt, ask in the CAB's office in Bariloche or at its information booth in Villa Catedral regarding the current condition of this route.

The day begins with a choice of two ski lifts that haul you from Villa Catedral to the start of the trek on the Cordón Catedral. The option we describe is the **Aerosilla Piedra del Cóndor** (adult/child US$2.50/2; open 10.30am-6pm Mon-Sun). An alternative, which cuts out even more walking, is the combination **Cablecarril y Aerosilla Lynch** (adult/child US$5.50/3.75; open 10am-5.30pm Mon-Sun), which goes to Refugio Lynch. If the fares, or the very idea of chairlifts, put you off, you can trek to Refugio

Lynch on a foot track that spirals up below the cable car. The trail is steep and exposed to the sun (carry water), and the climb takes around three hours. We only recommend this route for saving money or building character.

The chairlift heaves you up into the stony and sparsely vegetated alpine zone to **Piedra del Cóndor**. At 1759m this is the northernmost point of the Cordón Catedral, and offers an excellent unbroken panorama across Lago Nahuel Huapi. A rough road can be followed for 30 to 35 minutes around to **Refugio Lynch** (open year-round), at 2042m, where you can get meals and refreshments.

Continue southwestward along, or just to the left of, the bare ridge top, following yellow and/or red paint markings (lots of spots and dots on rocks) that lead up to the hump of **Punta Nevada**, where winter snowdrifts linger well into summer. There are fine views down to your right into the valley of the Arroyo Rucaco, whose stream meanders peacefully through alpine moors and over rock slabs before entering a gorge, and beyond to the great glaciers of Monte Tronador, which rises up on the western horizon. The route dips down to reach a small saddle, not far from the upper station of another ski lift, after 45 minutes to one hour.

Sidle rightward off the ridge to cross a scree slide, then make your way around below the rock spires of **Punta Princesa**. On your right the land falls away almost directly into the valley. Minor hand climbing is necessary as the route picks its way through short sections of rock blocks with small chrysanthemum bushes sheltering in the crevices. Keeping to this western side of the range, make your way on to reach the **Cancha de Fútbol**, one to 1¼ hours from the small saddle. At this sandy shelf surrounded by boulders, the 2388m Cerro Catedral Sur comes into view over to the south.

Prominent signs painted on rocks point left to 'Frey' (Refugio Frey) and right to 'Jakob' (Refugio San Martín on Laguna Jakob). Head down to **Refugio Frey** (bookings at the CAB in Bariloche ☎ 029 44-527966; sleeping space US$3, dinner

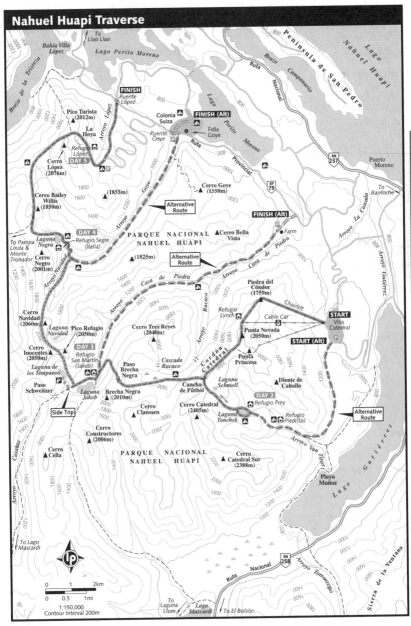

Nahuel Huapi Traverse

LAKES DISTRICT

Bahía Villa López

To
Llao Llao

Lago Perito Moreno

Brazo de la Tristeza

Peninsula de San Pedro

Lago Nahuel Huapi

Ruta Nacional

Brazo Campanario

FINISH
Puente López

Pico Turista
(2012m)
La Hoya

Refugio
López

Cerro
López
(2076m)

Colonia
Suiza
Puente
Goye

FINISH (Alt)
Felix
Goye

Arroyo López

Arroyo Goye

Lago Perito Moreno

Ruta Provincial

RN 237

Puerto
Moreno

To
Bariloche

Cerro Bailey
Willis
(1850m)

(1855m)

Cerro Goye
(1550m)

**Alternative
Route**

RP 79

Arroyo La Cascada

Arroyo Gutierrez

To Pampa
Linda &
Monte
Tronador

Laguna
Negra

Refugio Segre
(Italia)

DAY 4

PARQUE NACIONAL
NAHUEL HUAPI

Cerro Bella
Vista

FINISH (Alt)

Farm

Cerro
Negro
(2001m)

(1825m)

**Alternative
Route**

Arroyo Casa de Piedra

Casa de Piedra

Arroyo Navidad

Cerro
Navidad
(2060m)

Laguna
Navidad

Pico Refugio
(2050m)

Casa de Piedra

Arroyo Rucaco

Piedra del
Cóndor
(1759m)

Refugio
Lynch

Chairlift

Cable Car

START
Villa
Catedral

Cerro
Inocentes
(2050m)

DAY 3

Refugio
San Martín
(Jakob)

Cerro Tres Reyes
(2040m)

Arroyo

Punta Nevada
(2050m)

START (Alt)

Laguna
de los Témpanos

Paso
Schweitzer

Laguna
Jakob

Brecha Negra
(2010m)

Paso
Brecha
Negra

Cascada
Rucaco

Cancha
de Fútbol

Cordón Catedral

Punta
Princesa

Laguna
Schmoll

Diente de
Caballo

Side Trip

Cerro
Claussen

Cerro Catedral
(2405m)

Laguna
Tonchek

DAY 2
Refugio Frey

Refugio
Piedritas

**Alternative
Route**

Arroyo Casalata

Cerro
Cella

Cerro
Constructores
(2006m)

PARQUE NACIONAL
NAHUEL HUAPI

Cerro
Catedral Sur
(2388m)

Arroyo Van Titt

Playa
Muñoz

Lago Gutierrez

To Lago
Mascardi

0   1   2km
0   0.5   1mi

1:150,000
Contour Interval 200m

To
Laguna
Llum

Lago
Mascardi

To El Bolsón

RN 258

Ruta Nacional

Arroyo Tonnewai

Sierra de la Ventana

US$2.50-4; open year-round) as described (in reverse sequence) at the beginning of Day 2. Walking time from the Cancha de Fútbol to the *refugio* is 40 to 50 minutes.

The *refugio* stands at 1700m in a particularly scenic location on the eastern shore of **Laguna Tonchek**, looking out across the lake to the craggy spires of Cerro Catedral (Cathedral Mountain). The lake takes its name, which you may also see spelt 'Toncek', from the late Slovene andinist and CAB member Toncek Pangrec. The neat two-storey hut is built of local stone, and has sleeping space for 40 people upstairs. It can get very crowded, particularly during periods of poor weather in the main tourist season. There are sheltered but cramped and uneven **camp sites** in the *lenga* scrub just across the outlet creek on the southern side of the lake, and less sheltered but more spacious and level sites on open ground further round the southern shore.

Alternative Route: via Arroyo Van Titter
3½–4½ hours, 12km
This stage is longer than Day 1 and has no lifts to haul you up the mountain, but ascends at a more leisurely rate and is more sheltered. It is the only safe route when the high-level option is snowed over or icy.

From the CAB lodge at the southern edge of Villa Catedral, cut across the car park below a minor ski tow and take an old road up left to a signpost at the trailhead. The broad foot track goes southward through *ñirre* and *quila* scrub on a kind of wide terrace above Lago Gutiérrez, then rises gently into the forest below overhanging cliffs to a fork 1½ to two hours from the village.

Continue up, heading right (the left-hand route leads down to the lake), turning up northwest through moist forest, and cross the **Arroyo Van Titter** on a footbridge. The first authorised **camp sites** along the route are by the stream just after you cross this bridge. Ascend at a leisurely pace through the tall *lenga* forest with an understorey of herbs and wild flowers to pass **Refugio Piedritas** after 50 minutes to 1¼ hours. This quaint little *refugio* belongs to the local

Club Andino Esloveno and has been constructed by building a log wall across the opening of a large overhanging boulder just to the right of the path. Refugio Piedritas only has space for about eight people and is basic. You can find numerous good **camp sites** in the forest nearby.

Climb on through the forest, which soon changes into lower and denser *lenga* scrub, granting views of the peaks on the Cordón Catedral. The route crosses the now much smaller stream on stepping stones shortly before you reach **Refugio Frey**, beside Laguna Tonchek, after a final 50 minutes to 1¼ hours.

Day 2: Refugio Frey to Refugio San Martín (Jakob)
3½–5 hours, 8.5km
Make your way easily around either shore of Laguna Tonchek to its northwestern side, then begin ascending to the right (northwest). The path winds up the loose-rock slopes beside a splashing stream to **Laguna Schmoll**, a smaller and shallower lake that occupies a sparsely vegetated terrace opposite the impressive craggy columns of Cerro Catedral. Cross the tiny outlet and climb on more steeply into a rock gully. Early in the season, snow here may make this section dangerous. Look back for a final view of the lovely upper valley behind you, then continue up through a small sandy basin to reach the **Cancha de Fútbol** after one to 1½ hours.

A sign ('Jakob') and an arrow painted on a boulder indicate where the route descends into the next valley. Follow red splashes on rocks down a short way to the right, then traverse back briefly leftward. Now begin a long and very steep descent more or less straight down through dusty, raw talus, continuing down via a dry gully into the scrub. As the gradient eases, head off to the left along a good trail where beautiful *lenga* forest fringes the grassy valley floor. The path ducks in and out of trees to cross a stream below a cascade at an excellent official **camp site**, 50 minutes to one hour from the Cancha de Fútbol.

Make your way on gently upvalley through the forest, avoiding the soggy open area to the right. The route soon moves out into sporadic *ñirre* scrub, then crosses a stream coming down from the left. The Cascada Rucaco waterfall comes into sight on the slopes of Cerro Tres Reyes to the north, and red markings guide you up onto a flat, stony ridge dividing the upper valley. Behind you, on the adjacent range, the now familiar multisteepled form of Cerro Catedral rises up, looking just as spectacular from this angle. The track leads across the broad ridge top to a well signposted rock, then makes a final strenuous, but short climb west up through steep, loose rock to reach **Paso Brecha Negra** after one to 1½ hours. This is the broad ridge that connects Cerro Tres Reyes with Brecha Negra. There are superb views from here (better from a few paces downhill), with the *refugio* on Laguna Jakob clearly visible below to the southwest.

Sidle down towards the lake as far as a small outcrop, then descend steeply via (or beside) a loose chute of coarse gravel until below the scrub line. Turn left where the route meets the main trail coming up through the valley, and follow this through a few boggy areas to cross the small **Arroyo Casa de Piedra** on stepping stones just below where it leaves Laguna Jakob.

A short way on, the route intersects with the main path coming up through the valley. Follow this briefly to the left to **Refugio San Martín (Jakob)** *(sleeping space US$2, use of kitchen US$1, dinner US$4; open Nov-Apr)*, beside Laguna Jakob at 1600m, 45 minutes to one hour from Paso Brecha Negra. This timber and stone *refugio* stands near a tiny peninsula. It has a wood stove and can sleep 80 to 100 people. You can buy a few basic provisions and sweet luxuries from the hut warden. A much-needed toilet block was under construction when we visited. **Camping** is permitted in clearings in the *lenga* above the *refugio*; collect water from the spring water tap at the hut.

Side Trip: Laguna de los Témpanos

1–1½ hours return, 3.5km
This easy side trip from Refugio San Martín is not to be missed. From the camping area head up the steep ridge, then sidle on around westward over polished limestone slabs (note the scratch marks left by ice age glaciers) to reach Laguna de los Témpanos after 25 to 30 minutes. This spectacular little lake lies within a south-facing cirque with sheer rock walls that tower above its icy, blue waters. Return the way you came.

Day 3: Refugio San Martín (Jakob) to Refugio Segre (Italia)

5–7 hours, 8.5km
This section of the trek, following a high-level route, is harder and more hazardous than other stages. It should not be attempted unless the weather is very good. At any time – most commonly, early in the season (until about mid-December) – crampons and an ice axe may be needed to do the route safely. The hut warden at Refugio San Martín (who has photographs that clarify the route) can give further advice, and will ask you to fill in a form and hand it in on arrival at the other end.

Follow the Side Trip: Laguna de los Témpanos as far as a rocky spur that comes down from **Pico Refugio**, just before Laguna de los Témpanos comes into view. After carefully studying the route from this point, follow occasional cairns northeastward, with some scrambling as the ridge steepens, to meet a narrow ledge. Head left along the ledge for about 50m, then move up with care diagonally rightward through a steep couloir (rocky chute), which may be wet or snow-filled. After another 50m or so, ease back left across snowdrifts – if possible, below them – to gain the top of the ridge.

Taking care when negotiating more patches of old snow, head northwest along the ridge. After a short distance, a rocky pinnacle blocks the way. Avoid this by descending around to the right and traverse the slopes below the rock face. Continue through a stony area of gully cracks, where more snow may lie, towards an obvious narrow gap in the craggy range ahead, two to three hours from Laguna de los Témpanos. From here, move over onto the loose scree slopes on the eastern side of the range above Laguna Navidad. These lead to a low point in the main ridge line between Cerro

Inocentes and Cerro Navidad. From here, make your way 500m up a spur on scree to the summit of **Cerro Navidad**.

Head 400m down the ridge on the northern side of Cerro Navidad. From here a rough route can be followed northeast down more steep and unstable slopes into the narrow canyon at the head of the **Arroyo Navidad**. Late-lying snow may make this section tricky to negotiate. Crossing the cascading stream wherever necessary, follow it down to meet the main path coming up the **Arroyo Goye**, two to three hours on.

Follow red-paint markings up through *lenga* scrub, before beginning a steep, spiralling ascent adjacent to waterfalls where the Arroyo Goye spills over 300m cliffs. The path sidles on around westward over a low rock crest, from where Laguna Negra comes into view. **Laguna Negra** lies in a little trough directly below Cerro Negro (2001m), and was evidently named for its proximity to the black-rock mountain as its water is blue. To the north lies the paler-brown shale rock of Cerro Bailey Willis (1850m). Cut down leftward across the lake outlet to arrive at **Refugio Segre (Italia)** *(sleeping space US$2, use of kitchen US$1, dinner US$2.50; open Nov-Apr)* after a final 60 to 80 minutes. This two-storey concrete construction (whose bunker-like design can withstand heavy snows and small avalanches) lies at 1650m and has bed space for 60 trekkers. There are numerous sheltered **camp sites** hunkering in the scrub as you come over the rock crest just before arriving at Refugio Segre.

Alternative Finish: Refugio San Martín (Jakob) to Ruta Provincial 79

2¾–4½ hours, 13km

This is the normal access to Refugio San Martín and is the quickest exit route from the hut. It is also the final stage of the three-day trek known as the Circuito Chico.

Follow the well-travelled path down the true left (west) side of the **Arroyo Casa de Piedra**, crossing the stream just above a waterfall. Descend steeply in a series of switchback curves (known as Las Serpentinas) into the *lenga* forest, then more gently on past a side valley that ends in a large cirque at Laguna Navidad. From here, the route enters the drier central part of the valley (which apparently lies in the rain shadow of ranges to the west). The path leads through *mogotes*, *calafate* bushes and *ñirres* – typical dryland vegetation – to cross the stream on a rickety suspension bridge, 1½ to 2½ hours from the *refugio*.

Continue down the stony riverflats past where the Arroyo Rucaco flows into the main stream, then climb away left and drop back to the riverbank several times to avoid steeper banks before sidling gradually down into pleasant stands of *coigüe* trees, and some good **camp sites**, by the Arroyo Casa de Piedra after 50 minutes to 1¼ hours. The route soon leaves the riverside again, ascending briefly through the forest onto slopes covered by thickets of *retama* as it goes over into a 4WD track. Ahead of you, across Lago Nahuel Huapi, are the snow-capped mountains of the Sierra Cuyin Manzano. Pass by a tiny car park and a kiosk beside a farm, after which a proper road brings you down to intersect with the Ruta Provincial 79 after 30 to 45 minutes.

Those travelling in the reverse direction should watch out for a sign marking the start of the track beside Ruta Provincial 79; going uphill the trekking time is around six hours.

It's possible to walk from here to the holiday village of **Colonia Suiza** (p143) in 1½ to two hours (turn left and follow the road), but easier to wait for the No 11 bus from Bariloche, which passes this point five times daily (between 9.40am and 8.40pm) on the way to Colonia Suiza.

Day 4: Refugio Segre (Italia) to Refugio López

4–5½ hours, 7.5km

Head along the eastern lake shore, dotted with chrysanthemum bushes and yellow daisies, making your way on around the northern side of Laguna Negra over cracked rock and perhaps some snowdrifts. There is a short section of rock here (probably with a fixed rope to hang on to) that requires some careful downclimbing. From the far end of Laguna Negra, climb a short distance up to the right beside the small inlet stream, then cross to its true right side and head up a broad open rocky slope towards the low point in the ridge between Cerro Negro and Cerro Bailey Willis.

Head up right along the ridge (guided by a few cairns, canes and paint markers), over a knob and down to reach a gap on the southern side of Cerro Bailey Willis (where snow may lie well into the summer) 45 minutes to one hour from Refugio Segre. From here, the now familiar form of Cerro Catedral can be made out to the southeast beyond Laguna Negra. Sidle northward for a further 15 to 20 minutes, across a slope of coarse talus above a snow basin, to reach another small pass.

From the slopes of **Cerro Bailey Willis** you get an unobstructed panorama of the magnificent mountain scenery along the Chile–Argentina frontier. The great white rump of Monte Tronador, smothered by sprawling glaciers, completely dominates the views of the western horizon. The pointed peak visible to the north of Monte Tronador is Volcán Puntiagudo in Chile, and the highland lake perched in a depression to the southwest is Laguna Lluvú (or CAB; see Other Treks, p161).

Drop down north from the pass, descending briefly rightward through loose rock before you sidle along the left side of a green, boggy gully. In places the foot track is less definite, but the route is marked with cairns and occasional red-paint splashes on rocks. Follow these down left on to moist grassy meadows to cross a brook at the head of a tiny valley (the northern branch of the Arroyo Goye), 40 to 50 minutes from the pass. There is a small park-approved **camp site** here among low *lenga* forest.

Head on over a marshy clearing and up out of the *ñirre* scrub. The indistinct path leads northeast gently up the sparsely vegetated slopes to cross a small stream coming from an obvious rocky gap to the north. From this point, begin a very steep ascent up to the right via a gully of frost-shattered rock, whose large, loose, sharp fragments make the going strenuous (and slightly dan-

gerous), passing to the right of a rocky knob to reach a small dip in the range some way north of Cerro López's principal summit, 1½ to two hours from the camp site.

A short way northwest along the top of this ridge is a trig marker on the slightly lower summit of **Pico Turista**. This point offers another great panorama, which now includes Volcán Osorno (the perfectly symmetrical snowcapped cone visible beyond Monte Tronador in Chile), while to the north there are sweeping views across the islands, peninsulas and isthmuses that separate Lago Perito Moreno from Lago Nahuel Huapi. Condors often soar around these mountain tops.

Following paint arrows, drop down east from the dip in the ridge to skirt along the left side of a small glacial cirque known as **La Hoya**. A shallow tarn forms here once the snow melts, but by autumn this basin is normally dry and snow-free. Descend more steeply towards the *refugio*, visible far below you, downclimbing repeatedly at short sections of rock, to reach **Refugio López** *(sleeping space US$3, use of kitchen US$1, dinner US$2.50)* after 50 minutes to 1¼ hours.

The privately owned Refugio López is the most popular and accessible hut on this trek, and sits at around 1600m in a very scenic location overlooking Lago Nahuel Huapi. This two-storey red-brick building has modern amenities (but no hot showers) and there is sleeping capacity for 100 people. There are poor **camp sites** near the hut, or you can camp on a grassy area below a waterfall about 15 minutes down beyond the *refugio*. Refugio López stays open for the entire trekking season.

Alternative Finish: Refugio Segre (Italia) to Colonia Suiza
2½–3¼ hours, 12km
This is the usual access to Refugio Segre (Italia). It's also an easier alternative route out for trekkers who don't feel confident enough to tackle the high-level traverse of Day 3.

Head back down the switchbacks as described at the end of Day 3 to cross the Arroyo Goye and the Arroyo Navidad just above their confluence. The path dips down into the *lenga* forest beside the cascading stream to an official **camp site** after 40 to 50 minutes. Head gently downstream below high rock walls fronting the opposite side of the valley, crossing through a small area of *ñirre* and *quila* before you pass a side valley of the Arroyo Goye (barely visible through the trees).

Continue along the true-right bank, gradually moving down into evergreen forest dominated by *coigüe* to where the route joins a rough, disued road, one to 1½ hours down from the official camp site. At this point you'll see a signpost ('Picada a Laguna Negra/Refugio'), which indicates the way back up to the hut. Another trail branches off right (southeast) from here up to the 1550m lookout peak of Cerro Goye, a return side trip of 3½ hours.

Sidle down above the rushing stream through patches of exotic North American fir trees (which are spreading rapidly at the expense of the native forest), then turn right off the vehicular track at a gate and make your way along the right-hand side of a fence. The first part of this route ascends steeply; the last section takes you through stands of *ciprés de la cordillera* before dropping steeply through the *coigüe* forest to reach Ruta Provincial 79 at a parking area and a signpost ('Refugio de Montaña Laguna Negra...6 horas') after 35 to 45 minutes. Go left along this road, turning right into Felix Goye to arrive in **Colonia Suiza** (p143) a further 10 to 15 minutes on. Trekkers hiking up to Refugio Segre will find the signpost indicating the trailhead beside a black gate 400m east of the road bridge over the Arroyo Goye.

Day 5: Refugio López to Puente López

1½–2 hours, 3.5km
From just below the terrace of the *refugio* take a path that winds down through low scrub before joining a broad track that comes in from the right. This crosses two small streams at the source of the **Arroyo López** and meets the end of a road after 15 to 20 minutes. Follow the road past a small car park, then turn off left on to a signposted

foot track leading steeply down into the forest. The route twice crosses the road at hairpin bends, then leads down through previously fire-cleared slopes, now regenerating with *ñirre* scrub and thickets of spiny *crucero*. Here, avoid picking up trails which diverge rightward back on to the road, and continue down north into the forest. (If you follow the road, you'll end up about halfway along Ruta Provincial 79 between Puente López and Colonia Suiza).

The last section of the route follows the right side of the Arroyo López before coming to a picnic area and kiosk at **Puente López** after a final 1¼ to 1¾ hours.

Trekkers who do this stage in reverse order should reckon on taking two to three hours to reach Refugio López from Puente López.

Paso de las Nubes

Duration	2 days
Distance	23km
Difficulty	moderate
Start	Pampa Linda (p151)
Finish	Puerto Frías
Nearest Town	Bariloche (p113)
Transport	bus & boat
Summary Links two river valleys through saturated rainforest and below hanging glaciers at the foot of the mighty three-summit massif of Monte Tronador.		

The aptly named 1335m Paso de las Nubes (Pass of the Clouds) lies on a continental watershed, sending its waters into the Pacific on its southern side, via the Río Manso and Río Puelo, and into the Atlantic on its northern side, via Lago Nahuel Huapi. The route over Paso de las Nubes can be done as a trans-Andean trek by continuing over Paso de Pérez Rosales to the isolated village of Peulla on Lago Todos Los Santos in Chile (see the Alternative Finish, p156).

PLANNING

The trek follows a much travelled and generally well-marked path for most of the

Hear the Thunder

Monte Tronador's name means Mt Thunderer, and refers to the noise caused by repeated snow and ice avalanches that crash down from the mountain's extensive névés. Trekkers who spend any time observing Tronador's spectacular hanging glaciers are likely to hear confirmation of the name's suitability. Interestingly, the Mapuche people knew the mountain by the name of Anon, whose meaning is almost identical to the Spanish 'Tronador'.

way. Apart from a short section on top of Paso de las Nubes and the side trip to Refugio Otto Meiling, the route is completely within the shelter of the forest. Snow often lies on the pass well into January. On the section between the upper camp near Glaciar Frías and Laguna Frías, fallen logs and *quila* canes sometimes lie across the path; here the going is occasionally slippery after rain.

From Puerto Frías many trekkers continue into Chile via a good dirt road to Peulla on Lago Todos Los Santos (see the Alternative Finish, p156). This isolated 26km section across Paso de Pérez Rosales is inaccessible to outside traffic, and is travelled only by a regular bus service and occasional border-control vehicles.

The usual trekking time from Pampa Linda to Puerto Frías is two full days, but the recommended side trips to the Salto Garganta del Diablo or Piedra Pérez and Refugio Otto Meiling will lengthen the trek by one day each. These side trips begin and end in Pampa Linda, and so need to be done before you set out on Day 1 of the trek. Continuing to Peulla requires at least one additional (very long) day.

The trek can be done in either direction, although for transport reasons south-to-north will probably be the most convenient route.

When to Trek

This trek is best done between December and April.

What to Bring

Some form of alternative footwear suited to wet terrain, such as sport sandals, makes negotiating the *mallín* north of the Upper Río Alerce camp site less of a drama. As this is a frontier area, be sure to carry proper identification.

Permits & Regulations

All trekkers must register before the trek at the national park *intendencia* (administration centre) in Pampa Linda, and return their registration stub to the office at Puerto Blest on the way back to Bariloche after the end of the trek. No permit is required for the side trips to Salto Garganta del Diablo, and Piedra Pérez and Filo Clerk.

Maps

Recommended is the contoured 1:50,000 *Trekking 2* map in the Refugios, Sendas y Picadas series, which is an extract (with additional topographical information) from the larger-format colour 1:100,000 Refugios, Sendas y Picadas *Parque Nacional Nahuel Huapi*. This latter map covers a much wider area and is perhaps a better alternative if you plan further treks elsewhere in the park. Both are available from the CAB in Bariloche.

The Argentine IGM 1:100,000 map *Llao Llao* (Neuquén, No 4172-22) covers this area completely. However, this map (also used for the Nahuel Huapi Traverse) gives poor topographical detail and doesn't show the trekking route correctly.

A Chilean IGM 1:50,000 map, *Monte Tronador* (Section H, No 46), includes a good part of the frontier area on the Argentine side and is especially useful for trekkers who continue on to Peulla.

NEAREST TOWN & FACILITIES

See Bariloche (p113).

Pampa Linda

The trek begins at Pampa Linda, 77km by road from Bariloche via Villa Mascardi. *Guardaparques* at the national park office in Pampa Linda provide the latest information on trail conditions when trekkers register there.

Over the road from the national park office is the large **Camping Agreste Río Manso** (camping per person US$0.70), which has toilets and running water. Opposite is the very large CAB-run **Camping Pampa Linda** (camping per person US$2), which has better facilities including hot showers and a well-stocked kiosk. A short distance up the road towards Monte Tronador is **Hostería Pampa Linda** (☎ 02944-423757, 422181), which has a good **restaurant**.

Through summer, **Expreso Meiling** (☎ 029 44-467507; reservations at the CAB) runs regular buses to Pampa Linda and Cerro Tronador (US$5, 2½ hours), leaving at 8am, 9am and 10am from outside the CAB in Bariloche. One bus also leaves daily from **Transitando Lo Natural** (☎ 02944-423918; 20 de Febrero 25), opposite the CAB.

Peulla

For those continuing into Chile from Puerto Frías, there's a Conaf-run **camping ground** without facilities opposite the Conaf office in the village of Peulla, as well as the up-market but declining **Hotel Peulla** (☎ 065-258041; singles/doubles US$75/114), 1km from the dock.

From September to March a regular catamaran service departs from Peulla for Petrohué (US$32, 1¾ hours) at 3.30pm daily. At Petrohué minibuses to Puerto Montt meet the arriving boat.

GETTING TO/FROM THE TREK

The trek begins at Pampa Linda (p151) and finishes at Puerto Frías. From here a tourist boat across Laguna Frías to Puerto Alegre connects with a bus to Puerto Blest on a branch of Lago Nahuel Huapi. From Puerto Blest catamarans run across Lago Nahuel Huapi to Puerto Pañuelo (at Llao Llao). The last boat usually leaves Puerto Frías at 3pm. Trekkers can book this boat-bus-boat combination (US$10) and check departure times at the CAB in Bariloche or the CAB's *campamento móvil* (a kind of base camp) at the upper Río Frías camp site. From Puerto Pañuelo you catch the frequent local bus No 20 (US$0.70) for the final stretch back to Bariloche.

An extremely expensive (US$70!) bus service operates once daily Monday to Saturday in summer along the very scenic and otherwise untravelled 26km international road linking Puerto Frías to Peulla, so most trekkers who choose this alternative opt to walk (see the Alternative Finish: Peulla, p156). Remember that it is prohibited to bring most unprocessed foodstuffs into Chile.

THE TREK
Day 1: Pampa Linda to Upper Río Frías
4–5½ hours, 13km

The trek proper begins, as does the Side Trip to Refugio Otto Meiling (p155), with a walk of 30 to 40 minutes along the vehicle track from Pampa Linda to the **Río Castaño Overo**. Cross the river and continue up the vehicle track to a clearly signposted junction on a bend to the left a short distance above the river. Go right here and follow the remains of an ancient road northeastward to meet the **Río Alerce**. Apart from a short section where you have to climb over fallen logs at a tight bend in the river (while the old road simply fords and re-fords the milky waters), the route continues on gently up along the western bank. It goes through pleasant *coigüe* and *lenga* forest to reach the **Río Alerce camp site** at the edge of a *mallín* after a further one to 1½ hours.

Make an easy ford of the small Río Alerce and wade north for several hundred metres across sodden ground scattered with *ñirres* and thickets of *chapel*, a small shrub with fragrant white flowers. Pick up the path at the edge of the forest and begin a steadily steepening climb, making a few zigzags into the *lenga* scrub before the gradient eases. The route continues up more gradually, crossing a number of small streams and following cairns and paint markers northward over grassy alpine meadows to reach **Paso de las Nubes** after 1½ to two hours.

The 1335m pass is too scrubby to give any real vistas, but as you descend you pass small lookout points that grant a clear view down through the glacially formed valley ahead as far as the sombre-looking Laguna

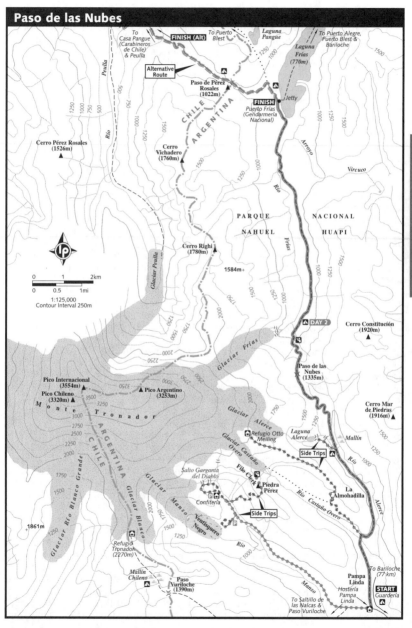

Paso de las Nubes

Frías. The descent is much steeper on this side of the pass. The path takes you directly down through moss-draped forest to cross a fast-flowing stream on stepping stones before coming out on to a small rocky outcrop.

Here you stand immediately opposite Glaciar Frías, an amazing icefall sprawling down from the névés on the eastern side of Monte Tronador. This glacier feeds a surging waterfall and numerous other smaller cascades that form the Río Frías, and drops large chunks of ice over a high cliff face. Drop down along the small rocky ridge to the valley floor, then recross the gravelly stream to arrive at the official, free **Upper Río Frías camp site**, 50 minutes to 1¼ hours from the pass. The CAB maintains a **campamento móvil** *(fixed tents per person US$2.50, dinner US$3)* here.

Side Trip: Salto Garganta del Diablo

3–4½ hours return, 17km

Although it follows an often dusty road for most of the way, this return side trip into the head of the Río Manso, at the foot of Monte Tronador, should not be missed (although you might consider hitching). For safety reasons the road is open only to upward traffic until 2pm and to downward traffic after 4pm. If you arrive with a return-day bus tour from Bariloche, the trip up to the Salto Garganta del Diablo will probably be included.

From Pampa Linda, walk northwest along the road past the *guardería* and *hostería*. Five minutes on, you pass the signposted path that's the turn-off to the Saltillo de los Nalcas (which is also the trail head for the route to Refugio Tronador – see Other Treks, p161). The road rises steadily beside the upper Río Manso, crossing the northern branch of the river shortly before it comes to a car park at a lookout point, one to 1½ hours on.

From here you get a sensational view up to **Glaciar Manso**, which ends abruptly at a hanging icefall above a 750m-high precipice on Monte Tronador. Blocks of ice that periodically drop off the icefall are smashed to pieces as they hit the ground, where the pulverised ice re-forms as another glacier. This is known as the **Ventisquero Negro** (Black Glacier) because the large quantities of moraine and broken rock that are mixed in with the ice give it a dark hue. A short trail leads down to the murky lake where the Ventisquero Negro ends.

Head on for 10 to 15 minutes to the **confitería** (small café/restaurant) at the end of the road; snacks and refreshments are available here. A foot track from the upper end of the car park here continues for a further 15 to 20 minutes up to the stream at the base of an impressive cirque at the head of the valley. Up to your left the long and spectacular waterfall known as the **Salto Garganta del Diablo** shoots down from the side of Glaciar Manso, while numerous other high cascades emerge from the icefalls up to the right. The agile can climb up to where the Salto thunders into a tiny chasm, spraying out mist that settles on the mossy rocks.

Trekkers who visit the Salto Garganta del Diablo should be mindful that there is a risk, although it is relatively low, of ice breaking off the hanging glaciers directly above and falling into the upper valley.

Side Trip: Piedra Pérez/Filo Clerk

1¾–2½ hours return, 3km

If you don't mind a strenuous climb, this 'side trip on a side trip', to a lookout point up on the ridge to the north of the route to the *salto*, is even more rewarding than the original.

From behind the *confitería* (see Side Trip: Salto Garganta del Diablo), head 50m right and downstream, crossing several small channels in the glacial stream. Pick up a graded foot track at the edge of the *coigüe* forest, and follow it as it snakes its way upward with the odd fallen trunk to clamber under or over. The route steepens as it rides a narrow spur covered with *lengas* up to the top of a broad ridge known as **Filo Clerk** (which is sometimes used by andinists as a route to the summits of Monte Tronador). Follow white paint markings a few hundred metres left (northwest) along the scrubby ridge above **Piedra Pérez**, a small but prominent tooth-shaped pinnacle visible from down in the valley, to reach a lookout point one to 1¼ hours from the *confitería*.

This part of the ridge offers a classic close-up view of **Glaciar Castaño Overo**. The crevasses and seracs of the glacier terminate in an impressive icefall that – like Glaciar Manso – hangs over a mighty precipice. Numerous meltwater cascades spill out from the edge of the ice. Visible on the ridge beyond the glacier is the path going up to Refugio Otto Meiling (see Side Trip: Refugio Otto Meiling), while to the southwest you should just be able to make out the old Refugio Tronador (see Other Treks, p161) on a high rock ridge just left of the Glaciar Manso icefalls. You also get an excellent view back into the upper valley of the Río Manso.

Return to the *confitería* via the ascent route.

Side Trip: Refugio Otto Meiling
5–6¾ hours return, 18km

This is another highly scenic return day or overnight side trip that is recommended to all trekkers. Note that the 4WD road above the Río Castaño Overo has been affected by landslides; the *guardaparques* at Pampa Linda have the latest information on the route.

After signing in at the *guardería*, take the vehicle track heading roughly north past a signposted trail diverging rightward up to Laguna Ilón (see Pampa Linda to Refugio López under Other Treks, p161). This 4WD road brings you through *coigüe* forest and small clearings intermittently strewn with the striking orange flowers of the *amancay* to reach the Río Castaño Overo after 30 to 40 minutes. Cross the small glacial river on a footbridge and continue a short way upstream to rejoin the 4WD road.

Bear left briefly along the road, which soon begins a steady winding ascent through attractive mature *coigüe* forest. Follow the vehicle track only for short sections (it has been cut by landslides further east), cutting between the long switchback curves on foot tracks to reach a signposted turn-off to Glaciar Castaño Overo. The return side trip to this glacier, which ends in a spectacular icefall, takes around one hour. After a

longish switchback in the road, continue up a steep network of often eroded foot tracks through *lenga* forest to reach the top of the ridge at an area known as **La Almohadilla**, 1¼ to 1¾ hours from the Río Castaño Overo.

Make your way gently up along this broad ridge top until the 4WD track ends at a grassy clearing near the upper limit of the *lenga* scrub. A well-marked path sidles on around to the left above high bluffs on the southern side of the ridge, giving wonderful views across to the adjacent Glaciar Castaño Overo and the various summits of Monte Tronador behind it. Cross back up to the right over a small snowfield before following large cairns and marker stakes up the bare, rocky ridge top to arrive at **Refugio Otto Meiling** *(sleeping space US$3, use of kitchen US$1.50, dinner US$4.50)* after one to 1½ hours.

Refugio Otto Meiling stands at an altitude of around 2000m, a short way below the permanent snow line, and has a loft with sleeping capacity for 60 people. Its location offers a superb panorama taking in Pampa Linda, Paso de las Nubes and Cerro Catedral to the east. There is space for several tents in the shelter of rocks near the *refugio*, where trekkers may camp with the permission of the warden in reasonable weather. This side of Monte Tronador is relatively sheltered from the westerlies, but it's still a windy site.

Descend by the same route.

Side Trip: Laguna Alerce
2 hours return, 2km

From the Upper Río Frías camp site, head up the true right bank of the Río Alerce to the base of a cliff on the left side of the gushing meltwater cascade. A steep climb over rock slabs leads into a tiny moraine-filled upper valley, which is followed (crossing the stream where necessary) to this impressive glacial lake lying directly under the hanging glacier known as Glaciar Alerce. Return the same way.

Day 2: Upper Río Frías to Puerto Frías
3¼–4½ hours, 10km

Pick up the trail below the camp site and begin the trek downvalley. This route avoids the open, waterlogged ground near the banks of the river by maintaining a slightly higher course along slopes on the eastern side of the valley through wet temperate rainforest dominated by *coigüe, mañío* and laurel. The moist conditions favour climbing epiphytes such as the *botellita* and the *estrellita*, whose delicate crimson flowers stand out on trunks.

The foot track is quite well maintained, with logs laid across boggy sections, as it leads through dense thickets of *quila* and *colihue* bamboo and negotiates numerous trees that have fallen across the way. The going is slow but not tedious, despite there being only the occasional glimpse through the trees of the range (usually snowcapped until midsummer) on the adjacent side of the valley. The path meets the Río Frías 2¼ to three hours from the camp site.

Follow the true right (eastern) bank of the river for 10 to 15 minutes, then cross its deep, murky waters on a large fallen log to halfway, then the rest of the way on a log bridge with handrails. Head on, close to the true left bank of the Río Frías at first, then leaving the river and coming on to a long-abandoned road just before you pass a memorial to members of the Argentine Gendarmería Nacional, who died in a plane crash here in 1952.

The route soon skirts the southwestern side of **Laguna Frías** to arrive at a small boat landing, a shelter with toilets and an outpost of the Gendarmería Nacional at **Puerto Frías** after a final 30 to 40 minutes. Laguna Frías is a superb example of a glacial trough and is surrounded by sheer-sided mountains that rise directly from the shore, giving it a dramatic fjord-like appearance. Trekkers continuing to Peulla in Chile pass through customs here (if you want to leave early it's possible to have your passport exit-stamped the night before). Those not going on to Chile begin the long trip back to Bariloche here by catching a boat to Puerto Alegre (see Getting to/from the Trek, p152).

There is a small **camp site** at Puerto Frías, just up from the jetty, but no roofed accommodation.

Alternative Finish: Peulla
6–9 hours, 26km
Be sure to have your passport exit-stamped at the *gendarmería* building before setting out.

Follow the good dirt road around the southwest side of Laguna Frías. The road climbs steadily in switchbacks to reach **Paso de Pérez Rosales** after 45 minutes to one hour. The pass lies in lush rainforest 1022m above sea level on the Argentina–Chile border.

Begin the descent into Chile past tiny *pampas* and an abandoned farmhouse on your left. There are excellent **camp sites** on little meadows 10 to 15 minutes down from the pass. The road gradually winds down through more dense forest of *coigüe* and *arrayán* to reach **Casa Pangue** after two to three hours. This post of the Carabineros de Chile looks up the valley towards the spectacular snowbound northern slopes of Monte Tronador. From here trekkers can opt to do the long (20km return) day trek up the gravelly east bank of the Río Peulla to the snout of the receding Glaciar Peulla.

Follow the road 3km downstream and cross to the southern side of the Río Peulla on a suspension bridge. The road heads west across the flat valley floor for two to three hours, before swinging around through a wide expanse of soggy grassland. Continue south for another 1½ to two hours to the Chilean customs post just outside **Peulla** (p152). Passports must be presented here and luggage may be inspected.

While in Peulla, stroll around to the **Cascada de los Novios** waterfall, or do the three-hour return trek up to **Laguna Margarita**. The tiny harbour is 1km on from the village.

Parque Nacional Alerce Andino

Ostensibly a reserve for the giant alerce, an extremely slow-growing native conifer (known to the Mapuche as *lahuén*), Parque Nacional Alerce Andino is in the precordillera, or Andean foothills, 25km east of Puerto Montt. Despite its proclamation as a national park in 1984, the area still attracts surprisingly few visitors.

Comprising 392 sq km, Parque Nacional Alerce Andino occupies much of the promontory between the broad bay of Seno Reloncaví and its elongated eastern arm known as the Estuario de Reloncaví. Here, the Pacific coast begins to break up into the maze of islands, fjords and channels that typify western Patagonia.

At the hub of the park, two small valleys (of the upper Río Lenca and the Río Chaica) run between granite ranges whose highest summits surpass 1500m. Although this rugged landscape bears the unmistakable signs of intensive glaciation during past ice ages – most notably its dozen or so beautiful glacial lakes – there are no glaciers left in Alerce Andino. On its northeastern side the park almost touches Lago Chapo, a natural lake whose water level has been raised as part of a hydroelectricity project.

NATURAL HISTORY

Luxuriant montane rainforest grows – at an almost visible speed – at all but the highest elevations. Two trees particularly favoured by Andino Alerce's moist and mild climatic conditions are the *tiaca*, whose elongated, serrated leaves bear a superficial resemblance to those of *raulí* (a beech species absent from the park), and the *ulmo*, which is found up to an altitude of 500m. When flowering in January and February, the *ulmo* is covered by fragrant blossoms. Hummingbirds, or *picaflores*, thrive on such nectar-bearing flowers, and because of their surprising lack of timidity these delicate birds can often be observed from close range. Unfortunately, *tábanos* also gain strength feeding on nectar, but soon start to crave the protein-rich blood of passing trekkers.

Other common tree species found in Alerce Andino include *coigüe de Chiloé*, *tepa*, *tineo*, *canelo*, *arrayán*, *avellano*, *ciprés de las Guaitecas* – and, of course, the majestic alerce. The area's relative inaccessibility has prevented major exploitation of its stands of giant alerces. The trees are now saved from the woodcutters, and the most ancient and massive specimens may exceed 4m in diameter and reach several thousand years of age.

Among the numerous creepers and vines of the rainforest understorey are the *copihue*, whose beautiful, large crimson flowers are the floral emblem of Chile. The related *coicopihue* has somewhat less exuberant red flowers, which are nevertheless quite lovely. Less discreet climbers are the *pilpil de canasta*, recognisable by its pinkish, tubular flowers, and the *voqui*, or *lilinquén*, a small bushy plant with alternate tear-shaped leaves that yields clusters of tiny (but unpalatable) deep-purple, cherry-like fruit. A similar-looking (although unrelated) species is the *quilineja*, or *azahar*.

Native fauna is much less conspicuous, but the shy pudu and the marsupial *monito del monte* are occasionally spotted in the forest. The vegetarian *coipo* and the carnivorous *huillín* are thought to inhabit Andino Alerce's lakes and streams. Catty cousins, the puma and the far smaller *huiña*, are the largest terrestrial predators.

CLIMATE

Parque Nacional Alerce Andino's proximity to the coast gives the area a mild maritime climate, but also high annual rainfall. Precipitation ranges from 3300mm in the lower sectors to maximum levels of 4500mm on the highest ranges, usually falling as snow down to 800m (or lower) in winter.

PLANNING
When to Trek

You are best to trek in Parque Nacional Alerce Andino between late November and mid-April. In January the *tábanos* are a nuisance.

Information Sources

There are three ranger stations in Parque Nacional Alerce Andino. The administrative office is at Guardería Correntoso, on the park's northern boundary, and Guardería Sargazo, which is 10km further along the road at the main entrance gate. The southern sector of the park is managed from Guardería Chaica.

LAKES DISTRICT

Permits & Regulations

There is a US$1.50 entrance fee to Parque Nacional Alerce Andino, payable when you sign in at Guardería Sargazo. Camping is only permitted at Campamento Pangal and Campamento Río Sargazo, and the only other place to stay is Refugio Sargazo, at the park entrance.

Laguna Fría

Duration	2 days
Distance	17km
Difficulty	easy–moderate
Start/Finish	Guardería Sargazo
Nearest Town	Puerto Montt (p114)
Transport	bus & walk

Summary Trek into the heart of the park, where massive and ancient alerces grow and charming lakes nestle in the cool, temperate forest.

Although the *guardaparques*, with the help of volunteers, do their best to keep Alerce Andino's foot tracks open, the ferocious growth rate of the southern Lakes District vegetation makes this a difficult task. This trek takes advantage of those tracks on which most attention is lavished. Even so, occasional fallen tree trunks have to be ducked or climbed over, and vigorous *quila* leans over the route in many places. Heavy winter snowfalls can flatten the *quila* canes, completely obscuring the path, and the trek's level of difficulty will depend largely on how recently track-clearing work has been done.

The difficulty of keeping tracks open means that an additional section between Campamento Pangal and Guardería Sargazo, and an alternative to that route via Refugio Pangal, were closed when we were last there. Park staff were optimistic that these tracks would eventually be reopened. Were this to happen, it would open up the way for a worthwhile longer trek of three days beginning and ending in Correntoso, which is accessible by bus from Puerto Montt. Plans to cut a foot track from Laguna Fría through to Lago Triángulo (in Alerce Andino's southern Chaica sector – see Lago Triángulo under Other Treks, p161), though, have been abandoned.

PLANNING
What to Bring

At the time of our research, several *refugios* in the park were either temporarily closed pending restoration works, or completely derelict. The main problem seems to be the prevalence in Chile of the hantavirus, which is carried by rodents, and the consequent need to rat-proof huts before opening them to the public. Trekkers must therefore carry a tent or do the trek in one longish day from a base at Refugio Sargazo.

Maps

Two IGM 1:50,000 maps cover the central part of the park: *Correntoso* (Section H, No 52) and *Lenca* (Section H, No 61). These maps do not accurately show local roads or trekking routes, but are otherwise reasonably accurate (note that on these maps the Río Lenca is incorrectly given as the Río Chaica and vice versa). The same is true of the JLM Mapas *Ruta de los Jesuitas* map (No 15), which includes a 1:50,000 (approximately) partial map of Parque Nacional Alerce Andino.

NEAREST TOWN & FACILITIES

Puerto Montt (p114) is the logical base for the trek and has the nearest well-stocked supermarkets. The village of Correntoso has a small grocery store selling basic provisions, which is likely to be your last option after leaving Puerto Montt. In the park itself there's nowhere to buy anything.

Refugio Sargazo

A former residence for *guardaparques* adjacent to Guardería Sargazo, where the trek starts and finishes, has been converted into a comfortable, basic **refugio** *(bunks US$3)*, with bathroom (cold water only) and kitchen. Camping is not permitted anywhere nearby, so the *refugio* is a valuable option for those without private transport who must walk from Correntoso.

GETTING TO/FROM THE TREK

To get there in a private vehicle, follow Ruta 7 – the Carretera Austral – east from Puerto Montt across the Río Chamiza to Chamiza, then head left up the Chamiza valley to the park. Vehicles can be left at the end of the public road, just outside the park entrance at Guardería Sargazo.

For those without private transport, the trek begins and ends with a road walk of about 13km between the village of Correntoso, 37km east by road from Puerto Montt, and Guardería Sargazo (see the Alternative Start, p160). Together the two companies

Buses Fierro and Buses JB run up to five buses daily (fewer on Sunday) to Lago Chapo, which pass through Correntoso (US$1.75, one hour). The last bus leaves the Puerto Montt bus terminal at around 5pm Monday to Saturday.

THE TREK
Day 1: Guardería Sargazo to Campamento Río Sargazo
1¾–2¼ hours, 4km

Follow the road 500m past Guardería Sargazo and pick up the signposted and substantially reinforced path leading off left

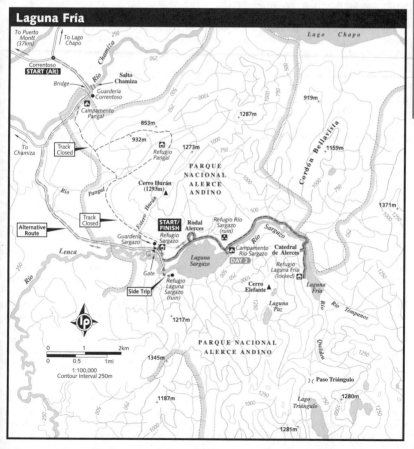

into the trees. The route climbs up past a forestry observation tower and over a low ridge, then dips gently around the rain-forested northern slopes just above **Laguna Sargazo** to pass a left-hand turn-off to an *alerzal* (a stand of alerces) known as the **Rodal Alerces** after 40 to 50 minutes. This is a rewarding short side trip to a small stand of particularly massive ancient alerces.

Make your way on through damp groves of leafy *tiacas*, which grant only the occasional unobstructed glimpse of the lake, and cut down across a small wash full of boulders. After finding the trail again in the scrub just up from the tiny rocky beach, climb on some way above the lake before you drop down again to a small, unofficial camp site and the reedy eastern shore of Laguna Sargazo after one to 1¼ hours.

Pick up the path in the scrub on the far side of this flat, boggy area and continue northeastward to the remains of an old orchard and the free **Campamento Río Sargazo**, with pit toilets, after 10 minutes or so.

Alternative Start: Correntoso
2¼–3 hours, 13km

From the bus stop in Correntoso (on the main road to Lago Chapo), take the turn-off leading east past wooden houses to cross the **Río Chamiza** bridge. Because water has been diverted for the hydroelectricity scheme on Lago Chapo, the once-powerful cataract known as the **Salto Chamiza** (Salto Correntoso on the JLM map) is now little more than a trickle. Continue along the road around a bend to reach **Guardería Correntoso** after 20 to 25 minutes, where you should sign in and ask the friendly and knowledgeable resident *guardaparque* for the latest information about tracks and *refugios* in the park. A few minutes farther along the road is the free **Campamento Pangal**, with toilets and plenty of grassy tent sites.

The road now continues gradually uphill for about 10km, and lies outside the park for much of that distance. There's no navigation required to speak of, and not much of interest to detain you until you come to the park entrance gate, **Guardería Sargazo** and the adjacent *refugio* (see Refugio Sargazo,

p158) after two to 2½ hours. Day 1 begins at the *guardería*.

Side Trip: Refugio Laguna Sargazo
50 minutes–1 hour return, 2km

This easy walk to the southwestern corner of Laguna Sargazo is worth doing even though at present it's not possible to stay at the hut. From Guardería Sargazo follow the road for 1.5km until it ends at a tunnel sealed by a locked gate. A path leads off right to meet the **Río Lenca** after a minute or two. Cross the river a short way downstream from here – an easy ford, since a weir just upstream diverts most of its water into the nearby tunnel. The path climbs up roughly eastward through the damp forest of *tepa* and *mañío*, then descends to the *refugio* after 25 to 30 minutes. This dilapidated shingled wooden shack stands just above a tiny beach on Laguna Sargazo. Return by the same route.

Day 2: Campamento Río Sargazo to Guardería Sargazo
4¼–5 hours, 13km

The continuation of the trek as far as Laguna Fría could be done at the end of Day 1 or even omitted (although it's hard to imagine why you'd come here and not go on). Leaving your packs at camp, continue northeast and almost immediately pass the largely demolished **Refugio Río Sargazo**. Built by a long-since evicted local settler, this shelter awaits rebuilding.

Proceed gently upvalley along the northern bank of the Río Sargazo through *quila* thickets, crossing several small side streams before a log bridge over the Río Sargazo after 35 to 45 minutes. The foot track, valiantly maintained in the face of overgrowth by vigorous bamboo, leads on up past a signpost pointing east towards another fine *alerzal*, the **Catedral de Alerces**, accessible just a short distance off the main track. Continue upstream to reach the lovely **Laguna Fría** 40 to 50 minutes after the Río Sargazo crossing.

Refugio Laguna Fría, in good condition but closed to trekkers at the time of research, is 300m on around the western side of the lake. Despite its name, which means 'Lake Cold', Laguna Fría is fine for swimming and is enclosed by various granite peaks visible only from the middle of the lake.

Return the same way to Campamento Río Sargazo to collect your packs, then reverse Day 1 to reach **Guardería Sargazo**, three to 3½ hours from Laguna Fría.

Other Treks

PARQUE NACIONAL LANÍN
Around Lago Lácar

An easy and convenient three-day route (two days if you get picked up in Pucará) for trekkers based in San Martín de los Andes leads around the southern shore of Lago Lácar. From the trailhead 2km south of Quila Quina (accessible in summer by regular buses and organised tours), a broad path climbs gently southwest to the eastern shore of Lago Escondido, where there is a park-authorised camp site. From a turn-off 1.5km before (east of) Lago Escondido, a trail climbs away north across a pass past Laguna Vizcacha and on down to Lago Lácar. The route then follows the lake's southern shore via Ruca Ñire and Pucará to Hua Hum, from where there are daily tourist boats and buses back to San Martín in summer. Trekkers can also arrange to be picked up in Pucará by one of the organised tours that explore Lago Lácar (including the nearby Termas de Queñi) in summer. Sendas y Bosques' 1:200,000 trekking map *Parque Nacional Lanín* shows the route.

PARQUE NACIONAL VICENTE PÉREZ ROSALES
Volcán Puntiagudo Lookout

Puntiagudo is a spectacular sharp volcanic plug whose distinctive form makes it easily recognisable from many places in the southern Lakes District. A long return day walk from Bahía Escocia (near the southern shore of Lago Rupanco – see Day 3 of the Termas de Callao trek, p139) follows a path south via a steep spur to a lookout point on the prominent volcanic ridge coming down from Puntiagudo's northeastern side. Two Chilean IGM 1:50,000 maps, *Cerro Puntiagudo* (Section H, No 35) and *Volcán Casablanca* (Section H, No 36), cover this trek but do not show its route.

Volcán Osorno to Refugio Picada

This short one- to two-day trek from Petrohué on Lago Todos Los Santos follows a marked trail around the northeastern slopes of Volcán Osorno

(2652m) to **Refugio Picada**. Ascents of Osorno are usually made from the Refugio Teski Club. The Chilean IGM 1:50,000 map *Petrohué* (Section H, No 44) covers this area of the trek but does not show the path.

Ralún to Ensenada Cayutúe

This easy return trek to Ensenada Cayutúe, an isolated southern arm of Lago Todos Los Santos, takes around three days. The route begins at a prominent road turn-off 2km east of the village of Ralún on Seno Reloncaví. The road passes farms before it terminates at a logging camp, from where a path climbs northward through the valley of the Río Reloncaví to the low pass of Portezuelo Cabeza de Vaca. From here, you descend to the lovely Laguna Cayutúe, then continue down the Río Concha to Ensenada Cayutúe. The recommended place to camp is at Laguna Cayutúe, on the other side of the inlet stream. The land fronting Ensenada Cayutúe is private property and camping there is not permitted.

Two Chilean IGM 1:50,000 maps, *Petrohué* (Section H, No 44) and *Cochamó* (Section H, No 53), cover the route. Ralún is about 95km east of Puerto Montt by road and can be reached by daily bus or ferry.

PARQUE NACIONAL NAHUEL HUAPI

The CAB and the staff at the APN Intendencia in Bariloche can advise you on other treks in the Nahuel Huapi area. The local publication *Las Montañas de Bariloche*, by Toncek Arko & Raúl Izaguirre, also contains many other good route suggestions.

Refugio Tronador (Refugio Viejo)

Refugio Tronador was the CAB's first *refugio* on Monte Tronador. Today, this small, arched-stone building (with room for 10 people) is also known as Refugio Viejo (Old Refuge), and has largely been superseded by Refugio Otto Meiling. Standing on a high ridge of the main Cordillera, Refugio Tronador offers superb views of both sides of the Lakes District. Five minutes west of Pampa Linda, the path (signposted 'Cascada de las Nalcas') leads off the road and across the young Río Manso. The route follows the Río Cauquenes up across Paso Vuriloche on the Argentina–Chile frontier to Mallín Chileno, a beautiful alpine meadow, then follows a rocky ridge northwest to the *refugio*, just a few paces inside Argentine territory at 2270m. The best map is the 1:50,000 *Trekking 2* map. The trek is recommended as an overnight trip. If the hut is full, Mallín Chileno is a good place to camp.

Cerro Volcánico

The climb to the 1861m summit of Cerro Volcánico is another excellent long day (or overnight) return trek from Pampa Linda. The route fords the Río Cauquenes where it leaves the path to Refugio Tronador (described previous) and follows a large side stream southward. A gentle climb eastward leads to Laguna La Rosada, from where the trail continues southwest through *mallín* meadows then on steeply through *lenga* forest on to a flat, windy ridge that gradually brings you up to the summit. Cerro Volcánico offers a fine view down to Lago Fonck and Lago Hess in the upper basin of the Río Manso between Cerro Cretón and Cerro Granítico. Use the 1:50,000 *Trekking 2* map.

Refugio Neumeyer

This easy and sheltered area makes a good option for two or three days trekking if the weather looks unstable. From Ruta Nacional 258 on the way to El Bolsón, a turn-off heads southwest up the Arroyo Ñirecó, before entering the broader side valley of the Arroyo Challhuaco. The road leads to Refugio Neumeyer, a well-equipped CAB hut, from where you can do a variety of nice day walks. Where the road crosses the Arroyo Ñirecó a foot track turns off to the right (west). A path continues along the eastern bank of the stream to Refugio Ñirecó, beside a *mallín* at the head of the valley. From here, a more difficult route leads west to a pass and follows the range north before descending via the Arroyo Melgurejo to Lago Gutiérrez. The best map is the 1:50,000 *Trekking 3* map. Refugio Neumeyer is accessible from Bariloche by private vehicle or tour bus (ask at the CAB office); you can walk to the trailhead in half a day.

Pampa Linda to Refugio López

This excellent four- or five-day trek is similar to the Nahuel Huapi Traverse, but much wilder. An old road leads from Pampa Linda across the Río Alerce, then climbs up between Cerro del Viento and Cerro Punta Negra to a minor pass. The descent dips north to Laguna Ilón, with a basic *refugio* on its northern shore. The route continues eastward between Cerro Capitán and Cerro Punta Negra, then descends past Laguna Jujuy to Laguna Callvu (Azul). From Laguna Callvu you go northeast via another gap south of Cerro Cristal, before dropping down to Laguna Lluvú (or CAB) and another basic *refugio*. From here the route descends to the Arroyo Lluvuco and crosses the Bailey Willis range to connect with Day 4 of the Nahuel Huapi Traverse (p148). Another possibility is to continue down the Arroyo Lluvuco to meet an old road leading northeast along the southern shore of Brazo Tristeza to Bahía López on Lago Nahuel Huapi. See the Paso de las Nubes trek (p150) and

the Nahuel Huapi Traverse (p142) for transport details. The 1:50,000 *Trekking 1* and *Trekking 2* maps cover the route.

Around Lago Mascardi

Lago Mascardi has a rough 'U' shape formed by two arms on either side of a peninsula. From the northeastern side of Lago Mascardi a path leads around the lake's western shore, cutting off the peninsula as it climbs to Laguna Llum, a tranquil lake surrounded by rainforest. The route continues over the main ridge north of Cerro General Justo, then drops back down to the lakeside. The route follows this western arm (Brazo Tronador) around to cross a footbridge over the Río Manso 1.5km before meeting the Pampa Linda road. Alternatively, trekkers can make their way up the Arroyo Callvuco (or Azul) to Laguna Callvu (or Azul) to meet the Pampa Linda to Refugio López route described previous. Use the 1:100,000 Refugios, Sendas y Picadas *Parque Nacional Nahuel Huapi* colour map. This is a two-day trek with a camp at Laguna Llum. The most reliable access is by daily buses between Pampa Linda (see Paso de las Nubes, p150) and Bariloche.

ASCENT OF VOLCÁN OSORNO (CHILE)

One of the great landmarks of the southern Chilean Lakes District, the perfect white cone of Volcán Osorno attracts considerable attention from serious mountaineers. Volcán Osorno's last major eruption occurred in 1835, and released a series of catastrophic floods and lahars (mud avalanches). The volcano has been more or less dormant since then, allowing extensive glaciers to re-accumulate around its upper slopes.

The climb to the summit, which takes two or three days, is normally undertaken from the *refugio* at 1180m on the western slopes of Volcán Osorno (outside Parque Nacional Vicente Pérez Rosales). At all times of the year crampons and an ice axe are required, and inexperienced climbers are strongly urged to make the ascent of the volcano with a professional local mountain guide.

A service road leads off the main Puerto Octay–Puerto Varas road, 2km north of Ensenada on the eastern shores of Lago Llanquihue, up to Refugio Los Pumas. The Chilean IGM 1:50,000 map *Las Cascadas* (Section H, No 43) covers the west side of Volcán Osorno and most of the ascent route. The adjoining map *Petrohué* (Section H, No 44) is also very useful.

RESERVA NACIONAL LLANQUIHUE (CHILE)

The roughly 300-sq-km Reserva Nacional Llanquihue forms a narrow band of wilderness stretching southeast from the southeastern corner of Lago Llanquihue along the north side of Lago Chapo almost as far as Seno Reloncaví. The 2015m Volcán Calbuco, in the north of the reserve, can be climbed in a two-day return trek from the Guardería Chapo, which is at the northern end of Parque Nacional Alerce Andino. The trek follows a path up the Río Blanco to a rustic Conaf *refugio* on the volcano's southern side. From here experienced climbers can tackle Volcán Calbuco, whose flat-topped summit is capped by a thick layer of glacial ice. The 1:50,000 Chilean IGM map *Correntoso* (Section H, No 52) covers the trek.

PARQUE NACIONAL ALERCE ANDINO
Lago Triángulo
Lago Triángulo lies in a deep fjord-like trough fronted by massive smooth granite walls in the southern (Chaica) sector of Parque Nacional Alerce Andino. It can be visited in an easy three-hour return trek through the rainforest from the car park at Lago Chaiquenes. The path leads briefly around the northern shore of Lago Chaiquenes, then follows the east bank of the Río Triángulo northward to the southern end of Lago Triángulo. Lago Chaiquenes is 17km by road from Lenca, a scattered village on Seno Reloncaví; there is a Conaf *guardería* 4km before Lago Chaiquenes. Lenca is on the Carretera Austral, and can be reached from Puerto Montt by several daily buses. There is no public transport to Lago

Chaiquenes, which makes a pleasant but long 4½-hour uphill walk from Lenca. The 1:50,000 Chilean IGM map *Lenca* (Section H, No 61) covers the route.

PARQUE NACIONAL CHILOÉ (CHILE)
The 430-sq-km Parque Nacional Chiloé, on the windswept western side of the large island of Chiloé, offers two excellent treks with wonderful coastal scenery of sandy beaches and estuarine lagoons set before a backdrop of densely forested hills. Due to the mild coastal climate, these treks can be undertaken at virtually any time apart from winter (June to September).

A two-day return trek leaves from the village of Chepu, in the park's northern sector, accessible by daily bus from Ancud. A good foot track can be followed south to a Conaf *guardería* and *refugio* by the Río Lar, where seal colonies inhabit the numerous rocky islets just offshore. The Chilean IGM 1:50,000 map *Chepu* (Section H, No 75) covers this route.

A more popular three-day return trek leads from the village of Cucao in the park's southern sector. Cucao is accessible by up to six daily buses from Castro. The route leads along lovely sandy beaches, past isolated farmlets and through wet rainforests as far as the Río Anay (which can be crossed to reach a wild surf beach). Two newly renovated Conaf *refugios*, at the Río Cole Cole and at the Río Anay, cost around US$10 per night.

Use two 1:50,000 Chilean IGM maps: *Río Anay* (Section H, No 86) and *Cucao* (Section H, No 95).

Central Patagonia

The Central Patagonian Andes are remote, often extremely wet and have considerable accessibility problems. Fewer roads (which are generally smaller and not often travelled) penetrate the Cordillera of central Patagonia and, especially on the Chilean side, trekking is limited by the lack of paths and by dense, impenetrable temperate rainforest. Despite this, trekkers adventurous enough to visit this thinly settled region will be rewarded for their perseverance by its wild and untamed nature.

GATEWAYS
Esquel (Argentina)

The dusty and windswept town of Esquel lies at the edge of the dry Patagonian *pampa*, just off Ruta Nacional 40 in northern Chubut. The local **tourist office** (☎ 02945-451927; W www.esquel.gov.ar; cnr Alvear & Sarmiento) is very efficient. The **Asociación de Guías de Montaña** (☎ 02945-450653; Ameghino 98) organises mountain guides and can give advice on trekking and climbing in the area.

Places to Stay & Eat Accommodation options include **El Hogar del Mochilero** (☎ 02945-452166; Roca 1028; camping per person US$3, dorm beds US$5) and the HI-affiliated **Parador Lago Verde** (☎ 02945-452251; e lagoverd@hostels.org.ar; Volta 1081; rooms per person US$15), which has nice rooms. **Residencial El Cisne** (☎ 02945-452256; Chacabuco 778; singles/doubles US$13/20) offers excellent rooms and has a communal kitchen. The three-star **Hotel Sol del Sur** (☎ 02945-452189; 9 de Julio 1086; singles/doubles US$23/46) has a buffet breakfast included in its rates.

La Trochita (☎ 02945-451484; 25 de Mayo 633) serves *parrilla* (mixed grills) and pasta, while **Don Pipo** (☎ 02945-453458; Fontana 649) has good pizzas.

Getting There & Away You can fly most days to Buenos Aires (from US$140) with

Cascading stream in Parque Pumalín, the world's first major private national park

- Tracing towering trunks of ancient alerces in Parque Pumalín (p167)

- Ambling through beautiful highland *lenga* forest on the way to Refugio Hielo Azul in the Comarca Andina (p171)

- Camping among *arrayán* trees beside Playa Blanca on Lago Futalaufquen in Parque Nacional Los Alerces (p177)

- Marvelling at the rock columns and turrets of Cerro Castillo from the upper Valle Parada in Reserva Nacional Cerro Castillo (p182)

Austral (☎ 02945-453413; Fontana 406). **LADE** (☎ 02945-452124; Alvear 1085) flies up to three times weekly to Bariloche (US$20), Neuquén (US$52), El Bolsón (US$18) and San Martín de los Andes (US$31).

From the **bus terminal** (Alvear), between Brun and Justo, there are daily buses to all major regional destinations, including

BRENT WINEBRENNER

CENTRAL PATAGONIA

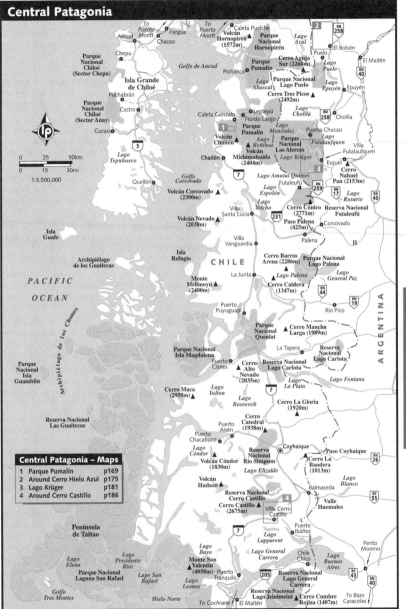

Central Patagonia

To Puerto Montt
Pargua
Ancud
Chacao
To Puerto Montt
Caleta Puelche
Volcán Hornopirén (1572m)
Parque Nacional Hornopirén
Lago Azul
RN 258
El Bolsón
Chepu
Golfo de Ancud
Pichanco
Parque Pumalín
Cerro Aguja Sur (2268m)
Puelo
Lago Puelo
El Maitén
Parque Nacional Chiloé (Sector Chepu)
Isla Grande de Chiloé
Puchabrán
Lago Abascal
Parque Nacional Lago Puelo
Lago Epuyén
RN 40
Epuyén
Parque Nacional Chiloé (Sector Anay)
Castro
Caleta Gonzalo
Leptepú
Fiordo Largo
Cerro Tres Picos (2492m)
Lago Cholila
RN 258
Cholila
Cucao
Parque Pumalín
Volcán Chaitén
Lago Menéndez
Puerto Chucao
Lago Futalaufquen
Villa Futalaufquen
5
Volcán Reñihue
Parque Nacional Los Alerces
Esquel
Cerro Nahuel Pan (2153m)
Lago Tepuhueco
Chaitén
Volcán Michimahuida (2404m)
Lago Krüger
Quellón
Golfo Corcovado
7
Lago Amutui Quimei
Futaleufú
RN 259
RN 17
Lago Rosario
RN 40
Volcán Corcovado (2300m)
Villa Santa Lucía
Lago Espolón
Cerro Cónico (2771m)
Reserva Nacional Futaleufú
Volcán Nevado (2038m)
231
Lago Yelcho
Paso Palena (425m)
Corcovado
Isla Guafo
Villa Vanguardia
Palena
CHILE
Cerro Barros Arena (2286m)
Parque Nacional Lago Palena
Isla Refugio
La Junta
Lago Palena
Lago General Paz
Archipiélago de los Guaitecas
Monte Melimoyú (2400m)
Cerro Caldera (1347m)
RN 44
PACIFIC OCEAN
Puerto Puyuguapi
RN 19
Río Pico
Parque Nacional Queulat
Cerro Mancha Larga (1989m)
ARGENTINA
Parque Nacional Isla Magdalena
Puerto Cisnes
Cerro Alto Nevado (2035m)
La Tapera
Reserva Nacional Lago Carlota
Reserva Nacional Lago Carlota
Parque Nacional Isla Guamblin
Cerro Maca (2958m)
Lago Yulton
Lago Roosevelt
7
Lago La Plata
Lago Fontana
Reserva Nacional Las Guaitecas
Cerro La Gloria (1920m)
Cerro Catedral (1938m)
Puerto Aisén
Puerto Chacabuco
Coyhaique
Paso Coyhaique
RN 26
Lago Cóndor
Reserva Nacional Río Simpson
Cerro La Bandera (1013m)
Volcán Cóndor (1830m)
Lago Elizalde
Lago Blanco
Volcán Hudson
Balmaceda
RP 55
Reserva Nacional Cerro Castillo
Cerro Castillo (2675m)
Villa Cerro Castillo
Valle Huemules
Península de Taitao
7
Puerto Ibáñez
Perito Moreno
Lago Bayo
Lago Lapparent
Lago Presidente Ríos
Lago General Carrera
Chile Chico
Lago Buenos Aires
RP 43
Lago Elena
Monte San Valentín (4058m)
Puerto Tranquilo
205
Reserva Nacional Lago General Carrera
RN 40
Parque Nacional Laguna San Rafael
Lago San Rafael
Lago Leones
Reserva Nacional Lago Jeinimeini
Cerro Cumbre Rojiza (1407m)
To Bajo Caracoles
Golfo Tres Montes
Hielo Norte
To Cochrane
El Maitén

0   25   50km
0   15   30mi
1:3,500,000

2
1
3
4

Central Patagonia – Maps

1	Parque Pumalín	p169
2	Around Cerro Hielo Azul	p175
3	Lago Krüger	p181
4	Around Cerro Castillo	p186

Bariloche (US$11, 4½ hours), Neuquén (US$30, 10 hours) and Buenos Aires (US$38, 20 hours). **Empresa Codao del Sur** *(☎ 02945-455222; Ameghino)* runs buses twice weekly to Futaleufú, in Chile (US$4, two hours). **Andesmar** *(☎ 02945-450143; w www.andesmar.com.ar)* goes daily to Osorno (US$26) and Santiago (US$40) in Chile.

Coyhaique (Chile)

Coyhaique sits in a sheltered valley behind ranges to the west. Coyhaique (coy-**aye**-kay; meaning 'landscape of lakes' in Tehuelche) marks the line of climatic transition between the moister western Patagonia and the drier eastern steppes. The mountains surrounding the city, which reach altitudes of almost 2000m, are green, forested and often snowcapped to the west, but become dry and barren a short distance to the east. Day treks in the scenic Reserva Nacional Coyhaique, 5km north of town, are worthwhile doing.

Information For general tourist information, visit **Sernatur** *(Servicio Nacional de Turismo; ☎ 067-240290; e infoaysen@sernatur.cl; Bulnes 35; open 8.30am-9pm Mon-Fri, 11am-8pm Sat & Sun in summer)*, just off the Plaza de Armas. Also visit the city website (Spanish-language) at w www.coyhaique.cl. The regional **Conaf office** *(Corporación Nacional Forestal; ☎/fax 067-231065, 232599; Ogana 1060)* is on the southern road out of town. The **Sodimac** *(☎ 067-231576; Baquedano 421)* hardware store sells white gasoline *(bencina blanca)* and some basic outdoor gear.

Places to Stay & Eat Accommodation options in Coyhaique include **Hospedaje Nati** *(☎ 067-231047; Simpson 417; rooms per person US$5)*. **Hostal Las Salamandras** *(☎ 067-211865; w www.salamandras.cl; Camino Teniente Vidal; dorm beds US$10, doubles with private bathroom US$23)* includes breakfast in its rate and is 3km from town on the road out to Coyhaique airport. **Residencial Carrera** *(☎ 067-236505; 12 de Octubre 520; rooms per person US$8)* and **Hospedaje Patagonia** *(☎ 067-231917; Freire*

119; rooms per person US$8) offer rooms with breakfast. **Hostal Bon** *(☎ 067-231189; Ignacio Serrano 91; rooms per person US$20)* charges a bit more but the rooms are more comfortable.

Cafetería Alemana *(☎ 067-231731; Condell 199)* serves cakes and espresso coffee. **Café Ricer** *(☎ 067-231622; Horn 48)*, just off the Plaza de Armas, serves excellent fish, steak and pasta dishes.

Getting There & Away Most buses leave from the **Terminal de Buses** *(☎ 067-211460)* at the bottom of Magallanes. Both **Buses Pudú** *(☎ 067-231008; 21 de Mayo 1231)* and **Buses Acuario 13** *(☎ 067-240990; Terminal de Buses)* run three or four weekly buses to/from Cochrane. **Transporte Don Carlos** *(☎ 067-231981; Subteniente Cruz 63)* runs buses to/from Puerto Aisén (US$2.50, eight times daily) and Cochrane (US$12, twice weekly). **Buses Daniela** *(☎ 067-231701; Baquedano 1122)* has four weekly buses running to/from Chaitén (US$22, 12 hours) and also runs eight buses daily to Puerto Aisén.

Navimag *(☎ 067-223306; Presidente Ibáñez 347; w www.navimag.cl)* and **Transmarchilay** *(☎ 067-231971; 21 de Mayo 417; w www.transmarchilay.com)* both run twice-weekly ferry services between Puerto Chacabuco (82km west of Coyhaique, near Puerto Aisén) and Puerto Montt (around US$55, 24 hours).

Transporte Don Carlos flies from Coyhaique to Chile Chico (US$30) almost daily, and to Villa O'Higgins (US$85) via Cochrane (US$60) on Monday and Thursday, returning the same day. **Aerohein** *(w www.aerohein.cl)* offers light-aircraft charters which can be useful if there are no seats available on other scheduled flights. Larger airlines use the airport at Balmaceda, 48km southeast of Coyhaique. From Balmaceda, **LanChile** *(☎ 067-231188; Moraleda 402)* has several flights daily to/from Puerto Montt (US$72) and Santiago (US$132), but there is only one flight weekly in each direction to/from Punta Arenas. **Sky Airlines** *(☎ 600-6002828)* flies several times weekly for similar fares.

Parque Pumalín

Chile's approximately 3450-sq-km Parque Pumalín extends some 150km south from the 42nd parallel (42°S) almost as far as Chaitén, and from the coast right to the Argentine border. Here, the wild, narrow strip of Chilean mainland is so broken up by fjords, steep-sided sounds and rugged rain-drenched mountains that no road has ever been built through it – this section of the Carretera Austral (Southern Highway) was considered simply too difficult and expensive to construct.

Parque Pumalín is the world's first and largest nongovernment 'national' park, having been established entirely by private land purchases (see the boxed text 'The Pumalín Story'). Much of the park's visitor infrastructure, including camping grounds, back-country camp sites and (especially longer-distance) trails, is being developed. Most of this is in Parque Pumalín's more accessible southern sector. Only several very short day treks have been featured in this edition (although we hope to give Parque Pumalín more extensive coverage in future editions).

The Pumalín Story

In 1990, Douglas Tompkins (cofounder of both The North Face outdoor-gear and Esprit clothing companies) bought a 170-sq-km ranch near Caleta Gonzalo on Fiordo Reñihue, north of Chaitén. Discreetly, Tompkins and his wife and business partner, Kristine Tompkins McDivitt, continued to buy up adjacent properties (largely through the US-based Conservation Land Trust), eventually acquiring over 3000 sq km of land in two large but separate northern and southern sections.

As their intention to establish a major national park became known, however, opposition to the project escalated. Chilean right-wing politicians, the military and members of the press declared this 'foreign-controlled entity' to be a danger to national sovereignty as it would effectively 'cut Chile in two'. Tompkins himself was savagely attacked for his 'atheistic' philosophy of Deep Ecology (which seeks to reinvent modern society based on respect for natural ecosystems). In a country where fishing, mining, logging and hydroelectricity generation are some of the most important regional industries, there was also – quite understandably – concern that the park would hinder economic development. Opponents were successful in blocking Tompkins' acquisition of a crucial central 300-sq-km parcel that would have created a contiguous (ie, unbroken) park stretching along the entire coast.

Despite this setback, Parque Pumalín has now become firmly established, with its transfer to a new Chilean-based park authority, the Fundación Pumalín (Pumalín Foundation). The park operates in a similar (if rather less bureaucratic) way to Corporación Nacional Forestal (Conaf)–administered national parks, with a system of local rangers. The foundation is developing a far-reaching management plan (stretching as far as 1000 years into the future!), according to which Parque Pumalín's primary function will be as a biosphere reserve. Scientific research is also a major priority. Although modest ecotourism projects and trekking trails are under construction or planned, most of the park is to remain inaccessible even to trekkers.

Scepticism among the local population has waned as employment opportunities unfold. Sustainable industries such as organic fish farming, horticulture, honey production and wool handicrafts are also being set up.

Parque Pumalín is an exciting project that conservationists all over the world are watching closely. Nonprofit organisations such as the World Land Trust and the Ecology Fund have copied the idea by acquiring land in parts of Africa and the Amazon basin to create large nature reserves. Meanwhile, Tompkins and McDivitt continue their capital-for-conservation endeavour through the Patagonia Land Trust, which has already purchased more than 1000 sq km of ecologically significant land across the border in Argentina.

CENTRAL PATAGONIA

These are three short but rewarding treks, which all begin quite close together from the Carretera Austral and can be done either individually, together over a long day, or over two days by camping at Camping Cascadas Escondidas or Laguna Tronador.

NATURAL HISTORY

Parque Pumalín has an extremely wet, but relatively mild, climate that nourishes some of the richest old-growth rainforests found anywhere in the southern Andes. All three *coigüe* (evergreen southern beech) species are present, and often dominate the forest canopy along with moisture-loving *arrayán*, *avellano*, *luma*, *ulmo* and *tineo*. *Canelo*, a member of the magnolia family that has distinctive white, sweet-scented flowers, and the coniferous Guaitecas cypress *(ciprés de las Guaitecas)* thrive near the coast. In places alerce forms small clustered stands (called *alerzales*) of ancient giant trees up to 4m in diameter. The *chupallita*, which belongs to the pineapple family, lashes its tiny roots onto the upper branches of rainforest trees. A native lizard known as the *largartija verde* lives in the shelter of the *chupallita*'s long saw-like leaves camouflaged by its scaly green skin. The vigorous *nalca* (or *pangue*) grows along streams, producing huge leaves at the end of a succulent thorny stem. The amphibious *coipo* inhabits the lower rivers.

More than 100 bird species inhabit Parque Pumalín (sometimes seasonally), including many species of aquatic ducks and geese and marine birds such as native herons.

PLANNING
Maps

The Chilean Instituto Geográfico Militar's (IGM) 1:50,000 *Fiordo Reñihue* (Section H, No 101) covers the treks but does not show trails (or even the Carretera Austral).

Information Sources

Parque Pumalín has **offices** in Puerto Montt (☎ 065-250079; *Buín 356*) and in Chaitén (p168). The park website is at **w** www.pumalinpark.org.

Permits & Regulations

Permits are not required to visit Parque Pumalín and there is no entry fee. Fires are prohibited outside camping grounds – they are *not* permitted in the back country. Camping is not permitted in the back country apart from at park-designated sites.

ACCESS TOWNS
Chaitén (Chile)

The tiny, unpretentious port town of Chaitén lies to the south of Parque Pumalín. The park's local **information centre** (☎ 065-731341; **e** pumalinchaiten@surnet.cl; O'Higgins 62) can advise visitors to the park. The **tourist office** (☎ 065-731310), on the esplanade at the end of Todesco, is open daily in summer.

Places to Stay & Eat Accommodation options in Chaitén include **Camping Los Arrayanes** (☎ 065-218202; *camping per person US$3*), 4km north of town. **Hospedaje Don Carlos** (☎ 065-731287; *Almirante Riveros 53; rooms per person US$7*) offers basic rooms with breakfast included. The Pumalín-affiliated **Hostal Puma Verde** (☎ 065-731184, 250079; **e** pumaverde@telsur.cl; O'Higgins 54; singles/doubles US$15/30) is next door to the park administration office. **Hotel Schilling** (☎ 065-731295; Corcovado 230; singles/doubles US$20/40, doubles with bathroom US$50) has a range of rooms available.

Canasto de Agua (☎ 065-731550; Prat 65) serves fine dishes (especially fish).

Getting There & Away Opposite the Parque Pumalín office, **Chaitur** (☎ 065-731429; **e** nchaitur@hotmail.com; Diego Portales 350) sells bus tickets and runs tours of Parque Pumalín as far as Caleta Gonzalo (p169). Buses run daily to Futaleufú (US$8, three hours) and further south along the Carretera Austral to Coyhaique (US$22, 12 hours).

In summer, **Transmarchilay** (☎ 065-270420; **w** www.transmarchilay.com) runs a ferry several times weekly between Chaitén and Quellón (US$13, five hours) on Chiloé.

Throughout the year, **Navimag** (☎ 065-253318; **w** www.navimag.cl) sails to/from

CENTRAL PATAGONIA

Puerto Montt and Chaitén several times weekly (US$19, 10 hours), and **Catamaranes del Sur** (☎ 065-482308; **w** www.catamaranesdelsur.cl) runs a faster twice-weekly catamaran service each way (US$26, four hours).

In Puerto Montt several small airlines – **Aeromet** (☎ 065-299400; Antonio Varas 215), **Aerochaitén** (☎ 065-253219; Quillota 127) and **Aerosur** (☎ 065-252523; **e** aerosur@telsur.cl; Serena 149) – have at least weekly flights to/from Chaitén (US$50).

Caleta Gonzalo (Chile)

This is a tiny ecotourism village on a scenic cove of Fiordo Reñihue, 60km north of Chaitén, where the Carretera Austral terminates. Parque Pumalín has an information centre and shop here. There are short nature trails and an organic farm nearby.

Places to Stay & Eat If you want a roof over your head, **Cabañas Caleta Gonzalo** (reservations **e** reservascaletagonzalo@surnet.cl) are seven comfortable, well-equipped cabins – without kitchen, however. Prices are US$47 for one person and go up to US$126 for five people in summer, or US$43 and US$114 in low season (1 March to 31 November). There are also sites at **Camping Caleta Gonzalo** (camping per site US$9). **Caleta Gonzalo Café** offers excellent meals and coffee.

Getting There & Away During January and February, **Navimag** (☎ 065-270420; **w** www.navimag.cl) operates a daily ferry service between Caleta Gonzalo and Hornopirén (US$13, five hours). **Buses Fierro** (☎ 065-253022) has bus connections between Hornopirén and Puerto Montt. **B&V Tours** (☎ 065-731390; Libertad 442) runs buses from Chaitén to Caleta Gonzalo (US$4, 1½ hours) at 9am on Monday, Wednesday and Friday, returning to Chaitén at 11am.

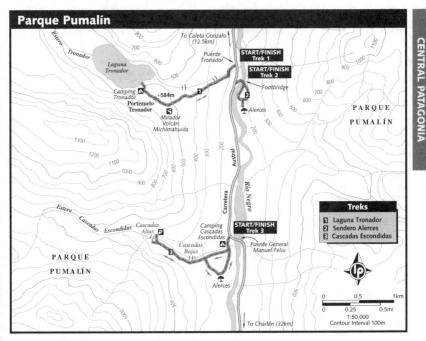

Parque Pumalín

Treks
1 Laguna Tronador
2 Sendero Alerces
3 Cascadas Escondidas

0   0.5   1km
0   0.25   0.5mi
1:50,000
Contour Interval 100m

To Caleta Gonzalo (12.5km)

To Chaitén (32km)

CENTRAL PATAGONIA

Laguna Tronador

Duration	2½–3½ hours
Distance	5km
Difficulty	easy–moderate
Start/Finish	Puente Tronador
Nearest Towns	Chaitén (p168)
	Caleta Gonzalo (p169)
Transport	bus or tour

Summary An energetic up-and-down trek (415m ascent/descent) to a jewel of a lake among luxuriant rainforest.

GETTING TO/FROM THE TREK

The trek begins and ends at the trailhead at Puente Tronador, a bridge on the Carretera Austral, 13km south of Caleta Gonzalo (35km north of Chaitén). There is limited parking space nearby.

Chaitur (see Getting There & Away for Chaitén, p168) does tours of Parque Pumalín (US$10), which usually stop at one or more of the trailheads for these treks. A charter costs around US$45 return; contact **Señora Avelina** (☎ 065-731745, 09-6721065) for more details.

THE TREK (see map p169)

Follow a stepped boardwalk up past cascades plunging into pools in the Estero Tronador. Soon you'll cross the stream on a suspension bridge over a spectacular little gorge. The well-routed track climbs steeply through fern forest of *canelo* over mossy roots, under trunks and up short ladders in places. Climb away left to a minor ridge top, then head rightward through stands of *mañio* and fragrant *tepa* to cross a small stream in a tiny open area.

Another steep climb brings you up to the **Mirador Volcán Michimahuida**, one to 1½ hours from Puente Tronador. From here, the volcano's domed snowy expanse is visible to the southeast. The route continues up gently past superb thick-trunked alerces (one is 1.3m in diameter) through the **Portezuelo Tronador**, a gap (around 545m) to the south of Point 585m.

Rest a while on the log benches here before you drop steeply down northwest to reach a tiny beach at the southern shore of **Laguna Tronador** (around 450m) after 15 to 20 minutes. The *huala*, or great grebe, is sometimes spotted on this beautiful lake, which is surrounded by almost sheer-sided ridges blanketed by rainforest. Hot weather, and – possibly – bothersome biting *tábanos* (horseflies), will quickly tempt you to take a cool dip in the deep water. **Camping Tronador**, about 50m around to the left, has two sites with tables and a pit toilet. Campfires are strictly prohibited.

Return via the same route.

Sendero Alerces

Duration	30–40 minutes
Distance	1.1km
Difficulty	easy
Start/Finish	Carretera Austral, 200m south of Puente Tronador
Nearest Towns	Chaitén (p168)
	Caleta Gonzalo (p169)
Transport	bus or tour

Summary A brief return trek to stands of glorious old alerces.

GETTING TO/FROM THE TREK

The trek starts 200m south of Puente Tronador (see Getting to/from the Trek for Laguna Tronador). There is limited parking space near the trailhead.

THE TREK (see map p169)

This short trek goes to what is probably the closest *alerzal* (stand of alerces) to any roadway – mainly because the road was built so recently. The path leads leftward from the road across a footbridge over the Río Negro, then cuts downstream to a first stand of tall alerces. Sadly, one of these superb trees has been partially stripped of its bark (used in an old method of caulking boats) and is unlikely to survive.

Continue on to a particularly enormous alerce, whose gently tapering trunk has a diameter of almost 4m at the base. A short way on, a little side trail leads over the trunks of long-fallen alerces to another small stand. When you're through marvelling at these wondrous trees, follow the trail around left, back over the footbridge and return to the Carretera Austral.

Cascadas Escondidas

Duration	1½–2 hours
Distance	3.5km
Difficulty	easy
Start/Finish	Camping Cascadas Escondidas
Nearest Towns	Chaitén (p168)
	Caleta Gonzalo (p169)
Transport	bus or tour

Summary Another short rainforest trek up to several 'hidden cascades' spouting into green rock pools.

NEAREST TOWNS & FACILITIES
See Chaitén (p168) and Caleta Gonzalo (p169).

Camping Cascadas Escondidas
This park-run **camping ground** (camping per site US$8.50) is at the end of a short access road, just north of the Puente General Manuel Feliu, a road bridge 14.5km south of Caleta Gonzalo (33.5km north of Chaitén). It has five excellent sites with shelters and picnic tables; there are toilets with cold showers.

GETTING TO/FROM THE TREK
The trek leaves directly from Camping Cascadas Escondidas. See also Getting to/from the Trek for Laguna Tronador).

THE TREK (see map p169)
Take the signposted track (opposite the camping ground toilet block) and cross the Estero Cascadas Escondidas on a footbridge. The trail climbs unobtrusively through the ferny, moss-draped forest to the left of the stream to a right turn-off. This leads down right via a ladder to a spectacular viewing platform at the base of the **Cascadas Bajas**, where the stream spouts through a crack in the rock and tumbles 25m down into a deep pool.

Climb on around past sitting benches above the waterfall to a left turn-off (which loops down for 15 to 20 minutes through stands of medium-sized alerces and back to the camping ground) and continue right. The gradient eases as you continue smoothly through thickets of *quila* (bamboo) and fragrant *tepa* forest to reach another right turn-off. This leads down across the stream and climbs briefly to the **Mirador Cascadas Altas**, a tiny lookout 'box' above a second waterfall that spills into a green, mossy pool. The main trail follows numerous ladders up until it ends at a final cascade that splashes over rocks into a smaller pool.

Return the same way (but via the alerces loop this time) to the camping ground.

Comarca Andina

The Argentine region known as the Comarca Andina del Paralelo 42 straddles the mountainous border with Chile along the 42nd parallel (42°S), which passes several kilometres south of El Bolsón and delimits Río Negro from Chubut. The Comarca Andina forms a band of rugged ranges with summits that easily top 2000m, covered by névés and glaciers, and long lateral canyons that descend eastwards to the steppes.

NATURAL HISTORY
Tall evergreen forest dominated by *coigüe* (spelt *coihue* in Argentina) grows in the moister valleys of the Comarca Andina, becoming increasingly species-rich the closer it gets to the Chilean frontier. Here, large pockets of typical Valdivian rainforest species such as *avellano*, *canelo*, *luma* and giant alerces grow.

The ranges' drier eastern slopes are covered by fragrant stands of Cordilleran cypress, or *ciprés de la cordillera*, and the understorey in these parts consists largely of thickets dominated by scrubby species such as *retama* and the leafless *crucero*, whose countless green stalky branchlets end in sharp spines.

Beautiful open deciduous forests of *lenga* mixed with *ñirre* (spelt *ñire* in Argentina) are found above 1100m. Despite the apparent biological paucity of these forests, the understorey harbours species such as *tihuén* (an alpine species of *quila*) and *traro*, a bush with clusters of large drooping dog-ear leaves at the ends of its branches. The *lenga* forest also provides an ideal habitat for the Patagonian red fox (usually called *zorro colorado* in Argentina), and Geoffroy's cat (*gato montés*), a shy 'mountain cat' that measures up to 1m from head to tail.

Two adaptable bird species, the small silvery-grey diuca-finch *(diuca)* and the rufous-collared sparrow, or *chinchol*, also dwell in these highland forests. The austral pygmy owl, or *chuncho*, makes up for its small size by its audacious (and occasionally aggressive) temperament. Larger birds of prey are the Andean condor and the black-chested buzzard-eagle, or *águila mora.*

CLIMATE
Visitors arriving from the nearby Argentine Lakes District will notice the dry, crisp continental climate. The high range of the Cordón Nevado acts as a surprisingly effective climatic barrier, filtering out much of the Pacific moisture carried by the westerly winds. Except for these loftier peaks close to the frontier, where rain and snowfall may exceed 3000mm annually, precipitation levels are relatively modest. Beyond the thin strip of mountains along the Cordillera, annual precipitation drops dramatically – in the valley of El Bolsón, to as little as 700mm. Summer temperatures are warm, but the frequent winds tend to prevent oppressively hot weather. In winter snow covers all areas above 800m.

INFORMATION
Books
Montañas de la Comarca, by Gabriel Bevacqua, is a Spanish-language guidebook that describes the best treks in the region.

ACCESS TOWN
El Bolsón (Argentina)
El Bolsón is situated in the southwest corner of Río Negro province in the broad basin of the Río Quemquemtreu between two high ranges (hence its Argentine Spanish name, meaning 'handbag'). As the self-appointed 'capital' of the Comarca Andina region, this small town offers a laid-back atmosphere ideal for relaxing after a hard week's trekking in the surrounding ranges.

Information El Bolsón's **tourist office** (☎ 02944-492604; e *sec_turismo@elbolson .com; cnr San Martín & Roca)* is near Plaza Pagano, the town's central park. The **Club Andino Piltriquitrón** *(CAP; ☎ 02944-492600; cnr Roca & Sarmiento; open 9am-noon & 8pm-9pm daily in summer),* almost directly west of the tourist office, operates a number of the *refugios* (huts) in the surrounding mountains.

Casa Cintia *(cnr Belgrano & San Martín)* and the **Patagonia Fly Shop** *(☎ 02944-1569 8595; San Martín 2087)* sell a small range of outdoor and fishing gear, as well as fishing licences.

Places to Stay & Eat About 1km south of the town centre by the Río Quemquemtreu is **Campamento Ecológico** *(☎ 02944-492954; e juliomus@hotmail.com; camping per person US$5, dorm beds US$7).* The homy, HI-affiliated **El Pueblito Albergue** *(☎/fax 02944-493560; e elpueblitobolson@ elbolson.com; dorm beds from US$6)* is 4km north of town, also by the Río Quemquemtreu.

Hospedaje Luz de Luna *(☎ 02944-491908; Dorrego; rooms per person US$8)* is near the river, and its rates include breakfast.

The Austrian-owned **Hostería Steiner** *(☎ 02944-492224; San Martín 670; rooms with bathroom US$15)* is at the southern edge of town.

La Tosca *(☎ 02944-493669; cnr Roca & Moreno)* serves café fare. **La Cocina** *(☎ 02944-491453; Sarmiento 2434)* is recommended for inexpensive grills.

Getting There & Away The following companies all have at least daily buses to Bariloche (around US$7, two hours): **Andesmar** *(☎ 02944-492178; cnr Belgrano & Perito Moreno),* **Via Bariloche** *(☎ 02944-491676; Roca 357),* **Don Otto** *(☎ 02944-*

493910; cnr Belgrano & Güemes) and **Charter SRL** *(☎ 02944-492333; cnr Sarmiento & Roca).* Via Bariloche and **Transportes Esquel** *(☎ 02945-453529; Alsina 1632, Esquel)* go to Esquel.

LADE *(☎ 02944-492206; San Martín),* between José Hernández and Azcona, has weekly flights to/from Bariloche (US$20), Neuquén (US$43) and Esquel (US$18).

Fran's Remises *(☎ 02944-493041; San Martín 2538)* has competitive taxi fares to trailheads.

Around Cerro Hielo Azul

Duration	3 days
Distance	33.5km
Difficulty	moderate
Start	Camping Hue Nain (p173)
Finish	Warton
Nearest Town	El Bolsón (p172)
Transport	bus or taxi

Summary An excellent trek linking two of the Comarca Andina's loveliest alpine valleys in the ranges visible from El Bolsón.

This route takes you into the cirque at the headwaters of the Río Teno, which is surrounded by craggy ridges with small glaciers, then leads into the Cajón del Azul, a deep gorge of the wild upper Río Azul. The trek includes a recommended day side trip, but it can also be further lengthened by several days by continuing up the Río Azul from the Refugio Cajón del Azul.

The trails are well marked (so route-finding should not be a problem). The trek is much easier in the direction described (ie, south to north).

PLANNING
When to Trek
The trek can normally be done from mid-November until late April. January and February can be hot and the *refugios* can be crowded, but – unlike in areas with moister climates to the north and on the other side of the Cordillera – there are few or no *tábanos* then.

What to Bring
There are two *refugios* on this trek, so it can be done without a tent – although this is not advisable in January, when the *refugios* are often full. Bring your own sleeping bag. Simple meals are available, as well as luxuries such as chocolate and beer.

Some sections of the route are scrubby or dusty, and wearing protective gaiters, or at least long trousers, will make your trek more comfortable.

Maps
Although it does not show the trekking route itself, the Argentine IGM's 1:100,000 map *El Bolsón* (Río Negro, No 4172-34) is relatively new and covers the area of the trek.

Permits & Regulations
Permits are not necessary for this trek, but camping is not permitted apart from at designated areas near the *refugios*. (If you *do* make an illicit camp, at least refrain from lighting a fire.) The route crosses private property in places, where trekkers should be particularly respectful.

NEAREST TOWN & FACILITIES
See El Bolsón (p172).

Camping Hue Nain
This camping ground *(☎ 02944-1563 8490; camping per person about US$3; open mid-Dec–early Mar)* at the start of Day 1 has sites with picnic tables right beside the Río Azul. There are hot showers and a small store.

There is no public transport to Camping Hue Nain, but it can be reached on foot from El Bolsón in about 2½ hours by first trekking west along Calle Azcuénaga and across the Río Quemquemtreu bridge. Turn right and follow the curving road up to a fork above the Río Azul, about 2.2km from town. Here, go right again and continue 4.8km to the driveway (on the left) leading down to Hue Nain. This turn-off is normally signposted only when the camping ground is open. If you come before or after the main tourist season, watch for the obvious gate and farmhouse – or ask a local. A *remís* (taxi) from El Bolsón costs around US$8.

GETTING TO/FROM THE TREK

The trek begins at Camping Hue Nain (p173). It finishes at the junction near Warton (also spelt Wharton), a farmstead 10km farther north along the Río Azul road. There is no public transport from this point either (although there is a store, from where you can call a taxi), but trekkers can continue on foot 1.4km east along the road to the intersection with the Mallín Ahogado road. From here, up to four buses daily run in a clockwise direction only around the 37km circuit road via Mallín Ahogado. For information call **La Golondrina** (☎ 02944-492557).

The friendly locals often pick up hitch-hikers, so you could also try thumbing a ride there and back, although the roads are usually very dusty.

THE TREK
Day 1: Camping Hue Nain to Refugio Hielo Azul

3¾–5¼ hours, 11.5km, 985m ascent

Trek upstream through the camping ground on the banks of the Río Azul, then cross the rickety (but safe) suspension bridge a short way above the river's confluence with the Río Raquel.

Go a few paces left (downstream), then cut back up right. Marked with yellow arrows on red-painted tin-tops nailed to trees, the track begins a long, often steep north-westerly ascent through *coigüe* to cross through a gate at a grassy shelf scattered with wild roses. Climb on through meadows overgrown with blackberry bushes across a trickling stream (the last water for some time) into dusty, steep slopes covered in Cordilleran cypress.

The gradient eases somewhat as you continue up into highland *lenga* and *ñirre* forest mixed with scrubby *retama*. After crossing a tiny *mallín* (wet meadow), head rightward along a ridge past the large boulder known as **Roca Grande** to reach a left turn-off, 1¼ to 2½ hours from the bridge. This short trail leads off for five minutes to a high precipitous bluff known as the **Mirador del Raquel**, which grants a fine view along the canyon of the Río Raquel towards Cerro Piltriquitrón.

Head on gently up the broad forested ridge among tall alpine *lenga* with a light *colihue* understorey, crossing through another gate to meet the small Río Teno. The path continues up smoothly beside this lovely little stream, passing the turn-off (right) to Cajón del Azul (see Day 2) before it turns off left alongside a brook to reach the **Refugio Hielo Azul** (*GPS 41° 53.292 S, 71° 38.346 W; camping per person US$1, dorm beds US$4, hot showers US$1, use of kitchen US$1, breakfast US$2, dinner US$4*), 1¾ to 2½ hours from the Mirador turn-off.

This CAP hut, built in 'log-cabin' style with trunks cut from the surrounding forest, stands at around 1300m in the beautiful upper valley of the Río Teno, enclosed by the high rock walls of a glacial cirque above which small névés are visible. It is frequently visited by local inhabitants such as the Patagonian red fox, and even the occasional puma has been known to pass by. It has sleeping space for up to 30 people. Depending on seasonal snow conditions, the *refugio* is generally staffed from early November to late April, but it is left open when the hutkeeper is absent. The surrounding **camping area** has picnic tables and fireplaces among *lenga* trees – collect your own firewood well away in the forest, not from the hut's supply.

Side Trip: Barda Negra

3½–5 hours return, 7km,
850m ascent/descent

This moderate–demanding return day trek from the *refugio* up to a lookout summit opposite 'blue ice' glaciers on Cerro Hielo Azul should only be done in fine weather. (The ascent of Cerro Hielo Azul itself, although a technically straightforward climb, involves crossing a small glacier with dangerous crevasses. It is suited only to parties with mountaineering experience and ice-climbing equipment.)

Cross a tiny wooden bridge over a streamlet at the edge of the *lenga* forest just a few paces on from the *refugio*. Head out directly into the amphitheatre through alluvial rubble and cross a second, somewhat larger stream, following this up until red

Around Cerro Hielo Azul

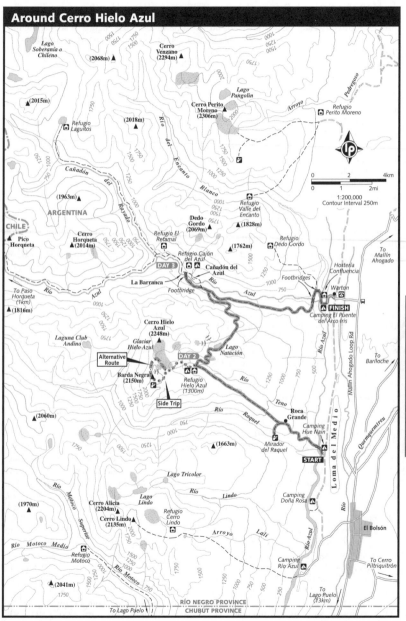

Lago Soberanía o Chileno

Cerro Venzano (2294m) ▲

(2068m) ▲

(2015m) ▲

Refugio Lagunitos ⌂

(2018m) ▲

Lago Pangolín

Cerro Perito Moreno (2306m) ▲

Arroyo

Refugio Perito Moreno ⌂

Pedregoso

To Mallín Ahogado

0   2   4km
0   1   2mi
1:200,000
Contour Interval 250m

Cañadón del Rosado

(1963m) ▲

ARGENTINA

Río del Encanto

Blanco

Refugio Valle del Encanto ⌂

CHILE

Pico Horqueta ▲

Cerro Horqueta ▲ (2014m)

Dedo Gordo (2069m) ▲

Refugio El Retamal ⌂

(1828m) ▲

(1762m) ▲

Refugio Dedo Gordo ⌂

Hostería Confluencia

To Mallín Ahogado

Refugio Cajón del Azul ⌂

DAY 3

Cañadón del Azul

Footbridges

Warton ⌂

To Paso Horqueta (1km)

Río Azul

La Barranca

Footbridge

Río Azul

Río Azul

FINISH
Camping El Puente del Arco Iris ⌂

(1816m) ▲

Laguna Club Andino

Cerro Hielo Azul (2248m) ▲

Glaciar Hielo Azul

Alternative Route

DAY 2

Lago Natación

To Bariloche

Barda Negra (2150m) ⌂

Refugio Hielo Azul (1300m) ⌂

Río

Mallín Ahogado Loop Rd

Side Trip

Río Raquel

Teno

Río Azul

(2060m) ▲

Río

Roca Grande

Camping Hue Nain ⌂

Loma del Medio

To Quemquemtreu

(1663m) ▲

Mirador del Raquel

START

Lago Tricolor

Río Lindo

Camping Doña Rosa ⌂

(1970m) ▲

Cerro Alicia (2204m) ▲

Lago Lindo

Refugio Cerro Lindo ⌂

El Bolsón

Cerro Lindo (2135m) ▲

Arroyo Lali

To Cerro Piltriquitrón

Río Motoco

Río Superior

Río Motoco Medio

Refugio Motoco ⌂

Río Motoco

Camping Río Azul ⌂

Río Azul

To Lago Puelo (13km)

(2041m) ▲

RÍO NEGRO PROVINCE

CHUBUT PROVINCE

To Lago Puelo

CENTRAL PATAGONIA

markings on rocks lead off to the right through a gravelly chute. The route leads on up a rocky moraine ridge to the base of cliffs rounded and smoothed by the action of glaciers. Here trekkers may spot the white *estrella de la cordillera* and the red bottle-shaped *voqui*, two hardy Andean wild flowers that grow sporadically on these otherwise bare slopes.

Sidle briefly left, back to the now cascading stream, and climb on steeply through the rock. Make your way over polished slabs littered with glacial debris to a milky-green meltwater lake at the snout of the small glacier known as the **Glaciar Hielo Azul**. Cross the turgid stream (the nascent Río Teno) to reach a waterfall spilling down from the left, one to 1½ hours from the *refugio*. From here the summit of Cerro Hielo Azul (2248m) is more clearly visible up to the right, above the broken-up ice on the upper part of the glacier.

Skirt the left-hand side of the Glaciar Hielo Azul, then cut up over the ice around a rock outcrop (marked by a prominent cairn) and climb on via the minor spur behind it into a snowy basin. (Alternatively, you can head directly up to the left of the waterfall through steep scree, but this is a route better taken on your way down.) The route ascends beside the small stream, crossing and recrossing as it rises steeply through (probably snow-filled) gullies and over loose rock. Where the stream ends, move rightward over persistent snow drifts to gain the ridge top (about 500m to the right of white veins of rock in the reddish-brown ridge forming a cross), continuing northwest along the snowy ridge to reach the 2150m summit of **Barda Negra** after one to 1½ hours.

Barda Negra offers a superb alpine panorama that takes in Cerro Piltriquitrón to the east beyond El Bolsón; Monte Tronador almost directly to the north; the perfect cone of Volcán Osorno to the northwest in Chile; and the distinctive triple summits of Cerro Tres Picos – the major landmark of the Comarca Andina – to the south. Laguna Club Andino can be seen in a deep glacial hollow to the northwest, and another, unnamed lake

is visible to the southwest. Trekkers also have an excellent chance of seeing condors swooping around the nearby mountain tops.

Return via the same route or take the alternative descent.

Alternative Descent: via Glaciar Hielo Azul
1¼–1½ hours, 2km, 350m descent
Although from below it looks quite difficult, this alternative descent is fairly straightforward. Taking this descent route adds an extra 30 minutes (or 500m) to the side trip. It calls for more care, however, and should not be done before mid-February because winter snows generally still hide the few (otherwise small and harmless) crevasses before then.

Head north over a tiny plateau, then follow the ridge through rock gaps to a low point between Cerro Hielo Azul and Barda Negra. Descend onto permanent snowfields, making your way down over a minor brown rock rib above a small lake dammed by the ice. From here continue along the right-hand (ie, southern) side of Glaciar Hielo Azul, keeping well away from the more crevassed ice over to your left. After you pass the large cairn on the rocky outcrop (see Side Trip, p174), cut down right off the ice and follow the edge of the glacier back to the waterfall near its snout.

Day 2: Refugio Hielo Azul to Refugio Cajón del Azul
3–4¼ hours, 10km, 135m ascent, 865m descent
Go back to the turn-off (signposted 'Lago Natación') 600m downstream from the *refugio* (see Day 1), then follow this rougher path across the Río Teno on a fallen-log bridge. Yellow-and-red marker plates lead on 300m downstream before cutting left directly up the slope to a shallow grassy lagoon. Drop gently northwest just left of a long *mallín* to reach a signpost *(GPS 41° 52.887 S, 71° 37.497 W)* in a grassy clearing near a snow-fed waterfall splashing over high cliffs on your left, 50 minutes to 1¼ hours from the *refugio*. From here, a brief side trip leads off northwest (left) 350m

through ñirre scrub to **Lago Natación**, a tarn with a rocky islet and muddy shores (which make it less appealing as a 'Swimming Lake').

Continue around northeast just above Lago Natación before descending through *lengas* mixed with bamboo to cross the cascading lake outlet (your last water for some way). The path lead up diagonally left over a minor crest onto high, open slopes of red-flowered *notro* and climbing orange *mutisias* overlooking the broad valley north of El Bolsón, 50 minutes to 1¼ hours from Lago Natación.

Begin the long, hot and dusty descent into the deep canyon, alternating between long leftward (northwest) sidles and short, sharp switchbacks. The path drops through fragrant stands of Cordilleran cypress towards the 2014m Cerro Horqueta and Dedo Gordo – the 2069m 'fat finger' peak on the opposite side of the valley – to meet a rough old 4WD track after one to 1¼ hours. This inconspicuous junction (*GPS 41° 51.150 S, 71° 36.530 W*) is marked only with a laconic 'H. A.' visible from upvalley.

Proceed left through tall *coigüe* forest for five minutes to meet the Río Azul again. The road fords the river here, but a good foot track continues 15 to 20 minutes upstream along its wild southern bank past small alerces and turquoise pools to cross the impressive 3m-wide, 40m-deep gorge known as the **La Barranca** on a footbridge. The path leads five minutes on through an orchard to the popular, recently extended, 45-bed **Refugio Cajón del Azul** (*camping per person US$1, dorm beds US$4, hot showers US$1, use of kitchen US$1, breakfast US$2, dinner US$4*). This homy hut stands at around 620m in a small open area of the valley, which is enclosed by incredibly steep rock walls. Hearty meals, like roast lamb with home-grown vegetables, home-baked bread and tasty home-brew beer, are available. Notify the friendly hutkeeper of your safe arrival, even if you are not staying at the *refugio*.

A popular two-day side trip leads upvalley to the rustic Refugio Laguitos at the head of the Cañadón del Rayado.

Day 3: Refugio Cajón del Azul to Warton

2½–3¼ hours, 12km, 150m descent

Retrace your steps to the 4WD track and follow it on downvalley past camping areas and occasional shacks along the Río Azul. After fording a cool side stream, the road climbs away rightward through low *maitén* to a high, dusty crest, then winds down to the Río Azul. Cross the river on a suspension footbridge just above its confluence with the smaller Río del Encanto Blanco, then cross the latter river on a second (equally rickety) bridge to reach the basic **Hostería Confluencia** (*camping per person US$1, rooms about US$4*) just downstream.

From here a road winds up around past **Camping El Puente del Arco Iris** (☎ 02944-1555 8330; [e] elpuentedelarcoiris@hotmail.com; *camping per person US$2*), which has pleasant sites with picnic tables, to meet a four-way intersection on the Río Azul road near the farm of **Warton**.

For trekkers going the other way, there are several signs at the turn-off – the most prominent reads 'Confluencia del Río Azul y Blanco'. You can phone for a prompt *remís* (taxi) at the small store on the northeast side of this intersection, or continue 1.4km ahead (east) to the Mallín Ahogado loop road, from where sporadic buses (see Getting to/from the Trek, p174) run back to El Bolsón.

Parque Nacional Los Alerces

The 2630-sq-km Parque Nacional Los Alerces lies to the west of the small city of Esquel in the north of Argentina's Chubut Province. Established in 1937 (concurrently with Parque Nacional Los Glaciares in southern Patagonia), the park protects – not always successfully, unfortunately – one of the largest and most beautiful tracts of Andean wilderness in central Patagonia.

The landscape in the northern half of the park is dominated by three major glacial lakes, Lago Rivadavia, Lago Menéndez and

Lago Futalaufquen (Big Lake in the Mapuche language), whose fjord-like arms stretch deep into the Cordillera. They are surrounded by several smaller, yet still quite sizable lakes, including Lago Cisnes and Lago Krüger. These lakes all drain southward via the huge hydroelectricity reservoir of Lago Amutui Quimei (formerly called Lago Situación) into the Río Futaleufú, which flows westward into Chile. Los Alerces' major lakes form a natural division between the dry, almost steppe-like eastern fringe of the park and the increasingly wet sector towards the west.

The scope for overnight trekking trips in Los Alerces is fairly limited, however, because the park's interior is closed to public access. (The only way to visit the restricted area is by taking a launch tour from Puerto Chucao on Lago Menéndez, which goes to a 2500-year-old stand of alerces.)

NATURAL HISTORY

Parque Nacional Los Alerces (like the national park of Alerce Andino in Chile) conserves some of the southern Andes' most majestic stands of giant alerces. The most eminent representative of the so-called Valdivian rainforest, the alerce grows throughout the southern Lakes District, but only occasionally reaches the enormous size for which it is so famous. The main prerequisites for this – mild conditions, deep and perpetually wet soil, absence of fire and lots of time – are fulfilled by several locations in the remote interior of the park. On the extreme northwest arm of Lago Menéndez are alerces aged well over 2000 years, but a single ancient specimen found on the lake's southwest arm is believed to be over 4000 years old.

Alerces are typically found growing in association with other rainforest trees. One species is the olivillo, or teque, which has pointed oval leaves whose undersides are lighter and often red-speckled, and produces small, round fleshy fruit. Also present are avellano, with shiny serrated leaves and white-spotted ash-grey bark, and tineo, instantly recognisable by its serrated, paired leaves. The holly-leafed taique, traumén

and tepú, a myrtle bush with small white flowers, are typical plants of the Valdivian forest understorey.

The lower, drier foothills on the park's eastern edge have some fine stands of coniferous Cordilleran cypress, often growing in loose association with the attractive maitén, which somehow resembles a cross between a willow and a peppercorn tree. The maitén, which was sacred to the local Mapuche people, is also an important winter fodder tree for wild animals such as huemul and guanaco. Bordering the lakeshores and the riverbanks are some superb examples of arrayán, a myrtle species that is recognisable by its striking reddish-orange bark and numerous twisted trunks. In summer the arrayán is covered by a profusion of white flowers.

Los Alerces' large lakes provide a habitat to many water birds. Visitors may spy the great grebe, or huala. The great grebe is brownish-grey with a long reddish neck and white underbelly, and feeds on a rich diet of fish, molluscs and aquatic insects in the many freshwater lakes in the park. It's often found with the red-gartered coot, or tagua, a black, yellow-beaked bird that builds a floating nest on lakes and still-water streams. The torrent duck, or pato de torrentes, is well adapted to fast-flowing rivers and streams, and is occasionally seen diving into white water in search of food. The colourful bronze-winged duck, or pato anteojillo, builds its nest on small islands.

In the forest trekkers will hear the distinctive chuckling warble of the chucao, which hides among the canes of the colihue bamboo, and may see the green-backed firecrown, or picaflor, a hummingbird that gorges itself on the nectar of the notro and the chilco. The austral parakeet, or cachaña, a green bird with a yellowish-red underbelly, is usually observed in pairs.

Predators found in the park include the puma, kodkod (or huiña) and two native foxes, the bluish-grey Azara's fox (zorro gris) and the brownish-coloured Patagonian red fox (zorro culpeo). The very lucky might even chance to spot the amphibious southern river otter, or huillín, which lives along the banks of the larger rivers and lakes.

CLIMATE

Parque Nacional Los Alerces is in a rain shadow, which is typical for areas in the lee of the Andes. Annual precipitation peaks at almost 4500mm in the ranges along Argentina's frontier with Chile, but declines progressively to a minimum of just under 800mm at the park's northeast boundary near Lago Rivadavia. A continental climate prevails, with occasional hot summer weather and crisp winters that can bring heavy snowfalls. Summer temperatures at Lago Krüger average around 20°C.

Permits & Regulations

All visitors to Parque Nacional Los Alerces must pay a US$4 fee at the park's north or south *portada* (entrance gate). On all routes, trekkers must set out before 10am in order to be sure of arriving back safely before nightfall.

Throughout Parque Nacional Los Alerces, camping is permitted only at organised camping grounds and the free park-authorised camping areas. Even for short treks, it is compulsory to sign in at one of the Administración de Parques Nacionales (APN) *guarderías* (ranger stations) before you set out.

Lago Krüger

Duration	4 days
Distance	44km
Difficulty	moderate
Start/Finish	Villa Futalaufquen
Nearest Towns	Esquel (p164)
	Villa Futalaufquen (p179)
Transport	bus

Summary A pleasant trek past lakeside beaches fringed by luxuriant forests on the southern shores of Lago Futalaufquen and Lago Krüger.

This is an out-and-back route that leads over an often windy pass (around 1050m) then down via a lovely little beach at the wild western end of Lago Futalaufquen to Lago Krüger. The trek can be shortened by taking a launch either to or back from Lago

Krüger. A recommended full-day side trip leads down past wild cataracts of the Río Frey to a lookout on the northern side of Lago Amutui Quimei.

Fallen logs and thickets of *colihue* may slow you down in places, especially on Day 2 (Playa Blanca to Lago Krüger). The route between Lago Krüger and Lago Amutui Quimei follows a disused road, where the odd collapsed bridge is a minor inconvenience.

PLANNING
When to Trek

The trek can normally be undertaken at least from late November until mid-April. The park authorities may close the route, however, when there is snow on the pass or after heavy rain.

Maps

Two Argentine IGM 1:100,000 maps, *Lago Rivadavia* (Chubut, No 4372-10) and *Villa Futalaufquen* (Chubut, No 2372-16), cover the trek, but do not accurately show the route.

Permits & Regulations

Before leaving for Lago Krüger, all trekking parties are required to register their details and obtain a permit at the APN information centre in Villa Futalaufquen or at Guardería Punta Mattos. You must normally set out from Villa Futalaufquen before 9.30am. Camping is permitted only at Playa Blanca (see Day 1) and at Refugio Lago Krüger (see Day 2).

NEAREST TOWNS & FACILITIES

See Esquel (p164).

Villa Futalaufquen

This scattered village is at the southeast corner of Lago Futalaufquen. The **APN's Centro de Informes** (☎ 02945-471020, 471015, ext 23), a museum and information centre, is open daily and sells fishing licenses. Villa Futalaufquen has a grocery store and a petrol (gasoline) station.

Camping Los Maitenes (☎ 02945-451003; camping per person US$5), 400m down from the information centre, has grassy sites with

CENTRAL PATAGONIA

hot showers and laundry facilities. The up-market **Hostería Futalaufquen** (☎ 02945-457008; w www.brazosur.com; doubles from US$140) is along the route of Day 1, 3km from the village at the end of the road (500m on from Puerto Limonao). The hostería has a **restaurant**.

Getting There & Away Villa Futalaufquen is most easily accessible from Esquel (p164). During summer, **Transportes Esquel** (☎ 02945-453529; Alsina 1632) runs two buses daily between Esquel and Lago Puelo (p190) through Parque Nacional Los Alerces, leaving in both directions at 8am and 2pm. From Esquel there is also one bus daily at 7.30pm that goes only as far as Lago Verde. From mid-March, the bus only runs several times a week. The fare to Villa Futalaufquen is US$3.

Around Lago Futalaufquen

Around the southern and eastern shores of Lago Futalaufquen are 11 free **camping areas** with no facilities. There are also a number of **camping grounds** (camping per person around US$3) and **hosterías** (self-contained 4- and 6-person cabins from around US$40): **Cabañas Las Cascadas** (☎ 02945-1568 0315), **Cabañas Futalaufquen** (☎ 02945-471008), **Hostería Quimé Quipan** (☎ 02945-454134), **Cabañas Los Tepúes, Hostería Pucón Pai** (☎ 02945-451381, 1568 2268), **Cabañas Tejas Negras** (☎ 02945-471046; e tejasnegras@ciudad.com .ar), **Refugio Bahía Rosales** (☎ 02945-471044) and **Hostería Cume Hue** (☎ 02945-453639, 450503).

GETTING TO/FROM THE TREK

The trek begins and ends at the village of Villa Futalaufquen (p179).

The trek can be shortened by taking a boat to/from Refugio Lago Krüger (see Day 1). The refugio runs a boat on demand to/from Punta Mattos (also called Punta de Matos, 21km north of Villa Futalaufquen), and charges US$20/30 per person one-way/return. The boat can be chartered by telephone, email or two-way radio – ask at ranger stations or at Fiunque Osuzt in Puerto Limonao.

Until recently, a launch ran daily from Puerto Limonao to Lago Krüger in January and February; it is possible that this service may resume in the future.

THE TREK
Day 1: Villa Futalaufquen to Playa Blanca

4¾–6¼ hours, 14km,
450m ascent/descent

After signing in at the APN information centre, follow the road (or alternatively follow a path slightly closer to the lake) around the southwest side of Lago Futalaufquen. Head left at a short road turn-off several hundred metres before Puerto Limonao, which soon ends at a small car park by the Arroyo de los Pumas after 30 to 40 minutes. Cross the small stream on a footbridge and head into the forest past a signposted trail leading off left to the **Cinco Saltos** (a series of waterfalls that can be visited in around 30 minutes return).

Continue trekking behind Hostería Futalaufquen (see Villa Futalaufquen, p179) to begin an undulating traverse up along the steep-sided lake through stands of Cordilleran cypress that gradually go over into coigüe. The path then begins a steady winding climb away to the left through clustered thickets of overhanging colihue, sidling on rightward over high slopes of ñirre and notro scrub, giving good views of Cerro Alto El Petiso and other peaks on the northern side of Lago Futalaufquen.

After turning northwest to cross a small stream, head up through a hollow covered with low, weather-beaten bamboo. The route skirts the lenga forest on the right-hand side of this shallow basin to reach a scrubby saddle (at roughly 1050m) overlooking a small cove in the lake immediately below to the west, 2¾ to 3½ hours from the Arroyo de los Pumas. Descend directly in steep, loose-earth zigzags before moving over to the left to reach **Playa Blanca** after a further 1½ to two hours. This idyllic little white-sand beach is fringed by lovely arrayán trees. There are idyllic **camp sites** here just back in the forest, but fires are not allowed.

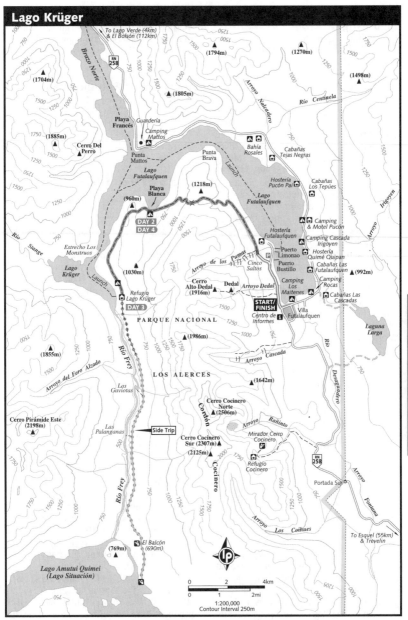

Lago Krüger

To Lago Verde (4km) & El Bolsón (112km)

RN 258

Braco Norte

(1794m)

(1270m)

(1498m)

(1704m)

(1805m)

Arroyo Nadadero

Río Centinela

(1885m)

Cerro Del Perro

Playa Francés

Guardería

Camping Mattos

Punta Mattos

Punta Brava

Bahía Rosales

Cabañas Tejas Negras

Cabañas Los Tepúes

Lago Futalaufquen

Playa Blanca

(960m)

(1218m)

Lago Futalaufquen

Hostería Pucón Pai

Arroyo Irigoyen

DAY 2
DAY 4

Río Stange

Estrecho Los Monstruos

Lago Krüger

(1030m)

Arroyo de los Pumas

Cinco Saltos

Cerro Alto Dedal (1916m)

Dedal

Arroyo Dedal

Hostería Futalaufquen

Puerto Limonao

Puerto Bustillo

Camping & Motel Pucón

Camping Cascada Irigoyen

Hostería Quimé Quipan

Cabañas Las Futalaufquen

(992m)

Camping Rocas

Camping Los Maitenes

Cabañas Las Cascadas

Refugio Lago Krüger

DAY 3

START/ FINISH

Centro de Informes

Villa Futalaufquen

Laguna Larga

PARQUE   NACIONAL

(1986m)

(1855m)

Río Frey

Arroyo del Foro Alzado

LOS   ALERCES

Arroyo   Cascada

Río Desaguadero

(1642m)

Las Gaviotas

Cerro Pirámide Este (2198m)

Las Palanganas

Side Trip

Cordón

Cerro Cocinero Norte (2506m)

Cerro Cocinero Sur (2307m)

(2125m)

Arroyo   Rañinto

Mirador Cerro Cocinero

Cocinero

Refugio Cocinero

RN 258

Portada Sur

Arroyo   Fontana

To Esquel (55km) & Trevelin

Río Frey

El Balcón (690m)

(769m)

Lago Amutui Quimei (Lago Situación)

Arroyo   Los   Coihues

0   2   4km

0   1   2mi

1:200,000
Contour Interval 250m

CENTRAL PATAGONIA

Day 2: Playa Blanca to Refugio Lago Krüger

2½–3¼ hours, 8km

Pick up the route again at the reedy far end of the beach. The often poor path leads away from shore through *coigüe* forest, where the distinctive call of the tiny *chucao* rings out from the *quila* underbrush and delicate white *palomita* orchids grow, thriving in the damp, humus-rich soil. After returning to the lakeside for some distance the route again moves away left, finally coming out onto a lovely pebble beach at **Lago Krüger**. The **Refugio Lago Krüger** (☎ 02945-452997, 471044; w www.lagokruger.com; rooms per person full board US$60) is 10 minutes on around past the camping ground and jetty at the lake outlet. After a complete renovation, the *refugio* has only two double rooms and one triple room, each with a private bathroom. Trekkers can also **camp** (camping per person US$10) by the lake a short way from the *refugio*.

Side Trip: Lago Amutui Quimei

5½–7 hours return, 27km

Follow the path from the southern side of the small clearing in front of the *refugio*. After a short distance, it goes over into a long-disused road which became obsolete after completion of the dam. This broad track leads smoothly down through tall *coigüe* forest into the valley of the **Río Frey**, which flows through a continuous series of white-water rapids. The route passes a sign-posted path turn-off leading down steeply to Las Gaviotas, a spot that is favoured by fly fishers, after 40 to 50 minutes.

Make your way on for 25 to 30 minutes past more anglers' pools known as Las Palanganas, proceeding smoothly through tiny meadows dotted with raspberry bushes and wild strawberries. Surrounding a glacial cirque up to your right stands the jagged 2198m peak of Cerro Pirámide Este. The old vehicle track climbs slightly over a crest, from where the reservoir of Lago Amutui Quimei comes into sight, then descends briefly to reach **El Balcón** after a further 1½ to 2 hours. Pairs of Andean condors often circle above this high open grassy shelf that looks out to the often snowcapped mountains

on the southern end of the lake. For better views continue for another 15 to 20 minutes to a higher knob on a minor peninsula.

Return to Refugio Lago Krüger via the same route.

Days 3 & 4: Refugio Lago Krüger to Villa Futalaufquen

7½–10 hours, 22km, 450m ascent/descent

These are a simple backtrack of Day 1 and Day 2. Some trekkers may opt to take the boat from Lago Krüger to Punta Mattos.

Reserva Nacional Cerro Castillo

Situated at roughly 46°S, the 1340-sq-km Reserva Nacional Cerro Castillo extends south from Lago Elizalde as far as the Río Ibáñez, southwest of Coyhaique in Chile's XI Region. The reserve is an area of heavily glaciated basalt ranges rising to over 2000m and covered by large névés and hanging glaciers, several of which creep right down into the valleys. Its highest point and key feature is the 2675m peak of Cerro Castillo, at the southern edge of the reserve.

NATURAL HISTORY

Reserva Nacional Cerro Castillo is an important sanctuary for the southern Andean deer, or *huemul*. Small numbers of this graceful but generally shy animal remain in the central part of the reserve, grazing in secluded upper valleys where recent glacial recession has led to recolonisation by palatable plant species. Other mammals sometimes spotted in the reserve include the *chingue*, or Patagonian skunk, and the small *zorro gris*.

Although uncontrolled burning has scarred a large part of the reserve's periphery, the interior remains relatively unspoiled. Open forests of *lenga* mostly cover the subalpine areas up to almost 1200m, generally with little underbrush. Ground-hugging forest plants, such as the devil's strawberry *(frutilla del diablo)*, the similar-looking Magellan strawberry *(frutilla de Magallanes)*, which produces pinkish edible berries, and the *brecillo*, whose purple berries are a favoured food of foxes and other native fauna, can be found on moister places.

The Chilean flicker, or *pitío*, is an endemic Patagonian woodpecker typically seen in the drier *lenga* forests found in the eastern sector of the reserve. The *pitío* has a greyish crown and brownish-black bands, but its creamy yellow face and upper neck make it easy to recognise. The great-shrike tyrant of Aisén, or *mero austral aiseño*, is a coffee-grey coloured subspecies endemic to the region.

CLIMATE

Situated well inland and largely sheltered from the far wetter coastal climate by high ranges to the west, Reserva Nacional Cerro Castillo has a continental climate. Annual precipitation levels are relatively moderate by the standards of western Patagonia, generally not exceeding 3000mm on the higher peaks. In the Valle Ibáñez to the south, the reserve borders abruptly on the drier *monte* terrain so typical of the Andes' eastern fringes, where rainfall is generally under 1000mm. Summers in the reserve are generally mild, with January temperatures only occasionally rising above 30°C. Winter can bring locally heavy snowfalls above 500m, and the first patches of permanent snow are encountered at a little over 1200m.

Around Cerro Castillo

Duration	4 days
Distance	62km
Difficulty	moderate–demanding
Start	Las Horquetas Grandes
Finish	Villa Cerro Castillo
Nearest Towns	Coyhaique (p166)
	Villa Cerro Castillo (p184)
Transport	bus

Summary A route through a raw alpine landscape where glaciers cling to craggy mountainsides and waterfalls tumble into the valleys.

Towering over the Río Ibáñez and the Carretera Austral, Cerro Castillo is the most prominent peak of the compact Cordillera Castillo. The mountain's Spanish name comes from its many striking basalt turrets and craggy ridges, which give it a strong resemblance to a medieval fortified castle. As a landmark of the Aisén region, this striking peak regularly attracts international climbers.

This trek leads along the first section of the Sendero de Chile in the Aisén region. Although this is an increasingly well-trodden route, it requires a good level of fitness and some care with navigation. The trek crosses glacier-fed streams in several places, although these are not normally large and can usually be forded without difficulty. Fallen branches and loose rock must also be negotiated.

PLANNING
When to Trek

The trek is best done from the beginning of December to the end of March (but up to a month earlier or later, depending on seasonal variations). Snow is likely to cover higher sections of the route at least until January.

What to Bring

There are no *refugios* for trekkers (although Conaf has plans to construct a *refugio* near Laguna Cerro Castillo), so it is essential that all parties carry a tent.

Maps

The Chilean IGM 1:50,000 series covers the area of the trek in three maps: *Lago Elizalde* (Section I, No 132), *Balmaceda* (Section I, No 133) and *Villa Cerro Castillo* (Section J, No 10). Although most of the route described here is not shown on these maps, they are still very useful.

Permits & Regulations

Permits are currently not required. Trekkers should leave their route details at the *guardería* at Laguna Chiguay or at the Conaf office in Coyhaique. A final section of the trek cuts through private property, where trekkers should be on their best conduct.

Due to an increasing numbers of visitors to this fragile area, please be especially mindful of your impact on the environment (see Responsible Trekking, p43). In particular, avoid

CENTRAL PATAGONIA

lighting campfires and be sure to carry out all your garbage – and perhaps that left by less responsible trekkers.

NEAREST TOWNS & FACILITIES
See Coyhaique (p166).

Laguna Chiguay
Laguna Chiguay is a small lake surrounded by exotic conifers beside the Carretera Austral, 6km north of Las Horquetas Grandes and 64km south of Coyhaique. Here, Conaf's **Guardería Chiguay** can give advice on the trekking route. The Conaf-run **Camping Laguna Chiguay** (camping per site US$8) has six sites with tables and fireplaces. Buses running between Coyhaique and Cochrane, Puerto Ibáñez or Villa Cerro Castillo all pass by Laguna Chiguay (but stop only subject to demand and seat availability).

Villa Cerro Castillo
On the Carretera Austral 98km south of Coyhaique, the tiny town of Villa Cerro Castillo (population 300) – not to be confused with its namesake farther south on the Torres del Paine road – lies almost below the majestic mountain itself. Near the village is an ancient rock-art site, painted by ancestors of the indigenous Tehuelche people.

Residencial El Custodio (O'Higgins; rooms per person around US$5) has basic rooms. **Residencial San Sebastian** (☎ 067-419200; Carretera Austral; rooms per person US$15), on the main road, offers somewhat better accommodation.

La Querencia (O'Higgins 460), where many buses stop, is the village's only restaurant.

Getting There & Away In Coyhaique, **Transportes Amin Ali** (☎ 067-419200; O'Higgins) runs buses to Villa Cerro Castillo (US$5.50, 2¼ hours) at 7am on Monday, Tuesday and Friday, returning to Coyhaique at around 11am the same day. Buses running between Cochrane (p197) and Coyhaique call in at Villa Cerro Castillo; going north, they generally arrive at Villa Cerro Castillo at around 1pm.

GETTING TO/FROM THE TREK
The trek begins at Las Horquetas Grandes, 75km south of Coyhaique. Las Horquetas Grandes is little more than a bend in the Senda Río Ibáñez (the name given to this section of the Carretera Austral) where two minor streams flow together. The Dirección de Vialidad has a small roadworks depot here on the west side of the road.

If arriving from Coyhaique, you can take buses going to either Cochrane or Puerto Ibáñez. The road is relatively good and the journey takes a bit less than two hours. In summer there are five Cochrane buses per week in each direction, usually departing around 8am. In Coyhaique private minibuses to Puerto Ibáñez often pick up passengers along Arturo Prat. Trekkers arriving from Cochrane or Puerto Ibáñez will disembark shortly after crossing the scenic Paso Las Mulas – but note that Las Horquetas Grandes is after (ie, downvalley from) Las Horquetas Chicas.

The trek ends at Villa Cerro Castillo

THE TREK
Day 1: Las Horquetas Grandes to Upper Río Turbio
3¾–5 hours, 18km, 240m ascent

Cross the bridge over the Estero Paso de Las Mulas, just above where the stream enters the Río Blanco, and then follow a dirt road down along the true left bank of the river. The road soon turns away westward past a farmhouse, winding on through open *lenga* forest before dropping gently down onto grassy flats beside the **Estero La Lima** after one to 1¼ hours. Make your way past a rustic *puesto* (outbuilding) and then cross the small side stream of the Estero Blanco Chico, heading on upvalley through streamside pastures to easily ford the shallow Estero La Lima itself after a further 30 to 40 minutes.

After crossing the Estero Aislado, which drains another tiny side valley to the north, the increasingly rough vehicle track skirts above a reedy lagoon frequented by black-necked swans to reach a fork after one to 1¼ hours. Here, take the left-hand branch, which avoids a *mallín* stretching along the poorly drained valley floor before it (almost imperceptibly) crosses a watershed to meet the **Río Turbio**, another 30 to 40 minutes on. This roaring white-water torrent flows through a wild upper valley below the Cordillera Castillo, whose towering peaks have been visible along much of your approach route.

Follow an indistinct 4WD track southwest along the broad gravelly valley floor below waterfalls spilling over sheer cliffs from hanging glaciers up to your right. Where the vehicle track finally peters out after 30 to 40 minutes, pick up a trail that continues into the *lenga* forest. The route crosses a clear brook before climbing gently rightward onto an open field of old glacial debris now covered by tussocky alpine grasses and *chauras* (which produce tasty white or red berries), a further 10 to 15 minutes on. There is scenic **camping** around this pretty head of the Río Turbio valley, where *huemul* sometimes graze.

Side Trip: Glaciar Peñón
1 hour return, 3.2km
The short side trip to this nearby glacier, which curls down from the heart of the Cordillera Castillo as the source of the Río Turbio, is recommended. Follow the river's boulder-strewn south bank west from the clear brook (see Day 1) for 20 to 30 minutes to a murky meltwater pool at the snout of the Glaciar Peñón. Only trekkers with the necessary experience should venture onto the ice itself.

Day 2: Upper Río Turbio to Laguna Cerro Castillo
4¼–5¾ hours, 14km, 775m ascent
Follow the trail on up southwest as the terrain steepens and the forest goes over into scrub. Higher up the path is less distinct, but the going is relatively easy close to the cascading stream. The route climbs on higher into a rocky gully, passing streamlets splashing down from a small névé up to the right before reaching **Paso Peñón** (1453m) after 1½ to two hours. Paso Peñón is a long, narrow gap filled by frost-shattered rock and accumulated winter snow (which may remain well

into February). From the southern end of the pass, the high, turquoise lake visible roughly southwest indicates the way ahead.

Descend cautiously onto steep and unstable scree-covered slopes, directly opposite spectacular icefalls gripping the raw eastern flank of Cerro Peñón that produce numerous meltwater cascades. Cut left across the glacial wash below to pick up random trails leading down the stream's forested left bank. After making a sometimes uncomfortable ford (which is easier where the stream briefly divides into two channels) you reach some reasonable **camp sites**.

Continue on downstream to arrive at the **Estero del Bosque** junction, just 1½ to two hours from Paso Peñón. Here, the eastern branch of the Estero del Bosque merges with the somewhat larger western branch before racing through a narrow canyon. Much of the forest around this stream junction has been flattened by winter avalanches sweeping off the southern side of Cerro Peñón, and is now too boggy to camp.

Head up along embankments on the true left (ie, northwestern) side of the west branch of the Estero de Bosque to meet a rocky streamway after 50 minutes to 1¼ hours, then move a short way up right where the trail ducks back into the weather-beaten scrub. The path continues upvalley for 10 or 15 minutes past excellent sheltered **camp sites** to cross a side stream spilling down in a large cascade fed by an icefall on Cerro Castillo Chico. It's well worth climbing either moraine ridge to reach several tarns on the shelf behind the waterfall; more adventurous and energetic trekkers can climb the loose bare slopes on the right for spectacular views.

Head on for a final 15 to 20 minutes up through streamside meadows interspersed with *lenga* thickets to arrive at **Laguna Cerro Castillo**. A stunning sight, the lake lies at 1275m above sea level in a deep glacial basin which is directly under the imposing Cerro Castillo. Hanging glaciers periodically drop ice blocks onto the rock cliffs below, where they shatter and occasionally hit the water. The open stony ground around the lake offers scenic but rather exposed **camping**.

CENTRAL PATAGONIA

Around Cerro Castillo

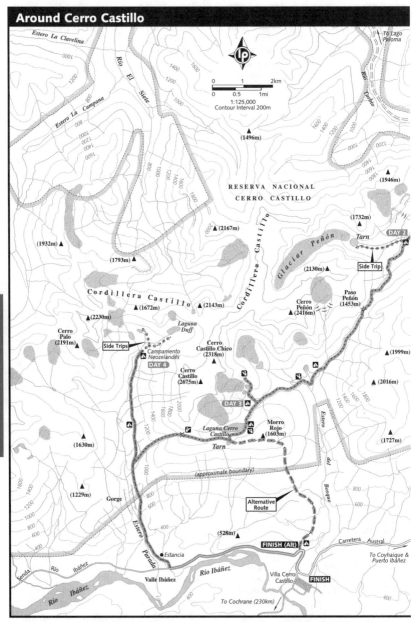

CENTRAL PATAGONIA

Estero La Clavelina

Río El Siete

Estero La Campana

To Lago Paloma

Río Turbio

1:125,000
Contour Interval 200m

0   0.5   1mi
0   1   2km

RESERVA NACIONAL
CERRO CASTILLO

(1496m)

(1946m)

(2167m)

(1732m)

Cordillera Castillo

Glaciar Peñón

Tarn

DAY 2

Side Trip

(1932m)

(1793m)

(2130m)

Cordillera Castillo

(1672m)   (2143m)

Paso Peñón
(1453m)

(2230m)

Laguna Duff

Cerro Peñón
(2416m)

(1999m)

Cerro Palo
(2191m)

Side Trips

Campamento Neozelandés

DAY 4

Cerro Castillo Chico
(2318m)

(2016m)

Cerro Castillo
(2675m)

DAY 3

Morro Rojo
(1603m)

Estero del Bosque

(1630m)

Laguna Cerro Castillo

Tarn

(1727m)

(1229m)

(approximate boundary)

Gorge

Alternative Route

Estero Parada

(528m)

FINISH (Alt)

Carretera Austral

To Coyhaique &
Puerto Ibáñez

Estancia

Río Ibáñez

Valle Ibáñez

Villa Cerro Castillo

FINISH

Senda

Río Ibáñez

To Cochrane (230km)

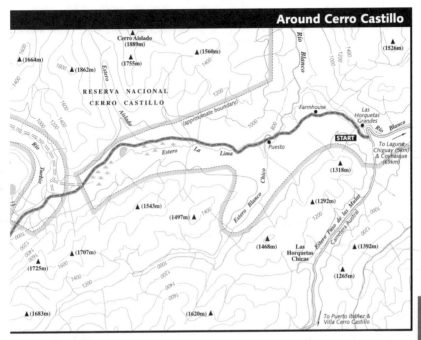

Around Cerro Castillo

CENTRAL PATAGONIA

Day 3: Laguna Cerro Castillo to Campamento Neozelandés

3½–4½ hours, 11km, 650m ascent

Cross the lake's outlet stream on stepping stones. Climb diagonally left along coarse, bare moraines to a very narrow shelf high above the lake and follow this around to reach a broad, flat **saddle** just west of Morro Rojo after 40 to 50 minutes. This spot offers a fine view to Cerro Castillo directly opposite (although you'll need a 28mm lens to get it all in one shot!). Trek a short way left across the saddle to a tarn, from where you can see the tiny town of Villa Cerro Castillo and down along the Valle Ibáñez as far as Lago General Carrera. (See also the Alternative Finish, p188.)

Continue westward along a shelf opposite the basalt turrets of Cerro Castillo, before climbing easily over boulder rubble to reach a rocky gap after 40 to 50 minutes. This ridge top overlooks the wild, forested valley of the Estero Parada, which is en-

closed by interesting jagged peaks. Most trekkers drop directly into the steep, scree-filled gully ahead, following its right side as it curves leftward into the trees to meet a prominent path coming up through the valley, 30 to 45 minutes on. A longer but less rough option is to climb north to a forested ridge, then follow it down to meet the path after 45 minutes to one hour.

Head upvalley through the *lenga* forest, passing some pleasant **camp sites** by the Estero Parada (not far downstream from where a large glacial tributary enters from an adjacent side valley) after 40 to 50 minutes. The path rises steadily onward, skirting soggy bogs close to the stream to arrive at **Campamento Neozelandés**, 50 minutes to 1¼ hours on. This is where a small mountaineering party from New Zealand established its base camp in 1976, making a number of first ascents in the area. This beautiful valley head is a great place to pitch your tent, but dry *and* level sites are limited.

Side Trip: Upper Valle Parada
2–3 hours return, 2–3km
The upper valley is enclosed on three sides by jagged summits of the Cordillera Castillo, and half a day or so might be spent exploring this area. **Laguna Duff**, a small tarn set in bare surroundings under Cerro Castillo Chico, can be visited from Campamento Neozelandés by heading up beside the narrow eastern branch of the Estero Parada. After the path peters out, continue over mossy slopes and glacial debris to the lake. On the west side of the valley, two more **lakes** formed by end moraines are best reached by crossing the east stream and heading around underneath the cliff face.

Alternative Finish: Laguna Cerro Castillo to Villa Cerro Castillo
3½–4½ hours, 11km, 1100m descent
A more direct (although not particularly rewarding) route down to Villa Cerro Castillo leaves from the saddle west of Morro Rojo (see Day 3). First contour eastward around Morro Rojo's southern side, before descending 1km along a steep spur to a prominent cairn. Here, move rightward and pick up an initially vague trail. The route improves as it leads down roughly southeast through regenerating forest into a fire-cleared area, then past a corral and a gate to meet a 4WD track. Follow this down past a farmhouse to the meet the Río Ibáñez road at the Estero del Bosque bridge, and continue as described on Day 4.

Day 4: Campamento Neozelandés to Villa Cerro Castillo
4–5 hours, 19km, 870m descent
Backtrack downvalley to the rocky stream gully where you first encountered the trail (see Day 3). After climbing over a minor ridge, follow the path across burnt-out slopes scattered with wild strawberries above where the Estero Parada races through a deep chasm. The route descends gently through pockets of *lenga* forest, before dropping rightward to the banks of the stream on the wide, open **Valle Ibáñez**. Now on the private property of an *estancia* (a large cattle or sheep property), cut down left across rocky pastures past a homestead sheltered by graceful poplars, 2¼ to three hours after you left Campamento Neozelandés.

Head slightly south of east along a farm track across rich grassy flats grazed by sheep and black-necked ibis *(bandurrias)*, then take a graded road on through *ñirre* scrub and *calafate* bushes to meet the **Río Ibáñez** after 40 to 50 minutes. The glacial waters of this large, swift-moving river flow through deep channels. Proceed on through a sandy plain to cross the Estero del Bosque on a bridge (where the Alternative Finish rejoins the route), and then continue on a short way down the road to arrive at **Villa Cerro Castillo** (p184) after a final one to 1¼ hours.

Other Treks

PARQUE NACIONAL HORNOPIRÉN
This 482-sq-km Chilean national park lies southeast of Puerto Montt near the village of Hornopirén on the Carretera Austral. The park centres round the 1572m cone of Volcán Hornopirén, whose name (a curious mixture of Mapuche and Spanish) means 'oven of snow'. A two-day return trek from Hornopirén follows a good horse trail through the forest along the western side of Volcán Hornopirén to the eastern shore of Lago Cabrera, from where there are good views across the lake to the superb 2111m Volcán Yate. Volcán Hornopirén can be climbed from its eastern side.

The Chilean IGM's 1:50,000 map *Volcán Hornopirén* (Section H, No 72) covers virtually all of the park; the adjoining map *Volcán Apagado* (Section H, No 71) is also useful. **Buses Fierro** (☎ 065-253022) runs daily buses between Hornopirén and Puerto Montt. The bus trip includes a ferry crossing between Caleta Puelche and Caleta La Arena on Estuario/Seno Reloncaví. The ferry runs on a two- or three-hourly schedule in either direction. You can also reach Hornopirén by a direct ferry (operated by the shipping company Transmarchilay) which departs daily from Angelmó in Puerto Montt.

PARQUE PUMALÍN
Río Ventisquero
A large tributary of the Río Puelo, the Río Ventisquero (Glacier River) drains the northeastern-

most area of Parque Pumalín. The beautiful valley of this river can be visited in a four-day return trek from the village of Llanada Grande, about halfway up the Río Puelo. A new road (which was originally scheduled for completion in 2001) is being pushed up the river to connect with a road in Parque Nacional Lago Puelo (p190) in Argentina. From Llanada Grande, it is a long day's trek upriver via El Puerto to the hanging bridge known as La Pasarela, which you cross before continuing with another long day's trek up the Río Ventisquero to Fundo Rincón Bonito, an isolated farm. (Another worthwhile one-day side trip from Llanada Grande goes to the impressive Lago Azul.)

There are several buses that run daily from Puerto Montt to the small town of Puelo at the mouth of the Río Puelo, but there is no public transport to Llanada Grande (though it is possible to fly in or trek there in around three days). Three Chilean IGM 1:50,000 maps cover the trek: *Llanada Grande* (Section H, 74), *Lago de las Rocas* (Section H, 84) and *Arroyo Ventisquero* (Section H, 83).

Lago Reñihue

Lago Reñihue is a large, remote lake at the headwaters of the Río Reñihue, which flows into Fiordo Reñihue near Caleta Gonzalo (p169). A six-day, 60km return trek from Caleta Gonzalo follows a foot track upriver past camping areas and excellent fishing spots to Lago Reñihue. The start of the route crosses private property, where trekkers should be on their best behaviour. Two Chilean IGM maps cover the route: *Fiordo Reñihue* (Section H, No 101) and *Pillán* (Section H, No 102).

Ventisquero Amarillo

The largest of several glaciers descending from the large névé on Volcán Michimahuida, the spectacular Ventisquero Amarillo can be visited in a two- or three-day trek from the village of El Amarillo, 25km south of Chaitén (p168). From Parque Pumalín's *guardería* (just 60m along the road to the Termas del Amarillo), a road turn-off goes to a camping ground (still under construction at the time of research). From here a foot track makes a long sidling climb over a saddle and down past an old *puesto* to the upper Río Amarillo. A route leads upvalley along the wide, gravelly flood plain to the snout of Ventisquero Amarillo, but it requires a serious wade of one of the river's several fast-flowing channels – a planned foot track would avoid any crossings.

Use the Chilean IGM's 1:50,000 map *Volcán Michimahuida* (Section H, No 111).

COMARCA ANDINA
Cerro Perito Moreno

This five-hour return trek begins from **Refugio Perito Moreno** (☎ 02944-493912). This hut at 950m belongs to the local CAP, and is 25km by road north of El Bolsón (p172). The route first climbs to the upper end of the winter ski lifts, then heads westward into the *lenga* scrub and crosses a plateau (at around 1600m) to reach the snout of the glacier on the side of Cerro Perito Moreno. The 2206m summit can only be reached by experienced climbers with proper mountaineering equipment, but from a lookout point on a spur a short way over to the left trekkers get an excellent view southward across the valley of the Río Encanto Blanco to the peaks around Dedo Gordo.

The 1:100,000 Argentine IGM map *El Bolsón* (Río Negro, No 4172-34) covers this area, but does not properly shows the route itself; see also the 'Around Cerro Hielo Azul' map (p175).

CERRO PILTRIQUITRÓN

Another of the Comarca Andina's key landmarks, the rump ridge of Cerro Piltriquitrón (pill-tree-key-**tron**) rises up directly east of El Bolsón. This panoramic 2260m peak can be climbed in a day trek from Plataforma del Piltriquitrón, at the end of the 10km access road (a taxi to here costs around US$10). A one-hour climb brings you to the **Refugio Cerro Piltriquitrón** (☎ 02944-492024; camping per person US$0.75, dorm beds US$2.50, meals US$4), a CAP hut at 1450m. A marked trail ascends on beside a disused ski lift, skirts away eastward, then climbs steeply through loose scree to the summit, giving superb views across Lago Puelo to Cerro Tres Picos and northward to Volcán Osorno and Monte Tronador.

The Argentine IGM's 1:100,000 map *Cuesta del Ternero* (Río Negro, No 4172-35) provides coverage of the trek.

CERRO LINDO

The glacier-crowned 2135m Cerro Lindo, which stands just less than 15km directly west of El Bolsón, can be climbed in a moderate three-day return trek. The path crosses the suspension bridge near the **Camping Río Azul** (☎ 02944-1560 2601) and climbs northwest through the forest. After descending steeply to cross the small Arroyo Lali (the last water until the *refugio*), continue up westward to reach the **Refugio Cerro Lindo** (camping free, beds US$3, meals US$4), a CAP hut that can get crowded in January. From here a rougher trail leads up to the summit of Cerro Lindo; the return trip takes around three hours. Recommended maps are as for the Around Cerro Hielo Azul trek (p173).

PARQUE NACIONAL LAGO PUELO

Centring round the 40-sq-km Lago Puelo itself, this small, 237-sq-km national park is 15km southwest of El Bolsón in the province of Chubut. The park administration centre or **Intendencia** (☎/fax 02944-499064) is at the village of Lago Puelo on the lake's northeastern shore.

Camping Lago Puelo (☎ 02944-499186; camping per person US$3) is in the village. The **Juana de Arco** (☎ 02944-493415; w www.inter patagonia.com/juanadearco) does launch trips around the lake, including to Río Turbio on the south shore (see Río Turbio & Cerro Plataforma below).

All of the longer treks starting in Parque Nacional Lago Puelo eventually lead outside the park boundaries. In addition to the routes outlined below, a once-popular four-day trek leads along the north shore into Chile then down the Río Puelo to Llanada Grande, but the road being built through this valley has lessened its remote appeal.

Two Argentine IGM 1:100,000 maps, *Cordón del Pico Alto* (Chubut, No 4372-3) and *Lago Puelo* (Chubut, No 4372-4), cover all of the park. In summer there are buses approximately every hour to Lago Puelo from El Bolsón.

Cerro Currumahuida

You can climb this peak (about 1200m) in around six hours return from the Intendencia. The route sidles along slopes on the eastern side of Lago Puelo, then climbs through stands of *coigüe* and Cordilleran cypress (higher up the forest has been largely destroyed by the fires of 1987) to the top of the range. A trek along (or near to) this ridge top to the summit of Cerro Currumahuida offers great views across Lago Puelo to Lago Inferior (in Chile), to Cerro Tres Picos to the southwest and Cerro Piltriquitrón to the northeast.

Río Turbio & Cerro Plataforma

The day trek to the Río Turbio leaves from the free camping area at El Desemboque, where the Río Epuyén runs into Lago Puelo; this is some 16km from El Hoyo, which is roughly 14km south of El Bolsón. The trail begins at the southern end of the beach, sidling up through burnt forest on the western slopes of Cerro Durrumbe before descending again to an APN *guardería* at the southeastern corner of Lago Puelo. From here launches run back across the lake to the jetty near the Intendencia on the northeast shore.

Cerro Plataforma, a flat-topped mountain well outside the park boundaries, where ancient marine fossils are found, can be reached in a three-day return trek from the *guardería*. The route turns southwestward, crosses the Arroyo Durrumbe and

climbs steadily up past little farms high above the valley of the Río Turbio; a final climb following red paint markings leads to the Cerro Plataforma. There are two rustic *refugios* along the route. Two Argentine IGM 1:100,000 maps, *Lago Puelo* (Chubut, No 4372-4) and *Lago Rivadavia* (Chubut, No 4372-10), cover this trek.

PARQUE NACIONAL LOS ALERCES

For all these routes, trekkers must begin climbing before 10am in order to return safely by nightfall.

Cerro Alto Dedal

The trek up to Cerro Alto Dedal (1916m) is the most popular in the park, and takes around seven hours return from Villa Futalaufquen. The signposted foot track leaves from the museum, and soon crosses the Arroyo Dedal (carry water from this stream as it is the last) as it climbs steeply out of the forest and follows a spur over Dedal (a minor point at around 1600m) to Cerro Alto Dedal. The summit offers great views northward across Lago Futalaufquen, east to Laguna Larga, south along the range to Cerro Cocinero (Situación) and southwest to the Cordón de los Pirámides.

The 1:100,000 Argentine IGM map *Villa Futalaufquen* (Chubut, No 2372-16) covers the area but does not show the route.

Refugio Cocinero

The trek up to this lookout point, which gives excellent views of a small glacier in the cirque between the northern and southern summits of Cerro Cocinero (Situación), is best done as an overnight trip. An unsignposted foot track leaves from the road 10km south of Villa Futalaufquen, first following the southern side of the Arroyo Rañinto. Head up left at the first large side stream you meet, crossing this several times as you climb steeply to reach **Refugio Cocinero**. This small hut has a fireplace and sleeping space for up to six people. Use the same IGM map as for the Cerro Alto Dedal trek.

Cerro Alto Petiso

The 1790m Cerro Alto El Petiso is the best lookout point in the park's northern sector, and you can visit it in a full-day trek of moderate difficulty taking around seven hours return. The trailhead is at Puerto Mermoud (where there is a historic wooden farmhouse built by the first settler in this area) on the western shore of Lago Verde. As a rule, trekkers must set out before 10am so that they have enough time to return safely by nightfall. The path climbs over a ridge, then follows the Arroyo Zanjón Honda up to its source at two tiny streamlets (the last running water). A final steep ascent along a spur leads to the summit, from where you get a superb panorama that includes Lago Menéndez, Lago Futalaufquen, Lago Rivadavia and the glacier-clad peak of Cerro Torrecillas. Use the same IGM map as for the treks mentioned earlier.

RESERVA NACIONAL FUTALEUFÚ

The 120-sq-km Reserva Nacional Futaleufú is directly southeast of the attractive village of Futaleufú, 160km from Chaitén in Chile. The reserve protects one of Chile's most northerly populations of *huemul*. A three-day circuit can be done from the bridge over the Río Futaleufú, 3km east of the Plaza de Armas in the village centre. The route leads up the Río Chico, then crosses a pass and descends along the Arroyo Quila Seca to meet the Río Futaleufú, following the river upstream back to the bridge. Another route goes up to the superb lookout summit of Cerro Cónico (2271m) on the Chile–Argentina border.

There are daily buses to Futaleufú from Chaitén. For more information contact Futaleufú's **tourist office** (☎ 065-721370; O'Higgins 596). Two Chilean IGM 1:50,000 maps cover the reserve: *Futaleufú* (Section I, No 11) and *Río Futaleufú* (Section I, No 24).

PARQUE NACIONAL QUEULAT

The 154-sq-km Parque Nacional Queulat lies southeast of the tiny town of Puyuguapi on Chile's Pacific coast. Its wet, maritime climate has produced vast glaciers and ice fields in the interior of the park, while the lower areas are vegetated by dense coastal rainforest. The administrative *guardería* for the park is at the end of a 2km turn-off, 25km south of Puyuguapi along the Carretera Austral. The *guardería* looks out towards the Ventisquero Colgante, a spectacular hanging glacier that drops great blocks of ice over a precipice several hundred metres high. There's a better lookout about 15 minutes on past the Conaf camping area. A harder return day trek continues across the suspension bridge and follows an increasingly overgrown path along the Río Ventisqueros to Laguna Témpanos, a small lake directly below the Ventisquero Colgante. The Chilean IGM 1:50,000 map *Puyuguapi* (Section I, No 61) covers the central part of the park around Ventisquero Colgante.

RESERVA NACIONAL RÍO SIMPSON

Reserva Nacional Río Simpson is a small reserve taking in the mountains to the west and northwest of Coyhaique. A three-day (37km) out-and-back trek leads up the Río Correntoso to a small lake at the foot of the craggy Cerro Catedral (not to be confused with its namesake, a peak in Argentina's Parque Nacional Nahuel Huapi). The trek begins at the Guardería Correntoso, accessible from 500m east of the Puente Correntoso, a bridge on the Coyhaique–Puerto Aysén road (Ruta CH 245), 22km from Coyhaique. Unfortunately, the trail has deteriorated badly in recent years, so until some serious maintenance is carried out (including replacement of footbridges) this route will remain virtually impassable. A two-day return trek from the Guardería Correntoso to the **Bosque Petrificado**, where small petrified stumps of ancient Guaitecas cypress are found, can still be done relatively easily.

One Chilean IGM 1:50,000 map covers the area: *Río Correntoso* (Section I, No 108).

CENTRAL PATAGONIA

Southern Patagonia

Southern Patagonia stretches south from the Península de Taitao and Lago Carrera/Lago Buenos Aires as far as the Straits of Magellan. Dominated by the two vast continental icecaps, the Hielo Norte and the Hielo Sur, this region is the most intensely glaciated part of South America. Unquestionably one of the world's most ruggedly beautiful places, southern Patagonia includes the internationally renowned Los Glaciares and Torres del Paine national parks.

GATEWAYS
El Calafate (Argentina)
El Calafate lies on the southern shore of Lago Argentino, and lives almost entirely from the booming tourism in the nearby vast Parque Nacional Los Glaciares. Day visits to Glaciar Moreno (including guided 'minitreks' on the ice), boat excursions across Lago Argentino to the snout of Glaciar Upsala and trips to the park's northernmost Fitz Roy sector all begin and end in El Calafate. The town's intrinsic attractions are limited, but there are far worse places to spend a day.

Information The **visitor centre** *(APN Intendencia; ☎ 02902-491755; Libertador 1302; open 8am-10pm daily Oct-May)* for Parque Nacional Los Glaciares is towards the western end of Av del Libertador, the main road through town. El Calafate's **tourist office** *(☎ 02902-491090; open 8am-10pm daily)* is at the bus station (Terminal de Omnibuses), a block uphill from the town centre.

The town website is at 🆆 *www.calafate .com.*

Supplies & Equipment El Calafate is the best place to stock up for treks in Parque Nacional Los Glaciares. Two of the biggest supermarkets are **La Anónima** *(Libertador 902)*, at the east end of town, and **Alas** *(9 de Julio 59)*; both open daily until late.

La Leyenda *(Libertador 1180; open 10am-1pm & 5pm-10pm daily)* sells white gas

NICK TAPP

Awe-inspiring ice towers and crevices on the broken surface of Glaciar Grey

- A surprise encounter with *huemul*, the rare Andean deer, near Glaciar Tigre on the trek to Laguna Tigre Sur (p203)

- Overnighting under the mighty Monte San Lorenzo at Refugio Toni Rohrer on the Campamento De Agostini trek (p199)

- Seeing Cerro Torre's chiselled form point skyward above a confluence of glaciers on the Laguna Torre trek (p210)

- Stupendous views from many angles of mighty Monte Fitz Roy (p212) and its satellite peaks

- Watching from the Torres del Paine lookout (p222) as dawn paints the sheer granite towers pink, then orange, then gold

- The first view over Glaciar Grey from Paso John Garner on the Paine Circuit (p223)

SOUTHERN PATAGONIA

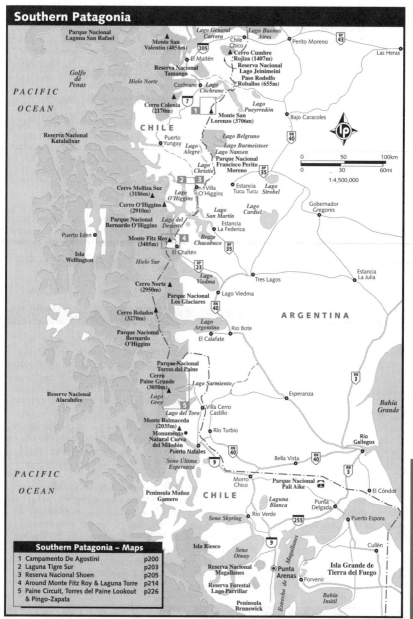

Southern Patagonia

PACIFIC OCEAN

Golfo de Penas

Hielo Norte

Parque Nacional
Laguna San Rafael

Monte San
Valentín (4058m)

Reserva Nacional
Tamango

El Maitén

RP 205

Lago General
Carrera

Chile
Chico

Lago Buenos
Aires

Perito Moreno

RP 43

Las Heras

Cerro Cumbre
Rojiza (1407m)

Reserva Nacional
Lago Jeinimeini

Paso Rodolfo
Roballos (655m)

Cochrane

Lago
Cochrane

RN 7

Cerro Colonia
(2170m)

Monte San
Lorenzo (3706m)

Lago
Pueyrredón

Bajo Caracoles

CHILE

Reserva Nacional
Katalalixar

Puerto
Yungay

Lago
Alegre

Lago Belgrano

Lago Burmeisteer

Lago Nansen

Parque Nacional
Francisco Perito
Moreno

RN 40

0   50   100km
0   30   60mi
1:4,500,000

Lago
Christie

RP 35

Cerro Melliza Sur
(3186m)

Lago
O'Higgins

Villa
O'Higgins

Estancia
Tucu Tucu

Lago
Strobel

Cerro O'Higgins
(2910m)

Parque Nacional
Bernardo O'Higgins

Lago del
Desierto

Lago
San Martín

Lago
Cardiel

Gobernador
Gregores

Puerto Edén

Isla
Wellington

Monte Fitz Roy
(3405m)

El Chaltén

Estancia
La Federica

Brazo
Chacabuco

RP 35

Hielo Sur

RP 23

Cerro Norte
(2950m)

Lago
Viedma

Lago Viedma

Tres Lagos

Estancia
La Julia

Parque Nacional
Los Glaciares

RN 40

ARGENTINA

Cerro Bolados
(3270m)

Parque Nacional
Bernardo
O'Higgins

Lago
Argentino

Río Bote

El Calafate

Parque Nacional
Torres del Paine

Cerro
Paine Grande
(3050m)

Lago Sarmiento

Esperanza

RN 3

Bahía
Grande

Reserve Nacional
Alacalufes

Lago
Grey

Lago del Toro

Villa Cerro
Castillo

Monte Balmaceda
(2035m)

Monumento
Natural Cueva
del Milodón

Puerto Natales

Río Turbio

RN 40

Río
Gallegos

RN 3

Bella Vista

PACIFIC
OCEAN

Seno Última
Esperanza

Morro
Chico

Parque Nacional
Pali Aike

RN 9

El Cóndor

Península Muñoz
Gamero

CHILE

Laguna
Blanca

Punta
Delgada

Puerto Espora

RN 255

Seno Skyring

Río Verde

RN 9

Cullén

Isla Riesco

Seno
Otway

Reserva Nacional
Magallanes

Punta
Arenas

Porvenir

Isla Grande de
Tierra del Fuego

Reserva Forestal
Lago Parrillar

Península
Brunswick

Estrecho de Magallanes

Bahía
Inútil

Southern Patagonia – Maps

(solvente) for stoves and a limited range of trekking equipment. **Paralelo 53** (☎ 02902-492596; 25 de Mayo 38) has a wider range of good-quality outdoor clothing, footwear, backpacks and accessories.

Various shops along Av del Libertador sell trekking maps.

Places to Stay & Eat El Calafate is well supplied with accommodation but demand can be fierce. Consider booking ahead.

The **Camping Municipal** (☎ 02902-491829; José Pantín; camping per person US$1.50) straddles the creek just north of the bridge into town and has hot showers.

Los Dos Pinos (☎ 02902-491271; w www .losglaciares.com/losdospinos; 9 de Julio 358; camping per person US$2.50, dorm beds US$7, doubles/triples US$16/24, with bathroom from US$25/30), three blocks north of Av del Libertador, has all manner of accommodation options.

The bustling HI-affiliated **Albergue Hostal del Glaciar** (☎/fax 02902-491243; w www.glaciar.com; Los Pioneros 251; dorm beds US$7, singles/doubles with bathroom from US$24/27) has triple and quad rooms as well, and is cheaper for HI members. Rates include breakfast. Los Pioneros is several blocks from the centre of town, east of the creek.

Albergue America del Sur (☎ 02902-493525; w www.americahostel.com.ar; Puerto Deseado; dorm beds US$8, doubles US$29) has well-designed four-person dorms and attractive communal areas. Room rates include breakfast. Cross the bridge heading east, go left on Coronel Rosales, then up the hill.

Amancay Hostal Patagónico (☎ 02902-491113; e amancayhostal@fibertel.com.ar; Gobernador Gregores 1457; doubles/triples US$28/35, 5-person room US$48) has a B&B feel with eight small but comfortable rooms.

Hostería Posta Sur (☎ 02902-492406; e hosteriapostasur@cotecal.com.ar; San Julián 490; doubles/triples US$50/67, 4-person apartments US$80), up towards Albergue America del Sur, is very nice indeed.

Fitz Roy or Paine?

Southern Patagonia's two big attractions for trekkers are undoubtedly the Fitz Roy sector of Argentina's Parque Nacional Los Glaciares and Chile's Parque Nacional Torres del Paine. Both offer spectacular treks through rugged glaciated landscapes, among sheer granite spires and wild forests. A trekking trip to the region would ideally visit them both, and proliferating transport services, as well as the development of the abridged Torres del Paine trek known as the W (see the boxed text 'The W', p230), make this ever easier to achieve. But if you really only have time for one of these great parks, how do you decide which one?

If you want a world-class long trek of a week or more, the Paine Circuit is the clear choice. Paine's *refugios* (huts) and catamaran services offer a level of trekker comfort not found in the Fitz Roy area – though comfort of this kind may not be everyone's cup of tea. Paine has the edge, arguably, for really big, accessible glaciers in action, right on the edge of the Hielo Sur. It has big, beautiful lakes, too, right in the thick of the trekking territory.

The Fitz Roy area is more compact and its treks shorter. Its glaciers are smaller but still spectacular, and many visitors here also make a day trip from El Calafate to the massive Glaciar Moreno. On the other hand, it has bigger mountains: Monte Fitz Roy is the highest peak in either park (at 3405m), and Cerro Poincenot and Cerro Torre likewise exceed 3000m in height; the only summit above 3000m in Torres del Paine is the main peak of Cerro Paine Grande. Where the Fitz Roy and Cerro Torre groups can't be beaten, in our view, is in their wonderful rock architecture and a climbing history that is almost without parallel, full of controversy, tragedy and achievement.

The choice, if you must make it, is yours. A final word of caution, though: if you simply must have sunshine and clear skies, the Costa del Sol is supposed to be nice.

Pietro's *(Libertador 1002; breakfast US$2.50, sandwiches US$1.50-3)* is a comfortable corner café for breakfast or something light to eat.

El Hornito *(Buenos Aires 155; pizzas US$1.50-7, pasta US$3-4)*, just south of the bus station, is a veritable museum of Patagoniana, and the food is good too.

La Tablita *(Coronel Rosales 28; mains US$1.50-4, parrillada for 2 US$10)* is not the only *parrilla* (grill restaurant) in town, but its mouthwatering meat meals are worth crossing the bridge for – and there are vegetarian dishes. Be early to beat the tour groups.

Getting There & Away Three airlines, **Aerolíneas Argentinas** *(☎ 0810-222 86527)*, **LAPA** *(☎ 0810-777 5272; Libertador 1015)* and **Southern Winds** *(☎ 0810-777 7979)*, offer a good range of flights between El Calafate and Buenos Aires (US$80, three hours, several daily), Bariloche (US$120, 1¾ hours, nine weekly), and Ushuaia (US$105, 1¼ hours, daily). **Aerovías DAP** *(☎ 02902-491143; Libertador 1329)* flies to Puerto Natales, Chile (US$50, 30 minutes, daily Monday to Friday).

The long-distance bus companies have offices at the bus station. **Cootra** *(☎ 02902-491444)*, **Turismo Zaahj** *(☎ 02902-491631)* and **Bus Sur** *(☎ 02902-491631)* all have services to Puerto Natales (US$15, five hours, daily). **Transportadora Patagónica** *(in Bariloche ☎ 02944-437699)* goes to Bariloche (US$42, 32 hours, daily) and **El Pingüino** *(☎ 02902-491273)* goes to Buenos Aires (US$46, 44 hours).

Puerto Natales (Chile)

Composed largely of imaginatively constructed corrugated iron buildings and stretching along the eastern shore of Seno Última Esperanza (Last Hope Sound), the windy town of Puerto Natales is the gateway to Parque Nacional Torres del Paine.

Information Puerto Natales' helpful **Sernatur tourist office** *(Servicio Nacional de Turismo; ☎ 061-412125; Costanera Pedro Montt; open roughly 8am-10pm daily in summer)* is about 1km north of the docks.

There's a **Conaf office** *(Corporación Nacional Forestal; ☎ 061-411438; O'Higgins 584)*, but information about Parque Nacional Torres del Paine is easier to come by out at the park itself or at **Andescape** *(☎ 061-412877; W www.andescape.cl; Eberhard 599)*, one of the two concessionaires that run the park's *refugios* (huts), or a tour agency such as **Turismo 21 de Mayo** *(☎ 061-411176; W www.chileaustral.com/21demayo; Eberhard 560)*. Andescape is the place to book *refugio* accommodation in Parque Nacional Torres del Paine.

Supplies & Equipment Buy all your supplies for Torres del Paine treks in Puerto Natales. The *refugios* in the park and the Posada Río Serrano (see Within the Park, p221), near the park administration centre at Lago del Toro, have small *almacenes* (stores) stocked with essentials and luxuries, but the range is limited and prices are high. Supermarkets near the centre of Puerto Natales include **La Bombonera** *(Bulnes 646)* and **Don Bosco** *(Baquedano)*.

Several stores along the streets south of the Plaza de Armas hire out trekking gear, but many trekkers rent tents, sleeping bags and stoves on the spot at *refugios* and camping grounds in the national park. For white gas *(bencina blanca)* and other fuel, try the **ferretería** *(hardware store; cnr Bulnes & Barros Arana)* down Bulnes towards the waterfront, which has some trekking clothing and equipment as well. Also try the **'trekking store'** *(Blanco Encalada 226)* in the centre of town, or **Servilaundry** *(Bulnes 513)*.

Bookstores, souvenir shops, trekking suppliers and Servilaundry all sell trekking maps of Torres del Paine.

Places to Stay & Eat If you're determined to camp, **Camping Josmar II** *(☎ 061-414417; cnr Arturo Prat & Esmeralda; camping per person US$3)* is central and reasonably well equipped if hardly rustic.

Puerto Natales is awash with budget *residenciales* (boarding houses or guesthouses). **Los Inmigrantes** *(☎ 061-413482; Ignacio Carrera Pinto 480; per person US$7)* is a good choice for trekkers who want to rent

SOUTHERN PATAGONIA

equipment or simply talk trekking. There are kitchen privileges, but no breakfast.

Hostal Don Guillermo *(☎ 061-414506; O'Higgins 657; singles/doubles US$12/21)* is a pleasant spot. Its small rooms have no windows, but the shared bathrooms are very clean.

Hostal Melissa *(☎ 061-411944; Blanco Encalada 258; singles/doubles US$14/28)* is in the thick of things opposite Andescape (see Information, p195), and has comfortable, compact rooms above a good, if smoky, **café**. Breakfast downstairs – at any hour if you're catching an early bus to the park – is included.

Concepto Indigo *(☎ 061-413609; e indigo@entelchile.net; Ladrilleros 105; rooms US$15-35)* has shared and private rooms, many with views over the sound, a bar and **restaurant** downstairs, and a climbing wall outside.

Hotel Lady Florence Dixie *(☎ 061-411158, 411943; w www.chileanpatagonia.com/ florence; Bulnes 655; singles/doubles from US$60/75)* has bright motel-style back rooms and smarter rooms above the street.

Masay *(Bulnes 427; pizzas US$3.50-5)* is a popular spot for sandwiches, hamburgers and pizzas.

La Tranquera *(Bulnes 579; mains US$3-8)* is unpretentious and friendly and serves standard nosh at reasonable prices.

Restaurant Última Esperanza *(Eberhard 354; mains US$4-11)* specialises in seafood and is good for a splash. The *cazuela* (soup; US$3.75) is a meal in itself.

Getting There & Away There is a small airfield a few kilometres north of town on the road to Torres del Paine. **Aerovías DAP** *(☎ 061-415100; Bulnes 100)* flies between Puerto Natales and El Calafate, Argentina (US$50, 30 minutes, daily Monday to Friday). The local office of **LanChile** *(☎ 061-411236; Tomás Rogers 78)* can help with flights from Punta Arenas to destinations including Santiago.

Puerto Natales has no central bus terminal, though several companies stop at the junction of Valdivia and Baquedano. **Buses Fernández** *(☎ 061-411111; Eberhard 555)*

has frequent buses to and from Punta Arenas (US$4, three hours) – book the day before. To El Calafate, Argentina (US$21, 5½ hours), **Turismo Zaahj** *(☎ 061-412260; Arturo Prat 236)* and **Bus Sur** *(☎ 061-411325; Baquedano 534)* have the most frequent (daily) service. Bus Sur goes on Monday to Coyhaique (US$48, 22 hours), heading first for Punta Arenas then transferring to another bus.

Many people arrive in Puerto Natales on the four-day, three-night ferry voyage from Puerto Montt through Patagonia's spectacular western channels. The MN *Magallanes* makes the return journey once a week, usually arriving in Puerto Natales on Thursday and leaving on Friday. Book at the Santiago office of **Navimag** *(☎ 02-4423120; w www .navimag.com; El Bosque Norte 440, 11th floor, Las Condes)*, or reserve via the Internet and confirm with the Santiago office. In Puerto Natales, Navimag is right by the ferry dock *(☎ 061-414300; Costanera Pedro Montt 262)*. Fares (which include meals) vary according to season, class of accommodation and view, but in high season (November to March), per-person one-way fares range from US$275 for a berth to US$1590 for an AAA single cabin.

Punta Arenas (Chile)

Punta Arenas is the largest city in southern Patagonia. Apart from some easy trekking in the low ranges of the Península Brunswick, it makes a poor base for trips into the Cordillera, but it is the regional transport hub, and there are plenty of interesting places to visit in and around the city. The **Museo Salesiano** *(Av Bulnes 374; admission US$2.50; open 10am-12.30pm & 3pm-6pm Tues-Sun)* has good exhibits on the mountaineer priest Alberto De Agostini and various indigenous groups.

Information The **Sernatur tourist office** *(☎ 061-241330; Waldo Seguel 689; open 8.15am-6.45pm Mon-Fri, to 8pm in summer)*, off Plaza Muñoz Gamero, publishes a list of accommodation and transport options. There's an **information kiosk** *(open 8am-7pm Mon-Fri, 9am-8pm Sat)* located in the plaza, and the **Conaf office** (☎ 061-223841; *José Menéndez 1147*) has details on nearby parks. **Hostería Las Torres/Fantástico Sur** (☎ 061-226054; *Magallanes 960*) manages Las Torres, El Chileno and Los Cuernos *refugios* and camping grounds in Parque Nacional Torres del Paine. There's an **Argentine consulate** (☎ 061-261912; *21 de Mayo 1878; open 10am-3.30pm Mon-Fri*), among others.

Places to Stay & Eat A private school, **Colegio Pierre Fauré** (☎ 061-226256; *Bellavista 697; camping per person US$4, singles with/without breakfast US$7/6*), six blocks south of Plaza Muñoz Gamero, operates as a hostel from December to February. Campers can pitch a tent in the side garden. All bathrooms are shared, but there's plenty of hot water.

Residencial Coirón (☎ 061-226449; *Sanhueza 730; rooms US$13*) is just across from the Fernández bus terminal. The sunny singles upstairs are the best deal, but all room rates include breakfast.

Hostal de la Patagonia (☎/fax 061-249970; *Croacia 970; singles/doubles US$31/50*) is a small, quiet and conscientiously run spot with perfectly adequate rooms that have private bathrooms. Breakfast is included.

Getting There & Away There are flights five times daily to Puerto Montt (US$140, 2¼ hours) and to Santiago (US$230, 4¼ hours) with **LanChile** (☎ 061-241100; *Lautaro Navarro 999*). **Aerovías DAP** (☎ 061-223340; *O'Higgins 891*) flies to Puerto Williams on Isla Navarino (US$70, 1¼ hours, daily Tuesday to Saturday) and Ushuaia, Argentina (US$108, one hour, twice weekly); luggage is limited to 10kg per person.

Punta Arenas had no central bus terminal at the time of writing. Most bus company offices are within a block or two of Av Colón. **Buses Fernández** (☎ 061-246242; *Pedro Montt 966*), **Bus Sur** (☎ 061-244464; *Menéndez 565*) and **Buses Pacheco** (☎ 061-242174; *Av Colón 900*) each have several departures daily to Puerto Natales (US$4,

three hours). Bus Sur goes to Coyhaique (US$44, 20 hours, twice weekly), and **Queilen Bus** (☎ 061-246242; *Pedro Montt 966*) and Buses Pacheco go to Puerto Montt (US$44, 30 hours, twice weekly) via Argentina.

Transbordadora Austral Broom's (☎ 061-218100; Ⓦ *www.tabsa.cl; Av Bulnes 05075*) ferries link several of Chile's southernmost ports. From the Tres Puentes ferry terminal north of town (get a *taxi colectivo* outside Palacio Mauricio Braun on Magallanes), the *Fueguino* sails every Wednesday to Puerto Williams, Isla Navarino (US$120/150 seat/bunk, 26 hours), and leaves Puerto Williams on the return voyage every Friday.

San Lorenzo Massif

Crowned by the 3706m Monte San Lorenzo – depending on definition, the Patagonian Andes' second- or third-highest summit – the San Lorenzo massif straddles the Chile–Argentina border a few dozen kilometres southeast of Cochrane. With its complex of towers and large glaciers, this isolated range is reminiscent of the Macizo Paine far to the south.

Monte San Lorenzo, still officially called Monte Cochrane in Chile (although that name is rarely used except on some government documents), is most easily accessible from its western (Chilean) side via private farms along the Río Tranquilo. The eastern (Argentine) side of the San Lorenzo massif enjoys much better environmental protection, however, being almost entirely within either Parque Nacional Francisco Perito Moreno (see Other Treks, p234) or the 140-sq-km former Estancia El Rincón, owned by the Patagonia Land Trust (a nongovernmental conservation organisation).

NATURAL HISTORY

Although rock and ice often block the way, the existence of several key passes and lower ridges in the San Lorenzo massif facilitates the biological communication between flora and fauna on each side.

The vegetation cover is determined mainly by microclimatic variations in precipitation along with exposure to the sun and savage drying winds. The upper valleys are largely covered by light Magellanic (southern Patagonian) forest of deciduous *ñirre* and *lenga*, with an understorey of *brecillo* and *chauras*, which produce bountiful red berries from late January. *Chilcas*, various species of native daisy-like shrubs, grow in the forest or on moist sunny sites. On the lower or exposed slopes, sparse vegetation more typical of the Patagonian steppes predominates, including tussock grasses and saltbush-like *mogotes*.

Although grazing cattle are the most dominant herbivore in Patagonia, *huemul* and occasionally even guanaco (Patagonian cameloid species, related to the llama) are sometimes seen on the Chilean side, crossing regularly from Argentina, stalked by the furtive puma. Trekkers may also be lucky enough to spot the shy Patagonian armadillo *(piche)*, which digs its burrow in soft earth.

The gregarious black-necked ibis *(bandurria)* is often seen in the lower valley and around moister areas, usually in flocks of a dozen or more, picking over the grassy areas with its long curved beak. The diminutive thorntail *(rayadito)* lives and nests among the *lenga* forests, feeding on the plentiful insects that hide in the trees' flaky bark. The cinnamon-bellied tyrant (called *dormilona rufa* in Spanish) inhabits the drier scrubland. Upland geese and flying steamer ducks visit the lakes and waterways. Andean condors are regularly seen circling high above the ridges.

CLIMATE

Exposed to the westerly winds due both to its unusual height and to the fact that it fills a 'gap' between the two great continental icecaps (the Hielo Norte and the Hielo Sur), the San Lorenzo massif is subject to changeable weather with sudden storms. Precipitation exceeds 4000mm on the higher summits and ridges – falling almost entirely as snow – which feeds major glaciers that splay down in all directions.

So-called ice mushrooms are created as the moist airstream randomly deposits crystals of ice in bizarre formations. Although situated too low to attract significant precipitation, the valleys surrounding the massif are buffeted by strong, dry winds, producing conditions similar to the steppes farther east.

ACCESS TOWN
Cochrane (Chile)

The very small town of Cochrane (population 3000) lies 340km south of Coyhaique on the Carretera Austral. There is a tourist kiosk situated on Cochrane's central Plaza de Armas. **Conaf** (☎ 067-522164; Río Nef 417), at the uphill edge of town, can give advice on treks in the area. The **Red de Turismo Río Baker** (☎ 067-522646; San Valentin 438) is a network of regional private tourism operators, ranging from camping grounds to fishing lodges. **Melero Ferreteria-Tienda** (☎ 067-522197; Golondrinas 148), on the Plaza de Armas, sells supplies and white gasoline.

At **Residencial Sur Austral** (☎ 067-522150; Prat 281; rooms per person US$7) the rooms are simple and clean, and breakfast is included in the cost. Other meals are available. **Hotel Wellmann** (☎ 067-522171; Las Golondrinas 36; singles/doubles US$25/ 35) has better rooms, and also has a good **restaurant**.

Getting There & Away Transportes Don Carlos, at Residencial Sur Austral (see Cochrane), has two flights each week between Coyhaique (US$60, around two hours) and Villa O'Higgins (US$50, around two hours), which (on demand) make a stop in Cochrane. Transporte Don Carlos, **Buses Los Ñadis** (☎ 067-522196; Río Maiten & Teniente Merino) and **Buses Acuario 13** (☎ 067-522143; Teniente Merino 481) each run three or four buses to and from Coyhaique (around US$12, eight hours) each week. Buses Los Ñadis also runs the once-weekly bus (US$9, six hours) to Villa O'Higgins. Charter vehicles *(fletes)* wait in front of Melero Ferreteria-Tienda's on the Plaza de Armas.

Campamento De Agostini

Duration	4 days
Distance	54km
Difficulty	easy–moderate
Start/Finish	Fundo Olivieo Paillacar
Nearest Town	Cochrane (p198)
Transport	bus

Summary A little-travelled route into a wild and remote upper valley from where De Agostini made his legendary first ascent.

The 'classic' route up to Campamento De Agostini (not to be confused with its namesake in Parque Nacional Los Glaciares) is only lightly travelled, mostly by andinists on their hopeful way to the summit. The trek follows old roads and a generally well-formed trail, and presents few difficulties – unless you want to continue to the summit of Monte San Lorenzo!

PLANNING
When to Trek
The trek can normally be done from early November until late April.

Maps
The route of the trek spreads over four Chilean IGM 1:50,000 maps, but, unfortunately, until now only two of these maps have been published: *Cochrane* (Section J, No 66) and *Lago Brown* (Section J, No 67). Fortunately, the area of the unpublished Chilean IGM maps is covered by one Argentine IGM 1:100,000 map: *Cerro Pico Agudo* (No 4772-27).

Permits & Regulations
As the San Lorenzo massif is a somewhat sensitive border area, climbers and trekkers are required to fill out a form detailing their intended route at the local office of the **Carabineros** (☎ 067-522313; *Esmeralda 522*), near the Plaza de Armas in Cochrane. While this wild frontier is patrolled only sporadically, anyone who crosses between Chile and Argentina without official permission is violating the law and, if caught, is certain to be forcibly expelled and/or fined.

As the trek is entirely within private property, do not camp anywhere along the route other than at the camping ground near the Fundo San Lorenzo farmhouse (see The Trek, Day 1) or at Campamento De Agostini (see The Trek, Day 2).

GETTING TO/FROM THE TREK
The trek begins at the Fundo Olivieo Paillacar, a farm at the end of the transitable road in the valley of the Río Tranquilo, 43km from Cochrane. From early December until early April, **Respuestos Moya** (☎ 067-522276; *Dr Steffens 147*) in Cochrane runs a 12-seat minibus to Fundo Olivieo Paillacar (US$4) on Monday and Thursday at 11am, returning at 1pm. (It is advisable to buy tickets in advance, but with sufficient bookings the minibus may run unscheduled trips.) From the approach road, there are spectacular views of the jagged ice-capped San Lorenzo massif. Fundo Olivieo Paillacar and Fundo San Lorenzo are in regular two-way radio contact with Cochrane, and can order a *flete* if the minibus is unable to take you.

THE TREK
Day 1: Fundo Olivieo Paillacar to Fundo San Lorenzo
4–5½ hours, 17.5km, 420m ascent
From where the minibus stops beside tall poplars sheltering the farmhouse, cross the Estero Plater (which flows through several stream channels that can often be jumped individually). Then follow a rough 4WD track that makes a long upward traverse northeast to high above the swampy, meandering Río Tranquilo under sharp towers of the Cordón Cochrane, a lateral range of the San Lorenzo massif. Across the valley are the less angular summits of the Cordón Esmeralda.

After two to 2½ hours, the old road turns abruptly around to the right away from the river, bringing the first direct views of Monte San Lorenzo, whose gleaming dome resembles an enormous cake smeared with thick white icing. Continue up southeastward among low *ñirres* and clearings scattered with *calafate* bushes to reach **Laguna**

SOUTHERN PATAGONIA

del Corazón, a small tranquil lake visited by flying steamer ducks, 50 minutes to 1¼ hours on.

Head up around the southwest shore of the lake, then cut on southeast across a broad plain strewn with *mogotes*. The 4WD track climbs through *lenga* forest to a ridge top before it sidles down left and fords the frigid, milky Río Tranquilo to terminate at the **Fundo San Lorenzo**, 1¼ to 1¾ hours from the lake. Particularly after midday, the river tends to be too high and fast-flowing for a comfortable wade across it, so head 400m upstream through the scrub to cross

on a sturdy (but makeshift) bridge over a narrow gorge.

Fundo San Lorenzo (☎/fax 067-522326; *Teniente Merino 750, Cochrane*) is a beautiful farm owned by Luis Soto and Lucy Gomez. No accommodation is available at the farmhouse itself, but there is scenic camping nearby (US$1.50 per person). Simple meals are served, and bread, pies and fruit conserves are sold – otherwise bring all supplies. Washing facilities are basic (cold!). Horses can be hired (US$16 per day) and, if pre-arranged, left at the Fundo Olivieo Paillacar.

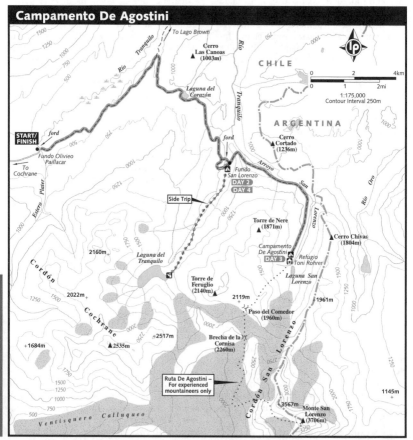

Campamento De Agostini

The scenic camping ground, just upvalley from the farmhouse under *ñirres* among moist meadows, looks south to hanging glaciers on jagged peaks at the head of the Río Tranquilo (see Side Trip). From here a six-hour side trip can be made up to Torre de Nere (1871m), a lookout that gives great views of the San Lorenzo massif and the distant Monte San Valentín.

Side Trip: Laguna del Tranquilo
3½–4½ hours return, 13km,
475m ascent/descent
Head upvalley past the camping ground along a rough road across wet pastures. This 4WD track cuts up left to slightly higher ground, passing through two fence gates among *calafate* meadows before it peters out at a 100m-wide gravel wash choking the *lenga* forest. Proceed along cattle trails across a small gully, then cut up rightward out of the trees through stabilising rubble to the end of a lateral moraine, one to 1½ hours from the farmhouse. Look up to spot circling condors.

Climb steeply, either along the crest of the moraine ridge or just left of it, to high above the raging Río Tranquilo, continuing well past where the forest begins to fringe the moraine until you get a near-full view of Laguna del Tranquilo, one to 1½ hours on. The grey waters of this bleak, forlorn lake fill a deep trough ringed by half a dozen glaciers clinging to the sheer walls of the valley. Slabs of ice erratically crash down onto the rocks below (occasionally even reaching the water), while waterfalls splash down from the snouts of the glaciers. When you've taken it all in, return via the ascent route.

Day 2: Fundo San Lorenzo to Campamento De Agostini
2½–3½ hours, 9.5km, 325m ascent
From the farmhouse, head northeast across open fields to the right of a stand of exotic pines, then cut back up steeply right over a ridge into lovely grassy meadows along the **Arroyo San Lorenzo**. Follow a foot track upvalley over beautiful grassy flats along the stream's true left (southern) bank towards Cerro Pico Agudo, a lone spiked

peak across the border in Argentina. After passing through a narrow gap, the route continues past the Portezuelo Arroyo San Lorenzo, an unobtrusive, scrubby saddle directly across the arroyo. (On the other side – in Argentina – is the former Argentine Estancia El Rincon, now owned by the Patagonia Land Trust).

Begin an initially gentle rise that steepens as you turn southward past where the stream races through a deep chasm. The gradient moderates again as you head on through several small meadows towards the looming colossus of Monte San Lorenzo to arrive at **Campamento De Agostini** (camping US$2 per person). Here, at around 1000m among *lenga* forest carpeted with low *brecillo* shrubbery, stands the basic original shelter (modified by generations of climbers) first built by Father De Agostini during his determined attempts on the summit. More enticing, however, is the excellent **Refugio Toni Rohrer** (US$3 per person). This is an excellent new wooden hut dedicated to a Swiss mountaineer who died climbing Monte San Lorenzo on 1 March 2000. It has a stove and a dining area with benches and tables; there is sleeping space in the loft for around 12 people. The *refugio* is left unlocked. Pay at the farmhouse. There are picnic tables outside in the forest for campers.

A path leads five to 10 minutes on upvalley to peter out among gravelly moraines overlooking Laguna San Lorenzo, a murky tarn fed by a glacier sprawling down from the northern summit of Monte San Lorenzo. From here, intrepid mountaineers continue southwest to the summit via the classic Ruta De Agostini (see the boxed text 'De Agostini's First Ascent', p202).

Days 3 & 4: Campamento De Agostini to Fundo Olivieo Paillacar
5½–7½ hours, 27km, 745m descent
Retrace your steps of Day 2 and Day 1, descending to Fundo San Lorenzo (two to three hours), then to Fundo Oliveo Paillacar (another 3½ to 4½ hours). To camp at Fundo Oliveo Paillacar, ask permission first.

Lago O'Higgins Area

The area around Lago O'Higgins, at the northeast edge of the Hielo Sur, is one of the wildest and most thinly settled parts of the Patagonian Andes. Despite its huge size (1013 sq km), Lago O'Higgins is merely the fifth-largest lake in Patagonia, yet its half a dozen long arms and mountainous peninsulas make it the most complex and interesting. The lake is shared fairly evenly between Chile and Argentina (where it is called Lago San Martín). With the completion of the Carretera Austral (Southern Highway) to Villa O'Higgins in 2000, and the continuing construction of a new road into Argentina along the Río Mayer, the Lago O'Higgins area is losing some of its isolation.

NATURAL HISTORY

Fashioned by enormous glaciers that once extended from the Hielo Sur far out into the Patagonian steppes, today this intensely glaciated landscape is largely covered by Magellanic forest of southern beech species, especially the deciduous *lenga* and *ñirre*. The area is one of the last strongholds of the *huemul* and breeding pairs are often encountered feeding on alpine grasses and mosses above the tree line. Also commonly sighted is the great Andean condor, which nests on high inaccessible cliff ledges.

CLIMATE

Chilled by winds blowing off the Hielo Sur and/or Lago O'Higgins, average summer temperatures in this area do not exceed 15°C. However, the mountains of the continental icecap catch much of the moisture in the westerly winds, leaving the area with modest rain and snowfalls. Annual precipitation at Villa O'Higgins is only 850mm, but rises to over 2500mm in surrounding mountains.

ACCESS TOWN
Villa O'Higgins (Chile)

Situated at only 265m above sea level on a windswept plain just north of Lago O'Higgins, Villa O'Higgins (population 500) is one of the most isolated settlements in Chile. This 'pioneer' village founded in 1967 comprises no more than a few street blocks. There is a small tourist information kiosk in the Plaza de Armas. For general information (Spanish-language) go to the village website at Ⓦ www.ohiggins.cl or contact the **municipal offices** *(municipalidad;* ☎ *067-211849)* on the east side of the Plaza de Armas. **Conaf** *(*☎ *067-211834; Lago Cisnes 101)*, right below the lookout tower *(mirador)*, can give advice on local treks.

Hospedaje Patagonia *(*☎ *067-234813; Río Pascua 1956; rooms US$7 per person)* includes breakfast in the room rate and serves basic meals. The **Hospedaje Apocalipsis 1:3** *(Pasaje Lago El Salto 345; rooms US$8 per person)* also includes breakfast in the room rate, and sells home-baked bread.

Getting There & Away A bus runs once a week in either direction between Cochrane and Villa O'Higgins (US$9, six hours). There are not many seats so it is advisable to book (and reconfirm) tickets well in advance.

De Agostini's First Ascent

In the late 1930s and the early 1940s, the already famous ecclesiastical andinist Father Alberto Maria De Agostini explored the valleys of the San Lorenzo massif in search of a viable route to the 3706m summit. In late 1943, at 60 years of age, the indefatigable De Agostini returned with two companions (Heriberto Schmoll and Alex Hemmi of the (Club Andino Bariloche) for a last attempt. Using his intuition as much as any topographical knowledge, De Agostini established a base camp in the upper Arroyo San Lorenzo. The climbing party headed southwest via Paso del Comedor and the Brecha de la Cornisa, then traversed across glaciers and over the northern summit to reach the main summit of Monte San Lorenzo on 17 December. In the five decades after De Agostini's epic first ascent, fewer than 10 other parties were successful.

Transporte Don Carlos (☎ 067-231981; Subteniente Cruz 63; Coyhaique) flies twice weekly to/from Coyhaique (US$85, around two hours) via Cochrane (US$45).

In summer, an irregular ferry runs roughly every 10 days in either direction across Lago O'Higgins between Bahia Bahamondes, 7km southwest of the village, and Candelario Mancilla (see Lago del Desierto, p234). For departure times call the municipalidad.

Laguna Tigre Sur

Duration	2 days
Distance	10km
Difficulty	moderate
Start/Finish	Puente Tigre
Nearest Town	Villa O'Higgins (p202)
Transport	bus or taxi
Summary	A simple trek that explores a wild, heavily glaciated upper valley frequented by huemul.

This short trek follows a rough, steep route to high tarns under small glaciers in the Cordón Nevado, whose snowcapped almost 200m peaks are visible to the northwest from Villa O'Higgins. The Cordón Nevado is exposed to severe winds and frequent rain or snowfalls (even in summer), so come well prepared.

PLANNING
When to Trek
The trek can normally be undertaken from early December until at least mid-April.

Maps
One Chilean IGM 1:50,000 map, Río Ventisquero (Section J, No 112), covers the area but shows neither the Carretera Austral nor the trekking route itself.

Permits & Regulations
No permit is required, but be mindful that the lower route crosses private property.

NEAREST TOWN & FACILITIES
See Villa O'Higgins (p202).

Cabaña Puente Tigre
This four-person cabin (still under construction at the time of writing), on the south side of the Puente Tigre, costs around US$20 per night. The owners are knowledgeable about

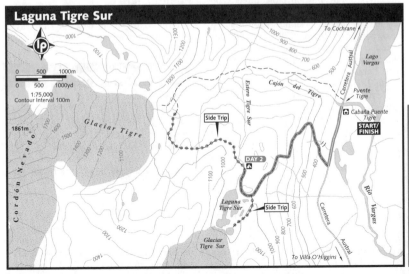

Laguna Tigre Sur

treks and climbs in the area. For more information, contact the *municipalidad* in Villa O'Higgins.

GETTING TO/FROM THE TREK

The trek starts at Puente Tigre on the Carretera Austral, officially given as 27.3km from Villa O'Higgins (but closer to 29km, according to other calculations). The only public transport is the weekly bus between Cochrane (p198) and Villa O'Higgins. The Don Carlos agent in Villa O'Higgins can organise a *flete* for around US$25 each way.

THE TREK (see map p203)
Day 1: Puente Tigre to Laguna Tigre Sur
2¾–4 hours, 5km, 565m ascent

Head 1.2km south along the Carretera Austral past the northern end of an elongated tarn to reach the 25.58km point (marked in paint by road workers) after 15 to 20 minutes.

Cross a tiny stream and head up northwest through forest of *coigüe de Magallanes* mixed with *canelo* and Guaitecas cypress. The route continues rightward up the slope out of the trees to cross a small stream above where it cascades in a waterfall. Wind your way on more directly up through small scrubby cliffs and over tiny terraces in the steep slope, before cutting back southwest (to the left of an obvious boulder on the ridge high above). The route ascends even more steeply to reach an isolated band of weather-beaten *ñirre* forest, 1¾ to 2½ hours after leaving the road.

Skirt southward below a rocky, glaciated ridge up to your right via an undulating ledge, from where you get a great view southeast along the swampy lower Río Mayer to Lago O'Higgins and across the valley to Lago Briceño, in a superb glaciated plateau. The route cuts up rightward (roughly west) over moraines past a tarn to reach the outlet of Laguna Tigre Sur, 45 minutes to one hour on from the *ñirre* forest. On moist, scrubby meadows downstream along the lake outlet are scenic **camp sites** looking out on glacier-shrouded peaks to the north – which can be ascended by experienced climbers.

Side Trip: Glaciar Tigre Sur
1–1½ hours return, 2km,
70m ascent/descent

From the outlet of Laguna Tigre Sur, climb south through gaps in the rock, where glacial ice has polished and scratched the black slab then scattered it with erratic blocks of granite. Yellow daisies shelter in the crevices. After 30 to 40 minutes you reach a turgid meltwater pool at the snout of Glaciar Tigre Sur, which drops icebergs into the lake down to your right. Return via the same route.

Side Trip: Glaciar Tigre
2–3 hours return, 5.5km,
140m ascent/descent

Ford the outlet 400m below the lake (a generally not too difficult crossing). Follow the outlet downstream to just before it begins to cascade into a steep gorge, then cut over left (northwest) through a minor gap in the ridge. The route continues around across small streams in moist meadows to near the snout of the **Glaciar Tigre**. The glacier's surging meltwater stream, which flows into the Cajón del Tigre, is usually too dangerous to cross.

Day 2: Laguna Tigre Sur to Puente Tigre
2¼–3 hours, 5km, 565m descent

Return via the route described in Day 1. Take care on the long, steep descent.

Reserva Nacional Shoen

Duration	2 days
Distance	13km
Difficulty	easy
Start/Finish	Villa O'Higgins (p202)
Transport	bus, plane or boat
Summary	A short trek that explores a wild, glaciated valley drained by a spectacular roaring torrent.

The approximately 60-sq-km Reserva Nacional Shoen (whose name means '*huemul*' in the language of the indigenous Tehuelche people) was initiated in 1995, though its establishment is still not finalised. The reserve takes in the ranges stretching east from Villa O'Higgins to the Argentine border. This pleasant out-and-back trek leads up the glacier-fed Río Mosco to a free Conaf *refugio*, so the trek can be done without a tent.

PLANNING
When to Trek
The trek can be (comfortably) done between early November and late April.

Maps
One Chilean IGM 1:50,000 map *Villa O'Higgins* (Section J, No J113) covers the route, but does not show either tracks or the *refugio*.

Permits & Regulations
No permit is required, but inform the ranger *(guardaparque)* in Villa O'Higgins before you set out.

THE TREK
Day 1: Villa O'Higgins to Refugio Río Mosco
2¼–3 hours, 6.5km, 250m ascent

From the Conaf ranger station *(guardería)*, follow a path left around picnic tables, then climb rightward to reach the **mirador** after five minutes. This lookout shelter (about 315m) gives a fine view across the village to the Cordón Nevado and Lago Ciervo. Red-white markings and arrowed posts lead southeast gently up through attractive forest of *canelo*, *lenga* and *coigüe de Magallanes*, where the delightful calls of tiny *chucaos* ring out in the underbrush, to a fork, 15 to 20 minutes on. (The yellow-orange marked left turn-off goes up to a lookout.)

Bear right and skirt a green, fire-cleared pasture above a small corral. Head rightward through scattered *calafate* bushes (that yield sweet berries in late February), then ascend a steep ridge overlooking the lower Río Mosco and the Brazo Norte Oriental (northeast arm) of Lago O'Higgins. The route begins a long, undulating traverse under the Cordón de Villa O'Higgins high above the roaring river, passing a second marked turn-off (that climbs to another lookout peak) just before it re-enters the unburnt forest, 30 to 45 minutes from the first turn-off.

Continue upvalley past a misty, mossy viewing point, where the torrential waters of the Río Mosco churn through a little

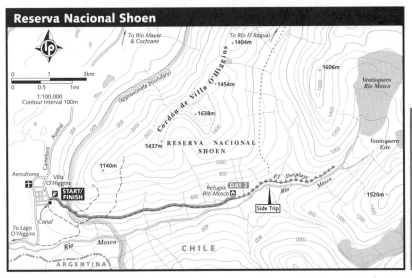

Reserva Nacional Shoen

gorge, to cross a narrow glacial side stream (sometimes tricky by midafternoon or after rain), 1¼ to 1½ hours on. From here you have views of a waterfall and a gleaming glacier in a side valley to the southeast, while pairs of condors circle above. The path first stays close to the furious, milky river, but soon climbs away left to arrive at the **Refugio Río Mosco** (GPS 48° 28.190 S, 72° 29.298 W) after a final 15 to 20 minutes. This new hut, at an elevation of around 485m, stands among lovely *lenga* forest – partly cut to build it! It has a fireplace and bunk space for six people. Get water from the stream 30m upvalley.

Side Trip: Ventisquero Río Mosco
3–4 hours return, 8km,
200m ascent/descent
This moderate–demanding route leads into a raw glacial landscape at the head of the valley.

From the *refugio*, head up the banks of the ever-angry Río Mosco past where a major glacier-fed tributary enters on the opposite side. The path leads on through a short section of avalanche-destroyed forest before crossing a log bridge over the stream draining the long side valley east of the Cordón de Villa O'Higgins, 30 to 40 minutes from the hut. (At this point, a very rough, unmarked route climbs steeply north, traverses high along the valley's west side through a pass, then follows the Río El Bagual to the Río Mayer road.)

Head around a large mossy boulder before cutting five minutes across the broad alluvial wash known as **El Desplaye**. Cairns and occasional paint markings guide you up over mossy slab-rock and eroding shale high above the river, granting views of surrounding snowcapped peaks and (behind you in the distance, just south of west) to the remarkable square-faced Cerro Melliza Sur (3186m) jutting abruptly from the Hielo Sur.

The route descends to the river, but you are soon forced to clamber back left again to avoid sheer slabs that meet the water. Continue on over bouldery moraine rubble beside the stream, where some messy

scrambling is required. The marked route peters out before it reaches the junction of the two stream branches emerging from the Ventisquero Río Mosco and Ventisquero Este, but there are some worthwhile views.

Return the same way.

Day 2: Refugio Río Mosco to Villa O'Higgins
2¼–2¾ hours, 6.5km, 250m descent
Retrace your steps as described for Day 1.

Parque Nacional Los Glaciares

Often considered the greatest single tract of remaining wilderness in the country, Argentina's vast Parque Nacional Los Glaciares in the south of Santa Cruz Province straddles the Hielo Sur, the largest icecap outside the earth's polar regions. Created in 1937 to protect a unique landscape totally dominated by ice age glaciation, Los Glaciares continues to exhibit a variety of remarkable and spectacular glacial phenomena. Parque Nacional Los Glaciares was declared a Unesco World Heritage area in 1982, and public access is tightly controlled and restricted to specific areas. The Fitz Roy sector at Los Glaciares' northern end is the only significant area where trekking is permitted.

Comprising an area of 4460 sq km, Parque Nacional Los Glaciares stretches 200km north to south along the eastern edge of the vast Hielo Sur between about 48°S and 51°S. Over a dozen major glaciers slide down eastwards from the Hielo Sur into Lago Viedma and Lago Argentino. These two enormous low-lying (roughly 200m above sea level) lakes extend well into the Argentine pampa, indicating the eastern extent of the ice age glaciers. Their numerous fjord-like arms, particularly those of Lago Argentino, reach westwards deep into the Andean Cordillera. Approximately a quarter of Los Glaciares' area – just how much is a contentious issue, since Argentina and Chile still disagree as to where the line of the international border should run – is covered by glacial ice.

One of Argentina's most famous natural landmarks, the spectacular Glaciar Moreno, lies in the southern sector of the park. Until recently, this glacier would periodically block off a major branch of Lago Argentino, creating a natural dam that built up behind the icy wall until the immense pressure of the backwaters eventually broke through it in a marvellous show of natural forces. Glacial recession (apparently caused by global warming) now seems to have stopped Glaciar Moreno's advance, however, and most Argentine glaciologists consider it unlikely that the glacier will return to its former behaviour in the near future.

At the far northern end of Los Glaciares lies one of the most magnificent and famous mountain areas in the Andes. Here the legendary diorite peaks of Cerro Torre (3102m) and Monte Fitz Roy (3405m) rise abruptly from the flat Patagonian steppes, attracting climbing expeditions from all over the world. Short lateral valleys lead into the ranges to the base of these peaks, giving trekkers relatively straightforward access to the finest scenery. This so-called Fitz Roy area includes the northernmost sector of Los Glaciares as well as the private land (largely belonging to the Estancia Ricanor) just outside the park's northern boundaries.

NATURAL HISTORY

Virtually all of Parque Nacional Los Glaciares' forests are a blend of two deciduous beech species, *lenga* and *ñirre*. Playing the role of postglacial colonisers (similar to that of birches in the Northern Hemisphere), *lenga* and *ñirre* have moved into new terrain left vacant by the receding glaciers. Growing sporadically in the forest are hardy wild flowers, including the *topa topa* and the *zapallito*, two low-growing, closely related annuals that produce one or two surprisingly large 'pea-like' flowers of a yellowish-red colour. Land orchids and species of oxalis may also be found. The *lenga/ñirre* (so-called 'Magellanic') forest forms a thin strip close to the Cordillera, which recedes into dry steppeland towards the east. This is because of the dehydrating effect of the incessant westerly winds that whip across the valleys and plains, carrying off moisture even as it falls as rain.

Scattered around the steppes are woody bushes such as *neneo rojo*, a dull-green, rounded shrub that brightens up the steppes with thousands of red flowers when in bloom, and *algarrobo patagónico* or Patagonian carob. *Hierba negra* or *mata barrosa*, a small misshapen umbelliferous small shrub that looks like scraggy fennel, is usually found growing in matted, windswept bushes known as *mogotes*. *Hierba negra* is often mixed with tough native tussock grasses called *coirones*. Other common steppeland species include the native Patagonian cactus and the *maihuén*, a more atypical member of the cactus family that grows in small mounds like spiny lawns.

Parque Nacional Los Glaciares boasts bountiful bird life, including Patagonia's two largest bird species. The flightless, ostrich-like *ñandú* (generally called the *choique* in Argentina, but known to English-speakers as Darwin's rhea) is sometimes glimpsed streaking across the steppes. More often spotted by trekkers is the great Andean condor, gliding with ease around the loftiest summits buoyed by mighty wings that have a span of over 2m. On the steppes you'll also find the *martineta copetona*, a black-crested ground-dwelling partridge whose plumage of fine black and ochre stripes camouflage it well. The *loica* is a meadowlark; the male is readily recognisable by his red breast and white slash above each eye. The *cometocino*, or *fringilio cordillerano*, a grey-hooded finch of the steppeland zone, typically builds its nest among the protective thorny branches of the *calafate* bush.

Another finch species, the *yal cordillerano*, is also generally found on the flat, dry lowlands, but prefers the highland environment. The austral blackbird *(tordo)* inhabits the Magellanic forests on the park's moister western side, retreating to the milder climate of the nearby Pacific coast for the winter. The *tucúquere* is a species of forest owl with twin crests above its eyes that look like feathery horns. Flocks of *cachañas*, a colourful and boisterous Patagonian parakeet that feeds on seeds, fruit and shoots, also visit Los Glaciares over the summer.

The guanaco forms herds mostly on the open steppes (where it can keep a lookout for pumas), but individuals sometimes move up into the mountains. The *huemul* survives in small remnant herds in certain areas of the park. Another gravely endangered native mammal is the *mara*, commonly known as the Patagonian hare, which still manages to survive despite the steady encroachment of introduced European rabbits into its steppeland habitat. The adaptable Patagonian red fox, or *zorro culpeo*, feeds mainly on these newcomers, and the numbers of this native fox are consequently quite high. It also preys on native animals like *chingue*, a Patagonian skunk with the characteristic black coat and white dorsal stripe.

CLIMATE

Parque Nacional Los Glaciares has a similar climate to that found farther north at the eastern rim of the Argentine Patagonian Andes. A major difference is that here the Hielo Sur completely blocks out the maritime influence, leaving a much more frigid continental climate. Closer to the great lakes of Lago Viedma and Lago Argentino a milder microclimate exists.

At El Chaltén, the average minimum/maximum temperature in February (summer) is 5/22°C. In August (winter), it is around 1/9°C. On the great icy expanse of the Hielo Sur, the average annual level of precipitation (falling almost entirely as snow) reaches 5000mm in places; this figure drops to little more than 1500mm on the forested Andean foothills, and to less than 400mm on the steppes at the park's eastern fringe.

The strong westerly winds are chilled and dry out as they blow over the Cordillera and continue in gusts across the steppes. Except for minor 'wind shadows' at the foot of the Cordillera, blustery winds blow almost incessantly throughout the summer. The cool, windy conditions prevent the development of summer thunderstorms, and the infre-

quent rain that falls often quickly evaporates again in the wind. Winter conditions are not as severe as you might think, because the winds that constantly blow throughout the summer months drop away from around May to the beginning of September.

PLANNING
When to Trek

Since large parts of Parque Nacional Los Glaciares receive heavy winter snowfalls, the recommended time to visit the park is during the summer season from November to April. If possible, stay away in January and the first half of February, when trails and camping grounds often become overcrowded.

Maps

Most recommended is Zagier & Urruty's 1:50,000 *Monte Fitz Roy & Cerro Torre Trekking-Mountaineering Minimap* or the same map with a Lago del Desierto map at 1:100,000, titled *Monte Fitz Roy & Cerro Torre Trekking-Mountaineering, Lago del Desierto Trekking-Travel Map*; both are available in El Calafate and many other cities in Argentine Patagonia. Less detailed but also useful is the Chaltén Outdoor 1:100,000 *El Chaltén, Fitz Roy – Torre* trekking map, which includes a rough El Chaltén map and trekking information.

Permits & Regulations

In order to protect the park's delicate environment, public access to Parque Nacional Los Glaciares is restricted. The only part of the park that is open for trekking is the northernmost Fitz Roy sector. Apart from supervised tourist launch excursions across Lago Argentino, venturing into the heart of Los Glaciares is not encouraged.

There is no charge to enter Los Glaciares' Fitz Roy sector, and trekkers do not require a permit. Trekkers may not stay longer than seven days at Campamento De Agostini or Campamento Poincenot.

Climbing permits (for mountaineers) are available without charge at the national park visitor centre in El Calafate and are valid for 30 days (after which they may be renewed once only).

ACCESS TOWN
El Chaltén (Argentina)

This still tiny town, spectacularly sited within view of Cerro Torre and Monte Fitz Roy, is experiencing a boom fuelled by budget travel. There's a variety of places to stay, several small supermarkets, and adventure tour operators galore, as well as a post office, **locutorio** (telephone office; Güemes; open until 11pm daily) and petrol (gasoline) station.

Information At the national park **visitor centre** (Centro de Visitantes; ☎ 02962-493004; open 9am-8pm daily in summer) on the southern side of the Río Fitz Roy bridge, helpful guardaparques are ready with park and accommodation information and a free map. The small **tourist office** (Güemes; open 9am-8pm Mon-Fri, noon-7pm Sat & Sun) is across the river from the park visitor centre at the southern edge of town. There is an informative town website at ⓦ www.elchalten.com.

The national park visitor centre has a list of accredited mountain guides. Some of El Chaltén's most experienced guides run

French Connections

Monte Fitz Roy itself may be named after an Englishman, but several names in the area have a decidedly French flavour. The tallest of Fitz Roy's neighbouring summits bears the name of Jacques Poincenot, an ill-fated member of the 1952 French expedition that first climbed Fitz Roy – Poincenot drowned while attempting to cross the Río Fitz Roy. Three flanking peaks are named in honour, not of climbers, but of three French aviators, Antoine de Saint-Exupéry (author of Le Petit Prince), Jean Mermoz and Henri Guillaumet, who pioneered flying routes across Patagonia as pilots for Aeroposta Argentina, the country's first airmail service. And somewhere in France must be a valley that gave its name to Fitz Roy's nearest neighbour to the north, Aguja Val de Vois. Even a street in El Chaltén is named after a Frenchman, Lionel Terray, one of two climbers who reached the summit of Fitz Roy on that first successful expedition.

guiding companies, including **Fitz Roy Expediciones** (☎/fax 02962-493017; ⓦ www .elchalten.com/fitzroy; Lionel Terray 212) and **Camino Abierto Expediciones** (☎/fax 02962-493043; ⓦ www.caminoabierto.com; San Martín).

Places to Stay & Eat El Chaltén has two free camping grounds: **Campamento Confluencia**, across the road from the national park visitor centre; and **Campamento Madsen**, at the north end of town, near where the main trekking routes begin. Both have very basic facilities – a pit toilet and little else – and become quite busy in January and early February. Trekkers should select tent sites with maximum shelter from the often very strong winds that sweep through the valley.

Camping El Refugio (☎ 02962-493007; San Martín; camping per person US$3) and **El Relincho** (San Martín; camping per person US$4) offer amenities including showers.

Numerous hostels include **Albergue Rancho Grande** (☎ 02962-493005; ⓔ rancho@ cotecal.com.ar; San Martín 635; dorm beds US$7), which has a busy **restaurant** (handy for breakfast or something to munch on while you wait for your Chaltén Travel bus), and **Albergue Los Ñires** (☎ 02962-493009; cnr Lago del Desierto & Hensen; dorm beds US$7, singles/doubles with bathroom US$22/32), which includes breakfast in its room rates and is located on the western edge of town with mountain views.

Hostería El Puma (☎ 02962-493017; Lionel Terray 212; singles/doubles with bathroom US$27/32) has a good library of Patagoniana and breakfast is included in the cost.

Posada Altas Cumbres (☎ 02962-493060; Lionel Terray 342; doubles/triples with bathroom US$35/43) is a friendly, newish place with good rooms. Rates include breakfast.

Small supermarkets for provisions include **El Súper** (Lago del Desierto), **El Gringuito** (San Martín) and a nameless **supermercado** (cnr Güemes & Lago del Desierto). The price difference is not as great as you might expect, but supplies are still cheaper in El Calafate.

Patagonicus (cnr Güemes & Madsen; pasta US$3-4, pizza US$2-7) is a nice place for light meals, cakes and good coffee.

Fuegia Bistró (☎ 02962-493019; San Martín; meat mains US$5-6, veg mains US$3-5) serves fine food in a smoke-free atmosphere, and is one of the few places in El Chaltén where you should book ahead.

Getting There & Away The 220km access route from El Calafate to El Chaltén goes north via the bitumen Ruta Nacional 40, then northwest via the unsurfaced Ruta Provincial 23. In summer at least five bus companies – **Cal Tur** (☎ 02902-491842), **Chaltén Travel** (☎ 02902-491833), **Interlagos** (☎ 02902-491179), **Los Glaciares** (☎ 02902-491158) and **Taqsa** (☎ 02902-491843) – run services from El Calafate to and from El Chaltén (US$13/26 one-way/return, four hours, once or twice daily each). All five companies have offices at the bus station in El Calafate. There is no problem breaking the journey, even if you want to stay a few weeks or more in the Fitz Roy area. Each bus line terminates at a different point in El Chaltén.

Hitching to El Chaltén outside the busy summer months is a lonely and unpredictable prospect (we don't recommend it as a rule).

Laguna Torre

Duration	2 days
Distance	19km
Difficulty	easy
Start/Finish	El Chaltén (p209)
Transport	bus

Summary Gaze up at the polished, vertical walls of the classic granite spire of Cerro Torre, one of mountaineering's most sought-after prizes.

This recommended short trek takes you to an exhilarating viewpoint opposite the 3102m Cerro Torre, which was for decades considered impossible to climb.

It is often done as a long return day trek, but a more leisurely two days are recommended with a night at Campamento De Agostini. The Sendero Madre e Hija alternative route (p211) provides a short cut between Campamento De Agostini and Campamento Poincenot and makes it possible to segue into the Around Monte Fitz Roy trek without returning to El Chaltén in between.

Winds of Change

You can still watch an Argentine cowboy (gaucho) drive a mob of horses at a canter down El Chaltén's unsealed main street, Av San Martín – but for how much longer? The winds of change are blowing through El Chaltén almost as hard as the fierce westerlies that raise dust storms from Av San Martín and routinely engulf Cerro Torre and Monte Fitz Roy in impenetrable cloud.

Little more than a decade ago El Chaltén housed the administration of Parque Nacional Los Glaciares' Fitz Roy sector and in summer catered to a trickle of visitors, most of whom were climbers. Two companies ran small buses from El Calafate a few times a week. And that was it.

Then the trickle began to grow. Now at least five bus lines each send one or more coaches to El Chaltén every day. There's a welter of accommodation options sprawling north across the plain, and a four-star hotel going up on a hill overlooking the town. Supermarkets, restaurants and a microbrewery have sprung up, a new sewerage system is under construction and the town is soon to be connected to the national gas grid.

The number of travellers has been kept somewhat in check by 188km of rough dirt road that links El Chaltén to Ruta Nacional 40, but this section of road is due to be surfaced in time for the summer of 2003–04. Just watch visitor numbers grow when there's a sealed road all the way.

Developments of this kind will make life easier for El Chaltén's hardy residents and visitors alike. There's even talk of a helicopter rescue service which, in time, will probably save trekkers' lives. But the winds of change sometimes create their own casualties, and who's blowing the wind? That's right: we are.

THE TREK (see map p214)
Day 1: El Chaltén to Campamento De Agostini
1¾–2¼ hours, 9.5km

The trek starts at the northwestern edge of El Chaltén. From a signpost on Av San Martín just south of Campamento Madsen, head west on Eduardo Brenner and then right to find the signposted start of the track.

The Laguna Torre track winds up westwards around large boulders on slopes covered with typical Patagonian dryland plants, then leads southwest past a *mallín* (wet meadow) to a junction with a trail coming in from the left (see Alternative Start) after 35 to 45 minutes.

Continue up past a rounded bluff to the **Mirador Laguna Torre**, a crest giving you the first clear view up the valley to the extraordinary rock spire of Cerro Torre standing above a sprawling mass of intersecting glaciers. The trail dips down gently through beautiful stands of stout ancient *lengas*, before cutting across open scrubby riverflats and old revegetated moraines to reach a signposted junction with the Sendero Madre e Hija, a short-cut route to Campamento Poincenot, 40 to 50 minutes on (see Alternative Route: Sendero Madre & Hija). Continuing upvalley, bear left at another signposted fork and then climb over a forested embankment to cross a small alluvial plain, following the fast-flowing glacial waters of the Río Fitz Roy, and arrive at **Campamento De Agostini** (formerly Campamento Bridwell), after a further 30 to 40 minutes. This free camping ground (with its pit toilet), the only park-authorised place to camp in the vicinity, is situated in a pleasant grove of riverside *lengas* below Cerro Solo.

Alternative Start
45 minutes–1 hour, 4km

From the southern end of El Chaltén, follow Av Lago del Desierto west past the edge of town, then drop to the riverbed and continue past a tiny hydroelectric installation. At a signpost the route climbs away from the river and leads on through scattered *lenga* and *ñirre* woodland (with the odd wire fence

to step over) before merging with a more prominent (signposted) path coming in from the right. Continue as for Day 1.

Side Trip: Mirador Maestri
1½–2 hours return, 5km

This wonderful trek leads to a lookout with grandstand views of Cerro Torre and its companion peaks and glaciers. It can comfortably be combined with either Day 1 or Day 2 (or both).

First head up northwest through barely vegetated glacial rubble to the top of the moraine wall damming Laguna Torre, a stark lake fed directly by Glaciar Torre, from which blocks of ice break off periodically and beach around the shore.

Make your way up northwards along the narrow crest of the moraine until about halfway around the frigid lake, then begin zigzagging up and diagonally leftwards. **Refugio Maestri**, a tiny A-frame 'bivouac' *refugio*, comes into view on a small terrace of dwarf *lengas*, and a little further on are the skeletal remains of another *refugio*. This lovely spot once served as a base camp for mountaineers, but the park authorities now prohibit overnight stays here.

The route emerges from the trees, climbing a short way up a moraine ridge to reach the unmarked **Mirador Maestri**, 50 minutes to 1¼ hours from Campamento De Agostini. From up here you get much enhanced views of the Cordón Adela, a serrated ridge that includes half a dozen snowcapped peaks between Cerro Grande (2751m) and Cerro Torre (3102m).

Retrace your steps to camp.

Alternative Route: Sendero Madre & Hija
1½–2 hours, 6km

This short cut between Campamento De Agostini and Campamento Poincenot makes it possible to link the Laguna Torre and Around Monte Fitz Roy treks without returning to El Chaltén in between.

From a signposted junction on the Laguna Torre track, climb steadily northeast until the track levels out after 30 to 40 minutes. Swing left at the top of the rise and continue to the southern end of Laguna Hija (Daughter Lake), where the track passes between it and the tiny Laguna Nieta (Granddaughter Lake). Head up the eastern shore of Laguna Hija until a strip of land on the left divides Laguna Hija from Laguna Madre (Mother Lake). Here the track starts to climb away from the shore and sidles around to meet the main track from El Chaltén to Campamento Poincenot at a signpost after a further one to 1¼ hours.

Day 2: Campamento De Agostini to El Chaltén
1¾–2¼ hours, 9.5km
Reverse Day 1 to El Chaltén.

Around Monte Fitz Roy

Duration	3 days
Distance	38km
Difficulty	easy–moderate
Start/Finish	El Chaltén (p209)
Transport	bus

Summary View mighty Fitz Roy and its spectacular satellites – one of the world's finest mountain landscapes – from many angles on this exploration of the beautiful surrounding valleys.

Easily the highest peak in the area, Monte Fitz Roy was first climbed in 1952 by a French expedition based at Campamento Poincenot. Even in these days of high technical climbing standards, its summit is still a highly prized objective. This trek takes you into the valleys surrounding Monte Fitz Roy and lets you view this classic Patagonian peak close-up from two high-level lookouts.

The local Tehuelche tribes venerated Monte Fitz Roy; its prominent form must have been a key landmark during their annual migrations from the Atlantic to the Cordillera. The Tehuelche called the mountain Chaltén (peak of fire), apparently in the belief that it was a volcano. Francisco Perito Moreno gave the peak its present (Celtic) name after Captain Fitzroy of the *Beagle*, who in 1834 accompanied Charles Darwin

up the Río Santa Cruz to within 50km of the Cordillera. Fitzroy (the original spelling of his name) and Darwin were presumably the first Europeans to view Monte Fitz Roy's classic 3405m summit of smooth, frost-polished granite.

The trek can be done in three days, either as described or by returning to El Chaltén along Ruta Provincial 23 (see Alternative Route: via Ruta Provincial 23, p217). Really, though, it deserves at least one additional day and probably more, to allow time for some of the attractive detours described and to give the bad weather that often obscures mountain views a chance to clear.

The well-trodden path up to Campamento Poincenot is marked with yellow-painted stakes and occasional red splashes on rocks, and – except for the short section leading out of the Río Blanco into the Valle Eléctrico – the remainder of the trek is easy to follow.

THE TREK (see map p214)
Day 1: El Chaltén to Campamento Poincenot
1¾–2¾ hours, 8km
The trek starts at the northern end of El Chaltén, at a signpost just beyond the entrance to Campamento Madsen. Climb to the right of a large rock outcrop onto open slopes of *mogotes* and tussock grasses giving fine views of the adjacent Cordón de los Cóndores. The route sidles on steadily upwards high above the braided gravelly channels of the Río de las Vueltas through pockets of *lenga* and occasional *coigüe de Magallanes*. After swinging around northwestwards through a minor saddle, head up beside the ravine of the Chorrillo del Salto to reach the signposted turn-off to Laguna Capri (see Side Trip: Campamento Laguna Capri, p213) after one to 1½ hours.

Make your way on upvalley through heathland scattered with stunted *ñirre* scrub past the signposted Sendero Madre e Hija, a short cut from Campamento De Agostini, diverging left (see Alternative Route: Sendero Madre & Hija, p211). Skirt along the left side of a broad boggy *mallín*, hopping across the tiny clear stream and following yellow-tipped marker stakes northwestwards through a band of Magellanic *lenga* forest. You will arrive at **Campamento Poincenot**, a free camping ground with pit toilet, 45 minutes to 1¼ hours from the turn-off to Laguna Capri.

Named in memory of a French mountaineer who died in 1952 while attempting to cross the Río Fitz Roy (see the boxed text 'French Connections', p209), this charming spot along the grassy (eastern) bank of the Río Blanco and on the treed terrace above the river looks up directly to the spires of the Fitz Roy massif. Campamento Río Blanco, on the opposite side of the river from Campamento Poincenot, is a base camp normally reserved for mountaineering parties.

Side Trip: Campamento Laguna Capri
20 minutes return, 1.5km
A tranquil lake with lovely little beaches, Laguna Capri sits before the jagged backdrop of the Fitz Roy massif. This recommended short side trip leads south from the

Climbing up a Storm

In 1959 the Italian alpinist Cesare Maestri reported that he and his Austrian companion Toni Egger had reached the summit of Cerro Torre. Egger, however, had been swept to his death by an avalanche on the descent – with the pair's camera, which would have contained the summit photos – and Maestri's claim aroused widespread scepticism. In 1970 Maestri returned with another party, hoping to put the matter beyond doubt, but provoked perhaps the bitterest controversy in mountaineering history by fixing hundreds of bolts with a portable compressor drill to reach the top of the rock – and then neglected to climb the unstable 'snow mushrooms' to the mountain's highest point. For many, the first undisputed ascent of Cerro Torre was achieved in 1974 by a subgroup of the Italian Alpine Club, the Ragni de Lecco (Lecco Spiders), led by Casimiro Ferrari.

signposted turn-off in the Chorrillo del Salto valley, up to the lake's northern shore, then dips left through the forest to reach the free camping ground of **Campamento Laguna Capri** after just 10 minutes. Other than Campamento Poincenot, this is the only place where trekkers are permitted to pitch tents along Day 1. Although Laguna Capri has no outlet its water is considered safe to drink, so please don't pollute the lake with detergents or soap, and use the pit toilet provided. To return to the main track, retrace your steps to a signpost, then take the left fork.

Side Trip: Laguna Sucia
1½–2 hours return, 5km
This spectacular lake can be reached on a track which begins 40m northwest of the footbridge over the Río Blanco and ends up following the river's bouldery bed. Laguna Sucia lies in a deep cirque under the towering granite 'needles' of **Cerro Poincenot** and **Aguja Saint Exupery**. Frozen white chunks periodically peel off the **Glaciar Río Blanco** icefall and plummet into the lake. The return journey follows the same route.

Side Trip: Laguna de los Tres
2–3 hours return, 5km,
450m ascent/descent
The obligatory trek up to this lake at the foot of Monte Fitz Roy will be another major highlight of your Patagonia trip. A predawn start will get you there for the scenic sunrise. From Campamento Poincenot cross the small river on a substantial footbridge to the mountaineers' base camp of **Campamento Río Blanco**, and there pick up a foot track leading off leftwards. Observe the signs and try to stick to the cairned route, which spirals up increasingly steeply west-southwest out of the trees and on over loose rocky ground to reach a low crest.

From here you get a sudden and stunningly close-up view of Monte Fitz Roy towering more than 2000m above the picturesque Laguna de los Tres, which lies in a glacial hollow immediately in front of you. Away to the southeast, beyond the nearby Laguna Madre and Laguna Capri,

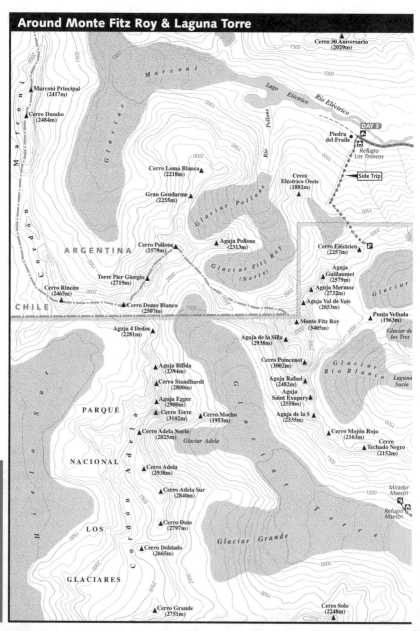

Around Monte Fitz Roy & Laguna Torre

Cerro 30 Aniversario (2029m)

Marconi

Marconi Principal (2417m)

Cerro Dumbo (2484m)

Glaciar Marconi

Lago Eléctrico

Río Eléctrico

Río Pollone

DAY 3

Piedra del Fraile

Refugio Los Troncos

Side Trip

Cerro Loma Blanca (2218m)

Cerro Eléctrico Oeste (1882m)

Gran Gendarme (2255m)

Glaciar Pollone

ARGENTINA

Cerro Pollone (2579m)

Aguja Pollone (2313m)

Cerro Eléctrico (2257m)

Aguja Guillaumet (2579m)

Torre Pier Giorgio (2719m)

Glaciar Fitz Roy (Norte)

Aguja Mermoz (2732m)

Cerro Rincón (2465m)

Aguja Val de Vois (2653m)

Glaciar

CHILE

Cerro Domo Blanco (2507m)

Punta Velluda (1963m)

Aguja 4 Dedos (2281m)

Monte Fitz Roy (3405m)

Glaciar de los Tres

Aguja de la Silla (2938m)

Aguja Bifida (2394m)

Cerro Poincenot (3002m)

Glaciar Río Blanco

Cerro Standhardt (2800m)

Aguja Rafael (2482m)

Laguna Sucia

Aguja Egger (2900m)

Aguja Saint Exupery (2558m)

PARQUE

Cerro Torre (3102m)

Cerro Mocho (1953m)

Agnja de la S (2335m)

Cerro Adela Norte (2825m)

Glaciar Adela

Cerro Mojón Rojo (2163m)

NACIONAL

Cerro Techado Negro (2152m)

Cerro Adela (2938m)

Glaciar Torre

Cerro Adela Sur (2840m)

Mirador Maestri

Refugio Maestri

Cerro Dato (2797m)

LOS

Cerro Doblado (2665m)

Glaciar Grande

GLACIARES

Cerro Grande (2751m)

Cerro Solo (2248m)

Hielo Sur

Cordón Adela

Cordón Marconi

SOUTHERN PATAGONIA

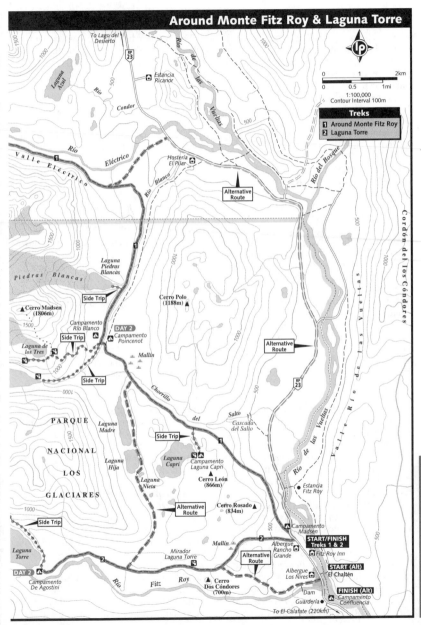

Around Monte Fitz Roy & Laguna Torre

Treks
1 Around Monte Fitz Roy
2 Laguna Torre

1:100,000
Contour Interval 100m

the enormous Lago Viedma spreads out into the dry steppes. Another wonderful viewing point can be easily reached by heading west around the shore of Laguna de los Tres to its outlet stream, then leftwards to a high precipice far above the cloudy-green Laguna Sucia.

For more superb vistas of Monte Fitz Roy, Cerro Madsen (1806m) can be climbed in a somewhat more difficult four- to five-hour return route that follows the spur just north of Laguna de los Tres.

Day 2: Campamento Poincenot to Refugio Los Troncos
2½–3½ hours, 11km

Cross the Río Blanco and find the sign-posted path just a short distance into the forest. The often vague route goes downstream along the western banks of the Río Blanco over eroding embankments and small gravel washes to meet a rubble-filled side valley after 35 to 45 minutes. From here, moderately agile trekkers can make a very worthwhile side trip to Laguna Piedras Blancas (see Side Trip).

Back on the main route, pick your way through the moraine debris and cross the gushing lake outlet stream. The trail then continues downvalley, skirting the edge of the rocky alluvial plain and occasionally dipping briefly left into the forest, and leaves Parque Nacional Los Glaciares at a stile over a wire fence. Where the valley fans out at its mouth, move away from the river towards hanging glaciers on mountains to the northwest to intersect with a more prominent foot track (which is indicated by red paint markings), 50 minutes to 1¼ hours on from the Laguna Piedras Blancas turn-off.

Head left (west) over rolling wooded slopes and through small fire-cleared pastures sprinkled with *calafate* bushes to enter the enclosed upper valley of the Río Eléctrico below high glacier-shaped cliffs after 30 to 40 minutes. The path proceeds gently up beside the rushing, murky-grey river through open, cattle-grazed *lenga* forest before cutting across a broad grassy meadow to arrive at **Refugio Los Troncos** (*camping per person US$3, dinner US$10*), a further 40 to 50 minutes on.

The *refugio* lies at the eastern end of **Piedra del Fraile**, a large erratic block (see the boxed text 'Signs of a Glacial Past', p22) in the middle of the flat valley floor below the 2257m Cerro Eléctrico. The whole of the Valle Eléctrico is private property (belonging to the nearby Estancia Ricanor), and the *refugio* is the only place trekkers are permitted to camp along the whole of Day 2. There are pleasant tent sites on watered lawns protected by Piedra del Fraile, cooking shelters, toilets and a hot shower. The resident caretaker sells essentials such as chocolate and beer.

A short pathway climbs up to the top of the rock for a great view upvalley to Lago Eléctrico, a dramatically bleak lake exposed to fierce and incessant winds blasting down from the nearby Hielo Sur. Lago Eléctrico can also be visited in around 1½ hours return by taking an easy trail across the moist river flats then over wave-like moraines to the lake's raw, glaciated southeastern shore.

Side Trip: Laguna Piedras Blancas
30 minutes return, 800m

Where the track on the west bank of the Río Blanco meets a rubble-filled side valley, follow cairns that lead up left around and over white granite boulders to **Laguna Piedras Blancas**. The heavily seraced **Glaciar Piedras Blancas** curves around from the eastern face of Monte Fitz Roy in a series of icefalls that sprawl down into this impressively bleak meltwater lake. Retrace your steps to the main track.

Side Trip: Cerro Eléctrico Lookout
7½–9 hours return, 8km,
1500m ascent/descent

This much longer and more difficult side trip (rated moderate–demanding) takes you well into the realm of the mountaineers, and should only be attempted during stable weather. Take the well-worn foot track southwest across the river flats, then up the steep southern side of the valley beside two streams that cascade down in the shape of a Y. When the gradient moderates, continue ascending steadily southwards to a rock bivouac on the lip of an impressive cirque filled by a small glacier after 1½ to two hours. Monte Fitz Roy can be seen towering above the back wall of this cirque.

The path leads slightly left, but after passing over a small spur it finally peters out. Head south along the bottom of reddish scree slopes with the glacier to your right for 30 to 45 minutes, bearing left where the cliffs up to your left suddenly change into black rock. Make your way up steeply to the right of the red rock over loose scree slopes into a small col, another 1½ to two hours on. Head east from the col and traverse the steep boulder slopes below a huge wedge-shaped rock, then ascend gradually to reach the lowest point of the main ridge of Cerro Eléctrico, 45 minutes to one hour on. From here there are utterly stupendous views towards Fitz Roy, Cerro Pollone and southwest over the Hielo Sur.

Return the same way.

Day 3: Refugio Los Troncos to El Chaltén

5–7 hours, 19km

Backtrack to El Chaltén via Campamento Poincenot (ie, Days 1 and 2 in reverse order). Without detours, this is comfortably done in a single day; alternatively, an additional night at Campamento Poincenot or Campamento Laguna Capri allows you to do side trips you missed on the outward journey or to spend more time in favourite places.

Alternative Route: via Ruta Provincial 23

4¼–5½ hours, 20km

Retrace your steps towards the Río Blanco and bear left at the trail junction, following signs eastwards through boulders and re-generating *ñirres*, and crossing several tributaries of the Río Eléctrico. The route swings northwest to meet Ruta Provincial 23, the main road through the Valle Río de las Vueltas, 1¾ to 2¼ hours from the *refugio*, at the Río Eléctrico road bridge.

Follow the gravel southeastwards across the Río Blanco after 1km, and past the turn-off to **Hostería El Pilar** (☎ 02962-493002; *singles/doubles US$44/58*), then around a tight, cliffed bend beside the river, edging on along a wide plain – your pace accelerated by gusty tailwinds – back into the national park. After two to 2½ hours the road passes the signposted trail to the Cascada del Salto, a waterfall spurting out of the gorge up to your right (reached in around one hour return). Proceed for another 30 to 40 minutes to reach **Campamento Madsen** at the northern end of El Chaltén.

Parque Nacional Torres del Paine

Parque Nacional Torres del Paine lies some 100km directly north of Puerto Natales in far southern Chile. Rising up from the flat steppes with breathtaking abruptness, the craggy mountains of Torres del Paine present an astonishing sight even when viewed from far off on the park's southeastern approach road. For more than 60 years before the establishment of the national park in 1959, the Torres del Paine area had been subject to often highly destructive grazing practices from which it is still recovering. The uniqueness of the area was fully recognised in 1978, when Torres del Paine was declared an international biosphere reserve by Unesco.

In recent years tourism has boomed in Torres del Paine, bringing infrastructure development, including new *refugios* and hotels. Increasing numbers of visitors have forced the park authorities to restrict public access to certain areas and tighten camping regulations, but this superb park unquestionably offers some of the best trekking in the world.

At roughly 51°S, Parque Nacional Torres del Paine takes in a remote area of 1814 sq km at the southeastern end of the Hielo Sur. To the north, Torres del Paine borders on Argentina's vast Parque Nacional Los Glaciares, and on its southwestern side it meets the much smaller Chilean Parque Nacional Monte Balmaceda.

SOUTHERN PATAGONIA

Torres del Paine was landscaped by the great glaciers of the Hielo Sur, which during the recent Pleistocene ice age extended right down to cover all but the highest ground and the park's most easterly areas. The great streams of ice have largely receded to the Hielo Sur, but today four major glaciers, Dickson, Grey, Pingo and Tyndall/Geikie – which are all appendages of this colossal block of ice – creep down into the park to terminate in deep meltwater lakes. The largest is the 17km-long Glaciar Grey, which disgorges huge icebergs into the turquoise waters of Lago Grey. The entire area of Torres del Paine lies within the basin of the Río Serrano, which drains southwards into the fjord-like Seno Última Esperanza.

Rising out of the largely flat and barren plains barely 300m above sea level, the roughly quadrilateral Macizo Paine (Paine Massif) forms the park's core and displays many of its most spectacular features. Numerous glacial lakes surround the Macizo Paine, principally Lago Grey, Lago Pehoé and Lago Nordenskjöld along its southern foot, while the somewhat smaller lakes of Lago Dickson, Lago Paine and Laguna Azul lie on the northern side of the massif. The park's largest lakes are Lago del Toro and Lago Sarmiento on its southeastern edge. The Macizo Paine is penetrated by the short but very deep valleys of the Río Francés and the Río Ascensio, which flow south into Lago Nordenskjöld.

At the southwestern end of the Macizo Paine stands the 3050m Cumbre Principal (main summit) of Cerro Paine Grande, the park's highest point and its only peak over 3000m. Cerro Paine Grande is capped by so-called *hongos de hielo* (ice mushrooms), a phenomenon seen in few areas outside the Patagonian Andes. Ice mushrooms form only at high elevations in subpolar regions, where moisture in the extremely intense winds freezes directly onto alpine rock. Just east of Cerro Paine Grande are the Cuernos del Paine, jagged turrets of a resistant layer of sedimentary black shale covering the granite base. At the eastern end of the Macizo Paine are three magnificent frost-polished 'towers' of granite, the Torres del Paine, from which the park gets its name.

How the towers came by their name is in some doubt. The word *paine* (**pie**-nee) means 'pale blue' in Tehuelche and may refer to the colour of the area's half-dozen or so large glacial lakes. The local Andean nomenclature often uses the names of andinists who achieved first ascents, and another theory says that Paine was the name of an early Welsh climber.

NATURAL HISTORY

Until the declaration of the national park in 1959 a large portion of the Torres del Paine area was grazed by cattle and sheep. Old fences and *puestos* (huts) are visible in places, and a local *estancia* (large cattle or sheep property) still runs some cattle – though not sheep, because they crop grass too close to the ground – in a small part of the park. The graziers' past use of fire to clear forest has greatly modified the landscape, and regeneration is occurring only slowly – a reminder of the destructive effect of fire in the Patagonian Andes.

Forests of *lenga* cover the moister interior areas of the park. On steeper slopes the trunks of these trees often take on a bow-like form, perhaps caused by the downward force of the heavy winter snows or the young trees' continual search for light. At lower elevations *coigüe de Magallanes* can also be found in the forest, although it rarely challenges the dominance of the *lenga* anywhere within the park boundaries.

Ñirre covers drier and well-drained slopes in the central part of the park. Daisy bushes including the *romerillo*, whose foliage has something of the appearance and smell of the rosemary bush, grow where the moist natural pasture meets the drier steppeland. Another daisy species found in this transition zone is the *chilco de Magallanes*, not to be confused with the common native species of fuchsia known simply as *chilco*.

The easternmost third of the park is covered by the *monte* vegetation characteristic of the lee of the Patagonian Andes. Here plants well adapted to the dry and extremely windy conditions, such as tumbleweeds *(mogotes)*, spinifex-like *maihuén*, the *cacto patagónico* or *yerba del guanaco*, the world's most southerly cactus, and clumps of native tussock grasses known as *coirón* are typical. A subspecies of butterfly, *Etcheverrius chilensis magallanicus*, lives among these steppeland plants, somehow managing to avoid being blown away.

The bird life in Torres del Paine is abundant and diverse. The park's lakes (particularly the saltwater ones such as Lago Sarmiento and Laguna Amarga) provide an ideal habitat for the *flamenco chileno* (Chilean flamingo). The only flamingo species found in Patagonia, the *flamenco chileno* eats aquatic insects and small molluscs, whose pigments are responsible for the striking pink colour of its plumage. Even more common is the *cisne de cuello negro*, a large white swan with a black neck.

Ducks such as the *quetru volador* (flying steamer duck), and the *caiquén* (upland goose), are often seen on Torres del Paine's lakes. In the fast-flowing rivers (such as the Río de los Perros), the now rather rare *pato de torrentes* (torrent duck), may occasionally be spotted swimming against the current in search of its prey, chiefly invertebrates and their larvae. Several species of heron, including the *garza grande*, are also found in lagoons and rivers.

Particularly on the drier eastern sectors of the park, several species of *chorlos* (plovers) can be sighted from time to time. These dry steppes are also the home of the *ñandú* which runs in a fast, zigzagging gait to outrun potential predators.

Condors are frequently sighted gliding effortlessly around the peaks. Identifiable in flight by their enormous size and distinctive splayed wing tips and white collar, these superb Andean vultures nest in inaccessible cliffs on the eastern side of (or even outside) the park. Condors will sometimes take small live mammals, and although they may attack a dying guanaco they prefer to feed on carrion. Other birds of prey that trekkers may observe are the *águila mora*, a handsome species of eagle, and hawks, harriers and falcons such as the *peuquito* and the *traro*, a species of *caracara*.

Guanaco graze on the grasslands in the eastern sector of Torres del Paine, and the park's less accessible western interior provides a refuge for small numbers of *huemul*. Such rich game sustains the puma, although trekkers are rarely lucky enough to catch even a fleeting glimpse of this discreet predator.

CLIMATE

Abutting the Hielo Sur, the western sectors of Parque Nacional Torres del Paine experience extremely unstable and often localised weather. Precipitation levels vary enormously over relatively short distances, and it is not uncommon to experience heavy downpours in areas closer to the icecap while sunshine is visible on the steppes just a few kilometres to the east. The highest precipitation levels, exceeding 4000mm, occur on the Hielo Sur (slightly west of the park's borders), dropping to about 2000mm around Refugio Lago Pehoé and under 800mm at Laguna Amarga. The mean annual temperature at Lago del Toro is only around 6°C, and summer days never rise much above 20°C. From October to April, but particularly from December to February, winds are almost unremitting and often extremely strong. The chilling effect of the freezing winds that blow off the great glaciers should not be underestimated.

PLANNING
When to Trek

The summer and early autumn season – from early December to late March – is the best time to trek in Parque Nacional Torres del Paine. Outside this period, areas above 500m (or lower) are subject to unpredictable and heavy snowfalls. The overwhelming number of visits to this extremely popular park are during the busy summer holiday season (January to mid-February), when the *refugios* are prone to overcrowding and the camping grounds can get cramped. During the winter season (from around May to mid-September), the severe Patagonian winds drop away almost completely, making winter trips to the park less extreme than might otherwise be expected.

Nonetheless, winter trekking should be confined to shorter low-level routes.

What to Bring

Trekkers seeking the greatest flexibility and safety in planning their itinerary should bring all camping equipment including tent, sleeping bag and stove. There are currently eight *refugios* for trekkers in Parque Nacional Torres del Paine, and it is possible to complete the Paine Circuit or the shorter W trek without carrying camping gear, by renting it each night at camping grounds adjacent to *refugios* and at the Andescape-run Campamento Los Perros – or indeed by staying in *refugios* most nights and camping, with rented gear, only at Los Perros. This, however, commits you to a fixed timetable using only those grounds, and rules out using intermediate camp sites. The day from Los Perros to Refugio Grey, in particular, would be a long one, and one we don't recommend.

Maps

The two best maps for all treks in the park are the JLM Mapas 1:100,000 *Torres del Paine Trekking Map* and the similar Luis Bertea Rojas 1:100,000 *National Park Torres del Paine Trekking Map*. Neither map is perfect – in particular, there are inaccuracies in the contours shown on the Rojas map – but both show adequate topographical detail, trekking routes with average times and the location of *refugios* and park-authorised camping grounds. Both are available at trekking suppliers and bookshops (*librerías*) in Puerto Natales and other towns throughout Patagonia.

Information Sources

The Torres del Paine *sede administrativa* (administration centre) and **visitor centre** (*open 8.30am-8pm daily*) is at Lago del Toro, beside the ruins of the original Estancia Paine building (which was destroyed in a fire in 1982).

For information about (or to reserve beds in) the *refugios* in the park, contact **Andescape** (☎ 061-412877; W *www.andescape .cl; Eberhard 599*) in Puerto Natales or **Hostería Las Torres/Fantástico Sur** (☎ 061-

226054; *Magallanes 960*) in Punta Arenas – and if you do plan to sleep in *refugios*, book ahead.

Climbers seeking permits to climb in the park can go through an adventure guiding outfit such as **Bigfoot Patagonia** (☎ 061-414611; W *www.bigfootpatagonia.com; Bories 206*) in Puerto Natales or start the process themselves by contacting the **Gobernación Provincial** (☎ 061-411423; *Eberhard 417, 2nd floor*), on the south side of the Plaza de Armas.

Permits & Regulations

All visitors to Parque Nacional Torres del Paine are required to register with Conaf at the park entrance gate at Laguna Amarga. Trekkers will be asked for details of intended routes. An entrance fee of US$11 for adult foreigners is payable here.

In order to protect the environment the park authorities restrict where you can trek and camp. Public access to many parts of the park is not permitted, and trekkers must not leave the official pathways. Camping is allowed only at designated camping grounds, and trekkers found pitching their tent outside these park-approved grounds are likely to be fined. The lighting of open fires is prohibited throughout the park. Given the continual rise in the number of trekkers visiting Torres del Paine it is important to follow these simple rules.

Supplies

It may be possible to leave well-packaged food at the administration centre or *guardería* for later treks, but don't count on it. During the busiest months (January and February) Conaf staff may be reluctant to store anything because of the lack of space available.

GETTING THERE & AWAY

Access to Parque Nacional Torres del Paine is usually via the road junction at Villa Cerro Castillo on the southeastern side of the park. The main park entrance gate is at Guardería Laguna Amarga, 116km by road from Puerto Natales; the park administration centre at Lago del Toro is a further

29km on from Guardería Laguna Amarga. The road is unsurfaced but well maintained. An alternative southern approach road leading around the western side of Lago del Toro is closed to public traffic, although local mountain-bikers use it.

Andescape (☎ 061-412877; Eberhard 599), **Buses JB** (☎ 061-412824; Arturo Prat 258), **Buses Fernández** (☎ 061-411111; Eberhard 555), **Fortaleza** (☎ 061-410595; Arturo Prat 234), **María José** (☎ 061-414312), **Bus Sur** (☎ 061-411325; Baquedano 534) and **Buses Gómez** (☎ 061-410595; Arturo Prat 234) each run one or more buses daily from late October until late April between Puerto Natales and the park administration centre (US$5.50 to US$8 one-way, 4½ hours). Most departures from Puerto Natales are at 7am or 2.30pm, and it takes 2½ to three hours to reach the entrance gate and another 45 minutes to the Refugio Pudeto boat landing. You can break your journey in the park for as long as you wish. The bus companies have different return departure times, but the earliest bus leaves the administration centre at 12.15pm.

A scenic alternative way to get to and/or from the park is by boat from Puerto Natales. **Onas Aventura** (☎ 061-412707; w www.onaspatagonia.com; Eberhard 599) and **Turismo 21 de Mayo** (☎ 061-411176; w www.chileaustral.com/21demayo; Eberhard 554) run daily trips by motor launch up Seno Última Esperanza to the foot of the Balmaceda and Serrano glaciers in Parque Nacional Bernardo O'Higgins, thence by Zodiac up the Río Serrano to the Torres del Paine park administration centre (US$85 one-way, six hours). Lunch is included.

GETTING AROUND

A return bus ticket from Puerto Natales to the park usually entitles you to travel short sectors on the main road through the park (with the same bus company) at no additional cost – so, for example, if you get off at Laguna Amarga and return there at the end of a trek, you can catch a bus from there to Pudeto or the administration centre on your original ticket. A ride with another bus company costs US$3.

A regular minibus shuttle service run by Hostería Las Torres meets buses at Laguna Amarga and ferries passengers along the 7km of unsealed road to the hostería (US$2, 15 minutes, five daily).

Trekkers who pay to camp or stay at any of the Fantástico Sur refugios (Albergue Los Cuernos, Las Torres or Albergue El Chileno) receive a voucher entitling them to a one-way trip with this shuttle.

Transfers by van or minibus within the park and its surrounds give additional flexibility in getting from one trek to another. Those specific to particular treks are detailed under Getting to/from the Trek. **Hostería Lago Grey** (☎ 061-410220, 410172; w www.austrohoteles.cl) will pick you up and drop you off practically anywhere in the park (US$5.50 to US$16 per person). Usually a minimum of three or four passengers are required.

From October to April **Hielos Patagónicos** (☎ 061-226054) runs a regular motorised catamaran across Lago Pehoé between Refugio Pudeto (a day shelter near Salto Grande) and Refugio Lago Pehoé (US$14 one-way, 30 minutes, three daily December to mid-March, two daily November and late March, one daily October and April). All buses call at the Pudeto landing en route to/from the administration centre.

Another launch runs across Lago Grey between Hostería Lago Grey and Refugio Grey (US$30 one-way, 1½ to two hours, twice daily). Contact the hostería for details.

ACCESS TOWN & FACILITIES

See Puerto Natales (p195).

Within the Park

In addition to the refugios and organised camp sites on the trekking routes, there are organised camping grounds within the park with toilets and hot showers: **Camping Las Torres** (camping free), among attractive lawns scattered with ñirres is just downhill from Hostería Las Torres.

Near the park administration centre is Conaf's basic **Refugio Lago del Toro** (mattresses US$5.50, hot showers US$0.70).

Just turn up and let yourself in; a *guarda-parque* collects fees. Also nearby is the **Posada Río Serrano** *(☎ 061-410684; dorm beds US$20, doubles with/without bathroom US$90/66)*, which offers genteel accommodation and has a good **restaurant** *(dinner US$12)*. Rates at the Posada include breakfast, there's an *almacén* on the premises and motorists can buy petrol (gasoline). Staff at *refugios* in the park can contact the Posada for you by radio.

Hostería Las Torres *(☎/fax 061-710050;* W *www.lastorres.com; singles/double US$155/ 176)*, accessible by road from Guardería Laguna Amarga, sits below the 2640m glacier-crowned summit of Cerro Almirante Nieto. It has a small shop and a **restaurant** *(dinner US$30)*. The trek to the Torres del Paine Lookout starts and finishes at the *hostería* and the Paine Circuit finishes there.

Hostería Lago Grey

This *hostería* *(☎ 061-410220, 410172;* W *www.austrohoteles.cl; singles/doubles S$173/ 199)* is located on the southern shore of Lago Grey, near the start of the Lago Pingo trek. It has a **restaurant** *(lunch or dinner US$24)*.

Torres del Paine Lookout

Duration	4½–6 hours
Distance	19km
Difficulty	easy–moderate
Start/Finish	Hostería Las Torres
Nearest Town	Puerto Natales (p195)
Transport	bus

Summary Visit the most spectacular lookout in Parque Nacional Torres del Paine, at the base of the granite towers that give the park its name.

This short trek should not be missed. The Torres del Paine stand just north of the Cuernos peaks within a deep valley of the Paine massif. The *torres* (towers) themselves are three-and-a-half distinctive pinnacles of hard Andean batholith rock, and are all that

remains of a great cirque that has been sheared away by the relentless forces of glacial ice. The summit of the tallest tower, the Torre De Agostini, stands 2850m above sea level and imposingly overlooks the intensely glaciated and barren surroundings 1500m below.

Apart from some minor rock-hopping on the final climb, this return trek follows a good and well-marked path for the whole way. The trek is easily combined with the Paine Circuit. If you can spare the time and the weather is favourable, it is worth spending a night close enough to be at the lookout at dawn.

NEAREST TOWN & FACILITIES
See Puerto Natales (p195) and Parque Nacional Torres del Paine (p217).

GETTING TO/FROM THE TREK
For details of how to reach the park entrance at Guardería Laguna Amarga see Getting There & Away (p220). Las Torres shuttle buses meet buses from Puerto Natales at Laguna Amarga and ferry trekkers and guests to the Hostería Las Torres, where the trek begins (US$2, 15 minutes, five daily). Trekkers staying at the Hostería Las Torres can ask permission to leave private vehicles there.

THE TREK (see map p226)
Follow the signposted road uphill past the Hostería Las Torres before dropping down to cross the Río Ascensio on a suspension footbridge. Continue across a small alluvial plain to where the 'Los Cuernos' path diverges left (see Paine Circuit, Day 8, p232). From here begin climbing northwestwards up an ancient heath-covered moraine ridge that lends a fine view south across Lago Sarmiento. Down to your right, the stream rushes through a gorge of layered black shale. The path traverses on into the valley along steep slopes high above the Río Ascensio, before moving down to meet the river again opposite the Fantástico Sur–operated **Albergue El Chileno** *(camping per person US$5, bunks US$17)*, one to 1¼ hours from the *hostería*.

Continue on up the western bank, gradually rising away from the river. Crossing several streams on log bridges and stepping stones, the trail brings you up through lovely stands of dwarf *lengas* (untouched by the fires that destroyed much of the forest farther down the valley) to arrive at **Campamento Torres** after 50 minutes to 1¼ hours. This is the main camping area for trekkers and mountaineers in the valley, and has the best and most abundant camp sites in the valley of the Río Ascensio. There's a toilet located at the back of the national park *guardería*.

Take the signposted path from the southern side of the small gully just *before* you reach the camping area. First follow the tiny clear stream up the left side of the regenerating glacial rubble and then follow the orange paint spots leading rightwards over bare boulders to arrive at the **Torres del Paine Lookout** at the top of the moraine wall after 40 to 50 minutes. This often windy spot lies immediately below the Torres del Paine, mighty columns of granite ringed by shelf glaciers whose meltwater streaks the rocks as it runs into the lake in the foreground – one of the Patagonian Andes' classic scenes.

Return downvalley by the same route.

Side Trip: Campamento Japonés
2–2½ hours return, 8km

This side trip takes you into the wild upper valley of the Río Ascensio. Pick up the initially vague trail at the lower edge of Campamento Torres. Follow cairns leading out over boulder rubble and across several channels of the cloudy glacial stream that descends from the lake at the foot of the Torres del Paine. The route rises mostly gently along the western side of the Río Ascensio before coming out onto an attractive forested flat after 50 minutes to 1¼ hours. Here you'll find **Campamento Japonés**, an old climbers' camp with a small, makeshift hut and various improvised plaques made from tin lids nailed to trees. From here a much less distinct route swings west as far as the head of the evocatively name Valle del Silencio.

Paine Circuit

Duration	8 days
Distance	104.5km
Difficulty	moderate–demanding
Start	Guardería Laguna Amarga
Finish	Hostería Las Torres
Nearest Town	Puerto Natales (p195)
Transport	bus

Summary Circumnavigate the Paine massif, from dry steppes through moist forests to highland moors and back again, with constantly changing views of peaks, lakes and enormous glaciers.

Truly one of the world's classic treks, the Paine Circuit is the longest and wildest route in the park, following the course of the Río Paine up to Paso John Garner, descending the Río Grey and skirting several of the park's spectacular lakes.

PLANNING
The full Paine Circuit as described takes eight days, although side trips and rest days might stretch out the trek to 10 days or more. Do not underestimate your trekking times, and be sure to carry enough supplies for a safe, comfortable trip. If you are unable to do the entire circuit, a shorter trek known as the W, taking around five days, is a recommended and increasingly popular alternative (see the boxed text 'The W', p230).

In most places the Paine Circuit is well enough marked (with orange stakes and paint) and trodden that serious navigational difficulties should not arise. The trail is less well maintained along the central section of the route, however, where fallen logs and boggy terrain make the going slower and more strenuous in places. Reliable bridges provide safe crossings of all larger streams.

The 1241m Paso John Garner lies in the remotest central section of the Paine Circuit. Although the crossing is technically very straightforward, this pass is exposed to strong, frigid westerly winds, which bring sudden snowfalls even in midsummer; at any time, but especially before December and after March, snow may close the pass completely. Even in recent years, inexperienced and/or poorly prepared trekkers have come to grief on Paso John Garner, so the crossing must be taken very seriously. Less dangerous but extremely bothersome (particularly during occasional windless moments in December and January) are the plagues of mosquitoes at some of the camping grounds along the circuit – carry some insect repellent.

Most parties trek the Paine Circuit in an anticlockwise direction, as it is described here. One disadvantage of an anticlockwise trek is that it requires a steep, slippery descent from Paso John Garner; balancing this, however, is the staggering view over Glaciar Grey from Paso John Garner, which is best appreciated after climbing from the east.

What to Bring

Thanks to the construction of new *refugios* in the park in recent years and the availability of camping equipment for hire at all *refugios* and at Campamento Los Perros, it is theoretically possible to trek the Paine Circuit without carrying a tent. This, however, means covering the most difficult and remote stretch of the circuit between Campamento Los Perros and Refugio Grey, including the crossing of Paso John Garner, in a long day. Some parties find this is beyond them and, since *refugio* accommodation must be booked in advance, face major disruption to their itineraries as a result.

In January and February the *refugios* are often very full. Campers should note that park authorities prohibit the lighting of camp fires along the entire Paine Circuit; trekking parties must use a portable stove or cooker

NEAREST TOWN & FACILITIES

See Puerto Natales (p195) and Parque Nacional Torres del Paine (p217).

GETTING TO/FROM THE TREK

The trek begins at Guardería Laguna Amarga, the main entrance point to Torres del Paine (see Getting There & Away, p220). It ends at Hostería Las Torres (see Within the Park, p221), from where Las Torres shuttle buses ferry trekkers to Guardería Laguna Amarga

(US$2, 15 minutes, five daily). Days 7 and 8 of the trek can be avoided by taking the catamaran from Refugio Lago Pehoé to Refugio Pudeto (see Getting Around, p221).

THE TREK (see map p226)
Day 1: Guardería Laguna Amarga to Puesto Serón
4–5¼ hours, 20km

Trek down to cross two road bridges over the Río Paine and continue a few minutes along to the right until a signpost indicates where the path leaves the road. Marked with orange-painted stakes and rocks, the trail moves well away from the Río Paine as it heads roughly north-northwest across the rolling grassy floor of the valley. After 1¼ to 1½ hours you pass a route leading off right. (This side trip takes less than 1½ hours return and leads almost directly east to the Cascada Paine, where the cloudy waters of the Río Paine drop 4m.)

The main path meets the Río Paine again 2km on, then continues upstream some distance above the river's steepening banks to reach a signposted trail junction (where the Alternative Start: Camping Las Torres intersects) after two to 2½ hours. Cut over left and through a gate to ford a shallow stream, then make your way approximately northwest across broad grassy riverflats scattered with ñirre woodland to arrive at **Puesto Serón** *(camping per person US$5)* after a final 50 minutes to 1¼ hours. This pleasant private camping ground has toilets, hot showers and good sites at the edge of a large, often windy pasture. Meals are available.

Alternative Start: Camping Las Torres
3¼–4 hours, 16.5km

This easy (and moderately scenic) short cut lets you combine the Torres del Paine Lookout trek with the Paine Circuit without returning to Guardería Laguna Amarga.

Take a 4WD track five minutes up the eastern side of the stream opposite Camping Las Torres past **Refugio Las Torres** *(bunks US$17)*. Just beyond the *refugio* a signposted path leads off to the right over grassed-over moraine mounds and through

The spectacular colours of the Torres del Paine at sunrise

Glaciar Grey and icebergs in Lago Grey, Paine Circuit trek

BRENT WINEBRENNER

Cuernos del Paine rising up above Lago Pehoé

CHRIS BARTON

Reflection of the spire of Cerro Torre (3102m)

BRENT WINEBRENNER

Camping by Lago Pehoé, Parque Nacional Torres del Paine

a tiny canyon, then climbs on gently across mostly open slopes scattered with *notro* bushes. Follow wire fences running below the steeper forested slopes up to your left, traversing high above the valley of the Río Paine as the route gradually swings from a north to a northwestward direction.

As you approach a broad flat plain beside the river, begin a northward descent to join with the main path from Laguna Amarga at a signpost after 2½ to 2¾ hours.

Day 2: Puesto Serón to Refugio Lago Dickson
4¼–5½ hours, 18.5km

From the old *puesto* head right beside a fence before continuing upvalley. The path first skirts broad waterlogged riverflats, where *caiquenes* and other water birds congregate in marshy overflow ponds. It leads on immediately beside the swift-flowing milky-blue river, then starts climbing away northwestwards through *ñirre* woodland to reach **Laguna Alejandra** after 45 minutes to one hour.

Make your way around the southern shore of this tiny horseshoe-shaped lake, before continuing up in a few wide switchbacks. A more gentle climb roughly westwards brings you into an indistinct saddle after 30 to 45 minutes. From this often gusty spot there is a wonderful panorama of Lago Paine, several hundred metres below you, and the impressive arc of jagged peaks along the Chile–Argentina frontier behind Lago Dickson at the head of the valley.

Begin a gradual traversing descent high above Lago Paine, rising and dipping continually as you head towards the glacier-crowned summit of Cerro Paine Chico 20km to the west. Because of their continual exposure to the wind and sun, these steep north-facing slopes are mostly covered with battered *calafate* bushes, *mogotes* and other well-anchored plants. After sidling gently down through the light forest above boggy *mallines* where the Río Paine enters the lake you arrive at **Campamento Lago Paine (or Coirón)**, one to 1¼ hours on. This free area is the only alternative camp site on this stage of the trek. The best spots are mainly on the other side of the stream.

It's advisable to boil drinking water unless you fetch it from well upstream. Please go well downstream – ie, *not upstream* – and at least 30m from the waterway to defecate.

Follow the path roughly west-southwest through stands of *ñirres* and open grassland dotted with wild daisies, keeping a good distance from the Río Paine to avoid marshy areas along its banks. Magnificent views of the mountains ahead, from the 2197m Cerro Trono Blanco in the Cordillera Paine to Cerro Ohnet to the northwest, open out as you go. After crossing through previously burnt-out *lenga* forest now slowly regenerating, the path climbs an old moraine ridge, suddenly bringing Lago Dickson into sight. The ridge top offers a wonderful view across the lake to Ventisquero Dickson, whose white icy mass sprawls down from the Hielo Sur to calve in its greenish-grey waters.

On a lakeside meadow immediately below you stands Andescape's **Refugio Lago Dickson** *(camping per person US$5, bunks US$14.50)*, which should be reached two to 2½ hours after leaving Campamento Lago Paine. There are hot showers for *refugio* guests and cold ones for campers, flush toilets, tables and an *almacén*; cooked meals and hot drinks are served.

Day 3: Refugio Lago Dickson to Campamento Los Perros
3¼–4¼ hours, 9km

Follow the trail as it loops around southwestwards through low forest onto the steep embankment of the **Río de los Perros** (River of the Dogs), which is supposedly named after a herder's dogs which drowned in its fast-flowing waters. Make your way on upwards well above the rushing river (which is initially heard but not seen), remembering to look back for your last views across the lake to Ventisquero Dickson, its snout ringed by floating ice debris. Shortly after passing a tiny peat bog, from where you get the first views upvalley into the wildest and least accessible section of the Paine Circuit, the route comes to the Río Cabeza del Indio. Cross this large side stream on a log bridge 1¼ to 1¾ hours from the *refugio*.

SOUTHERN PATAGONIA

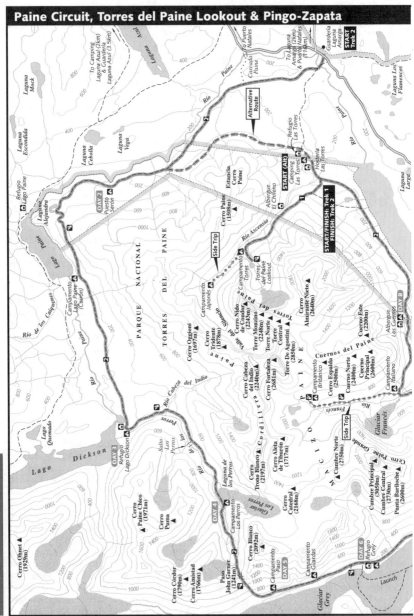

Paine Circuit, Torres del Paine Lookout & Pingo-Zapata

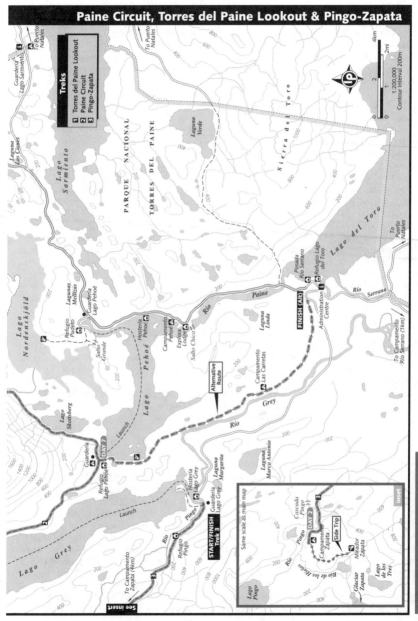

Paine Circuit, Torres del Paine Lookout & Pingo-Zapata

Treks
1 Torres del Paine Lookout
2 Paine Circuit
3 Pingo-Zapata

The path undulates southwestwards through stands of *coigüe de Magallanes* to pass **Salto Los Perros** in a thunderous chasm after 20 to 25 minutes. Delicate ground orchids thrive here. Continue upvalley through attractive open *lenga* forest in long, virtually flat stretches interrupted only by very short steeper climbs to cross a suspension bridge spanning the Río de los Perros, a further 1¼ to 1½ hours on.

Head up through regenerating glacial debris, then climb the end-moraine that dams **Laguna de los Perros**. A small glacier calves directly into the lake, and blocks of ice float in its frigid waters. The route now follows the top of the moraine wall before leading off right across river flats to arrive at **Campamento Los Perros** *(camping per person US$4.50)* 30 to 40 minutes on from the suspension bridge. This Andescape-operated camping ground, situated in the forest near the confluence of the valley's two uppermost stream branches, has toilets, cold showers and a shelter to cook in. Meals are available, there is camping equipment for hire, and there is also a small (and expensive) *almacén*.

Day 4: Campamento Los Perros to Campamento Paso

3¾–5½ hours, 12km, 680m ascent, 800m descent

This day takes you into very exposed terrain well above the tree line. Trekkers should not cross the pass alone or in poor weather.

Not far above where the large side stream (coming from a glacier between Cerro Paine Chico and Cerro Cóndor) enters, cross the main stream on a small bridge. Make your way upvalley along an often very muddy path through stunted forest to recross the stream at a little chasm, one to 1¼ hours from the camping ground.

Follow the stream briefly to the tree line, then pick up cairns leading away to the left (roughly west-southwest) up over sparse alpine grasses. The route then ascends more steeply to cross a tiny tumbling brook, climbing on over barren rock slopes. To the north a small crevassed glacier, which is the source of the valley's uppermost stream, descends from Cerro Amistad. Watching

out carefully for marker stakes and the occasional paint markers, ease leftwards to reach **Paso John Garner** after one to 1½ hours.

The pass lies at 1241m above sea level, and is the highest point on the Paine Circuit. From up here trekkers get their first awe-inspiring view across Glaciar Grey, whose enormous fractured mass of ice chokes the valley ahead, while in the other direction you can see back down the valley towards Lago Paine. The almost gale-force westerlies that blast through this low point in the range may make it hard to enjoy the views for long.

Zigzag a down short way down from the pass, then follow the trail markings that lead diagonally down left into the uppermost wind-whipped *lengas*. The route first drops sharply through this robust alpine scrub, then moves steadily downward through evergreen *coigüe* forest. An extremely steep descent – a very slippery section after recent rain – brings you to the former site of Campamento Paso, 1¼ to two hours from Paso John Garner. *Cachañas* frequent this area during the summer. The relocated **Campamento Paso**, a free, park-approved camping ground with a flush toilet and a three-sided shelter, lies a further 30 to 40 minutes south, just beyond a log bridge over a substantial stream.

Day 5: Campamento Paso to Refugio Grey

2¾–4 hours, 10km

Begin contouring roughly southeastward through the forest to reach a ravine, which is being heavily eroded by a small torrent. At various times metal railings, fixed ropes and wooden ladders have been erected here to help trekkers cross, but since these aids don't hold for long in the loose eroding rock you may have to negotiate this somewhat dangerous obstacle using your own wits.

Continue on, rising and dipping along the steep slopes high above Glaciar Grey to enter a second ravine, which should be easier to cross than the first. Along much of this section fires have killed most of the young trees which had been slowly regenerating after the original forest was burnt out decades ago, but the route gradually leaves the fire-damaged area behind as it leads through pleasant *coigüe* forest to arrive at **Campamento Guardas**, two to three hours on from Campamento Paso. This free camping ground with a flush toilet and a three-sided cooking shelter offers the only authorised camping between Campamento Paso and Refugio Grey. A pretty cascade on the lower side of the camping ground provides uncontaminated water. A short, unmarked trail leads from Campamento Guardas to a lookout which gives wonderful views across the glacier.

The route now takes an undulating course past Glaciar Grey, whose mighty snout (divided into two by a large rock outcrop, a so-called nunatak) forms the northern end of **Lago Grey**. The unstable, 200m-thick wall of ice continually sends large blocks – some as big as a house – plunging into the freezing waters. Driven by the strong winds, these icebergs sail across the lake before stranding around the shoreline. The best vantage points to view this spectacle can be reached via short side trails passed just before the main path cuts up behind a minor peninsula.

Descend gently to a signposted path junction and proceed briefly right to arrive at **Refugio Grey** *(camping per person US$5, bunks US$14.50)*, 45 minutes to one hour down from Campamento Guardas. This modern Andescape-run *refugio*, with toilets and hot showers, looks out towards Glaciar Grey from a lovely little lakeside meadow with its own pebble beach. An adventure guiding company, **Bigfoot Patagonia** (W *www .bigfootpatagonia.com)*, operates 'ice hikes' on Glaciar Grey from a base in a corner of the camping ground. Unless strong winds or icebergs make the trip too dangerous, a tourist launch operates from the dock near the Hostería Lago Grey (at the southern end of the lake) to Glaciar Grey, calling in at Refugio Grey (US$30 one-way, twice daily).

Day 6: Refugio Grey to Refugio Lago Pehoé
3–4 hours, 11km, 300m ascent/descent
Return to the junction a few minutes up from the *refugio* and follow the main path

on behind a long rock rib. After descending slightly past a large waterfall and crossing its raging torrent on a bridge over a tiny gorge, the route continues leftwards up a steep, muddy slope equipped with handrails. Accompanied by the sharp ice-shrouded peaks of Cerro Paine Grande jutting up to the left, you now begin a steady upward traverse via narrow glacial terraces covered with the prostrate, heather-like *brecillo* high above Lago Grey to cross a saddle after two to 2½ hours.

Make your way on around the left side of a little lake perched scenically above Lago Grey and then descend southeastwards through a broad dry gully vegetated with *maihuén* and *mogote* bushes to reach an *almacén* and a toilet block situated in an attractive grassy plain at the northwestern shore of **Lago Pehoé**, one to 1½ hours on. Away to the right, looking out across the brilliant turquoise lake, stands Andescape's **Refugio Lago Pehoé** *(camping per person US$5, bunks US$14.50)*. Cooked meals and hot drinks are available at the *refugio*. The old *refugio*, just to the left, now serves as a national park *guardería*. Places to camp spread towards the lake – most of them are shielded by wind barriers from the strong gusts that would otherwise flatten many tents.

Except when strong winds or mechanical breakdowns stop it from operating, a motorised catamaran runs between Refugio Lago Pehoé and Refugio Pudeto (US$14 one-way, about 40 minutes, three daily). The boat landing is to the right, beyond the *refugio*.

Alternative Finish: Lago del Toro
4–5½ hours, 17.5km
Climb over a minor ridge at the western edge of the grassy plain, beyond the *refugio*, sidling up and down around the mostly steep lakeside to reach a tiny bay opposite some islets after 45 minutes to one hour. Rising up dramatically from the brilliantly turquoise waters of Lago Pehoé, the black slate and granite summits of the Cuernos del Paine now appear from a particularly scenic aspect.

Cut southeastwards away from the lake, first over ancient moraine mounds now covered with grasses and light scrub, then across a broad pampa to meet the broad, cloudy-green **Río Grey** (the outlet of Lago Grey). Follow the undulating path downstream along the river's often steep banks, climbing high to avoid cliffs before you drop down to the riverside to reach **Campamento Las Carretas**, a free camping ground in a slight depression (giving shelter from winds), after 1¾ to 2¼ hours. It's not all that nice, since past fires have killed off the *ñirres* here.

The route now breaks away from the Río Grey, turning gradually eastwards as it crosses a wide expanse of windy steppes, where flocks of *bandurrias* and, occasionally, small groups of *ñandú* may be observed. (Trekkers heading in the other direction are almost certain to encounter strong northwesterly headwinds along this section.) Where the path brings you to a road (to Lago Grey), turn left and trek along trails not far to its left to arrive at the administration centre at Lago del Toro after a final 1½ to 2¼ hours. This is where buses to the park from Puerto Natales terminate (see Getting There & Away, p220).

Day 7: Refugio Lago Pehoé to Albergue Los Cuernos

3½–4½ hours, 13km

Pick up the path near the *guardería*, heading around the steepening lakeside before you

---

The W

When the previous edition of this book was written, the trek known as the W did not even have a name. Now authorities estimate that about half of all people who trek in Parque Nacional Torres del Paine do the W.

The key to the W is the trail along the northern shore of Lago Nordenskjöld that links the Valle del Francés directly with the Río Ascensio valley and the Torres del Paine lookout. A *refugio* and camping ground have opened beside the trail at Albergue Los Cuernos, which makes it possible to cram many of the Paine Circuit's attractions into a trek of five days or even less, with the option of *refugio* accommodation every night.

The W visits all the scenic highlights of the southern side of the Paine Circuit, including the Valle del Francés and the Torres del Paine lookout. It omits the crossing of Paso John Garner, with its breathtaking views across Glaciar Grey, and the more remote northern stages of the circuit which for many trekkers come as an unexpected delight.

The W is named for the rough approximation to the letter W that it traces out on the map. Variations are possible, in particular for trekkers who carry a tent and camping gear, but a standard itinerary might go something like the following. For full descriptions of all sections of the route, see Torres del Paine Lookout (p222) and Paine Circuit, Days 6–8 and Side Trip: Valle del Francés (p223).

Day 1: Puerto Natales to Refugio Grey

Take the bus from Puerto Natales to Pudeto and the catamaran from Pudeto to Refugio Lago Pehoé. Trek to Refugio Grey (11km).

Day 2: Refugio Grey to Refugio Lago Pehoé

Take in views of the snout of Glaciar Grey from viewpoints beyond Refugio Grey. Trek back to Refugio Lago Pehoé (13km). Trekkers with a tent might push on to Campamento Italiano.

Day 3: Refugio Lago Pehoé to Albergue Los Cuernos

A long day (25km approximately). Trek to Campamento Italiano and up the Valle del Francés to Campamento Británico and the nearby *mirador*. Trek back down the valley and continue to Albergue Los Cuernos.

break away north-northeast to reach **Lago Skottsberg**. The route gently rises and dips around the western side of this windswept lake under small hanging glaciers that slip down the southern flank of Cerro Paine Grande. Climb over a minor crest with the help of some stretches of duckboards, and continue past a smaller lake on your right to meet the **Río Francés** on its true right bank. Head upstream to cross the river in two bites, on a footbridge across a secondary braid, then a suspension bridge over the main branch, and enter the popular free camping ground known as **Campamento Italiano** after two to 2½ hours. Level camp sites and a pit toilet are just a couple of minutes downstream.

Continue trekking downstream and then swing to the east below the imposing Cuernos del Paine with fine views back up the Valle del Francés. After rounding a shoulder to bring the *refugio* ahead into view, the track continues on, descending to the rocky northern shore of Lago Nordenskjöld, which it then follows, crossing a couple of small streams, to reach **Albergue Los Cuernos** *(camping per person US$5, bunks US$17)* after 1½ to two hours. This camping ground can be a very windy spot and there are not many sheltered tent sites available. Campers are allowed to use the toilets and showers located in the Fantástico Sur-operated *refugio*, and meals and hot drinks are available.

The W

Day 4: Albergue Los Cuernos to Albergue El Chileno
Trek to Albergue El Chileno and from there to the Torres del Paine lookout and back (roughly 23km).

Day 5: Albergue El Chileno to Puerto Natales
Trek approximately 5km to Hostería Las Torres (with the option of trekking an extra 9km and making a dawn visit to Torres del Paine Lookout beforehand). Take the shuttle to Guardería Laguna Amarga and the bus to Puerto Natales.

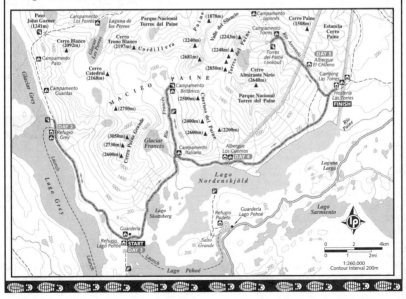

Side Trip: Valle del Francés

3–4 hours return, 12km,
520m ascent/descent

This superb side trip into the valley between the Cuernos del Paine and Cerro Paine Grande is not to be missed – not even if you've almost completed the Paine Circuit and think you've seen all of the park's wild wonders! A good way to do it is to combine Day 6 with the first part of Day 7, and after a night at Campamento Italiano either spend an entire day exploring the Valle del Francés, or visit the valley and continue to Albergue Los Cuernos the same day.

Head upstream through Campamento Italiano, then follow paint markings leading through boulder rubble up to your right to gain a lateral moraine ridge. The route traces this forested ridge top, then drops down left-wards past where the Río Francés shoots through an awesome water slide, before climbing on through the woods to reach an open area that serves as a natural lookout.

Here you get exciting views of **Glaciar Francés**, whose hanging icefalls cling to the sheer black-rock east face of Cerro Paine Grande. At the least predictable moments whopping hunks of ice dislodge and crash noisily into the valley, their shattered fragments then re-forming into a small glacier which finally melts into two murky pools. Southwards, the view stretches beyond Lago del Toro on the park's southern periphery.

Head on into the upper valley, rising more gently now beside the stream through lovely alpine *lenga* forest. After crossing a water-logged grassy area, from where you get a fine view of the ice-formed 'horns' of the Cuernos del Paine up to your right, the path re-enters the forest to reach **Campamento Británico**, without facilities, after 1½ to two hours.

From Campamento Británico a foot track continues for 10 to 15 minutes to a **mirador** with grandstand views of the peaks surrounding the head of the valley. Backtrack down the Río Francés to Campamento Italiano. For the really eager, further rough tracks lead beyond the **mirador** to the north-east, up a gully past another fine viewpoint, and northwest, up to two attractive tarns near the tree line at the head of the valley.

Day 8: Albergue Los Cuernos to Hostería Las Torres

2¾–4 hours, 11km, 160m ascent,
100m descent

Cross the stream on a substantial bridge behind the *refugio* and head east over a headland. After climbing steadily above Lago Nordenskjöld, the track levels out and passes alongside a compact cliff line, then through a gap after 40 minutes to one hour.

Continue roughly northeast, crossing an eroded stream gully and another headland before coming to a large stream in a wide stony gully after 35 to 45 minutes. Go upstream if necessary to hop across several minor braids, then down to track level to cross the major branch with a single strand of fencing wire tensioned between metal stakes to hang on to. This can be a daunting prospect after rain or warm weather (which increases the melt rate of the small glacier that feeds the stream).

Continue past a signposted short cut to Albergue El Chileno on the left. Use the stepping stones to cross the tiny outlet stream of a little lake. After another 'El Chileno' signpost just past the lake, the route winds through a small valley beside a sizable stream hidden in *lenga* on the left. Splash across the stream where it emerges into the open and regain the track, which leads around a moraine and across a grassy plain to cross the Río Ascensio suspension bridge. Continue to **Hostería Las Torres** (see Within the Park, p221) after 1½ to 2¼ hours.

Pingo-Zapata

Duration	2 days
Distance	28km
Difficulty	easy
Start/Finish	Guardería Lago Grey
Nearest Town	Puerto Natales (p195)
Transport	bus & van

Summary Head up a tranquil forested valley to view two glaciers on the edge of the Hielo Sur.

This trek takes you up the valley of the Río Pingo, beyond Lago Grey in the wild western sector of Parque Nacional Torres del

Paine. Here Glaciar Pingo and Glaciar Zapata spill down from the edge of the Hielo Sur to give rise, respectively, to the Río Pingo and its tributary the Río de los Hielos. The valley sides are covered with attractive stands of open Magellanic forest, and along the undulating riverbanks are thickets of *calafate* bushes which in February and March produce abundant berries. Small numbers of *huemul* thrive in the isolation of the Pingo area.

PLANNING

The simple return trek to Campamento Zapata follows a marked and very well trodden path – if anything, too well trodden by horses – and presents little route-finding difficulty. The gradient rises gently along the course of the river, and there are no really strenuous sections. Mosquitoes can be quite a problem here in late December and January.

At the time of writing, a crucial footbridge over the Río de los Hielos had still not been replaced several years after it was destroyed by a flood. The park authorities have no immediate plans to rebuild this bridge, and in its absence – although some intrepid trekkers wade the icy waters – the Río de los Hielos should be considered unsafe to cross. This means that Lago Pingo, into which Glaciar Pingo calves in spectacular fashion, must be viewed from a distance. Easily visited on a side trip, though, is the smaller but still impressive lake, fed by Glaciar Zapata, that is the source of the Río de los Hielos.

The trek takes two days, but an extra day to explore this lovely area is time well spent. Trekkers should sign in and out at the beginning and end of the trek at Guardería Lago Grey.

NEAREST TOWN & FACILITIES

See Puerto Natales (p195) and Parque Nacional Torres del Paine (p217).

GETTING TO/FROM THE TREK

The trek begins from the car park of Guardería Lago Grey. This is at the southern end of Lago Grey, 18km on from the park administration centre at Lago del Toro, where buses to the park from Puerto Natales

terminate (see Getting There & Away, p220), and about 1km beyond Hostería Lago Grey (p222). Irregular minibus or van transfers bridge the gap between Lago del Toro and the trailhead (US$5.50 to US$6.25 per person, minimum three passengers). Transfers are best organised at least a day ahead. One driver often waits for custom at the administration centre; or call **Hostería Lago Grey**.

THE TREK (see map p226)
Day 1: Guardería Lago Grey to Campamento Zapata
3¾–4¾ hours, 14km, 330m ascent, 230m descent

From the car park below the *guardería* take the signposted foot track upstream along the western side of the river to reach **Refugio Pingo** after 30 to 40 minutes. This basic tin hut has a pit toilet and sleeping space for eight trekkers. Continue upvalley, climbing away from the Río Pingo through grassy meadows (granting views of Cerro Paine Grande to the northeast), thickets of thorny *calafates* and patches of mature forest. The trail returns to the riverside just before it passes the signposted turn-off to the Cascada Pingo, 2½ to 3¼ hours on from Refugio Pingo; this waterfall can be visited as a 15-minute side trip.

Make your way on for 30 to 40 minutes to **Campamento Zapata** at the edge of a grassy open riverflats. A cosy wooden *refugio* which stood here and once served as a *puesto* for the Estancia Paine was destroyed by fire late in 2002. Although there are attractive spots all along the Río Pingo valley, the only park-approved camping grounds are here and at Refugio Pingo.

Side Trip: Mirador Zapata
1½–2 hours return, 4km, 100m ascent/descent

This rewarding return trek follows a signposted and cairned route southwestwards from Campamento Zapata across a bare stony valley, then swings to the south into *lenga* and climbs to a lookout point after 35 to 45 minutes. From here there are views across to Glaciar Zapata, which ends above a meltwater cascade that feeds a small unnamed lake. This lake in turn drains into the Río Pingo via the short-lived Río de los Hielos. For more extensive views which include Glaciar Pingo and Lago Pingo to the northwest, follow a faint cairned track south above the lake to reach the crest of a moraine in a further 20 minutes. Retrace your steps to Campamento Zapata.

Day 2: Campamento Zapata to Guardería Lago Grey

3¼–3¾ hours, 14km, 230m ascent, 330m descent

Retrace the route of Day 1. The gradient is mostly downhill and the going is consequently easier.

Other Treks

RESERVA NACIONAL LAGO JEINIMEINI

Reserva Nacional Lago Jeinimeini (hey-ni-may-ni) lies in the forested ranges between the semi-arid country around Lago General Carrera to the north and the equally dry steppes of the Valle Chacabuco to the south. Lago Jeinimeini lies in the heart of this large reserve, approximately 60km by road south of the town of Chile Chico on Lago General Carrera.

From north of the guardería on the northern end of Lago Jeinimeini, an easy day trek can be made west to Lago Verde, a spectacular lake enclosed by high glaciated cliffs. From Jeinimeini's eastern shore, another much longer track (for a moderate three-day trek) leads south up the Estero San Antonio to an attractive pass then continues down the Estero La Leona to eventually reach the Valle Chacabuco, which is run as a vast *estancia*. At present the road ends at Lago Jeinimeini, but in time it will be extended along the route of the present foot track so that it connects with the Chacabuco–Paso Rodolfo Roballos road.

The Chilean IGM 1:50,000 map *Lago Verde* (Section J, No 49) covers the key area around Lago Jeinimeini. There is no regular public transport up to Reserva Nacional Lago Jeinimeini, although in summer there is just enough traffic to make hitching a ride possible (ask at the Conaf office in Chile Chico).

RESERVA NACIONAL TAMANGO
Tamango Circuit

The small, 83-sq-km Reserva Nacional Tamango, immediately north of Cochrane (p198) at the west-

ern end of the Cordón Chacabuco, is one of the principle reserves for the endangered huemul. This surprisingly wild and attractive range can be visited in a three-day (33km), easy–moderate circuit from the Guardería El Hungaro, 6km from Cochrane.

The circuit leads via Laguna Tamango (from where more experienced trekkers can climb the 1722m Cerro Tamango in a six-hour side trip) to Lago Elefantita. From here, you can either traverse southwest high above Lago Cochrane to back to the Guardería El Hungaro or follow the shore to the Guardería Embarcadero, just 3km from Cochrane.

Red de Turismo Río Baker (☎ 067-522646; *San Valentin*) in Cochrane runs several camping grounds with cabins along Lago Cochrane's shore. One Chilean IGM 1:50,000 map, *Valle Chacabuco* (Section J, No 57), covers the park. A free brochure map available at Conaf's Cochrane office shows trails accurately.

PARQUE NACIONAL FRANCISCO PERITO MORENO

The 1150-sq-km Parque Nacional Francisco Perito Moreno is situated roughly 250km directly southwest of the provincial town of Perito Moreno in Argentina's Santa Cruz Province. The park is a superb wilderness enclosed by eight major lakes that reach out into the Patagonian steppes from the park's mountainous interior. The northern part of Parque Nacional Francisco Perito Moreno almost touches the Monte San Lorenzo massif (p197).

For more information, contact the **park administration** (☎ 02962-491477) in the small town of Gobernador Gregores 225km from the *guardería* near the east end of Lago Belgrano.

The park's interior is relatively difficult to reach, as fast-flowing streams and sheer rock walls around lakes block the way in places. In addition, public access is not permitted to a newly declared biosphere reserve (reserva natural restricta).

An easy overnight trek goes to Lago Azara from the end of the road near Cerro Mie. The track leads five hours around the southern side of Lago Belgrano to **Puesto del Nueve**, a rustic hut that serves as a good base for exploring the area. A four-day return trek from the former **Estancia El Rincon** (now owned by the Patagonia Land Trust, which is negotiating this property's transfer to that national park) leads up via the Río Lácteo (shown on IGM maps as 'Río Late') to a *refugio* at around 1000m. From here, a more difficult route climbs to two high glacial lakes known as Lagunas Los Tempanos.

The park has minimal tourist infrastructure, but **Estancia La Oriental**, which lies inside the park, and the nearby **Estancia Menelik**, offer accommodation in the medium price range.

The Argentine IGM's 1:100,000 maps *Lago Belgrano* (Santa Cruz, Nos 4772-33 & 4772-32) and *Monte Tetris* (Santa Cruz, No 4972-3) cover the park.

Visitors without their own transport will find Parque Nacional Francisco Perito Moreno a difficult place to get to. It may be possible to charter (or hire) a vehicle from either Perito Moreno or Gobernador Gregores.

PARQUE NACIONAL LOS GLACIARES
Lago Toro

Lago Toro's raw setting makes it a worthy objective for this two-day trek. The route begins behind Guardería Chaltén, leading southwards across a footbridge then southwest to a shallow lake on a little plateau looking out towards Cerro Huemul. From here you drop down to a private hut on the northern bank of the Río Tunel, and follow the trail upstream to Lago Toro, at the snout of the Glaciar Río Tunel below high craggy peaks. There is a tiny *refugio* near where the river leaves Lago Toro. Camping is permitted here, although there are nicer sites farther downstream.

Experienced trekkers can continue up to Paso del Viento at the edge of the Hielo Sur, a trackless route that takes another long day. Cross a short section of the lower Glaciar Río Tunel (there are no crevasses on this part of the glacier), continuing around a tiny lake at the snout of a second glacier before you ascend steeply southwest over scree slopes to the pass.

LAGO DEL DESIERTO

The 12km-long Lago del Desierto is outside Parque Nacional Los Glaciares, 37km north of El Chaltén. Until recently, it was the source of a long-running border dispute, but in 1995 an international tribunal accepted Argentina's claim to the whole Lago del Desierto area. A recommended two- or three-day trek begins where the road ends at the lake's southern end. A foot track crosses a bridge over the outlet and leads around the eastern shore to a *gendarmería* at the northern end of the lake, where there's free camping. From here, trekkers can continue two days north across the Chilean border to the isolated farm of **Candelario Mancilla**, from where an irregular ferry runs across Lago O'Higgins to Villa O'Higgins (p202) approximately every 10 days. The most useful map is Zagier & Urruty's *Monte Fitz Roy & Cerro Torre Trekking-Mountaineering, Lago del Desierto Trekking-Travel Map*, with a 1:100,000 insert showing the route. Various companies run minibuses from El Chaltén to Lago del Desierto (US$8 same-day return, US$14 if you break the trip at the lake).

PARQUE NACIONAL TORRES DEL PAINE (see map p226)
Laguna Verde

This is a longish one-day trek to a large shallow lake where bird life and guanacos can be observed. Just north of the Río Paine bridge (2.5km north of the administration centre) a foot track climbs northeast and leads across the windy steppes to Laguna Verde. At the southeastern corner of the lake are a hostería and a (currently closed) Conaf guardería. There's nowhere to stay other than the hostería, and camping is not permitted.

LAGUNA AZUL TO LAGO DICKSON

This four- or five-day trek leaves from Guardería Laguna Azul (or you can take a short cut north from Guardería Laguna Amarga) and largely follows a 4WD track (used to transport goods to Refugio Lago Dickson). The track goes to a *refugio* on the northern side of Refugio Lago Paine and continues to a lookout near the northeastern head of Lago Dickson, from where you can view the spectacular Ventisquero Dickson from quite close up. This route gives far better views of the Macizo Paine than the parallel section of the Paine Circuit (which leads via the Río Paine's southern banks along the foot of the massif), but requires backtracking.

Salto Grande & Cuernos Lookout

From the Pudeto boat landing a 1½- to two-hour return trek leads via the nearby surging falls of Salto Grande (where the Río Paine enters Lago Pehoé), to a lookout point from where there are classic views across Lago Nordenskjöld to the Cuernos del Paine, which rise imposingly immediately north of the lake.

Tierra del Fuego

Tierra del Fuego, the largest of South America's islands, is a southern extension of the Patagonian mainland. Its northern half is covered by arid steppeland devoted to sheep grazing and oil production, but farther south this dry, flat land gradually changes into undulating terrain of shallow lakes and extensive peat bogs before meeting what remains of the Andean Cordillera in the south of the island. Rising at the mighty Darwin Range (Cordillera Darwin), these so-called Fuegian Andes form a narrow line of mountains that becomes progressively lower with increasing distance to the east.

The Isla Grande (Great Island) is divided into more or less equal Chilean (western) and Argentine (eastern) sections by an arbitrary north–south border that cuts across the Fuegian Andes at right angles. Only the northernmost part of Chilean Tierra del Fuego has been settled to any extent, and the far south remains an almost uninhabited and largely inaccessible wilderness. Argentine Tierra del Fuego, on the other hand, has a much higher population, with roads penetrating all but its more remote corners.

GATEWAY
Ushuaia (Argentina)

The duty-free city of Ushuaia, whose name means 'bay that runs to the west' in the language of the indigenous Yaghan people, stretches along the Beagle Channel directly below the snowcapped summits of the Fuegian Andes.

Information The **tourist office** (☎/fax 02901-424550; San Martín 674; open 8am-10pm Mon-Fri, 9am-8pm Sat, Sun & holidays) is very helpful, and the **Club Andino Ushuaia** (CAU; ☎ 02901-422335, e cau@tierradelfuego .org.ar; Fadul 50; open 10am-12.30pm & 2pm-9pm Mon-Fri, 10am-2pm Sat in summer) sells maps and guidebooks, and organises treks and climbs. A popular short trek near Ushuaia is the one up to the Glaciar Martial (see Other Treks, p258).

Peat ponds and moors of the Valle Carbajal on the Sierra Valdivieso Circuit

- Adventuring through the heart of the Argentine Fuegian Andes in the Sierra Valdivieso (p239)

- Spotting condors gliding around the Cordón Vinciguerra from the Paso de la Oveja (p246)

- Taking in the marvellous views and spectacular wilderness on the Dientes Circuit (p253), the most southerly trek in the world

The **APN office** (Administración Parques Nacionales; ☎ 02901-421315; e pntf@tierra delfuego.org.ar; San Martín 1395; open 9am-4pm Mon-Fri) can give advice on trekking in Parque Nacional Tierra del Fuego. **Compañía de Guías de Patagonia** (☎ 02901-432642; e lacompania@arnet.com.ar; PO Box 147 (9410)) organises a wide range of short and multiday treks around Ushuaia. **Deportes**

Todo Terreno (☎ 02901-434939; e dttush@ infovia.com.ar; San Martín 1258) sells a small range of outdoor gear, including tents and ice-climbing tools. **Casa Fueguia** (☎ 02901-430767; San Martín 1240) sells white gasoline (as diluyente industrial).

Places to Stay & Eat The CAU's **Camping Pista del Andino** (☎ 02901-435890, 1556 8626; Av Alem 2873; w www.lapistadelandino .com.ar; camping per person US$3), several kilometres northwest of the centre, up near the lower chairlift station (phone for a free pick-up), has tent sites with good facilities.

Refugio del Mochilero (☎ 02901-436129; e refmoch@infovia.com.ar; 25 de Mayo 241; dorm beds US$13) can organise tickets and tours. Climbers and trekkers won't mind walking four blocks uphill to the **Nido de Cóndores** (☎ 02901-437753, 1561 8426; Gobernador Campos 783; doubles US$20), whose young owners know the Fuegian Andes intimately; room rates include breakfast. The **Posada Costa Serena** (☎ 02901-437212; e mcsuarez@ciudad.com.ar; Roca 129; singles/doubles from US$17/24) is centrally located opposite the Aerolíneas Argentinas office.

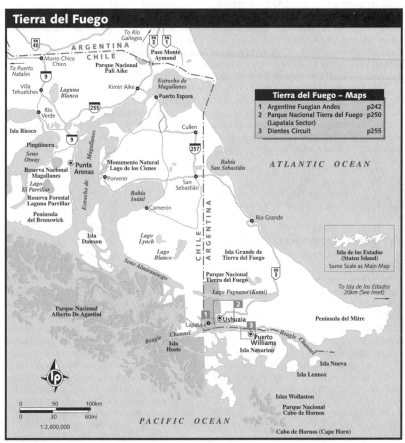

Tierra del Fuego

Tierra del Fuego – Maps	
1 Argentine Fuegian Andes	p242
2 Parque Nacional Tierra del Fuego	p250
(Lapataia Sector)	
3 Dientes Circuit	p255

La Rueda (☎ 02901-436540; San Martín 193) does great all-you-can-eat parrillas (mixed grills) for US$7. **Casa de los Mariscos** (☎ 02901-421928; San Martín 232) serves fish and seafood dishes from around US$5.

Getting There & Away In January and early February, airline and bus tickets to/from Ushuaia may be booked out many days ahead – reserve and reconfirm well in advance.

Southern Winds (☎ 02901-437073; Maipú 237), **Aerolíneas Argentinas** (☎ 02901-421091; Roca 116) and **LAPA** (☎ 02901-432112; 25 de Mayo 64) all fly daily to Río Gallegos (around US$60) and Buenos Aires (from around US$120). LAPA and Aerolíneas Argentinas fly to El Calafate from around US$70, but **LADE** (☎ 02901-421123; San Martín 542) has flights from around US$50. **Aerovías DAP** (☎ 02901-431110; 25 de Mayo 64) flies on Monday and Wednesday to Punta Arenas (US$117 one-way), returning to Ushuaia (US$108 one-way) the same day. **Via Patagonia** (☎ 02901-426010; Rosales 281) flies to Punta Arenas and El Calafate.

Tolkar (☎ 02901-431408; Roca 157) sells bus tickets to Río Grande (US$6, three hours), Río Gallegos (US$16, nine hours) and Punta Arenas (US$22, 11 hours).

Argentine Fuegian Andes

Sandwiched between Lago Fagnano (also known by its indigenous Ona name, Lago Kami) to the north and the Beagle Channel to the south, the Argentine Fuegian Andes form an arc of rugged wilderness stretching around the regional capital of Ushuaia. With few summits exceeding 1500m, the mountains of Argentine Tierra del Fuego lack the altitude, extent and savage scenery of Chile's Cordillera Darwin, but are far more accessible and enjoy a less extreme climate than the glacier-smothered ranges on the Chilean side.

Intense ice-age glaciations have so shaped these ranges that they resemble scaled-down versions of far higher mountain massifs. As you trek through deeply carved glacial valleys and over passes separating jagged peaks ringed with glaciers, it's easy to forget the Argentine Fuegian Andes' relatively low elevation. The upper limit of alpine vegetation is around 600m, and the permanent snow line is only several hundred metres above this.

Adventurous trekkers will appreciate the numerous excellent off-track routes that make the Argentine Fuegian Andes such an exciting area to explore.

NATURAL HISTORY

The moist Fuegian forests are less dense than those farther north, with numerous kinds of low herb-like plants but little real underbrush. The southern beech species lenga is dominant higher up, where soils tend to be shallower, but coigüe de Magallanes, (locally called guindo), is more common lower down.

A typical herb-like plant of these subantarctic forests is the devil's strawberry (frutilla del diablo), which grows close to the ground and produces miniature, but inedible, bright-red berries on tiny brush-like branchlets. The Magellan strawberry (frutilla de Magallanes) is surprisingly similar in appearance, but is most easily distinguished by its 'real' berries, whose look and taste is actually more akin to that of raspberries. Thickets of calafate and miniature ferns cover the ground in open, more well-drained areas. Sundews grow in the acidic soils low in nutrients, but these delicate plants are able to supply their needs by trapping small insects with their sticky, tentacle-like branchlets. Another carnivorous plant is the flor del pantano, which has violet flowers.

Numerous species of lichens and mosses are found growing on tree trunks, including the parasitic cabello de ángel, a member of the mistletoe family. The llao-llao or Indian bread (pan del indio), a parasitic fungus, produces spongy yellow clustered balls on the branches of southern beech species, and was eaten by the indigenous peoples of Tierra del Fuego. The luminous orange jelly-like growths you may see on fallen trees are another interesting type of fungus, which accelerates the rotting of the dead wood.

Poor drainage favours the development of sphagnum bogs, known as *turbales*, which cover extensive areas of the valley floors. Sphagnum bogs form beautiful, spongy golden-red peat mounds that are often dry enough (but tiring) to walk on. Thick deposits of peat have accumulated – to a depth of 5m in places – and this material is cut commercially (chiefly for use as plant potting mix).

Although more at home on the open plains of northern Tierra del Fuego, the ashy-headed goose (*cauquén*, or *canquén* in Chile) is found in the Fuegian Andes. This native goose has an orangey-brown head and upper neck, and bluish-grey body plumage interrupted by brown stripes on its breast. Trekkers have a better chance of sighting the upland goose (*caiquén*). The female upland goose looks similar to the ashy-headed goose but is somewhat larger and darker, while the male has a white head, breast and underbelly. A common seabird is the dolphin gull, a species endemic to southern Patagonia and Tierra del Fuego.

Guanaco are common throughout the Argentine Fuegian Andes and their trails often provide excellent natural walking routes. The Fuegian fox *(zorro fueguino)* is a subspecies of the Patagonian red fox (now also introduced from the mainland). It is the only fox native to Tierra del Fuego, and lives its furtive existence in field and forest.

Regrettably, North American beavers now inhabit most forested streams all over Tierra del Fuego. The gnawed tree stumps and the animals' often surprisingly high dams are a constant hindrance and eyesore. Reindeer have also been introduced to the Fuegian Andes, but fortunately their numbers have stayed low enough to keep them a novelty.

CLIMATE

Somewhat sheltered by the much higher mountains to the west and by other, lower ranges on the Chilean islands of Isla Hoste and Isla Navarino to the south, the Argentine Fuegian Andes have a relatively moderate maritime climate considering their subantarctic latitude. Average annual precipitation levels are 1500mm, though there is considerable variation between the higher ranges and valleys. Subantarctic conditions concentrate the climatic zones into narrow altitude bands, which are reflected in the local vegetation and low permanent snow line. Because of the southerly latitude, the Fuegian winter (from late May until early September) brings heavy snowfalls – even down to sea level.

PLANNING
Maps

The Zagier & Urruty 1:50,000 *Ushuaia Trekking Map* covers most of the eastern Argentine Fuegian Andes, showing all important routes quite accurately. This new colour map is sold locally in bookstores and at the CAU in Ushuaia (see Information, p236).

Books

Guía de Sendas & Escaladas de Tierra del Fuego, by Luis Turi and Carolina Etchegoyen (available in local bookstores and from the CAU), includes treks throughout the Argentine Fuegian Andes.

The Uttermost Part of the Earth, by E Lucas Bridges, tells the fascinating story of the pioneering Bridges family, who established Estancia Harberton, the first farm in southern Tierra del Fuego. A reprint is sold in local bookstores.

Sierra Valdivieso Circuit

Duration	4 days
Distance	48.5km
Difficulty	demanding
Start	Ruta Nacional 3 (16km from Ushuaia)
Finish	Posada del Peregrino
Nearest Town	Ushuaia (p236)
Transport	van or taxi
Summary	An adventurous trek through the heart of the Argentine Fuegian Andes, crossing superb rugged wilderness in splendid isolation.

Extending eastward along the southern side of Lago Fagnano (Kami) from the boundary of Parque Nacional Tierra del Fuego to the landmark summit of Monte Falso Carbajal (1250m), the Sierra Valdivieso arguably offers the most scenic wilderness trekking in the Argentine Fuegian Andes. The numerous (now mostly quite small) glaciers and névés of this jagged range are remnants of far larger glaciers that reshaped the landscape during past ice ages, gouging out countless alpine lakes and tarns. Connecting many of its tiny valleys are gentle passes that serve as convenient crossing routes between the raw ice-clad peaks.

This route is mainly open trekking – through clearings and moors or above the tree line – where markings are minimal (though they are more reliable at crucial junctions).

PLANNING
When to Trek

The Sierra Valdivieso Circuit can normally be done between early December and late March, although in some years the trekking season lasts longer.

Conditions in April can also be quite mild, but any breakdown in the weather so late in the season is likely to bring snowfalls down to at least 300m.

What to Bring

Apart from the Refugio Bonete a few hours from the start, there are no huts or any other reliable shelter along the trek, so it is essential that all parties carry a good tent. There is much waterlogged ground (caused in part by the vandalistic work of introduced North American beavers), so it is advisable to wear well-waterproofed boots on the trek.

Permits & Regulations

No permit is required to trek the Sierra Valdivieso Circuit. Trekkers *are* permitted to camp where the route transits the eastern fringe of Parque Nacional Tierra del Fuego – despite a general ban on overnight trekking in the park – but should be mindful of their impact on the environment at all times (see Responsible Trekking, p43). The final section of the route crosses private land, where camping is not allowed.

NEAREST TOWN & FACILITIES

See Ushuaia (p236).

Hostería Kauyeken

This upmarket place (☎ *02901-433041;* ✉ *kauyeken@cotelnet.com.ar; singles/doubles from US$40/55)* is 500m south from where the trek finishes on Ruta Nacional 3 (12.5km from the centre of Ushuaia), right at the western foot of Monte Olivia.

GETTING TO/FROM THE TREK

The trek starts on Ruta Nacional 3, right where the gas pipeline *(gasoducto)* crosses under the road, roughly 16km northeast from Ushuaia (or 3km from Refugio Altos del Valle, see p245). Yellow *'Peligro'* ('Danger') signs on both sides of the road indicate this point. (Also look for a blazing mark with yellow paint on a tall *lenga* tree.) There is plenty of car parking space beside the road.

The trek finishes back on Ruta Nacional 3 near the Posada del Peregrino, a youth rehabilitation centre at the turn-off to the Turbera Valle Carbajal, 13km northeast from Ushuaia. If no public transport is available, you may be able to telephone for a taxi *(remís)* at the Posada, back at the Turbera (see Day 4) or at the Hostería Kauyeken. Traffic is busy enough to make hitching a reasonable proposition. Otherwise, the 13km walk back to Ushuaia takes around three hours.

Both trailheads can be reached from Ushuaia by (irregular) minibus, which runs

> ## Warning
>
> The Sierra Valdivieso Circuit follows a largely unmarked and little-trodden route through rugged and challenging country. It is therefore suitable only for fit and self-reliant parties with good navigational skills. Even summer weather is highly erratic, with sudden southerly storms – be alert to changes in the weather. Streams (especially the Río Olivia) become difficult to cross safely after rain. Parties should carry at least two extra days of supplies in order to wait for better weather and/or for stream levels to fall.

from the corner of Maipú and 25 de Mayo to the *refugios* along Ruta Nacional 3 (around US$4). **Remises Carlitos** *(☎ 02901-422222; San Martín 995)* charges around US$8 for a taxi (up to three people) in either direction.

THE TREK (see map p242)
Day 1: Ruta Nacional 3 to Refugio Bonete
1½–1¾ hours, 4.5km, 140m ascent
Especially if you set out early, this section may be too short for one day, so trekkers may opt to continue into the upper Río Beban.

From where the route leaves Ruta Nacional 3 *(GPS 54° 43.465 S, 68° 10.071 W)*, head down 50m past a rustic tin shelter to meet a muddy, eroded 4WD track. Follow it around through a little meadow to cross the small Río Esmeralda on a ruined old bridge (made passable by stacked logs) after 10 minutes. Walk northwest along a grassy old road through regenerating *lenga* into a *mallín* (wet meadow), 25 to 30 minutes on. Head 200m through this wet bog before cutting left, back into the forest. The route continues through more forest and soggy areas, turning gradually northeast towards the dominant 1118m summit of Cerro Bonete to cross a small open stream basin with a large beaver dam after 40 to 50 minutes. (Here a rough trail goes off east to the Refugio Altos del Valle, see p245).

A gentle climb north brings you to **Refugio Bonete** *(GPS 54° 42.048 S, 68° 10.070 W)*, 10 minutes on, at around 320m on a minor ridge under its namesake mountain. This simple hut has a potbelly stove – the gas stove is only for emergencies – and one two-berth bunk plus a loft with sleeping space for about four people. There is no charge to use the *refugio*. There is no toilet, so please 'go' well downhill, and collect water upstream from the brook 100m north of the hut. A local Fuegian fox passes the *refugio* on its regular patrols.

Day 2: Refugio Bonete to Salto del Azul
4½–6 hours, 14km, 510m ascent
Make your way northwest – from here on there will often be no real track, just a rough route – towards the 1039m 'sentinel' peak of Punta Navidad. Skirt small moors (avoiding

ridges covered in *coigües* up to the right), following an undulating terrace above the Río Beban past a waterfall into a flat valley basin. Continue for 500m until you are under high bluffs on Cerro Bonete's west side, then ford the small river and head into *lenga* forest. The route cuts rightward, back to the stream, rising on past a large broken beaver dam to cross a side stream *(GPS 44° 40.709 S, 68° 10.648 W)*. (A route variant climbs its true left (north) bank of the side stream to a crest, then drops to meet the main route above the camp sites.)

Proceed towards Monte Falso Carbajal (1250m), at the head of a superb side valley completely enclosed by craggy rock walls with hanging glaciers. Where the stream divides, climb away via its northwestern branch (with fine views south to the jagged 1331m Monte Olivia) to reach some excellent **camp sites** in an isolated clump of *lenga* forest, 1¾ to 2¼ hours from the *refugio*. Here the stream flows through tiny tarns hidden in a field of bouldery moraine debris.

Continue up along the often marshy true right (south) bank of the stream to a flat slab on a gravelly wash, then cut up steeply left through an obvious chute of brittle white shale and ease back right to reach **Paso Beban Este** (around 830m) after 50 minutes to 1¼ hours. This eastern pass gives a good view south down a wild little valley to Laguna Paso Beban, a small lake perched slightly above tree line under the craggy Tres Picos. Traverse on around rightward over the coarse scree and snowdrifts, then cut up directly into **Paso Beban Oeste** (around 850m) after 15 to 20 minutes.

Apart from a large cairn (and some distasteful graffiti painted on rocks) you can't see much from this pass. Descend northwest into the valley of the **Río Torito**, mostly along the boggy right side of the small stream (but crossing where necessary) until you meet a side stream coming down from the north (right). Here, it is probably best to cross the Río Torito and climb around through open areas in the scrub on its true left side (although a route continues down through wet forest on the stream's right bank) to reach a beaver pond *(GPS 54° 38.738 S, 68° 15.223 W)*.

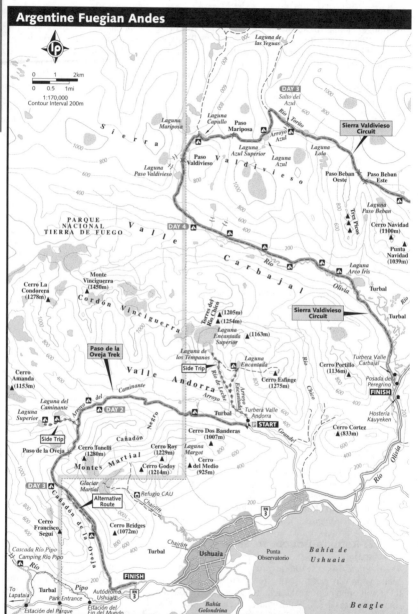

Argentine Fuegian Andes

0 1 2km
0 0.5 1mi
1:170,000
Contour Interval 200m

Laguna de las Yeguas

DAY 3
Salto del Azul
Río Torito

Sierra Valdivieso Circuit

Laguna Mariposa

Laguna Capullo

Paso Mariposa

Arroyo Azul

Laguna Azul Superior

Laguna Azul

Laguna Lola

Sierra

Paso Valdivieso

Laguna Paso Valdivieso

Valdivieso

Paso Beban Oeste

Paso Beban Este

Laguna Paso Beban

Tres Picos

Cerro Navidad (1100m)

Punta Navidad (1039m)

PARQUE NACIONAL TIERRA DE FUEGO

Valle

DAY 4

Carbajal

Río

Laguna Arco Iris

Olivia

Turbal

Río

Turbal

Cerro La Condorera (1278m)

Monte Vinciguerra (1450m)

Cordón Vinciguerra

Torres del Río Chico (1205m) (1254m)

Laguna Encantada Superior (1163m)

Sierra Valdivieso Circuit

Paso de la Oveja Trek

Laguna de los Témpanos

Side Trip

Laguna Encantada

Río de Leche

Cerro Esfinge (1275m)

Turbera Valle Carbajal

Cerro Portillo (1136m)

Posada del Peregrino

FINISH

Cerro Amanda (1153m)

Valle Andorra

Caminante

Arroyo

del

Arroyo Encantada

Río

Chico

Río

Grande

Hostería Kauyeken

Laguna del Caminante

DAY 2

Laguna Superior

Side Trip

Turbal

Turbera Valle Andorra

P START

Olivia

Paso de la Oveja

Cañadón

Negro

Cerro Tonelli (1280m)

Cerro Roy (1229m)

Cerro Dos Banderas (1007m)

Laguna Margot

Cerro del Medio (925m)

Cerro Cortez (833m)

Montes Martial

Cerro Godoy (1214m)

DAY 3

Glaciar Martial

Alternative Route

Refugio CAU

Chairlift

Cañadón de la Oveja

Cerro Francisco Seguí

Cerro Bridges (1072m)

Chairlift

Turbal

RN 3

Cascada Río Pipo
Camping Río Pipo

Río

Ushuaia

Punta Observatorio

Bahía de Ushuaia

FINISH

RN 3

Autódromo Ushuaia

To Lapataia

Turbal
Park Entrance

Pipo

Estación del Parque

Estación del Fin del Mundo

Bahía Golondrina

Beagle

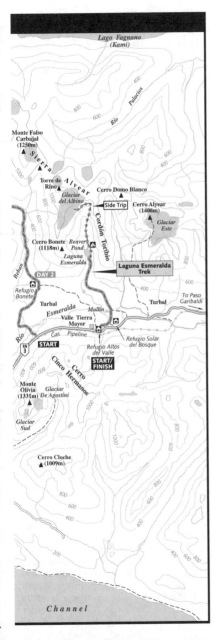

Follow a minor ridge until it peters out at some more beaver dams, then make your way around through trees killed by the inundation to reach the **Salto del Azul**, a waterfall spilling down from the left, 1½ to two hours from the (western) pass. **Camp sites** can be found around attractive meadows here.

Day 3: Salto del Azul to Central Valle Carbajal

5½–7¾ hours, 14km, 550m ascent, 700m descent

This is a long day that can be broken by camping en route – the sites above Laguna Capullo are recommended.

Hop across the **Arroyo Azul** on rocks and head 1.25km on downvalley to the end of the higher of two boggy terraces, just before the Río Torito curves right *(GPS 54° 38.021 S, 68° 17.525 W)*. Climb steeply roughly southward through *coigüe* scrub and tiny shelves covered in heath-like *brecillo* to a prominent boulder (marked by a cairn), from where views open out down along the marshy lower valley to Bahía Torito on Lago Fagnano (Kami).

Continue around rightward up through sloping clearings on a broad spur to reach a tiny cascade near a beaver pond, then cut up directly over a rocky crest to reencounter the Arroyo Azul (crossed lower down) at a small grassy plateau. The route follows the splashing stream up to **Laguna Azul**, a blue lake in a raw basin below rugged glaciated peaks, 1½ to 2¼ hours from Salto del Azul. Scenic but at best semisheltered **camp sites** can be found here.

Walk around to lawns along Laguna Azul's southwest inlet, then head up this stream into a rocky gully. The route climbs briefly left onto a broad rock rib, which it follows up west before ascending directly into **Paso Mariposa** *(GPS 54° 38.543 S, 68° 19.171 W)*, one to 1½ hours from the lake. Marked by another large cairn, this high, often windy gap (not much under 1000m) lies between bands of white and grey shale rock. It offers wonderful vistas east and west across the surrounding Argentine Fuegian Andes, including Laguna Azul

Superior behind and Laguna Mariposa ahead. (Note that there is a slightly lower pass 600m to the south, which is a better route alternative only if you are doing the trek in the opposite direction.)

Make an initially steep descent across a raw scree basin, then drop left beside a streamlet to reach the (rather uninteresting) **Laguna Capullo** after 30 to 45 minutes. Crossing several inlets, head briefly around the lake's southern shore before you cut up left to a grassy shelf with nice **camping** among the boulders. The route climbs on steeply southwest over green carpets of *azorella* and on up left via a grassy chute to a high rocky crest. From here there is a wonderful view north across four lakes, including **Laguna Mariposa** (almost 200m directly below you), to the picturesque Bahía de los Renos on Lago Fagnano (Kami).

Now above the tree line, head southward over an undulating panoramic terrace past two deep pools, then follow the outlet of the second pool down into the upper valley. The route cuts up past tarns in scrubby alpine meadows to cross **Paso Valdivieso** (also known as Paso de las Cinco Lagunas), 1¼ to 1¾ hours from Laguna Capullo. The cairn here *(GPS 54° 39.268 S, 68° 21.422 W)* is at roughly 700m, although the lowest point is actually some way over to the right. The pass lies directly below a long shelf glacier whose tumbling meltwater streamlets flow both north and south of the watershed. To the southwest, Monte Vinciguerra can be identified beyond the Valle Carbajal.

Walk down past a rocky outcrop, then descend steeply rightward to Laguna Paso Valdivieso. Follow a well-defined trail around the lake's eastern shore, making your way down beside the cascading outlet stream. Cross to the right bank when you come to the first patches of taller scrub before dropping into the light forest to meet the **Río Olivia** about halfway along the Valle Carbajal, 1¼ to 1½ hours from Paso Valdivieso. Extending from near Lago Alto in the heart of Parque Nacional Tierra del Fuego, this deep wild valley separates the Sierra Valdivieso from the Cordón Vinciguerra.

Camp sites can be found around here, although sites along the forested river flats farther downvalley are even more pleasant. (Trekkers coming the other way should turn up northwest where the glacier above the pass comes into sight at GPS 54° 40.792 S, 68° 20.908 W.)

Day 4: Central Valle Carbajal to Posada del Peregrino
5½–7 hours, 16km, 100m ascent, 180m descent

Begin the long stretch down through the lovely wild Valle Carbajal. Avoiding occasional areas of beaver activity, follow rough trails through the *lenga* forest (with abundant *chauras* and the native Magellan strawberry) along the northern bank of the meandering river. Excellent **camp sites** are passed almost continually. The route leads into the increasingly extensive belt of moors (*turbales*) towards the valley mouth, crossing five larger side streams (which often meet the main valley in high waterfalls as they gush down from 'hanging' side valleys up to your left), before it finally turns away along a forested lateral moraine *(GPS 54° 41.995 S, 68° 14.809 W)* after three to four hours.

This low ridge ends at the large peaty pond of **Laguna Arco Iris**, after 25 to 30 minutes. (Trekkers heading in the other direction should look out for a large marker pole where the path enters the forest here.) Head around the spongy western shore, from where there are great views across the lake to the majestic 1331m Monte Olivia, and then make a (usually knee-deep) ford of the Río Olivia *(GPS 54° 42.480 S, 68° 13.711 W)*, 20 to 25 minutes on.

A muddy path (often confused by cattle trails) now takes an up-and-down southeastward course, avoiding the vast rusty-red moorland dotted with little ponds that stretches along the broad valley junction by staying in the forest. The route continues as a rough road after passing a (locked) gate, crossing through drying racks stacked with cut peat to reach buildings of the **Turbera Valle Carbajal**, 1½ to two hours from the ford. Be on the lookout for possibly unfriendly dogs here. Recross the **Río Olivia** on the road bridge and continue through another locked gate to arrive back on Ruta Nacional 3 at the **Posada del Peregrino** (see Getting to/from the Trek, p240) after a final 10 minutes.

Laguna Esmeralda

Duration	3–4 hours
Distance	9km
Difficulty	easy
Start/Finish	Refugio Altos del Valle (p245)
Nearest Town	Ushuaia (p236)
Transport	van or taxi

Summary An excellent day trek (or a short overnight trek) to a lovely subalpine lake below the tiny 'icecap' of the Glaciar del Albino.

One of the most popular day treks near Ushuaia, the trek up to Laguna Esmeralda involves a minimal ascent and descent. It makes an excellent medium-length day trek from a base in Ushuaia or from one of the *refugios*, or a short overnight trek (with a camp at the lake and a side trip to Glaciar del Albino).

The first section of the route leads over several converging cross-country skiing and dog-sledding runs. As signage is inadequate, it is easy to lose your way – if only momentarily. Note that teams of huskies are trained on these trails even in summer; if you encounter a team of dogs, step off the trail and let them pass.

PLANNING
When to Trek
The trek is normally easily passable at least from late November to mid-April. Early in the season (or after heavy rain) the trail can be wet and boggy in places.

NEAREST TOWNS & FACILITIES
See Ushuaia (p236).

Refugio Altos del Valle
The trek begins and ends at Refugio Altos del Valle *(☎/fax 02901-422234, [e] gatocu ruchet@hotmail.com)*, a small winter skiing

and dog-sledding centre just off Ruta Nacional 3, about 19km from Ushuaia, where in summer dorm beds cost around US$8 (without breakfast) and basic meals are served.

Several other similar *refugios* exist further along Ruta Nacional 3, including **Refugio Solar del Bosque** *(☎ 02901-43527; [e] solarbosque@tierradelfuego.org.ar)* 650m further on.

In summer, **Transporte Pasarela** *(☎ 02901-421735; cnr Maipu & 25 de Mayo)* runs shuttles to Lago Fagnano (US$25) at 10am; these pass by Refugio Altos del Valle (US$10), returning in the evening. Otherwise, taxis in Ushuaia charge a fixed-rate fare to the *refugio*. **Remises Carlitos** *(☎ 02901-422222; San Martín 995)* charges around US$10 (up to three people) in either direction. There is free car parking on the turn-off just before the *refugio*.

THE TREK (see map p242)
From just before the *refugio*, follow the (unsignposted) old bulldozed track off left directly into a little clearing. Continue off rightward, to meet a trail crossing the path. Go right here, proceeding to a more prominent dirt road, where you should turn left (the right option goes to Refugio Solar del Bosque).

Head north towards the Sierra Alvear's spectacular skyline of jagged peaks and gleaming glaciers – most strikingly, the 1406m Cerro Alvear itself, to the northeast. The route leads through fields dotted with fleshy-leafed daisies to cross a streamlet on a broad bridge just before passing a (right) trail turn-off. Bear leftward and continue across a small *mallín*, then cut away rightward past another (right) turn-off (marked with white arrows on a red background) where you enter the trees. After a gentle climb through the open *lenga* forest you come out into a peaty bog along the Río Esmeralda.

The wet, muddy track cuts up through this into the tiny valley beside the river, climbing over a crest to arrive at **Laguna Esmeralda** (Emerald Lake), 1½ to two hours from the *refugio*. This bluish-green lake lies almost directly under Glaciar del Albino (see Side Trip), whose cloudy meltwater gives the lake its attractive colour, and is fringed by lovely white-pebble beaches. Ashy-headed geese can sometimes be spotted around the north shore. There are secluded **camp sites** at the northeast end of Laguna Esmeralda.

Return via the same route.

Side Trip: Glaciar del Albino

3½–5 hours return, 7km,
600m ascent/descent

This moderate–demanding route is recommended to trekkers with extra time – and energy.

Head 10 minutes around the east shore of Laguna Esmeralda, then continue into the upper valley past a large beaver pond. This unmaintained but generally well-trodden foot track leads alongside the stream past excellent **camp sites** situated on small flats in the *lenga* forest to a large bivouac rock immediately below the scrub line. Ascend directly into this moraine-filled gully – there is often a followable path – past where the stream cascades down over slabs up to the left.

When you reach the grey rock *(GPS 843m; 54° 40.344 S, 68° 07.840 W)*, climb steeply west through loose rock beside a streamlet to reach a somewhat larger stream on a rocky shelf. Cross this stream and head 50m along the shelf, then find your way up over the red rock slab. Some minor hand-climbing may be required. Although there is no serious exposure to a fall, this calls for some care. The route cuts up to a rock outcrop at the edge of the **Glaciar del Albino**, 1¼ to 2½ hours from the lake. This small glacier lies between impressive peaks and offers a mountaineer's perspective on the Esmeralda valley far below.

The ice near the rim is not crevassed, and it is safe to walk about 50m up for a view across the glacier to an iceberg-filled lake created by a high moraine wall – but only properly equipped and/or guided trekkers should consider venturing beyond this point.

Return via the same route.

Paso de la Oveja

Duration	3 days
Distance	31.5km
Difficulty	moderate
Start	Turbera Valle Andorra
Finish	Ushuaia (p236)
Transport	taxi

Summary A trek around the Montes Martial through idyllic valleys covered by beautiful forests and areas of Fuegian moor.

The increasingly popular trek over the Paso de la Oveja connects the two valleys that surround the Montes Martial. Rising abruptly from the Beagle Channel directly behind Ushuaia, this short range remains an undisturbed wilderness despite its proximity to the booming city.

The side trip to Laguna Encantada and Laguna de los Témpanos is highly recommended, and can be done (before the trek proper) in one or two days as individual day treks or a short overnight trek.

PLANNING
When to Trek

The route is normally in condition from mid-November until mid-April. Early or late in the season, heavy snow may lie on the pass.

Permits & Regulations

Although a ban on overnight trekking applies elsewhere in Parque Nacional Tierra del Fuego, the Paso de la Oveja route is permitted as only a short section of the circuit that transits the park's eastern fringe. However, trekkers must first obtain a permit from the APN office in Ushuaia (p236).

In addition, be particularly mindful of your impact on the environment when passing through this area (see Responsible Trekking, p43). Note that campfires are not permitted anywhere along the Paso de la Oveja route.

The side trip to Laguna de los Témpanos and the final part of the route cross private land, where trekkers must be on their best behaviour.

GETTING TO/FROM THE TREK

The trek starts near the Turbera Valle Andorra, 9.5km from Ushuaia in the lower Valle Andorra. The (left) turn-off is 5km from the centre of town on Ruta Nacional 3. There is no public transport, but taxis *(remises)* will drive you there. **Remises Carlitos** *(☎ 02901-422222; San Martín 995)* charges around US$6 (up to three people). Otherwise, it's at least a three-hour walk from Ushuaia.

The trek finishes near the Autódromo Ushuaia, a car-racing track just north off Ruta Nacional 3, 6km west from the centre of Ushuaia. Buses running to/from Parque Nacional Tierra del Fuego (p250) pass by this point and can be flagged down. Otherwise, it's an easy walk back to town.

THE TREK (see map p242)
Day 1: Turbera Valle Andorra to Upper Arroyo Grande

2¾–3½ hours, 11km, 85m ascent

From the small car park at the locked road gate into the Turbera Valle Andorra (a peat-cutting operation), walk through the pedestrian gate on the right – the sign warning you not to enter does not apply to foot traffic – and follow the road for five minutes, almost until it ends at some shacks by the Arroyo Grande.

Turn left along an unsignposted old 4WD track that leads upvalley through tiny pastures, grazed by horses, above drying racks stacked with 'bricks' of cut peat along the river. Continue on through *coigüe* forest, then (where the old 4WD track peters out) drop slightly rightward to reach a small meadow *(GPS 54° 45.358 S, 68° 21.003 W)*, still just outside the national park boundary, 50 minutes to 1¼ hours from the road. There are pleasant **camp sites** here (although irresponsible visitors have left behind garbage).

Follow the path up leftward to cross and recross the stream coming from the **Cañadón Negro**, then head northwest through a broad gap on the south side of a long forested ridge. The route continues along the edge of the valley, usually just high enough to avoid spongy moors over to the right. There are unsatisfying views north to the snowy summits of the Cordón Vinciguerra as you continue westward through open *lenga* forest in earshot of the roaring river.

After cutting through small grassy *mallines*, turn slowly southwestward and rise, still only very gently, over timbered flats beside the river. Dip over shallow channels to avoid low cliffs shortly before you cross to the true left bank of the **Arroyo del Caminante** not far upstream from where it meets the branch draining the valley to the northwest to form the Arroyo Grande *(GPS 54° 45.228 S, 68° 25.152 W)*, 1¾ to 2¼ hours from the national park boundary. There are pleasant **camp sites** both before and after this easy crossing.

Side Trip: Laguna Encantada & Laguna de los Témpanos

4¾–6¼ hours return, 13km,
730m ascent/descent

This can be done as a long day trek, as an overnight combination – by camping at Laguna Encantada, then trekking to Laguna de los Témpanos the next day – or broken into two separate day treks.

Walk down to the buildings of the Turbera Valle Andorra on the south bank of the tranquil **Arroyo Grande** (see Day 1). Cross the river in a normally shallow wade (a suspension bridge that was here some years ago has now been removed).

A trail laid with cut logs – the sleepers remaining from a narrow-gauge rail line used to transport timber out of the valley until the 1940s – leads upstream through soggy green river flats grazed by flocks of upland geese to enter the forest at a stand of *ñirres (GPS 54° 45.352 S, 68° 18.798 W)*. Cut gently upward through the trees to cross a stream (the outlet of Laguna Encantada), then almost immediately steer around to the right and climb more steeply to reach a trail fork (at approximately 335m), 40 to 50 minutes after crossing the river.

Continue up northeast into a tiny side valley. The gradient remains fairly steep as you ascend on through highland *lengas* past a discreet (left) turn-off, but moderates as you rise through scrubby meadows to reach

Laguna Encantada, 45 minutes to one hour from the trail fork. This 'enchanted' lake lies at around 550m in a grassy bowl headed by a horned peak (1163m) above high cliffs with a long cascade streaming down (from the unseen Laguna Encantada Superior). On the lake's east side stands the 1275m Cerro Esfinge, which can be climbed (by first following the lake's southeast inlet, then cutting up to the right) for sensational views.

There are scenic (unlevel and only semi-sheltered) **camp sites** on the west side of the outlet, and sheltered sites in the scrub a little over halfway around the lake's west side.

Return to the trail fork at around 335m, 30 to 40 minutes from Laguna Encantada, then go right and head northwest through tall *lenga* forest. This muddy but initially well-graded path sidles gently upward, gradually turning northward as you climb over a spur to enter a tiny side valley. Make a rising traverse below occasional cliffs to meet the **Río de Leche** (at about 530m), following the cascading stream up briefly before you cross it on a flat grassy shelf, 40 to 50 minutes from the fork. The route climbs through moraine rubble well above the stream to reach **Laguna de los Témpanos** (around 715m), 20 to 30 minutes on.

Alternatively, from Laguna Encantada descend a short way past the streamside meadows to the discreet turn-off noted on the way up. A short cut then climbs 250m from here to Laguna de los Témpanos over a distance of 2km, in 45 minutes to an hour. Turn up right (west) and climb steeply up over the grassy ridge top. The route traverses northwest up the ridge's left side, high above glowing red moors in the Valle Andorra, to reach a cairn on a minor rock outcrop at 680m *(GPS 54° 44.426 S, 68° 19.413 W)*, then cuts down to rejoin the main route at the grassy shelf by the Río de Leche.

Although – despite its Spanish name – there are no icebergs in the lake's cloudy waters, the smooth snout of **Glaciar Vinciguerra** creeps right down into this awesome meltwater tarn from the ice-smothered mountain above. Climbers have built low rock shelters where **camping** is possible (though not really recommended). The ice can be reached by heading around the lake's east side past a large polished slab.

When you're done, head down to the trail fork at 335m and retrace your steps to the Turbera Valle Andorra.

Day 2: Upper Arroyo Grande to Upper Cañadón de la Oveja

2½–3¼ hours, 6.5km, 465m ascent, 250m descent

The gradient steepens gradually as you head around southward to recross the small but rushing Arroyo del Caminante (just above its confluence with the smaller stream coming from Paso de la Oveja) on a makeshift log bridge after 30 to 40 minutes. Follow the often muddy track on up to reach the unmarked right turn-off going to Laguna del Caminante (see Side Trip, p249) at the upper scrub line *(GPS 54° 45.765 S, 68° 25.908 W)*, 10 to 15 minutes on. Climb for another 15 to 20 minutes through alpine meadows beside the stream to a marker stake under the pyramid-like crags of Cerro Tonelli (1280m).

From this point you can either ford the stream and follow its east (true right) bank, staying close to the stream as you rise through the narrowing talus-filled gully into **Paso de la Oveja** (around 800m), or continue up the west side of the stream, then climb and make a higher traverse around into the pass. Both routes take 50 minutes to 1¼ hours. Marked by a chest-high cairn, Paso de la Oveja (also known as Paso del Caminante) lies directly under the spires of Cerro Tonelli and brings into view two towering twin peaks (both just over 1200m) in the valley ahead. There are also more fine views back northward to the glacier-clad summits of the Cordón Vinciguerra. Condors can sometimes be observed gliding around these ranges.

Descend past a cirque on Cerro Tonelli's western side to cross the tiny stream emerging from the scree. The best route follows the steep left bank of the stream down around to the left to reach a route fork *(GPS 54° 47.062 S, 68° 26.846 W)* at the scrub line in the upper **Cañadón de la Oveja** (see Alternative Route) after 35 to 45 minutes. Scenic **camp sites** can be found here in the low vegetation under half a dozen cascades spilling over green, grassy cliffs. (If walking the other way, note that this is the last camping until well beyond the pass.)

Side Trip: Laguna del Caminante
1–1¼ hours return, 3.5km,
110m ascent/descent
The short easy side trip to this serene lake should not be missed. From the unmarked turn-off mentioned in Day 2, the well-trodden route sidles northwest over grassy slopes under cliffs, then climbs above the tumbling **Arroyo del Caminante** to a grassy shelf. Cut down rightward on a steep, muddy path and cross the main inlet below a waterfall to reach **Laguna del Caminante**. Various excellent **camp sites** can be found in the *lenga* forest fringing meadows on the lake's south shore, from where the tops of the Cordón Vinciguerra are just visible.

From the grassy shelf above the lake, you can continue southwest to the slightly higher **Laguna Superior** (an additional 35 to 45 minutes and 2km return), which lies under Cerro Amanda and Cerro Tonelli. This lake also offers scenic **camping**.

Retrace your steps to the main route.

Day 3: Upper Cañadón de la Oveja to Ushuaia
4½–5½ hours, 14km, 785m descent
At the left (east) side of the valley, climb diagonally leftward up over coarse talus to a minor rocky spur *(GPS 54° 47.203 S, 68° 26.227 W)* just before a stream gully coming down from a cirque on the south side of Cerro Tonelli. The route now begins a traverse along the steep scree slopes (at just over 500m), high above the scrubby, waterlogged meadows of the valley floor, towards Isla Navarino beyond the Beagle Channel. Opposite you are craggy 1200m peaks with 500m walls spouting waterfalls. Watch for yellow marker posts and/or occasional yellow paint markings that lead rightward down along the edge of a coarse talus field to a poorly marked trail junction in the forest, one to 1½ hours from the camp

in the upper valley. The right branch leads 100m down to the stream, which can be crossed to reach some idyllic **camp sites** on grassy meadows *(GPS 54° 47.983 S, 68° 25.646 W)* under Cerro Francisco Seguí.

Continue down through *guindo (coigüe)* forest above the stream, which here flows within a gully. Despite muddy sections and occasional fallen logs, the going is fairly easy, and you reach a gate marking the boundary of private land at the end of the deep, enclosed canyon *(GPS 54° 49.207 S, 68° 24.718 W)*, one to 1¼ hours on.

Follow a grassy farm track around southwest (towards the airport) gently down over pastures scattered with *calafate* and native daisy bushes, passing a blue shack – the dogs here are usually kept chained – to reach another (locked) gate along the turn-off to the **Autódromo Ushuaia**, 150m from Ruta Nacional 3, after 30 to 40 minutes. (Trekkers going the other way should take the turn-off just east of the **Club Hípico** and climb over the gate marked with blue stripes. Alternatively, you can continue past the speedway, then follow the stream up to the start of the canyon.)

Alternative Route: Low-Level Trail
1½–2 hours, 3.5km
This slower and less scenic route may be a better bad-weather option. It is very boggy and scrubby in places, though generally quite pleasant going.

From the route fork in the upper Cañadón de la Oveja, skirt the talus for 300m, then duck rightward into the brush. The sometimes indistinct route leads downvalley beside or near the stream (which you should not have to cross) through open *lenga* forest and lovely grassy flats to meet the main high traverse route below a coarse talus field. Now proceed as described in Day 3.

Isla Navarino

Isla Navarino lies on the Beagle Channel just to the south of the Fuegian 'mainland'. This large island (measuring almost 100km

Parque Nacional Tierra del Fuego – Lapataia Sector

Parque Nacional Tierra del Fuego forms a 630-sq-km strip of rugged mountainous country stretching northward along the Chilean frontier from the Beagle Channel to well beyond Lago Fagnano (Kami). The national park begins just 10km west of Ushuaia, and is surrounded by even more expansive areas of Fuegian-Andean wilderness. Only shorter day treks are possible in the park's southernmost (Lapataia) sector.

Maps

Either the Zagier & Urruty 1:50,000 *Ushuaia Trekking Map* (see Maps, p48), or the simple maps of Parque Nacional Tierra del Fuego available free of charge from the APN or tourist office in Ushuaia are sufficiently accurate for the routes described in this boxed text.

Permits & Regulations

A fee of US$4 is payable at the park entrance.

Apart from this southernmost (Lapataia) sector of the park and the Paso de la Oveja route (p246), trekking is prohibited in Parque Nacional Tierra del Fuego unless you are accompanied by a park-approved guide (such as from the Compañía de Guías de Patagonia – see Ushuaia, p236). Absolutely no public access is permitted in two biosphere reserves (known as *reservas estrictas)* on the Chilean border – an area on the south side of Lago Fagnano (Kami), and the peninsula between Bahía Lapataia and the Beagle Channel.

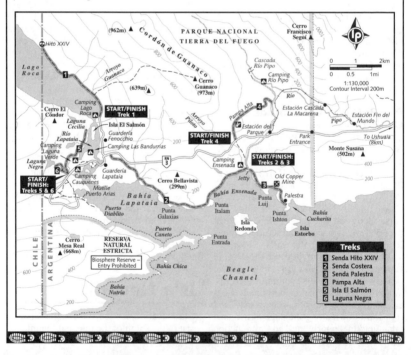

Parque Nacional Tierra del Fuego – Lapataia Sector

Nearest Facilities

There are five free, basic camping grounds (without facilities) that are often crowded in summer. **Camping Ensenada** is 6km from the park entrance and nearest the Senda Costera; **Camping Río Pipo** is 6km from the entrance near the Pampa Alta trail. **Camping Las Bandurrias**, **Camping Laguna Verde** and **Camping Cauquenes** are on islands in the Río Lapataia.

In addition, **Camping Lago Roca** *(camping per person US$5)*, at Lago Roca's southern end, has good facilities, including a store.

Getting There & Away

There are several buses that run daily from the corner of Maipú and 25 de Mayo in Ushuaia (US$10 return – even if you stay a few days). A tourist train, **Tren del Fin del Mundo** *(☎ 02901-431600; W www.trendelfindelmundo.com.ar)*, runs between Estación del Fin del Mundo, 8km west of Ushuaia, and Estación del Parque, on the Río Pipo near the road to Bahía Ensenada (adults/children US$20/6 return). **Remises Carlitos** *(☎ 02901-422222; San Martín 995)* charges around US$15 (up to three people) one-way for a taxi to Lapataia.

Warning

Occasional blooms of native marine algae, a phenomenon known as red tide *(marea roja)*, can contaminate molluscs (such as clams and mussels) with a powerful toxin that is deadly to humans even in small doses. For this reason it is both illegal and extremely unadvised to eat shellfish taken from anywhere along the shore of the Beagle Channel.

Senda Hito XXIV

From Camping Lago Roca, a popular 8km (four-hour) return trek leads around beautiful Lago Roca's northeast shore to Hito XXIV – that number is *veinticuatro* in Spanish – the boundary post which marks the Argentina–Chile frontier. It is illegal to cross the frontier, which is patrolled regularly.

Senda Costera

This 7km (four-hour) trek leads west from Bahía Ensenada along the coastline past old middens (archaeologically important mounds of shells left by the indigenous inhabitants) to meet Ruta Nacional 3 a short way east of the park administration centre at Lapataia.

Senda Palestra

This 4km (three-hour) return trek from Bahía Ensenada follows a path eastward past a disused copper mine and to the popular rock-climbing wall of Palestra near a disused *refugio*.

Pampa Alta

The low heights of Pampa Alta (around 315m) grant some long views across the Beagle Channel to Isla Navarino and Isla Hoste. This lookout point is reached on a 3.5km path that leaves the Ruta Nacional 3 1.5km west of the Río Pipo and Bahía Ensenada road turn-offs.

Isla El Salmón & Laguna Negra

From the road 2km southwest of Lapataia, a trail leads north along the western side of the Río Lapataia to reach a fishing spot opposite Isla El Salmón. Laguna Negra, a lovely lake in the forest, is easily accessible via a 1km circuit loop at a signpost 200m past the trail to Isla El Salmón.

by 40km) is a superb subantarctic wilderness of rugged windswept ranges rising to over 1000m and alpine moors. The craggy Cordón de los Dientes divides Isla Navarino into two (not quite equal) halves and shelters the island's narrow northern coastal strip from southerly storms. The larger southern half of Isla Navarino is an open expanse of subantarctic tundra, dotted with hundreds of moorland ponds and a number of larger lakes, including Lago Windhond and Lago Navarino.

NATURAL HISTORY

Physical isolation and severe climatic conditions on Isla Navarino have affected the island's wildlife. The only true forests are found close to sea level or on more sheltered north-facing slopes. There is less diversity of tree species compared with areas further north, with deciduous *lenga* and the evergreen *coigüe de Magallanes* predominating. Where exposure to the elements becomes extreme, vegetation is reduced to beautiful stunted forms. Waterlogged peat bogs and attractive mossy lawns compete with the forest at all elevations.

There are no native land-dwelling predators on Isla Navarino, although introduced stray and feral dogs are beginning to have a severe impact on the local ecology. The ground-dwelling flightless steamer duck, a large bird that forages in small flocks on meadows or along streams – often well away from the protection of any sizable body of water – is being particularly severely affected. The upland goose *(caiquén)* also lives and nests on the island in open areas close to water. The male upland goose has white and grey plumage, while the female is coffee-black. Isla Navarino's open alpine scrublands provide a favourable summer habitat for the fire-eyed diucon *(diucón)*, an uncommon small grey-breasted bird with blackish-brown wings and red eyes, and an endemic southern subspecies of the yellow-bridled finch *(yal cordillerano austral)*.

Isla Navarino's guanacos are larger and heavier than those found either on the Fuegian or South American mainland. This appears to be the result of the absence of predators – even the indigenous Yaghan (or Yamana) people were essentially seafaring nomads less skilled in hunting agile land-dwelling animals.

Unfortunately, runaway dogs seem to be causing an alarming decline in guanaco numbers, though at least they may also be helping to control Isla Navarino's introduced North American beavers. Andean condors are surprisingly numerous on Isla Navarino, perhaps because dead beavers supply them with plenty of carrion.

CLIMATE

Isla Navarino has a stark subantarctic climate similar to that of the adjacent Argentine Fuegian Andes, though its mountains are somewhat more exposed to the fierce gales that frequently sweep in from the moody seas immediately south of the island. The Cordón de los Dientes shelters the northern coast of Isla Navarino from these southerlies, receiving up to 2000mm in precipitation annually. This falls fairly evenly throughout the year, but winter brings snowfalls right down to sea level. In the mountains, summer (December, January and February) temperatures average around 8°C – still less extreme than might be expected this far from the equator.

ACCESS TOWN
Puerto Williams (Chile)

Puerto Williams lies about midway along Isla Navarino's north coast on the Beagle Channel, 60km east of Ushuaia. A Chilean naval base and minor fishing port (known for the king crabs, or *centollas*, caught in the surrounding sea canals), Puerto Williams is the most southerly town in the world. Essential trekking provisions can be bought at the general store in Puerto Williams, although the range is limited.

The **tourist office** (☎ 061-621140) is on the tiny Centro Comercial square. About 3km west of Puerto Williams across the Río Róbalo, is **Parque Etnobotánico Omora**, set up to protect and study the ecology of the world's most southerly forests. Omora welcomes visitors and has several short interpretive trails.

Places to Stay & Eat Both the **Refugio Coirón** (☎ *061-621225*; e *coiron@simltd .com*; *Ricardo Maragaño 168*; *rooms with breakfast per person US$10*), which trekkers favour, and the cosy **Hostal Pusaki** (☎*/fax 061-621116*; e *hostalpusaki@ze.cl*; *Piloto Pardo 222*; *rooms per person US$12*) offer use of a kitchen.

Restaurante Cabo de Hornos (☎ *061-621232*; *Ricardo Maragaño 146*) has a varied menu. The bar at the **Club de Yates Micalvi** (☎ *061-621041*), Puerto Williams' legendary yacht club, is a lively place after 9pm.

Getting There & Away There are daily flights (except Sunday) to/from Punta Arenas (US$71) with **Aerovías DAP** (☎*/fax 061-621051*; w *www.aeroviasdap.cl*; *Centro Comercial*); the checked baggage limit is 15kg (US$1.50 per extra kg). **Aeroclub Ushuaia** (☎ *02901-421717*; w *www.aero clubushuaia.org.ar*) operates charter flights to Puerto Williams from Ushuaia from US$100 per person (plus US$13 taxes per flight).

Transbordadora Austral Broom (☎ *061-218100*; w *www.tabsa.cl*) operates the *Ferry Fueguino* which runs from Punta Arenas to Puerto Williams; the ferry departs from Punta Arenas on Wednesday evening and returns from Puerto Williams the following Friday evening (US$120/150 one-way, 26 hours).

Disagreements between Argentine and Chilean maritime authorities have prevented a regular ferry service between Ushuaia and Puerto Williams for decades – a perennial on-again, off-again affair. If and when the ferry begins operating again, the one-way fare is likely to be around US$40.

Boats can be chartered from Ushuaia (p236) – ask there at the tourist office, the harbour, the Refugio del Mochilero or the Nido de Cóndores – for around US$100. Private yachts on their way to and from Cape Horn or Antarctica pass through Ushuaia and/or Puerto Williams, and it is often possible to hitch (or pay for) a ride on one of these boats.

Taxi Navarino (☎ *061-621387*; e *serenap@ starmedia.com*) does trekker shuttles.

Dientes Circuit

Duration	5 days
Distance	53.5km
Difficulty	moderate–demanding
Start/Finish	Puerto Williams (p252)
Transport	boat or plane

Summary This most southerly trek in the world leads around the spectacular rock towers of the Cordón de los Dientes.

The Dientes Circuit (Circuito Dientes de Navarino) leads around the jagged pinnacles known as Los Dientes de Navarino through a spectacular wilderness with raw rock ranges and hundreds of lakes. The Dientes are the highest summits on Isla Navarino, and are identifiable landmarks from around the island and from the Beagle Channel.

There are many naturally boggy areas, but in places beavers have flooded the forested valleys with their (usually shallow) dams.

Cairns and painted red horizontal stripes on a white background (with numbering that corresponds to the route description in the Bienes Nacionales brochure – see Books & Maps, p254) now reliably mark the circuit. The Dientes Circuit is normally done over four or five days in a clockwise direction. The trekking days laid out here are suggestions only; as good camp sites can be found along much of the route, parties can move at their own pace. Numerous additional side trips (such as to the Mirador de los Dientes, Lagunas Chevallay, Laguna Alta or even to Lago Windhond) could lengthen the trek by days.

PLANNING
When to Trek
The trek is best done from early December to the end of March, although – provided the weather cooperates – more experienced and well-prepared parties can go at least a month earlier or later.

What to Bring
There are no *refugios* (or any other buildings) along the route and it is essential that parties carry a good tent. Often, only semi-sheltered camp sites are available.

Books & Maps

The Chilean Ministerio de Bienes Nacionales (Ministry of National Resources) has recently produced an excellent bilingual (Spanish-English) colour brochure titled *Circuito Dientes de Navarino* that gives a careful route description of the trek and includes a contoured map (at a scale of approximately 1:121,000). This brochure and map are available in Punta Arenas (p196) from the **Bienes Nacionales office** (☎ 061-221651; Av España 981) but are hard to find on Isla Navarino itself – although places like the Refugio Coirón in Puerto Williams (p252) may have a copy that can be photocopied.

Two Chilean IGM 1:50,000 maps also cover the Dientes Circuit: *Puerto Williams* (Section L, No 190) and *Lago Windhond* (Section L, No 203). Although these maps fail to show many lakes and do not indicate the circuit route, they are otherwise quite accurate and very useful.

Permits & Regulations

No permit is required and there are few regulations, but be sure to leave your details, including expected return date, either where you are staying or at the Gobernación Marítima office above the waterfront.

THE TREK
Day 1: Puerto Williams to Laguna del Salto

4–5¼ hours, 12km, 710m ascent

The first section of the walk takes a cleared track up to Cerro Bandera. This is a popular day walk for locals. With light daypacks, the trip to Cerro Bandera can be done in around four hours return (carry water).

Walk along the street (Calle Teniente Andrés Muñoz Henríquez) out of town past the Entel telecommunications station to **Plaza de la Virgen**, a small park at a road junction. Take the left road (signposted 'Acceso al Sendero de Chile') and follow it gently up (past a turn-off going to a navy installation) through *canelo* and *coigüe* scrub beside the small **Río Róbalo** to a car park at a tiny dam (the town water supply), 35 to 45 minutes from Puerto Williams. A short path crosses a footbridge below the spillway

cascade to a picnic area with tables and fireplaces known as the Mirador Cascada – some people also **camp** here.

Two signposted paths leave from immediately above the car park. Disregarding the left branch (which goes eastward to Refugio Valle Ukika), take the right trail (signposted 'La Bandera') and continue for 10 minutes along the river to a fork (see Alternative Route, p256). Here, bear left and follow horizontal red stripes on a white background (the markings of the Dientes Circuit) up increasingly steeply southeast through the Magellanic *lenga* forest. Fifty minutes to 1¼ hours on, the trees give way to wind-battered beech brush. A direct 20- to 30-minute climb straight up the grassy slope leads to **Cerro Bandera** (620m). More a broad ridge top than a summit as such, Cerro Bandera (Flag Mountain) was given its name when a large sheet-metal Chilean flag was erected here in the early 1980s during a tense period of military confrontation with Argentina. Cerro Bandera overlooks Puerto Williams and gives magnificent views stretching out along the Beagle Channel to Ushuaia and beyond.

Marker stakes and large cairns lead on along the exposed, stony plateau – first south, then southwest – across a small stream (the only water between the car park and Laguna del Salto). Cut rightward and begin a scenic undulating traverse just above the scrub line over scree slopes alternating with areas of green, lawn-like *azorella* mounds and heathy *brecillo*. There are fine views across the lake basin of the upper Valle Róbalo to craggy peaks in the Cordón de los Dientes. When you reach a

Warning

This trek into the wild interior of Isla Navarino should not be taken lightly. Although somewhat protected by the mountains further to the west, the island experiences constantly unstable and often savage weather, with strong winds and summer snowfalls. Most of the route is above the tree line in exposed terrain, where careful navigation and route-finding is required.

Dientes Circuit

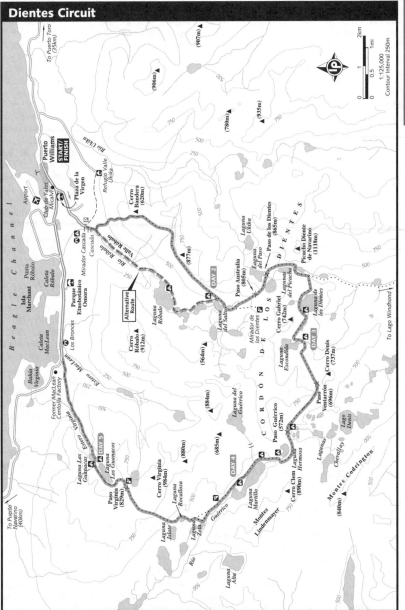

slope of loose, coarse talus coming down across the trail, descend right in tight switchbacks via a tiny rock knob to reach the shore of **Laguna del Salto** (474m), two to 2½ hours from Cerro Bandera.

Semisheltered **camp sites** can be found around the lake's southeast and northern shore. Aim to have minimum impact on this fragile, heavily used area and carry out all (perhaps including other peoples') rubbish. Pairs of Andean condors (which apparently nest in the impressive bluffs at the head of Laguna del Salto) can often be seen gliding high above.

Alternative Route: via Valle Róbalo

3¼–4¼ hours, 10.5km, 455m ascent
This lower route is less scenic but more sheltered, and may be a better option in bad weather. It is less trodden, however, and there are more fallen trunks across the path.

Turn right at the trail fork 10 minutes up from the car park (see Day 1), and follow markings of blue horizontal stripes on a white background southwest up very gently through the *coigüe* and *lenga* forest. This sometimes rough path leads along the true right (east) bank of the Río Róbalo to reach **Laguna Róbalo** after 1½ to two hours. This large lake offers pleasant **camping** and good views of the Dientes de Navarino. The route continues around the lake's southeastern shore past another small tarn in the low forest, then climbs slightly southeastward past the shore of another unnamed lake to reach **Laguna del Salto**, 50 minutes to 1¼ hours from Laguna Róbalo.

Day 2: Laguna del Salto to Laguna Escondida

3¼–4¼ hours, 9km, 560m ascent
Walk around to the cascading lake inlet, then head up steeply through this stream gully to a flat grassy area. The route climbs on via a minor ridge, cutting left across the stream before ascending through a rocky gap (sometimes called **Paso Primero**, although it is not a true pass) to reach a tiny shallow tarn on a barren shelf. Head up alongside the now trickling stream until it

disappears at another tarnlet, then swing around left (eastward) up over rubble to arrive at **Paso Australia** (805m), 50 minutes to 1¼ hours from Laguna del Salto. Marked by a large cairn, the pass lies below the towering rock 'teeth' of the Dientes de Navarino and overlooks **Laguna del Paso**, filling in a deep glacial trough.

The route cuts down rightward over persistent snowdrifts towards the gap visible at the head of the lake. Traverse around high above Laguna del Paso over scree slopes and rock ledges to reach this **Paso de los Dientes** (865m) after 30 to 40 minutes. The pass grants your first views south over Isla Navarino's spongy lowlands towards the mountainous Peninsula Hardy on neighbouring Isla Hoste and the misty islands around Cape Horn.

Drop gently past a tiny névé up to your right and skirt the left side of the elongated upper lake of the **Lagunas del Picacho**, between the spectacular east wall crowned by several rock pinnacles touching 1000m and the **Picacho Diente de Navarino** (1118m) – the island's highest summit on your left. The route leads around the west shore of the (smaller) lower lake to reach a signposted junction, 25 to 30 minutes from the pass. From here a rougher track continues down south to Lago Windhond.

The circuit route (signposted simply 'C. D. N.') turns away westward (right), climbing across a minor ridge before it cuts down through *lenga* scrub to reach **Laguna de los Dientes** after 30 to 40 minutes. Trace the beaver-chewed shoreline for 15 to 20 minutes around to an inlet stream on its northwest side, where you will find scenic **camp sites** *(GPS 55° 01.044 S 67° 41.087 W)* with views over this sizable lake to the Dientes peaks.

Climb moderately northwest through a tiny side valley past small tarns to a minor watershed under the impressive rock pinnacles of **Cerro Gabriel**, where the starkly beautiful **Laguna Escondida** suddenly appears. Laguna Escondida (Hidden Lake) is enclosed on three sides by reddish craggy peaks and fringed by scree slides. Descend almost to a rocky bluff, then cut down left

Icebergs in Lago Grey and peaks above the Valle del Francés, Parque Nacional Torres del Paine

Glaciar Piedras Blancas drops towards the valley of the Río Blanco, Parque Nacional Los Glaciares

The harbour city of Ushuaia (Argentina) below the summits of the Fuegian Andes

The craggy Cordón de los Dientes on Isla Navarino, Tierra del Fuego

and follow the sometimes bouldery (but always beavered) shore to the lake outlet, 40 to 50 minutes from Laguna de los Dientes. The exposed camp sites here are not recommended, but there is sheltered **camping** a few minutes downstream.

Day 3: Laguna Escondida to Laguna Martillo
3–4¼ hours, 8km, 240m ascent
Follow the lake outlet 10 minutes down past small beaver ponds before cutting rightward over the stream. The route sidles on west through low *lenga* forest along the edge of tilted cliffs above more beaver dams into the head of a tiny side valley, then ascends a small ridge to reach **Paso Ventarrón** *(GPS 55° 01.350 S, 67° 43.413 W)*, one to 1½ hours from Laguna Escondida. This windy saddle at 696m lies on the north side of **Cerro Denis** (737m) and is marked by a high cairn. Paso Ventarrón looks out southwest across the wild enchanting basin of the **Lagunas Chevallay** towards the mildly contoured Montes Codrington (named by Captain Fitzroy of the HMS *Beagle* after one of his crew, although Fitzroy almost certainly intended the more striking Dientes).

About Those Names...

In 2001 Chile's Ministerio de Bienes Nacionales (Ministry of National Resources) officially remapped and marked the Dientes Circuit, applying names to features according to the simple principle of usage. Names that had been tentatively given to lakes and passes in previous editions of this guidebook (simply so that readers could identify them more easily) were taken up as official nomenclature. New names were given to a number of key features on the circuit that had remained nameless – from Paso Australia to Laguna Zeta – but Bienes Nacionales also added a Cerro Clem and Montes Lindenmayer. I swear I had nothing to do with it – fame just creeps up on you when you're least expecting it, I suppose.

Clem 'Monty' Lindenmayer

Do not head directly down the slope, but first walk five minutes along the ridge before you begin a long descending traverse northwest over coarse talus into the *lenga* scrub to reach a first beaver dam. The route circles around the edge of this peaty basin above tarns and past fair **camp sites** on occasional drier flat areas to the end of an elongated lake. Here, cut up rightward through a bouldery chute and follow red markings up to **Paso Guérrico** (also called Paso de la Hermosa). This pass (572m) gives a fine view over Laguna Hermosa (Beautiful Lake) to Cerro Clem, the sharp southern summit of the Montes Lindenmayer (see the boxed text 'About those names...').

The path first heads down southwest, traversing some way above the initially steep scrubby sides of Laguna Hermosa before it drops to the lake and continues around to reach the lake's northern shore, 1½ to two hours from Paso Ventarrón. There is scenic semisheltered **camping** among the *lenga* scrub on both sides of the outlet. The ashy-headed goose (*canquén*) can sometimes be spotted paddling around the picturesque islet in this kidney-shaped lake. Make your way on down the stream's true right bank for 20 to 25 minutes to arrive at **Laguna Martillo** (Hammer Lake). Better **camp sites** can be found a short way back from this southeastern shore.

Day 4: Laguna Martillo to Laguna Los Guanacos
3½–5 hours, 10.5km, 420m ascent
Head around the right (northeastern) side of Laguna Martillo past sporadic **camp sites**, climbing over a small peninsula to reach a tiny clearing on the lake's northern 'hammerhead' section after 30 to 40 minutes. Proceed for five minutes to the outlet (the Río Guérrico) and head downvalley through soggy meadows on the stream's northern side under an impressive row of rock spires in the Montes Lindenmayer to reach **Laguna Zeta** (424m), 30 to 40 minutes on.

Follow a small inlet stream of this Z-shaped lake southeast for five minutes to rejoin the marked route (which takes a more difficult short cut over scrubby ridges without passing Laguna Zeta). Continue northwest past a beaver pond to **Laguna Rocallosa** *(GPS 54° 58.999 S, 67° 47.425 W)*. The route skirts the north shore of this small, elongated lake before rising over a crest into a waterlogged basin and climbing to a marker cairn on a small rock outcrop above **Laguna Islote** *(Islet Lake; GPS 54° 58.575 S, 67° 47.802 W)*.

Cut up diagonally rightward into low *lenga* forest, then make a very steep and muddy ascent directly against the slope to finally reach a grassy ledge beside a streamlet. (Due to heavy erosion this rather unsatisfactory section of the circuit may be rerouted at some future time.) Climb on, still quite steeply, through a grassy chute out of the trees, then traverse up northward to meet a stream coming from a broad barren plateau *(GPS 54° 58.037 S, 67° 47.440 W)*. There are more marvellous views back south to the rugged Montes Lindenmayer and Laguna Alta (High Lake), a hanging lake with an outlet cascading into the Valle Guérrico, and northwest (along the Beagle Channel) to Ushuaia and the Cordillera Darwin. Peaks on the neighbouring Isla Hoste also stand out.

Head up about 50m to the right of the stream past icy tarns, continuing northeast across the barren sloping plateau to reach **Paso Virginia** (829m), 1½ to 2¼ hours from Laguna Zeta. This point, the highest on the circuit, gives new vistas northeast across the Beagle Channel. Directly ahead the land falls away abruptly into **Laguna Los Guanacos**, a classic glacial lake in a deep, spectacular trough.

Keeping well away from the often dangerously corniced precipice rim, walk 100m rightward to where red markings lead down through bluffs. The route then makes a rapid sliding descent through coarse, loose scree slopes almost to the base of a permanent icy snowdrift on your left. Continue up around over talus fields on the northwest side of Laguna Los Guanacos to reach the lake outlet, 50 minutes to 1¼ hours from the pass. On the opposite bank are scenic **camp sites** sheltered by low scrub (and by the enclosed lake basin itself).

Day 5: Laguna Los Guanacos to Puerto Williams

4–5½ hours, 14km, 530m descent

Drop steeply along the true left (west) side of the **Estero Virginia** (the lake outlet) into the trees, crossing the tumbling stream immediately before you come out onto the boggy terrace surrounding **Laguna Las Guanacas** after 15 to 20 minutes. There are excellent **camp sites** here at the edge of the *lengas*.

Head around the right (eastern) shore, then continue down across another terrace with several more beaver ponds. Follow an often vague and sometimes rough trail on down through *coigüe* forest along the right (east) bank of the stream, eventually coming out onto a tiny wet clearing covered with big, fleshy-leafed daisies *(GPS 54° 56.686 S, 67° 44.002 W)* just where the valley begins to open out, one to 1½ hours from Laguna Las Guanacas.

Cut over rightward into fire-cleared slopes overlooking the picturesque Bahía Virginia and Caleta MacLean, and move down northeast through regenerating slopes of red *chauras*, *calafate* bushes and clover. In places stock trails confuse the route, which follows a ridge above an abandoned seafood-processing plant (the former MacLean Centolla factory) to meet Isla Navarino's north coast road at the **Estero MacLean** after a final 45 minutes to one hour. Just across the road bridge is **Los Bronces**, a picnic area (where trekkers have been known to camp).

From here, it's a pleasant 7.5km (two- to 2½-hour) walk east along the road past the Parque Etnobotánico Omora back to **Puerto Williams**. Occasional vehicles usually stop (even for trekkers who are not actually hitching).

Other Treks

Yendegaia

Yendegaia is a large property of almost 400 sq km on Bahía Yendegaia at the eastern edge of the Cordillera Darwin, at the extreme southeast corner of Chile's half of the Tierra del Fuego mainland. This former *estancia* was purchased some years ago with the assistance of the Conservation

Land Trust, and is being set up as a private 'national' park (along similar lines to Parque Pumalín, p167) by the Fundación Yendegaia, which now administers the area. The construction of trekking trails and other infrastructure including a information centre, *guardería* and camping facilities is planned for Caleta Ferrari, at the northwestern end of Bahía Yendegaia.

Nearby trekking possibilities include Ventisquero Stoppani, from where treks can be undertaken to Lago Zorros and Glaciar Darmoor. A more adventurous possibility is an eight-day trek north to Caleta María, near the mouth of the Río Azopardo – the outlet of Lago Fagnano (Kami) – where there is an aerodrome.

Although it is only 20km west of Lapataia in Argentina, Yendegaia is an extremely remote region without road access – the Fundación Yendegaia is fighting a projected road continuation south from Lago Blanco. The Transbordadora Austral Broom's *Ferry Fueguino* running between Punta Arenas and Puerto Williams (p252) will let you off or pick you up at Yendegaia for an additional fee of US$10. There is an airstrip. Compañía de Guías de Patagonia (see Information, p236) does guided trekking tours to Yendegaia.

Apart from aerial photographs, the best topographic map is the Chilean IGM's 1:250,000 *Canal Beagle* (No 5469), still only available in the rough 'preliminary' series.

Glaciar Martial

This is a popular half-day outing to a small glacier on the upper northern slopes of the Montes Martial right above Ushuaia. You can walk to the start of the trek (7km from town) by taking San Martín west and continuing to ascend as it zigzags (there are many trekker short cuts) to the ski run. At this point either take the **Aerosilla** *(US$6; open 10am-7pm)* or walk another two hours to the snout of the Glaciar Martial. Minivans leave from Maipú and 25 de Mayo every half-hour from 10am to 6.30pm (US$5 return). The treeless upper slopes offer excellent views across the Beagle Channel to Isla Navarino. The trek can be lengthened by continuing over the saddle and dropping down to intersect with the route through the Valle Andorra described in the Paso de la Oveja trek (p246).

Estancia Túnel & Estancia La Segunda

This easy–moderate four-day coastal trek begins from the bridge on the lower Río Olivia, and leads to isolated ranches on the Beagle Channel east of Ushuaia. First take the Ruta Nacional 3 southeast to the trout hatchery *(estación de piscicultura)*, 6km from the centre of town, then cross the Río Olivia and continue past Estancia Río Olivia. The route leads on for 9km around the steep-sided coastline to Estancia Túnel, from where it is possible to continue for a further 10km to Estancia La Segunda.

The Camino del Atlántico road being built (gradually) along the coast will eventually make this route obsolete as a trek. The road currently reaches the lighthouse at Punta Escarpados, 3km before Estancia Túnel. Use Zagier & Urruty's 1:50,000 *Ushuaia Trekking Map*.

Travel Facts

TOURIST OFFICES
Local Tourist Offices

In both Chile and Argentina, there are well-organised tourist offices *(oficinas de turismo)* in all regional centres and many larger towns, often located on the main plaza or at the bus terminal. During the summer months (December to February) temporary tourist offices often operate in quite small towns. Staff are generally helpful and often know some English. Local tourist offices can supply lists covering accommodation in all price ranges; tourist maps and pamphlets are generally available free of charge.

The Chilean national tourist service, **Sernatur** (W *www.sernatur.cl*), has offices in many larger centres. For information on trekking in local parks and reserves contact the local office of **Corporación Nacional Forestal** *(Conaf;* W *www.conaf.cl).* For on-line tourist information on Chile go to W www.visit-chile.org. Specific email enquiries can be directed to E infochile@ chiletourdesk.com.

The Argentine national tourist agency, **Sectur** *(*W *www.sectur.gov.ar),* can provide general online information about Argentina. For information on trekking in national parks contact the local office of the **Administración de Parques Nacional** *(APN;* W *www .parquesnacionales.gov.ar).*

Details of local tourist offices are given under the Gateway, Access Town and Nearest Town headings in the regional chapters.

Tourist Offices Abroad

National airlines and the embassies of Chile and Argentina (see Embassies, p261) represent the tourist offices abroad.

VISAS & DOCUMENTS
Visas

For entry to both Chile and Argentina, citizens of most western European (including European Union) countries as well as citizens of Australia, Canada, New Zealand and the United States do *not* require a visa for stays of up to 90 days. (Note that this may not immediately apply to all of the 10 countries due to join the European Union in 2004.) Entry requirements may change over time and you should check on the current situation before departing.

As obtaining a visa for stays of longer than 90 days can be time consuming and expensive, most trekker-travellers arrange their trip so that they cross into the neighbouring country before their 90 days is due to expire then simply return to be granted another stay of up to 90 days.

Onward Tickets

In theory, nonresident foreigners entering both Chile and Argentina are required to have an onward ticket, though this is not usually controlled.

Travel Insurance

Buy a policy that generously covers you for medical expenses, theft or loss of luggage and tickets, and for cancellation of and delays to your travel arrangements. Check that your policy doesn't exclude trekking as a 'dangerous activity' and that it includes the cost of rescue. If you intend to undertake activities such as mountaineering (whose definition may include various kinds of activity using ropes or ice-climbing equipment), you will probably need to pay for additional coverage.

Buy travel insurance as early as possible to ensure you'll be compensated for any unforseen accidents or delays. If items are lost or stolen get a police report immediately – otherwise your insurer might not pay up.

Driving Licence & Permits

Formally, you must have an international or inter-American driving permit to supplement your national or state driving licence. In practice, police rarely examine these documents closely and generally ignore the latter. They do not ignore registration, insurance and tax documents, which must be up to date.

Travel Discounts

The International Student Identity Card (W www.isic.org) can help travellers obtain discounts on public transport and museum admissions. Travellers over the age of 60 can sometimes obtain senior citizen discounts on museum admissions and the like when photo ID is shown.

EMBASSIES
Chilean Embassies

Argentina (☎ 011-4827020, W www.emba jadadechile.com.ar) Tagle 2762, CF 1425, Buenos Aires

Australia (☎ 02-6286 2430, W www2.emba chile-australia.com) 10 Culgoa Circuit, O'Malley, ACT 2606

Canada (☎ 613-235 4402, W www.chile.ca) 14 13–50 O'Connor St, Ottawa, Ontario K1P 6L2

France (☎ 01 44 18 59 60, W www.amb-chili.fr) 2 Av de la Motte-Picquet, 75007 Paris

Germany (☎ 030-726203-50, W www.emba jadaconsuladoschile.de) Mohrenstrasse 42, 10117 Berlin

New Zealand (☎ 04-471 6270, W www.emb chile.co.nz) 19 Bolton St, Wellington

United Kingdom (☎ 020-7580 6392, W www .echileuk.demon.co.uk) 12 Devonshire St, London W1G 7DS

USA (☎ 202-785 1746, W www.chile-usa.org) 1732 Massachusetts Ave, NW, Washington DC 20036

Argentine Embassies

Australia (☎ 02-6273 9111, W www.argentina .org.au) John McEwen House, Level 2, 7 National Circuit, Barton, ACT 2600

Canada (☎ 613-236 2351, W www.argentina -canada.net) 90 Sparks St, Suite 910, Ottawa, Ontario K1P 5B4

Copies

All important documents (passport, credit cards, travel insurance policy, driving licence etc) should be photocopied before you leave home. Leave one copy at home and keep another with you, separate from the originals.

Another way of storing your travel documents is with Lonely Planet's free online Travel Vault. Create your vault at W www .ekno.lonelyplanet.com.

Chile (☎ 02-6331076, W www.embargentina.cl) Miraflores 285, Santiago

France (☎ 01 45 53 33 00, W www.embafracia -argentina.org) 6 Rue Cimarosa, 75116 Paris

Germany (☎ 030-22668930/24, W www.argen tinische-botschaft.de) Dorotheenstrasse 89, 3 Stock, 10117 Berlin

Ireland (☎ 01-269 4603, e feirla@mrecic.gov.ar) 15 Ailesbury Dve, Ballsbridge, Dublin 4

New Zealand (☎ 04-472 8330, W www.arg.org .nz) 142 Lambton Quay, Wellington

United Kingdom (☎ 020-7584 6494) 65 Brook St, London W1Y 1YE

USA (☎ 202-238 6401, W www.embajadaar gentinaeeuu.org) 1600 New Hampshire Ave, NW, Washington DC 20009

Embassies in Chile

Australia (☎ 02-5503500, W www.argentina .embassy.gov.au/quienes/cl) Isidora Goyenechea 3621, 12 & 13 Floors, Las Condes, Santiago

Canada (☎ 02-3629660, W www.dfait -maeci.gc.ca/chile) Nueva Tajamar 481, 12th Floor (World Trade Center), Torre Norte, Santiago

Germany (☎ 02-4632500, W www.emba jadadealemania.cl) Las Hualtatas 5677, Vitacura, Santiago

France (☎ 02-4708000, W www.france.cl) Av Condell 65, Providencia, Santiago

Ireland (☎ 02-2456616, e aylwin@netline.cl) Isidora Goyenechea 3162, 8th Floor, Oficina 801, Las Condes, Santiago

New Zealand (☎ 02-2909802, e nzembassy chile@adsl.tie.cl) El Golf 99, Oficina 703, Las Condes, Santiago

United Kingdom (☎ 02-3704100, W www .britemb.cl) Av El Bosque Norte 0125, Santiago

USA (☎ 02-2322600, W www.usembassy.cl) Av Andrés Bello 2800, Las Condes, Santiago

Embassies in Argentina

Australia (☎ 011-4779 3500, W www.argentina .embassy.gov.au/quienes/ar) Villanueva 1400, 1426 Buenos Aires

Canada (☎ 011-4808 1000, W www.dfait-mae ci.gc.ca/argentina) Tagle 2828, C1425EEH Buenos Aires

Germany (☎ 011-4778 2500, W www.embaj ada-alemana.org.ar) Villanueva 1055, C1426BMC Buenos Aires

France (☎ 011-4515 2930, W wwww.embafran cia-argentina.org) Cerrito 1399, 1010 Buenos Aires

Ireland (☎ 011-5787 0801, ⓔ info@irlanda
.org.ar) Av del Libertador 1068, 6th Floor,
(Edificio Bluesky), C1112ABN Buenos Aires
New Zealand (☎ 011-4328 0747, ⓦ www
.nzembassy.com/argentina) Carlos Pellegrini
1427, 5th Floor, CP1011 Buenos Aires
United Kingdom (☎ 011-4808 2200, ⓦ www
.britain.org.ar) Dr Luis Agote 2412,
C1425EOF Buenos Aires
USA (☎ 011-5777 4533, ⓦ http://usembassy
.state.gov/buenosaires) Av Colombia 4300,
C1425GMN Buenos Aires

CUSTOMS

Except during busy periods, clearing customs
is generally fairly fast and hassle-free in both
directions between Chile and Argentina.

Note that it is prohibited to enter Chile
carrying dairy products or any kind of
unprocessed food or agricultural product –
even if they are of Chilean origin. This
includes foodstuffs such as honey, milk
powder, salami or mushrooms (dried or
fresh). Foods like packaged soups or dried
pre-prepared meals or canned fish are OK.
This is particularly important if you buy
food in Argentina with the intention of
doing a trek immediately after arriving in
Chile. At an increasing number of border
posts luggage is unloaded and scanned before passengers may proceed. Fines may be
imposed for infringements.

MONEY

It is important that you carry at least one alternative form of payment, including a
credit card, travellers cheques or cash. Although the euro (€) has gained some ac-
ceptance as an alternative, the US dollar
(US$) remains the Latin American 'shadow
currency' of choice. All prices in this guidebook are quoted in US$.

Currency

Although their relative values are vastly different (see the Exchange Rates table), both
Chile and Argentina use a currency called
the peso. In both countries, a simple dollar
sign ($) is often used to show prices in local
pesos.

The Chilean peso (CLP) comes in notes
of the denominations 500, 1000, 5000,

10,000 and 20,000 pesos. Coins are in one,
five, 10 and 100 peso denominations.

The Argentine peso (ARS) is made up of
100 centavos. Coins come in denominations
of one (rare), five, 10, 25 and 50 centavos,
and one peso. Notes come in denominations
of two, five, 10, 20, 50 and 100 pesos. Formerly pegged 1:1 to the US dollar, the Argentine peso was floated in early 2002. Its
value has since dropped massively against
most other currencies, generally making Argentina a cheaper place to travel in than
previously.

Exchange Rates

The fall of the US dollar and rise of the euro
has readjusted exchange rates considerably
in recent years. For latest rates go to the online currency converter at ⓦ www.oanda
.com.

country	unit		CLP	ARS
Australia	A$1	=	$476	$1.89
Canada	C$1	=	$519	$2.05
euro zone	€ 1	=	$823	$3.26
Japan	¥100	=	$600	$2.37
New Zealand	NZ$1	=	$423	$1.67
Switzerland	Sfr1	=	$532	$2.11
UK	UK£1	=	$1,168	$4.62
USA	US$1	=	$719	$2.85

Exchanging Money

Banks in Chile and Argentina exchange foreign currencies at reasonable rates. Exchange bureaus *(casas de cambio)* can be
found in tourist towns and larger regional
centres, and tend to give somewhat better
rates than banks. Most larger hotels will exchange US dollars in cash (though rarely in
travellers cheques).

ATMs Automatic teller machines (ATMs, or
cajeros automáticos) can now be found even
in many small towns throughout Chile and
Argentina. Some ATMs, especially in Argentina, will dispense cash in US dollars.
Most ATMs operate under the Cirrus/Maestro
system that allows you to withdraw cash directly from your home bank account. ATMs
are generally a more secure, convenient and
cheaper way to access your travel money

than using travellers cheques or credit cards – but don't rely on them entirely.

Credit Cards Another way to avoid carrying too much cash on you is to use a credit card. In both Chile and Argentina, Master-Card is the most widely accepted credit card, followed by Visa. American Express and Diners Club are also valid in many places. Note that there is sometimes a surcharge *(recargo)* – typically around 5% – for purchasing on credit card; stores in Argentina often give a discount for cash payments instead.

Credit cards can be used for cash advances at ATMs, but you may end up paying a high commission (up to 6%) after currency conversions and service fees are factored in. Also, the amount you eventually pay may be based on the exchange rate some weeks after the purchase itself.

Travellers Cheques In remote areas of southern Chile and Argentina exchanging travellers cheques for a reasonable rate is not always easy to do. In addition, heavy commissions are often charged on travellers cheques. Although it's quite possible to get by without using them at all, carrying some of your money in travellers cheques is advisable.

On the Trek

Except for more popular routes that have *refugios* (huts) or other trekking infrastructure (such as the Nahuel Huapi Traverse or the Paine Circuit), there isn't usually much need for – or even opportunity to spend – money on the trek itself. At times trekkers may need cash to pay for camping or even to buy produce like cheese, bread or eggs from farms along the way. It's nevertheless advisable to carry plenty of cash if you expect to be away from towns for a lengthy period of time.

Costs

At the time of writing, Argentina was somewhat cheaper than Chile, although major price readjustments after the massive devaluation of early 2002 (when Argentina became

very cheap) have already occurred. However, Argentina's continuing economic uncertainty could see its peso strengthen or weaken considerably against other currencies.

For obvious reasons, the more time you spend in the wilds the cheaper your trekking holiday will be, but the minimum you can realistically budget for per month is around US$300.

item/service	cost (US$)
camping ground (per person)	3.00
hostel (dorm bed)	6.00
budget room (per person)	10.00
bus ticket (200km)	5.00
1L of milk	0.55
loaf of bread	0.80
espresso coffee (per cup)	1.20
simple meal	6.00

Tipping & Bargaining

Although many local patrons seem to disregard this, it is customary to tip about 10% of the bill in restaurants, except for family-run establishments. Taxi drivers don't expect tips, but it's customary to round up to the nearest peso if the difference isn't much.

At times it's worth bargaining for your hotel room, charter boat or taxi, but don't expect to beat the starting price down by more than about 20%.

Taxes & Refunds

In Chile, it is sometimes possible to legally avoid the 18% Impuesto de Valor Agregado (IVA, or value-added tax) by paying for (usually more upmarket) accommodation in US-dollars cash. In Argentina, foreign visitors may obtain refunds of the IVA on purchases of Argentine products of US$70 or more at certain participating stores upon their departure from the country.

See also Departure Tax (p267).

POST & COMMUNICATIONS
Post

Although the postal services in Chile and Argentina are decidedly better than in most other Latin American countries, they are inefficient by the standards of Western Europe and North America.

Bulky or heavy items not needed on your trek can be mailed ahead to a poste restante *(lista de correos)* address and collected later. You can receive mail via *lista de correos* at any Chilean or Argentine post office. Instruct your correspondents to address letters clearly and to indicate a date until which the post office should hold them; otherwise, they may be returned or destroyed. In Chile there is usually a small charge on poste restante services, about US$0.25 per item. In Argentina post offices have imposed heavy charges, up to US$1.50 per letter.

Chilean post offices maintain separate lists of correspondence for men and women so check both if your correspondent has not addressed the letter 'Señor', 'Señora' or 'Señorita.' There may be particular confusion if correspondents use your middle name, since Chileans use both paternal and maternal surnames for identification, with the former listed first.

Bus companies will transport unaccompanied baggage *(encomiendas)* for a reasonable fee, though usually not across international borders.

International parcel postage is expensive in both Chile and Argentina and costs around US$10 per kg for airmail (surface mail is not available to many regions).

Chile Although delivery is slow, Chile's postal service, **Correos de Chile** (w *www .correos.cl)*, is fairly dependable. The post restante service is quite well organised, but mail is normally only kept for 30 days.

A 20g airmail letter to anywhere in South America or to the USA costs US$0.40, and to anywhere in the rest of the world costs US$0.45.

Argentina The Argentine postal service, **Correo Argentino** (w *www.correoargentino .com.ar)*, is expensive and unreliable. Mail sometimes gets 'lost' in transit, so anything of value is best dispatched from Chile. The same goes for the poste restante system.

A 20g airmail letter to within Argentina costs US$1.20, to anywhere in the Americas US$1.40 and to the rest of the world US$1.75.

Telephone

The telephone systems in both Chile and Argentina are now very modern and relatively inexpensive. Public telephone offices *(centros de llamados* in Chile and *locutorios* in Argentina) can be found around the centres of all cities and – even very small – towns. Most street telephones take phonecards, some also accept coins, while some take coins only. Reverse-charge or collect *(cobro revertido)* calls overseas are simple to make, as are credit card calls. Calls are charged on a timed basis. Per-minute rates from public telephone offices to the United States and Europe are generally from around US$0.40 per minute, but higher to Australia and many other places.

Area codes are used throughout the Patagonian Andes and you'll need to dial them first before dialling the telephone number, except when you are within the area code. Area codes begin with ☎ 0. If dialling from abroad, dial the country code, then the area code without the ☎ 0, then the local number.

Chile's national telephone code is ☎ 56. Argentina's national telephone code is ☎ 54.

Useful Phone Numbers		
	Chile	Argentina
emergency	☎ 133	☎ 107
police	☎ 133	☎ 101
directory assistance	☎ 103	☎ 110

Phonecards Called *tarjetas telefónicas,* phonecards are widely available and made by many companies in many price ranges.

Lonely Planet's ekno Communication Card, specifically aimed at travellers, provides competitive international calls (avoid using it for local calls), messaging services and free email. Visit w www.ekno.lonely planet.com for information on joining and accessing the service.

Mobile Phones Chileans and Argentinians widely use mobile (cell) phones. The larger telephone companies – **Entel** (W *www .entelphone.cl)* and **Telefónica** (W *www.tele fonica.cl)* in Chile; **Telefónica de Argentina** (W *www.telefonica.com.ar)* and **Telecom Argentina** (W *www.telecom.com.ar)* in Argentina – rent out mobile phones from around US$30 per month.

Coverage is almost complete in cities and larger towns, but although mobile phones sometimes work in parts of national parks or reserves close to highways or settled areas, the network is generally too limited to be a reliable form of communication on the treks.

Satellite (World) Phones Although heavy and extremely expensive, satellite (world) phones allow trekkers to make calls from *anywhere*. Satellite phones cost from around US$1500 to buy or US$250 per month to rent, plus from US$2 per minute to use – you also pay for incoming calls.

Companies like **Nextel** (W *www.nextel .com)*, **RentCell** (W *www.rentcell.com)* and **Worldcell** (W *www.worldcell.com)* rent out international and satellite phones.

Email
Finding access to the Internet is usually not a problem except in the most out-of-the-way places. Internet cafés are common and many public telephone offices also offer Internet access; many offer broadband connections. Rates are typically from around US$1 per hour (but much higher in touristy or remote places). Note that on Spanish keyboards the '@' symbol (called *arroba*) is made by holding down the Alt key and typing 64.

TIME
Normally, Argentina is three hours behind Greenwich Mean Time (GMT) and Chile is four hours behind GMT. However, in Chile Daylight Saving Time runs from the first Sunday on or after 9 October until the first Sunday on or after 9 March. In Argentina, Daylight Saving Time is not observed at all. This means that for most of the trekking season the two countries share the same time (ie, three hours behind GMT). In recent years, Chile has extended the period of Daylight Saving Time by up to one month due to power shortages.

Note that 24-hour times are normally used in bus timetables etc.

ELECTRICITY
Chile and Argentina use the same round, twin-pronged power plug, and run a 220-volt current. Today, even the smallest and most isolated townships have a reliable electricity supply.

BUSINESS HOURS
In general, bank opening hours are from 10am to 4pm, and offices are normally open from 9am until noon, and then from 2pm to 7pm. In some of the bigger cities supermarkets and larger shops often stay open throughout the day, but in the more remote areas, even in the cool south, the siesta break can be as long as four hours. Government offices and many businesses have adopted a more conventional 8am to 5pm schedule.

In summer, tourist offices in larger centres are generally open daily, at least from 9am to 6pm; in smaller towns tourist offices are usually closed on Sunday (sometimes also Saturday).

Ranger stations and information centres in national parks and reserves are usually open daily, but regional Conaf and APN offices are generally open Monday to Friday from 9am to 5pm or 6pm.

PUBLIC HOLIDAYS
Many religious and national holidays are celebrated in both Chile and Argentina (including Easter and Christmas), when government offices and businesses are closed. (If the holiday falls on a day in the middle of the week or on the weekend, it's often moved to the nearest Monday.) In addition, the general summer holiday (vacation) period begins around Christmas and continues until mid-February. Some provincial or regional public holidays are also celebrated locally.

The following national public holidays fall within the extended summer season:

Todo Los Santos (All Saints' Day) November 1
Inmaculada Concepción (Immaculate Conception) December 8
Navidad (Christmas Day) December 25
Año Nuevo (New Year's Day) January 1
Semana Santa (Easter Week)
Día de las Malvinas (Malvinas Day; Argentina only) April 2
Día del Trabajor (Labor Day) May 1
Glorias Navales (commemorating the naval Battle of Iquique; Chile only) May 21
Revolución de Mayo (May Revolution of 1810; Argentina only) May 25

Getting There & Away

South America is really only accessible by air. The most direct international routes to Chile and Argentina by air are via the national capitals of Santiago and Buenos Aires. Although getting to the region is relatively expensive, there are direct overseas air connections from North America, the UK, Europe, Australasia and South Africa, as well as virtually all South American countries. Alternatively, you can fly in to a neighbouring country, such as Brazil, Bolivia or Uruguay, then continue overland to Chile or Argentina.

Warning

The information in this section is particularly vulnerable to change: prices for international travel are volatile, routes are introduced and cancelled, schedules change, special deals come and go and rules and visa requirements are amended. You should check directly with the airline or a travel agent to make sure you understand how a fare (and ticket you may buy) works and be aware of the security requirements for international travel.

The upshot of this is that you should get opinions, quotes and advice from as many airlines and travel agents as possible before you part with your hard-earned cash. The details given in this section should be regarded as pointers and are not a substitute for your own careful, up-to-date research.

AIR
Airports & Airlines

Chile's main international airport is **Aeropuerto Internacional Arturo Merino Benítez** (☎ 02-601 9709) in the suburb of Pudahuel, Santiago.

Argentina's main international airport is **Aeropuerto Internacional Ministro Pistarini** (☎ 011-4480 0235), commonly known as Ezeiza, 35km southwest of central Buenos Aires. Most domestic flights use **Aeroparque Jorge Newbery** (☎ 011-4771 2071), commonly known as Aeroparque, close to central Buenos Aires – remember this if you have an onward connection.

Airlines operating to Chile and Argentina include:

Aeroflot (W www.aeroflot.com)
Aerolíneas Argentinas (W www.aerolineas.com.ar)
Air Canada (W www.aircanada.ca)
Air France (W www.airfrance.com)
Air New Zealand (W www.airnz.com)
Alitalia (W www.alitalia.com)
American Airlines (W www.americanairlines.com)
Avianca (W www.avianca.com)
British Airways (W www.british-airways.com)
Copa (W www.copaair.com)
Iberia (W www.iberia.com)
Japan Airlines (W www.jal.co.jp)
KLM (Royal Dutch Airlines; W www.klm.com)
Korean Air (W www.koreanair.com)
Lacsa (W www.taca.com)
LanChile (W www.lanchile.com)
LAB (Lloyd Aéreo Boliviano; W www.labairlines.com)
Lufthansa (W www.lufthansa.com)
Malaysia Airlines (W www.malaysiaairlines.com.my)
Pluna (W www.pluna.com.uy)
Qantas (W www.qantas.com.au)
SAS (Scandinavian Airlines System; W www.scandinavian.net)
South African Airways (W www.flysaa.com)
Swiss (W www.swiss.com)
TAM (W www.tamairlines.com)
TAP (Air Portugal; W www.tap.pt)
United Airlines (W www.ual.com)
Varig (W www.varig.com)
VASP (W www.vasp.com.br)

Departure Tax

Departure taxes on international flights out of Chile and Argentina are usually included in the ticket price. As some international passengers have been double-charged for airport taxes at Buenos Aires (Ezeiza) airport in recent years, recheck with your travel agent that all taxes are included in the price.

In Chile, departure tax is around US$18 for international flights and US$8 for domestic flights. Argentina levies a tax of around US$17 for international flights.

Special Fees Passengers *arriving* at Santiago airport – but only in Santiago – on passports of the following four countries must pay a special fee (valid for the life of the passport): United States, US$100; Canada, US$55; Australia, US$30; and Mexico US$20. Leave the receipt stapled into your passport.

The UK

From London, British Airways flies direct to both Santiago and Buenos Aires. Iberia/ LanChile have daily connections to Santiago via Madrid and Aerolíneas Argentinas

Best-Value Air Tickets

For short-term travel, it's usually cheaper to travel midweek and to take advantage of short-lived promotional offers. Return tickets usually work out cheaper than two one-ways.

Booking through a travel agent or via airlines' websites is generally the cheapest way to get tickets. However, while online ticket sales are fine for a simple one-way or return trip on specified dates, they're no substitute for a travel agent who is familiar with special deals and can offer all kinds of advice.

Buying tickets with a credit card should mean you get a refund if you don't get what you paid for. Go through a licensed travel agent, who should be covered by an industry guarantee scheme.

Whatever your choice, make sure you take out travel insurance (see p260).

flies to Buenos Aires. Varig has several daily connections to both Santiago and Buenos Aires via Río de Janeiro and/or São Paulo.

Continental Europe

From their hubs in Madrid, LanChile and Aerolíneas Argentinas fly to Santiago and Buenos Aires respectively; Iberia also flies daily to both Santiago and Buenos Aires. These airlines have connector flights from major European cities such as Amsterdam, Frankfurt, Paris, Rome and Zurich. From Paris, Air France flies direct to Buenos Aires, and TAM Meridional and Varig fly to Buenos Aires via São Paulo.

Other major airlines that fly from continental Europe to Santiago and/or Buenos Aires include Aeroflot, Alitalia, KLM, Lufthansa, Pluna, TAP (Air Portugal), SAS (Scandinavian Airlines System) and Swiss.

The USA

The national carriers, LanChile and Aerolíneas Argentinas, have many (including code-shared) flights to Santiago and Buenos Aires from many larger hubs, including Dallas/Fort Worth, Los Angeles, Miami and New York. Other airlines that fly to Santiago and Buenos Aires include American Airlines, British Airways, Japan Airlines, Korean Air, LanChile, LAB (Lloyd Aéreo Boliviano), United Airlines and Varig.

For the cheapest flights try Lacsa, which flies from Los Angeles and Miami to Santiago and Buenos Aires (in both cases via San Jose and Lima), Copa, which flies from Los Angeles to Buenos Aires via Panama City, or TAM, which flies from Miami to Santiago and Buenos Aires via São Paulo.

Canada

Air Canada and LanChile both have almost daily connections from Toronto to Santiago and Buenos Aires via São Paulo and Dallas/Fort Worth. Other airlines, including American and Continental, have connections in New York, Miami and Los Angeles.

Australia & New Zealand

There are several options. You can fly LanChile and Qantas, which have a code-shared flight three times weekly from Sydney to Santiago via Auckland.

Qantas also flies from Sydney to Tahiti twice a week to connect with LanChile's Tahiti–Easter Island–Santiago service, which has connections to Buenos Aires – a tempting flight if you want to see Easter Island or Tahiti. Air New Zealand does the same from Auckland.

Yet another way to get to Buenos Aires is to travel via the US (San Francisco, Los Angeles or Miami) with United Airlines.

Asia & Africa

Carriers serving Santiago and Buenos Aires directly from Asia, usually via North America, are Japan Airlines and Korean Air. Malaysia Airlines/South African Airways has twice-weekly connections from Kuala Lumpur to Buenos Aires via Cape Town and Johannesburg. Varig and VASP have good connections via Río de Janeiro or São Paulo.

South America

The main national carriers of Chile and Argentina, LanChile and Aerolíneas Argentinas, fly to/from most important capitals and other major cities (including all those mentioned below).

In addition, Varig flies daily to both Buenos Aires and Santiago from Río de Janeiro and São Paulo. From Lima (Peru) LanChile, Taca and Lacsa fly most days to Santiago and Buenos Aires. There are also regular flights from Bogotá (Colombia) with Copa and Avianca. From La Paz (Bolivia), LAB (Lloyd Aéreo Boliviano) flies daily to Buenos Aires and Taca flies several times weekly to Santiago.

LAND

Many travellers arrive by land from neighbouring Bolivia, Paraguay, Brazil and Uruguay. There are many possible routes.

Border Crossings

Bolivia From Bolivia there are a number of routes into Chile. Bolivia has a long border with Chile, but most of the land traffic is between La Paz and Arica in Chile's far north. From La Paz there are bus services to Arica.

The main road link between Bolivia and Argentina goes via La Quiaca/Villazón on the northern border in Jujuy Province. From Villazón there are daily buses to the Argentine provincial capitals of Salta and Jujuy.

Brazil Travellers coming from the north usually make the crossing from Brazil into Argentina at the spectacular Iguazú Falls. Regular buses leave from the Brazilian side of the falls at Foz do Iguaçu to Puerto Iguazú in Argentina.

Peru Where Peru's southern border meets Chile is the point of entry for many travellers. There are two ways of entering Chile from Peru. The only overland route is from the southern Peruvian town of Tacna to Arica in the far north of Chile. Arica can be reached daily from Tacna by either bus, train or taxi.

Uruguay Border crossings from Uruguayan cities to Argentine cities include Gualeguaychú to Fray Bentos, Colón to Paysandú and Concordia to Salto.

Car & Motorcycle

The Panamerican Hwy runs south from Santiago right through the heart of the Chilean Araucanía and Lakes District.

In Argentina, the two principle road routes into Patagonia are Ruta 40 and Ruta 3. The classic Ruta 40 runs south along the eastern Andean foothills, linking Mendoza

---

Baggage Restrictions

Airlines impose tight restrictions on carry-on baggage. No sharp implements of any kind are allowed onto the plane, so pack items such as pocket knives, camping cutlery and first-aid kits into your checked luggage.

If you're carrying a camping stove you should remember that airlines also ban liquid fuels and gas cartridges from all baggage, both check-through and carry-on. Empty all fuel bottles and buy what you need at your destination.

to Zapala (then continues south via Esquel, Perito Moreno and El Calafate). Ruta 3 runs south from Buenos Aires along the Atlantic coast to Viedma (then continues south via Comodoro Rivadavia to meet the Ruta 40 near Río Gallegos).

Bus

Long-distance buses run very frequently from Santiago to important cities along the Panamerican Hwy, including to Los Ángeles (from US$10), Temuco (from US$12), Osorno (from US$13) and Puerto Montt (from US$14). Most long-distance buses for southern destinations leave from Santiago's **Terminal de Buses Sur** (☎ 02-776 0645; *Alameda O'Higgins 3848*).

Buenos Aires is much further from the Andes, but in summer there are regular bus departures from Buenos Aires' **Retiro bus terminal** (☎ 011-4310 0700), next to Retiro train station, to Patagonian destinations including Bariloche (US$35), Esquel (US$38), Zapala (US$33) and Neuquén (US$30).

Train

Chile's **Empresa de Ferrocarriles del Estado** (*EFE;* ☎ 02-3768500; [W] *www.efe.cl*) operates a once-daily rail service in either direction between Santiago and Temuco. Trains leave from Santiago's Estación Central at 9.30pm and from Temuco at 9pm (both services US$11/14 2nd/1st class one-way, 12 hours).

There are no direct rail services from Buenos Aires to cities in the Patagonian Andes, although it is possible to first travel by bus to the city of Viedma (950km south of Buenos Aires), then take the **Tren Patagónico** (☎ 02920-422130, 427413) to Bariloche. Trains leave Viedma on Wednesday and Sunday at 6pm, and return from Bariloche on Tuesday and Friday at 6pm (US$9/21/32 tourist/Pullman/cabin one-way, 16½ hours).

Getting Around

Chile and Argentina have modern, efficient and reasonably cheap long-distance public transport. In most cases, getting to or from treks by local public transport is easy.

AIR

In Argentina, Aerolíneas Argentinas (including its subsidiary, Austral) has the most extensive network of flights, but LADE (Líneas Aéreas de Estado) links many of the important destinations along the Patagonian Andes (such as Bariloche and El Calafate) and in Argentine Tierra del Fuego (such as Ushuaia). Small regional carriers like TAN and AIRG (formerly LAPA) tend to be somewhat cheaper and often fly routes that are more convenient to trekkers in Patagonia.

In Chile, the overwhelmingly dominant national airline, LanChile (including LanExpress), flies between all main regional cities. Several small regional airlines, such as Aerovías DAP and Don Carlos, service remoter areas of central and southern Patagonia. (Since the demise of ALTA, however, central and southern Patagonia are connected only by once-weekly LanChile flights between Punta Arenas and Balmaceda (Coyhaique), so it is usually necessary to fly in/out of Balmaceda via Puerto Montt.)

Airlines operating in southern Chile and Argentina include:

Aerolíneas Argentinas ([W] www.aerolineas .com.ar

Aerovías DAP ([W] www.aeroviasdap.cl)
Don Carlos ([W] www.doncarlos.cl/avion.htm)
LADE (Líneas Aéreas de Estado) ([W] www.lade .com.ar)
LanChile ([W] www.lanchile.com)
Sky Airline ([W] www.internationalms.com/ skyairline)
Southern Winds ([W] www.sw.com.ar)

Air Passes

Air passes are tailored to travellers who want to jet around a country or region in a short time, and are therefore less suited to trekkers. In both Chile and Argentina, special air passes (which must be purchased with an intercontinental air ticket outside either country) are available to foreign tourists.

The 30-day Visit Argentina Airpass is valid on the entire domestic network of both Aerolíneas Argentinas and Austral. This pass costs US$400 for three flight coupons, plus US$165 for each additional coupon. A coupon covers one flight of any distance (in some cases including a *direct* connection).

LanChile's one-month Visit Chile Airpass is valid for the whole LanChile domestic network (except flights to Easter Island). It costs US$250 for three flight coupons, plus US$60 for each additional coupon (or US$350 and US$80 if you do not arrive with LanChile).

BUS
Except in parts of southern Argentina and Tierra del Fuego (where flying often works out cheaper) bus travel is likely to be the main form of intercity transport for trekkers. Buses are fast and services are generally frequent, and major companies such as **Andesmar** (w *www.andesmar.com.ar*), **Igi-Llaima** (☎ *045-210364; Miraflores 1513, Temuco*) and **JAC** (w *www.jac.cl*) have modern comfortable coaches.

There are bus stations in all the large provincial cities, and these serve as departure and arrival terminals for virtually all local and long-distance services. On well-travelled routes there is a considerable difference in ticket prices between bus companies, so it usually pays to compare prices. On international routes, always remember that a bus service across the border will usually be much more expensive for the distance travelled than a combination of regular buses.

CAR & MOTORCYCLE
Particularly for trekkers who intend to visit out-of-the-way areas (such as Parque Nacional Perito Moreno), the advantages of having your own means of transport are considerable. Road tolls are charged on some sections of the Panamerican Hwy in southern Chile. Apart from the main highways, roads in the south are usually unsurfaced.

Petrol (gasoline – called *bencina* in Chile and *nafta* in Argentina) prices average around US$0.90 per litre in Chile. It is heavily subsidised in Argentina's Patagonian provinces (Neuquén, Río Negro, Chubut, Santa Cruz and Tierra del Fuego), where it only costs around half as much – about US$0.50 per litre – as in other parts

of Argentina. Carry extra petrol when travelling in remote areas.

See Driving Licence & Permits (p260).

Road Rules
In Chile, speed limits are 50km/h in towns and 100km/h in rural areas – regularly enforced by heavy fines. Argentine highways have a speed limit of 80km/h and some have been raised to 100km/h or more, but few drivers observe such regulations. In Chile, the legal blood-alcohol limit for drivers is 0.05%; in Argentina, the limit is 0.08%.

BICYCLE
Bicycling – especially mountain biking – is increasingly popular in Chile and Argentina, and many foreigners also pedal their way around. When planning your route through Argentine Patagonia pay special attention to prevailing wind directions, which in summer tend to blow from the east to northeast. The frustration of pedalling against eastern Patagonia's strong and incessant head winds leads some cyclists to give up. There are bicycle shops in all the larger cities, but in out-of-the-way places spare parts can be hard to find.

HITCHING
The Spanish term for hitching is *viajar a dedo,* literally 'to travel by finger'. Hitching in Chile and Argentina is reasonably reliable along the main routes during the busy summer holiday period, but remember that for many local backpackers hitching is the only affordable way to see their country, so try not to compete with them for rides unless there is no other viable means of transport.

On lonelier stretches of road you may have to wait a long time – even days – for a ride, but drivers in remoter regions are more inclined to stop.

Warning

Hitching is never entirely safe in any country and we don't recommend it. Women travelling alone should be extremely cautious about hitching anywhere.

BOAT

In southern Chile, sea-based transport is very important, and boats are still the only means of access for some isolated settlements. Long-distance ferries *(transbordadores)* run by the companies **Navimag** (W *www.navimag .cl*) and **Transmarchilay** (W *www.transmarch ilay.com*) ply the beautiful fjord-studded coast south of Puerto Montt. Navimag's *Magal-* *lanes* runs between Puerto Montt and Puerto Natales weekly in either direction, while the *Evangelista* runs between Puerto Montt and Puerto Chacabuco. See also Local Transport.

LOCAL TRANSPORT
Boat

In addition to maritime traffic, regular ferry services on many of the large lakes of

---

Border Crossings

The best way to see the Patagonian Andes is probably to start in the north and work your way southwards, crossing between Chile and Argentina a number of times. There are many border crossing points. Some good options are listed here.

Temuco to Zapala This road route goes across the Paso de Pino Hachado among lovely araucaria forests via Curacautín near Reserva Nacional Malalcahuello-Nalcas and Parque Nacional Conguillío. Buses run at least daily.

Pucón to Junín de los Andes This attractive but largely unsurfaced road route across Paso Mamuil Malal gives access to Parque Nacional Villarrica and for the ascent of Volcán Lanín. It is served by buses running between Temuco and San Martín de los Andes.

Puerto Fuy to San Martín de los Andes A scenic route first by ferry across Lago Pirehueico (accessible by daily bus from Panguipulli) then by bus via Paso Huahum to San Martín de los Andes.

Osorno to Bariloche The most important international route in the Lakes District, and usually the quickest way across the border. A good surfaced road goes via Entrelagos across the Paso Puyehue and around Lago Nahuel Huapi. Numerous international buses run this route.

Petrohué to Bariloche This slower (usually two-day) tourist route takes several boats through superb Lakes District scenery. It is available as a package (sold as the 'Cruce de los Lagos' by tourist agencies in Puerto Montt and Bariloche) from around US$60, including meals and accommodation.

Futaleufú to Esquel This remote, scenic route from a popular white-water river centre leads to the gateway for Argentina's Parque Nacional Los Alerces. Minibuses run most days in summer.

Coyhaique to Río Mayo An unsurfaced route via Paso Coyhaique to a village on Argentina's Ruta 40. There are several international buses per week in either direction between Coyhaique and Comodoro Rivadavia on the Atlantic coast.

Chile Chico to Los Antiguos Popular with travellers heading to the Argentine town of Perito Moreno. It goes east along the southern shore of Lago General Carrera (whose name changes to Lago Buenos Aires at the Argentine border).

Cochrane to Bajo Caracoles The most isolated of the international pass routes, and leads through the Valle Chacabuco across Paso Rodolfo Roballos. There is no public transport and traffic is extremely thin.

Puerto Natales to El Calafate A key route between the gateway towns to Torres del Paine and Los Glaciares national parks. Buses run daily throughout the summer.

Puerto Natales to Río Turbio An uninteresting route but may be your fastest way of getting to Río Gallegos. Frequent buses run across the border.

Punta Arenas to Río Gallegos Follows the coast of the Straits of Magellan before heading inland at the border, and passing the turn-offs to the Laguna Azul and Pali Aike reserves. There are frequent buses.

Puerto Williams to Ushuaia This route across the Beagle Channel is the most southerly border crossing possible. Various boat and plane options exist, and a ferry service (which has operated at times in the past) may resume in the future.

southern Chile and Argentina are an important means of transport for most travellers. In some cases, such as on Lago Nahuel Huapi in the Argentine Lakes District, these are mainly tourist boats. In other lakes such as Lago Pirehueico in the Chilean Lakes District and Lago General Carrera in central Patagonia, ferry services are quite simply the most practical form of transport.

In a few cases – the access to the Termas de Callao (p135) for example – the best way to get to a trek is by chartered boat. You will have to negotiate payment and transport yourself.

Taxi

Sometimes chartered taxis (called *fletes* in Chile and *remises* in Argentina) are the best way of getting to the start of the trek. Out of season, it may sometimes be necessary to hire a taxi if tourist buses are no longer running. Especially in Argentina (such as in Ushuaia and El Bolsón), fixed prices apply to certain trailheads. Expect to pay from around US$10 per 20km by taxi.

Language

WHO SPEAKS WHAT WHERE?

Both Argentinians and Chileans speak Spanish, or *castellano*, the term generally preferred over *español* in the Americas. In the cities quite a number of people know some English, but in the countryside this is rare. In certain parts of the south, small but influential communities of German, Italian, English, Croatian and even Welsh settlers continue to speak their languages. In some areas indigenous tongues still survive, the most notable being the Mapuche dialects of the Lakes District. Most Mapuche Indians are now able to speak Spanish as well as or better than their traditional languages.

LATIN AMERICAN SPANISH

On the whole, Spanish is not difficult, and you should try to gain some knowledge of simple conversational Spanish before you travel. Being able to communicate even at a very basic level with locals will be helpful and satisfying. Despite the common Hispanic colonial past of Chile and Argentina, there are major differences between the forms of Spanish spoken in each country.

For a more comprehensive language guide, pick up a copy of Lonely Planet's pocketsized *Latin American Spanish phrasebook*. The compact *University of Chicago Spanish-English, English-Spanish Dictionary* is another useful resource.

Pronunciation

c   as the 's' in 'see' before **e** and **i**; elsewhere, as English 'k'

h   invariably silent

j   a guttural version of English 'h'

ll/y   as the French 'j' in Jean-Jacques or, more strongly, as the English 'j' in Jessie Jackson

ñ   as the 'ny' in 'canyon'

Local Spanish

Argentine Spanish has been heavily influenced by Italian immigration, which has given this dialect a pleasant, melodic sound. Another strong characteristic of Argentine Spanish is the continued universal usage of the archaic word *vos*, meaning 'you'. *Vos* (pronounced 'boss') completely replaces *tú* as the familiar singular form.

Chilean Spanish is invariably spoken rapidly, and often has a high-pitched, lilting intonation that makes it immediately recognisable. Having been described as the 'Australians of the Spanish-speaking world', many Chileans speak without appearing to move their mouths very much, and often mumble or swallow their words. Chileans have developed a great amount of local idiom and slang.

The different national forms of Spanish extend more or less right down into Patagonia, where many words of indigenous origin that describe things peculiar to Patagonia, such as *mogote*, referring to the native cushion plants, and *puelche*, a warm wind that blows across the steppes from the north.

Greetings, Civilities & Basics

Good morning.	*Buenos días.*
Good afternoon.	*Buenas tardes.*
Hello.	*Hola.*
My name is ...	*Me llamo ...*
What's the time?	*¿Qué hora es?*
Where are you from?	*¿De dónde es Usted?*
Do you live here?	*¿Vive acá?*
Wait for me here.	*Espéreme aquí.*
It's a very beautiful spot.	*Es un lugar muy lindo.*
I'm sightseeing.	*Estoy paseando.*
We're getting to know the area.	*Estamos conociendo (la zona).*
See you later.	*Hasta luego.*
Goodbye.	*Adios/Chau.*
Farewell.	*Que le vaya bien.*
Yes.	*Sí.*
No.	*No.*

Getting Around

When does the next bus leave for ...?
   ¿Cuándo sale el próximo bus/colectivo a ...?
I'd like to charter a boat/taxi.
   Quisiera contratar un bote/remise.
Come to pick us up in five days.
   Venga a buscarnos en cinco días.

Can you take me to ...?
¿Puede llevarme a ...?
I'd like to get off at the turn-off.
Quisiera bajar en la bifurcación.
I'll hitchhike.
Viajaré a dedo.
We're leaving tomorrow.
Partiremos (vamos a partir) mañana.

first	*primero*
last	*último*

Around Town

I'm looking for ...	*Estoy buscando ...*
a bank	*un banco*
a chemist/ pharmacy	*una farmacia*
the market	*el mercado*
the post office	*los correos*
a telephone	*un teléfono*
phone call	*llamada (telefónica)*
person to person	*persona a persona*
What time does it open/close?	*¿A qué hora abren/cierran?*

Accommodation

hotel	*hotel/hospedaje/ pensión/residencial*
single room	*habitación sencilla*
double room	*habitación doble/ matrimonial*
What does it cost?	*¿Cuánto cuesta?*
May I see it?	*¿Puedo verlo?*
per night	*por noche*
too expensive	*demasiado caro*
cheaper	*más económico/barato*
the bill	*la cuenta*

Food & Drinks

I'm a vegetarian.	*Soy vegetariano/a.*
I don't eat/drink ...	*No como/tomo ...*
I'm allergic to nuts/peanuts.	*Soy alérgico/a a las fruta secas/los maníes.*
water	*agua*
purified water	*agua purificada*
bread	*pan*
meat	*carne*
cheese	*queso*
eggs	*huevos*

Signs

Entrada	**Entrance**
Salida	**Exit**
Información	**Information**
Abierto	**Open**
Cerrado	**Closed**
Prohibido	**Prohibited**
Comisaría	**Police Station**
Servicios/Baños	**Toilets**
Hombres/ Caballeros/Varones	**Men**
Señoras/Damas/ Mujeres	**Women**

milk	*leche*
juice	*jugo*
vegetables	*hortalizas/legumbres*
fish	*pescado*
coffee	*café*
tea	*té*
beer	*cerveza*

Time, Days & Numbers

Eight o'clock is *las ocho*, while 8.30 is *las ocho y treinta* (eight and thirty) or *las ocho y media* (eight and a half). However, 7.45 is *las ocho menos quince* (eight minus fifteen) or *las ocho menos cuarto* (eight minus one quarter).

Times are modified by morning *(de la mañana)* or afternoon *(de la tarde)* instead of am or pm. Use of the 24-hour clock, or military time, is also common, especially with transportation schedules.

What time is it?	*¿Qué hora es?*
It's one o'clock.	*Es la una.*
It's two/three o'clock.	*Son las dos/tres.*
At three o'clock ...	*A las tres ...*
today	*hoy*
tomorrow	*mañana*
yesterday	*ayer*
Monday	*lunes*
Tuesday	*martes*
Wednesday	*miércoles*
Thursday	*jueves*
Friday	*viernes*
Saturday	*sábado*
Sunday	*domingo*

1	uno
2	dos
3	tres
4	cuatro
5	cinco
6	seis
7	siete
8	ocho
9	nueve
10	diez
11	once
12	doce
13	trece
14	catorce
15	quince
16	dieciséis
17	diecisiete
18	dieciocho
19	diecinueve
20	veinte
21	veintiuno
22	veintidós
30	treinta
31	treinta y uno
40	cuarenta
50	cincuenta
60	sesenta
70	setenta
80	ochenta
90	noventa
100	cien
101	ciento uno
102	ciento dos
200	doscientos
1,000	mil
1,100	mil cien
2,000	dos mil
100,000	cien mil

Emergencies

Help!	¡Socorro!/¡Auxilio!
Help me!	¡Ayudenme!
Thief!	¡Ladrón!
Fire!	¡Fuego!
police	gendarmería (Arg)/ carabineros (Ch)
doctor	doctor
hospital	hospital
Leave me alone!	¡Déjeme!
Go away!	¡Váyase!
I've been robbed.	Me han robado.
They took my ...	Se me llevaron ...
money	el dinero
passport	el pasaporte
bag	la bolsa

influenza	gripe
a migraine	jaqueca
snow blindness	ceguera de nieve
sore throat	dolor de garganta
sprain	una torcedura
a stomachache	dolor de estómago

I can't move my ...	No puedo mover mi ...
I have a pain in my ...	Me duele mi ...
ankle	tobillo
arm	brazo
back	espalda/columna
elbow	codo
foot	pie
knee	rodilla
leg	pierna
neck	cuello
shoulder	hombro
throat	garganta

antibiotics	antibióticos
antiseptic	antiséptico
bandage	vendaje
dizzy	mareado/a
medicine	medicamento
ointment	pomada
pills/tablets	pastillas
pregnant	embarazada

Health

I'm sick.	Estoy enfermo/a.
I need a doctor.	Necesito un doctor.

I have ...	Tengo ...
asthma	asma
a blister	una ampolla
a cold	un resfrío
dehydration	deshidratación
diarrhea	diarrea
epilepsy	epilepsia
fever	fiebre
frostbite	congelación
a headache	dolor de cabeza

Difficulties

We've lost the way.
  Hemos perdido el camino.
I'm looking for ...
  Estoy buscando ...

Is it dangerous?
  ¿Es peligroso?
Can you help me?
  ¿Puede ayudarme?
I'm thirsty/hungry.
  Tengo sed/hambre.
Can you repair this for me?
  ¿Puede arreglarme ésto?
I don't understand.
  No entiendo.
Please speak more slowly.
  Por favor, hable más despacio.
Does anyone here speak English?
  ¿Hay alguien aquí que hable inglés?

TREKKING
Preparations
Where can we buy supplies?
  ¿Dónde podemos comprar víveres?
Can I leave some things here a while?
  ¿Puedo dejar algunas cosas acá por un rato?
Where can we hire a mountain guide?
  ¿Dónde podemos alquilar un guía de montaña?
I'd like to talk to someone who knows this area.
  Quisiera hablar con álguien que conozca este sector.
How much do you charge?
  ¿Cuánto cobra Usted?
We are thinking of taking this route.
  Pensamos tomar esta ruta.
Is the trek very difficult?
  ¿Es muy difícil la caminata?
Is the track (well) marked?
  ¿Está (bien) marcado el sendero?
Which is the shortest/easiest route?
  ¿Cuál es la ruta más corta/más fácil?
Is there much snow on the pass?
  ¿Hay mucha nieve en el paso?
We'll return in one week.
  (Volverémos/Vamos a volver) en una semana.

Weather
What will the weather be like?
  ¿Qué tiempo hará?
Tomorrow it will be cold.
  Mañana hará frío.
It's going to rain.
  Va a llover.
It's windy/sunny.
  Hay viento/sol.

It's raining/snowing.
  Está lloviendo/nevando.
It has clouded over.
  Se ha nublado.
The rain slowed us down.
  Nos atrasó la lluvia.
At what time does it get dark?
  ¿A qué hora cae la noche?

clear/fine	*despejado*
cloud	*nube*
fog/mist	*neblina/niebla*
frost	*helada*
high tide/low tide	*altamar/bajamar*
ice	*hielo*
overcast/cloudy	*nublado*
rain/to rain	*lluvia/llover*
snow/to snow	*nieve/nevar*
spring melt/thaw	*deshielo*
storm	*tormenta/tempestad*
summer	*verano*
good/bad weather	*buen/mal tiempo*
whiteout/clag	*borrina/encainada*
wind	*viento*
winter	*invierno*

On the Trek
How many kilometres to ...?
  ¿Cuántos kilómetros son hasta ...?
How many hours' walking?
  ¿Cuántas horas son caminando?
Does this track go to ...?
  ¿Va este sendero a ...?
How do you reach the summit?
  ¿Cómo se llega a la cumbre?
Where are you going to?
  ¿A dónde va Usted?
May I cross your property?
  ¿Puedo cruzar su propiedad?
What is this place called?
  ¿Cómo se llama este lugar?
We're doing a hike from ... to ...
  Estamos haciendo una caminata desde ... a ...

hut warden	*guarda de refugio*
park ranger	*guardaparque*

Directions
circuit	*circuito*
highway	*carretera*
path/trail	*sendero/picada/senda*
road/vehicle track	*camino*
route (unmarked)	*huella/ruta*

shortcut	*atajo*
sidewalk/footpath	*vereda*
adjacent	*al frente*
ahead/behind	*más adelante/atrás*
ascent/descent	*subida/bajada*
before/after	*antes/después (de)*
below/above	*debajo/encima de*
beside	*al lado de*
between	*entre*
early/late	*temprano/tarde*
east/west	*este/oeste*
flat/steep	*llano/empinado*
height/depth	*altura/profundidad*
here/(there)	*aquí/(acá/allá)*
high/low	*alto/bajo*
(to the) left/right	*(a la) derecha/izquierda*
near/distant	*cerca/lejos*
north/south	*norte/sur*
on the other side of	*al otro lado de*
southern	*austral/meridional*
towards/away from	*hacia/desde*
up/down	*arriba/abajo*

Map Reading

Do you have a better map?
  ¿Tiene un mejor mapa?
Can you show me on the map where we are?
  ¿Puede señalarme en el mapa dónde estamos?

altitude difference	*desnivel*
contour lines	*curvas de nivel*
frontier mark	*hito*
map	*mapa/carta*
metres above sea level	*metros sobre el nivel del mar (msnm)*
spot height	*cota*
tree/timber line	*nivel del bosque*

Camping

Where is the best place to camp?
  ¿Dónde está el mejor lugar para acampar?
Can we put up the tent here?
  ¿Podemos armar la carpa acá?
Is it permitted to make fire?
  ¿Está permitido hacer fuego?
There is no firewood.
  No hay leña.
I have a gas/petrol stove.
  Tengo un calentador (Arg)/*anafe* (Ch) *a gas/bencina/nafta.*
I'm going to stay here two days.
  Voy a quedarme dos días aquí.

Trail Terms

bivouac	*vivac*
to camp	*acampar*
campfire/fireplace	*fogata/fogón*
camping area	*campamento/campismo*
camp site	*sitio (de acampar)*
firewood	*leña*
rubbish	*basura*
signpost	*cartel indicador*
traverse	*traversía*
to walk/go on foot	*caminar/ir a pie*

Clothing & Equipment

altimeter	*altímetro*
anorak/rainjacket	*campera/chaqueta impermeable*
backpack/rucksack	*mochila*
batteries	*pilas/baterías*
billy/cooking pot	*olla*
(boot) laces	*cordónes (de bota)*
(walking) boots	*botas (de caminar)*
camp stove	*calentador* (Arg)/ *anafe* (Ch)
candles	*velas*
canteen/water bottle	*cantimplora*
cap/beanie	*gorro*
carabiner	*mosquetón*
compass	*brújula*
crampons	*grampones/trepadores*
gaiters	*polainas*
gas cartridge	*cartucho de gas*
gasoline	*gasolina/nafta* (Arg)/ *bencina* (Ch)
gloves	*guantes*
ice axe	*piolet, piqueta* (Arg)
kerosene	*parafina/kerosén*
pocketknife	*cortaplumas*
provisions/food supplies	*víveres/abastecimientos*
rope	*cuerda*
runners/sneakers	*zapatillas*
sleeping bag	*saco de dormir*
sleeping mat	*colchoneta aislante*
sunglasses	*gafas de sol*
tent	*carpa*
torch/flashlight	*linterna*
trekking stocks	*bastónes*
white spirit	*bencina blanca*

Natural Features

Andean meadow	*alpage/coironal*
avalanche	*alud/avalancha*
bay/cove	*bahía/caleta*

LANGUAGE

beach	playa
bog/swamp	pantano/mallín
branch of a lake/ river	brazo
brook	riachuelo
cairn	mojón/pirca
cave	cueva/caverna
chasm	abismo
cliff	acantilado/barranco/ farellón
coast, shoreline	costa
(snow) cornice	cornisa (de nieve)
crag	peña/peñón
crater (of a volcano)	caldera
creek/small river	estero/arroyo
crevasse	grieta
drainage basin	hoya/cuenca
face of a mountain	muralla/vertiente
fjord/sound	fiordo/seno
forest	bosque
frontier/border	frontera/límite
gap/narrow pass	portillo/pasada
glacier	ventisquero/glaciar
gorge/canyon	cajón/barranco/ garganta
hill	morro/colina/loma
hillside/ mountainside	faldeo/ladera
iceberg	témpano
island	isla
lake	lago/laguna
landslide	derrumbe
location/spot	lugar/paraje
lookout	mirador
moor	turbal/mallín
moraine	morrena
mountain	cerro/montaña/monte
mountain chain	cordillera/cordón
national park	parque nacional
névé/permanent snowfield	neviza/campo de nieve
outlet stream	desagüe
pass	paso/portezuelo/abra
pinnacle	pináculo/aguja/diente
plain/flat terrain	llanura/planicie
plateau/tableland	meseta
range/massif	sierra/mazico
rapid	catarata
reserve	reserva
ridge/spur	filo/espolón/cresta
river	río/quebrada
river bed	cauce/lecho
riverbank/shoreline	ribera/orilla

scoria	escoria
scrub/underbrush	matorral/sotobosque
slope/rise	cuesta/pendiente
source of a stream	nacimiento
spring	fuente/manantial
steppe/plain	estepa/pampa
stone/rock	piedra
strait	estrecho
stream junction	horqueta/confluencia
summit/peak	cumbre/cima/pico
thermal springs	termas/aguas calientes
torrent/gushing stream	chorro
valley	valle
volcano	volcán
waterfall	salto (de agua)/cascada

Artificial Features

border post	aduana
bridge/footbridge	puente/pasarela
ditch	zanja
farm	finca/chacra (Arg)/ fundo (Ch)
fence	cerco/alambrado
firebreak	cortefuego
homestead	caserío
house/building	casa
hut/mountain shelter	refugio
jetty/landing pier	muelle
lighthouse	faro
park entrance	entrada del parque
ranch	estancia
ranger station	guardería
ski lift/ski tow	aerosilla/andarivel
ski run	pista de esquí
stockyard/corral	galpón
town/village	pueblo/aldea

Vegetation

branch	rama
bush/shrub	arbusto
flower	flor
grass	pasto
leaf	hoja
lichen	liquen
moss	musgo
root	raíz
tree	árbol

Wildlife

| beaver | castor |
| cat | gato |

cow/cattle	*vaca/ganado bovino*	*cautín*	a native duck
deer	*ciervo*	*che*	people
dog	*perro*	*co*	water
duck	*pato*	*coli/colu*	brown
eagle	*águila*	*copa*	green
fish	*pez*	*cuel*	hill
flea	*pulga*	*cura*	rock/stone
fly	*mosca*	*cuy cuy*	log bridge
fox	*zorro*	*filu*	snake
frog	*sapo/rana*	*futa*	big
hare/rabbit	*liebre/conejo*	*gol*	stake/stick/pole
hawk	*halcón*	*huapi*	island
horse	*caballo*	*hue*	place/location
horsefly	*tábano*	*hueico*	tiny lake/puddle
seagull	*gaviota*	*huille*	south
sheep	*oveja*	*huiqui*	thrush
swan	*cisne*	*iñim*	bird
trout	*trucha*	*lafquén*	sea/lake/plain
vulture	*buitre*	*leufú*	river
wild pig	*jabalí*	*lemu*	forest
woodpecker	*carpintero*	*llanca*	a semiprecious blue stone

MAPUCHE & TEHUELCHE

Although there's absolutely no need to learn any Mapuche or Tehuelche, the significance of certain place names (particularly in the Araucanía and Lakes District) will be clearer if you're able to decipher a few words of indigenous origin. Two good locally available dictionaries are the *Diccionario Mapuche Español* (Siringa Libros, Neuquén) and the *Diccionario Lingüistico-Ethnográfico de la Lengua Mapuche* (Editorial Andrés Bello, Santiago de Chile), a very recent Mapuche-Spanish-English title by prominent Chilean linguist Maria Catrileo.

Most spellings given below are as used in local place names. They reflect the sounds of Spanish, and some of the words differ both in spelling and pronunciation from the original Mapuche.

lonco	head
mapu	land
mahuida/mavida	mountain
mallín	moor
mañque	condor
mapu	land/earth
milla	gold
nahuel	tiger/jaguarete
ñamcu	eagle
ñiri	fox
pangi	puma
poco	frog
pile/pilén	frost/ice
pire	snow
pillán	volcano
puelche	warm northerly wind in Patagonia
púlli	mountainside
quilla	moon
repú	path/track
traful	confluence/river junction
tromén	cloud
tue	ground/soil

antu	sun/day
buta	large/great
cacique	Indian chief
calfu	blue

Glossary

The following words or terms have been used throughout the text as defined below.

aduana – border or customs post (Spanish)

aerosilla – chairlift

Aisén – also spelt Aysén; Chile's wild and thinly-settled XI Región in central Patagonia

albergue – hostel (Spanish)

alerce – large conifer mainly found in wet areas of the Lakes District

alerzal – a stand of *alerces* (Spanish)

almacén – small store that sells provisions (Spanish)

amphitheatre – rounded glacial cirque enclosed by high rock walls

Andean – pertaining to the Andes, the world's longest and second-highest mountain range

andinist – Andean mountaineer

APN – Administración de Parques Nacionales; the national-park authority of Argentina

araucaria – tree whose umbrella-like form graces the forests and ridge tops throughout the Araucanía; known in Argentina by the *Mapuche* word *pehuén*

Araucarian – see *Mapuche*

arrayán – native myrtle with orange-red bark, usually found growing on water-logged sites

arroyo – stream or creek (especially in Argentine Spanish)

asado – whole sheep or calf grilled on a spit around a large open charcoal fire; popular in Argentina

bahía – bay (Spanish)

bandurria – black-necked ibis; often seen on pastures or wetlands throughout Patagonia

biota – flora and fauna of a national park or other area

bushbashing – trekking on *off-tracks* through (dense) forest

CAB – Club Andino Bariloche; the largest mountain club in South America

calafate – thorny bush of the *Berberis* genus, common in southern Patagonia

caminata – trek or hiking trip (Spanish)

camino – road, but locally sometimes also used to mean 'foot track' (Spanish)

camping ground – place offering organised camping; camping grounds generally have basic facilities such as toilets and showers, and may charge a fee

camping libre – free camping area without facilities (used mainly in Argentine national parks)

camp site – used in each trekking stage of this guidebook for any suitable place where camping is allowed; a camp site may be 'wild' (if local regulations permit this), at a camping area designated by the park authority, or at a camping ground

CAP – Club Andino Piltriquitrón; the local mountain club in El Bolsón

Carabineros de Chile – Chilean police force (also responsible for patrolling the frontier and for immigration control)

Carretera Austral – 1137km unsurfaced 'Southern Highway' that runs south from Puerto Montt to Villa O'Higgins in southern Aisén

casa de cambio – currency exchange bureau

casa de familia – private household that takes in paying guests

centro de inform – information centre (Spanish)

cerro – mountain summit (Spanish)

chaura – species of low erica-like shrub that produces edible berries

chilco – native Patagonian fuchsia species

Chilote – inhabitant of the island of Chiloé

Chubut – Argentina's central Patagonian province, centred around the Río Chubut

chucao – small ground-dwelling bird often heard (sometimes seen), mainly in forests of the Lakes District and central Patagonia

cirque – high rounded precipice, formed by the weathering action of ice and snow, typically found at the head of a small alpine valley

club andino – mountain club (literally 'Andean club'; Spanish)

club de montaña – a mountain club (Spanish)

Codeff – Comité Nacional Pro Defensa de Fauna y Flora; conservation organisation based in Santiago de Chile

coigüe – group of three evergreen species of southern beech; known as *coihue* in Argentina

colectivo – in Argentina, a public bus; in Chile, a shuttle taxi that stops to pick up passengers (Spanish)

colihue – native bamboo species

Comarca Andina del Paralelo 42 – Andean region centred around the Argentine town of El Bolsón

Conaf – Corporación Nacional Forestal; Chilean forestry and national-park authority

confitería – small café-restaurant (Spanish)

contour – to move along a slope without climbing or descending appreciably

Cordillera – the long chain of the Andes

Cordillera de la Costa – range of lower mountains running between the Andean Cordillera and the Pacific coast

crevasse – deep fissure in a glacier

downclimb – descent that is steep enough to require trekkers to use their hands for support and/or safety

entrada – entrance gate (Spanish)

estancia – large cattle or sheep property (Spanish)

estero – stream or creek (especially Chilean Spanish)

filo – ridge or spur (Spanish)

4WD track – rough road suitable only for four-wheel drive vehicles

fumarole – vent near or on a volcano from which gases and steam are emitted

fundo – farm, normally smaller than an *estancia* (especially Chilean Spanish)

gaucho – Argentine cowboy

Gendarmería Nacional – Argentine equivalent of the Chilean Carabineros

geyser – vent emitting hot water and steam, can sometimes erupt violently

glaciar – glacier (Spanish)

glissade – snow-sliding technique used to descend snow slopes

GPS – Global Positioning System; device that calculates position and elevation by reading and decoding signals from satellites

gringo – term (not necessarily disrespectful) for a foreigner of northern European descent (Spanish)

guanaco – Patagonian cameloid species (related to the llama)

guardaparque – national-park ranger (Spanish)

guardería – national-park ranger station (Spanish)

Hielo Norte – the northern continental icecap, which lies entirely within the Aisén region of Chile

Hielo Sur – the larger southern continental icecap

hito – (natural or artificial) surveying point that marks the international border (Spanish)

hospedaje – small, usually family-run, hotel (Spanish)

hostal – hotel (Spanish)

hostería – similar to a *hospedaje* (Spanish)

huaso – Chilean cowboy; in its wider sense, *huaso* simply means a country person

huemul – rare species of native Andean deer

icecap – vast dome-shaped glacier covering a mountain range in high-precipitation regions (see Hielo Norte, Hielo Sur)

icefall – very steep broken-up section of a glacier

IGM – Instituto Geográfico Militar; military cartographic institutes in both Chile and Argentina

intendencia – Argentine term for the administration centre of a national park

lago/laguna – lake (Spanish)

lenga – most common deciduous species of southern beech

librería – bookstore (Spanish)

Magallanes – Chile's southernmost XII Región, which includes Chilean Tierra del Fuego

Magellanic forest – southern Patagonian forest (composed mainly of *lenga* and *ñirre*)

mahuén – plants of the genus *Mahuenia*, a rather atypical member of the cactus family, which grow in spiny, lawn-like mounds in dryland areas

mallín – area periodically inundated and typically covered by open swamp vegetation

Mapuche – group of ethnically related tribes that inhabit(ed) both sides of the Andes of northern Patagonia

mara – Patagonian hare

menú – fixed-price meal (Spanish)

meseta – tableland

mirador – lookout or viewing point (Spanish)

mochilero – backpacker (Spanish; as in English, the word doesn't tell you whether the person concerned is trekking or simply using a backpack as convenient travel luggage)

mogote – species of tumbleweed found in dry areas of eastern Patagonia; also known as *mata spinosum*

monito del monte – mouse opossum; small marsupial that inhabits the forests of the Araucanía and Lakes District

monte – term used in Argentina to describe the scrub-covered hill country fringing the eastern Patagonian *precordillera*; also used more generally to mean 'mountain summit', when it is synonymous with the Spanish *cerro*

moraine – rock debris carried by glaciers and dumped as the ice melts

msnm – *metros sobre el nivel del mar*, or 'metres above sea level' (Spanish)

ñandú – native ostrich of the Patagonian steppes; also called *rhea*

névé – permanent snowfield in the high alpine zone (French)

ñirre – small deciduous southern beech species; spelt *ñire* in Argentina

Nothofagus – botanical name of the southern beech genus, the most dominant trees of the Patagonian Andes

notro – also called *ciruelillo*, a common shrub that produces flamboyant red flowers

off-tracks – (trekking routes) not following any real walking track

out-and-back – trek whose route involves backtracking

outlet – place where a stream flows out of a lake

pampa – field or meadow; also used in Chile and Argentina to describe the vast steppes of eastern Patagonia (Spanish)

parque nacional – national park (Spanish)

party – used in this guidebook to mean a group of two or more trekkers

Patagonia – trekker's paradise

pehuén – see *araucaria*

pensión – boarding house or guesthouse (Spanish)

peter out – to gradually disappear (of a path or route)

petro – small biting gnat; usually found in lowland areas grazed by livestock

picada – foot track, usually less well-defined (mainly Argentine Spanish)

pilme – see *petro*

playa – beach (Spanish)

pobladores – the gradual regeneration of vegetation cleared by settlers

portada – national-park entrance gate (Argentine Spanish)

portería – national-park entrance gate (Chilean Spanish)

precordillera – Andean foothills that fringe both sides of the main range, the *Cordillera* (Spanish)

proveeduría – canteen or small store (such as at a camping ground or *refugio*) that sells basic provisions

puente – bridge (Spanish)

puesto – small hut or primitive shelter, usually on a more remote part of an *estancia*, where ranch workers can sleep a night or two (Spanish)

puma – South American mountain lion (related to the cougar of North America)

quila – collective term (of Mapuche origin) for about half a dozen species of vigorous native bamboo

quincho – communal shelter at camping grounds (Spanish)

reducción – Indian reservation (Argentine Spanish)
refugio – mountain hut or 'refuge' (Spanish; pronounced ref-oo-he-o)
remís – taxi (Argentine Spanish)
reserva nacional – national reserve (Spanish)
reserva natural estricta – restricted area of national park where public access is strictly controlled, and generally allowed only under the supervision of national-park personnel (Spanish)
residencial – boarding house or guesthouse (Spanish)
rhea – English word for *ñandú*
río – river (Spanish)
ruca – traditional thatched house of the *Mapuche* people

scree slide – slope of loose rock (known as scree or talus), below steep rocky mountainsides prone to weathering
scrub line – low, weather-beaten brush (usually *lenga*) on a high mountainside
seccional – *guardería* subordinate to the main APN *intendencia* (Argentine Spanish)
senda/sendero – path or foot track (Spanish)
serac – large, prominent block of ice typically seen on steep glaciers or icefalls (French)
Sernap – Servicio Nacional de Pesca; the Chilean authority responsible for regulating commercial and recreational fishing
Sernatur – Servicio Nacional de Turismo; the organisation which runs tourist offices in Chile
sierra – mountain range (literally 'saw'; Spanish)
southern beech – see *Nothofagus*
stage – individual section of a longer trek

switchbacks – sharp bends in a path that takes a winding route directly up or down a steep slope

tábano – collective term for two or more kinds of blood-sucking horseflies that infest forested areas in the Araucanía and Lakes District from early summer to midsummer
tarn – small highland lake
taxi colectivo – see *colectivo*
Tehuelche – an indigenous people who inhabited the steppes of southeastern Patagonia
termas – thermal springs (Spanish)
trailhead – point from which a trekking route begins (eg, a car park, roadside, or national park ranger station)
trans-Andean – leading across the main range of the Andes
tree line – the altitude (which drops steadily from north to south) above which trees can no longer survive due to the severity of the climate
true left/true right – 'true' indicates the side of a river (or valley) from the perspective of a trekker facing downstream (or downvalley)

Valdivian forest – from the local Spanish term *bosque valdiviano*, this is the species-rich temperate rainforest that grows in the wettest areas of Andean foothills of the Lakes District and the north of central Patagonia
ventisquero – alternative word for glacier (Spanish)

wild camping – pitching a tent outside a camping ground or a national park–authorised camping area

XI Región – see *Aisén*
XII Región – see *Magallanes*

Lonely Planet Guides by Region

Lonely Planet is known worldwide for publishing practical, reliable and no-nonsense travel information in our guides and on our Web site. The Lonely Planet list covers just about every accessible part of the world. Currently there are 16 series: Travel guides, Shoestring guides, Condensed guides, Phrasebooks, Read This First, Healthy Travel, Walking guides, Cycling guides, Watching Wildlife guides, Pisces Diving & Snorkeling guides, City Maps, Road Atlases, Out to Eat, World Food, Journeys travel literature and Pictorials.

AFRICA Africa on a shoestring • Botswana • Cairo • Cairo City Map • Cape Town • Cape Town City Map • East Africa • Egypt • Egyptian Arabic phrasebook • Ethiopia, Eritrea & Djibouti • Ethiopian Amharic phrasebook • The Gambia & Senegal • Healthy Travel Africa • Kenya • Malawi • Morocco • Moroccan Arabic phrasebook • Mozambique • Namibia • Read This First: Africa • South Africa, Lesotho & Swaziland • Southern Africa • Southern Africa Road Atlas • Swahili phrasebook • Tanzania, Zanzibar & Pemba • Trekking in East Africa • Tunisia • Watching Wildlife East Africa • Watching Wildlife Southern Africa • West Africa • World Food Morocco • Zambia • Zimbabwe, Botswana & Namibia
Travel Literature: Mali Blues: Traveling to an African Beat • The Rainbird: A Central African Journey • Songs to an African Sunset: A Zimbabwean Story

AUSTRALIA & THE PACIFIC Aboriginal Australia & the Torres Strait Islands •Auckland • Australia • Australian phrasebook • Australia Road Atlas • Cycling Australia • Cycling New Zealand • Fiji • Fijian phrasebook • Healthy Travel Australia, NZ & the Pacific • Islands of Australia's Great Barrier Reef • Melbourne • Melbourne City Map • Micronesia • New Caledonia • New South Wales • New Zealand • Northern Territory • Outback Australia • Out to Eat – Melbourne • Out to Eat – Sydney • Papua New Guinea • Pidgin phrasebook • Queensland • Rarotonga & the Cook Islands • Samoa • Solomon Islands • South Australia • South Pacific • South Pacific phrasebook • Sydney • Sydney City Map • Sydney Condensed • Tahiti & French Polynesia • Tasmania • Tonga • Tramping in New Zealand • Vanuatu • Victoria • Walking in Australia • Watching Wildlife Australia • Western Australia
Travel Literature: Islands in the Clouds: Travels in the Highlands of New Guinea • Kiwi Tracks: A New Zealand Journey • Sean & David's Long Drive

CENTRAL AMERICA & THE CARIBBEAN Bahamas, Turks & Caicos • Baja California • Belize, Guatemala & Yucatán • Bermuda • Central America on a shoestring • Costa Rica • Costa Rica Spanish phrasebook • Cuba • Cycling Cuba • Dominican Republic & Haiti • Eastern Caribbean • Guatemala • Havana • Healthy Travel Central & South America • Jamaica • Mexico • Mexico City • Panama • Puerto Rico • Read This First: Central & South America • Virgin Islands • World Food Caribbean • World Food Mexico • Yucatán
Travel Literature: Green Dreams: Travels in Central America

EUROPE Amsterdam • Amsterdam City Map • Amsterdam Condensed • Andalucía • Athens • Austria • Baltic States phrasebook • Barcelona • Barcelona City Map • Belgium & Luxembourg • Berlin • Berlin City Map • Britain • British phrasebook • Brussels, Bruges & Antwerp • Brussels City Map • Budapest • Budapest City Map • Canary Islands • Catalunya & the Costa Brava • Central Europe • Central Europe phrasebook • Copenhagen • Corfu & the Ionians • Corsica • Crete • Crete Condensed • Croatia • Cycling Britain • Cycling France • Cyprus • Czech & Slovak Republics • Czech phrasebook • Denmark • Dublin • Dublin City Map • Dublin Condensed • Eastern Europe • Eastern Europe phrasebook • Edinburgh • Edinburgh City Map • England • Estonia, Latvia & Lithuania • Europe on a shoestring • Europe phrasebook • Finland • Florence • Florence City Map • France • Frankfurt City Map • Frankfurt Condensed • French phrasebook • Georgia, Armenia & Azerbaijan • Germany • German phrasebook • Greece • Greek Islands • Greek phrasebook • Hungary • Iceland, Greenland & the Faroe Islands • Ireland • Italian phrasebook • Italy • Kraków • Lisbon • The Loire • London • London City Map • London Condensed • Madrid • Madrid City Map • Malta • Mediterranean Europe • Milan, Turin & Genoa • Moscow • Munich • Netherlands • Normandy • Norway • Out to Eat – London • Out to Eat – Paris • Paris • Paris City Map • Paris Condensed • Poland • Polish phrasebook • Portugal • Portuguese phrasebook • Prague • Prague City Map • Provence & the Côte d'Azur • Read This First: Europe • Rhodes & the Dodecanese • Romania & Moldova • Rome • Rome City Map • Rome Condensed • Russia, Ukraine & Belarus • Russian phrasebook • Scandinavian & Baltic Europe • Scandinavian phrasebook • Scotland • Sicily • Slovenia • South-West France • Spain • Spanish phrasebook • Stockholm • St Petersburg • St Petersburg City Map • Sweden • Switzerland • Tuscany • Ukrainian phrasebook • Venice • Vienna • Wales • Walking in Britain • Walking in France • Walking in Ireland • Walking in Italy • Walking in Scotland • Walking in Spain • Walking in Switzerland • Western Europe • World Food France • World Food Greece • World Food Ireland • World Food Italy • World Food Spain **Travel Literature:** After Yugoslavia • Love and War in the Apennines • The Olive Grove: Travels in Greece • On the Shores of the Mediterranean • Round Ireland in Low Gear • A Small Place in Italy

Lonely Planet Mail Order

Lonely Planet products are distributed worldwide. They are also available by mail order from Lonely Planet, so if you have difficulty finding a title please write to us. North and South American residents should write to 150 Linden St, Oakland, CA 94607, USA; European and African residents should write to 72-82 Rosebery Ave, London, EC1R 4RW, UK; and residents of other countries to Locked Bag 1, Footscray, Victoria 3011, Australia.

INDIAN SUBCONTINENT & THE INDIAN OCEAN Bangladesh • Bengali phrasebook • Bhutan • Delhi • Goa • Healthy Travel Asia & India • Hindi & Urdu phrasebook • India • India & Bangladesh City Map • Indian Himalaya • Karakoram Highway • Kathmandu City Map • Kerala • Madagascar • Maldives • Mauritius, Réunion & Seychelles • Mumbai (Bombay) • Nepal • Nepali phrasebook • North India • Pakistan • Rajasthan • Read This First: Asia & India • South India • Sri Lanka • Sri Lanka phrasebook • Tibet • Tibetan phrasebook • Trekking in the Indian Himalaya • Trekking in the Karakoram & Hindukush • Trekking in the Nepal Himalaya • World Food India **Travel Literature**: The Age of Kali: Indian Travels and Encounters • Hello Goodnight: A Life of Goa • In Rajasthan • Maverick in Madagascar • A Season in Heaven: True Tales from the Road to Kathmandu • Shopping for Buddhas • A Short Walk in the Hindu Kush • Slowly Down the Ganges

MIDDLE EAST & CENTRAL ASIA Bahrain, Kuwait & Qatar • Central Asia • Central Asia phrasebook • Dubai • Farsi (Persian) phrasebook • Hebrew phrasebook • Iran • Israel & the Palestinian Territories • Istanbul • Istanbul City Map • Istanbul to Cairo • Istanbul to Kathmandu • Jerusalem • Jerusalem City Map • Jordan • Lebanon • Middle East • Oman & the United Arab Emirates • Syria • Turkey • Turkish phrasebook • World Food Turkey • Yemen **Travel Literature**: Black on Black: Iran Revisited • Breaking Ranks: Turbulent Travels in the Promised Land • The Gates of Damascus • Kingdom of the Film Stars: Journey into Jordan

NORTH AMERICA Alaska • Boston • Boston City Map • Boston Condensed • British Columbia • California & Nevada • California Condensed • Canada • Chicago • Chicago City Map • Chicago Condensed • Florida • Georgia & the Carolinas • Great Lakes • Hawaii • Hiking in Alaska • Hiking in the USA • Honolulu & Oahu City Map • Las Vegas • Los Angeles • Los Angeles City Map • Louisiana & the Deep South • Miami • Miami City Map • Montreal • New England • New Orleans • New Orleans City Map • New York City • New York City City Map • New York City Condensed • New York, New Jersey & Pennsylvania • Oahu • Out to Eat – San Francisco • Pacific Northwest • Rocky Mountains • San Diego & Tijuana • San Francisco • San Francisco City Map • Seattle • Seattle City Map • Southwest • Texas • Toronto • USA • USA phrasebook • Vancouver • Vancouver City Map • Virginia & the Capital Region • Washington, DC • Washington, DC City Map • World Food New Orleans **Travel Literature**: Caught Inside: A Surfer's Year on the California Coast • Drive Thru America

NORTH-EAST ASIA Beijing • Beijing City Map • Cantonese phrasebook • China • Hiking in Japan • Hong Kong & Macau • Hong Kong City Map • Hong Kong Condensed • Japan • Japanese phrasebook • Korea • Korean phrasebook • Kyoto • Mandarin phrasebook • Mongolia • Mongolian phrasebook • Seoul • Shanghai • South-West China • Taiwan • Tokyo • Tokyo Condensed • World Food Hong Kong • World Food Japan **Travel Literature**: In Xanadu: A Quest • Lost Japan

SOUTH AMERICA Argentina, Uruguay & Paraguay • Bolivia • Brazil • Brazilian phrasebook • Buenos Aires • Buenos Aires City Map • Chile & Easter Island • Colombia • Ecuador & the Galapagos Islands • Healthy Travel Central & South America • Latin American Spanish phrasebook • Peru • Quechua phrasebook • Read This First: Central & South America • Rio de Janeiro • Rio de Janeiro City Map • Santiago de Chile • South America on a shoestring • Trekking in the Patagonian Andes • Venezuela **Travel Literature**: Full Circle: A South American Journey

SOUTH-EAST ASIA Bali & Lombok • Bangkok • Bangkok City Map • Burmese phrasebook • Cambodia • Cycling Vietnam, Laos & Cambodia • East Timor phrasebook • Hanoi • Healthy Travel Asia & India • Hill Tribes phrasebook • Ho Chi Minh City (Saigon) • Indonesia • Indonesian phrasebook • Indonesia's Eastern Islands • Java • Lao phrasebook • Laos • Malay phrasebook • Malaysia, Singapore & Brunei • Myanmar (Burma) • Philippines • Pilipino (Tagalog) phrasebook • Read This First: Asia & India • Singapore • Singapore City Map • South-East Asia on a shoestring • South-East Asia phrasebook • Thailand • Thailand's Islands & Beaches • Thailand, Vietnam, Laos & Cambodia Road Atlas • Thai phrasebook • Vietnam • Vietnamese phrasebook • World Food Indonesia • World Food Thailand • World Food Vietnam

ALSO AVAILABLE: Antarctica • The Arctic • The Blue Man: Tales of Travel, Love and Coffee • Brief Encounters: Stories of Love, Sex & Travel • Buddhist Stupas in Asia: The Shape of Perfection • Chasing Rickshaws • The Last Grain Race • Lonely Planet ... On the Edge: Adventurous Escapades from Around the World • Lonely Planet Unpacked • Lonely Planet Unpacked Again • Not the Only Planet: Science Fiction Travel Stories • Ports of Call: A Journey by Sea • Sacred India • Travel Photography: A Guide to Taking Better Pictures • Travel with Children • Tuvalu: Portrait of an Island Nation

LONELY PLANET

You already know that Lonely Planet produces more than this one guidebook, but you might not be aware of the other products we have on this region. Here is a selection of titles that you may want to check out as well, available wherever books are sold:

Buenos Aires
ISBN 1 74059 022 8
US$14.99 • UK£8.99

**Healthy Travel
Central & South America**
ISBN 1 86450 053 0
US$5.95 • UK£3.99

**Latin American Spanish
Phrasebook**
ISBN 1 74059 170 4
US$7.99 • UK£4.99

**Ecuador & the
Galapágos Islands**
ISBN 1 74059 464 9
US$21.99 • UK£13.99

Peru
ISBN 0 86442 710 7
US$17.95 • UK£11.99

**Argentina Uruguay &
Paraguay**
ISBN 1 74059 027 9
US$24.99 • UK£14.99

Colombia
ISBN 0 86442 674 7
US$19.99 • UK£14.99

South America on a Shoestring
ISBN 1 86450 283 5
US$29.99 • UK£17.99

Bolivia
ISBN 0 86442 668 2
US$21.99 • UK£13.99

**Trekking in the
Central Andes**
ISBN 1 74059 431 2
US$19.99 • UK£14.99

Chile & Easter Island
ISBN 1 74059 116 X
US$21.99 • UK£14.99

Index

Bold indicates maps.
For a full list of maps, see the
Table of Maps (p3).
For a full list of treks, see the
Table of Treks (pp4-5).

Bold indicates maps.
For a full list of maps, see the Table of Maps (p3).
For a full list of treks, see the Table of Treks (pp4-5).

Bold indicates maps.
For a full list of maps, see the
  Table of Maps (p3).
For a full list of treks, see the
  Table of Treks (pp4-5).

Boxed Text